PRODUCING
VIDEOS

a complete guide

x2-10

third e

MARTHA M

ALLEN&UNWIN

First published in 1997

This edition published in 2010

Allen & Unwin
83 Alexander Street
Crows Nest NSW 2065
Australia
Phone: (61 2) 8425 0100
Fax: (61 2) 9906 2218
Email: info@allenandunwin.com
Web: www.allenandunwin.com

Cataloguing-in-Publication details are available
from the National Library of Australia
www.librariesaustralia.nla.gov.au

ISBN 978 1 74237 056 9

Index by Puddingburn Publishing Services
Set in 9.75/12 pt Stempel Schneidler by Bookhouse, Sydney
Printed in Singapore by KHL Printing Co Pte Ltd
10 9 8 7 6 5 4 3 2 1

With thanks to my parents
Marie and George Mollison
who gave me wings
and taught me how to use them.

(Photo by Marjorie Holmes)

CONTENTS

ACKNOWLEDGMENTS

Thanks to Jim Tumeth, Rowan Ayers and Ian Stocks for their contributions to the previous incarnation of this book, *The AFTRS Guide to Video Production*.

Thanks also to the staff of the Australian Film, Television and Radio School (AFTRS) and other industry professionals who read and commented on the text, helped me find materials, and graciously posed for photographs: Tony Atkins, Gilda Baracchi, Sara Bennett, Tony Bosch, Ian Bosman, Rod Bower, Peter Butterworth, Helen Carmichael, Rebecca Chiu, Ian Clark, Ken Crouch, Hilton Ellingham, Julian Ellis, Barry Fernandes, Chris Fraser, Serge Golikov, Trevor Graham, Marguerite Grey, Ernst Hadenfeld, Phillippa Harvey, Sara Hourez, Colin Kemp, Elisabeth Knight, Anna Lang, Ben Lay, Gerry Letts, John Lonie, Vicki Lucan, Yvonne Madon, Tony Mandl, Peter Millyn, Marilyn Murphy, Jane Paterson, Grahame Ramsay, Helen Salter, Wayne Smith, Faye Starr, Fiona Strain, Alistair Thornton, Jason Wheatley and Annie Wright.

Additional thanks to the other media professionals who've advised and assisted me: Katrina Beck, Lester Bostock, Barbara Bishop, Kathryn Brown, Peter Chvany, Ian Collie, Rebecca Gerendasy, Marsha Della-Giustina, the late Ernst Hadenfeld, Lawrie Hill, Tom Kingdon, Darrell Lass, Brian McDuffie, Byron Minger, Randolph Sellars, Paul Sosso and Cathy Zheutlin.

Larger text contributions were made by Luke Barrowcliffe, Usha Harris, Jerry and Machelle Hartman, Don Bethel, Tom Jeffrey, Harry Kirchner, Chris Peckham, Meredith Quinn and John Sirett. A range of imaginative learning activities were provided by Rachel Masters.

Ian Atkinson, Rob Davis, Richard Fitzpatrick, Peter Giles, Phillippa Harvey, David Jahns, Sebastian Jake, Bruce McCallum, Dominique Morel, Bill O'Donnell, David Opitz, Silvia Pfeiffer and Charlie Tesch all helped me come to terms with new methods and equipment.

Michelle Blakeney, Barbara Bishop, Irena Boboia, Kimberley Brown, David Cameron, Nancy Clover, Erik Fauske, Richard Fitzpatrick, Edis Jurcys, Walter Locke, Graeme MacLeod, Don Pollock, Grahame Ramsay, David Shaheen, Keith Smith, Neil Smith, Rob Stewart, Peter Thurmer, Arlington Community Media Inc. (ACMi), Central TAFE Perth, Metro Screen <www.metroscreen.org.au>, The Madeleine School, Portland Community College and Portland Community Media all supplied large numbers of vivid photos.

And very special thanks to Meredith Quinn, publisher of the first edition, Miranda Douglas, designer of the first edition, Elizabeth Weiss, publisher of the second and third editions, Colette Vella, Ann Savage, Sue Jarvis, Ann Lennox and Clara Finlay, my understanding and intrepid editors, Sophia Barnes, publishing assistant, Simon Paterson, Lisa White and Michael Killalea, designers, Anthea Stead, illustrator, John Buckingham and Edis Jurcys, photography, Sky Cooper, Photoshop, and David Jahns and Phil Cooper, technical graphics.

Finally, a warm tribute and smile to the tips providers, who've generously contributed their kernels of wisdom:

Andrew Abernathy, Channel Seven Townsville, Townsville, QLD, Australia

Caite Adamek, Film and Video Editor, Sydney, NSW, Australia

Leone Adams, ABC TV, NSW Training Coordinator, Sydney, NSW, Australia

Doug Adler, Videographer, Portland, OR, USA

Marjorie Anderson, National Coordinator Aboriginal Employment and
    Development, ABC TV, Sydney, NSW, Australia

Ian Andrews, Metro Screen, Paddington, NSW, Australia

Gilda Baracchi, Producer, Sydney, NSW, Australia

Luke Barrowcliffe, Goorie Vision, QLD, Australia

Claire Beach, Edmonds-Woodway High School, Edmonds, WA, USA

Jason Benedek, Tin Sheds, University of Sydney, NSW, Australia

Sara Bennett, Editor, Australian Film Television and Radio School

Don Bethel, Consultant, Television Production Techniques, Sydney, NSW,
    Australia

Barbara Bishop, Independent Producer, Winthrop, MA, USA

Jeff Bodmer-Turner, Manchester Memorial School, Manchester, MA, USA

Julie Booras, Offspring Productions, Lynnfield, MA, USA

Ian Bosman, Gaffer, Australian Film Television and Radio School

Josephine Bourne, Producer, Townsville, QLD, Australia

Melissa Bourne, Editor, Melbourne, VIC, Australia

Ken Bowley, University of Wollongong, NSW, Australia

Carol Brands, Curtin University of Technology, Perth, WA, Australia

Kathryn Brown, Director, Sydney, NSW, Australia

Kimberley Brown, Editor/Camera Operator, Vancouver, BC, Canada

David Cameron, Charles Sturt University, Bathurst, NSW, Australia

Helen Carmichael, Scriptwriting, Australian Film Television and Radio School

John Carroll, Charles Sturt University, Bathurst, NSW, Australia

Pam Carsten, Portland Community Media, Portland, OR, USA

Sandra Chung, ABC TV, Training and Development, Sydney, NSW, Australia

Peter Chvany, Emerson College, Boston, MA, USA

Ian Clark, Video Maintenance, Australian Film Television and Radio School

Paul Clark, Manchester Memorial School, Manchester, MA, USA

Hart Cohen, University of Western Sydney–Nepean, Sydney, NSW, Australia

Lester Crombie, Queensland School of Film and Television, Brisbane, QLD,
    Australia

Rob Davis, Editor, Digital Dimensions, Townsville, QLD, Australia

Marsha Della-Giustina, Emerson College, Boston, MA, USA

Tracy Dickson, College of the Southwest, Roma, QLD, Australia

Miranda Douglas, Publishing, Australian Film Television and Radio School

Shaun Edwards, Cape York Indigenous Theatre Troupe, Cairns, QLD, Australia

Hilton Ellingham, Props and Staging, Australian Film Television and Radio
    School

Julian Ellis, Cinematographer, Australian Film Television and Radio School

Philip Elms, Media Resource Centre, Adelaide, SA, Australia

Lee Faulkner, Queensland University of Technology, Brisbane, QLD, Australia
Erik Fauske, Portland Community College, Portland, OR, USA
Barry Fernandes, Sound, Australian Film Television and Radio School
John Fiddler, Producer, Reel Image, Brisbane, QLD, Australia
Carl Fisher, Murriimage, Wolvi via Gympie, QLD, Australia
Richard Fitzpatrick, Camera Operator, Digital Dimensions, Townsville, QLD,
    Australia
Jeanne Flanagan, Independent Producer, Somerville, MA, USA
Bernadette Flynn, Griffith Film School, Griffith University, Brisbane, QLD,
    Australia
Joseph Ford, Royal Melbourne Institute of Technology, Melbourne, VIC,
    Australia
Chris Fraser, Cinematographer, Australian Film Television and Radio School
Clint Ganczak, Final Cut Pro Users Group, Portland, OR, USA
Denise Galloway, University of South Australia, Underdale, SA, Australia
Rebecca Gerendasy, Producer, *Cooking Up a Story*, Portland, OR, USA
Peter Giles, Head of Digital Media, Australian Film Television and Radio School
Mark Gingerich, Final Cut Pro Users Group, Portland, OR, USA
Serge Golikov, Post Production Supervisor, Australian Film Television and Radio
    School
Trevor Graham, Documentary Filmmaker, Australia
Nigel Graves, Scriptwriter, Sydney, NSW, Australia
Jeff Grinta, Producer/Director, Vancouver, WA, USA
Ernst Hadenfeld, Engineer, Australian Film Television and Radio School
Antti Hakala, Actor, Turenki, Finland
Usha Harris, International Communications, Macquarie University, NSW,
    Australia
Phillippa Harvey, Editing, Australian Film Television and Radio School
Philip Hayward, Macquarie University, North Ryde, NSW, Australia
Alan Hills, Queensland School of Film and Television, Brisbane, QLD, Australia
Colin Holmes, Videographer, Canberra, ACT, Australia
Sara Hourez, Special Projects, Australian Film Television and Radio School
Rich Howley, Video Trainer, Somerville, MA, USA
Hsing Min Sha, Independent Producer, Somerville, MA, USA
Jan Hudson, Videographer, Sydney, NSW, Australia
Ian Ingham-Young, Academy of Photogenic Arts, Sydney, NSW, Australia
David Jahns, Editor
Stephen Jones, Australian Film Television and Radio School
Edis Jurcys, Photographer/filmmaker, Portland, OR, USA
George Karpathakis, Edith Cowan University, Perth, WA, Australia
Judi Kelemen, Newton Cable TV, Newton, MA, USA
Donna Kenny, The Video History Company and Center for Recording Life
    Stories, Florence, MA, USA
Colin Kemp, Engineering Department, Australian Film Television and Radio
    School
Tom Kingdon, Director, Emerson College, Boston, MA, USA
Harry Kirchner, La Trobe University, Bundoora, VIC, Australia
Stewart Klein, Scriptwriting, Australian Film Television and Radio School

Elisabeth Knight, Directing, Australian Film Television and Radio School
Ben Kreusser, Portland Community Media, Portland, OR, USA
Debra Kroon, Northern Territory University, Darwin, NT, Australia
Anna Lang, Directing, Australian Film Television and Radio School
Darrell Lass, Production Designer, Sydney, NSW, Australia
Julian Lauzzana, Videographer, Portland, OR, USA
Ben Lay, Editing, Australian Film Television and Radio School
Gill Leahy, University of Technology, Sydney, NSW, Australia
Sue L'Estrange, Videographer, Sydney, NSW, Australia
Gerry Letts, Operations and Facilities, Australian Film Television and Radio
    School
David Leonard, Executive Producer, Sydney, NSW, Australia
Walter Locke, Community Outreach Coordinator, Arlington Community Media
    Inc. (ACMi), Arlington, MA, USA
John Lonie, Scriptwriting, Australian Film Television and Radio School
Bruce McCallum, Technician, Sony Australia
Penny McDonald, Filmmaker, Sydney, NSW, Australia
Brian McDuffie, Director, Sydney, NSW, Australia
Shane McNeil, Flinders University, Adelaide, SA, Australia
Graeme MacLeod, Film and TV, Central TAFE, Perth, WA, Australia
Tianli Ma, Videographer, Portland, OR, USA
Yvonne Madon, Scriptwriting Dept, Australian Film Television and Radio School
Clodine Mallinckrodt, Director, Boston, MA, USA
Tony Mandl, Gaffer, Australian Film Television and Radio School
Peter Millyn, Production Accountant, Australian Film Television and Radio
    School
Byron Minger, Director/Editor, M3 Productions LLC, Portland, OR, USA
Dominique Morel, High Performance Computing Support, James Cook
    University, Townsville, QLD, Australia
Steve Morrison, University of Western Sydney–Nepean, Sydney, NSW, Australia
Lyvern Myi, Media Resource Centre, Adelaide, SA, Australia
Andy Nehl, Head of Television, Australian Film Television and Radio School
Rob Nercessian, Videographer, Sydney, NSW, Australia
Bill O'Donnell, Television Technician, James Cook University, Townsville, QLD,
    Australia
Florence Onus, School of Indigenous Australian Studies, James Cook University,
    Townsville, QLD, Australia
David Opitz, Metro Screen, Paddington, NSW, Australia
Steven Parris, Edmonds-Woodway High School, Edmonds, WA, USA
Jane Paterson, Sound Dept, Australian Film Television and Radio School
PC Peri, Producer, Portland, OR, USA
Rachel Perkins, Producer/Director, Australia
Gordon Peters, Cameraman, Channel 7 News, Bundaberg, QLD, Australia
Alan Petschack, Videographer, Bellingen, NSW, Australia
Silvia Pfeiffer, CEO, Vquence Pty Ltd, Sydney, NSW, Australia
Peter Poire-Odegarde, Portland Community Media, Portland, OR, USA
Donald Pollock, University of La Verne, CA, USA
Meredith Quinn, Publishing, Australian Film Television and Radio School

Jeremy Reurich, Technical Trainee, Australian Film Television and Radio School
Tim Rooney, Portland Community Media, Portland, OR, USA
Cameron Rose, Video Art Society, University of Tasmania, Hobart, TAS, Australia
Adrian Rostirolla, Editor, Metro Screen, Paddington, NSW, Australia
Neal Ruckman, Portland Community Media, Portland, OR, USA
Randolph Sellars, Director and DOP, Portland, OR, USA
David Shaheen, Methuen High School, Methuen, MA, USA
Danny Sheehy, Queensland School of Film and Television, Brisbane, QLD,
    Australia
John Sirett, Producer, Sydney, NSW, Australia
Ian Slade, Southern Cross University, Lismore, NSW, Australia
Keith Smith, Edith Cowan University, Perth, WA, Australia
Neil Smith, t.a.v. productions, Adelaide, SA, Australia
Wayne Smith, Props and Staging, Australian Film Television and Radio School
Paul Sosso, Producer and Editor, Portland, OR, USA
Ed Spencer, Portland Community Media, Portland, OR, USA
Beryl Stephens, Videographer, Sydney, NSW, Australia
Rob Stewart, Northern Melbourne Institute of TAFE, Collingwood, VIC,
    Australia
Mark Stiles, Writer and Filmmaker, Sydney, Australia
Fiona Strain, Editor, Australian Film Television and Radio School
Sharon Taylor, Public Relations and Marketing, Australian Film Television and
    Radio School
Charlie Tesch, Independent Producer, Somerville, MA, USA
Mark Tewksbury, The Nine Video School, Brisbane, QLD, Australia
Alistair Thornton, Props and Staging, Australian Film Television and Radio
    School
Peter Thurmer, Hamilton Secondary College, Mitchell Park, SA, Australia
Christine Togo-Smallwood, School of Indigenous Australian Studies, James Cook
    University, Townsville, QLD, Australia
Francis Treacey, Deakin University, Clayton, VIC, Australia
Gypsy Rose Tucker, Scriptwriting, Australian Film Television and Radio School
Jim Tumeth, Training Development, Australian Film Television and Radio School
Mandi Vernoy, Final Cut Pro Users Group, Portland, OR, USA
A.J. Von Wolfe, Final Cut Pro Users Group, Portland, OR, USA
John Waikart, Satellite News Gathering KGW, Portland, OR, USA
Lindsay Ward, School of Information Technology, James Cook University,
    Townsville, QLD, Australia
Peter Watkins, Educational Media Services, University of Western Sydney,
    Macarthur, NSW, Australia
Brian Williams, Western Australian School of Art and Design, Northbridge,
    WA, Australia
Jason Wheatley, Educational Media, Australian Film Television and Radio School
Alison Wotherspoon, Flinders University, Adelaide, SA, Australia
Cathy Zheutlin, Producer, *Holy Rascals, The World's Kitchen*, Portland, OR, USA

GREETING

Hello to you, Aspiring Videomaker!
    You're about to learn a skill which will give you both satisfaction and unexpected challenges. You'll find yourself looking at film and television differently, and even real life will sometimes get a frame around it in your eyes.

The book you're holding is an attempt to pass on to you the things I can tell you about video. I've tried to write it so it feels more like I'm right there talking to you rather than like I think I'm some remote authority on the subject. I hope you find it easy and fun to read.

As with any communication, you have a right to ask about me, so you can decide how to weigh up what I've written. But as books aren't geared up for two-way communication, I'll take that step for you.

For 28 years I've been working in video, and it's opened many doors for me that would never have opened otherwise. I've lugged gear to cover a wide range of events—cultural, political and personal—in Australia and the United States, and in Kenya and China as well.

As a teacher of video, I've helped other people develop the tools to tell their own stories—some heartfelt, some fantastical, some straight, some quirky. I've been a sort of midwife of the medium. On screening days, and even at rough-cut sessions, I've felt wonder and awe at the imaginativeness and uniqueness of the stories newly born.

At times I've been entrusted with telling other people's stories. To do this, I've been invited into the lives and perspectives of people from many backgrounds. I've always walked away a richer person.

I've found enormous satisfaction working with Indigenous Australians, whose many stories are emerging and altering forever the consciousness of people worldwide and the accepted definition of what it means to be Australian.

No teacher comes from nowhere, and I owe my own formation as a video person to the Somerville Producers Group, in Somerville, Massachusetts, USA. SPG is a constantly evolving collection of people who, as a group, have maintained the longest-running public access cable TV show in America.

I had lots of practical experience working for Adams Russell Cable TV in Norwood, Massachusetts. The Women's Video Collective, from the Boston area, was the enabling group for many intense video experiences, including covering the Women's Encampment for a Future of Peace and Justice in Seneca, New York in 1983, and the International Women's Conference in Nairobi, Kenya in 1985.

When I struck out on my own as a videomaker, I had the privilege of making a documentary on the experience of a special sector of US women. It's called *The Invisible Force: Women in the Military.*

In Australia, I came to teach short courses for the Australian Film Television and Radio School (AFTRS). It was through this connection that I was invited to teach video in Ngukurr in East Arnhem Land. Then followed opportunities to do video training with Indigenous Australians in Tennant Creek, Katherine, Alice Springs and Sydney.

I've worked as a video teacher at the University of Technology, Sydney, and the University of Newcastle, and taught within the Koori TV Training Course and the Indigenous TV Training Course, both run at the Australian Film Television and Radio School and later at Metro Screen.

In 1995, Director David Wang and I took a team of Indigenous Australian students to southwest China to make a documentary on the women of the Dai ethnic minority, who live in the mountains of Yunnan Province.

For five years, I taught video at the School of Indigenous Australian Studies at James Cook University in Townsville.

Since then, I've worked extensively on refugee stories, I've been very active with video clubs and have run many workshops, including lots of weekend video retreats for people to have fun shooting scripted dramas tailored to specific locales.

Martha Mollison with L–R: Sean Renfrey, Juan-Carlos Martinez, Teshome Teseme, Stephen Plumridge and Laura O'Neill, *Ethiopian Australian Story.*

I'm indebted to people all along the way who've taught me what I didn't know, shown me how to do new things, and shared their ideas and methods generously—and their anecdotes and laughter as well.

It's a great feeling to be part of an international network of media teachers who are passionate about what they do, and committed to helping others build their skills so they can tell their own stories.

In every edition of this book, many, many video teachers have participated by offering their training tips. The book is better for it, but the thing that makes me happiest is the feeling that this book, in some small way, reflects the breadth of people out there trying to bring media literacy and accomplished storytelling within the grasp of all those who seek it.

So seek on and build your skills. You have stories to tell which are both uniquely yours, and also reflective of the times and culture from which you come.

The more stories that get told, the richer we all will be.

Martha Mollison

P.S. Please send your own pictures and tips to my website, <www.marthamollison.com>.

THE CAMERA

The way to learn video is by doing it. So swing that camera up to your eye and have a go! You can't hurt the camera, unless you drop it or get it soaked.

You already know plenty about screen images: you know what you like, what you don't like, and what you want to see from your shoot.

Now—how to get it.

The most effective way to learn video is to make a start and then ask the questions you need as you go along. No one can learn a hundred buttons at once, so work at your own pace.

Usually you'll be working in a group, so what one person forgets, another person generally understands and can explain. Don't be afraid to ask other people—next time you may remember something that they've forgotten.

Most people start off thinking that video production is about technical knowledge. Of course that's part of it. But almost no one produces a video on their own.

Jason Sharp tries out the P2. Central TAFE, Perth.

Everyone finally concurs that the shot is right. Tianli Ma on camera, Tristian Spillman on sound and Erik Fauske teacher, Portland Community College.

Video work is group work, and it relies on the combined efforts of a good team. When the crew members communicate well with each other, and everyone feels their contribution is needed and respected, people really start to fire with creativity.

That lifts the production to a higher level.

Okay, where to start . . .

Sharon Thomson heads out with a DVCAM. (Courtesy of Portland Community Media)

The Power Supply

There are two ways to power up the camera. You can either use a battery or you can connect the camera to the electrical outlet on the wall, using the AC adaptor.

The Camera Battery

Most cameras operate on rechargeable batteries. These are usually NiMH (nickel metal hydride) batteries or lithium ion batteries. Both types are much lighter in weight and run for longer than the old NICAD batteries, which are now out of favour due to the toxic heavy metal, cadmium, that they contain.

Lithium ion batteries have the added advantage of being totally free from developing a *memory*. The dreaded memory effect causes a battery which is repeatedly used for a short time and then recharged again to start acting like a short-term battery. Hopefully you won't encounter this problem, but if you do, you should know that 'memorised' batteries can regain their full power by being totally drained and totally recharged several times in a row.

The camera and battery are designed so you can only attach the battery to the camera in the right way. If you try to do it upside down or backwards, it won't go. This leads us to:

THE FIRST LAW OF VIDEO

If it doesn't go easily, don't force it.

In video, everything is made to insert or connect easily. If you're having trouble connecting something, you're doing it wrong.

If you think pushing harder will do the trick, you're doubly wrong.

If you try to force something in video, you'll break it.

If you learn nothing else on the first day, learn this.

Photo courtesy of Metro Screen.

The metal contacts must make the right connections in order to pass their power.

If you look at the battery, which is a dark and uninspiring lump of a thing, you'll see that it has little metal contacts on it somewhere. They're the gateway for the battery's stored electrical power to get into the camera. These contacts must connect with their counterparts on the camera.

In many compact consumer cameras, it's necessary to swing the camera eyepiece out of the way before you can line up the battery correctly for attachment.

Both the camera attachment spot and the battery will have arrows to guide you, and you can expect to hear a satisfying little click when the battery locks into place, but it's a good idea when you're new at this to give the battery a little wiggle just to make sure it's secure.

When you want to detach the battery from the camera, look for a little button called *battery release* or *eject*. It's usually very close to where the battery connects to the camera. When you push it, the battery attaching lock will be released and the battery can be removed.

Of all the various and sundry extra bits in video, the battery looks the most robust. But there are ways you can damage it.

When connected correctly, the battery won't wobble.

How to Avoid Battery Problems

1. **Don't drop it.**

   The cells inside can be broken by shock. Then the battery won't work.

2. **Don't short-circuit it by allowing a metal object to touch it across its contacts.**

   So would you carry it in your pocket with lots of loose change?

3. **Don't expose it to fire or water.**

4. **Allow time to 'break in' new batteries.**

   New batteries are in a discharged condition when sold. You should plan to do an overnight (twelve-hour) charge on a new battery before you have to use it. It can take two to four times of fully charging and fully discharging a new battery before it's 'formed'.

   If your charger stops before your new battery is fully charged, don't worry— that's quite a common occurrence. Just remove the new battery from the device and reconnect it. Charging should start up again.

5. **Exercise the batteries.**

   Batteries should be used every two or three weeks to stay in good shape. They self-discharge over time, so if they've been idle for a while you may need to break them in again.

6. **Store batteries in a cool, clean, dry place.**

7. **Clean dirty battery contacts with a cotton swab and alcohol.**

8. **Don't leave it behind.**

   Batteries are unobtrusive little numbers and fade into the surroundings quite easily. It's not at all hard to leave one under a chair, on top of a piano or on the floor of a car.

   The problem is, their appearance belies their value. Unlike the AA cells in your digital stills camera, video batteries are expensive to replace.

Battery End Game

Batteries do eventually die. After 500–800 charge/discharge cycles, or a couple of years of regular use, they'll start showing their age by reduced running times. (Don't we all?) At that point you should plan on replacing them.

If you borrow a battery that doesn't last very long at all, it's good video manners to let the equipment store know that it's suss. You wouldn't want to get it again, would you?

Don't just chuck batteries in the bin.

When you get rid of batteries DO NOT throw them in the trash; DO NOT burn, break, compact or compost them. Batteries should be recycled correctly or returned to the place from which you bought them.

NICAD batteries contain cadmium, which is toxic and environmentally hazardous. These batteries should NEVER be sent to landfill.

With NiMH batteries, the nickel component is semi-toxic and large amounts of the electrolyte can be hazardous to the environment.

Although Li-Ion batteries don't contain metallic lithium and aren't an environmental risk, they do contain recyclable materials and are accepted for recycling.

For help locating your local recycling facility, contact:

- *Australia:* MRI Australia, Battery World
- *New Zealand:* Exide Technologies, and <www.medichem.co.nz/battery-disposal.htm>
- *USA and Canada:* call Portable Rechargeable Battery Association at 1-800-822-8837
- *United Kingdom:* BatteryBack.org.

Charging a Battery

Your camera kit will come with a battery charger. Sometimes the charger is a separate unit, sometimes it's combined in the same piece of equipment as the AC adaptor (more about that in a minute), and sometimes the battery can be recharged while in the camera.

Charging a battery is simply a matter of connecting the battery to the charger, plugging the charger into an electrical socket and turning it on. In some cases you'll also have to move a switch to *charge*. A light will come on to show that it's charging, and the light goes off when the battery is fully charged. On some chargers a red light will come on when a quick charge is happening, and a green light will come on when it's a trickle charge. A quick charge can get a battery fairly rapidly up to a usable level of power and can save the day when on a shoot. But whenever possible you should let your batteries get the full trickle charge.

Batteries take much longer to recharge than they do to use (a one-hour battery may take three hours to charge), so it's a good idea to charge your batteries the night before your shoot. It's no good having your crew waiting around while you try to will your battery charger to work faster.

Another thing to know: an AC adaptor/charger can only do one thing at a time. If you're using it to power the camera, it can't simultaneously be charging a battery for you. If it's charging a battery, you can't use it to run the camera.

Time for a tea break? Many's the time batteries have been charged under the table in a cafe. Just don't go off without them!

Charging a battery always takes a lot longer than using one.

Battery Behaviour

Like many of us, batteries work well when they're in comfortably warm surroundings. A battery will last less time if used in a very cold setting. So for those shoots of skiers and ice skaters, take more batteries.

Also like many of us, batteries lose energy when left on their own. So a charged battery left in the

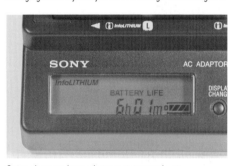

Some chargers have a battery status read-out.

storage room will gradually lose power. For maximum battery strength, it's best to charge up your batteries the day before, or on the day of, your shoot.

The AC Adaptor

Portable video equipment is designed to operate on battery power, so you can be mobile and take the camera wherever you want to get your story.

That means the camera is made to use direct current (DC) electricity, because batteries supply DC power.

But the power points (electrical sockets) in buildings supply a different sort of electricity, called alternating current (AC). The camera can't accept AC.

So in order to use wall current, you need to use an AC adaptor—which does just what its name implies: it changes AC to DC.

You plug the adaptor into the wall and it takes the alternating current up the cord from the power point, changes it from AC to DC in the little intermediary box, and then sends the direct current along the other cord into the camera.

Just one caution: to avoid giving the camera a power surge, which could damage it, make sure that before you plug things together you turn all the power switches off. Connect the AC adaptor to the wall and the camera, then power up in this order:

The AC adaptor converts the electricity from the wall socket into the DC current your camera needs.

1. Turn on the wall power point.
2. Turn on the AC adaptor.
3. Turn on the camera.

Why Use an AC Adaptor Instead of Batteries?

1. To save your batteries.

Since batteries have a limited life span, it's sensible to use them only when you need them.

2. To ensure that your power doesn't cut out at a critical point in your shoot.

Scenario: The bride and groom have stood patiently through all the wedding ritual and are just about to exchange their promises when—oops—the camera shuts off. While you scrabble through your bag for the other battery, they say their words, and you're finally recording again just in time for their exit.

Other Power Supply Aids

When you're on the go with a shoot, the last thing you want is to be stopped by lack of battery power.

AN ADAPTOR FOR THE CIGARETTE LIGHTER OF A CAR

An optional video accessory is a little adaptor which plugs into the cigarette lighter of a car and extracts 12 volts of usable current.

If your genre is road movies, this may be just the thing to liberate you from standard sockets and keep your show on the road, so to speak.

Check the length of the cable on the adaptor before you head out, though. The cord tends to be fairly short, so it can keep you closer to your vehicle, and passing trucks, than you might otherwise choose.

An extension cord can usually be purchased or soldered together by a helpful technician. Then you can get whatever shots you require.

Another handy use for the cigarette adaptor is to power your battery charger as you move from one production site to another.

A car cigarette lighter still has a use in this post-smoking era.

DUAL BATTERY CHARGER/HOLDER

With a dual battery charger/holder, it's possible to be using two batteries on your camera at once. This gives you more time to record without stopping. In fact, you can even take one battery out of the holder and replace it with a fresh one without stopping your recording. So I guess you could go on like this for hours.

The battery charger/holder clips onto your belt, and, because it uses lithium ion batteries, it doesn't drag you down like the old battery belts did.

This system is great if it's imperative that your recording not stop and you're in a situation where you can't use AC power.

Getting to Go

Once you've supplied an electrical source to the camera, find the power switch and turn the camera on.

Now remove the lens cap and right away you should see a picture in the viewfinder.

If you see a bright blue screen but don't see a picture, check again that you've turned the power switch to *Camera* rather than *Play* or *VCR*.

Hang on, what if it's on *Camera* but you don't have any picture in the viewfinder, just some words?

Don't panic, you may have a camera with a lens *flap* instead of a lens cap! Find the lever and open it up. Voila! A picture.

If your viewfinder image looks like a dark night of the soul, remove the lens cap.

If you have a lens flap instead, flip the lever to open up the lens view.

The Electronic Viewfinder (EVF)

The electronic viewfinder is inside the eyepiece. It's a tiny monitor which shows you what the camera is 'seeing'. It allows you to establish and frame the shot you want to record.

The viewfinder's picture may be in black and white, even though the camera is producing a colour signal. But aside from this, one of the beauties of video is that 'what you see is what you get'. So if you've got a good picture in the viewfinder, you're pretty well assured that you're recording a good picture.

Except . . . some viewfinders have brightness and contrast controls.

The EVF gives you your camera's view of the world.

EVF Brightness and Contrast Controls

Because any knob on shared equipment is subject to random tweaking, it's always possible that the person before you has turned the brightness or contrast up or down and the viewfinder is giving you an image that is darker or brighter than what the camera will be recording.

To ensure that the viewfinder is working for you, rather than tricking you, always adjust it to the camera's colour bars at the beginning of your shoot.

Using Colour Bars to Normalise the Viewfinder

Colour bars display a standardised video test signal, which has a number of uses. They really are in colour if you see them on a monitor or record them, but they may be black and white in your camera viewfinder.

Look for a switch on your camera labelled *Bars* and flick it on. In a black and white viewfinder you'll see seven or eight vertical stripes. They should range from peak white on the left, through descending levels of grey, to black on the right.

In a colour viewfinder they start with white on the left and show stripes of yellow, cyan, green, magenta, red, blue and finally black. If they don't, the viewfinder is incorrectly set and needs to be adjusted.

To normalise the viewfinder, turn the brightness and contrast controls until the stripes look the way they should. Once you've adjusted your viewfinder to show this standard signal correctly, then you know that what you see is what you get.

If you can't get colour bars to show correctly, it can indicate problems with the colour part of the video signal, and a technician may need to make internal adjustments to the camera to align the colours correctly.

With these colour bars, the stripes from left to right are white, yellow, cyan, green, magenta, red and blue, with black on the bottom. On a black and white viewfinder, the bars are in descending shades of grey.

Are You Left-eyed or Right-eyed?

Most likely you can't answer this because it's something you've never had to know. Oddly enough, your *eyedness* (is that a word?) doesn't necessarily conform to whether you're left-handed or right-handed.

Jacqueline Antoinette checks whether she's right-eyed . . .   . . . or left-eyed.

But there's sufficient variation in people that camera manufacturers have taken account of it. The viewfinder on some cameras will slide left and right to get to your preferred eye, once you untighten a little knob located near it.

Check it out. Which is more comfortable for you: to look through the viewfinder with your right eye or your left eye? Whatever works, that's the way for you. The soft eyecup is often removable, so you can turn it around the other way if you're left-eyed. It's a fiddly thing to get off and on, but you can do it with gentleness and patience. Actually, gentleness and patience are useful in lots of video tasks.

Once you know whether you're left-eyed or right-eyed, always take the time to adjust the viewfinder so it works best for you.

And Now a Word From Your Viewfinder: OSD

The viewfinder displays various words and symbols which are referred to in techie alphabet-speak as OSD, simply meaning *on screen display*. These advise you about such things as battery strength, brightness level (*f* stop), shutter speed, present and remaining record time, white balance, whether you're in manual or auto mode, and whether you're recording or not.

It's a good idea to read the camera manual's page on these OSD messages, so you're not the last one to know what your camera is trying to tell you.

Mini DV cameras contain many functions and settings you can access and adjust via the menu button on the camera, some of which you may never need to use. While most people have a natural aversion to reading the manual and can usually get the camera to work without referring to it, it's worthwhile reading it to see what these functions are, as some of them may well be useful to you. It also pays to be very careful that you don't accidentally switch on some camera settings or functions, or that they haven't been left switched on by someone else who used the camera before you.

Andy Nehl, Head of Television, AFTRS.

You should routinely check through all this information at the beginning of each shoot; then, if you find that the displays are annoying or covering important parts of your shot, you can turn off some or all of them.

The *Date and Time* display is notorious for tricking people. Be sure to read your manual to see whether you're burning that date and time into the image you're recording or if you're just seeing it as EVF information. In home videos for the family, the date and time can solve disputes over when a shot was recorded, but if you're shooting drama, you don't want it marring your scene.

Note: Your camera has a *pre-installed battery* which keeps track of the date and time, but it can wear down if the camera isn't used for more than three months. You can recharge this battery by running the camera via the AC adaptor for 24 hours.

Your viewfinder also displays many *menus* which can be activated by a little *menu* button somewhere on the outside of the camera.

These menus give you lots of choices for different settings for both recording and playback. You usually scroll through these menus by rotating a little dial on the outside of the camera and then register the choices you want to activate by pressing in on the dial. Sometimes menus are operated by the LCD touchscreen.

The Diopter

The *diopter* seems to be the best-kept secret in video! It's the lens in the viewfinder's eyepiece and it lives right behind that soft rubber eyecup.

Some plain-English camera manuals refer to the diopter as the *viewfinder lens*.

Whatever it's called, you need to use it. Getting the diopter correctly adjusted for your eyesight can make or break your ability to get clearly focused shots.

This lens can be moved forwards and backwards, in relation to the viewfinder's screen, in order to suit the eyesight of each user.

Whenever it's your turn to use the camera, the first thing you should do is adjust the diopter to your own eyesight, so you can see the camera's image clearly. Otherwise, how can you know if you've got the picture in focus or not?

Your first step is to find the darn thing! People don't know about it partly because they don't notice it. It's very discreetly tucked away.

On some EVFs the diopter is adjusted by sliding a little button on the underside of the viewfinder.

On very compact cameras, you will have to pull out the top of the viewfinder tube to even find this little button. If you're the sole user of a camera, you can adjust the diopter and push the extended section back in and never have to reset it. It will stay the way you left it.

On other cameras, there's a ring behind the eyecup that you turn to control the position of the diopter.

On still others, there's a ring that you loosen which allows you to pull out the tube holding the diopter and set it to the right position, then you carefully tighten the ring down again to hold the diopter in place for you during the shoot.

Use this tiny knob, located on the underside of the viewfinder, to adjust the diopter.

Pull the tiny viewfinder outward to reveal the diopter adjustment dial.

To adjust this diopter, unscrew the tightening ring and extend the eyepiece towards you, then tighten the ring again.

How to Make the Diopter Adjustment

The first thing to do is to make sure the main camera lens is zoomed out all the way to the wide angle position. That way, the camera's focus will not be an issue.

Then put your eye to the eyepiece and tweak the adjustment knob so the lens moves forward and back until you see the clearest possible image.

It helps to look at something with a sharply defined outline, like the edge of a door, or at the camera messages on the screen.

Once you have it right, secure the diopter in that position.

Dai girls use the viewfinder to review a scene for the documentary *Dai Women Speak*, Xishuangbanna, China. (Photo by Michelle Blakeney)

Changing the EVF to Distance Viewing Mode

On older camera models, the diopter and eyecup are mounted on a hinge so they can be swung aside, allowing you or your actors to stand back and watch the miniature viewfinder screen from a distance.

Diopter closed for handheld operation.

Diopter open—an option for tripod operation.

The LCD Screen

The LCD (liquid crystal display) screen is a flipout screen which gives you a larger version of your viewfinder image, and it's in colour. This is a relief to many people because they can feel more confident about their white balance (discussed in Chapter 2).

Many people also prefer the LCD screen because, quite simply, they can see their picture better. On long drama takes or long shoots in general, it can be much less stressful to be able to stand back and watch your shot from a comfortable distance than to have to keep one eye pressed to the viewfinder while the other closed eye starts to spasm from fatigue.

The LCD screen is easier for most people to use. Valarie Giarrusso captures a winter scene. Methuen Community TV. (Photo by Nancy Clover)

Jan Hudson avoids sun glare with a screen hood velcroed to her LCD screen.

Silvia Pfeiffer checks Benjamin's shot for *The Lizard of Oz*.

Andy Nehl,
Head of
Television,
AFTRS.

If you're walking and following an actor or shooting tracking shots, always look at the flipout screen rather than through the viewfinder. You'll get a steadier picture.

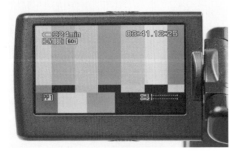

Use colour bars to adjust your LCD screen for brightness and contrast. (Courtesy of Metro Screen)

Sunlight poses a problem for LCD screens, however. On a bright day outdoors it can be harder to see the image, but you can fix this problem with an inexpensive screen hood. There are various commercial models which attach by elastic or Velcro. You can even make your own.

For those who are more visually challenged, some screen hoods come with a 2× magnifier as well.

Bright days and other screen reflections can also send you back to your viewfinder with a renewed appreciation for it.

On most cameras, only one screen is active at a time, but some cameras allow you to have both running at once. Of course, this uses more battery power, so you should have a reason for doing it.

If you're handholding the camera, you may prefer to work with the viewfinder next to your eye. But if you want to show your footage to others—perhaps your actors in order to discuss their performance—the LCD screen makes it possible to go out recording without an additional field monitor.

The LCD screen also allows directors to easily check each camera operator's shot before calling 'action'.

A minor drawback of an LCD screen is that it uses more power than the viewfinder, so if you're running out of batteries, you can squeeze out a little more time by turning off the LCD screen.

LCD Brightness

Many LCD screens present a falsely bright image, perhaps to counteract the sunshine problem. This can make you think your picture is okay when it's actually recording a bit on the dark side. Just as with the viewfinder, the LCD screen can have a brightness control. If your camera has a colour bars display, always use it to normalise your LCD screen. Then you can decide whether or not you need more light.

LCD Gymnastics

LCD screens not only open out so more than one person can view the image, they can also flip over so the person in front of the camera can see their own image if desired.

When left is right and right is left, show them what they're used to seeing.

When you flip the LCD screen over, it can automatically flip the image as well, so it's right side up for the viewer in front of the camera.

And just so your actor or presenter doesn't get confused, the screen can be set to show that person a mirror image, rather than the true TV image.

Why? Because we're all used to looking in mirrors and seeing our left hand on the left side of the mirror, and if we move to the right, the mirror image moves to the right of the mirror, too. But in real life, when we're viewed by someone else, they see our left hand on their right side, and so on. That's the way the TV image is, too. But people aren't used to seeing their TV image, and it can get them all flustered when they move one way and the LCD screen shows them moving the other way.

The LCD screen can be angled so you can frame your image from below or above, whatever is needed to get that shot.

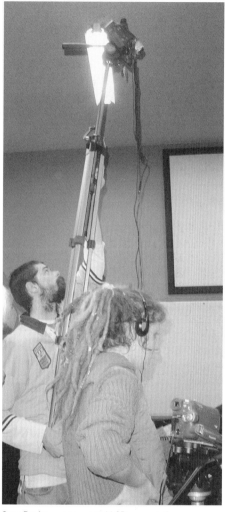

Sean Renfrey uses a rotated LCD screen to frame a very high-angle shot for *Ethiopian Australian Story*.

LCD Controls

Some inexpensive video cameras have LCD screens with touchscreen controls built into them. This may make for compact design, but anything that requires you to push on the LCD screen while actually recording is a liability. For example, if you're nudging the screen in order to change the focus, it will jar the camera and thereby diminish the smoothness and usability of your work.

LCD screens can also have many other controls on their surrounding plastic frame, like adjustment for sound volume and brightness/contrast controls.

What controls do you have for your LCD screen? What controls are around the edge of it?

What other camera controls are nearby?

The Zoom

The zoom is a complex lens system which gives you instant gratification.

It allows you to alter the image you see, continuously varying it from a wide-angle shot, all the way through to a close-up, and back again. It's the control that most fascinates new users, and consequently their first videos can induce motion sickness in their audiences.

Wide-angle coverage

Telephoto coverage

Wide-angle view

Telephoto view

Lens Angles

Wide angle: With a wide-angle lens the camera gathers an image from a large vertical and horizontal field.

Telephoto angle: With a telephoto lens the camera gathers an image from a much narrower *angle of view*. It allows the camera to show an enlarged view of a small detail, even from quite a distance.

> Avoid full telephoto handheld shots. Telephoto magnifies everything, including camera wobble.

Philip Elms,
Media Resource Centre.

Zoom Lens

The zoom lens is actually a number of individual lens elements mounted within one unit in the lens barrel of the camera.

The front and back lens elements remain stationary while the middle elements can be moved forwards and backwards, allowing the camera view to range from wide angle to telephoto, and to reproduce every stage in between.

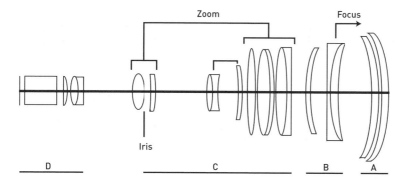

A Fixed front elements

B Movable group for internal focusing

C Optically compensated zoom movement for 10:1 ratio

D Fixed rear group

Elements in a zoom lens.

Zoom Ratio

The zoom ratio is the degree of difference between the *widest* shot and the *tightest* shot that the particular zoom lens can handle.

Consumer-level cameras may have a 6:1 zoom ratio; better cameras have a 10:1, 14:1 zoom or greater.

An *optical zoom* is achieved by the use of physical lenses and gives good results through its entire range.

A *digital zoom* operates by producing a digital enlargement of a section of the image. This can give dramatic results, but the image can look odd, like a mosaic. You may find it's wiser to turn off the digital zoom so you don't get this effect.

Telephoto wide angle

Andy Nehl,
Head of
Television,
AFTRS.

Don't use the 'Digital zoom' setting available on many cameras. Make sure it's turned off in the menu. If you want to zoom further into the image than the lens is capable of by itself, you can do this in postproduction.

Your useful zoom range may not be as fantastic as you once thought, because camera promoters add both the optical and digital zoom ratios together when designing their ads.

When recording a zoomed-in image, you'll find your picture can get very shaky and it's advisable to stabilise your camera somehow. It's a good idea to use a tripod.

When doing shots from a very great distance, you may need a zoom lens with a higher zoom range. Kimberley Brown, Pangnirtung, Nunavet, Canada. (Photo by Silvia Cloutier)

Automatic Zoom

The zoom-control button operates the automatic zoom, which is powered off the camera battery. It's labelled W (wide angle) on one side and T (telephoto) on the other. By pressing the T side of the switch you cause the camera to zoom in all the way to give you a close-up (a *telephoto* or *tight* shot). Pressing the W lets you zoom out all the way to a wide shot.

On some cameras, the zoom control is touch sensitive, which means the harder you press, the faster the angle will change.

Auto zoom rocker switch.

The advantage of using the auto zoom is that it produces such a smooth transition from one shot size to another.

There are two quite minor concerns in using the auto zoom.

1. The little motor that operates it can make a faint whirring sound which can be picked up by the camera mic in an extremely quiet shot.
2. The motor uses battery power. If your battery is nearly flat, it may be silly to waste power on the auto zoom.

Auto/Manual Zoom Control Switch

On some cameras you can change the zoom over to manual operation by flipping another one of those discreet little switches lurking somewhere near the lens barrel.

Once you change over to manual mode, the auto zoom control is disempowered, and the zoom is operated by turning the zoom ring on the lens barrel.

You must flip this switch back again to restore the zoom to auto mode. When the zoom is in auto or remote mode, you can't zoom manually.

Manual Zoom

You can operate the zoom manually by turning the zoom ring on the camera lens barrel.

Usually there's a little stick jutting out from it, which makes it easy to find and latch onto.

It takes some practice to get a manual zoom to look smooth, but on the other hand, if you want some weird effects—like a jagged zoom or some lightning in-and-out changes—hand-controlling it is the way to go.

Manual zoom does not cause a drain on your camera battery.

The best way to keep the camera steady without a tripod is to shoot everything on wide angle. Forget about the zoom—move in physically closer to the subject and suddenly your shots will look a lot steadier.

Mark Tewksbury, The Nine Video School.

Use this switch to set the zoom to auto or manual control.

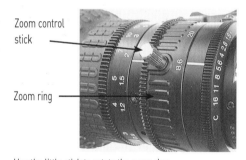

Zoom control stick

Zoom ring

Use the little stick to rotate the zoom ring.

The Iris

The camera iris is the mechanism that controls the amount of light entering the camera.

The size of the opening in the iris (the *aperture*) can be varied to let in greater or lesser amounts of light, depending on the brightness of the scene, and the quality of the image you seek to record.

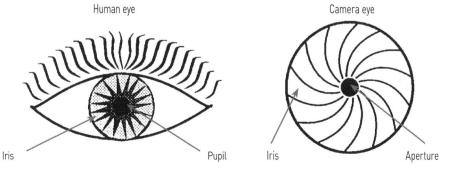

Human eye   Camera eye

Iris   Pupil   Iris   Aperture

The camera iris system is similar to that of the human eye.

F Stops

The size of the aperture (opening) is measured in *f stops.* A common range of *f* stops is:

f 1.4, f 2.8, f 4, f 5.6, f 8, f 11, f 16 and f 22.

This numbering system is confusing because the smallest number (*f 1.4*) means the largest opening, and the biggest number (*f 22*) means the smallest opening.

Just memorise this: the bigger the number, the smaller the hole.

The system is calibrated so that moving from one iris setting to the next either doubles or halves the amount of light admitted to the camera.

For example, moving from *f* 22 (the smallest opening) to *f* 16 (the next opening) doubles the amount of light entering the camera.

Conversely, moving from *f* 16 to *f* 22 halves the light entering the camera.

And so on through all the *f* stops.

Just as with the human eye, the smallest aperture opening is used under the brightest light, and the largest aperture opening is used under low light conditions.

The human eye pupil at a sunny beach.

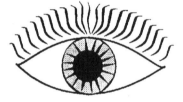

The human eye pupil in a dark room.

For the best picture results, medium *f* stop settings are preferred (especially *f* 5.6). To be able to use them, you may need to add lights to your scene.

Note: Images shot with large aperture openings have less *depth of field*. This affects the focus of your shot. (See Depth of Field in Chapter 2.)

Choosing the Iris Control Mode

The iris can be assigned to either automatic or manual control. Some cameras also allow remote control of the iris.

In multi-camera situations, the technician adjusts the iris settings of all the cameras via their CCUs (camera control units) from the studio control room or OB (outside broadcast) van.

There may be a switch on your camera for selecting the iris control mode, or it may be a selection within the *Camera* menu.

If it's a switch, slide the button to A for automatic control, to M for manual control and to R or S (servo) for remote control.

Automatic Iris or AEC (Automatic Exposure Control)

You'll probably find that your camera will be in auto iris mode when you turn it on.

In auto iris, the camera uses its own inbuilt sensor (a type of light meter) to measure the incoming light. Then the auto iris circuitry averages the variations in brightness and applies a formula to select the appropriate *f* stop.

Much of the time the auto iris chooses the best aperture setting. In scenes with a low *contrast ratio*—where there's not a huge difference in brightness between the light and dark areas of the picture—the system works the best.

> *Luminance:* Look at whites. Push the iris until the whites begin to flare and then wind back a little. In the absence of a zebra function in the camera, this will give a fast, usable video level.
>
> **Jason Benedek,** Videographer.

The formula is oriented to deal with the majority of video images, which have a brighter top than bottom due to the presence of some amount of sky or a well-lit upper background. The light level from the top of the image is therefore given somewhat less weight in the calculation than that from the bottom of the image.

However, sometimes the auto iris gets tricked.

In images with a high contrast ratio, where there's a substantial part of the picture which is much darker or much lighter than the rest, the calculated formula doesn't give the best result.

> Are you driving the camera or is the camera driving you? Automatic settings put you on automatic. Take control of the camera and practise 'active' cinematography!
>
> **Keith Smith,** Edith Cowan University.

For example, in a wide shot of a performer dressed in white, who is on a dark stage, the auto iris could open up due to the general darkness and give you an overly bright image of a flaring costume with no detail.

Conversely, with a subject in a very bright surrounding, the auto iris could close down and leave you with a subject that is dark and shows little detail.

Auto Iris Mistakes

A person in front of a window or a bright sky becomes a silhouette because the auto iris closes down too far in response to the incoming light.

A person in front of a whiteboard or white wall becomes a near-silhouette because the auto iris closes down too far in response to the reflected brightness of the background surface.

A person in front of a very dark background can look bleached out if the auto iris opens up too much in response to the large section of darkness.

What's the Zebra?

Your camera may have a zebra function. If you choose to turn it on, you'll see thin black and white stripes on the overly bright parts of your LCD or viewfinder image. These stripes don't get recorded, but they're a warning that you may want to close the iris down a little or change the way you've lit your shot.

On this Sony DVCAM, the manual iris is operated by the silver knob.

On manual iris, you decide. Katrina Beck, Metro Screen.

Sunlight on your azaleas can make for an overly bright picture. If you see zebra stripes, you might close down your camera iris a bit.

Manual Iris Control (Exposure)

If you choose to operate on manual iris, you will need to decide which iris setting to use for each shot. You select the light level (*Exposure, f* stop) to suit the part of the picture which is most important, and to give your image the overall look you want.

You need to be careful to match this look to that of the other shots of the same location which will come before and after it in the planned edited sequence. In other words, you need to maintain *lighting continuity*. You don't want a room to pulse light and dark from shot to shot!

You switch to manual iris by either choosing it within the *Camera menu* or pressing the button labelled *Exposure* on the outside of the camera.

Then the LCD or viewfinder screen will display an *f* stop reading, or a meter which shows you your relative bright-to-dark setting. You can vary the iris setting by turning a little dial or knob on the outside of the camera.

If you're uncertain, you can start out by using auto iris mode on your shot and seeing what the camera circuitry chooses, and then switching to manual iris to do your own finetuning.

Some cameras have a *push auto iris* button. When you press it, the auto iris function takes over and selects an iris setting, and when you let go of it, the iris stays at that setting but the camera returns to manual iris mode. This button is useful for quick referencing.

Manual iris poses a challenge if, in one shot, you're following a subject through changing lighting conditions. Auto iris might be better for this. In fact, some cameras give you a choice of reaction times on auto iris adjustments. In the *Camera menu* you can select Fast, Middle or Slow.

Manual iris is especially useful in shots that have a high contrast ratio, and where large dark or bright sections of the image might trick the auto iris into choosing an undesirable aperture setting.

Button Vertigo?

If you're starting to feel boggled by all these buttons and choices, just start off by using the 'Easy' setting on your camera. This will lock all functions to automatic and you can move on to manual settings when you feel ready.

The High-speed Shutter

Another control over the amount of light used to form the picture is the *high-speed shutter*.

This control allows you to grab each frame of video at a specified speed. It's a good tool for videoing fast action, such as sport or dance.

If you look frame by frame at fast action recorded at the standard shutter speed, you'll see that each individual frame of video has a blurred image because the subject is moving faster than the camera can capture it. When you play back this image, it looks fine because the eye gets the sensation of speed and you don't notice the blurs.

But if your aim is to analyse the motion carefully, to improve your golf swing or find out just where that gymnastics tumble went wrong, you need to see the image clearly in each frame.

You can achieve this by increasing the shutter speed. The speeds available in high-speed shutter mode vary from camera to camera, but you'll notice you can get speeds from 1/50 sec. to 1/8000 sec. on some cameras.

As you increase the shutter speed, you increase the speed of action which you can capture clearly. This lets you record an exact unblurred image in every frame.

However, because you're recording very tiny grabs of time with this method, using high-speed shutter means that you'll have gaps in the action. When you play back something which was recorded

Action shutter: I use high-speed shutter when I'm shooting sports in particular because it enhances subject movement and decreases depth of field. Beware of using shutter under fluorescent lighting as it can alter white balance noticeably (especially while spooling).

Gordon Peters, Cameraman, Channel 7 News, Bundaberg.

Walter Locke ready for capturing fast action shots. (Courtesy of Arlington Community Media Inc. [ACMi])

in high-speed shutter, it will look stilted because there's a distinct jump from each frame to the next. There'll be no blurring in the image to smooth those transitions. You'll have more of a high-speed *stutter*.

The other important factor is that the higher the shutter speed, the less amount of light can get into the camera to form the image. So the faster the shutter speed, the darker the picture will be. For this reason, high-speed shutter works best in a brightly lit space, and is pretty useless in darker areas.

Confusing Buttons

You may find that high-speed shutter and manual iris control are operated by the same button on your camera. This double-function button can cause disasters for the inexperienced user.

If you're trying to alter the manual iris setting but are changing the high-speed shutter by mistake, you may get quite mystified by what you see happening to your image.

If you find the picture getting much darker than you think it should be, check whether you're accidentally altering the high-speed shutter. This is one instance when studying both your camera manual and the markings on your camera body makes good sense.

Gain

Sometimes you're in a low-light situation where even the largest aperture opening isn't good enough and you just can't add lights—either you don't have them, there's nowhere to plug them in, or the person in charge of the space has said no.

In a case like this, you can make use of the *gain* function.

The gain allows the camera to electronically boost the brightness level of the signal it is processing.

Gordon Peters, Cameraman, Channel 7 News, Bundaberg.

Don't use gain unless you have to. Gain should be called grain because that's what it does to your video.

It does this internally—with no added light—and the picture is more acceptable.

There's a trade-off for boosting the gain, though. Your picture will look grainier and it won't copy or edit as well.

Often cameras have these gain settings:

0 dB   which means there's no additional gain inserted, operation is normal.

6 dB   which means the video signal is boosted a bit. Try to get by with this level if you can.

12 dB   which means the gain is boosted quite a lot. This can give you a very grainy picture (covered with random red dots) and should only be used when it's essential to get the shot. It won't edit well.

18 dB   occurs on only some cameras. Be very reluctant to use this one. Wait until you have to record paintings in a cave!

Richard Fitzpatrick, Cameraman, Digital Dimensions.

On a lot of the digital cameras, we shoot on –3 dB. It gives you better definition.

Your camera may allow you to select other gain settings via the camera menu—for example, 3, 6, 9, 12, 15 and 18. Some cameras even have hypergain—36 dB.

Before you go boosting the gain, though, make sure you really are on the largest aperture possible and not accidentally on high-speed shutter.

Night mode will give you an image in very dark circumstances, but it will look overall green and can be quite jumpy. Good for spy movies!

Inserting the Videotape

There's a button on the camera labelled *open/eject* or just *eject*. Once you push it or slide it sideways, you can gently pull open the side of the camera. You may hear a cute little 'bing', and the tape carriage will rise up and pop open. (Some tiny cameras open out the bottom instead of the side.)

You insert the videotape cassette into the carriage slot, making sure that the arrows on the cassette are pointing towards the inside of the camera and the clear plastic windows on the tape cassette are facing the outer cover of the camera.

Then you gently press the tape carriage closed (noting the spot which says 'press here' or 'don't press here') and the tape carriage clicks shut and then retracts back into the camera body of its own accord. (DON'T push it in!) You'll hear a marvellous series of little whirrs and clicks. When they finally stop, the cassette is loaded and the videotape inside has been laced up around the head drum. Then you snap shut the outer casing.

The camera is now ready to record an image.

To get the tape out of the camera, press the same eject button and reopen the camera's side. You'll hear some more whirring and clicking and you'll be re-presented with your tape.

The tape will only go in if it's oriented correctly.

Inserting the Disk or the Flash Memory Card

If your camera records to an optical disk, you follow a similar procedure but with fewer clicks and pings.

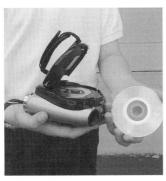

The camera records on mini DVDs.

Jake loads his camera.

Jake Perry records playground scene with Oscar Boots.

Flash memory card. (Courtesy of University of La Verne, California)

Take care not to put your fingerprints on the disk, and always put the disk back in protective casing once you remove it from the camera.

If your camera records to a flash memory card, find the right slot, orient the card correctly and slip it in.

Laura O'Neill does interior shots for *Ethiopian Australian Story.*

Hard Drive Cameras

If your camera records to an internal hard drive, you don't need to insert anything BUT you should make sure that you've got enough space on the drive for your shoot. Going out with a hard drive loaded with material you don't want to erase because you haven't yet downloaded it is…well, I'll let you finish this sentence.

Recording

Your camera's power switch may have a dial with a number of positions on it. First off, you should set this dial to *Camera* (not *Lock* or *Photo* or *VCR*).

First turn the camera on.

Set the power switch to camera, not VCR.

Then slip your right hand up under the camera grip strap and use your thumb to press the little flat record button.

This is a most unsatisfying button. It barely moves. It never clicks aloud or gives your thumb a sensation that it's affected anything underneath it. It gives no sign of response at all.

Consequently people sometimes think that they need to hold it down to keep the recording going. This isn't true.

Once you press the button, you should see a message in the viewfinder which confirms that the camera is recording—usually it's the letters REC—letting you know for sure this show is on the road.

As soon as the camera is recording, you should move your thumb aside so you don't accidentally put the camera in and out of record mode by unconsciously changing the pressure of your thumb. (It's a sensitive switch, even though it's unsatisfying.) Even if you like special effects, you don't want to strobe things now.

There's often a thumb rest next to this smooth switch, and sometimes it's ridged so you can easily feel the difference. That's where your thumb should be for the rest of the recording session.

So there you go!

The camera is recording and you now know how to zoom in and out, and how to change the brightness of the image by either adjusting the aperture or engaging the gain.

Stopping the Recording

You stop recording by putting the camera into pause mode. This is done by re-pressing that smooth little record button near your thumb.

When you pause a tape camera, the tape will remain laced around the heads in exactly the same position, waiting for you to begin your next shot. If you press the record button again, the camera will make a beautiful, technically clean edit and the transition (change) to the next shot will look as good as if it had been edited in a proper edit system.

In-Camera Editing

You can make use of the camera's capacity to do clean edits by planning out every shot of your program ahead of time, and then recording your material step by step in the exact program sequence.

You can put together a whole piece this way, and save yourself heaps of time in the edit room. But you have to be quite good at your camera work so every shot is acceptable.

And you have to move quickly through your shot list, because the camera won't stay in pause mode for long.

After about five minutes, the camera will go out of pause mode and into stop. In stop mode the videotape is no longer laced around the record heads, and the tape is ready to be ejected from the camera.

If you go back into record mode from stop mode, the tape may not lace up on the record heads in exactly the same position, so instead of a clean edit point there will be a visual disturbance between the previous shot and the next one.

When you're doing in-camera editing, a glitch like this mars your product.

However, being disciplined with in-camera editing can liberate you from hours and hours of editing on those home videos.

Looking up HD lens. (Courtesy of Metro Screen)

You take one good shot, then pause and line up your next good shot before pressing record, then pause again to line up and focus the next shot, and press record again and so on through the birthday party, family reunion or whatever. That way you can make the relatives happy by giving them all DVDs of the event without committing yourself to a nightmare of editing out useless shots and other camera mistakes.

Rachel Masters, Corporate Training Coordinator, SBS.

Watch out! Some cameras backspace a little before they begin to record. You can test if your camera does this by recruiting the help of a friend and getting him/her to count to ten, on camera. At ten, you pause the camera. Then ask your friend to begin counting again, and you recommence recording. When you play back the tape, you'll see how many seconds the camera has cut out, and then you'll know what its 'roll-up time' is.

Rollback Time

Something to be careful about with in-camera editing on a tape camera is *rollback time*.

Just like your car at an intersection, cameras can't go from stop to record speed in an instant. So when you go from pause to record, they roll the tape backwards a little, come forwards getting up to speed, and then go into record mode when they're synched up to the signal of the previous shot and just *before* the tape gets to the end of the recorded signal.

This means that you lose a little bit of the video at the end of the previous shot. It also means that the recording doesn't happen exactly when you press the record button.

So you need to allow for both of these things.

First, always shoot a video *buffer*—that is, a little bit more video than you need at the end of the shot. If you're working with a presenter, train this person to finish the commentary, then just stand still so you don't get sideways eye motions or other silly face or body movements during that buffer time. You've seen those reporters on TV who go into freeze mode at the end of their report?

If you're recording an action, keep recording for a bit after the action is completed.

Then know your camera. Work out how long it takes to get into record mode once you press the record button. Once you're sure of how your camera handles rollback, don't give the signal for speech or action until after those seconds are over. That way, your in-camera editing will work, and you won't have a story which is missing bits, as if some mysterious video moths chewed holes in it when you weren't looking.

Standby

Some cameras go into standby mode to save battery power if they haven't been used to record anything for a few minutes.

In standby, the viewfinder goes black but the camera is still receiving a little power. To get it going again, press the standby switch and the camera should come fully on again immediately. Or on some cameras you just lightly touch the LCD screen to wake them up.

Other cameras go to *Stop* and turn themselves off.

Playback Mode

You can use the camera as a playback machine, too. Once you finish recording, turn your power switch dial to the *VCR* or *Play* position.

Now you can operate all the same functions you have on your home VCR: play, fast forward, rewind, search forwards, search backwards, pause and stop.

You can watch the playback in the tiny viewfinder, on the LCD screen, or you can connect the camera to a monitor or TV and watch it all on the big screen.

To send the image to a monitor, use the AV cord that came with the camera. It's that triple cord which has three RCA connectors at one end but only one mini connector at the other end.

Connect the single end to *AV out* on the camera. You may have to look hard for this connection point. It's often hidden away behind a little unobtrusive door.

Now attach the yellow connector at the other end to *video in* on the monitor. That cord will convey the picture. For sound, attach the red and the black (or white) connectors to the two *audio-in points* on the monitor. If the monitor has only one *audio-in*, well, you can only use one connector, or you can get a Y-Connector to combine the two signals.

Connection points can be at either the back or the front of the monitor. If you have two sets of inputs, you'll need to select Video 1 or Video 2 to select the correct input for your signal.

Make sure the TV/monitor is turned on and is set to the video (auxiliary) channel—not to a TV station—and press play on your camera.

Hey, how's that? Are you thrilled? It's such a high the first time anyone gets picture and sound!

If you found that you had stretches of video which surprised you, long shots of your own feet and the pavement as you walked along, and then

Joe Clover plays back his shots to make sure he has all he needs. (Photo by Nancy Clover)

nothing of the shot you thought you'd gotten, don't panic. It's just that you fell into the most common of all video traps: recording when you thought you were in pause, and not recording when you thought you were on. You know what we call those shots? Spare *foot*age!

Have you had enough? If so, close the book and have a good play with the camera. That's the surest way to learn.

If you can deal with more at this point, the next chapter addresses quite a few more camera essentials, like focus, depth of field, colour temperature, white balance, black balance and the use of filters.

2

IMAGE CONTROL

Now you know how to get the camera up and running, the next step is to be able to get the image that suits your production.

There are a number of variables in recording a video image. The most obvious one is focus—you can have an image that's clear, soft or downright blurry. There are times when you might want each of these. But you need to have enough knowledge of the camera so you can *choose* the image quality, rather than getting lumbered with results you don't want.

Adjusting the focus so it's just right. (Courtesy of Film & TV, Central TAFE, Perth, WA)

Focus

In a correctly focused image, the *subject* looks sharp and clear, and has well-defined edges. This applies whether you're doing a panorama scene or a close-up of a tiny detail.

If other parts of the image are softer or blurry, the well-focused part draws the viewer's attention to the subject of the shot.

Focus is directly related to the distance between the subject and the camera lens.

If the camera is moved closer to the subject, or if it is moved further away, the focus setting may have to be changed.

Automatic Focus

Your camera will probably be in auto focus mode when you turn it on. That means the camera will adjust the focus for you, from shot to shot.

When you're just learning to handle the camera and taking your first images, it's easier to use auto focus. But as your confidence increases, you should learn to manually focus the camera for those times when auto focus can't give you what you want.

HOW DOES AUTO FOCUS WORK?

Auto focus works by sending an infra-red beam out from the front of the camera. The beam hits the 'subject' and bounces back to a beam sensor, also on the front of the camera. Then the auto focus circuitry calculates the distance between the subject and the camera and adjusts the lens accordingly.

The problem is that the system has no judgment. Auto focus has no way of knowing what your subject is, so it assumes that your subject is in the centre of the frame. In most cases this is a safe assumption. Some cameras have a couple of settings, so you can choose for auto focus to work using the exact centre of the picture or using a wider general centre area. However, if your subject isn't within those confines, auto focus will set the lens according to whatever *is* in the centre of the frame, no matter how irrelevant that object is.

That's why there are many times when auto focus gives you the wrong focus setting. For example:

With a landscape shot, the infra-red beam goes out and never comes back. Malcolm Foreman on a doco shoot for tav productions, The Grampians, VIC. (Photo by Neil Smith)

FOCUSING FOR TOO CLOSE A DISTANCE

There's a chain link fence between you and the geese at the animal park. The camera is resting on your shoulder. As you breathe, the camera moves slightly up and down. With each breath, the heavy-gauge chain link fence wire crosses the centre of the frame.

Result: The focus keeps shifting between your close-up of the goose and a sharp picture of the fence wire. Your audience feels confused and nauseated.

   OR

You're at the top of a tower building doing a cityscape shot. The windows haven't been washed for a long time.

Result: The camera focuses on the window dirt rather than the Opera House.

FOCUSING FOR TOO GREAT A DISTANCE

You have positioned the art gallery curator at the left side of the frame, and asked her to gesture towards a statuette beside her at the right of frame. But in centre frame, quite a distance in the background, there's a small decorative table against a wall.

Result: The beam targets the table, and the camera focuses clearly on it, while the presenter and the statuette are fuzzy in the foreground.

Never shoot on auto. There's a tiny chip in your camera which will guess what you're shooting. But in your head you have the best computer that can be made by unskilled labour.

Tim Rooney, Portland Community Media.

SEARCHING FOR FOCUS

You're doing a pan along a line of people in the cafeteria, but you feel self-conscious about being there with the camera so you're standing at the other side of the room. This means you've had to zoom in all the way to get the close-up face shots you want for your story.

The students are standing in clusters, rather than in a rigid primary school type line, so some are closer to you and some are further away. During your pan, as each person crosses the centre of frame, the auto focus gets a message that the distance to the subject has changed.

Result: The focus control is continually *searching*, moving the lens in and out. The shot looks ridiculous. Again, your audience is nauseated.

OTHER AUTO FOCUS GREMLINS

Autofocus can give you the wrong results if:

Something passes between you and your subject.
Your image has very bright lights in it.
Your subject has very reflective surfaces, like chrome or glass.
Your image has very little contrast.
Your subject is on a slant away from you.
You're operating in low light.

TECHNICAL DIFFICULTIES

You can also get auto focus problems if:

Something (e.g. your hand) is blocking the sending or receiving of the beam.
Or the beam sensor gets dirty.

Paul Sosso,
Editor/
Producer.

You need to know your camera. If you don't, you're setting yourself up for problems in postproduction.

So, although people are often delighted that their cameras have auto focus, using it sometimes gives them poor results.

However, if your eyes have difficulty seeing the image clearly on the small viewfinder, or even the LCD screen, and you understand how auto focus works and make sure you allow for its limitations, it can be a useful tool.

Nevertheless, if you can see clearly, you're better off learning how to focus and relying on your own skill.

Colin Holmes,
Videographer.

Use the camera on automatic until you see what it can do; then practise, practise, practise until you can find all the buttons (exposure, shutter speed, white balance, focus, etc.) without reference to the manual.

Face Detection

Face detection is a feature that allows the camera to recognise a human face when it's in your image and automatically adjust focus, colour control and brightness so the face is clear and sharp. It's claimed that face detection will work in group shots of up to eight faces.

Manual Focus

To switch your camera to manual focus mode, you'll need to find the right switch, button or menu item. Make a quick examination of your camera body, including the side section revealed when you open the LCD screen. If you don't find anything labelled *Focus*, haul out your camera manual and search the index for the page on manual focus.

Once you switch the camera to manual focus you should see an indication in your viewfinder and on your LCD screen. You might see *MF* or there might be a tiny symbol of a hand with an *F* in it or a symbol of a mountain range.

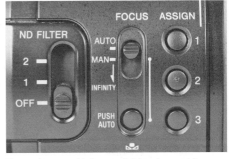

Note: You can't switch to manual focus if your camera is set to 'Easy' mode or is in auto lock mode.

Next, you need to find the method for changing focus.

You need to move this focus switch to get manual focus.

Changing the focus is accomplished by altering the distance between the camera's lens and its light-gathering surface inside the body of the camera.

To do this, the lens is eased forward or back until the right focus is achieved.

You adjust focus by turning the focus ring located at the front end of the lens barrel. Or your camera may have a small dial that you rotate to make your image come in clear.

If you're unlucky, it could be a matter of pushing a spot on your LCD screen. (Groan!)

Settings for different distances between your subject and your camera are usually written in both metres and feet and range from about 1 metre (3 feet) to infinity.

To change the focus, turn the focus ring at the front of the lens barrel.

Though some people may use these numbers when shooting a rehearsed movement (as in a drama), most people just adjust the focus until the subject looks clear to them on the LCD screen or on their larger field monitor.

How to Manually Focus a Video Camera

Zoom in and focus—it's as simple as that.

Imagine that you're taping an interview with someone and you want to be able to alternate between a long shot, a close-up and a mid-shot. Because you'll be recording non-stop through the whole interview, you'll need to avoid any awkward moments when your subject is out of focus.

Before you do any recording, this is how to ensure good focus for all your shots:

1. Set up your camera in relation to your subject.
2. Zoom in all the way to the eyes or mouth of your subject.
3. Adjust the focus until the image is as clear as possible.
4. Zoom out.

You're now ready to shoot. You'll find that the image is correctly focused for every type of shot of that subject.

Zoom in and focus. Allan Collins, freelance cinematographer.

For correct back focus, the white line should usually be aligned with the triangle.

Kimberley Brown, Editor/ Camera Operator.

Fifty per cent of the job is having creative knowledge and 50 per cent is having technical knowledge. There's a good balance between the two.

As long as both you and your subject stay at the same distance from each other, you won't have to focus again.

Fixing a Back Focus Problem

If you've zoomed in and focused clearly, but you find that as you zoom out the image goes out of focus, then you have a back focus problem. This is a hazard exclusive to zoom lenses.

On a consumer-level camera, you won't be able to do this adjustment, but on a more expensive camera you may be able to.

The back focus adjustment is done at the back of the lens barrel, near the camera body. Because most of the time the back focus lens is meant to stay in one place, you have to untighten a little lever in order to move this ring.

To adjust the back focus, zoom in on your subject again and make certain that it's in clear focus. Then zoom out all the way and turn the back focus ring until you get as sharp a picture as possible.

Once you're happy with the adjustment, carefully twist the lever back in tight so the back focus doesn't get accidentally disturbed.

Macro

Macro allows you to get a clear focus on subjects that are within 1 metre (3 feet) of the camera.

On consumer-level cameras, to get macro to work, you just need to remember two things:

1. Make sure the camera is in auto focus mode.
2. Zoom out all the way. (I know this is a bit counter-intuitive.)

Then you can move your camera right in so the lens is almost touching your subject and you can still get a beautifully clear shot.

Macro is great for shots of flowers, the lettering on wedding invitations, tiny details on objects or anything else that you want to enlarge on the screen.

On professional cameras, the macro adjustment ring is sometimes located right next to the back focus ring, and people do mistakenly untighten the little back focus lever and turn both rings around together. Needless to say, this creates more focus problems.

To use macro, the zoom still needs to be in the wide angle position (zoomed out all the way).

Then all you do is turn the macro ring until you get a clear focus on your subject, or that part of your subject you want to show clearly.

The one thing you have to watch when using macro is that putting the object so close to the lens tends to block out the light needed to illuminate it. Careful positioning of a side light, or working near a window, can help.

Don't be tempted to move an intense light in too close to the camera, though. You could melt your lens hood—I've seen it happen!

MAKE FRIENDS WITH MACRO. Once you get to know macro you'll use it often. I named my dog Macro. I use macro to ensure an accurate rack-focus without changing my framing. Set up your shot, then focus on your background with your focus ring. Engage macro and adjust it until your foreground object is in focus. Reverse the technique for a rack-focus from foreground to background. This method, as opposed to a regular rack-focus, minimises any change in framing. Macro will also give you a great focus effect when you zoom.

Gordon Peters, Cameraman, Channel 7 News, Bundaberg.

Will Miller uses macro focus to shoot *The Adventures of Harry the Horse*.

Close-up of Harry's face. Harry gets his 15 minutes of fame.

The Connection Between Zoom and Focus

Once you've had some practice operating the zoom and the focus, you'll probably notice there's a connection between the two.

In the wide-angle view (zoomed out all the way), you can turn the focus ring or dial all the way around in either direction and see very little change in the clarity of the image in the viewfinder. You'll probably find the picture looks pretty good no matter what the focus setting.

But in telephoto (zoomed in all the way), you'll see that a very slight movement of the focus control

When possible, stay zoomed out all the way and move your camera closer to the subject, rather than moving in. This will result in a larger depth of field, which will improve focus/sharpness of your shot, improve exposure by letting more light in, and minimise shaking. Zooming in has the opposite effect—lets LESS light in, magnifies shaking, and reduces depth of field.

David Shaheen, Videographer/ Teacher.

Courtesy of University of La Verne, California.

makes a dramatic change to the image, and that it will vary from being sharp and clear to being entirely blurry. In fact, there will be only one position where the focus looks right.

In practice, this difference means that focusing is far more critical in telephoto than in wide angle.

Good Focus Practice

When you have only one subject and it's staying still—and so are you—you can set the focus by zooming in and focusing on your subject at the beginning of your shot (or your shoot) and know that it will be right for any zoom position you later choose.

In a situation where each shot is done at a different distance to the subject, you need to check your focus again each time.

If your subject is moving, you need to have learned for sure which way to turn the focus ring so the shot comes rapidly into focus. You don't want to be searching back and forth for focus while recording your shot.

Focusing for More Than One Subject

Often, however, there'll be more than one subject which you're expected to cover.

Have a look at the next drawing, shown in the 'plan' convention—which means it's shown as if you're viewing the scene from above.

This drawing indicates that each person or object which is the same distance away from the camera will require the same focus setting.

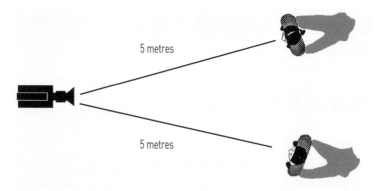

5 metres

5 metres

Same distance to subjects = same focus setting.

However, if you have more than one subject and they're at different distances from the camera, the correct focus adjustment for each close-up will be different, and you'll have to rehearse your shots carefully so you can smoothly refocus as you change from one person to the next.

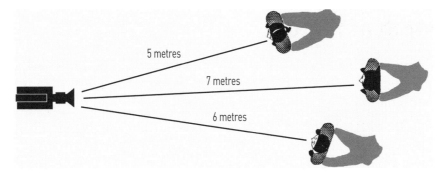

Different distances to subjects = refocus for each subject.

Focus Emergencies

If your subject makes a sudden, unrehearsed movement, and you're zoomed in for a close-up, most likely your shot will go blurry. Zoom out immediately and stay on wide angle until the person settles down into a new position. Only then will it be prudent to attempt another close-up requiring careful focus.

Push-Auto Focus

Some cameras have a *push-auto focus* button. If you need to find focus very quickly, you can engage the camera's auto focus function briefly by holding in this button. The camera will do its best to find the right focus. When you release the button, the camera's focus stays where it is, and the focus mode goes back to manual.

If your subject keeps moving, stay on wide angle.

Difficult Focus Situations

In a pre-rehearsed action with a moving subject, reference to the focus ring markings might help you guarantee a clear focus when the subject reaches its final predetermined position. However, you may still find that following by eye and synchronising the movement of the focus ring with the changing image in the viewfinder is the most practical and effective method of operation. Remember, in video what you see is what you get.

With subjects that constantly move, such as dancers, close-ups in good focus are nearly impossible. Only with very careful rehearsals could you expect to do well-focused close-ups. This is due to depth of field.

NAIDOC Day performance at Long Bay Gaol, Sydney, NSW. (Photo by Michelle Blakeney)

Depth of Field

You now know that focus is related to the distance between the subject and the lens. There will be one focus setting which is the best for a subject at any particular distance.

But it's also true that both before and after this position (both closer and further away) there's a certain range of distance within which focus is still acceptable. This range, from front to back, is known as the *depth of field*.

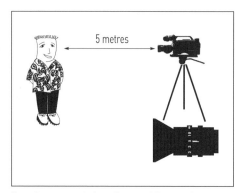

Focus is set correctly for a distance of 5 metres from the camera.

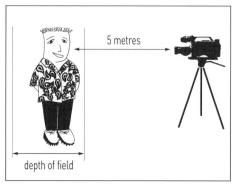

The depth of field is the range of distance, both front and back of the subject, within which focus is acceptable.

Lens Angle Affects Depth of Field

Wider lens angles give a greater depth of field. This means that when the camera is zoomed out all the way, your subject will be able to move forwards and backwards across a considerable range and still be in focus.

Narrower lens angles (especially telephoto) give a smaller depth of field. As you zoom in, the range of acceptable focus for your subject will decrease. When you're zoomed in all the way on a close-up shot, the depth of field will be smallest.

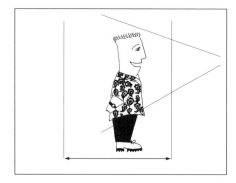

Depth of field on wide angle (zoomed out).

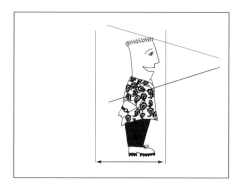

Depth of field on telephoto (zoomed in).

Iris Setting Also Affects Depth of Field

The wider the aperture (the more open the iris), the smaller the depth of field.

This means focus will be more problematic in low light conditions where the iris will need to be opened wide. You'll find that your subject won't be able to move forwards or backwards very far without going out of focus.

Depth of field with a wide open iris.

Depth of field with a nearly closed iris.

Telephoto Lens and Wide Open Iris Combined

The combination of telephoto lens (zoomed in all the way) and a wide aperture (big iris opening) gives you the smallest depth of field of all.

This is the hardest situation for shooting action over which you have no directorial control, because very small movements forwards or backwards will cause focus difficulties.

For example, if you're taping a singer in low light at a night-time outdoor concert, and you have the lens in telephoto to give you a close-up of his face on the screen, you'll find that if he sways only slightly forwards or backwards with the feel of the music, he'll go in and out of focus.

There's not much you can do. Your work will look awful and people won't be able to understand why you didn't just focus the camera.

Don't hang back and zoom way in. It's preferable to get close to the stage so you have a better depth of field. Johnny G., Dorado. (Photo by Ben Lipsey)

To retrieve the situation, you can stay on a wider angle shot, and then move your camera in closer to the stage when that song ends. But it's times like this that make you wonder why you got into video in the first place.

> **For better depth of field in low light conditions, you should try to either get in close to your subject so you can stay on the wide-angle lens, or add lights so you can use a smaller aperture.**

Desperately Seeking Depth of Field

On the other hand, sometimes you may *want* a narrow depth of field. Because many of the new consumer-level cameras have lenses that give a very deep depth of field, doing a pull-focus can be hard to set up. However, if you add a neutral density filter, you can aim to get to *f*2.8 so you'll have shallower depth of field and then do some arty shots.

Aperture Priority/Shutter Priority

Some cameras are automated to the extent that you can decide what function you want most and set that one, and the camera will adjust all the other function settings accordingly.

For example, if your main concern is to freeze the motion in the image because you're a physiotherapist or sports teacher and you're doing motion analysis, you can tell the camera to prioritise the high-speed shutter setting. The camera will then adjust the iris and other functions to suit the high-speed shutter setting you've selected.

On the other hand, if you're mainly concerned with getting the greatest depth of field because you're videoing dancers who will be coming forwards and backwards in the frame and you need them to always be in focus, you can tell the camera to prioritise the aperture setting, and the camera will make all the adjustments needed to the other functions.

Ernst Hadenfeld, former Chief Engineer, AFTRS.

Another solution to improve depth of field under low light levels is to increase the camera's video gain from 0 dB (normal operation) to +6 dB or +12 dB. In the +6 dB setting you can increase the iris setting by a factor of 2, for instance from *f*2.8 to *f*4.0, without lowering your camera's video signal.

Colour Temperature

Different light sources have different colour temperatures.

We don't notice this because our eyes automatically adjust to the light source we're in and they represent colours correctly most of the time. (Still, if you're older than Generation X, you may have had the experience of going to a shopping mall wearing a red shirt and having it appear to turn purplish once you got inside.)

The colour temperature of light is measured in degrees Kelvin, which is written as K.

Colour Temperatures of Different Light Sources

Incandescent lights for video studio use have a standard colour temperature of 3200K. Portable video lights also run at about 3200K. This light has a reddish tinge to it.

Common home light bulbs are incandescent, too, but usually have a lower rating, like 2850K.

Fluorescent lights have a wide range of colour temperatures, but the ones video people come across frequently are those used in schools, which are usually around 4200K, and have a greenish tinge.

CFLs (*compact fluorescent lights*) have about the same colour temperature as the common incandescent home light bulbs they are replacing. But they can also be purchased in higher Kelvin temperatures for *bright white* and *daylight*.

Sunlight spans a wide range of colour temperatures, but in the middle of a clear sunny day it's generally about 5500–6500K, and skylight can be upwards of 10 000K. This light has a bluish tinge to it.

A CFL (compact fluorescent light) runs much cooler and longer than a normal tungsten bulb, but it can have a similar colour temperature.

However, you know from your own experience that *dawn and dusk* have redder light. As the sun goes down, your image will shift in colour unless you counteract this.

On cloudy days the colour temperature outdoors can be as high as 7000K.

Shade colour temperatures are different from the sunny positions next to them, so you need to allow for this when you move from one recording position to another.

The *sodium vapour* lamp used for street lighting produces a broken-spectrum light that will drastically affect the colours of your image. You may choose to avoid such lamps.

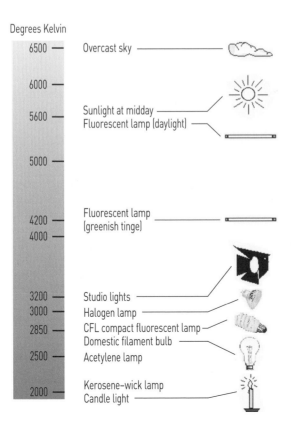

Degrees Kelvin

6500 —	Overcast sky
6000 —	
5600 —	Sunlight at midday / Fluorescent lamp (daylight)
5000 —	
4200 —	Fluorescent lamp (greenish tinge)
4000 —	
3200 —	Studio lights
3000 —	Halogen lamp
2850 —	CFL compact fluorescent lamp
	Domestic filament bulb
2500 —	Acetylene lamp
2000 —	Kerosene–wick lamp / Candle light

The Filter Wheel

Some cameras come with an inbuilt filter wheel that allows you to insert a colour filter behind the lenses, in the pathway of the light entering the camera. Its dial is usually found on the left side of the camera, close to the front.

The usual filters are 3200K for use with studio lights, 5600K for daylight, 5600K+ 25% ND (see below) for very bright daylight and C for closed.

You operate the filter by rotating the small serrated filter wheel dial until the number of the filter you choose appears to your view. Most often, there's a little list near the filter wheel to remind you which number goes with which filter.

The ND Filter

ND means *neutral density*. A neutral density filter reduces the *amount* of light passing through it without changing the *colour* of the light. When an ND filter is combined with a 5600K filter it's useful for 'taming' the overly bright areas of an image.

On very glary sunshiny shoots, like midday football games where the players have white on their uniforms, and for beach shoots and water shoots, the brightness of the light reflected off the white areas produces 'hot' spots in your image, and causes the iris to close down. The camera then registers these spots as *peak white* (the top level of brightness it can handle) and is forced to alter the black level of the image in compensation. Why?

This is due to the *contrast ratio*. The camera can only reproduce a certain range of gradations between white and black. When the peak white level is set unusually high, the details in the picture which would normally have appeared grey are lost to the viewer because they get reproduced as black. The definition in the darker, shadowy areas of the picture just can't be seen anymore.

Using an ND filter on a bright day allows you to get a fuller, more satisfying image which retains detail in the darker areas.

ND filters are available in different strengths, to suit different shooting conditions. Because there are lots of very bright shooting circumstances like snow, sand and water, it would seem that all cameras sold should come with an ND filter. But they don't.

If your camera doesn't have one, you can buy an ND filter from a camera shop and attach it to your lens barrel on bright days. You simply unscrew the lens hood, screw on the ND filter, and then put the lens hood back on.

Joseph Ford,
RMIT.

Chant this like a mantra every time you put your eye to the viewfinder: FILTER, FOCUS, FRAMING, *F*-STOP, CHECK, DOUBLE CHECK!

Don't forget to remove the ND filter when you're shooting indoors and in darker circumstances, or it will cause you to have to open your iris up more than you might like.

Choose the Filter First

If your camera does have a filter wheel, be sure to set the filter to the correct position *before white balancing* the camera. This will give you better colour results.

White Balance (WB)

Video cameras are made to reproduce colours accurately, but to do this they must be electronically alerted to the colour temperature of the light which is illuminating the subject. This is called *white balancing* the camera.

(You know how some labels never seem to fit quite right? I've always thought this process should be called *colour balancing*, because it's the colours that are being adjusted, but I guess it's called white balancing because the signal is being correctly referenced to white.)

How to Do a Manual White Balance

1. Set your camera to manual white balance mode. If the WB switch on your camera is on *Preset*, the camera can't do a manual white balance, so make sure to check the WB switch position.
2. Zoom in on a white card that is under the same light as your subject will be *or* put the white lens cap on and point the camera towards the source of light that will illuminate your subject.
3. Hold the white balance button down for a second or so (on some cameras), or until you get the *white balance completed* message in the viewfinder (on other cameras).

Storing a White Balance Setting

If your camera has the labels WB1 and WB2, it can remember two white balance settings at the same time, which can be very convenient if you're rushing through a shoot with both indoor and outdoor shots.

Bronwyn Gell does a white balance on the white lens cap. Hamilton Secondary College, Mitchell Park, SA.

Do a proper white balance under one of the light conditions with the switch set to WB1, and then do a second white balance under the other light condition with the switch in WB2. The camera will hold the memory of both white balances.

You won't have to re-white balance every time you change location, but you will have to remember to flip the switch from one setting to the other before you start shooting after each change.

Preset Mode

Some cameras have a *preset* white balance setting. In a situation where you're using only 3200K studio lights, you can switch the camera to *Preset* 3200K and you won't have to white balance.

Gordon Peters,
Cameraman,
Channel 7
News,
Bundaberg.

FROM A TO B: Most broadcast cameras have three white balance settings: Preset, WB1 and WB2. A handy trick is to white balance WB1 for light and WB2 for shade. This technique is sensational for days when patchy cloud interferes with the sunlight.

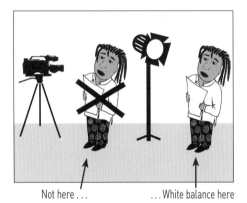

Not here . . .   . . . White balance here

Caution: Studio lights tend to slip to lower colour temperatures as they get older, so if you find that the colours in your shot look slightly off, do a manual white balance.

White Balance Mistakes

When you white balance, be sure to hold the white card under exactly the same light conditions your subject will be under. If the card is held closer to the camera, so it's not really in the shot's light, the camera may be influenced by some other light source and give you the wrong colour result.

You should always white balance the camera at the start of your shoot, and you must do it again any time you change light sources. If you don't, your picture could be tinged with an unrealistic colour.

If you're indoors and go outside without re-white balancing, the bride's dress will change from white to blue as she emerges from the church door.

If you're outdoors and go in without doing a white balance adjustment, your characters will suddenly look quite ruddy and the surrounding room will have a golden glow. (Sometimes you may do this deliberately—say you're shooting a breakfast scene and want it to have extra warm tones.)

If you go from the sun to a shade house and forget to white balance, darker-skinned people could appear to have bluish skin.

Once, the most frustrating thing about making a white balance mistake was that you were stuck with it—you couldn't correct it later. No matter how beautiful your shot was, it would look odd and unprofessional if its colour was off. Now, with digital editing systems, corrections can be made in postproduction. Don't let this knowledge make you get careless, though. It's ALWAYS easier to shoot something right than to have to fix it in postproduction! It's easier in time, money and stress—all important things to consider.

Problems with Automatic White Balance

Many cameras have an auto white balance function which continually assesses white balance and adjusts it automatically, even when you're in record mode. As long as your subject remains under only one light source, your picture will look okay.

However, if you pan from one colour temperature to another, as you would if you were panning across a classroom, from students who are illuminated by the overhead fluorescent lights to students lit by the sun coming through the window, the auto white balance mode will cause your picture to change colour in mid-shot as it senses the second light temperature. Again, that's not a professional-looking shot.

For the director, it's decision time:

- Is that pan really necessary?
- Or could you use just one wide shot?
- Or should you go for two separate shots, one white balanced for the students lit by the fluorescent lights, and a second shot white balanced for the students over near the windows who are lit by sunlight?

Creative Use of White Balance

You can deliberately trick the white balance of a camera by white balancing while showing the camera another colour. Then you can get some wild-looking pictures!

Throwing the white balance off deliberately like this will make the camera reproduce white as some other colour and change every other hue as well.

Chrominance: Skin tones are always my bottom line. You can cheat the white balance (by balancing on shades other than white) to give people warmer, colder or stranger looks. You may need to open the iris or lower the shutter speed for the camera to be able to balance on hues other than white, but it can produce the effect you're after—and remember to be consistent for continuity's sake.

Jason Benedek, Videographer.

You can *warm up* your video images by white balancing with a *quarter blue* gel or an *eighth blue* gel, instead of *white*, when manually white balancing.

Peter Thurmer, Hamilton Secondary College.

Black Balance

Some cameras also allow you to do a black balance. Usually this is done by flicking the white balance toggle switch in the other direction to the setting labelled BB. The camera will close its iris and balance its colour to the black it 'sees' within itself. You know it's finished when you get the 'completed' signal in the viewfinder. Black balancing should be done before white balancing, at the beginning of each shoot.

It's not necessary to black balance again when you re-white balance on the same shoot, but it doesn't do any harm.

Lens Hoods

The lens hood is a soft plastic, hard plastic, rubber or metal device attached at the front of your camera lens. It's used to shade the lens from sunlight, so you don't get flares in your image or small coloured artefacts from the sun hitting tiny dust particles on the surface of your lens.

Lens hoods come in many sizes and shapes. Your camera may have come with one, but if you attach a different lens to your camera, you may want to buy a different lens hood. Deep hoods are used for telephoto lenses and shallow ones for wide

Eddie Hanham uses his specially shaped lens hood, shooting a scene for *The Rainbow Boughquaker.*

Lyvern Myi,
Media Resource
Centre.

Avoid some lens flare by using your hand as an extension of the rubber lens hood.

angle lenses. You can get petal-shaped ones to give you better flare protection without impinging on the corners of your shot.

There are lots of lens hoods available via the internet, but you may have greater success the first time if you take your camera to a shop and try them for size before you buy one. The same goes for filters, unless you're certain of the size you need.

Filters

Filters are glass disks that screw on to the front of your lens barrel and alter the light entering the camera, thereby affecting the image the camera produces.

There's a wide variety of filters available from photography stores, and many are the right size for your video camera.

By using filters, you can make almost any alteration to the colour or distinctness of your image that you can imagine.

Colour Filters

There are filters that add a uniform colour across the whole image. You can use these to 'warm up' or 'cool down' the tone or mood of the image.

Or you can give the image an overall colour wash—make it magenta, yellow, green . . .

Graduated Filters

Some filters have a colour that is darker at one edge of the filter disc and lighter at the other, changing its depth of colour evenly across the filter.

These give a more intense colour to the top, bottom or side of your image (depending on how you orient the filter in relation to the lens), but contribute a tinge of that colour throughout the whole image.

Graduated filters can be used to intensify the sky colours on sunsets, for example.

Bi-coloured Filters

There are filters that can add two different colours to your image. They can simultaneously enrich the blue of the sky and the green of the land—or whatever you choose. You have to construct your shot to match the filter, though, or you may get a colour in the wrong place.

Star Filter

A star filter turns any very bright spot in your picture into a star (e.g. lights, headlights, reflections off glass). Some people like them and some people hate them, so they should be used with discretion.

They can make a group of children holding candles and singing carols look like they've just arrived from another sphere. Great for special effects on holiday tapes.

Polarising Filter

A polarising filter reduces or cuts out bright reflections and glare. It can let your camera see the fish swimming beneath the surface of a brightly reflective pool. It can heighten the drama of cumulus clouds in a bright sky.

Polariser: a polariser is an attachable lens filter which reduces reflection and glare from smooth surfaces like glass or water. Colours are more vivid when a shot is polarised. I ALWAYS use a polariser when I'm shooting outside.

Gordon Peters, Cameraman, Channel 7 News, Bundaberg.

Because a polarising filter is directional, you can adjust the degree of effect you want. If you want to get rid of all the glare, orient it one way; if you want to get rid of just some, give it a bit of a turn. You can keep turning it until it gets rid of no glare at all.

A polarising filter has no effect on colour balance.

Multiple Image Filter

If you're into drastically altering your picture, you can use filters that multiply your image across the screen.

So instead of one red Ferrari driving in, you can have five. And they can be driving in the top, bottom, sides and centre of your screen.

UV Filter

An ultraviolet (UV) filter absorbs ultraviolet radiation beyond the visible spectrum. A UV filter doesn't alter your image, but it's an inexpensive and effective way to protect your lens from dirt, fingerprints, raindrops, scratches and other damage. Lots of people keep a UV filter on their camera all the time, knowing that if it gets damaged it's far cheaper to replace it than it is to get a new camera lens. If you have a new camera, this should be the first filter you buy.

Digital Effects

Your camera has its own digital effects built in. A common range of in-camera effects are: sepia tone, black and white, mosaic, posterisation, cometing, negative image and mirror image doubling. However, all of these can be added at the editing stage as well.

With digital editing, your original video footage isn't degraded or shredded by the editing process, so good shots can be used again and again on many projects in the future. Over time, you're very likely to go back to a previous project to get some good shots you need for a new edit.

Bearing that in mind, weigh this up: although this time you want a certain effect on your shot, for another project you may not want that effect.

Another consideration with an effect like strobing is getting the timing of the effect just right.

Strobe is a series of still frames which are grabbed as the video is recording in real time. It gives the effect you may have seen when dancing under strobe lights. The speed of the strobe is variable, so it can be a rapid series of short quick shots, resulting in very little picture information being missing, or the individual freeze frames can be longer in duration, thus blocking out large chunks of the intervening action.

Say you want to strobe your friend as he plays his guitar and his offsider dances. If the strobe starts in the right spot it could look great. But if the strobe starts a mini-second earlier or later, the whole strobe can look awkward and less appealing.

Previewing the strobe effect before editing it can help you find exactly the best place and time to start the effect.

But if you've shot it strobed in the first place, you just *don't have* the missing bits, and you're stuck with whatever way it happened at the shoot.

Neal Ruckman,
Producer.

Shoot clean. Don't use in-camera effects.

With any of these effects, once they're recorded as part of the image, you can't get them off. That's why it's more prudent to shoot footage plain to start with, and add the effects in postproduction.

However, if you don't have access to video editing, or if you're shooting material for fun and laughs and you have no plan to use it in another way later, go ahead and add all the effects you want.

Superimposed Text

Nearly any camera these days allows the operator to add titles while taping. The titles can be an opening name for the program, like 'Lisa's Birthday Party' or 'Jack and Ginny's Wedding'. Spiffier set-ups can do rolls on the screen, so end credits can rise across the image, like you see on TV. Some cameras are even able to do key effects, so you can superimpose a sort of stencil of one image over another one. There's lots of scope for creativity with this.

But again, if you shoot things plain, you can still add titles in the editing phase.

Other Image Changers

There are many semi-transparent things which you can put in front of the lens. If the material is very close to the lens, so the lens can't focus on it but looks through it, you can get some cool effects.

One or two layers of black silk stocking stretched tightly across the lens (held in place with an elastic band or tape) can beautifully soften the image, making it look more romantic—good for topics dealing with memories, dreams, nostalgia.

If no one has black silk stockings (and who does these days?) try anyone's semi-sheer pantyhose and see what you get.

Other good materials to try are lightweight gauzes, and very fine fabrics.

And then there's the age-old trick with Vaseline (petroleum jelly). You smear Vaseline around the outer edge of a clear glass filter or a UV filter—NOT your camera's lens—and then attach this in front of your camera lens. You'll get an image with soft edges all around, like a photographic vignette—again, good for dreams and memories.

Use your imagination. Try lots of things. Create your own look. Be an initiator in the screen world!

Cleaning the Lens

No matter whether you want to reproduce life in the natural colours you see, or alter the image to make your own unique aesthetic statement, you need a clear lens. If there are fingerprints, dust, smoke, fluff, pollen, sea spray or hairs between the world and the camera, the truth of the image will be reduced, due to an inglorious lack of good housekeeping.

The first way to keep the lens clean is to put the lens cap on whenever the camera isn't in use. Shelter the camera from blowing dust, smoke and grit. Don't let sea spray or rain drops get to it. Don't let that toddler, with her peanut butter-smeared fingers, run up and touch it.

But sometimes lenses do get dirty, and you need to clean them before your next shoot.

Remember: Glass scratches easily. There are sharpnesses that you wouldn't suspect in ordinary cloth and paper tissues. So always clean your lens with the tissues that are sold in photography stores especially for lens cleaning.

You can buy a lens-cleaning kit. It has a soft brush for clearing away any major dust and grit. And it has a small bottle of lens cleaning fluid and the special super-soft tissues.

1. Brush or blow away any movable debris.
2. Wet the tissue with a few drops of lens cleaning fluid.
3. Start cleaning at the middle of the lens and make circular motions with the tissue until you gradually work your way to the outer edges.
4. Repeat the circular cleaning until the fingerprints and other marks are gone.
5. Don't try to scrub off the purplish coating! It's supposed to be there! It helps reduce unwanted internal light reflections in the lens system and also helps reduce flare.

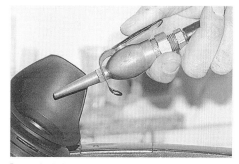

Pressurised air can remove fine particles from the lens without scratching it.

Suggestions from Rachel Masters

The Macro Lens

Practise using the *macro* lens of a camera by taping a short collage piece—no longer than 60 seconds or 20 shots—using in-camera editing. Shoot macro shots of interesting colours, shapes, features and textures. If you frame the shot very tightly, it will be hard to tell what each surface belongs to. What does the texture of brick look like in a close-up? What about grass? Try to shoot contrasting colours and textures and observe closely the way the light affects the focus and depth within the frame. Explore the use of focus. Perhaps you can save this original vision for an editing exercise later on.

Image Altering

Try putting an old mirror tile in a bucket of water and shooting the mirror reflection through the ripples in the water. Frame out the bucket so the final image is just the reflection.

Experimenting with Creative Images

Test the effects of shooting through glass, net, nylon, gauze, coloured plastic or the bottom of a glass tumbler.

Shoot through a frame made of aluminium foil, or through a long tube. Or cut out a paper mask frame and attach it to the front of the camera.

COMPOSITION AND FRAMING

3

Video is limited to presenting a flat image within a rectangular frame, and it's through this peephole that directors seek to convey to other people a believable three-dimensional world.

In the video past, now referred to as SDTV (Standard Definition TV), the frame had an invariable *aspect ratio* of 4:3. This meant that however wide the image was, its height was only three-quarters of that measurement.

Widescreen was the new kid on the block, with an *aspect ratio* of 16:9, more like the shape of the image at the movies.

Then came HDTV (High Definition TV), also shot in 16:9. But HDTV has a higher *resolution*, which means that the HDTV image has more picture information in it than SDTV.

Can these different frames mesh? And is framing up a shot different now?

When a 16:9 image is shown on a standard 4:3 screen, there are black bars across the top and bottom of the screen. This resulting image is sometimes referred to as *letterboxing* because the image appears as if it's seen through a wide slit which runs across the width of the screen.

Should they shoot 4:3 or 16:9? (Courtesy of University of La Verne, California)

**Richard
Fitzpatrick,**
Camera
Operator,
Digital
Dimensions.

Widescreen can be
upconverted to HDTV, but
it will never be as good as
something which was sourced
on HDTV.

The general public hates
letterboxing. They feel they're
not getting the whole picture.
But they are; it's just smaller
so you can show the entire
width of the shot. It's the
difference in the shape of the
16:9 frame that necessitates
the black bars at the top and
bottom.

Cinema mode on mini DV
cameras is bogus widescreen.
You get the look but you're
losing 25 per cent of your
vertical resolution. However,
you can buy a 16:9 optical
converter for your camera,
which lets you shoot true
16:9 and not lose the vertical
resolution. That will produce
a picture which looks fine on
widescreen TV.

Your camera may be switchable between 4:3 and 16:9 (*cinema*). If you choose to shoot in *cinema*, your image will have black bars across the top and bottom of the picture when it's shown on a standard TV set.

Some people like the *cinema* look and shoot this way to be arty. Others don't like to lose any part of the screen to black bars.

HD camera viewfinders can show you the 4:3 frame, in case you need to allow for it when you frame your shot.

Visual Language

In most screen productions, both time and space are compressed. But viewers are still meant to understand the story and become immersed in its telling.

A tall order? Yes. But over the years a vocabulary and grammar of visual images—a visual language—has developed. Knowing and using this language helps directors and camera operators convey their thoughts and their stories.

Composition

Part of visual language is screen *composition*.

Composition deals with the way the parts (*elements*) of the picture are arranged in relation to each other, and where each one appears on the screen.

The image can be made to look crowded or spacious, elegant or confusing. Some ways of arranging a picture are considered more beautiful than others, or more dynamic.

There are known ways to lead a viewer's attention into a picture and to guide the eye's gaze around the various parts of it.

Aesthetic and dramatic statements can be made by the specific arrangement of the elements in an image.

Julian Ellis,
Cinematographer.

What is your shot trying to say?

Shot Sizes

Another part of visual language involves *shot sizes*. Shot size is related to how much of the picture is filled by the subject.

When the subject fills the picture, it's considered to be a *closer* shot, even if the camera itself was located quite a distance away.

When the subject is just a small element in the picture, it's considered to be a *longer* (further away) or *wider* shot.

The size of the shot is important to the meaning of the shot, and to the meaning of the shots that come before or after.

There are standard shot sizes which directors call upon. The way a director chooses to use—or alter, or distort—these accepted shot sizes is part of the style and the meaning of the story.

Framing

A third part of visual language is the *framing* of the shot.

Framing refers to where the edges of the shot are placed.

You can compare it to the frame of a picture on the wall. If the framing is *tight*, there's not much space surrounding the subject. If the framing is *loose*, the edges of the picture are a little further out from the subject than they are in a conventional shot of that size.

The aspect ratio you use will definitely have an impact on how you frame your shots.

The frame can be placed in accordance to normal television practice, or it can deliberately be readjusted to make a statement using visual language.

For example, if a character in a drama is always framed at the very edge of the shot, or half out of it, it can visually underscore a view of this person as being marginal or eccentric.

In this way, the frame can contribute to the overall meaning of the piece.

Paul Gamst and Charlie Neff check framing choices for the next shot. (Courtesy of University of La Verne, California)

You've got to keep in mind the 4:3 screen when you frame a shot in widescreen, so the 4:3 shot can be used for those people who still have the standard TVs. The widescreen camera has a 4:3 safety zone which you can call up on the viewfinder to check how your framing will work on standard TV.

Richard Fitzpatrick, Camera Operator, Digital Dimensions.

The sooner we get out of the 4:3 world the better, because it's a different feel for composition.

Tianli Ma checks framing choices for the interview while the lighting is set up, Portland Community College.

Composition

By Tom Jeffrey, Producer/Director

The art of composition is in arranging the elements of a scene so the totality of the picture yields the desired effect.

In most cases, the aim is for a balanced and visually pleasing image, but sometimes a disharmonious composition is used to reinforce the tension or drama of the storyline.

In composition, there's nothing which is absolutely right or always wrong.

Balance

Balance depends on a number of factors, such as the size of the subject, the subject's position within the frame and the relationship of it to other objects or subjects.

Balance is usually desirable, but shots can be balanced and dull. A series of shots where the subject is always positioned in the centre of the frame won't hold the viewer's interest for long.

Angled shots often give more drama and dimension than full frontals.

Horizon or Horizontal Lines

In most pictures, there is a horizon line. The simplest horizon line will divide the picture into two equal parts. This can be very boring to the eye.

Boring   Preferred   Preferred

Vertical Lines

Similarly, a vertical line which divides the frame into two equal parts can be quite uninteresting. Shifting the emphasis of the verticals to the left or the right creates increased interest.

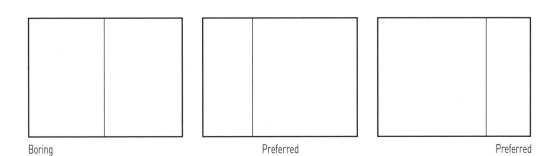

Boring   Preferred   Preferred

Thirds

From these ideas on horizontal and vertical lines, we can reach the notion of dividing the frame into *thirds*.

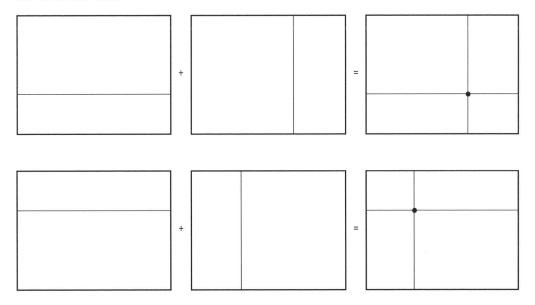

Where the lines intersect can be points of interest.

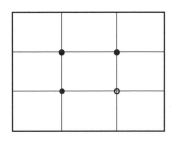

Diagonal Lines

Lines which dissect the frame at angles can heighten interest, heighten tension or increase the strength of a point of interest in the picture.

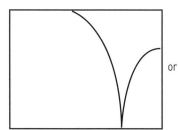 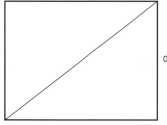 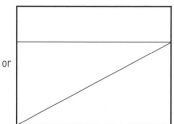 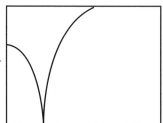 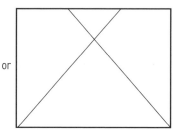

or

or

Diagonals can also curve.

or

Triangles

Triangles can give strength to a picture.

The face forms a natural triangle.

A group of people can make one too.

The classic mother and baby may be the best-known compositional triangle.

Perspective

Perspective, in its simplest descriptive form, is a combination of vertical and diagonal lines which give a three-dimensional look to the two-dimensional picture—creating a feeling of distance or space.

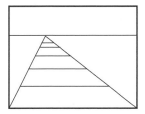 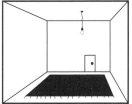

When directing, remembering the rules is very important, but also always remember that if the idea works for the script in hand, then it is right, so do it.

Ian Ingram-Young, Academy of Photogenic Arts.

Comparisons in Framing

Consider the following examples of possible shot compositions and framings. Don't have all the main picture elements equi-distant from each other.

Not so good   Preferred

To add visual interest and a sense of depth, arrange your subjects at different distances from the camera, taking care they don't conceal each other.

Not so good   Preferred

Left/right symmetry can be boring. Balance the elements in the frame in an asymmetrical fashion.

Not so good   Preferred

Keep the horizon above or below the centre of the frame.

Not so good   Preferred

When the subject is in the distance, a secondary object in the foreground can emphasise depth.

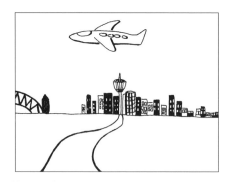

Not so good   Preferred

Parallel horizontal lines can shorten perspective and reduce the sense of depth. Try to place a diagonal against a horizontal.

Not so good   Preferred

Shooting two-dimensional objects, like paintings or signs, from a side angle will produce a distortion. Shoot them straight on unless the distortion is desired.

Not so good   Preferred

Composition for Reverse Shots for Dialogue

The subject facing the camera should get about two-thirds of the screen space.

Main shot   Reverse shot

Shot Sizes

The shot is the basic building block of a screen production. Through a succession of shots, the story emerges.

You might consider each shot to be like a phrase or sentence in a written text. Each shot is important and should be carefully designed to *say* what it's meant to say.

Choosing the right *shot size* is one of the key decisions the director makes. It's no good having a deep emotional scene shown in such a long shot that the people's facial expressions can't be interpreted. And it's no good having a shot so close that important body action is happening outside the frame.

The illustrations opposite show the standard shot sizes used in broadcast television. A fluent understanding of these shot sizes will help you plan your coverage, fill out your storyboard and call the shots on the day of the shoot.

You don't have to stick to these shots exactly. You can have a 'tight mid-shot' or a 'loose close-up'. But these terms give you a common set of reference points, shared by other people in the industry, which allow you to communicate the scenes in your head to the camera operator and other members of your crew.

As you can see, shot sizes are defined in relation to the human figure. With the exception of the term *close-up*, these terms aren't applied to other objects. You can't have a mid-shot of a car, for example—regardless of how personal your relationship is with your car!

There's one other shot size not shown here. It's the *wide shot*. The wide shot is the unhindered view you get looking at a scene. It can be very wide, like a view of the Sydney Harbour Bridge, or smaller, like the front of a cafe. In a wide shot, it's possible to see many human figures.

Richard Fitzpatrick, Camera Operator, Digital Dimensions.

Underwater camera work was traditionally wide shots, following shots. Now we apply standard shot sizes to build story sequences. Anyone who wants to do nature filming should apply the same traditional film techniques that are used in drama—that is, build up visual sequences. That's what producers look for in demo reels and in programs.

Very long shot (VLS)

Long shot (LS)

Medium long shot (MLS)

Mid-shot (MS)

Medium close-up (MCU)

Close-up (CU)

Big close-up (BCU)

Extreme close-up (ECU)

Framing

Here are some guidelines to consider when framing your subject.

Head Room

Shots of people are usually framed with a small amount of space above their heads. This space is called *head room*.

Shots need to have sufficient head room because when the top of the head is right against the top of the frame, it can produce a claustrophobic impression.

The most common framing error made by beginners is to put the subject too low in the picture, leaving heaps of head room. If nothing important is happening in the part of the frame that's above the head, this is wasted screen space and you could more productively either tilt down to show more of the person's body, or zoom in to give the viewer a better look at the subject's face.

Too little head room   Too much head room   Preferred

If the person isn't framed properly s/he will appear to head-butt the frame or to be hanging by the neck.

The Eyes

Generally speaking, you should aim to put the subject's eye level about two-thirds of the way up the screen.

The eyes play a very important role in communication, and eye signals and eye orientation are very closely connected to culture.

Although it's standard practice in television to use close-ups of subjects facing directly to the camera, with their eyes looking straight down the lens barrel, this is culturally inappropriate in many societies, including for some Indigenous peoples.

Because it's unacceptable in some cultures for a younger person to meet the eyes of an older person, the full-on gaze of an older person looking out from the television screen can cause some younger viewers to avert their eyes. If it's important for your audience to continue watching the screen, it makes sense to arrange your shot so they can comfortably do so.

It may be more acceptable to have the elder shown in three-quarter face (i.e. looking slightly away from the camera), or even in profile, so their eyes aren't directed straight at the viewer; in this way, the scene reflects the image the audience would normally see in daily life.

When you're making a program, consider the cultural mores of your subject and the needs and responses of your anticipated audience.

The Mouth

The mouth is also an important element in communication. The shot should usually be framed so the audience can get a good view of moving lips, so the mouth shouldn't be part-way off the screen.

Because many people watch mouth movements when they're listening to a person speak, profile shots—which show only the side of the mouth— can reduce the viewer's ability to catch the words the person is saying.

Any program which is aimed at an audience that includes hearing-impaired people (in fact, this is *every* audience) should be made with thought given to the placement and visibility of the talking mouth on the screen.

When framing an individual for a 'talking head' interview, place the tip of the subject's nose in the centre of the screen. This works equally as well if the subject is facing in any direction and also works if the shot is medium close-up, close-up, or extra close-up! It satisfies the need for looking room and the rule of thirds. It's quick and easy.

John Sirett, Videographer.

Looking Room/Talking Room

When a person is framed so they are looking off screen, there should be more space in front of the person's face than behind the head. This front space is called looking room.

When people are talking to someone off screen, as in a three-quarter close-up of a person in a talk show situation, there should be space in the frame in front of each of them for their words to flow out of their mouths. It may sound silly, but if the edge of frame is close to the front of their faces, it feels to the viewer as if their words will hit a brick wall and go nowhere.

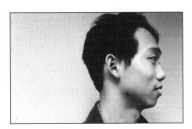

Not enough looking/talking space

Preferred

Walking Room

Similarly, a person walking across the screen needs to have walking room at the front.

Keeping walking room requires well-timed panning on the part of the camera operator. It's easy to go a little too slow and have the person appearing to head into a rigid barrier (the edge of the frame), and then jerk the frame over to try to catch up. This looks daggy. Shots with planned movements like this should be well rehearsed before they're recorded.

The concept of walking room also applies to other human movements, like skating, swimming, skiing and so forth.

And it also applies to vehicular movement—planes, trains and automobiles.

Framing for Widescreen

If you're shooting in widescreen (16:9), most of the same ideas on composition apply but in addition you have to consider who your audience will be. Will they be viewing your material on widescreen? Or will they still have to see it on standard 4:3 screens?

Some images just don't convert well from wide screen to 4:3.

This shot was framed for wide screen, the 16:9 aspect ratio.

A 4:3 centre cut of this frame looks ridiculous.

Some editors will pan and scan it into two shots like this.

Appropriate Size

Make sure the subject is shown at an appropriate size, so sufficient detail can be seen and important parts aren't chopped off by framing that's too tight.

Too small   Too tight   Preferred

Inclusiveness

Make sure that important elements are shown completely.

Element cut off   Element fully within frame

Masking

Don't let one important element obscure another main element, or its value will be reduced.

Element obscured   Preferred

Many thanks to Tom Jeffrey for his help in the preparation of this chapter.

4 THE CAMERA'S VIEW

The image is produced not only by the size and framing of the shot, and the arrangement of the elements within it. It's also greatly affected by *where* the camera is: its position relative to the subject, its height, its closeness to the action, and whether it's moving or not.

Edis Jurcys in the Gaza Strip, working on *Compassionate Listening* between Israeli and Palestinian people.

Chris Fraser,
Cinematography
Department,
AFTRS.

When there are people in the shot, the shot can support a bit of a shake. Shots with nobody in them should be dead steady.

Handholding

There are definite advantages to handholding. The camera is able to move fluidly through the location and even the action, changing its point of view, responding quickly to the unexpected, and even interacting with the subjects.

But there are difficulties with handholding, too. In the hands of a beginner, the resulting image can be shaky when the operator is standing still, and jerky when s/he attempts to walk.

A picture recorded with the lens on wide angle will look less bad, but if there's any attempt to use telephoto, the image will be unacceptably jittery.

A steady handheld camera can add production value to your program and save you time in the edit suite. A handheld moving camera allows you to capture action that might otherwise have taken a number of camera set-ups. Effectively you're editing in-camera, going from wide shot to close-up and back again, changing subjects, changing points of view, etc. With handholding you're able to follow actors and action, and shoot in confined spaces, saving time on location.

Andy Nehl, Head of Television, AFTRS.

Steadicam

Many people dream of getting a steadicam to smooth out their moving shots.

The original steadicam was a harness contraption that held the camera on a jointed arm, isolated from the movements of the camera operator. The view taken by a steadicam seemed to glide through the world, without the jolts of the operator's footsteps, or the rise and fall of the operator's shoulder as s/he breathed.

Steadicam revolutionised filmmaking from 1976 onwards, and was intrinsic to new styles in TV, like the NBC series *ER* and music videos.

Steadicams used to be so expensive it was a rare organisation that could build one into an annual budget round. Newer steadicams go for $600 or less, but that might still break the bank.

S-o-o-o-o . . . you should get *very* good at handholding. Practice does help. There are ways of steadying the camera by supporting your camera-holding arm with your other arm or by holding the camera with both hands and pressing your elbows into your chest for a firm shooting base.

And there are usually other objects nearby which will help you steady your shot. Rest your camera on a fence post, a stone wall, the roof of a car, a tabletop, a boulder, whatever you can find that's strong enough and that's less likely to wobble or move than you are.

There are also ways to walk more smoothly, by keeping your knees loose and slightly bent, so they absorb the shock of each footstep rather than transferring the jolt up through your body to the camera. You may look like a silent-film comedian, but people won't laugh when they see your footage. What's better, they won't moan or reach for the motion sickness tablets.

Chris Fraser demonstrates the use of an original steadicam, AFTRS.

You can stabilise the camera by propping your camera arm against your fist in your armpit. Allan Collins, Cinematographer.

There are even ways of breathing more shallowly so your shoulder doesn't rise and fall so much. In fact, for brief shots some camera operators take a big breath beforehand and don't breathe until the shot is finished.

Image Stabiliser (Steady Shot or Shake Reduction)

The image stabiliser in your camera is designed to reduce jiggly camera work by adjusting away your own personal shakiness. (This might sound good after a big night out.)

You may find you can choose different degrees of stabilisation:

- *Hard:* Gives a strong compensation for bumpiness, but doesn't work too well with panning shots.
- *Standard:* Activates the circuitry for normal handheld shake.
- *Soft:* Leaves a slight unsteadiness in case you still want a bit of that handheld look.
- *Wide Conv:* To be used with a wide conversion lens.

Optical image stabilisers (OIS) are built into the lens and are the preferred type. It is claimed that some can keep a recording steady even when using the telephoto setting or when shooting video from a moving car or train, when the bumpiness has nothing to do with your own skill as an operator.

Digital image stabilisers are built into the camera circuitry. They work by comparing each frame to the one that came before and compensating for slight changes in framing by drawing on a buffer of pixels recorded outside the visible frame.

The image stabiliser is an option that can be turned on and off, except in locked modes like *easy recording.*

It's recommended that you turn the image stabiliser off if you're using a tripod. This will reduce battery usage and prevent some erratic effects which can happen when the camera is stable.

There is an *Image stabilisation filter* in some digital editing programs. It also works by comparing one frame to the next, but it degrades the image slightly by either reducing the size of the frame to compensate for missing picture information or by inventing pixels by extrapolation.

As with any other aspect of video, it's best to get your image as right as possible during the shoot!

Gordon Peters, Cameraman, Channel 7 News, Bundaberg.

Avoid an erratic or volatile background as too much movement will distract the viewer from the talent, or make the talent look silly. Our junior cammo once shot an interview at a steam train launch. The conductor was positioned so that steam from the train appeared to be emanating from his ears.

Stationary Camera

If the camera doesn't have to move around or through the action space, then the best idea is to stabilise it firmly in one spot. A good-quality tripod is probably the go.

For any shots which require absolute stillness of the camera, like telephoto shots and macro shots, the tripod is close to essential.

The Tripod

The tripod is a three-legged structure (as its name implies) that telescopes down to a small size for transporting, but can be made into quite a tall camera support if needed.

Like some funny android, the tripod doesn't have much to it—it's all legs and head.

Tripod Construction

There's variety in the shape and material of tripod legs. There are the rugged, heavy wooden ones, and the lighter metal ones. Some tripods are absolutely spindly. These were designed to be used with lightweight stills cameras, not video cameras.

The first consideration in choosing a tripod is whether it's strong enough to support a camera of the size you're using—and whether it has sufficient weight in itself to keep a gust of wind from blowing it over once the camera is attached to it.

When shooting while walking, open both eyes to avoid collisions.

Lyvern Myi, Media Resource Centre.

The second consideration is whether it pans and tilts smoothly. Don't use one that requires you to unlock the tilt mechanism by twisting the panning lever's handle. These give you terrible picture results because every time you want to change the tilt, that twisting motion puts a horizontal jerk into your picture. Many of the cheaper tripods have this obnoxious problem. Okay for stills, not okay for video.

The third consideration is how heavy the tripod is, and how far you'll have to carry it. Unless you've got a Rambo on your crew, you may not want to take a heavy one on a long bush trek.

Hold the camera nice and still, and then move it around slowly.

David Cox-Taylor, Production Assistant.

It can be a very great boon if the tripod comes in its own little dufflebag, with a strap. Some tripods have a handle attached to them—that's a help, too.

When buying a tripod, the tendency is to go for a cheap one, probably because so much money has to be sunk into the camera. But a tripod that is stiff or hard to use, and adds jerkiness to your shots, is not worth the savings.

Make sure the steadyshot or stabiliser is switched on. While stabilisers and steadyshots will degrade your image quality very slightly, this minor degradation is far outweighed by the smoothness that they add to handheld shooting. Optical stabilisers are better than digital stabilisers so if you have a choice when purchasing, hiring or borrowing a camera, go for one with an optical stabiliser. If you are shooting on a tripod, turn the stabiliser or steadyshot off.

Andy Nehl, Head of Television, AFTRS.

The Legs

You'll find, along the three collapsed legs, a series of knobs, enlarged wing nuts, or some other form of release mechanism. Wherever you find one, that's an expansion point for the tripod leg. There are one, two or three of these for each leg, depending on the style of tripod. The expansion points allow you to open the tripod up to be

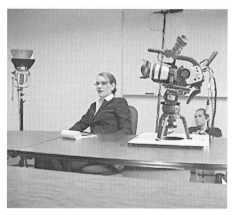

To get an eye-level camera angle around the boardroom table, the camera was mounted on a high hat (or hi-hat). Leah Polacco, actor, *Dot Com Dementia*.

Lengthen the tripod legs evenly before you open them. Gunther Hang, AFTRS.

very tall, set it to a medium height, or even use it at a very low level. In fact, tripods can be purchased in different sizes, from tall to *baby legs*. For table work, you can even buy the head mount without any legs at all.

One of the tricks of using a tripod is lengthening all the legs evenly. If the legs are uneven, then the platform at the top where you attach the camera won't be level, and your shot will be slanted in relation to the horizon or the walls of the room you're in.

One effective way of evenly lengthening tripod legs is to lay the closed tripod across your lap, then extend all three legs so the feet are flat against your outheld palm. If they're even when the legs are closed, they'll be even when the tripod is set up.

The leg procedure goes like this:

1. Loosen a leg.
2. Lengthen the leg.
3. Retighten the leg.
4. Roll the tripod over to do the next leg.

Step 3 is the important one. It's so easy when you're rushing or momentarily distracted to forget to tighten one of the legs!

Then what can happen? You can attach the camera to the tripod top, turn to get a battery out of the bag, and look back to see the untightened leg collapsing and the camera beginning to topple (or worse).

So: . . . Loosen . . . Lengthen . . . Tighten.

The Feet

At the base of the tripod legs are what we might call the feet. Some tripod models give you a choice of feet. You can use the round rubber bottoms, or you can screw them upwards to reveal pointy metal ends; on other models, there are metal claws that you can flip downward. Choice of feet, like your choice of shoes, is based on common sense. Which tripod feet would you use on the polished wooden floor of a library? Which feet would you use at the soccer field?

Setting Up

When you set the tripod up, it's a good idea to spread the legs out fairly wide so it has a good stable base. It's more stable to have the legs extended a bit further and

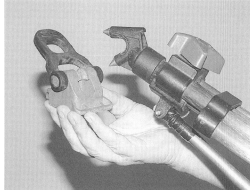

Tripod foot with rubber pad.   Tripod foot with spiky point.

the feet out wider (if there's space where you're operating) than it is to have the legs precariously close together.

Most tripods have a way of stabilising the spread of the legs, with straps, chains or connecting strips. If your tripod doesn't have any way of keeping the legs from sliding further out, you can build a wooden triangle to set the legs in. Oddly enough, this triangle is called a 'spreader'.

On some tripods, tightening the bolts at the apex (top) of the legs also stops them from spreading.

The Head

Some cheaper tripods have a fixed head attached at the top of the legs, but professional tripods usually have a head that attaches via an adjustable, swivelling ball-and-cavity system. This lets the operator level the camera platform independently of the legs, and check its levelness by using the spirit level gauge on the side of the head.

Attaching the Camera

There are a number of ways that cameras can be attached to tripods.

Basic tripods have heads with a tightening system consisting of a bolt, operated by a small and large knob beneath the mounting platform and a separate lever. With that system, you line up the hole on the bottom of the camera with the bolt protruding through an opening on the mounting platform. For some people, this can be quite tricky. Part of the problem lies in supporting the weight of a heavy camera with one hand while peering under the camera to see the camera hole, and the other part is in lining up the bolt to thread in correctly. Also, there never seem to be many turns of thread to grab on to the camera.

You're not always going to have level ground. (Photo by Michelle Blakeney)

With this system, once you have the positioning right, you tighten the smaller bottom knob first, then the wider one, and finally you swing the lever across to do the last tightening. (Make sure you start with the lever moved to the untightened side, so it has somewhere to go when you need to use it for the final tightening.)

An easier design is if your camera comes with a mounting plate. In that case, you screw the lightweight mounting plate onto the receiving bolt on the tripod head. Once you're sure that the camera plate is firmly on (give it a wiggle and check to see whether you can see any air between the underside of it and the tripod head), then you can snap the camera into place.

Ian Slade, Southern Cross University.

In this age of lighter digital cameras, tripods may seem to have almost become irrelevant. Image stabilisers can smooth out the camera operator's excitement in capturing the action. Stabilisers are good for dealing with small amounts of camera movement, but only up to a point. After that, image quality is what is being sacrificed to keep the image steady.

People often choose lightweight tripods. This is fine if you're not wanting to pan and tilt with accurate beginnings and endings to your shots. The choice of a rock-steady tripod and fluid head that offers smooth variable dampening in pan and tilt should be the start of wonderful relationship between what you see in the viewfinder and what the audience gets to see. You'll get steady images when you need them, and of course when you don't you can go back to wobble cam.

So choose a tripod that can handle a little more than you're asking it to carry. Then the image quality will come with practice—no more blaming the tripod.

Screw the mounting plate on tight.

Carefully insert the camera into the mounting plate and lock it in place.

Give it a wobble to make sure it's secure.

Tracy Dickson, College of the Southwest, Queensland.

Never leave a camera unattended on a tripod.

Insert the camera into the positioning slots at the back and front of the mounting plate, flip the lever at the front of the plate, and it should be locked in.

Be sure to position the camera correctly—it *is* possible to do it wrong and still flip the locking mechanism.

So never let go of the camera until you've given it a little shake to see whether it's firmly attached.

Another way to attach a camera is when the tripod itself comes with a *quick release* plate. This is a small plate that you screw onto the bottom of your camera, and then the plate fits into a receiving slot on the tripod head. Again, there's a locking lever—this time to hold the plate firmly in place.

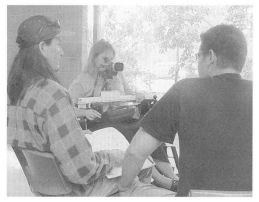 

Leanne Holland uses a special tripod head support made for her wheelchair by Joe Conway, while she interviews Marty Adams and Kingi Tahana, James Cook University.

Tripod Head Moves

Although the tripod holds the camera in one place, the camera can still be moved to vary its view from that one spot, similar to the way we can move our heads on our shoulders. The smoothest moves are done with a fluid-head tripod.

Pan

Panning refers to rotating the camera in the horizontal plane—that is, to the left or right. Panning is used to follow an action, survey a scene or show where one person or object is in relation to another.

Some things to keep in mind when preparing to pan:

1. Make sure the horizon line will be level at both the beginning and the end of the pan. It will go out of whack part-way through if your tripod is on a slight slant.

2. Record a few seconds with the camera still before starting the pan, and continue to record more with the camera still after you've finished the pan. This is necessary for editing. It's generally not acceptable to begin or end an edit in the middle of a pan.

When panning, try to frame in such a way that, if your shot was still-framed, you would be happy with it.

Chris Fraser, Cinematography Department, AFTRS.

A simple method of tripling your shots is employable when panning. Instead of just recording a pan, let your camera roll for an extended period prior to and after panning. This technique really pays off in edit because you end up with a pan and two static shots, increasing your options.

Gordon Peters, Cameraman, Channel 7 News, Bundaberg.

I find it easier to get a smooth pan by twisting the tripod head itself, rather than using the extension handle.

Richard Fitzpatrick, Camera Operator, Digital Dimensions.

When panning, try to start and end on a well-framed and composed shot.

Philip Elms, Media Resource Centre.

For smooth panning: Pulling on a large rubber band attached to your pan handle can eliminate jerkiness.

Beryl Stephens, Videographer.

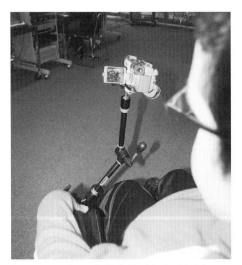

A camera attachment for Kevin Hatch's wheelchair lets him stay on the move with video. Methuen High School, Massachusetts. (Photo by Nancy Clover)

3. The speed of the pan should be slow enough so the audience can absorb the information and fast enough to prevent the audience from getting bored with the shot.

4. When you have enough time, it's a good idea to redo the pan at different speeds and in different directions, so there's more choice when it comes to the edit.

5. *Unwinding a pan*: Whether using a tripod or handholding, always move your body from an uncomfortable position to a comfortable one. This means you should stand facing the end point of your pan, then turn the camera and your body towards the starting position, with your feet still facing the end of the shot. Doing the pan from this position means that it will get easier for you as you move through it, and helps avoid that awkward, shot-ruining camera jerk just at the end of a beautifully executed pan.

Tilt

Tilting is the vertical movement of the camera, when you tip the camera lens up and down from a fixed position.

The tilt is used to emphasise height or depth, to follow an action, to survey the face of a building or the length of a human body, and to show the relationship between one place or object and another.

Zoom

When you have a camera attached to a tripod, it's often easier to change the camera's shot size by zooming than by actually moving.

You may zoom to prepare for your next shot, or you may zoom while you're recording.

It's easy to overdo recorded zooming, though. Despite the fact that it tends to fascinate the novice camera operator, too many zooms can irritate the viewer and make editing the shots difficult.

Zooming in and out frequently is called *tromboning*.

Combining a Tilt With a Zoom

With experience, you'll see that zooming in or out changes the height of your subject in the frame, so in order to keep a consistent framing, you'll need to combine a tilt with your zoom. If you rehearse the shot before you launch into recording it, you'll get better results.

Motivation for a Camera Move

Something within your shot can motivate a camera move. Your viewer can develop a desire to have a question answered. For example:

'What is that object in the distance?'
or
'What is that child playing with?'

This gives the shot motivation to zoom in so the eye can see more clearly.

'Where is that person going?'
or
'What's at the other end of that bridge?'

This gives the shot motivation to pan left or right.

'How tall is that building?'
or
'Whose feet are these?'

This motivates a tilt upward.

Kimberley Brown, Camera Operator and Editor.
(Photo by Henry Naudluk)

I don't ever lock a tripod off unless an effect (animation, superimposition) hinges on it. You never know when an action or gesture will extend beyond the area it took place in during rehearsal/blocking. You need to keep the flexibility to follow it and capture it all. This applies even to tighter frames of people talking, moving, gesticulating.

Jason Benedek, Videographer.

Moving the Camera

Many directors prefer to use a static (stationary) camera. It gives good control over the image and it's still possible to produce strong feelings of movement within the shot by carefully orienting the fixed camera in relation to the action.

However, as we all know, sometimes you just have to move.

If you want walking or tracking shots, it's better not to use the viewfinder at all because your head moves up and down as you walk, as will the camera if you have it up to your eye. Hold the camera away from your head in a comfortable position and imagine there's a line running straight through the camera out of the middle of the lens—you point this imaginary line at the centre of the shot you want to frame. You then put your effort into holding the camera steady as you walk. This is also a safer thing to do because you can see where you're going and are less likely to walk into things.

Andy Nehl,
Head of
Television,
AFTRS.

The Dolly

The terms *dolly* and *track* have become blurred, and the word *track* is now used to cover all these movements. Few people use the word *dolly* nowadays.

Chris Fraser,
Cinematography
Department,
AFTRS.

A dolly is a unit with wheels on it, to which a tripod can be attached. Once the tripod is on a dolly, it can be moved along smoothly in any direction.

When a director wants a camera operator to move the camera in closer to the subject or to back away from it, the expressions used are *dolly in* and *dolly out.*

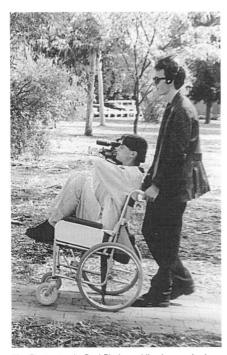

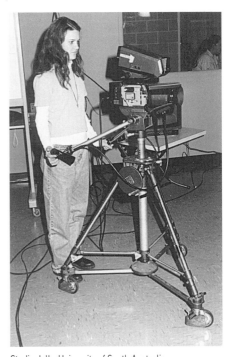

Alex Dunton tracks Paul Pledger while also monitoring the actor's wireless mic, Hamilton Secondary College, Mitchell Park, SA.

Studio dolly, University of South Australia.

When a director wants the camera to be moved to the left or to the right, the expressions used are *track left* and *track right*.

If you need the dolly to stay fixed in one spot, you can lock the wheels by stepping on the footbrake above each one.

Tracking shots can be used to move the camera alongside, or to the front or back of, a walking figure or a moving animal or object.

With the camera moving, it's possible to keep the subject the same size in the shot, even though the subject's relationship to the background is changing.

A wheelchair is wonderfully manoeuvrable and can get through some small passageways.

Other camera-moving possibilities are: a baby pram, a supermarket trolley, the equipment trolley from the media store (though these can give a pretty rough ride, maybe worse than handholding), a slow-moving automobile, a child's wagon (again, could be bumpy), a merry-go-round, rollerskates, rollerblades and a skateboard. Can you think of others?

With the last three you definitely need a competent rider. The idea is to provide a moving camera *support*, not a camera death ride.

For a ground-level tracking shot, a camera strapped to a skateboard and rolled along can be quite effective.

It's great to be creative, but whatever camera-moving device you use, think safety first for both the operator and the equipment.

Students from the University of La Verne, California, get a move on.

A wheelchair can make a great dolly and tracking device, and can be bought cheaply secondhand.

Peter Thurmer, Hamilton Secondary College.

Andy Nehl's Camera Moves from a Fixed Position

If you're going to use camera movement and vary the shot as part of your shooting style while your subject is not moving, you can achieve a range of variation in your shots with a steady moving image by standing on the one spot and moving your body with large, flowing movements.

If you place your feet about 1 metre (1 yard) apart, by bending one knee and moving down and forward over it, holding the camera in front of you, you can achieve about a metre of forward movement, which can vary the shot significantly if your subject is close and you're on full wide-angle lens.

By keeping the balls of your feet on the same spot and pivoting around to bending the other knee, as you turn you can achieve a relatively smooth handheld pan through 180 degrees.

This position also allows you to move up and down.

It's worthwhile practising it so you can get good at smooth movements. It's also worthwhile blocking through these kinds of shots before you shoot them if you have time.

Andy Nehl demonstrates his fluid method of camera movements, all of which arise from a fixed position.

Tracks

A very few video training centres have access to a dolly and track system. The tracks may not take you far, but it's a great ride!

L-R: Peter Watkins, Hunter Cordaiy and Colin Barton record a scene from *Our Heritage of Learning—The History of Education in Bankstown*, University of Western Sydney.

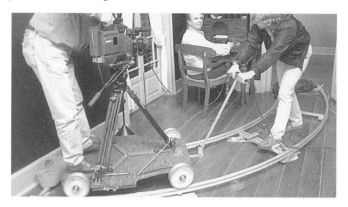

Checking out the potential of a wavy tracking shot, Film & TV, Central TAFE, Perth.

Testing the effect of circling an actor, using the Panther dolly, Film & TV, Central TAFE, Perth.

Barbara Bishop, Independent Producer.

One thing I like at Wakefield Community Access TV is a camera mounted on a 10 foot boom pole with a camera monitor at eye level. The camera can swing around, up and down, whatever, with a very smooth movement. They use it for opening and closing shots for serious programs and kids love it for music videos.

Cranes

Cranes are used to lift the camera to great heights, and lower it down again.

They're good for long shots which survey the scene, or the shot which brings the viewer down from a high perspective and into a locality.

The thought of having a crane on a shoot is seductive, but as with other seductive thoughts, there are important second thoughts about what it means for both the personal safety of the camera operator and the survival of the project budget.

Tony Bosch with a Piccolo crane, AFTRS.

At Wakefield Community Access TV in Massachusetts, a camera mounted on a boom pole gives great 3D control of the camera, with a sense of freedom and flight.

Using a Spotter

Though this fancy gear may be absolutely fabulous, you can still move the camera by walking with your own two feet.

One popular video shot shows a presenter walking through an environment towards the camera. This necessitates the camera to be moving backwards. Possible? Yes. Safe? It has to be. You can do it—here's how: use a spotter.

A spotter is someone who walks with the camera operator, but this person is walking forwards while the camera operator is walking backwards. Keeping a hand lightly on the elbow of the camera operator, a spotter indicates by slight squeezes when to stop and start and can grab the camera operator should s/he stumble.

Needless to say, the terrain should be checked out before the shot is attempted so both the camera operator and the spotter have seen the potential hazards. And there's nothing wrong with a couple of walk-throughs before the actual recording.

The spotter doesn't speak, so as not to mar the soundtrack. It's all a matter of trust and light touches.

People will often forget that time you got the perfect shot, but they will never forget that time you dropped the camera.

Gordon Peters, Cameraman, Channel 7 News, Bundaberg.

Spotter Jake Perry assists Padraig Gillen to track backwards safely while presenter Allison Darne walks forward. The Madeleine School, Portland, Oregon.

Camera Angles

The height of the camera and the angle at which it views the subject can subconsciously affect how the audience perceives the subject. The camera's angle of view can resonate with meanings in the viewer's life experience.

Eye level

High angle

Low angle

Rima Tamou and Murray Lui on location at the Three Sisters for a University of Western Sydney co-production, Katoomba, NSW.

High Angle

When the camera is high in relation to a human subject, so it's tilted downwards to get its shot, the perspective is similar to that of an adult looking at a child.

This angle of view tends to diminish the authority of the person in front of the camera. It can make that person look inferior, and give the viewer an impression of their own superiority.

A high-angle shot is useful when doing a long shot of a larger scene because it can show the relationship of the various elements in the scene, giving a sense of the geographical layout of the location, and showing action in greater spatial depth.

A very high-angle shot is called a 'bird's eye view'.

A high tripod doesn't have to mean a high angle. Here the tripod is high enough to get over the heads of the crowd, but the camera is still only eye-level to the stage floor. (Courtesy of Arlington Community Media Inc. [ACMi])

Ruth Janszen taping kid action on location for *Promise*, Berrima, NSW.

Low Angle

With a low-angle shot, where the camera is looking upwards at the human subject, the camera's view is like that of a child looking up at an adult, or an underling looking up at a figure of power.

Mark Tewksbury, The Nine Video School.

A fly on the wall—most shots are from the objective point of view, like the view of a fly on the wall. But the common fly doesn't always hover at eye level. Make your camera work more interesting by shooting above or below eye level.

This camera angle can make the subject look more dramatic, and give the person an aura of authority or grandeur.

Low-angle shots are useful for eliminating unwanted background elements, or for separating the subject from the background. They can heighten the sense of size and, in some cases, speed.

They're also useful for dramatising a point of view—of a child, or a dog, say.

Don't look down on your subject.   Go for a neutral angle.

Neutral Angle

A neutral-angle shot puts the viewer's perspective on an equal par with the subject, so there's no subliminal commentary going on in the visual language of the program.

Cathy Zheutlin uses a low tripod to get a neutral shot of Rami Shapiro and Prasanna for *The Wisdom Keepers*.

As a general rule, shoot with the camera at full wide and frame your shot by physically moving closer to the subject rather than zooming in. The wider you are, the steadier your handheld shot will be; the more you zoom in, the shakier your shot will be. The exceptions would be if you can't move in physically closer, or the value of the close-up to the story you're telling outweighs the negative of the shakiness of the shot.

Andy Nehl, Head of Television, AFTRS.

Unintended Angles—Handholding

When a person is handholding, the camera's view is the same as their own. When a tall person is holding the camera, it's higher off the ground than when a short person is holding it. If the operator is unaware of this, unintended messages can be introduced into the look of the image.

Short people need to stand on a box to avoid getting that up-the-nostril shot. Tall people need to lower themselves so the tone of their footage doesn't always look down on their subjects.

An up-the-nostril shot! (Photo by Bob Humphries)

Unintended Angles—Tripods

If people aren't aware of the meaning of camera angles, they set the tripod to the height that's comfortable for them.

So when someone's shooting an interview of seated people, the shot gets done from a high angle because the camera operator is standing. This usually gives a diminished look to the interviewee.

Or when someone is shooting a standing presenter, the shot gets done from whatever height works for the camera operator, rather than from a neutral angle at the height of the presenter's eyes. Learn to ask yourself: What is the *right* angle for this shot?

Sue L'Estrange,
Video Teacher.

Choose an interesting angle.

Creative Angles

You may come across a situation where you just can't get the angle you need without doing some good lateral thinking.

Alan Petschack was observing a little petting corral of baby farm animals. He wanted to get close-up neutral shots of them, but as an adult he wasn't allowed to step inside. That didn't stop him, though.

With his camera on the tripod, he held it over the fence and upside down, so the camera was nearly touching the ground—down at eye level with the chicks! Then, in the editing system, he inverted the picture and had the footage he wanted.

If they won't let you in with the chicks . . .   . . . use some creative thinking . . .   . . . to find a way to catch their eye anyway.

Choosing the Right Lens

Your video camera will have a zoom lens so you can take shots from a distance, and it's also likely to have a macro lens for close-ups. But sometimes the work you choose (or get asked or told to do) requires specialist equipment. Sorting out what gear you need is a job for the time period known as preproduction. You don't want to get to the job and then realise you haven't got what it takes (literally or otherwise).

But how can you know what to choose if you don't even know what's out there? Here are some interesting possibilities.

For wildlife photography, you'll need the ability to do super zooms and super close-ups.

This long, slim lens is called a probe lens. It allows you to get in extremely close for wonderful shots which fill the screen.

Eyeballing a snake. Richard Fitzpatrick uses a probe lens for Digital Dimensions.

The baby turtles dashing to the sea and onto the TV screen. Digital Dimensions.

The endoscope lens is very tiny and comes on a long flexible head with a light mounted next to it.

The endoscope lens attaches to the front of the camera lens, shown here by Julian Ellis, Cinematographer.

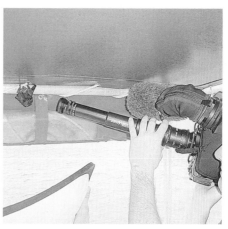

A tiny bat takes refuge on the dive boat of Digital Dimensions.

Richard Fitzpatrick, Camera Operator, Digital Dimensions.

Some of the animal behaviour shoots I do can take months, but I may only be shooting once a week.

An endosope lens comes with a fibre optic internal reflection cable mounted next to the lens.

The cable can be bent any which way and still send light through it. The light-able end is mounted right next to the lens so you can get into very tiny spots where you couldn't video otherwise. You attach the endoscope lens to the front of your camera.

Choosing the Right Camera

This is called lipstick cam—it fits in your handbag!

When the camera needs to work inside very tiny places, you can use a *lipstick cam*.

Lipstick cam is very useful in wildlife photography. For example, you can drill a hole in the side of a box in which an animal is giving birth, and insert the lipstick cam through the hole to video the process without disturbing the animal. Lipstick cam can use a variety of lenses, including wide angle.

If the camera must soar, here's one way to do it.

Helicopter cam. (Photo by Digital Dimensions)

If you're making sports videos, especially of extreme sports, there are *wearable* POV (point of view) flash memory cameras that resist shock, dust and water and give options in resolution and frame rates (30, 25, 24, 15 fps).

Tim Rooney, Portland Community Media.

Bells and whistles don't mean anything if the story can't stand on its own.

Getting critical footage doesn't always wait for a specialist camera. Your mobile (cell) phone may record an event that no one else can catch, or a moment in life you want to remember forever. It's the image that counts, however you get it.

Caring for the Camera

Caring for the camera is largely common sense. But for those for whom common sense is commonly absent, try to remember these few things:

Don't EVER let it get wet. This could mean carrying a spare (clean) garbage bag with you on every shoot so that if it starts to rain you can cover it for the run back to the car.

If you're working in the Tanami Desert, you don't need to take the bag for rain protection, but then again, you may need it for the next rule.

Keep the camera away from sand, dirt, smoke and other airborne particles. Grit can scratch the lens and cause problems with the tape transport system. The salt in seaspray is corrosive.

Keep it fairly cool. Don't ever leave it in a hot car, especially not where the sun can get to it. Don't leave it too close to video lights or a wood stove.

Carry the camera by its handle, not by its viewfinder or microphone!

Don't knock the camera into things, or allow it to bang around in the back of the car while driving to the next shoot.

When moving between very different temperatures, allow the camera some time to adjust to the new situation. Going from an airconditioned room to a humid outdoors area can cause condensation to form on the lens and the electronics. This has to dry off before the camera is able to operate.

Don't use the camera near TV transmitters, portable communication devices and other sources of magnetic or electric radiation. These can cause disturbance to your picture and may even permanently damage the camera.

Fine dirt on the lens, or salt spray if you are shooting at the beach, may not be visible on the flip-out screen but will show up more easily on the B&W viewfinder in the eyepiece if your camera has one. It sounds obvious, but it's worthwhile to remember to visually inspect the front of the lens regularly to make sure it's clean. Lens-cleaning tissues are cheap from any camera store and a very worthwhile addition to your camera kit.

Andy Nehl,
Head of
Television,
AFTRS.

Suggestions from Rachel Masters

Look at the shapes the body naturally makes and interchange these with shapes found naturally in the environment. Do the fingers on your hand remind you of anything? Are they like the branches of a tree? What about the freckles on your friend's face? Are they similar to a pebbled path? The angle of a beautiful aquiline nose may remind you of the corner edge of a roof. Shoot a collage video intercutting these images together. Be imaginative—look at things in a new way. Have fun!

5 TELLING THE STORY

There's another kind of angle to consider when you're making a story for the screen: the inner perspective on the action that you want the viewer to experience. Where you put your viewer psychologically is very much a part of how you tell the story, and it affects what your viewer will think and feel.

Shooting a comedy piece for Adelaide Crows *Best and Fairest*, with former Crows player Rod Jamieson, shot by Mal Foreman, directed by Graham Peach, John Cowan on audio. (Courtesy of tav productions)

The Inner Perspective

Objective View

An objective camera views the action impersonally, as if through the eyes of an unseen, outside observer.

Objective camera angles are good for giving an overall view of what's happening. They're frequently used in news reports and documentaries.

Subjective View

Subjective shooting brings the viewer into the scene. The camera lens becomes the eye of a person able to move through the action, and therefore able to observe it from many different angles. The audience tends to feel more involved with this kind of camera work, rather than stuck on the sidelines or in front of the stage.

Subjective camera work is much more common in recent years, and has been highlighted in TV shows like *NYPD Blue* and *Blue Heelers*.

Some people say this style of camera work, which evokes being present in the scene, is a result of the rise of home videos. People have become used to shots recorded by a camera operator who's a member of the family which is celebrating the wedding or travelling through the theme park.

Your camera viewfinder doesn't take the place of your eye. Look around, make sure you see the whole picture.

Tim Rooney, Portland Community Media.

When you're operating a camera, you should always remember that, as you move your camera, you are moving your audience.

Ian Ingram-Young, Academy of Photogenic Arts.

POV

POV stands for *point of view*. It's the most subjective camera view of all. The POV shot is taken from the perspective of one of the participants in the action, perhaps the presenter in a travelogue, or one of the characters in a drama.

Always keep a spare tape hidden in your car. You never know when you'll come across some great video!

Andrew Abernathy, Channel 7 TV.

The POV is very powerful, because it shows the viewer everything from the 'head' of someone inside the program. It's also very limited because it can't look neutrally at what's happening. It can't step outside the action for a more objective assessment.

With POV camera work, you can take your audience on a ride, whether in a plane or on a rollercoaster in an IMAX cinema, or a descent into fear or grief. Be careful with it.

Children in Sandy Tindall's class, Years 5, 6 and 7 at Mabuiag Island State School, worked with Josephine Bourne on a short video documentary on diabetes.

Consider how you can introduce variety into the POV. Could you have some shots through a window? Frank McLeod and Beryl Stephens set up a shot for *The Rainbow Boughquaker*.

**Josephine
Bourne,**
Producer.

When you're introducing kids to the creative medium of film or video construction:
- Don't freak out if you're not where you want to be at, at any given time; you have to let them lead you a little.
- Be aware that as the experienced filmmaker you're going to feel a little out of control. There's a brief moment when you have to give them control, yet still guide them to achieve their vision and maintain quality.
- *Remember:* It's a creative thought process. You can't always tell them what their vision should look like. Once you take away their creative freedom, it's no longer fun. This isn't to say that working with this medium is not hard work. What I'm trying to say is that it can be fun, so why not allow for it to be?

Your Own Perspective

Another choice you have is to be clearly autobiographical in your work, and to include yourself as the person speaking.

Your camera's remote control unit allows you to start and stop recording despite being at a distance from the camera.

You have plenty of stories to tell from your own perspective. Hannah Westerman, Methuen High School, Massachusetts.

This sort of recording is especially nice when sending messages to loved ones, or when making your own brand of video diary of your thoughts and feelings. Under such circumstances, people often prefer to have privacy rather than speak with a camera operator in the room.

One helpful hint is to monitor your shot throughout the taping session. It's so easy for you to unconsciously shift your position a bit while speaking and later find that the shot looks poorly framed, or that your head has left the picture entirely!

You can flip the LCD screen over to keep an eye on things if you're close to the camera, or you can add an auxiliary monitor for more distant viewing. If you add a monitor, take care to place it very close to the camera lens so that your eyeline can be consistent. If you're looking away to check your shot, you may look shifty-eyed to your viewer.

Remote Operation

There are many other uses for remote operation. It can work in circumstances when getting the view you want is not something you would normally be able to do. For example, you may want to capture some great close-up shots of the wild birds at the birdfeeder.

If you set up your camera on a tripod near the feeder, put the camera on wide-angle lens so focus isn't a problem, and then settle yourself in a comfortable chair on the other side of the verandah, you could get some absolutely wonderful footage. It may take a few attempts to get the aiming and framing right, and the birds will have to become accustomed to the new weird object near their feeder, but patience does have its rewards in video.

You may find that remote operation works better with your family, too, if they tend to freeze up when you approach them with a camera on your shoulder. The main trick is to remember to keep the lens on wide angle.

The Historical View

Photographs from the past, from many other people's perspectives, are often important in telling a story. You can incorporate old photographs into your video very easily.

All you do is pin the outer edges of each photo carefully to some cork or other upright backing, put the camera on a tripod, zoom in until the picture fills the frame, and shoot.

There's a huge range of wonderful materials kept in people's homes, even in old coffee tins in the attic!

Photos don't need to look like still images when transferred to video. You can add liveliness by moving the camera through the picture—panning across a row of basketball players, for example, or starting in close on someone in a group shot and zooming out to show everyone else.

Julie Booras and Jodie Cutter select photos for the video *The Story of Nana*, produced by Offspring Productions, Lynnfield, Massachusetts.

There are a couple things to bear in mind when shooting photographs. You have to make sure there's enough light on them. Mounting them near a window helps, as does working in a studio situation where there's good lighting.

If the photos have a glossy surface, your light may cause unwanted reflections, which will show up as white spots on the picture. Getting rid of unwanted reflections is a matter of fiddling with the light and the placement of the photos, and sometimes with the angle of the camera.

Plan. Plan, plan, plan and plan. That is where the real work lies. Editing is the magic, the rest will fall into place.

Claire Beach, Videographer/ Teacher.

Of course, if you have access to a good scanner, you could turn the photos directly into digital files and import them into your edit program that way. Then you can pan and zoom on them within your photo program or video editing software.

Video cameras can also shoot in *photo mode*. You can pad your historic video with your own stills of generic scenes which seem timeless (that ocean shore, that stand of trees) and discreetly mix them in with the archival footage. Or use them as part of a montage for an opening sequence or a segue from one segment to the next.

Planning both drama and camera direction requires careful visualisation. If you don't know what you want, how can you hope to create it?

Ian Ingram- Young, Academy of Photogenic Arts.

For a more historical look, you can add a sepia or black and white effect.

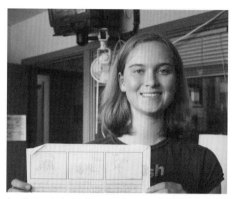

Amelia Ley took the time to make a storyboard. (Courtesy of Portland Community Media)

It's essential to storyboard your scenes before the day of the shoot. If you're working with an editor, have him/her look over your storyboards and give you feedback.

Julie Booras,
Offspring
Productions.

It helps to think of the shot *before* and the shot *after* each shot—when visualising, scripting, shooting, editing— whenever.

Denise Galloway,
University of
South Australia.

When you're thinking of a shot, first of all you have to ask, 'Is it going to cut?'

Julian Ellis,
Cinematographer.

The Storyboard

One sign of a beginner in video is the person who thinks s/he can just *wing it* on the day.

'I'll just shoot what's happening,' or 'I'll get what moves me at the time.'

A more experienced person knows that having a shooting plan will make the success of the end video far more likely.

One kind of shooting plan is the *storyboard*.

A storyboard is a series of drawings that clearly shows the expected camera coverage for a shoot. It's drawn out shot by shot—looking rather like a comic strip—and amounts to a paper edit of the project.

The storyboard is drawn up during preproduction, and then carefully discussed and revamped until the director feels satisfied that the coverage is complete and that, once shot, the images will be able to be edited.

Working things out carefully before the heat of the moment gives the director the mental space to imagine creative shots, and to check whether there are any gaps in the coverage or places where there may be *jump cuts* that require the shooting of *cutaways* or *cut-ins*.

Jump cuts occur if two similarly composed shots of the same subject are edited in next to each other. The effect is disconcerting because the subject appears to suddenly jump to the new position. There are ways to plan your shots to avoid jump cuts in the edit suite:

1. Make a major difference in shot size for any two shots which will be adjacent in the final edit. For example, follow a long shot with a medium shot or follow a close-up with an MCU. This can be done either by moving the camera nearer to the subject (or further away), moving the subject, or zooming in or out.

2. Change the camera angle between shots. For example, go from full face to half-profile or from eye level to a lower or higher angle shot.

3. Shoot cutaways to use where similar shots must go together.

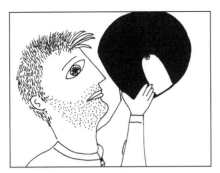

CU Biker puts helmet on.

LS Biker rides towards camera, race banner in b/g.

MS Profile biker rides to screen right.

VLS Biker rides to screen right.

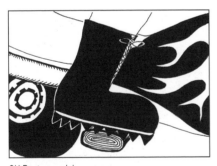

CU Boot on pedal.

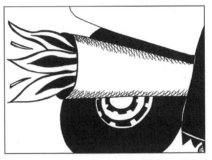

CU Exhaust pipe.

LS from rear, Biker rides towards finish line.

CU Biker's head as he passes the finish line flag.

Never cut from this . . .

. . . to this (jump cut).

It's okay to cut from this . . .

. . . to this (change of angle and size of shot).

Or cut away from this . . .

. . . to this . . .

Rachel Masters, Corporate Training Coordinator, SBS.

One thing to remember about video: if you haven't shot it, you can't edit it. Make sure you're thinking about alternatives both before and during the shoot, and be sure to shoot enough material.

. . . to then return to this (cutaway shot covers jump cut).

Crossing the Line

In any scene you shoot, there's an imaginary 180 degree line called the *action axis line*. It runs along the path of the dominant action. This action may be moving people or vehicles, or the eyeline between the characters in the scene.

If the camera shoots the action from one side and then crosses over the line to the other side for a different shot, the subjects will jump from one side of the frame to the other when the two shots are edited together.

Or the vehicle or moving person will appear to reverse direction.

During an action sequence, for example, continuity of screen direction is important. It tells the viewers where they are. Break that illusion and viewers will become disoriented and distracted and the edited sequence becomes nonsense.

How can you avoid 'crossing the line'?

1. Draw the imaginary action axis line on your storyboard picture before shooting a scene. This will show you the limits of your camera positions.

2. Then always make sure that, if the subject appears on the left side of the screen in one shot, it also appears on the left side in the next.

3. Be sure that people or objects only change direction if they're seen to do so in a shot, *or* if there's a neutral shot edited in between the shots that shows a reversal.

A neutral shot shows the action headed straight towards the camera or straight away from it.

Directors don't always worry about crossing the line anymore. Watch the Bathurst car races—the cars go in all directions. Who cares? We all know that they're going in the same direction. It's far better to place your cameras where they get the best shot, and assume your audience is visually literate.

Chris Fraser, Cinematography Department, AFTRS.

If you establish your scene with the interviewee on the right...

...then how can he flip to left of screen in his single?

...and how can the interviewer suddenly appear on the right in hers?

Thanks to Laudie Porter and Cody Rosebrook, The Madeleine School Tech Club, Portland, Oregon.

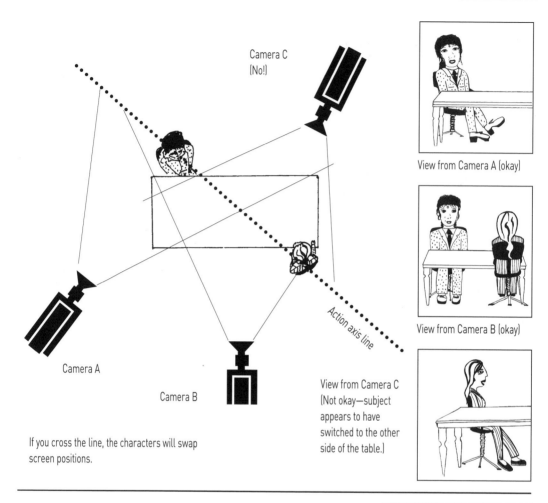

Camera C
(No!)

Camera A

Camera B

Action axis line

View from Camera A (okay)

View from Camera B (okay)

View from Camera C
(Not okay—subject
appears to have
switched to the other
side of the table.)

If you cross the line, the characters will swap
screen positions.

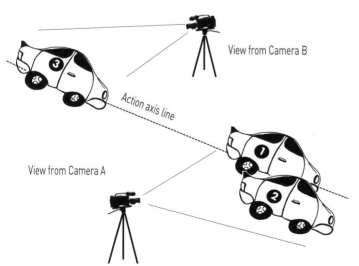

View from Camera B

Action axis line

View from Camera A

Camera A

Camera B

Are they going in the same direction?
How can a viewer make sense of this
footage?

Once you've chosen your establishing shot . . .

. . . make sure all your singles match it . . .

. . . by staying on the same side of the action axis line.

Suggestions from Rachel Masters

SHOT ANGLE

Choose something very mundane and ordinary like a garbage can. Shoot the garbage can from as many different angles as you can think of—high, low, standing, sitting, overhead, underneath, and POV from the inside of the garbage can.

When you play the video back, ask yourself, 'How does the angle affect the content?' That is, how does it affect the way you *understand* the shot? Does a low angle make the garbage bin look large, intimidating or imposing? Does a high angle make it look small and insignificant? What does the world look like from inside the garbage can? (Don't forget to leave the lid off—it can get pretty dark in there!)

DEPTH

An interesting video makes you feel involved: you feel like you go inside the picture, inside the frame. To explore depth, go to a park and videotape a friend walking *towards* the camera from a way-off point in the distance, the point of infinity. Then tape the friend walking away from the camera, starting by entering the frame from behind the camera. View these shots back. Are you exploring the full depth and scope of the frame?

EXPERIMENTING WITH IMAGES

If it's a cloudy day, prop the camera on its end and place a small sheet of glass across the lens. Then gently drop lightweight things on the glass. Try flowers, leaves or even worms! Look at how the strength of the light can make the images on the glass appear almost transparent. How does this influence the audience's point of view of the objects?

UNPREDICTABILITY

Exciting vision is often unpredictable. Shoot several shots where people enter the frame from different sides. (For example, a head pops up from the bottom of the frame, or two hands come in from the left and right sides of the frame.) Watch your shots back. Have you discovered the six types of screen space? (Left, right, up, down, from behind the camera, coming towards the camera.)

STORYBOARDING

Draw up a series of images for a short drama. Explore a range of options. How would it affect the story if you edited the images in a different order?

REVERSING THE ORDER

Another interesting exercise is to attempt to tell your story backwards. Is it possible to begin your story with the last scene? How does this affect the way the audience will interact with your story? Will the audience view your characters differently?

PLANNING A SHOT SEQUENCE

Practise shooting a scene that happens only once. Plan a short video of 60 seconds featuring a person eating an icecream. The scene starts with the icecream in a wrapper and ends when the wrapper is dropped into the bin. As the icecream will melt fairly quickly, you'll need to plan the scene carefully before you start shooting—it could get expensive doing reshoots. And everyone has a limit on how much they can eat! Think about continuity during the planning of the shoot. The aim is to show the action without any jump cuts. You'll need to shoot cutaways to help link the shots together.

VIDEO FORMATS

6

Before high definition TV (HDTV) came in, the hype was that it would end the problem of there being many different video formats. Alas, we now have more than ever. Old video doesn't die, it just begs to be *up-converted*.

In the beginning there were many designs for television, but the National Television Standards Committee settled on one unifying standard for within the United States. This is called the NTSC (I'm sure you can see why) and it worked well enough. But there were problems with colours shifting, so detractors sometimes refer to it as 'Never Twice the Same Colour'.

Television presents one still picture after another.

Later, two other systems were developed in Europe. SECAM (Système Electronique Couleur Avec Memoire) was developed in France, and PAL (Phase Alternate Line) was developed in Germany. PAL corrected for the colour errors found in NTSC. Some people refer to PAL as 'Perfection at Last', but there are detractors to everything and it has also been called 'Pay for Added Luxury'.

So then what? You guessed it. Germany began using PAL, as did the United Kingdom, most of Western Europe, Australia, New Zealand, much of Asia including China, also Brazil and parts of Africa. Basically, these countries were the trading partners of the original adopters, who were out to on-sell their TV hardware.

France and the Soviet Union adopted SECAM, and then sold their systems throughout Eastern Europe and to many other countries in western Africa.

NTSC was adopted in most of the Americas, and in Japan and the Philippines.

So the variation in television standards goes back to the politics and trading patterns of the post-World War II Cold War era, when television broadcast stations were first being set up around the world. Unfortunately, those patterns (divisions) deeply affected the ability of the world's people to communicate with each other via television.

Although these TV standards had some things in common, there were enough differences that you couldn't play a program on one that had been made on another.

What Is a Frame?

The term *frame* comes from film, where you can actually see each separate and complete picture by holding a strip of processed film up to the light. You see what's within the boundary chosen by the camera operator, no more and no less.

Although video technology is different and you can't see pictures when just looking at recorded videotape, a *frame* is still the term used for one complete picture.

Remember making your own little pencil and paper *movies*, by drawing stick figures in different positions on the corner of your school notebook pages and flipping through them quickly when the teacher wasn't looking? Film and video operate on the same idea.

In film, the viewer is shown 24 complete pictures (24 *frames*) per second. In video, the *frame rate* is slightly faster. In both PAL and SECAM, the frame rate is 25 frames per second. NTSC has a frame rate of 30 frames per second (well, 29.97 to be exact).

Horizontal Scan Lines

Each video frame is actually made up of many *horizontal scan lines* of picture information.

In PAL and SECAM, it takes 625 horizontal lines of picture information to make up one single frame of video. In NTSC, the picture is composed of 525 horizontal lines. In the days of tube television, the horizontal line information was gathered over mini periods of time by a scanner passing quickly, again and again, across the light-gathering surface in the camera. Each scan covered a slightly different portion of the picture. Bright spots resulted in more electricity, darker spots resulted in less.

Did you ever use a 'magic' paintbrush when you were a kid? You dipped it in water and drew it across the page of a special colouring book and it would reveal a hidden picture? If you had that experience, you might find it easier to understand about a picture being revealed line by line, and, by extension, a frame being made up of scan lines. If you didn't have that experience, maybe you'll find it replicated one day on YouTube!

These days, the camera's incoming light is focused onto a photosensitive CCD (charge-coupled device). The CCD is a semiconductor and is often referred to as a *chip*. Some cameras have only one CCD, and others are three-chip cameras. In this case, more *is* better because three-CCD cameras handle colour much more accurately.

The CCD converts the light into electrical information, which is output from the CCD and can be either recorded or transmitted, or both.

Some recent cameras are using CMOS image sensors, in place of CCDs.

In any case, the picture information is still presented as a *raster*, a rectangular grid made up of horizontal lines of pixels. But our eyes don't see the video image as 625 (or 525) separate lines. Instead, we perceive one whole, unified picture.

With many lines in each frame, and many frames in each second, we're tricked into thinking we're seeing whole images actually in motion. (So, in a way, video is a double con.)

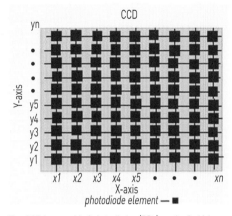

The CCD has a grid of photodiodes (PDs), each of which collects light information for one tiny segment of the image.

CMOS is the new generation of image-sensing devices.

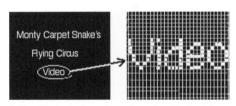

L: The video image is made up of a series of horizontal lines of picture information. R: Enlargement of detail.

What Is Interlace-scan? What Are Fields?

PAL, NTSC and SECAM were all designed as *interlace-scan* systems.

With interlace-scan, each complete frame of video is separated into halves, into what are called *fields*. Each *field* is made up of half the horizontal lines of picture information—but not the top half and the bottom half, or the right half and the left half.

The first field is made up of all the odd-numbered lines of the frame (lines 1, 3, 5, 7 and so on), so it's known as the *odd field*.

The second field is made up of all the even-numbered lines of the frame (lines 2, 4, 6, 8 and so on), so it's called the *even field*.

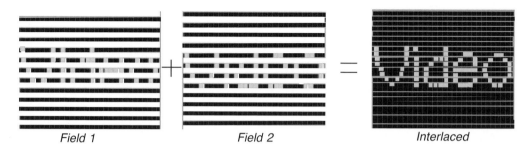

Field 1   *Field 2*   *Interlaced*

Two fields make one complete frame of video.

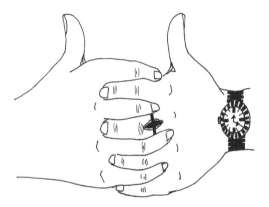

The lines of the two fields interlace, like these fingers, to form one complete frame of video.

When each frame is reassembled from its two fields, a line from the first field is followed by a line from the second field, and that's followed by a line from the first field, and so on.

You may wonder why anyone would bother inventing such a system. But by presenting each video frame as two separate fields, this doubles the apparent image presentation rate. So instead of seeing 25 complete *frames per second* (in PAL or SECAM) or 30 complete frames per second in NTSC, we see 50 (or 60) *fields per second*.

If you're naturally a numbers person, you'll see that the field rate in these systems corresponds to the electricity used in their originator countries. Germany's electrical system is 50 Hz (50 cycles per second) and in the United States the mains electricity supply is 60Hz (60 cycles per second). These field rates are not just random.

With rapidly appearing fields, once again our eyes are tricked, and the prize for this effort is that the image doesn't seem to flicker.

All three major formats of standard definition TV (SDTV) with the old 4:3 aspect ratio are *interlace-scan*. But that doesn't mean the method has been discarded. Some HDTV video is also interlace-scan. Interlace-scan formats are indicated with a diminuitive 'i'.

480i means 480 horizontal lines in an interlace scan (SDTV: NTSC Standard Definition TV).

1080i means 1080 horizontal lines in an interlace scan (HDTV: High Definition TV).

Progressive Scan (Non-Interlace) Has No Fields

Some more recent formats of video use *progressive scanning*. Progressive scanning means that the horizontal lines are scanned in sequential order and the entire image is presented as a whole each time. Computer screens use progressive scanning.

There are no fields, only complete frames with progressive scanning. Therefore it is a *non-interlace* system.

An advantage of progressive scanning is that the total picture information can be presented twice as often as with interlace-scan, so that's 50 times per second with PAL and 60 times per second with NTSC. This makes for a crisper image and more clarity when there's lots of movement on the screen, as in sports.

Progressive scan formats are indicated with a 'p', as in 720p, 768p and 1080p.

Nearly all digital TVs use progressive scanning, though some networks broadcast in interlace-scan and some in progressive-scan. Thankfully, digital TVs can handle both broadcast types.

PAL (PHASE ALTERNATE LINE)

The PAL signal's frame is composed of 625 lines, and the signal runs at 50 Hz, which is 50 fields per second, 25 frames per second. PAL is used in Afghanistan, Algeria, Andorra, Angola, Argentina, Australia, Austria, Azores, Bahrain, Bangladesh, Belgium, Bosnia and Herzogovina, Brazil, Brunei, Cameroon, China, Cook Islands, Croatia, Denmark, Ethiopia, Finland, Gambia, Germany, Hong Kong, Hungary, Iceland, India, Indonesia, Ireland, Israel, Italy, Jordan, Kenya, North Korea, Kuwait, Laos, Lebanon, Lesotho, Liberia, Macedonia, Malaysia, Maldives, Malta, Mozambique, Namibia, Nepal, Netherlands, New Zealand, Nigeria, Norway, Oman, Pakistan, Papua New Guinea, Paraguay, Poland, Portugal, Qatar, Romania, San Marino, Montenegro, Serbia, Seychelles, Sierra Leone, Singapore, Slovenia, Somalia, South Africa, Spain, Sri Lanka, Sudan, Swaziland, Sweden, Switzerland, Tanzania, Thailand, Tonga, Turkey, Uganda, United Arab Emirates, United Kingdom, Uruguay, Vanuatu, Vietnam, Yemen, Yugoslavia, Zambia, Zimbabwe.

SECAM (SYSTÈME ELECTRONIQUE COULEUR AVEC MEMOIRE)

The SECAM signal's frame is also composed of 625 lines and the signal runs at 50 Hz, which is 50 fields per second, 25 frames per second. SECAM is used in Albania, Armenia, Azerbaijan, Benin, Botswana, Bulgaria, Burkina Faso, Burundi, Central African Republic, Chad, Democratic Republic of Congo, Egypt, Equatorial Guinea, France, Gabon, Georgia, Greece, Iran, Iraq, Kazakhstan, Kyrgyzstan, Latvia, Madagascar, Mali, Mauritania, Mauritius, Mongolia, Morocco, New Caledonia, Niger, Russia, Rwanda, Saudi Arabia, Tajikistan, Togo, Tunisia, Turkmenistan, Ukraine, Uzbekistan.

BOTH PAL AND SECAM

Cyprus, Czech Republic, Djibouti, Estonia, Ghana, Lithuania, Luxembourg, Monaco, Senegal, Slovakia, Syria.

NTSC (NATIONAL TELEVISION STANDARDS COMMITTEE)

The NTSC signal's frame is composed of 525 lines and the signal runs at 60 Hz, which is 60 fields per second, 30 frames per second. NTSC is used in Antigua and Barbuda, Bahamas, Barbados, Belize, Bolivia, Burma, Canada, Chile, Colombia, Costa Rica, Cuba, Dominica, Ecuador, El Salvador, Fiji, Grenada, Guatemala, Guinea-Bissau, Guyana, Haiti, Honduras, Jamaica, Japan, South Korea, Marshall Islands, Mexico, Micronesia, Nicaragua, Palau, Peru, Philippines, Puerto Rico, Suriname, Trinidad, United States of America, Venezuela.

This list is from a wall chart supplied by Video 8 Broadcast in Sydney, NSW, Australia. As countries continue to upgrade their systems, please check the internet for the latest information.

Resolution: What Are All Those Numbers?

The resolution of an image is basically a measure of how much picture information is available. The term *resolution* is used in relation to both image capturing (cameras) and image display (TVs).

In digital video, the resolution is determined by how many *pixels* (picture elements) there are to handle the picture data.

The video image is rectangular in shape, so it has both width and height. Resolution is normally expressed by two numbers that give the number of horizontal pixels (the width) and the number of vertical pixels (the height) in the grid.

Although the entire frame of SDTV video is made up of 625 (or 525) horizontal lines, not all those lines are used for the actual picture.

In broadcast, some of the non-picture lines are used for transmitting other data, like closed captioning. The horizontal non-picture area is that black band which you could see on your old TV if the picture started flipping up or down.

So when resolution is mentioned, the numbers are smaller than the total number of horizontal lines in the signal. The result of this is that standard definition PAL format is referred to as having 576 horizontal lines of available picture information (not 625). NTSC has 480 horizontal lines of resolution (rather than 525).

When referring to resolution, it's the convention to write the width number first and the height number second. So PAL is written as 720 × 576. This means a viewable picture dimension of 720 pixels across by 576 horizontal lines. NTSC is written as 640 × 480. This means a viewable picture dimension of 640 pixels in width by 480 pixels in height.

(Yes, it *is* confusing, because the height is the number of horizontal lines, which feels like it would have to do with width. Some things you just have to work to understand or swallow hard and memorise them.)

HDTV (all in wide screen)

- **720p:** The picture is 1280 × 720 pixels, at 60 *complete* frames per second.
- **1080i:** The picture is 1920 × 1080 pixels, at 60 *interlaced* fields per second (30 *complete* frames per second).
- **1080p (or 1080p60):** The picture is 1920 × 1080 pixels, sent at 60 *complete* frames per second. (Blu-ray players, video game consoles).

Signal Compatibility

If you're using just your own camera and home editing system, or if your media centre was careful to buy all the same-format cameras, then compatibility isn't likely to be a problem for you. *But* if several people are contributing to a project and they're using different cameras, recording in different formats, signal compatibility can become a nightmare. Somehow you will need to agree what format you'll edit your project in and then convert all the signals to the same master format. You also need to make sure your chosen format and timeline match—but we'll deal with that later in the editing chapter.

The only things the same these days are the frame *sizes:* 1920 × 1080 and 1280 × 720 are the HD sizes in both worlds. But the frame rates are all over the place. NTSC countries still shoot 23.98, 29.97 or 59.94 and broadcast 29.97 or 59.94. Film still shoots at 24 (or 23.98), and the PAL countries use 25. But it can be 1080p25, or 1080i50, or 720p50, and cameras can shoot 720p25, so there's still all of the conversion headaches we've always had.

David Jahns,
Editor.

There are many different forms of HDTV, but it's only the progressive scan format that allows full backward compatibility with other HD formats and standard definition formats like PAL and NTSC, both widescreen and 4:3.

Richard Fitzpatrick,
Camera Operator, Digital Dimensions.

The difference in picture resolution is quite dramatic going from one format to another. You can see this by multiplying out the horizontal and vertical pixel counts to get the overall resolution number. As you can see, HD formats have massively more picture information than SD formats.

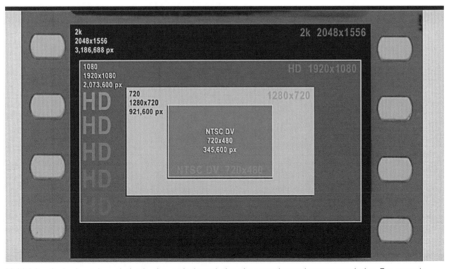

Multiplying the horizontal resolution by the vertical resolution gives you the total screen resolution. For example, a 1080p screen has 1920 horizontal pixels by 1080 vertical pixels and this equals 2073600 pixels. (Graphic by David Jahns)

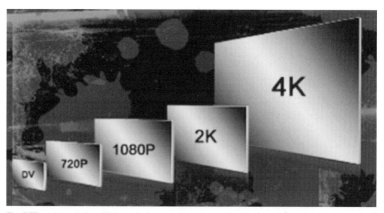

The RED cameras bring video resolution to a heretofore unheard of level. (Graphic by David Jahns)

RED One, capable of recording at resolutions up to 4096 horizontal by 2304 vertical pixels, directly to flash or hard disk digital storage. It features a single Super 35-sized CMOS sensor. (Courtesy of RED Digital Cameras)

RED Camera—4K digital:

- Uses 35 mm lenses.
- Shoots 4K images.
- Can be down-converted to 2K, 1080, 720, NTSC, PAL, etc.
- Records to hard drive or flash drive.
- Much cheaper than ViperCam or 35 mm film—could change moviemaking as we know it.
- Workflow can be very tricky—4K is a lot of data; few systems can handle it.
- HD delivery—easiest workflow: renders out 1080 quicktimes; use those as masters.

Up-Converting and Down-Converting

David Jahns, Editor.

Showing an SD signal (cable TV, DVD) on an HDTV is basically like watching a quicktime in full screen mode on your computer. It scales it up to fill the screen, but it's not really 'up-converting', which implies adding pixels to create a higher resolution.

The number of pixels on a TV display grid is fixed (e.g. 1920 × 1080 in HD), so the best resolution possible is also fixed. TVs will scale the incoming signal to fit the screen's pixels. A signal with higher resolution has to be *down-converted* to be shown on the screen. This picture will still look good.

Up-converting a signal from a lower resolution can yield less favourable results, because the required additional picture information is just plain missing and has to be interpolated (invented from surrounding information).

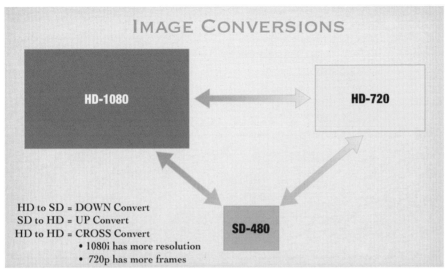

Graphic by David Jahns.

Composite Video

The composite video signal is the one most home users deal with.

This is the entire picture signal (picture only, no audio) and it's carried on one cable, often a simple RCA cable which is colour-coded yellow at its end connectors.

Actually, you could send the video signal on any RCA cable—white, red or black-ended—if you didn't have a yellow-ended one. The colour coding simply helps people get both ends of the same cable connected to the right positions when dealing with three-strand video and audio cables. It's simply a convention that yellow is for video and the red- and white-ended cables carry the audio signals.

Component Video

The component video signal is the video signal separated into its component parts. These are referred to as RGB for red, green and blue, which are the primary colours of video. (But not the primary colours of paints, which are red, yellow and blue, as you remember correctly from kindergarten.)

The component video signal is carried on three cables (or a one-to-three cable), normally colour-coded with red, green and blue connectors at their ends. The red cable carries the red part of the signal, the blue cable carries the blue part of the signal, but the green cable carries BOTH the green part of the signal AND the luminance information (the black and white picture information).

When would you use component video?

David Jahns,
Editor.

Component video is the best analogue format, so, basically—use it whenever you cannot use a digital signal . . . for whatever reason.

Maybe you have a camera with an HDMI (high definition multimedia interface) output, but your capture card has only an SDI (serial digital interface) input. Chances are, both devices will have component video ports, so the best (and sometimes only) way is to convert it to analogue out of one device and back into the other. In the HD world, at least.

In the SD world, legacy BetaSP decks and even modern SD DVD players, for example, do not have digital ins or outs, so the component video will look *much* better than Composite, or S-Video.

S-Video

S-Video is the Super VHS (SVHS) signal. S-Video travels within one special outer cable using several inner wires and it comprises two parallel signals, one for the *luminance* (brightness) and one for the *chrominance* (colour). SVHS handles video colour more accurately than normal VHS did.

The RF Signal

You may have noticed that you can connect the entire TV signal (both video and audio) into your television using just one cable, as with the set-up for cable TV.

This shielded coax cable is called an RF cable (RF stands for *radio frequency*). In this case, the entire video and audio parts of the TV signal have been converted into a radio frequency. This is how the TV signal travels through the atmosphere.

The RF cable connects to the socket called *Antenna in* or *RF in* on your television.

RF signals are usually received on Channel 0 or Channel 1 on your TV. If you select one of these channels and the signal appears there but it isn't clear, adjust the finetuning control on your television.

If the signal doesn't appear at all, check that you have the TV/VCR switch in the correct position on your TV or remote control.

Colour

Video colour is the result of additive colour mixing.

This means that the three primary colours (red, green and blue) can be combined in various percentages to produce all the other colours. Surprisingly, green and red produce yellow!

Colour Bars

You may have noticed that these primary and secondary colours in this additive colours chart are the same as those that appear in *colour bars*, the test signal used for lining up a signal in preparation for recording or broadcast.

Colour Variables

The three variable characteristics of the colour signal are referred to as luminance, hue and saturation.

Luminance

The term *luminance* refers to brightness. When a colour is very luminous, it approaches peak signal level (it can appear white). When it's very non-luminous, or dark, it approaches the black level of the signal.

Hue

The term *hue* has the meaning that we generally give to the word 'colour'—that is, red, green, blue, yellow, and so forth.

Saturation

The term *saturation* refers to the richness of the colour present. Pastel colours are less saturated than vivid colours. Highly saturated colours can seem cartoon-like, and in fact are often used in animation and graphics.

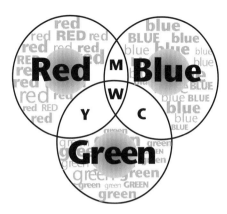

Red + Blue = Magenta, Red + Green = Yellow, Green + Blue = Cyan, all colours together = White.

From left to right: white, yellow, cyan, green, magenta, red, blue. Black is at the bottom.

Video and Film

Because of the difference in frame rates, film and video aren't perfectly compatible. Sometimes people transfer film to PAL video using variable-speed projectors and speeding the film projection up to 25 frames per second. This works fairly well, though it causes a minor shift in the audio.

Some video cameras now allow for variable frame rates and can be adjusted to shoot slightly more slowly, at 24 frames per second.

In NTSC, with its 30 frames per second, the difference between video and film is greater, so trying to speed up the projector yields a more drastically altered screen product.

Transfers from film to television are made using a device called *telecine*. Telecine equipment corrects for the difference in frame rate between film and video.

Thanks to Ernst Hadenfeld, David Jahns and Phil Cooper for their help in the preparation of this chapter.

VIDEO STORAGE: THANKS FOR THE MEMORY

7

Digital video is wonderfully transferable. It can be recorded and stored in many ways: in magnetic media (videotape and hard drives), in optical media (CD, DVD, Blu-ray) and in solid-state media (flash memory).

And it can be transferred without loss of signal accuracy from one medium to another or compressed to take up less space if required.

Garrett Gutierrez, University of La Verne, California.

For example, you might record to *videotape* in your camera, download your footage into the *hard drive* of your computer, put a small amount of that footage onto a *flash memory stick*, take it to your video partner's place, transfer the digital files to his/her *external hard drive* where all the project footage is being collected, complete the edit there together on that *computer hard drive*, then save the finished program to *DVD* and send it out to your friends.

Videotape

The oldest medium for video recording and storage is videotape. This is a magnetic medium that successfully made the transition from analogue to digital recording and remains with us today.

There are many current digital tape formats including:

- HDV/DV tape
- MiniDV tape
- Digital8
- DVC HD
- DVC PRO
- DVC PRO HD
- DVCAM
- HD CAM
- HD CAM SR
- Digital Betacam
- D-5.

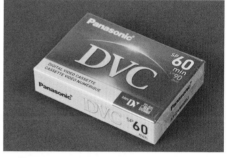

MiniDV tape.

Some older analogue formats, like VHS, may no longer be on the shelves in the malls, but there are still lots of those tapes lying around, and never fear: you can still edit that footage by using an *analogue-to-digital converter* to get it into your editing system (see Chapter 10, Editing: Getting More Technical).

Anatomy of Videotape

> VHS is dead. And what a lot of space those analogue VHS cassettes take up!
>
>
>
> **Alan Petschack**, Videographer.

Videotape is made using a clear plastic polymer ribbon as the base. This allows the tape to be thin, strong and durable.

On the recordable side, the plastic is coated with very tiny metal particles which are sensitive to magnetism. Videotape manufacturers continue to try to make these particles smaller, more uniform in size and shape, and pack them in more densely to achieve a better image with higher *resolution*. Some tapes are labelled MP (metal particle) and some are ME (metal evaporated).

These magnetic particles are suspended in a *matrix* or *binder* (if you cook, you can think of it as a sort of batter) which holds them together and keeps them attached to the plastic tape. There are other ingredients in this layer as well. For example, a lubricant can be included to help the tape pass easily over the record heads. Each tape manufacturer's 'recipe' is better guarded than Aunt Milly's prize-winning pumpkin scone mix.

On the back side of the tape, there's a fine coating of carbon material. Because carbon does not respond to magnetic fields, this coating helps prevent a bleed-through of the recorded magnetic signal from one layer of tape to the next as the tape gets rewound.

The carbon is also a dry lubricant which buffers the layers of tape from each other, reduces tape drag and prevents the layers from sticking together.

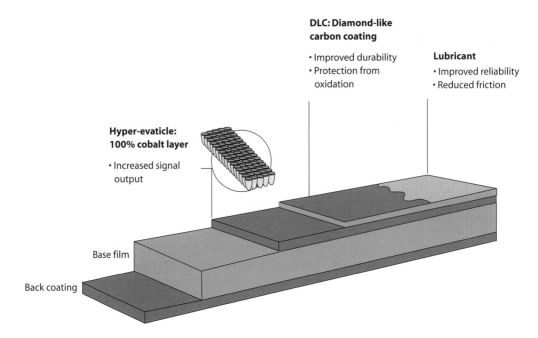

DLC: Diamond-like carbon coating
• Improved durability
• Protection from oxidation

Lubricant
• Improved reliability
• Reduced friction

Hyper-evaticle: 100% cobalt layer
• Increased signal output

Base film

Back coating

Advanced Metal Evaporated (AME) tape. (Courtesy of Sony)

The Smart Cassette

Some video cassettes (like DVCAM and miniDVCAM) have an IC memory chip which allows a person to mark shots while out in the field shooting. There's enough memory to mark OK/NG (for *okay/no good*) along with the timecode in and outs, the reel number, scene number and take number.

Why? Because when the tape goes back to the edit suite, the computer edit system will then only copy into itself the ones marked good, so no time is wasted in transferring unusable material. These same tape brands can be purchased without the chip, for less money.

Videotape Quality

Tapes are labelled with a confusing array of names. A basic rule of thumb is this: if the tape has the word 'standard' in it, it's a lower grade of tape. Even if it's called 'Super High Grade Standard', it's still in the standard category.

Please use quality videotapes! Not rubbish from the supermarket.

Peter Watkins, Educational Media Services, University of Western Sydney.

Cheaper tapes tend to have poor-quality cassette housing and an inferior coating of the magnetic layer, so they record with lots of *dropouts*. You may find that's acceptable for off-air recording of TV shows or movies you'll view just once. But why waste your time and energy shooting a project onto inferior material? The difference in cost is nothing compared with the effort of the shoot.

Many people claim it's best to pick a single brand of tape and stick with that for all your work. Most people claim you should buy a known, reputable brand.

Videotape Recording: It All Happens at the Gap

Video recording occurs when the record heads in the camera magnetise the metal particles on the videotape.

The record heads are very small and mounted on the outer edge of a circular, polished metal *head drum*.

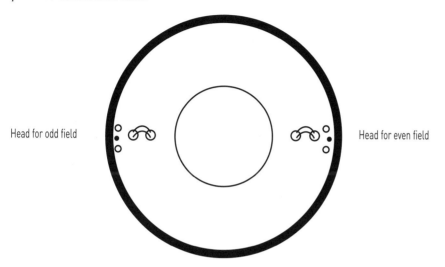

Head for odd field   Head for even field

The two heads are mounted on opposite sides of the head drum.

This drum spins rapidly during the recording process and the videotape is drawn across it. As the tape moves through the magnetic field at the head gap, the metal particles on it get aligned into a distinct pattern. Once the tape has passed away from the record heads, the particles are outside the range of the magnetic field, so they stay in that pattern. This pattern is the picture information.

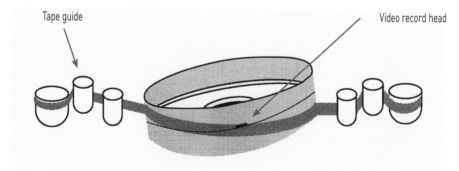

Tape guide   Video record head

The videotape is drawn across the spinning head drum at a high speed.

If a record head becomes clogged with anything, the recording no longer happens from that head.

Because the heads both read and write (that is, they both record and play back the video), it's also true that if a head gets clogged during playback, the playback doesn't look right.

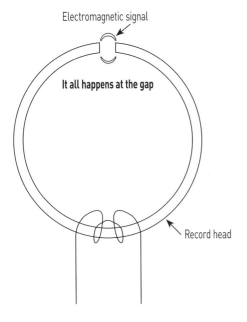

Electromagnetic signal

It all happens at the gap

Record head

Occasionally you can fix a head clog by running the tape forwards and backwards a few times in search mode. This can sometimes dislodge the offending particle and send it on its way.

If that doesn't work, you'll need to clean the heads—carefully! Technicians generally advise people not to use head-cleaning tapes because they're abrasive and can damage the record heads.

If you do use a commercial head-cleaning tape, be sure to follow the directions carefully and don't assume that if running it for ten seconds will be good, then twenty seconds will be better.

If two or three passes with the head-cleaning tape doesn't work, you should have the heads cleaned manually by someone who knows what they're doing, and who has the right cleaning fluid and chamois or non-fibrous cleaning tips to use.

Cotton buds are a bad choice for cleaning video heads because the cotton fibres themselves can get caught in the head gap, compounding the problem.

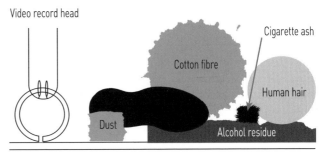

Video record head

Cigarette ash

Cotton fibre

Human hair

Dust

Alcohol residue

Plastic tape base

Watch out! Lots of little things can clog the video heads.

When cleaning video heads, it's easy to damage them if the cleaning implement is moved up and down, perpendicular to the direction of the head travel. Hold the cleaning material stationary against the heads and rotate the head drum backwards and forwards by hand.

Ian Clark,
Maintenance
Technician,
AFTRS.

Care of Videotapes

KEEP THEM IN A CLEAN AND DRY ENVIRONMENT
The biggest threat to the life of a videotape appears to be the effect of humidity on the binder. The binder can absorb moisture from the air and this causes the tape to distort, producing errors in playback.

At its worst, it causes the magnetic layer to become sticky and break away from the plastic ribbon-like base. This is referred to as *sticky tape syndrome*. The recording layer will start to fleck off, causing dropouts, a dirty tape path in the camera or VCR, and *clogged heads*. If you're trying to play back a tape in very hot, muggy weather, you may well have difficulties.

It's sometimes possible to temporarily restore a tape with sticky tape syndrome by baking it! But you have to know how. This is not as simple as baking that readymade chocolate chip cookie dough.

Dust, cat fur, carpet fluff, pollen, human hair, sawdust, cigarette smoke and ash—think of all the airborne particles that could stick to a videotape. Wherever something has stuck onto the tape, it prevents the playback heads from reading the video signal properly.

Whenever the tape path becomes dirty, it should be entirely cleaned, including all the record heads and pinch rollers. If it isn't cleaned, the muck just gets transferred to the next unlucky tape and your problems multiply. You could end up damaging a prize tape by being careless about what you played before it. Grit and sand, due to their size and sharpness, can actually slice into a videotape as it runs through a machine.

So don't set your unprotected tapes down on grass, dirt, sand, shedding carpets, and so forth. Don't put one down on a counter where there was a sugar doughnut a minute ago, or where someone was just spooning out the coffee.

> As good as they are, digital tapes are not infallible. They are still prone to stretch, dirt and jamming, and can be accidentally erased.

Philip Elms, Media Resource Centre.

Try Not to Drop Them

Tapes are surprisingly slippery little things, especially if you're carrying a stack of them around and they're not in their cases.

> *Scenario: It's late at night, you're trundling out of the edit room, bleary-eyed and brain-fried. A tape in the middle of your stack enters another reality, suddenly auto-ejecting, like an air force prototype, and all the others spew out after it in a spasm of catapulting black plastic.*

Though videotapes are made from quite durable plastic, if they land smack on a corner, especially onto concrete or another hard surface, the corner can sometimes break off.

Trying to salvage the situation by putting your videotape into another cassette housing is a nightmare of flying springs and little metal bits, and can most gently be described as utter insanity.

You don't need that aggravation, nor do you want to risk losing your recorded material.

Keep Them Away from Magnets

Because the recorded video signal is merely an arrangement of magnetic particles, any other strong magnetic field can *erase* that signal by pulling the magnetic particles into a different alignment.

You may not have horseshoe magnets lying around on your coffee table, but don't forget that televisions, VCRs, speakers, electric motors, power transformers

Penny McDonald,
Film and Videomaker.

Always label your tapes. Any unlabelled tape is in danger of being reused.

Hey, what are those tapes doing on top of your TV?

and computers generate magnetic fields and might erase your tapes without giving you any warning.

Though most home equipment has shielding to keep its magnetic fields from affecting other things, sometimes there's leakage.

There is a small amount of demagnetisation which will happen just from the general atmosphere.

Thank goodness this was just a dub and not the master!

Keep Them Cool

Heat can damage tapes. Extreme heat can ruin them.

The temperature in a closed car in the sun can reach over 50°C (120°F).

A risky place to put videotapes is on the shelf beneath the rear window of a car. If it's not hot that day, it may be the next, and what if you forget they are there?

Keep Them Upright

Have you ever seen the deformation that can happen to a roll of cellophane tape? Over time, the tape can droop downward from the spool, morphing from a flat reel to a cone shape.

A videotape left on its side can suffer from tape droop, too. Then when you go to play it, the tape isn't lined up right for the tape path and it can get edge damage, which will knock out your time code or soundtrack or more.

So videotapes should be stored standing upright, like books on a shelf, or stored on their spines (which makes it easy to read their labels if they're kept in a drawer) but never lying flat on their large surfaces.

Rewind Them After Use

Always rewind the tape after use, as this prevents it getting a bend in the middle of the program material. A rewound tape, with its outer edge covered by the clear plastic leader, is also less susceptible to absorbing moisture.

Retrieving Material from a Damaged Tape

If you suspect that playback problems are due to damaged tape, you can check it out this way. On one of the four thinner sides of the tape cassette, there's a door that opens to allow the tape to wrap around the record heads. Near every door is a little secret button which pushes in or slides sideways, unlocking the door and allowing it to swing open and reveal the videotape.

It's important not to touch the tape with your fingers, because natural skin oil and dirt will stick to the tape and then get conveyed into your video equipment, generally gumming up the works.

If you do find a scratch along the tape, or the bottom or top edge is ruffled, or the tape is wrinkled, you've got problems. Whatever was recorded on that section won't play back properly again.

It's not a good idea to put a damaged tape into a camcorder or VCR. A new tape will cost you less than $20, but repairing fragile heads that got yanked by a wrinkle could cost you hundreds. If the tape is damaged, throw it away.

If the tape contains critical recorded material that you can't do without, you can make a copy on some machines using this method:

1. Start by determining the start and end points of the wrinkle, ruffle, scratch or whatever. Put your damaged tape into a source machine and note the time code (or zero the counter) where the damage begins. Rewind the tape to wherever you want to begin the transfer. Then put the source machine into *play* and the record machine into *record*.
2. Press *stop* on your source machine just before you get to the damaged section, and *pause* the record machine.
3. *While in stop, fast forward* the source machine until you're sure you have passed the damaged part. In *fast forward* mode the damaged tape will not be in contact with the heads. DO NOT use search mode! If you can see the image on the player monitor, you're in search mode, and using this drags the damaged tape even faster across the fragile heads, increasing the likelihood of damage.
4. Return the source machine to play mode when it's reached good tape again, and put the record machine back into record mode to copy the rest of the footage to the end of your video.
5. Then throw the damaged tape away. Or if you're into the unusual, use it for streamers at your next party.

Warning: Some machines do keep contact with the heads in fast forward and rewind modes—so check out your VCR before you begin this process.

Archiving Videotapes

You may be surprised at the thought of yourself as an archivist, but it doesn't take long to get quite a stock of recorded tapes, and presumably you want them to stay in good condition.

It's recommended that you keep them in a cool, dry (low humidity), dust-free storage space and away from direct sunlight. NOT in metal cabinets— remember they're magnetic particles. NOT in sealed plastic bags—there should be airflow around them so they don't experience dampness. They shouldn't be on the floor, in case of flooding.

I used the software program ScenalyzerLive to catalogue each of my miniDV tapes. It creates thumbnails when it detects a new scene. This makes it easier to recall the tape contents. I enter a description into an Excel spreadsheet so that I can search keywords when I am searching for footage.

Alan Petschack, Videographer.

You should 'repack' archived tapes at least every three years to release any stress which has built up due to moisture absorption. Some people do this by fast-forwarding and rewinding them. Other people do this by playing them, which is claimed to be a more gentle way of repacking them.

It's not such a great idea to put old tapes in pause mode for long at all, as this can scrub down the magnetic layer and degenerate the image stored there.

If you find they've grown some mildew or other fungus (as I did once, to my horror) you need to have them professionally cleaned.

Your original footage, your *masters*, should always be copied straight away so you have *security dubs* (or *secondary masters*) of your material. The masters and security dubs should be kept in separate places—separate buildings, if possible—in case of fire and other unexpected major damage.

> I actually prefer tape because of its archival nature.

Don Pollock,
University
of La Verne,
California.

You should make sure that the record tab is broken off your masters or the slider has been moved to the locked or 'save' position.

Longevity of Videotape

How long is a piece of string? VHS tapes are now well over 30 years old. Some still play fine, others are hopeless. Even if you keep your tapes in very good conditions, you probably shouldn't count on going more than ten years, maybe less, before you make copies of your footage onto new tapes or into other storage media.

AIT Series (1–5) of Tapes for Data Storage

Sony's AIT (advanced intelligent tape) format is designed for backup and archiving. It features WORM (write once read many) technology. Information in these tape cartridges cannot be wiped out or changed. It requires a special drive to use it, so you can't just pop one of these tapes into your VCR.

The claim is that these tapes will last 30 years and can allow 30000 end-to-end passes. Access to the stored data is through use of the MIC (memory in cassette) chip, which allows for fast searching and fast loading of the material. It's cheaper per gigabyte than optical storage media (CD, DVD) and each cassette has a far higher capacity.

You can plug the LaCie Rugged Hard Disk Drive into almost any computer for backup, video storage and large data volume exchange. With its rubber bumper it's suited to extreme conditions. (Courtesy of LaCie)

Hard Drives

Another form of magnetic storage is found both inside your computer (the *hard drive*) and in portable forms, called *external drives* or *portable hard drives*. You can increase your available memory in two ways. You can add boards to the inside of your computer. Internal hard disk drives slot into a 'bay' and are connected by ribbon and power cables to the mother board. Or you can just plug in external hard drives, usually through the USB connection.

A hard drive also has a record head like a videotape recorder does, but unlike with videotape, the head doesn't come into direct contact with the platter onto which the information is written. When the hard drive is on, the platter spins at high speed and the head glides over the top of it, able to randomly access any section of it. If the hard disk is jolted, the record head could bang into the delicate magnetic surface of the disk and permanent damage can result. If this 'crash' happens in the directory region of the hard drive, then the information on the disk may no longer be accessible.

Because a hard disk crash can be so disastrous, always have your footage backed up on another hard drive or in some other storage medium. This is a good reason to keep your master tapes, if you're still using tape.

The LaCie Little Big Disk Quadra can store 500 GB and 1 TB. Its aluminium heatsink body requires no fan, so it's silent. (Courtesy of LaCie)

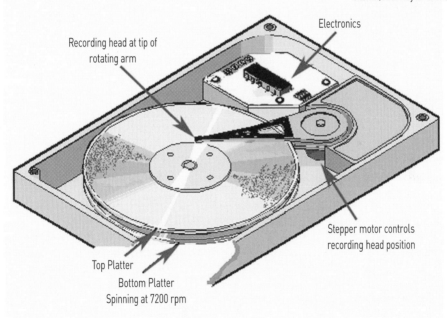

Recording head at tip of rotating arm

Electronics

Stepper motor controls recording head position

Top Platter

Bottom Platter
Spinning at 7200 rpm

To avoid damage, be sure to follow the correct procedure before turning off or disconnecting your hard disk.

When the hard drive is correctly *put away* before it's turned off or disconnected from your computer, the head is moved out of range of the platter and safely *parked*.

When in sleep mode, your computer should also park the record head.

It's important to not cut power to a hard drive without going through the correct shutdown procedure. You don't want to stop it from finishing writing any data that

Back it all up, and back up the backup.

Peter Chvany, Facilities Manager, Emerson College.

Your first drive won't be your last.

might still be cached either by the computer or the hard drive because that data could be lost.

Hard drives can store your video footage either in full quality or in whatever level of compressed version you send to them, and a good-sized hard drive can store the information of several videotapes.

Hard drives are usually referred to by the amount of memory they provide, and they have increased dramatically in their storage capacity and come down considerably in price.

Once an 80 GB hard drive was considered good, but now you can purchase 250 GB, 500 GB, 750 GB, 1000 GB (a Terabyte) and even more.

To help you understand this storage terminology, here's a quick tour of computer memory terms.

A *bit* is the basic unit of measurement. A bit stores just one value, either a 1 or a 0, which are the only numbers in the binary system computers use (1 = on and 0 = off).

A *byte* is made up of eight bits, so depending on the way the bits are arranged, it can store any one of 256 values (2 to the power of 8). (A *nibble* is four bits—you don't need to know this, but I like the word myself.)

A *kilobyte (KB)* is roughly 1000 bytes. Technically it's a little over that amount; it's 1024. This is arrived at by taking 2 to the power of 10, but for our purposes 1000 is close enough. Kilobytes are often referred to as Ks. Text files tend to be in Ks.

By the same token, a *megabyte (MB)* is roughly a million bytes. (People talk about *megs*, meaning megabytes.) Graphic and picture files are often in megs.

A *gigabyte (GB)* is roughly what Americans call a billion, and what Australians call a thousand million. So that's what people mean when they say *gigs* (unless they're musicians!). Video files are generally gigabytes in size. Despite the 5:1 compression, one hour of DV video takes about 13 GB to store.

A *terabyte (TB)* is a trillion bytes.

You just basically need to remember that a meg is a lot bigger than a K, a gig is way bigger than a meg, and a TB is unbelievably huge.

Lindsay Ward,
School of
Information
Technology,
James Cook
University.

You know how the saying goes—the amount of data we want to store is always just that little bit more than the amount of storage space available.

A RAID

A RAID (redundant array of independent disks) can store terabytes of data. With its two or more identical drives it can simultaneously store on one and do a mirror backup on the other, or it can write across all disks for higher speed.

A Server

In a media centre situation, computer editing facilities can be networked so video footage can be stored on the high-capacity servers, rather than on each individual computer's hard drive. Then the footage can be made accessible to all, which is a system that works well for distributing editing exercises to lots of learners. Alternatively, each person's video files can be kept on the server but be password protected so they are only available to the person or team responsible for shooting them.

The LaCie Hard Disk MAX can handle terabytes of data and operate in either RAID 0, for high capacity, or in RAID1 (SAFE) which does simultaneous backups for high security.

IceCube and Other Drive Holders

The IceCube isn't a drive itself, it's an external drive *holder* designed for desktop operation and portable use. Though it's well known, it's just one of many external hard drive-holder brands. You can put drives of different sizes in it, according to your needs. If you buy a holder and hard drive separately, make sure they're compatible in both size and connection ports.

At some public access sites in the States, they encourage people to use their own home computers for editing, so they sign out a hard drive for a month or so at a time, and expect the finished product to be turned in on that!

Barbara Bishop, Independent Producer.

You can also *daisy chain* external hard drives, which means you can attach two or more together via their in and out connection ports, and have a string of them all connected to your computer at once. This will increase your storage space without using up more connection ports on your computer.

Alternatively, you can use a USB2 hub to connect various sources to your computer via just one port.

The IceCube is *hot swappable*, which means you can disconnect one and connect another through the FireWire port while your edit session is running, without any problem to the computer in recognising the new drive.

The Clearlight is a smaller version of the IceCube and is handy for use with laptops.

Small drives can be *phantom powered* by your computer, which means the computer can supply the electricity to operate them. But bigger drives need to be plugged into the wall current.

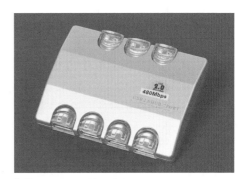

As they say, any port in a storm...

Connection Ports

External drives can be connected to computers via cables attached to their connection ports. When purchasing an external drive, be sure to match the ports on your computer with the ports on your potential external drive.

Be very wary of how many devices you attach to your computer editing system. The computer will be phantom-powering them. It can handle a moderate load, but it can't run your refrigerator.

Bill O'Donnell, Video Consultant.

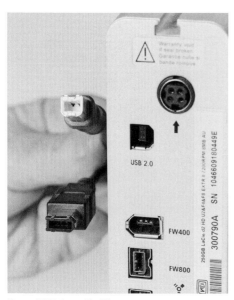

Upper: USB2, lower: FireWire.

USB (UNIVERSAL SERIAL BUS)

This connection was designed to be the standard connection for a wide variety of computer *peripherals*, including the mouse, keyboard, digital stills camera, flash memory and some hard drives. This is the slowest of the connections you'll come across on a hard drive.

FIREWIRE (APPLE) OR iLINK (SONY)

Firewire 400 (known technically as IEEE 1394 interface) was released in 1995 and designed as a higher-speed connection, to supersede the SCSI bus (Small Computer System Interface). Since then, it has been upgraded and is available in FireWire 800, which is much faster and has a different shaped connection port, but it remains backward compatible.

PC users can buy a PCI (peripheral component interconnect) board interface with FireWire ports so they can use FireWire for capturing their video.

USB2

This is the newer, much faster USB connection. Though USB 2.0 is a 480 Mbps interface and FireWire 400 is a 400 Mbps interface, due to differences in their architecture, FireWire 400 performs overall at a faster rate.

SATA

The very high speed SATA (Serial ATA drive) connector is said to have a transfer rate of 150 MB/sec. (Note the capital *B* here, this means mega*bytes*, not megabits, as in the earlier speeds mentioned previously.)

Care of Hard Drives

As with videotape, there are certain things to bear in mind to keep them running well:

1. Don't move the hard drive while it's in use. This can cause the record head to crash into the magnetic disc and damage it.
2. Don't place it near strong magnetic forces, such as speakers, magnets and electric motors.
3. Consider connecting it to a surge protector and power stabiliser.
4. Give it some air space at the back so its ventilation system can keep it cool.
5. Keep it switched off when not in use.
6. Always quit from your drive correctly according to your computer operating system. Don't just unplug it or switch it off.
7. Don't rely on one drive as your sole archive. Always back up your data somewhere else. Hard drives do die, very suddenly and unexpectedly.
8. Plan to replace your drive every few years.
9. Defragmenting the drive now and then can help improve access times.

HDD Cameras (Hard Disk Drive)

Some video cameras record on non-removable hard drives, and some have removable hard drives. These hard drives vary in both physical size and storage capacity.

HDD cameras also differ in the method in which they record the video signal. Some record in MPEG2 and some record using the AVCHD format (see page 127). A very few are selectable and record in both. Both of these compression formats are greater than miniDV, so you can put lots of video on the drives, but the quality is less.

Sometimes their recording format is referred to as 'DVD level' in the advertisements, which sounds okay, as we're used to watching good quality on

The Canon Legria HG21 HD HDD has 120 GB of storage. (Courtesy of Canon)

DVDs. But it means the video is already highly compressed as you record it. Your editing system might compress it further, and your DVD burning program will compress it even further again. How far down do you want to go?

Be very careful when you purchase an HDD camera to be sure the video can be exported from the camera into your computer! Watch out for cameras using file formats that are incompatible with your computer editing system. Some cameras use their own proprietary editing software that comes with the camera or is downloadable from the internet, but which just won't interface with your own, nor will it have the power of the edit system you already have.

Hybrid Cameras

And then there are the *hybrid* cameras which come with both hard drive recording and removable flash memory cards. Presently the size of the hard drives exceeds by a wide margin that of the flash memory cards.

External Hard Drives for Field Recording

The EDIROL F-1 by Roland is a device designed specifically for people who want or need to accelerate their production work flow by getting footage to other hard drives at the time of recording.

This device captures HDV or DV directly to a shock-resistant and removable floating hard drive,

Sony HDR-SR12 120GB HD Hybrid Camcorder: You can record for up to 14.5 hours and use the memory stick for transferring video and stills to your PC for editing, emailing or printing once you're done. (Courtesy of Sony)

while at the same time you can record directly to videotape in the camera as a backup or as a master tape, depending on how you think about it.

Skip transferring files back in the edit room; record directly to external drives in the field. The EDIROL F-1. (Courtesy of Roland Systems Group US)

The EDIROL F-1 can be used as a separate piece of equipment or it can be part of a camera. (Courtesy of Roland Systems Group US)

CD or DVD: How to tell them apart? Read their label.

The Edirol F-1 has two channels of additional audio inputs, too, as well as multiple power supply options, and remote control via LAN (local area network). You can review your clips via the RGB (red green blue) output and it comes with software so you can do basic editing and file management in the field.

Optical Media: CD, DVD, BD (Blu-ray Disc)

CD and VCD (Video Compact Disc)

CD is the early form of optical recording media. A CD is a polycarbonate disc, with a reflective layer over it (usually aluminium but sometimes gold) which is covered by a protective lacquer layer. CDs are 12 cm wide and 1.2 mm thick.

VCDs are the later version of CDs, designed for the storage of digital data. A VCD can hold up to 800MB of information and is recorded using MPEG1. The quality on a VCD is like that of VHS.

The data on a CD is recorded in tiny pits along a spiral track which starts at the centre and works its way outward. The information is written and read back by a red laser beam.

DVD (Digital Versatile Disc or Digital Video Disc)

DVD is a big advance on CD when it comes to storage capacity. Though the discs are the same size, a DVD can store 4.7 GB on a single-layer disc and up to 18 GB on a double-layered, double-sided disc. Single-layer discs are labelled SL and double-layer discs are labelled DL.

DVD also relies on a red laser to read and write the data, but it has a shorter wavelength than for CDs, and it uses a smaller pit size and a smaller track pitch than CDs, so more data can be recorded on it. There are three competing formats for DVD: DVD-R, DVD+R and DVD-RAM. The *R* means read only.

There are further disc types, which relate to the previous formats: DVD-RW and DVD+RW. The *W* means the disc is rewritable. The claim is that it's rewritable 1000 times.

Though these DVD formats aren't compatible, the format war is pretty much over because newer devices will play all the formats and are referred to as DVD+RW.

Unlike videotape, DVDs also support features such as menus, selectable subtitles, multiple camera angles and multiple audio tracks. A DVD allows you to go directly to the segment you want to view.

It's not so easy to get files off a DVD, though. You might need to get a DVD ripper, which can be downloaded from the internet.

DVD Structure

A DVD is made of two polycarbonate discs, bonded together. On a single-sided disc, one disc contains the laser guiding groove, coated with the recording dye and a silver alloy or gold reflector, and the other one is just smooth. The second disc helps make the DVD more rigid and it builds the width up to the standard CD size. Double-sided discs have two grooved recording sides, so the disc must be flipped to access the data on the other side.

A *dual-layer* disc has a second physical layer within the disc itself which is accessed by shining the laser through the first semi-transparent layer. There can be a slight hesitation in playback when shifting from one layer to the other. There are two recording methods for these. *Parallel track path* (PTP) has both layers start at the inside diameter (ID) and end at the outside diameter (OD). This system is used with DVD-ROM. *Opposite track path* (OTP) has the lower layer start at the ID and the upper layer start at the OD, where the other layer ends. This is used on many DVD-Video discs.

MiniDVD

MiniDVDs are just 8 cm (3 inches) across and are used in some video cameras for recording directly onto discs, which can then be put into a computer, for editing without the download time.

Storage capacity is:

- single-sided, single layer: 1.4 GB
- single-sided, double layer: 2.66 GB
- double-sided, single layer: 2.8 GB
- double-sided, double layer: 5.2 GB.

Blu-ray Disc (BD)

Blu-ray, also known as Blu-ray Disc (BD), provides more than five times the storage capacity of DVDs, even though it's still the same size. A Blu-ray disc can hold up to 25 GB on a single-layer disc and 50 GB on a dual-layer disc.

Blu-ray gets its name from the blue-violet laser it uses. This laser has a much shorter wavelength than the red one used for DVDs, so it can be focused with greater precision, allowing data to be packed more tightly and stored in less space.

Blu-ray products can be backward compatible with CDs and DVDs through the use of a BD/DVD/CD compatible optical pick-up unit.

Sony flash memory card for EX-1 and EX-3 cameras. This is an 8 gig card. They come in bigger flavours too. (Courtesy of University of La Verne)

With a USB flash memory key on your key ring, you're ready to download files anywhere.

The Canon Legria FS100 has a built-in SDHC card slot. (Courtesy of Canon)

Don Pollock, University of La Verne, California.

The workflow is very different. You need to download the cards to a computer on location and you'd better be sure to back up. So now you need a laptop on location and two hard drives and an extra crew member to do the downloading so you can free up the cards to keep shooting.

Blu-ray was developed to enable recording, rewriting and playback of high-definition (HD) video, as well as storing large amounts of data.

Pioneer has announced an advanced Blu-ray disc with a storage capacity of 500 GB by using 20 layers.

Care of Optical Media

The main damage to optical discs is mechanical. Be sure to put each disc back in its container when it's not in use. Having lots of discs lying around out in the open on your computer desk or editing space is just asking for scratches and other damage.

When mailing discs, it's far better to use the hard plastic jewel cases than the soft paper or cardboard sleeves, and it's better to use a mailing box rather than a flexible envelope because the discs can crack and break if handled roughly. Once broken, the disc can't be played.

Solid-State Media: Flash Memory

Flash memory is known as *solid-state* memory because there are no moving parts involved in either recording or playback—everything is electronic instead of mechanical. Because flash memory has no moving parts, it's noiseless. It also allows faster access and is lighter in weight and smaller in size than hard drive memory.

Flash memory for video cameras comes in cards. For transferring data between hard drives it can be either in memory sticks which plug into USB drives, or in cards that plug into slots.

Flash memory is highly resistant to vibration and humidity, and it uses less power than disc recording. It is claimed that it has a much longer life—up to 100000 record and playback times. And it uploads files at a faster speed.

However, flash memory is still much more expensive per gigabyte than hard drive memory. Until cost and capacity are improved, solid-state devices might mainly be used for short-term storage and data transfers.

Flash Memory Cameras

Video cameras that use flash memory can take one or two cards which can be removed and used to transfer recorded video into computers or other devices. Flash memory sticks don't come in very large capacities yet, so cameras which record exclusively to flash memory must use very high compression rates.

Using cards is a faster process of transferring material into the edit system, and you don't have to pay for tapes to shoot on as the media is reusable a large number of times.

Don Pollock, University of La Verne, California.

Which leads us to one of the key ideas in digital video storage: *compression*.

Compression

In any video picture, there are many tiny bits of picture information, some of which are repetitive.

This pretty scene can be greatly compressed without any noticeable loss for the viewer.

To understand this, imagine a scene with a little pond surrounded by trees in full leaf. The surface of the pond is mostly blue, the trees are mostly green. When this image is electronically scanned, the data produced says, in effect:

Green, green, green, green, green, green, green, green, green, green, green, for a horizontal line across the wooded area.

And blue, blue, blue, blue, blue, blue, blue, blue, blue, blue, blue, blue, blue, blue, blue, for a similar horizontal line across the pond.

Of course, the trees have trunks which are also evident, and there may be ducks on the pond. But still, *much* of the additional picture information, on any given horizontal line, is a repeat of the same.

So, instead of wasting storage space by repeating so much of the data, there's a way to electronically say *ditto* (*compressing* the data) when storing the picture information, and a corresponding way to uncompress the picture correctly when it has to be displayed.

Thus:	green	In effect becomes:	green
	green		"
	green		"
	green		"
	green		"

In a way, compression is like a ditto formula, which saves lots of storage space.

Not all subjects compress as well. Simple shots with large areas of uniform colours compress well. Very intricate areas with a lot of small details aren't as successful. For example, a presenter giving the news in front of a fixed background compresses better than a shot with lots of varied colour and movement in it.

HD TAPE/FORMAT COMPATIBILITY MATRIX

	1080p					1080i			720p			Comp	Color Samp	Data Rates Mb/s
	23.98	24	25	29.97	30	25 50	29.97 59.94	30 60	50	59.94	60			
HD-CAM SR	√	√	√	√	√	√	√	√	√	√	√	2.7:1	4:4:4 4:2:2	880 440
D5-HD	√	√	√	√	√	√	√	√	√	√	√	4:1	4:2:2	210
HD-CAM	√	√	√	√	√	√	√	√				4:1	3:1:1	140
DVCPRO HD						√	√	√	√	√	√	7:1	4:2:2	100
HDV*	JVC					√	√	√	√	√	√	20:1	4:2:0	25
AVCHD*	?	?	?	?	?	√	√	?	√	√	?	30:1	4:2:0	18

* HDV & AVCHD are new formats with low cost cameras, but be aware that they can be very difficult to work with in post production, and new products are being introduced every day.

How much compression can your project (and client) live with? (Graphic by David Jahns)

Digital video cameras compress video as they record it. The standard compression rate for DV is 5:1. You may also hear the expression 'DV25'. This comes from the fact that DV compression is at a fixed rate of 25 megabits per second. So right from the start with digital video, you're dealing with a compressed image.

When the signal is passed into a computer, it can be compressed even further, in order to reduce the file size and save on the use of the hard drive's memory.

What is a Codec?

A *codec* is what compresses and decompresses video signals. Get it? **Co**mpresses and **dec**ompresses. A codec can be a piece of hardware that can be purchased on its own. It's sometimes inbuilt in equipment like DV camcorders and capture cards. A codec can also be software.

Some codecs operate with a fixed compression rate, and some have the ability for the compression rate to be varied, and set as needed by the operator.

With a variable codec, you can choose whatever compression rate you want to work with. When starting your edit, you may want to enter large amounts of footage into the computer as possible source material. This can be fairly highly compressed. But in the end, you should do your final cut from files that are entered into the computer as less compressed video. This way, your final product can assembled, stored and output at the best quality your system can deliver.

What is AVCHD?

AVCHD is a high-definition (HD) video recording format which records 1080i and 720p signals onto DVDs, SD memory cards and hard drives. It's more efficient than previous codecs such as MPEG2, which has been the standard compression for DVDs. Blu-ray uses AVCHD.

Merits and Disadvantages of Different Data Storage

Of course, people wonder which is the best medium for recording and storing video when there are so many options available. Although I don't think there's one definitive answer, here are some things to think about.

Cost Per Gigabyte

Videotape still has the edge here.

Ease of Use for You

Some videographers have no problem with using cables to hook up a camera to a computer, while others just leave their cable set-up ready for their return, or even use a separate camera or player for downloading.

> When the project is finished, how do you archive your HD dailies? You could burn them to Blu-ray if you have that capability. You could burn to a DVD, but then you won't be in HD.

Don Pollock, University of La Verne, California.

Some people have the time to download video from tapes and other people are far happier to pop in a miniDVD disc or a flash memory and go straight from there.

Weight is a big consideration, especially for older, younger and differently abled people. The super-light flash memory palmcorders could be a big advantage here.

Accessing particular shots in your footage is quicker and easier on any other medium than it is on videotape.

Not all hard disk drive (HDD) cameras download easily into your computer.

Flexibility

Hard drives allow random access so you can quickly locate desired material, delete unwanted files, and rearrange playback sequences. There's no need to be fast forwarding or rewinding tape while referring to your logging sheet.

With some flash memory systems, both video and still pictures can be recorded on the same medium, which can be a handy aspect.

Some systems allow for recording and storing at variable compression rates, and that delights certain users. But others are into point-and-shoot and don't even want to think about that number stuff.

For people who are doing a joint project, it's a big advantage to have a portable hard drive to move large amounts of footage from one editing site to another. Memory sticks just don't cut it yet with big amounts of video.

External drives are restricted in data flow speed by the type of connection used.

Security of Recorded Video

If you're the sole user of a video camera, then security of recorded material is probably not an issue. But when a camera is shared among family or friends, or borrowable from a media centre, security of data looms large.

It's better if you can remove your material from the camera before someone else gets to use it, so no one can see it, if it's private or confidential, and no one can access it for their own purposes and give you problems resulting from loss of control of your shots. It goes without saying that you don't want your footage recorded over.

In the days of tape, media centres issued students with tapes for the semester and hopefully they were bulk-erased when returned. As tape costs came down, students chose (or were required) to buy their own stock. So all but the forgetful or chronically disorganised took their tapes out of the camera and went home with them. Their material was theirs alone.

Hard drive cameras present new problems because it's not so easy to be always dumping off the last recording session, and there's the added hazard of losing original material if there's a computer failure and the copying process doesn't work; however, no one knows this until the camera's drive has been erased. Oh dear.

Flash memory and DVD cameras are a mix of possibilities. A flash drive or miniDVD disc for every user might be possible and material can be taken away on it. But is this what people are doing?

Printing on paper lasts hundreds of years. What digital device beats that? Margaret Miller enjoys the 'video' of her own imagination.

Robustness of the Storage Medium

Which would you rather drop—a videotape, a DVD, a memory stick or a hard drive? Which can take more heat or humidity?

Videotape is known to be affected by humidity and to develop sticky tape syndrome or grow mould.

Optical media can get scratched or cracked.

Hard drives (as we've all experienced?) can just up and die for no apparent reason.

Archiving

Archiving media relies on two general factors: device obsolescence and materials durability.

Those who have been working in digital video for some years will recall many magnetic media storage devices which have passed into obscurity. Who now uses zip drives, orb cartridges or bricks?

Whatever the merits of a medium, if there are no longer devices to play it, the material stored on it is lost.

Manufacturers make all sorts of claims about durability when they introduce a new technology. But it's time that tells. Some 30-year-old VHS tapes still play, some don't.

Claims are made that DVD-R and DVD+R can last for 30–100 years, and *up to* 30 years for DVD-RW, DVD+RW and DVD-RAM. But many factors affect the life of a DVD: the sealing method, the reflective layer, the organic dye, the manufacturer and the method of storage.

Given a situation of damage, with videotape you might lose a few seconds of footage, but not the entire recording. With scratched DVDs and those spirit-plummeting hard drive crashes, you know all is lost.

Thanks to David Jahns, Phil Cooper, Peter Chvany, Bill O'Donnell and Lindsay Ward for their help in the preparation of this chapter.

8 EDITING BASICS

Whatever computer editing software you use, you can expect it to do certain basic operations. The opening screen may look quite different from one to the next, but the essential functions are the same.

Though learning the first system may be a steep climb for you, especially if you're not familiar with computers, every one after that will make more sense because you'll know what to look for.

Editing class with Tim Rooney at Portland Community Media.

Some editing programs come bundled with other software when you buy a new computer. So they're free and they're good ones to start learning on. iMovie comes with Macintosh computers; Windows Movie Maker comes with other PCs.

As you expect more from your editing system, you'll probably move on to a program that you have to pay for, because it will have more features and you can perform more complex edits. Some well-known editing programs are:

- Final Cut Pro <www.apple.com/finalcutstudio/finalcutpro>
- Adobe Premier <www.adobe.com/products/premiere>

- Vegas Video <www.sonycreativesoftware.com/vegaspro>
- VideoStudio Pro <www.corel.com>
- Pinnacle Studio <www.pinnaclesys.com/PublicSite/us/Home>
- Edius HDStorm <desktop.grassvalley.com/products/HDSTORM/index.php>
- AVS Video Editor <avs4you.com/AVS-Video-Editor.aspx>.

When you're deciding which one to buy, you'll no doubt consider price, but also check to make sure that the package you buy is able to import the file format from your camera and that it can output the type of file you want for your end product.

When setting up an edit system, make sure you consider ergonomics. A monitor should be at your comfortable eye level. You shouldn't be tilting your head up or down to see it, or your neck will revolt.

Rob Davis,
Editor, Digital Dimensions.

Basic Editing Functions

Your edit program will do these things:

1. Capture footage from your camera and other sources.
2. Store the footage so you can access it for editing.
3. Let you name and sort the shots into categories which make sense to you.
4. Provide a workspace (usually called a *timeline*) where you can put your shots into an order.
5. Provide a way for you to adjust the volume of the sound (audio).
6. Have a viewing space where you can look at your program as it stands.
7. Give you a range of possible transitions (like fade and dissolve) for going from one shot to the next.
8. Allow you to import and use still photos.
9. Allow you to import and use music and sound effects.
10. Allow you to add simple titles.
11. Possibly give you a choice of some special video effects you can add to your shots.

Capture and Import

When you're bringing video footage into your edit system directly from your camera, it's called *capturing*.

When you're bringing in video files from another project, or bringing in photos or audio files, it's called *importing*.

Wherever you are, you can be editing. Working at sea. (Courtesy of Digital Dimensions)

Capture

To capture the footage from your camera, you need to first connect the camera to your computer. This is done using a FireWire (iLink) cable. Then turn your camera on

and finally open your editing software. You should get a message indicating that the computer can 'see' the camera. If not, check the cables again, and confirm that the camera is indeed on. The camera should be in playback mode unless you want to do a live capture right there and then, without going through a recording process.

Note: If you're using video that has been recorded onto a DVD or flash memory card, you will need to insert that medium into the correct slot or disc holder on your computer and go from there.

Capturing from videotape happens in *real time*—that is, an hour of video will take an hour to capture if you don't stop and start it.

The most *basic capture* is to take in whatever is on your recording, from beginning to end. You can just start the capture and walk away for a while, letting the program do its thing. In a busy life, this is an attractive option. The disadvantage is that you could be capturing stuff you won't want and using up more hard drive memory than necessary.

Your edit program might automatically break the footage into individual shots (*clips*) wherever you have put the camera into pause mode. This is a handy feature and it makes the material more manageable.

Cathy Zheutlin prepares to capture video for *Holy Rascals.*

First thing to do when you start a non-linear edit is to look at the tapes. Second thing to do is log them. Third thing, look at them again. Fourth thing is a paper-edit. Fifth and final thing, turn on the computer.

Francis Treacey, Deakin University.

Some programs give you the choice of either capturing all the footage directly to the timeline, or sending it into a holding space from which you pick and choose the bits you want.

Say you've recorded a family birthday party. You could choose to put your whole recording straight onto the timeline since it's an event that has a clear chronological order which your viewers know and expect. You'll probably just want to eliminate the bad shots (or indiscreet comments) and give it out to everyone. A few cuts here and there, some titles, some music and you're done.

Familiarity with the footage is always helpful. If tapes are captured in their entirety, then knowing the shot order via timecode logs and visually allows you to quickly locate them using the play head tool.

Philip Elms, Media Resource Centre.

But if you want to do lots of rearranging of shots, it's easier if you store your footage into the *clip viewer* (or *browser,* or whatever your program calls it).

Once all your shots are captured, you can recognise them by the *thumbnail* that represents each one. The thumbnail is a tiny image that usually shows the first frame of each shot. This doesn't always work as a good shot identifier, but your program should allow you to choose a different frame to be the thumbnail image, if that's the case.

You'll also have the option of giving names to your shots. Naming needs to be done carefully.

You can label your shots as anything you choose, but it has to make enough sense that you can easily find what you're looking for later. Unless you have a photographic memory, don't go for something like: skiing 1, skiing 2, skiing 3, skiing 4!

The names should clarify the content of each shot, so something like ski rack on car, chairlift wobbling, Mt Hood Meadows practice run, race with Dieter, would be more useful.

On some systems, you can have the clips list out in several different ways. For example, you can view your shots by small or large thumbnails, or if you're a text-oriented person they can be listed alphabetically by title, by date recorded or by length of clip, and you can switch between these ways as needed.

Another capture method is *capture now*. With this method, you sit with the edit system and tell it when to start and stop capturing. If you've looked at your footage first and done a basic *log* (list, map) of it, you'll have a good idea of what you want to keep and what's useless to you.

As much as possible, break your material into small segments as you capture it. Then it will be easier to trim and manipulate during the editing phase. You could bring in each take or usable shot individually, or by each script segment. Very long slabs of video will require lots of cutting up later.

If you're not a prepare-first person, you can still sit and do capture now on the fly, but it won't be totally quick because you'll be rewinding and forwarding as you decide what to keep or not to keep.

Another way is to *batch capture*. Not all systems do this, but yours might.

With this method, you go through your footage and mark all the start and end points of the shots you want to capture. Then you tell the computer to begin; again, you can do something else for a while. With capture now and batch capture you only expend hard drive memory on the shots you want to keep.

Import

One of the beauties of video has always been that you can use footage over and over again in different ways, for different projects. Once you've captured

When capturing footage, it's better to capture it in sections rather than as a whole. If you do it in sections, later when you want to make space on your hard drive you can selectively delete some of your media files.

Melissa Bourne, Editor.

Everything is marked, everything is clear, everything has a folder to go in.

Tim Rooney, Portland Community Media.

Make your project so that someone else can open it and figure it out. Label *everything* in an obvious way.

Peter Poire-Odegarde, Portland Community Media.

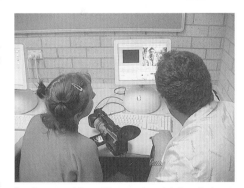

Your best use of time while capturing might be to look at your footage.

During postproduction, one often asks, 'What went wrong?'

Everyone has problems or makes mistakes. The real trick is to learn from your experience.

Rachel Masters, Corporate Training Coordinator, SBS.

Rob Davis,
Editor, Digital
Dimensions.

To capture many shots at
once, you can do a *batch
capture*. If there's a break in
your timecode, you can't batch
capture across the break.

**Melissa
Bourne**, Editor.

When capturing, keep in mind
that you want to organise
files not only for your own
understanding but just in
case you got sick and needed
someone else to edit, they
would be able to continue
where you left off.
Professionally, it will save
money and time.

Your project can include photographs, music, sound
effects, graphics, video from other sources, film converted
to video, and the list goes on. Julie Booras at work in her
studio for Offspring Productions, Lynnfield, Massachusetts.

Tim Rooney,
Portland
Community
Media.

Never have anything called
untitled. Untitled means
*this is something you will
never find when you need it.*

your footage, you can access it again from your hard
drive and import it into any other project.

You can also import graphics, photo files and
audio files into your edit program. In fact, iMovie
is set up so it automatically links to both iPhoto
and iTunes, which is very convenient.

When you get more advanced, you can export
still frames to Photoshop, alter them and bring them
back into your project in their new glory.

You can also import an entire previous edit into
a new project, but the catch is that it may come
into your project as a unified whole. The shots may
no longer be separate, and you may not be able to
easily split the audio from the video.

Handling Your Media

As your video data is stored 'in a black box'—in
other words, you can't actually get your hands on
it as you could with analogue tapes—it's essential
for you to understand where it is on your hard drive
and how to get to it.

Clips and Bins

Each section of video and audio that you've
captured and labelled is referred to as a *clip*, and
it's represented in your clip viewer or browser by
a thumbnail or title.

Each clip can be selected and played independently of any other clip. And you can choose to sort
your clips by categories, and group them in *bins*.

The terms *clip* and *bin* come from the days of
actual film editing, but if you're familiar with word
processing, a clip is rather like a document and a
bin is like a folder.

So you might find it useful to put all the clips
of the actual hockey game in one bin, the cutaways
of the crowd in another bin, the graphics you've
designed for the project in a third bin and so on.

The decision as to which bin to put a shot
in needn't be agonising; by making a copy you
can store a clip in more than one bin. But getting
organised means that when the time comes to edit,
you don't have to look through all your shots to
find something.

Know Where Your Media Is Stored

Sometimes people get confused between the clip icons and the stored media files. The media files are the actual video data, and they're what take up the huge amount of storage space on your hard drive. The clip icons are merely the in and out points of the various shots in your stored media. In a sense, they're pointers for the computer to find the images, but not the images themselves.

So if you decide to delete your material from the computer and you just delete the clip icons, the computer will still be burdened with the huge files of your images.

On the other hand, if you delete the digitised media and save the clip icons, you'll have no images for the computer to go to.

Destructive and Non-destructive Edit Programs

Entry-level editing systems handle captured media in a way that is simplified for beginners. All the media is significantly *compressed* and *captured directly into* the project you're working on, rather than into a dedicated space (*scratch disk*) on your hard drive.

Programs like this are referred to as *destructive*, because your media files can be changed or gotten rid of from within the project.

If you cut a clip into pieces, it stays cut (unless you do an undo on it). Any clips or trims that you put into the trash bin within the project get deleted entirely from your drive when you empty the trash. If you delete the project, everything is gone—clips and media files both.

As long as you don't trash them, you can access these clips again, either from your clip viewer or your timeline, for use in other projects.

The good thing is that you don't have gigabytes of footage lurking unseen in the bowels of your computer, and the bad thing is that if you copy a project, it duplicates EVERYTHING, all the media files, thus doubling the used storage space.

With the more complex systems like Final Cut Pro, your media files are stored on a *scratch disk*, which is a section you designate on your computer's hard drive or another hard drive. You establish the

Envision what your hard drive will look like when you're done and start there: voiceover folder, soundtrack folder, raw images, ready images, graphics in progress.

Tim Rooney, Portland Community Media.

File structure is huge. Put every asset you're using into your project file. By this I mean the media, render files, music, graphics, everything, not just the go-to icons. Don't have your project's assets spread across several drives.

Paul Sosso, Editor/ Producer.

It's possible to be doing basic cut-and-paste editing in a few minutes, but if you don't know the structure of the data management in the computer (i.e. where rendered files, master clips, etc. reside) it's possible to delete the wrong information and something you've spent ages on can disappear in a keystroke.

Rob Davis, Editor, Digital Dimensions.

Editing class. (Courtesy of Portland Community Media)

location of the scratch disk in the program *preferences* or your program will default it to a section called Final Cut Pro Capture Scratch.

Your clips stay there unless you move them or deliberately put them in the main trash and empty it. You can't even accidentally delete them by clicking on them and pressing delete. So that's good, because they're protected. It's also good because you can use them again and again by importing them into new projects.

Scratch Disks					

Scratch Disks						
Video Capture	Audio Capture	Video Render	Audio Render			
☐	☐	☐	☐	Clear	Set...	12.9 GB on Macintosh HD/Users/m...l Cut Pro Documents
☑	☑	☑	☑	Clear	Set...	28.3 GB on Martha's LaCie Disk
☐	☐	☐	☐	Clear	Set...	6.0 GB on USB Disk
☐	☐	☐	☐	Clear	Set...	<None Set>

☐ Capture Audio and Video to Separate Files

Waveform Cache: Set...   12.9 GB on Macintosh HD/Users/marthamol...ments/Final Cut Pro Documents
Thumbnail Cache: Set...   12.9 GB on Macintosh HD/Users/marthamol...ments/Final Cut Pro Documents
Autosave Vault: Set...   12.9 GB on Macintosh HD/Users/marthamol...ments/Final Cut Pro Documents

Minimum Allowable Free Space On Scratch Disks: 800 MB
☐ Limit Capture/Export File Segment Size To: 2000 MB
☑ Limit Capture Now To: 15 Minutes

Cancel   OK

You choose where your media files will be stored. Your project scratch disk can be on your computer drive or on an external drive.

If you begin a project and then move the media files to another location or change their name on the scratch disk, your project won't be able to find them and you'll have to do a reconnecting procedure.

Melissa Bourne, Editor.

Organisation and naming of files are very important. If files go off-line it's much easier to find them and reconnect.

With the scratch disk system, once a clip has been imported into your project, you can cut it up in all different ways, and the original clip remains whole and hearty on your scratch disk. So this style of media handling is call *non-destructive*.

The *full* version of Final Cut Pro has a Media Manager which does many wonderful things, including allow you to selectively delete unwanted footage from *within* your stored media clips. This helps reduce the burden on your hard drive.

For example, say you have 50 seconds of a child playing in the waves at the beach, but the first part is out of focus, in the middle the camera wanders off the child and the end is all jerky because the wave splashed you. Still, there are parts of the shot which are (you decide modestly) GREAT. Media Manager lets you delete the bad bits from within the shot and keep the good bits. Gone off the drive, not just gone out of your project.

What's in a Name?

Here's a trap I've definitely learned the hard way: when you're importing media files, make sure you open and name a project FIRST before you import the clips into that project. If you're rushing or not paying attention and import them without assigning them to a named project, they'll come into your general scratch disk as *untitled*.

It's a good idea to also give them individual clip names as you go.

Of course, you can still import *untitleds* into a program you begin later, and the computer can find them despite their apparent anonymity UNTIL the day you're running short of space on the hard drive and you decide to do a spring clean.

'What's all this untitled stuff?' you ask yourself, forgetting that rushed project from a few months ago. So you hustle them into the trash and press Empty Trash with a self-satisfied flourish, feeling you're finally getting on top of this scratch disk business!

Voilà! More space, yes, but next time you go to play that earlier project, there will be red lines through the files (indicating clips have gone off-line) and it won't be able to play . . . because the underlying media clips are *gone*.

Getting Started

Set-up

Before you begin to do any editing, your application must be set up correctly for your project. Though your edit program comes with default settings, they may not be right for you. In fact, they could be very, very wrong.

For example, the program settings might default to NTSC when you're working in PAL. This will become obvious if you start editing without checking, because each clip you put into your sequence will generate a *render* message.

In Final Cut Pro, the render message is a red line along the top of the clip's position in the timeline. FCP is a powerful program and can do standards conversion for you (change PAL to NTSC), but it will take lots of time and it won't be an improvement for your video. If you're shooting in PAL, your timeline should be PAL.

Audio/Video Settings

Summary \ Sequence Presets \ Capture Presets \ Device Control Presets \ External Video \

Sequence Preset: DV NTSC 48 kHz Superwhite [⬍]

Use this preset when editing with DV NTSC material with audio set to 48KHz (16bit for DV). Use this to match graphics to source material with very bright exposure.

Capture Preset: DV PAL 48 kHz [⬍]

Use this preset when capturing PAL material for DV FireWire input and output using DV FireWire.

Device Control Preset: Non-Controllable Device [⬍]

This Device is not able to be controlled.

External Video: Apple FireWire PAL (720 x 576) [⬍]

(Create Easy Setup...)

(Cancel)   (OK)

What's wrong with this picture? The sequence (timeline) is set for NTSC, but the capture preset and the playback are both set for PAL. Though device control is available for the camera being used, the device control setting is at 'No controllable device'. In short, this is a mish-mash—an edit set-up bound for disaster. Don't be afraid to learn about settings—it's essential to your set-up and it should become clear to you before too long.

Audio Video Settings and Preferences

George Karpathakis, Edith Cowan University.

Don't be too hasty to start an edit session—check your preferences before you begin and save angst later!

There are essential choices to make before you start editing. These are the *AV settings*, like what format is the sequence (timeline) set to, what is the capture setting, and what is the format for playback. You want to make sure you remember to set these correctly.

And then there are the less essential preferences, like how often your project will be automatically saved, the default duration of freeze frames and the colour-code settings. These are entirely discretionary—for example, you can opt to mark clips green for good shot, yellow for cutaway shot, blue for voice is good but vision is poor, or whatever you choose. Some people will make use of these additional features and other people won't, but if you ignore them there's no harm done to your capacity to edit.

Melissa Bourne, Editor.

Before starting a project, make sure all your preferences match the format of your footage and your scratch disk is allocated to the right folder. Sometimes people assume it will automatically correct itself. Or they may start editing with footage that has been captured as a 16:9 but be putting it into a timeline set at 4:3. What happens is your footage will be letterboxed and if you try to copy it to a second sequence with the correct setting of 16:9, you may find that it will squish your letterbox footage into a 16:9 sequence. You may have to start the edit all over again, a mistake you do not want to make.

Editing the Clips

At last! Getting going with the editing!

Basic editing involves three main tasks: choosing, sequencing and trimming.

Moving clips to the Timeline

Most of the time you'll have some idea of the order you want for your project, either because you've been working from a script or because you're editing an event that has its own natural progression.

You get the basic structure happening by putting the clips (or shots) in the desired order on your timeline or editing space. This is so simple—you just click on the clip and drag it into the timeline and let go: *drag and drop*.

If you decide you want to change the order, that's simple—just drag the clips around to new places and drop them there. The other clips will either obligingly dodge out of the way, or you can push them aside to make space for the new arrivals.

> Three things the editor has to keep in mind about each cut:
> 1. **content** (what's in the cut)
> 2. **context** (what cut precedes this one and what cut will come after it)
> 3. **contact** (how long to keep it on the screen before the next cut).

Danny Sheehy, Queensland School of Film and Television.

Trimming clips

Most clips will need a little trimming at the beginning and end. You can do this before you put them on the timeline and you can also do it when they're already in the timeline. Generally, you just push in the ends of a clip to shorten them to the right spot. Or you can use a cutting tool from your virtual toolbox (a razor blade icon for some) to trim off the unwanted edges.

In some programs, you adjust a rectangular selecting tool so it covers just the range of frames you want. Or you can also mark in and out points with a marking tool or enter timecode ins and outs.

Edit systems are designed so there are at least three ways to do anything, so you can choose the way that's most comfortable and efficient for you. Don't worry if someone else tells you to do it differently—if your way works, it works.

You might be a person who mainly uses the mouse. Other people like to use keyboard commands and shortcuts. Some rely on the menu bar. It doesn't matter: it's your choice.

Undo

If you make a move that you regret (don't we all?), in video you just click the *Undo* command and you're back to where you were before. In fact, you can undo and undo and undo if you need to. The number of times you can undo is something

> If you are using editing software such as Final Cut Pro/Express for the first time, edit a one-minute silent picture sequence first. This way you can learn the picture editing features first, then proceed towards adding music and narration.

Usha Harris, International Communications, Macquarie University.

Doug Adler,
Videographer.

Making a video in non-linear editing is like making a meal. Collecting your media clips is like putting ingredients in the cupboard. Your editing decisions in the timeline are like your recipe. The beauty is that you can mess with the recipe or throw it away and start again, and your ingredients are still there.

you can set in preferences in some systems. If you undo too many times, you can hit *redo* to get back where you want to be.

If your edit system will display a *history* of the decisions (commands) you've been making, you don't have to go back one step at a time, but just look through the history list until you find where you want to get to, and you can go there in one click.

Making the Most of a Clip

You may find that within one clip you have several usable shots. For example, say you were at the markets and kept the camera rolling as you walked around. Out of the jumble of jerks and blurs and people walking in front of the lens, you might have a wonderful few seconds of a child licking an icecream cone, a decent pan of some handcrafted goods, and an exciting few seconds by a diablo spinner. In this clip, it's not just the ends that need trimming; the whole clip needs to be dissected to produce the bits you want for your edit.

One method, in iMovie, is to bring up the clip in the viewer and then make your way through it using the command *split video clip at playhead*, which means that a break will be made in the clip at whatever frame is currently showing.

Kevin Hatch works on his editing project. Methuen High School, Massachusetts. (Photo by Nancy Clover)

As you progress through the clip, you get more and more smaller clips which you can sort and trim as needed, and you can put the unwanted video scraps in the trash bin. In this destructive method, your original clip is mincemeat, and you're left with selective fragments of it, which you can use wherever you choose. You can also make copies of the bits and pieces so you can use them multiple times in your timeline. (Some people like to build a video stutter of an action by repeating a small clip several times, to make their audience laugh.)

If you decide you've thrown away something you need, you can get it back by clicking on a remaining fragment of the original clip and using *restore clip*. This will give you the original clip in its entirety if it's still in the trash bin on your screen. However, if you've emptied the trash bin, the contents will have been erased from your hard drive and you'll have to reimport the material to get it back.

Final Cut Pro has a different method of handling clips of inconsistent quality. You play the clip in your viewer and mark the in and out points of the first usable video section, then use the command *make subclip*. This saves the in and out data for that part of the original clip and you store that subclip as a separate item in the browser. Moving along, you

Philip Elms,
Media Resource
Centre.

Learn where the save button is and use it every five minutes or so. If the worst happens, at least you will not lose too much work.

make subclips of the other fragments you want to keep. Once done, the browser still has the main clip in its entirety, and all the little subclips as well.

Getting a Closer Look

You'll often need to take a closer look at the timeline, especially if there's a quick flash of black between clips or an audio blip you're having trouble with.

Look around: there will be a way to *zoom in* so you can see your project as close as frame by frame, which is immensely handy for doing fine cutting.

You can also *zoom out* to have the whole sequence displayed on the screen at once.

A movable bar allows you to quickly scroll through your project to locate sections you want to work on or review.

You can go straight to any part of the timeline you choose and play from there, by clicking the play head icon at the desired starting spot.

If editing for 4:3 from 16:9 footage, you can 'pan and scan' in the digital edit system, to frame the 4:3 shot however you want it, or you can set the system to just 'centre cut' by default. But I think that to pan and scan within a shot is just sacrilege. It goes against the original artistic side of the composition.

Richard Fitzpatrick, Camera Operator, Digital Dimensions.

Multiple Video Tracks in the Timeline

Your edit screen may be able to show more than one video track for your sequence, and in some systems you can add and add and add both video and audio tracks.

With multiple tracks, you can layer the video to make more complex shots, with titles, effects and even additional composited elements.

The order of the layers does matter. What's on top is what plays.

Multiple tracks helps in another way. If you're not sure which cutaway to choose for a particular spot, you can place various cutaways in the same timeline position but on different tracks, and then by turning tracks on and off you can play each version until you decide which one works best.

If you're still unsure which version is preferable, you can call up the various possibilities to show your editing partners when they return from that inexplicably lengthy coffee break.

Another opinion can help you decide what works. (Courtesy of Portland Community Media)

If you have different aims for different audiences, you can save several versions within the same project. Then, when you output for one audience, you turn on only the tracks you need.

Not saving regularly is a guaranteed strategy to make your computer crash.

Jeff Bodmer-Turner, Manchester Memorial School, Massachusetts.

When you output for another audience, turn on the tracks which work for their edit version.

Programs with just one video track will still allow you to do a few layers, adding titles and effects by dropping them right on top of the clip within that single track.

Getting Rid of the Shakes

A new feature is *video stabilisation*, which can go a long way towards eliminating that shaky handheld, or jeep-bounced, image that has marred so many videos in the past. Unless your script requires a short sequence with a point-of-view action shot, your audience will appreciate your using this to give them a smoother ride through your program.

Speed Changes

Pretty much all the edit systems provide the tools to make your clip run different degrees of faster or slower. Some even allow reverses for fun like divers flying back up to the diving board, cats flipping back up onto the couch, or more gross shots like food exiting mouths—well, I won't go on.

The higher-end editing programs allow you to make very controlled motion changes within a clip. So you can accelerate that dirt bike coming towards the jump, slow down its rise into the air to a breathcatching near-stop, and then speed it up again on the descent.

Keyboard Shortcuts

A.J. Von Wolfe,
Videographer.

'Command S, Command R!'
Always.

As you get more familiar with editing, you'll find that you can speed up your work by using keyboard shortcuts for the operations you perform frequently. The one you'll need most is *Save*.

On Final Cut Pro you control playback options with JKL: J plays backwards, K stops play and L plays forwards. JJ plays backwards double speed, LL plays forwards double speed.

'Command S (Save), command R (Render)' is a terrific sequence, because it saves your edit before beginning to render.

I've learned this one the hard way, because I've found crashes happen more frequently when rendering than otherwise and I'm heartily sick of redoing complex effects just to lose them unsaved in a crash.

Using keyboard shortcuts is one way to be using both of your hands. Too much mouse control can leave one arm very sore!

**Mark
Gingerich,**
Portland Final
Cut Pro Users
Group.

You can work faster if you take advantage of keyboard shortcuts. In higher-end programs (Apple's Final Cut Pro and Adobe's Premier Pro, for example) these shortcut key combinations can be viewed in a 'Preferences' or 'Tools' menu. You can print out a list of the shortcuts and use it as reference while you're learning them. In Final Cut Pro if you go to the Tools Menu: Keyboard Layouts: Save Grid as Text you can save a text file of all the current keyboard layout keys . . . nice. But, we're visual people, that's why we are excited about VIDEO right!? It's a visual medium! So try this out: Go to the Tools Menu: Keyboard Layouts: Customise. The Keyboard Layout Editor pops up. Now, maximise the Keyboard Layout Editor by dragging the lower right corner of the window, then take a screen shot and print that off for a nice visual version.

A few useful Final Cut Pro keyboard commands:

Space bar	Play or Stop playing
I	Marks in point
Option I	Clears in point
O	Marks out point
Option O	Clears out point
M	Inserts a marker for any reason
Command +	Zoom in
Command −	Zoom out
Up arrow	Next cut
Down arrow	Previous cut
Home	Beginning of sequence
End	End of sequence
Left arrow	Back one frame
Shift left arrow	Back 10 frames
Right arrow	Forward one frame
Shift right arrow	Forward 10 frames
Command L	Create or break the link between audio and video
Control G	Removes gap between clips (this is my personal favourite).

For right-handed people, the home position in digital editing is with your *left* hand on JKL and your right hand on the mouse.

Tim Rooney, Portland Community Media.

With Final Cut Pro, an *autosave vault* will be saving your project as you go along. In preferences you set the frequency with which it saves. Ten minutes? Twenty minutes? Five minutes? How much can you bear losing?

The autosave vault shouldn't replace good manual saving habits, but after a crash it can retrieve a terrible situation by taking you back to its most recent save.

Akira Haga, from Waseda University, Japan, shows good hand positions for efficient editing. (Courtesy of Portland Community Media)

Transitions

A transition is a digital effect that gets you from one shot to the next.

The Straight Cut

A *cut* is when the picture goes totally from one shot to the next in a clean and immediate change. You get this transition by placing one clip snug up to the next one on the timeline. It's a term held over from film editing, where editors do literally cut the film between frames and then attach the next shot to where the cut was made.

A cut is also the transition the camera produces when you go in and out of pause mode.

If the change in brightness from one shot to the next is very dramatic, like going from a really dark scene to a very bright one, the edit point may jolt the viewer. In that case, it's best to change the edit points, if possible, to make the change less stark—unless you want to make a point by emphasising the contrast.

Mark Gingerich, Portland Final Cut Pro Users Group.

Usually it works well to change shots at the end of a spoken phrase, when the viewer has heard a complete thought or is ready for something new. Sometimes that doesn't work though, based on the footage or how the end of the take goes. If this is the case, you can look for natural distractions in the footage to help with the transition.

The Dissolve

After the straight cut, the most commonly used transition is the *dissolve*, which is a mix of the video from the end of one shot and the beginning of the next. As one picture gets weaker, the other one gets stronger. At the halfway point, or mid-dissolve, both pictures are visible at half-strength. At the end point, the first picture is gone and the second one is full-strength on the screen.

There needs to be enough frames at the beginnings and ends of your clips to allow for dissolves and other transitions to happen without eating into the important parts of your shot. This is why you shoot with some extra frames at the beginning and end of each shot, and why you capture your clips into the computer with *handles* (extra frames at each end). Handles that are one second long will usually be enough.

If you just haven't got enough of a handle, another possibility is to dissolve between a freeze-frame and a moving image.

Tom Kingdon, Emerson College.

The dissolve is so accessible now that students resort to it too frequently and have all but lost the sense of how to make an effective straight cut. The cut is still the strongest and most versatile transition and, unless you are working with music or want to achieve a special effect (like the passing of time) you should use it 99 per cent of the time.

A dissolve can soften a cut that would otherwise be too harsh. Experimenting with the timing and previewing a few possibilities will help you get it just right. Sometimes it needs to be long and languid and other times a very quick one is just enough.

Dissolves are often used in dance and music pieces, and in some transitions in drama. The speed of the dissolve affects the overall mood and flow of the piece.

The Fade

Another old faithful is the *fade*, which is actually a particular kind of dissolve. You can fade to black, white or another colour, and then fade up again to the next shot.

In visual language, a fade is understood to indicate the passage of time or a change of place.

The fade to black is frequently used at the end of a production, and a fade up from a black, white or coloured screen is a common transition for opening shots.

Fades can be recorded in-camera by using the fade function or by simply closing down the manual iris or reopening it, but if you do it in the edit suite you have more control over its timing and placement.

The Mix

Mixes are like dissolves, but they don't necessarily go all the way. You can mix a shot in part-way and keep it for a while, then back it out again. For example, you have a flamenco dancer positioned mid-screen. After a while, your main camera is cued to move subtly to the left and a close-up of the guitarist's hands playing the music appears in the upper right, then it fades out again just as the dancer becomes especially energetic.

> Digital editing *is* faster and easier, but the creative process is still the same as working in analogue. Like all artistic processes, it's still labour intensive.

Christine Togo-Smallwood, Producer.

The Wipe

Wipes are transitions which cause one picture to replace another by moving at full strength across the screen in any one of many selectable geometric patterns. You can wipe vertically from left to right or from right to left. Horizontally, too. You can have a circle opening in the middle, a diagonal, squares, bars, sawtooth patterns—and many many more.

> The perfect time to make a shot change is when the viewer is distracted. If they don't notice your edit you've done your job well. Here's an example: Let's say you're shooting a wide shot of someone walking down the sidewalk. You're shooting from the other side of the street and a car rumbles by. You might initially want to toss the footage and do a second take because 'That darn car ruined everything.' But . . . as the car crosses, blocking the frame, this is a perfect time to cut to another shot. Maybe to a close-up shot of the person walking or maybe something completely different. Basically you can use the car like a wipe transition.

Mark Gingerich, Portland Final Cut Pro Users Group.

Entry-level editing systems often have a giddy range of wipes at your fingertips. You pick from what's there, like in a lolly shop.

The more complex systems give you the tools to design your own wipes and other transitions. Sometimes this is a great creative freedom. Other times it's just a much more labour-intensive way of getting your project something flashy.

If you design a wipe or other transition that you like, save it in your *Favourites* file so you can use it again later.

Applying Transitions

In most cases, applying a transition to an edit point is as easy as moving a clip to the timeline. Again, you just drag and drop it onto the junction of your shots. Some transitions can be played back right away. These are referred to as RT (real time). Others need some time to be *rendered*.

> If you do something you're really excited about, save it immediately.

Fiona Strain, Editor.

Rendering means that the computer has to invent the needed frames to achieve the effect. Since the blended video doesn't exist, the computer has to make a new frame for each stage of the transition.

You can render each transition as you go along, you can render the last few you've done while you take that phone call, or you can do your whole edit and then ask the edit system to render all. Everyone finds their own way of dealing with rendering.

Audio

Video people tend to be visually oriented and think of sound second, alas! But with bad sound, people won't watch your piece.

Field Audio

Field audio is what you recorded along with your video. It could be the general surrounding sound or it could be audio from an interview mic, but it's what will come in with your images during capture.

On some edit systems, this audio will be embedded in the clips when you drag them into the timeline.

On higher-end systems, the video and field audio can be separated (*unlinked*) and handled each on their own.

It will often be the case that you'll want to have some sound segments play back with a different video clips. That's fine. Even on entry-level systems, you can *extract audio* to separate them out and move them to where you want them on your audio tracks.

Charlie Tesch, Somerville Producers Group.

You can't do anything without good audio: it's the most important thing and it's the hardest part. If you can hear it but you can't see it, it still works. If you can see it but you can't hear it, it's useless.

Moving a strip of audio which includes someone speaking can give you grief, though, because you'll lose *lip sync* and the mouth actions will no longer match the sounds. That's fine if you're not going to use the vision anyway, but generally it's better not to move dialogue away from its source video. If you do, it can take a lot of time and heartache to put it back to its correct face position.

More advanced systems will actually tell you how many frames you've moved the audio, so that's a huge advantage for correcting a lip sync mistake.

Melissa Bourne, Editor.

Check the tape and the format before capturing. If the audio has been recorded at 32 kHz but the timeline was 48 kHz, it plays fine in the edited sequence but when you're exporting your audio will not be in sync.

Clip Volume

The most likely adjustment you'll make to the audio is the volume, making the soundtrack louder or softer.

There will be a volume line across the length of your clip which you can move up and down. This line isn't always visible: you may have to find the command to make it appear. Once you find it, you can raise and lower the volume level of each single clip or you can combine the clips into a group and affect them all equally.

By making a bend in the volume line at either end of the clip, you can fade the sound in and out. And you can lower the audio in places within a clip so sound from another source, like the voiceover, can be heard. Some programs call this manipulating *rubberbanding*.

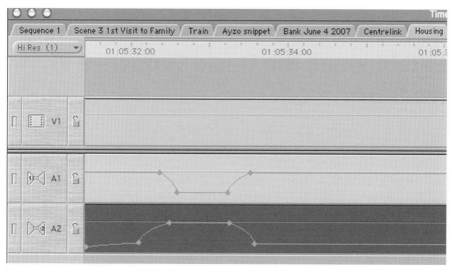

When the location sound on track 1 (A1) is faded down, the music on track 2 (A2) is raised to fill the aural gap. A2 fades down when A1 is needed at full strength again.

Audio Waveform

If your edit system can show you the waveform of your audio clips, you can cut with more precision. You can see just where that nasty sound problem is and eliminate it. You can find the exact beginning and ending of voiceover pieces.

A Word About Logging

A *log* is a map of the video material you have.

In a short project, if you've viewed your footage and have a good memory, you may be able to recall your material in detail.

In a long project, filing your shots into marked bins, like putting all the cutaways together, will be very useful. Good naming practices help, too.

If you have lengthy interviews, you'll save lots of heartache and lost time re-listening if you make at least a dot-point list of the speaker's points in the order they were spoken.

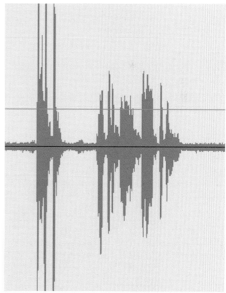

With this waveform you can see that there's a general level of background noise in the room, then there's a loud cough by the presenter and *then* the commentary begins. Of course, you want to start your edit after the cough, and with this graphic read-out you can finetune just where to make the cut.

You can break the entire interview up, making each topic into a chronologically numbered subclip, or you can scroll through the entire interview clip, using a log to locate the sound bites you need.

How you log isn't so much a matter of right and wrong ways, as finding what works for you as an editor.

Establishing the Basic Sequence of the Story

Your first task is to get the essential shots in the right order.

Let's say your project is documentary style, a series of comments made by people who were videoed on location.

First, the best and most usable comments should be chosen and the script order decided upon.

There will be many waffly statements and repetitions, and people may jump back late in their interviews to expand upon a topic they covered at the beginning. So, to be frank, you'll begin with an audio jumble. That's okay, that's normal.

Phil Cooper edits *Sleep Apnoea Solutions.*

The initial editing is a matter of selecting the sound snippets you want to use and putting them in the right sequence on the timeline.

Eventually, you'll get to the point that your story is being told in a way that flows and makes sense. But the resulting vision will be full of jump cuts.

Never fear, you can conceal these edit 'seams' by putting video 'patches' over the edit points—a bit like clever sewing. This is where many of your cutaways can be used. (Let's hope you remembered to get them.)

If you don't have enough cutaways (also called *B-roll* from the old analogue days), you may need to send someone out to get more. Or you may be able to edit in still photos and graphics to smooth out the picture flow. Sometimes problem-solving like this results in an enhanced edit product because you're compelled to use more resources.

Another option is to use digital transitions where you've made cuts. A dissolve can soften a jump between two very similar images. A wipe can get you past the more glaring shot changes.

Warning: There will be times and topics where this reassembling of speech can be offensive to the person interviewed. If you don't want to misguide your audience about *exactly* how the person answered, let the cuts remain apparent in the video. A fade to black, or white, and back again gracefully acknowledges where a cut has been made.

If, instead, your project was a scripted drama, the initial work is more in choosing the right takes than in establishing the order of shots. But there will still be lots of juggling of both video and audio. The best delivery of a line can easily happen in a take when the camera jolted or was out of focus, so sometimes a cutaway to another character can recover the situation. Or you can try starting a line from one actor while showing the other character who's being addressed. This can let you ease past a visual mistake.

Voiceover

You may feel that your project needs a voiceover to put the video in context or to give an overview or commentary on the action. It's handy to do this audio segment next, though you can forge your soundtrack in any order you choose.

You might have recorded commentary in bits as you went along. Maybe a friend was describing a process as you shot it, or perhaps you recorded the guide as you walked through Jenolan Caves. Now your job will be to find the fragments you want to use and string them together in a good order. Be discerning: you don't need to use everything, and there will always be parts where the audio is muffled or it's marred by other people's comments or coughing and so on.

And relax, you don't need wall-to-wall talking. Let your edit breathe!

When you're editing, remember you are the entertainer and people are going to watch what you're producing, so be single-minded and think of the audience, who are easily bored.

Rob Nercessian, Videomaker.

When recording whilst travelling on small planes or helicopters, I attach a small lapel mic to my camera and place the mic head so it's cushioned between my ear and the earpiece of the headphones that are included in the tour to enable the pilot to converse with the passengers. By doing this, I have been able to record the voice of the pilot as he points out places of interest and avoid the deafening noise of the engine.

Jan Hudson, Videographer, South West Sydney Video Club.

Once you've put the various dialogue and voiceover segments onto one of the audio tracks in your timeline, you can go through your field audio and make it rise and fall in between these segments. This gives a feeling of life and depth to your video without drowning out your speaker. (That waterfall sound would be nice coming up between two observations by the guide standing in front of it.)

Voiceover is often done after the fact, either in an impromptu fashion in response to watching the video edit, or as a carefully crafted script. When recording this sort of voiceover, use a good mic and eliminate any background sounds that you can. Although you could just speak into the computer's built-in mic, both the volume level and the quality of the audio will be lower and you'll pick up the sound of the computer's fan in the background.

Colour-Coding Clip Icons

When you have many shots (20+) in a single category, like lots of cutaways of the kids playing at the campground or dancers at the Oktoberfest, it can be hard to remember which ones you've already used in your edit and which ones you haven't. But even a brief cutaway used twice in a short piece stands out like a sore thumb. Final Cut Pro lets you assign a colour to clip icons, so if you make each one orange, or whatever, as you use it, then your list of uncoloured options diminishes as you progress through the edit and you'll find you're spending less time searching fruitlessly through your bins.

Sound

There are many other sound sources to employ besides the field audio you got on the day.

Music

Music livens up a video and carries your audience along with it, affecting viewers' emotional reactions to the images and enhancing their pleasure and understanding of your movie.

Usually you add the music to a separate audio track in your timeline so you can run it behind everything else that's happening, and raise and lower it so it fits glove-like around your voiceover and field sound.

However, in the production of an MTV-style music clip, the order of your work flow reverses. The music is the first track you lay down and then everything else gets added to meld with (or counterpoint) the rhythm, beat and words of the music.

The Case of the Vanishing Music

You can import music into your edit from CDs. (Copyright questions will be dealt with later.) But a pitfall is this: If you add the music to your project by importing it directly into your edit from the CD, when you take the CD out of the computer the music will disappear from your edit! This is because the edit program can no longer find the music. You need to copy the music into your computer hard drive (iTunes does very well here) and from there import it into your project. Then the music stays with the computer when the disc moves on.

Sound Effects

Your edit system is likely to have a library of special effects that you can use. Though they'll be pretty standard, your audience might just love them—especially if you use them in surprising ways. Fire engine, thunder, horses hooves, car engine, doorbell, etc. What if you put a lion's roar where that baby yawns? You can insert any audio you want to liven up your project.

Audio Filters

The audio filters that come with your system can be used to clean up your sound or to enhance it. You can get rid of some unwanted frequencies, add reverberation and many other effects. This is covered in more detail in Chapter 14, Sound Postproduction.

Titles

Title-making is available on every editing program I know of. Some programs get far more into it than others, with a rich stable of fonts and backgrounds, but you can count on being able to add a title page, a credit scroll (that's those rising credits like you see at the end of films), a crawl of words across the bottom of the screen (CNN style), an identifier (as talk shows put up across the chests of their guests) and possibly various other text additions, like a music clip style lower left corner segment.

Your titles can flash onto the screen, twist, twirl, arrive in snaky waves, typewriter in, etc., etc. Lots of fun to play around with.

You'll have controls to fix the length of time it takes for them to arrive and depart, and how long they'll remain on the screen.

For people who just can't get enough of text effects, you can add on another program like Boris Calligraphy, Graffiti, RED or Blue. These can generate 2D and 3D text with automation.

> Make sure you check the title safe reference line when adding text. Having titles part-way off the screen is an easy mistake.
>
>
>
> **Melissa Bourne**, Editor.

Boris Blue can do 3D warping and shading of text elements and can render titles with scene reflection, texture mapping and imported video. Boris comes bundled with some edit programs.

Once you've made a title, be sure to store it in your browser or favourites bin so you can access it again. You could well want to use the title as a template for similar titles further into the project, or even in another project, so having the colours, font and spacing saved will be a big timesaver.

Special Effects = Altered Images

You can expect to get at least a few video special effects which you can add to your images. Here are some of the most common ones. (You'll find your camera can do some of these, too.)

Negative

The *negative* button will cause your image to be produced in its colour opposites. Not quite the same as a photographic negative, because video colour opposites are different, but you get the idea.

Invert

Invert, as you've probably guessed, presents your image upside down. (Remember Alan Petschack's shot of the baby chicks?)

Monochrome (Mono)

By pressing the *mono* button, you can turn your image into black and white.

Paint

The *paint* effect simplifies the colour values in the image by reducing the number of tones. All the shades of a colour within certain ranges are reproduced as one flat tone, so as you increase the paint effect the picture looks more and more like a paint-by-numbers oil painting or a poster. (On some mixers it's called *posterisation*.)

If your image starts to remind you more of your elderly uncle's lounge room paintings than of a chic poster, you might reconsider using it.

Mosaic

The *mosaic* effect breaks the whole image into rectangles, like mosaic tiles. When a small amount of mosaic is dialled up, the image is only slightly affected, but when it's fully applied, the image is no longer recognisable. Mosaic can come with horizontal and vertical controls which operate independently of each other, so you can have tall thin tiles, or short fat ones, or square ones.

Compression Effects

There are a number of variations possible with compression circuitry. For one thing, you can have the image squeezed thin so two images can appear side by side on your screen. Or it can look flattened, so two squashed images can sit atop each other on your screen.

Mirror

The *mirror* effect compresses the image vertically or horizontally, so it fits into half the screen and then fills the other half of the screen with its mirror image.

Multiple Image

Your image can be made smaller while retaining its original internal dimensions. So you can have several of the same image appear on one screen at the same time.

Themes

A good tape is a finished tape.

Hsing Min Sha, Independent Producer.

iMovie now comes with themes so you can pick an overall style and look for your home video. It will make your opening shot and all the rest of your video hang together with the appearance of a photo album or bulletin board or many other homespun or hot looks. They're like an extension of the DVD opening page idea.

For a project made for a class exercise, teachers may not think the Maclook is evidence of sufficient creative effort on your part, but a home user can get lots of kudos simply by tapping into the work of a professional designer.

Themes are integrated into your program with one click, and eliminated as easily, so you might like to survey the options to get the idea, anyway.

Time Needed for Editing

Editing always takes much longer than you'd expect. As a rule of thumb, people say an hour of editing is needed to cut one minute of finished product.

This ratio helps get a perspective on things, though there will be some minutes which may take you three hours (and leave you wondering where the time—and your sanity—went) and other segments will flow smoothly and quickly.

It's usually a timesaver to edit with a partner at first, because the operation that one person forgets, the other person might remember.

Tip: Don't promise anyone you'll be home from editing before midnight!

Figure out what your pain threshold is—how many hours/minutes of work could you bear to re-do? Then use an alternating backup system: save to drive A, next time to drive B, then to drive A again, so any file corruption won't wipe your project out.

Jason Wheatley, Educational Media.

Human Care

Editing is exhausting, especially when you're a beginner. If you stay in the edit room too long, you're likely to start feeling weird effects, like headache, nausea and the sense that your brain has been scrambled.

Four-hour editing sessions are plenty long enough until your system gets used to it. For some people, four hours will always be pushing the limits of what they can stand.

Plan your editing sessions according to what your body tells you, and not just what the facility will allow.

Also, take care to sit as far from the monitors as you can, so you don't get a dose of invisible but unwanted radiation.

Philip Elms,
Media Resource
Centre.

Output more than one master in multiple formats. Each master will be of the highest quality possible and saves dubbing sub masters later if needed.

Finally

Keep dated versions of your edits so you can easily find the one that you need to work on.

Further Help

Go through whatever manual came with your edit program. Yes, bite the bullet!

Another option is *The Missing Manuals* (see <http://missingmanuals.com>). This book series goes from iMovie 1 through iMovie HD and iDVD 5—start with the one you need.

Screen Media Arts, by Hart Cohen, Oxford University Press, 2008—this book goes over both screen theory and the production process and has a DVD that instructs on Final Cut Pro editing.

Also check out all the Visual Quickstart guides on Final Cut Pro editing by Lisa Brennais. These are available on Amazon.com.

EDITING CONCEPTS

How often have you been watching a TV show when someone has exclaimed, 'The editing is fantastic!'

Probably not very often. Maybe never. People notice great camera work, they get drawn into a captivating storyline, they like exciting soundtracks . . . but good editing, even great editing, often goes unnoticed.

Rob Davis is definitely an AVID man. Digital Dimensions, Townsville, QLD.

Good editing, like good sewing, appears seamless. The material flows fluidly before the eyes, one scene into the next, and the viewer is unconscious of the shot changes, unless they're deliberately attention-getting.

A good way to begin noticing shots and shot changes is to turn the sound down completely on your TV and just watch the visuals. Without the soundtrack propelling you along, you'll be able to pay much more attention to the length of the shots, the types of shots used, the points at which the shots change, and the kinds of changes employed. In fact, you may start to notice the editing for the first time (and you'll never be so visually innocent again).

Through editing, time is manipulated to encompass a span of minutes, hours, days or longer within a short sequence of shots. Sometimes it's millennia in space odysseys. Yet the meaning remains comprehensible and we accept it without question. Why?

There are certain picture signals that over the years have come to hold accepted meanings for audiences. The erudite way to talk about this is to refer to the *conventions of screen language*.

No one needs to tell you that a fade to black, followed by a fade up to another image, indicates either the passage of time or a change of location. Through repeated use, the fade has come to mean a break, or disjuncture, in time and space.

Editors make use of the accepted conventions of screen language to assist them in telling their stories. With the exception of sports and incredibly hot-breaking news stories, viewers just don't have time to watch screen stories in real time.

So *time shortening* is one of the major functions of editing.

Time Manipulation

Jump Cuts

If an editor simply chops out sections of footage of an event, the result is a *jump cut*. The person on the screen is suddenly in a different position from where he or she was a milli-second ago. Though what is being said on the soundtrack may make sense, the viewer will experience a momentary visual disturbance, because in our real-life experience people don't make lightning rearrangements of their posture or their position in space.

If you cut from this . . .   . . . to this . . .   . . . to this, your speaker will appear to jump through his talk.

If these three shots are edited together as is, the viewer will see the speaker appear to jump from one shot to the next.

Now the truth is that, with most interviews, the editor must shorten a person's responses to a handful of their most relevant sentences. So a half-hour of rambling becomes two minutes or less of succinct commentary.

The editor does this by removing all the waffle. The best sentences are selected and assembled into a coherent sequence of thoughts, but this often results in a series of visual jumps at the edit points.

Sometimes jump cuts are allowed to be shown in late-breaking news stories, when immediacy trumps finesse, and editors don't seem to worry about jump cuts in music clips and montages. But in smooth conventional storytelling, they're generally considered to look jarring and unprofessional.

Noddies

It's acceptable style in news and current affairs to acknowledge the presence of the interviewer. This makes the editor's job easier.

The audience understands the interviewer's role as twofold: asking the right questions and reacting to the answers. So the camera operator is instructed to tape the interviewer asking at least the key questions and then some *noddies* (reaction shots) showing the interviewer reacting to the comments of the person being questioned. Reaction shots usually include smiles, thoughtful expressions, quizzical looks, sometimes sceptical looks or surprise, and nods that indicate agreement or a signal to the person to continue speaking.

Use a noddy to get smoothly from the first shot of your interviewee to the second one.

The reality of shooting is that, for efficiency's sake, ordinary interviews are usually covered with only one camera, so the questions and the reaction shots are taped after the interview has ended, usually after the VIP has left the room.

Until a presenter becomes used to pumping out these visual artefacts, or *noddies*, it's easy to feel silly sitting and smiling and nodding to a camera which has been repositioned behind the interviewee's empty chair.

> When shooting noddies, check that your eye lines and screen direction are correct.

Julie Booras, Offspring Productions.

But, forced or ridiculous as the process may seem, noddies give the editor a variety of shots to cover the jump cuts at the necessary edit points, and allow the edited sequence to flow along rather than to hobble.

In effect, when the viewer's attention is directed to the interviewer and then back to the VIP, it's no surprise to see a head tilted at a different angle or an arm in a different position. That's the way things are in life; the jolt is gone.

Note: Directors must make sure that the presenter's eyeline is correctly oriented to where the face of the interviewee was during the taping session, or the noddies will be unconvincing to the audience.

Also, care should be taken that the questions are repeated exactly as they were asked during the interview, and that any additional questions which were not on the planned interview script, but were thrown in on the spur of the moment, are remembered and re-asked.

Cutaways

A *cutaway* is any visual that bears some relationship to the sequence being edited.

Cutaways are frequently used to cover an edit point which would otherwise be a jump cut, and often a cutaway assists the meaning of the video by illustrating, augmenting or even contradicting what the interviewee or commentator is saying.

They're useful for shortening the length of a scene because they shift the viewer's attention to something else, and when the editor cuts back to the original scene, real time can be accepted to have passed.

Gordon Peters, Cameraman, Channel 7 News, Bundaberg.

OVERSHOOT. It's always better to have too much overlay than not enough. Any unused vision may come in handy for graphic backgrounds, DVD menus, Special Features or for filling the gaps you hadn't anticipated.

Noddies are a particular type of cutaway, but the options seem endless. For example, in an edit of a person speaking about the environment, cutaways could include shots of the bush, rivers, the sea, wildlife, traffic, buildings, the sky, and so on.

The more relevant and high quality the cutaways, the better the edited sequence will look. Steady camera work (involving the use of a tripod) is desirable.

Generally, people want to shoot their own cutaways on location to go with their story. But at a pinch, someone else, or a stock footage supplier, may have a good usable shot.

Because viewers assume a link between the soundtrack and the cutaways, there are ethical considerations in using cutaways. It's unfair to throw in a shot that alters the meaning of the story being told, unless it's clear to the viewer that the edit is not a faithful account. This is why TV broadcasters are supposed to label and date stock footage when they drop it into a fresh news story.

Cut-ins

A *cut-in* is a closer look at something that is within the scene being shown. It could be a close-up of an object, a hand performing an action, or a vase of flowers on an elegant table setting—anything that is a detail from the wider shot.

A cut-in is used in the same way as a cutaway, allowing time to be shortened by focusing the viewer's eye on a finer point, while the editor adjusts the scene or removes footage from the shot material and returns to the story at a different point in time.

If you use a cut-in to a smaller part of the frame, you can cut back out to a different shot without jolting the viewer's perception.

Exit and Entrance

Another way to shorten time without a jump cut is to have the actor fully leave the frame during a shot, then cut to a different scene and have the actor enter the new one.

Almost any amount of time or space can be eradicated, as long as an exit and entrance are clearly shown.

For example, a surfer lifts her board and walks out of the water and out of frame. In the next shot, the surfer is getting into a car. Whether she's leaving a nearby parking lot or has just hiked 300 steep steps up a cliff, the time is equally gone, yet the story thread is intact.

But, exit and entrance shots work only if the footage was shot that way in the first place, and our surfer exits leaving a clean frame or enters into a clean frame. Getting the screen direction to match is a help too.

So the choices available in the edit suite hark back to the skill of the director.

You'll need to edit an interview down to its best points. Michelle Blakeney interviews mothers in a schoolyard in Ginghong, China, for *Dai Women Speak*. (Photo by Gill Moody)

> The best way to learn how to shoot is to have to edit your own stuff.

Martha Mollison, Videographer.

Parallel Action

When two characters in two different places are shown alternately in an edited sequence, two aspects of the story can be developed at once and the switching from one to the other works for the editor the same way that a cutaway does. Great chunks of time and action can be eliminated through the use of parallel action. So:

Long shot (LS): Semi-trailer zipping down the highway on a rainy night, past the turn-off for Port Hedland.

Dissolve to *close-up* (CU): Truck driver rubbing his eye.

Mid-shot (MS): Young woman tucks small child into bed.

Mid-shot (MS): Truck driver lifts mug of coffee in roadside cafe in Karratha.

Medium close-up (MCU): Young woman in nightdress stares out window at blowing trees.

The truck driver has travelled more than 200 kilometres in five shots, and we've travelled the distance between him and his home twice.

Establishing Shots

An *establishing shot* is a fairly wide shot that shows the viewer the general surroundings in which the characters find themselves. It can be the very first shot used in an edited sequence, to let the audience get oriented to the overall setting and understand the action within its broader context.

> Like good camera work, editing should be invisible so the viewer can concentrate on the story.

Mark Tewksbury, Nine Video School.

Sometimes the establishing shot is used later in a sequence, when the aim is to tantalise the viewer as to where the action is taking place, or give a jolt or surprise. This works well with suspense and comedy.

Master Shot Coverage

One day in the edit suite you may feel like that old-timer informing the tourist, 'You can't get *there* from *here* . . .'

Sometimes there are essential bits of footage which just weren't shot. Or there's a continuity problem, so the shots which were supposed to go together just can't be linked.

Then it's handy to have a long shot, which is a master shot showing the entire action from the viewpoint of an outside observer. This can be used to bridge the gaps.

It's another example of how successful editing relies heavily on well-planned coverage on the day of the shoot.

Visual Transitions

A *shot transition* is the way an editor makes the change from one shot to the next, choosing from a swag of possibilities, including cuts, fades, dissolves, mixes and wipes.

The type of shot transition chosen is related to the style of the piece being cut. A car chase scene would probably work well with lots of fast cuts, whereas a ballet dance flourishes with slow dissolves.

Flashy wipes are often used on game shows, children's programs and advertising. Some people love them, some hate them. It's a question of style.

As an editor, you decide what transitions are appropriate for your piece.

Audio Transitions

The audio track often unifies the edited piece, providing the information backbone of the story to which the pictures relate—or, in the case of MTV, the musical engine on which the images ride.

Though in the field the sound is recorded along with the picture, the relationship of the two is often altered during editing. There are various techniques for linking the audio and the video.

Video Precedes Audio

Video precedes audio means that the picture starts first, and then the related sound begins.

So you could see a shot of a person talking, while you hear the voiceover introducing who the person is, and then you begin to hear the words the person is actually saying.

Audio Precedes Video

Audio precedes video means that you hear the sound first, and then you see the pictures related to the sound.

So you might be watching a presenter talk about an arts festival and, while she's still speaking, you begin to hear some music softly playing in the background. As she finishes her remarks, the music becomes louder and then the picture changes to the dance piece she was introducing.

To have the music begin while the presenter is still speaking, place the presenter's words on one audio track and the music on the other track, then fade the volume on each track up and down as needed.

Rolling In the Audio

Of course, the simplest thing is to have the sound and picture begin together at the edit point. One good trick to know is about *rolling in* the audio. If the sound is fairly loud on the field audio you're editing in, sometimes it will sound too abrupt at the cut. So what you do is pull down the audio at the start of the new clip, let the edit begin and then raise the volume (either quickly or slowly) until you get to the end level you want, thus rolling-in the sound.

Fading the Audio In or Out

At other times it works well to have the audio volume set at zero, and then fade the sound up from silence after the cut begins and the picture is on screen.

It can also work, at times, to fade the sound out before the edit ends.

Another good idea is to bring in music before the image appears, thus setting an emotional tone to lead the viewer into the story.

Jessica Gould and Camilla Havmoller finetune their class project, Griffith University, Brisbane.

Music and Dialogue Together

A common problem is for the music to be fighting with the dialogue during playback.

Professionally recorded music has a lot of oomph to it, so it needs to be kept very low if it's to coexist well with dialogue, which is often recorded at a lower level.

Of course, you never put a song with words in it against a dialogue track because the words will jar against each other, resulting in an audio muddle. Keep those lyric-rich tracks for times when a speaker doesn't need to be heard.

Audio Wash

Music run at a very low level in the background of your video is called an *audio wash*. It's great for giving a richer, more robust feel to your soundtrack.

Movement

Far more moving shots are used these days. The effect is great when it's well done because it adds such dynamism to a program. Even static studio interviews employ frequent camera moves, panning across the seated guests and rising and descending for no apparent reason other than to keep the audience stimulated by activity in the visual field.

If you want your frames to have lots of movement, guarantee that they're shot that way. Planning ahead is the key. Take the time to imagine fully how you'd like your edit to look. Then make sure you get a selection of moving shots recorded at different speeds, some lightning pans (very fast), some leisurely ones, some from left to right, others from right to left. That way, when you get into the edit room, you'll have lots of choices.

Sara Bennett,
Editing
Department,
AFTRS.

Planning pays off. Don't be a bull at the gate. Think before you cut and even then don't be surprised if other members of the creative team can think of other/better ways of doing it. That's editing!

I once watched a home movie of someone's trip to Alaska. The landscapes were breathtaking, one after another. Unbelievable mountain views. But every single one was panned from right to left, until the repetition of the camera work overpowered the brilliance of each view. Some variety of approach would have helped a lot.

Don't be too shy to ask a few people to look at your work while you're editing. Often someone will spot a cut which doesn't work well, or where the movement is just wrong, though you haven't noticed it yourself.

You can tinker with movement within the shot by engaging the slow motion, fast motion and reverse functions in the edit system.

Continuity

Continuity means that one shot follows another in a way that seems smooth and logical. There are many kinds of continuity. Continuity of sound, lighting, performance level, story, props . . .

Glasses shouldn't get inexplicably fuller, scarves shouldn't be on and off and on again, the furniture shouldn't rearrange itself in a blink, the sun shouldn't rise twice in a day.

As you edit, sometimes things just won't cut right for continuity reasons. Then you'll have to find a way around it.

Pace

The *pace* of a piece relates to the speed with which the audience moves through the material. Some programs benefit from a brisk pace, with short shots, many shot changes and lots of action on the screen. Other pieces call for a more gentle pace, lengthy shots and slow dissolves.

Pace can change within a piece, and often that wild chase scene at the end of an action feature has much faster cuts than the character development scenes at the beginning.

Pace should change with some flow and rationale, however. You don't want your audience to feel like they're on a journey with someone just learning to use the clutch.

Pace, like almost everything else in editing, relies on the right footage having been shot in the first place.

> Editing gives your work rhythm; this is measured in heart beats, not frames.

Cameron Rose, Video Art Society, University of Tasmania.

How can an editor produce a one-minute car chase scene, with a shot change every two seconds (yes, divide two into 60 seconds), unless the field footage includes 30 good shots? Since not all shots are good, and not all good ones will be usable, considerably more than 30 shots need to be taped. Directors take note.

Pace is something that's very hard to judge as you're initially sequencing your shots on the timeline because you're just too close to each edit. You need to look at a whole sequence in one hit, perhaps after you've had a break, in order to assess whether the pace is right for that segment.

Creative Considerations

By Sara Bennett, Editing Department, AFTRS

Once you get familiar with the basics of editing, the process will change from being an activity which is governed by concerns about 'Which button do I push next?' and you'll feel ready to move on to the next challenge.

With basic cutting experience behind you, and more complex material available to you, the process can become quite exciting, creative and satisfying. Some people say that it's the second chance to 'write the story', only this time it's with pictures and sounds.

And, just as with writing, editing is often a long, slow process where a small change of emphasis makes a very big difference.

> An editor is concerned with the flow of the program, the pace, rhythm and timing.

Phillippa Harvey, Editing Department, AFTRS.

It's always revealing, when a group of students is given the same five shots which contain the same two lines of dialogue, to see how many variations they come up with. Multiply that a few hundred times and you'll see why it can take six months to a year to edit a feature film!

So you should never think that your first version is your last. It's always worth trying to think of other ways of using the material, other ways of telling the story.

Shooting Ratios

The *shooting ratio* is the relationship between how much footage you shoot and how much footage is used in the final edited product.

With pre-scripted and rehearsed material, like drama or training tapes, the shooting ratio should be fairly low, like 6:1. This means you may do several takes of a shot, but you know what shots to do. For a one-hour piece, you shouldn't have much more than six hours of raw footage, if that.

With less predictable genres, like documentary, the shooting ratio can be as high as 20:1.

Take care not to wildly overshoot. Having heaps of vaguely conceived footage is a logging and editing nightmare.

Harry Kirchner, La Trobe University.

That sunrise shot you spent three hours setting up for might look fantastic, but if it doesn't end up serving the film as a whole, you might have to grit your teeth and be prepared to leave it on that virtual cutting-room floor.

Francis Treacey, Deakin University.

If you are asking me if I think you should leave a shot out of the edit, then you already know the answer: cut it!

Editing Tips

- Be ruthless in your edit decisions. Never edit a poor shot into a final product. It brings down the tone of your work very quickly. A few wobbly, out-of-focus, or wrongly white-balanced shots will make your product look amateurish, no matter how good the rest of your shots are.
- Let go of things. Don't include a shot because it's your favourite, or because it took you forever to do. Use it only if it works.
- Cut concisely. Let the shot speak, then move to the next one. Shots that drag on just dull the flow.
- Don't cut into or out of a partially completed pan, tilt or zoom. Let the camera movement run its full course.
- Don't put too many camera movements close together unless you're serving motion sickness tablets to your audience.
- Take care that the audio tracks don't fight each other.

Suggestions from Rachel Masters

IMAGE ORDERING

How does rearranging the order of the images affect the story?

Editing equipment is often in high demand. It's a good idea to try to get your head around the concepts of ordering and sequencing images well before you go into an edit suite.

Here's a game you may have played as a kid. First of all, draw a series of images on single sheets of paper—perhaps a woman on one, a dog on the next, a house, a butcher's shop, a butcher, a bone, a street and a hat.

Now lay the drawings out on the floor. Ask someone to narrate a story using the pictures, and you arrange (*sequence*) the drawings in the order of the story. For example, start with the butcher's shop. The *dog* looks through the window and barks at the *butcher*. There's a *woman* wearing a *hat* inside the shop. She feels sorry for the dog and buys him a *bone*. The woman and the dog walk down the *street* together towards the woman's *house*.

Now ask someone else to rearrange the drawings to tell a different story, starting with the woman. A *woman* is walking down the *street* when she is chased by a snapping *dog*. A *butcher* comes running out of the *butcher's shop*, brandishing a *bone* like a club to chase away the dog. The feral dog jumps at the butcher and tries to bite him, but only gets his *hat*. The dog runs away.

There could be so many different versions using these images. Another could start with the butcher. The *butcher* is in his shop. The *woman* is a shoplifter and hides a *bone* for her *dog* under her *hat* when the butcher isn't looking.

Use your imagination—everyone should be able to think of a new story with the same pictures. Some stories may not need all the pictures.

When you tell your story, are you telling it from the point of view of the woman? The dog? The butcher? Are you using an objective or subjective point of view?

10 EDITING: GETTING MORE TECHNICAL

You can get started with editing without reading this, but as you get more skilled this chapter may help you.

Platforms

Once you get past editing for yourself or for your coursework, it will be time to consider how your future videos will be shown to others.

The *platform* you use will affect both who will see your work, and how you actually set up to edit it.

Think like an editor! Paul Sosso, Portland, Oregon.

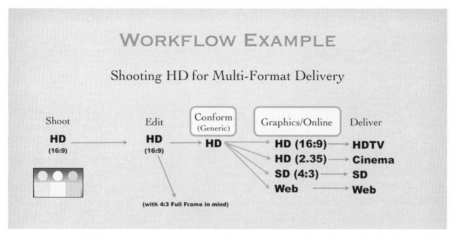

WORKFLOW EXAMPLE

Shooting HD for Multi-Format Delivery

Shoot	Edit	Conform (Generic)	Graphics/Online	Deliver
HD (16:9)	HD (16:9)	HD	HD (16:9)	HDTV
			HD (2.35)	Cinema
			SD (4:3)	SD
			Web	Web

(with 4:3 Full Frame in mind)

Within one project, you may be asked for multi-platform delivery. Graphic by David Jahns, Editor.

Are you making a video that you'll distribute on DVD? Blu-ray?
Is it a product for email or mobile (cell) phone delivery?
Will you be posting your video to the internet?
Is it going to be broadcast on television using high-quality tape?
Or is this one for your grandmother, who can handle her VHS machine and sees no need to make changes?

Formats

If you're using other software to add graphics to your project, make sure the settings of the graphics match the settings of your footage.

Melissa Bourne, Editor.

If you're producing a video entirely on your own, it's likely to all be shot on one camera—yours. But as soon as the project becomes more complex, with footage from additional people, you're likely to run into format differences.

You may have a nifty new high definition (HD) digital video camera, and you're confident it will be great for capturing the main bands at the Spring Music Festival—great colour reproduction, good in low light, easy to move around with, and so on. But three friends are coming along on the roadtrip/camp-out with you and they've all volunteered to help make the documentary.

One friend has a standard definition camera that can be switched to 16:9, one has her aunt's Super VHS which still works great but can only do 4:3, and one has a digital stills camera and a good eye, so you're hoping for some electric photos for a montage opening. This is a recipe for a weekend of excitement, energy and creativity, followed by a very challenging edit. But that may be okay.

When you pool resources to shoot dramas for fun, you take what formats you can get. At least come to an agreement on 4:3 or 16:9.

If you need to use some footage that was shot in analogue video (e.g. SVHS), use an analogue-to-digital converter. You can also use it to output digital video to analogue-format tapes.

David Jahns,
Editor.

Mastering a show in 1080p24 (23.98) will allow for the cleanest conversions to other formats (cinema, SD-NTSC, 720p60, etc . . .) from that one version.

Before you start to edit, you'll have to choose just one format for your timeline. You do this either in the edit program's preferences or in the opening dialogue box. Once chosen, it's pretty final. You can't change a timeline format once there are shots on it.

If you start with a timeline in HD, all your clips must be either originated in HD or up-converted to HD. If you start with your timeline in NTSC standard definition, that's what your finished program will be.

Anything that is dragged to the timeline that doesn't match the chosen format will have to be converted (rendered). Some conversions yield happier results than others.

If you find you've made a mistake and chosen the wrong timeline, or forgotten to choose and ended up with the default one and it doesn't work for your production, you basically have to start again. (Sigh!)

PAL users beware: some editing programs default to NTSC. You'll know there's a problem with the timeline settings if all your PAL clips say they need to be rendered. The sign of needing rendering can be a red line across the top of the clip once it's put on the timeline.

S.D. "TAPE" FORMATS

Format	Compression	Color Space	Signal
DigiBeta	1.6:1	4:2:2	NTSC/PAL
DV50	2.5:1	4:2:2	NTSC/PAL
BetaSP	Analog		NTSC/PAL
DVCAM	5:1	4:1:1 4:2:0	NTSC PAL
miniDV	5:1	4:1:1 4:2:0	NTSC PAL
DVD	20:1°(variable)	4:2:0	NTSC/PAL 24 frame 16:9 or 4:3
3/4"	Analog		NTSC/PAL
VHS	Analog		NTSC/PAL

Within standard definition there are plenty of variables. (Graphic by David Jahns)

18 DTV Standards - U.S. Broadcast Formats

Format Level	Vertical Pixels	Horizontal Pixels	Pixel Shape	Aspect Ratio	Scan Mode	Frame Rates	NTSC Rate
HD	1080	1920	Square	16:9	Progressive	24	23.98
HD	1080	1920	Square	16:9	Progressive	30	29.97
HD	1080	1920	Square	16:9	Interlaced	30 (60i)	29.97
HD	720	1280	Square	16:9	Progressive	24	23.98
HD	720	1280	Square	16:9	Progressive	30	29.97
HD	720	1280	Square	16:9	Progressive	60	59.94
ED	480	704	Rectangular	16:9	Progressive	24	23.98
ED	480	704	Rectangular	16:9	Progressive	30	29.97
ED	480	704	Rectangular	16:9	Progressive	60	59.94
ED	480	704	Rectangular	4:3	Progressive	24	23.98
ED	480	704	Rectangular	4:3	Progressive	30	29.97
ED	480	704	Rectangular	4:3	Progressive	60	59.94
ED	480	640	Square	4:3	Progressive	24	23.98
ED	480	640	Square	4:3	Progressive	30	29.97
ED	480	640	Square	4:3	Progressive	60	59.94
SD	480	704	Rectangular	16:9	Interlaced	30 (60i)	29.97
SD	480	704	Rectangular	4:3	Interlaced	30 (60i)	29.97
SD	480	640	Square	4:3	Interlaced	30 (60i)	29.97

It's not just the frame rates that vary; even the pixel shapes are different, which will impact on any graphics.
(Graphic by David Jahns)

Settings

Don't freak if you have material in more than one format—people manage to edit great shows with multiple-source formats all the time. You just need to watch what you're doing. Go carefully through the import settings and timeline options, and choose the ones that will work for your particular collection of format types.

Advertising producers have to deal with signal compatibility all the time.

David Jahns, Editor.

I recommend the Creative Cow website (<www.creativecow.net>). It has terrific industry news and the most helpful forums for everything from cameras to editing software. Creative Cow forums have helped me resolve a number of very tricky technical issues—the people who look after the forums, and the forum members, are very helpful and quick to respond.

Caite Adamek, Film and Video Editor.

Variety Is the Spice of—Editing? The Chilli Perhaps!

Okay, so an Australian video buff and an American met while on holidays on a Greek island. They travelled together for a few days, admired each other's footage and agreed to share it. They promised to send each other an edit of their times together. Maybe they promised more, but we won't go into that.

Once back home again, they each went to do their editing and found they had to make lots of adjustments to put the footage together.

FRAME DIMENSIONS
One had shot in 4:3 and the other had done widescreen.

SD or HD
The 4:3 was standard definition and the widescreen was high definition.

PROGRESSIVE OR INTERLACED?
The 4:3 was interlaced, but the HD was progessive (1080p).

FRAME RATE
One person's footage was PAL (25 frames per second) and the other's was NTSC (29.97 frames per second).

COMPRESSION
One camera shot at 7:1 compression rate and the other at 5:1.

AUDIO BIT RATE
They both recorded their audio at 16 bit. Hooray! There was some compatibility!

What would an editor do with these variables?

David Jahns,
Editor.

Yeah—that's quite a doozy! Mixing and matching just about everything, eh?

It depends on what you're hoping to deliver—an HD Blu-ray? Standard Def NTSC DVD? PAL DVD? Or simply a web video to share on YouTube?

The short answer is . . . if you're only looking for web-quality video to share with friends, then Final Cut Pro will be fine at dropping everything into a timeline and rendering it, and the consumer editing systems will basically do the same thing.

If you really want it to look nice at DVD or HD quality, then everything should be converted to match formats—probably using Compressor to up-convert the PAL to the HD, cropping it to 16:9, and editing in HD.

The HD footage will look very good, and the PAL won't look as good—but that's to be expected in such a scenario. If you converted the HD to PAL and edited PAL, it would probably look as good as the original PAL footage, but not any better.

It's also a big variable as to whether you would choose to de-interlace the PAL footage to better match the progressive frames or not. Personally, I probably would, but without actually seeing the footage, I couldn't say for sure what the best scenario would be.

Learn to think like an editor!

I have noticed that some people save multiple projects instead of creating sequences within the project. Only save it as a separate project if you are to work with a later version of Final Cut and then move to an earlier version. This might happen if you're working from home and yours is a later version and the computer at work or uni is an earlier version, or vice versa.

Melissa Bourne, Editor.

Userbits

Userbits are an additional part of the timecode information on tapes, and with them you can discreetly store data like the recording date, the site, the camera operator, the camera number (especially useful for multi-cam shoots) and other things that you choose.

Userbits don't allow the use of many characters, but by setting up simple codes where a number stands for something (like 4 = anemones at the Barrier Reef) you can set up a searchable database of your recordings. So years later you can still find the tape with that elusive wildlife shot on it.

Userbits can only be recorded at the time of shooting, so preplanning is needed to use them most effectively. They can help you in editing, but only if they were recorded in the first place.

Compression (Data Bit Reduction)

Compression means taking the amount of data in the video signal and reducing it so the file size is smaller—that is, the amount of data is less.

The *first compression* happens inside the camera, usually without you being actively involved. The higher-quality cameras employ less compression and the cheaper cameras use more:

- HD-CAM compresses the image it captures by a ratio of 4:1
- MiniDV compresses 5:1
- AVCHD—some flash memory cameras—compress 30:1.

So, right from the start, the image you record is less than the image your great lens could see.

The *next compression* is controlled by you and your edit system. This is the compression rate you choose for importing your footage into your hard drive. You choose the rate of compression based on whether you want low-quality video for doing your initial editing or high-quality video for your final editing.

For getting started, for your rough cut, you can use greatly compressed video because the quality of the signal isn't so important at this stage. What is important is that you have access to all your shots—anything that might possibly be useful for your project.

For the fine cut, you can reimport the required footage at a higher quality (a lower compression rate).

Don't get confused here—lower compression means a higher level of detail and a better quality of image.

If you wait to import the highest-quality images for the fine cut, each frame will require more storage space in your hard drive. But because you've made your final edit decisions and have eliminated many of the shots that were previously under consideration, it shouldn't be a problem. Hopefully, the total data of the final high-quality shots will demand less storage space than was needed for storing all your lower-quality captures.

If you have boundless hard drive space, you can save some time by importing all your video at full quality right from the start.

Then, if you have a full Media Manager function, you can later get the edit program (in Final Cut Pro) to delete from your drive any footage not used in your final edit.

Because the editing workflow has changed from former days, and now the rough cut seems to morph over time directly into the final cut, being able to import everything at full quality is handy. But drives do cost, and people have to work around what's available to them.

The *third compression* decision comes when you export your project from the timeline.

You can elect to export your project as full-quality video. If you're exporting to a master videotape, use the highest quality you can. On the other hand, video for the web can be compressed 50:1 or more. Get clear on the requirements of your distribution path.

Gordon Peters, Cameraman, Channel 7 News, Bundaberg.

LABEL YOUR MEDIA. Editors tend to become emotionally fragile when they have to spool through wilds in search of specific vision. This is when the need for labelling and shotlisting media becomes painfully evident. If possible, consolidate your media to reduce edit suite clutter (and free up recording media).

Q: What compression types does Portland Community Media accept?
A: H.264, .AVI, .MOV, Mpeg2, and DV.
                                              (From PCM *Advice to Producers*)

The *fourth compression* happens when you put your project into an authoring program so you can burn it to DVD or a Blu-ray disc. It may be imperative that your very complex 78 minute show be compressed to fit on a single DVD. Your authoring application can do this compression for you, or you can fiddle with the compression settings yourself.

Compression, like much in life, is a bit of a juggling act. You want to keep the highest possible quality at the lowest memory cost. The trick is to wind back the file size to the point where the loss of quality is still invisible to the viewer.

It's a choice between whether you want speed of download or great images. (Graphic by David Jahns)

Compression Methods

Deciding what kind and level of compression to use is connected with knowing how your viewer will see your product. Anything viewed on a full-screen TV will need bigger file sizes than something viewed in a tiny window on a website.

Reducing Frame Size

One method of compression is to reduce the size of each frame. This achieves quite dramatic results. A 320 × 240 image uses only a quarter the number of pixels as a 640 × 480 picture.

If you're authoring for the web, it works fine to send smaller frames. People are used to accepting pictures that don't fill their computer screens and they're generally impatient with slow downloads, so they may not wait if it's looking discouraging to them. This is the era of Macvideo—it's expected to be fast.

Reducing Frame Rate

Another compression method is to adjust the number of fields or frames per second. Some systems allow the editor to capture or output less than the 25 (or 30) frames in each second of video.

Video with a frame rate of 15 frames per second will look fairly smooth to the eye, but it will be using only half the storage rate of the normal (NTSC) signal. A similar calculation can be applied to PAL video, of course.

Frame rate reduction does not allow the editor to do frame-accurate editing, because some of the frames on which the editor might choose to perform a cut won't be available.

Images compressed by frame rate will also suffer a bit in the playback of motion.

Frame reduction is probably more useful when editing or exporting for the web than for products for more demanding platforms. For higher-quality delivery, this is not a desirable way to edit.

Reducing the Colour Information

Another factor that the compression inventors have taken into consideration is that the human eye is less sensitive to changes in colour than it is to changes in brightness. So lots of colour information can be discarded before the compression becomes noticeable to the viewer.

Colour compression does produce some artefacts (visible degradations of the image), however. These show up most on sharp colour boundaries, like white text on a dark background.

Lossy vs Lossless Methods

When a signal is compressed, then decompressed, then compressed again, repeatedly, it does begin to degrade. But most editing processes don't require repeated conversions.

Some codecs are 'lossy', which means the image will degrade. The 'lossless' ones aren't supposed to degrade at all.

Codecs

A codec is a compression algorithm—a formula for compressing a signal. (Codec is one of those words made from other words: **co**mpression and **de**compression.)

Different codecs have different uses and advantages and disadvantages.

- MJPEG   Used for general applications.
- MPEG1   Used for CD-ROM and the web.
- MPEG2   Used for DVD and satellite TV, can handle both standard definition and high definition video.
- MPEG3   Used for high-quality digital sound.
- MPEG4   Used for interactive multimedia, and can be played out at differing rates, depending on the acquiring source (computer, mobile phone).
- DV   A very good codec for video editing.

Intra-frame Compression vs Inter-frame Compression

INTRA-FRAME COMPRESSION

With *intra-frame compression*, each single video frame is compressed separately.

Intra-frame compression is good for editing because every frame is available and complete in itself; thus every frame is considered a key frame, and edit systems can use any one of them for making a cut.

Intra-frame editing compression is measured in *bits per frame*.

INTER-FRAME COMPRESSION

Inter-frame compression operates differently. It works on the fact that much of the data from one video frame to the next is the same. Inter-frame compression just stores the *differences* from one frame to the next.

There are three kinds of frames in inter-frame compression. (Just skip this bit if your brain is in overload, but hang in there if you like knowing the tech stuff.)

First, there's the *I frame*. This means *intra-frame*, which is just like the normal DV frame. This type of frame has the largest amount of data.

Then there's the *P frame*, standing for *predicted frame*. It's arrived at by referencing it to the frames that came before it. A P frame can be less than a tenth of the size of the frame that came before it.

And there's the *B frame*. The B stands for *bi-directional*. B frames are calculated from the frames that come before them and after them and they're very low bit-rate frames.

So MPEG2 is said to have an *IPB format*. (I'm SURE I don't have to explain why this is so.) A compressed IPB video signal could look something like this:

I-P-P-P-P-B-B-B-B-P-B-B-B-I-P-P-P-P-B-B-B-B-P-I-P-P-P-B-B

The *I frames* have to recur every now and then so there isn't a problem with accumulated error, which could cause unacceptable distortion of the original signal.

Inter-frame compression is good for exporting video. Its value is especially in being low bit rate, and its output stream is measured in bits per second.

Inter-frame compression isn't so good for editing because some edit systems can only cut on a complete frame and, as you have seen, the I frames only occur now and then. You can cause an I frame to occur, but the more you do that, the less value there is to inter-frame compression.

UPLINKING VIDEO TO THE WEB: It's important to know what player you'll be using on the web (flash, Quicktime, etc.) and then from there on it's all about codecs and what can give you the best quality for the file size. The one pointer I received from a mentor was to purchase stand-alone compression software for the job rather than use the software bundled with editing programs. There's a lot of computations that go into creating a good looking export and a company that specialises in that part of the workflow will do it better than anyone else.

Mark Gingerich, Portland Final Cut Pro Users Group.

Audio

Editing audio well relies largely on your ears, but some basic technical knowledge will help you deal with camera and edit system settings and compatibility problems.

Bit Rates

The *bit rate* is the number of bits of audio information gathered at each measurement.

Your camera set-up menu will give you the choice of recording audio at different bit rates. DON'T go for 12 bit, always choose 16 bit audio.

Although it's true that 12 bit audio will take up less space and give you a smaller file size, 16 bit is the minimum you need for good sound quality. Recording 12 bit audio is a false economy.

If you're using audio that was recorded by someone at 12 bit by mistake, you may have trouble with it.

To handle this situation, you could try unsampling it. This doesn't always work well, but some systems can handle it okay.

Sample Rates

The *sample rate* is the number of times per second the audio is measured.

If you're using 16 bit audio, it could have a sample rate of 44.1 kHz (that's 44,100 samples per second) or 48 kHz (that's 48,000 audio samples made per second).

44.1 kHz is the standard sample rate for CD audio. 48 kHz is the typical DV/pro video/digital TV sample rate. With added bandwidth and capacity on Blu-ray, you're now seeing the advent of 96 kHz audio at 24 bits. The higher the bit rate/sample rate, the more accurate the audio—but you also get larger amounts of data, which equates to bigger file size.

Paul Sosso,
Editor/
Producer.

Stereo Pairs

Be conscious of how your audio has been recorded.

You could find that you have the exact same audio on both audio tracks. This would be the case if you recorded just from your camera mic, or if you used one auxiliary mic and assigned its sound to both channels equally. A giveaway is when both audio tracks have waveforms that look identical. If this is the case, you could choose to delete one track so your audio mix is simpler.

If you've used two mics in the same sound environment, you may notice that their waveforms are similar in shape, but one has more amplitude (i.e. it's bigger) than the other. This could happen if you used one mic that was much better at picking up sound than the other one was. There's no harm in this situation, but you might choose to delete the weaker signal channel.

Edit systems usually import the audio linked with the video (though there are commands which let you import video only or audio only).

Upon import, the two channels might be linked to each other as well. This means that if you move one channel, or raise or lower the volume on one channel, the same thing will happen with the other channel automatically. This is called a *linked stereo pair*.

Before they edit their project together, some people forget to check their audio inputs. They have forgotten to separate inputs if different mics were used, or failed to make them into a stereo pair. They spend so much time fixing it later.

**Melissa
Bourne**, Editor.

In order to have fuller control over your audio, find the command that will let you link and unlink your audio tracks. This way you can move audio separate from video, and you can move and act upon each audio track on its own if you need to.

Manipulating the Video

Digital editing allows changes to video that could only be wished for in an earlier day, or done at a huge price in high-end postproduction. That's great.

But every change you make to your video takes editing TIME. So correcting mistakes still doesn't come cheap.

Reflect upon any video repairs you're making in your current project and try to eliminate the need for them next time around.

However, if your footage is great to begin with, there are some nifty things you can do with it to construct even more striking images.

> Acquisition is key. For every little thing you screw up in acquisition, you're adding exponential time in post.

Paul Sosso, Editor/ Producer.

Cropping the Image

Your picture might benefit from a slight tweak in the framing—getting rid of the edge of that silver camera case in the lower left corner, for example, or that boom mic hovering just above the presenter's hat.

You can selectively shift the boundaries of the frame, moving in the top, bottom, left or right sides, or any combination, by using the crop tool. Slight adjustments usually work out without harming your picture quality.

If you need to change the frame shape from wide screen to 4:3, you can employ centre crop. This works, as long as your camera operator shot with 4:3 centre cutting in mind. Otherwise, you may lose some important part of the image when you cut off the left and right sides of the frame.

Resizing

Sometimes you want to make an image smaller, so you can put two or more images on the screen at once. Or you want to have space to the left or right for a credit roll. Reducing the image size works if the image is a close shot and not too complicated. Very busy shots or long shots might lose too much of their impact by reducing their size.

Going bigger can also be done, but it's trickier because as you expand the image you blow up the pixel data and your picture quality could start being compromised. Again, less is more with this. You can pretty much rely on your eyes if you have a good monitor.

> When it comes to colour correction, find the white in the image. By using RGB in the colour correction folder, take out as much blue from the white area as you can, then play around with the red and green to make the white patch as white as you can get it. Some people have an eye for it; some just learn with the more projects they do.

Melissa Bourne, Editor.

Overlays: Changes in Opacity

When something is opaque, it means you can't see through it. Each video clip, when it's placed on the timeline, is fully opaque.

When you decide to make more complex images, why not try combining two or more clips on the screen at once? This is done by putting the clips in the same position on the timeline, one above another. If you can't see where to do this, just try dragging a clip down to the timeline and hover it above the spot. With Final Cut Pro, another video track will suddenly appear for you.

When doing colour correction, get the whites right first, then get the contrast, then work on the colours.

Rob Davis,
Editor, Digital
Dimensions.

Now the way it works is that the edit program will prioritise whatever is currently on the uppermost video track, whether you have two or ten or more. So, if you play the timeline you'll only see the top clip because it will be opaque *until* you alter its opacity.

There's an opacity line that can be turned on. You'll then see the line on the clip itself, and you can raise or lower it to make the clip more or less transparent. As you experiment, you'll begin to see the image which is directly beneath it in your stack. To see a clip further down in the pile, you need to alter the opacity of each clip above it.

If you change the order of the track stack, you'll change the output image.

You can change the opacity for the duration of the whole clip, or you can alter it at different points in the clip, so your top clip can become less opaque and then more opaque as the clip unfolds.

Ever wanted to make a ghost appear and disappear within a shot?

Or perhaps simulate a memory coming and going in the character's mind?

Key Effects

Key effects work like stencils. You can overlay one clip above another, and the gaps created by the key effect applied to the top clip will be filled in by the content in the corresponding segments of the bottom clip. This is another form of basic compositing, but if you've been around the medium for a while, key effects are probably something you've experienced in the past; it's just that before you needed a vision mixer to produce them.

Compositing

Once you're into manipulating the content of clips, you're ready for compositing. This means combining various picture *elements* (pieces) within one frame. Composited images are great for intros and outros of a show, but have their place wherever the image from a single clip just won't do—or would be enhanced by additions.

It ain't the paintbrush, it's the artist.

Paul Sosso,
Editor/
Producer.

Here's an example of a simple bandaid-type composite: your period drama occurs in a field fringed by trees. The acting is great, you're very enthused, but once back in the edit suite, you see that there's a recycling bin way in the back at the treeline; nobody noticed it during the shooting.

You can take the clip with the offending bin—fortunately it's only seen for a few frames—and do a cut-out of the bin. Then you stack the clip with the bin cut out on top of the clip with the bin present and slide the clip with the bin present slightly to the right or left, so the hole in the upper clip is filled with more of the general tree line and—BIN GONE! Hopefully no one will notice the patch. Tinker until you get it right.

Here's an example of a reverse situation. You have a shot of a rabbit, but you wanted to have more rabbits in the picture—pesky things, they kept running away! You make a careful cut-out of the one rabbit and overlay that opaque cut-out in several different positions of the image on track above track, altering its size, and sometimes flipping it left to right to make some variety. The edit program will show every rabbit as being present in the frame of the main clip which is at the bottom of the stack. And there you have it—a plague of rabbit clones!

Buoyed by these baby-step successes, you can move on to inventing frames with all manner of elements added to them. The elements need not come from video clips, either. Digital photos, clip art, scanned images and many more can be woven into your digital tapestry.

The tools you have now, you can do so much with. The low-end application now is the high-end application of fifteen years ago.

Paul Sosso,
Editor/
Producer.

When you don't have a deadlined project on the boiler, play around with compositing so you can offer yourself as an increasingly skilled editor for your next team project or paying client.

I was working on a full-length student film (mostly colour correcting and compositing) and I was responsible for creating the DVD version as well. I was highly frustrated for ages because it was a Noir film, in black and white, but once I exported it using my editing software the blacks were so crushed that it caused a lot of the shots in the movie to become a muddy mess. And then encoding it onto a DVD only made that problem worse.

Using a program like Compressor or Sorenson's Squeeze to create the final output, instead of your main editing software, can create a higher-quality and more accurate render, whether it's for a DVD or the web. Once I did that, my final video looked 100 times better. And everyone was very happy with the results.

Mandi Vernoy,
Final Cut Pro
Users Group.

Motion Paths and Key Frames

You can have a shot change in size and position and move through the frame.

You can have several different shots moving around the frame at once.

You can make a montage so that a head shot of each actor, or a representative shot of each scene, grows from nothing to full screen, then recedes back to occupy a quarter (or any fraction) of the screen, until finally you have a frame with all of them coinciding.

You can have multiple video and non-video-generated elements, people or creatures that never met in real life, twirling, changing size, even distorting and changing shapes as they interact within the frame.

You do this by defining a *motion* path and setting *key frames* for every element or clip you're using.

As with everything else in your edit system, there will probably be three ways to achieve this. The simplest one will be to engage the motion path mode and click and drag your clip or element through its choreography. Every change, whether for size, motion or distortion, becomes a key frame for playback.

Usually there's a read-out that will show you schematically where every key frame is. Then you can make adjustments by adding and deleting them for each clip or element.

Keyboard Mapping

Keyboard mapping lets you customise your keyboard, assigning shortcuts to any menu commands you choose. If using shortcuts is your editing style, this is your opportunity to greatly enlarge their potential.

You can also have different virtual keyboards, so if you use auxiliary programs frequently, say *After Effects*, you can have a keyboard set-up which works for that, as well as one for your normal editing. In fact, you can have several. The AVID system is good for this.

To find out more about keyboard mapping, visit: <www.geniusdv.com/weblog/archives/mapping_menu_commands_to_an_avid_keyboard.php>.

Editing: Way of Life? Obsession?

For some people, video is addictive. Once started, it's an intense hobby or a new career or an obsession.

Editing is a very powerful activity. A chance in life to play demi-god or at least CEO. And there's always more and more to learn and be able to do.

When your edit application is no longer adequate to your desires, there are many other supplementary programs into which you can move your project and refine it further. A few are:

- After Effects
- Motion
- Colour
- Boris Calligraphy
- ProTools.

Thanks to David Jahns, Paul Sosso and Rob Davis for their help with this chapter.

MICROPHONES

11

What people notice first about video is the image. That's what the cameras are designed to do well; that's what most camera advertisements stress.

But if the soundtrack on your project is poor or annoying, people will turn away very quickly.

Recording good-quality sound requires you to look beyond the camera.

This is because almost all cameras are equipped with *omnidirectional microphones*, and the *omni* is the least useful to you for getting clear and controllable sound.

There are many other *mics*, each designed for specific recording needs. Their cables can be plugged into your camera where it says *mic in*.

Usually just plugging the mic in will override your camera mic, but on other cameras you have to move a switch from *internal mic* to *external mic* in order for the sound from the external (*auxiliary*) mic to be recorded.

Pick-up Patterns

Each microphone is classified by its *pick-up pattern*, which is the range of directions from which it's designed to pick up sound well.

Omnidirectional

Omni means 'every'. An *omnidirectional* microphone picks up sound from all directions—in front of it, behind it, above, below, and from all sides.

An omni is the type of mic to choose to record

Vox populi at the University of La Verne, California.

ambient sound, which is the sound coming into a scene from all directions. An omni would capture the general atmosphere of a street market day—all the voices mingling, the wind chimes, the poultry squawking, the buskers, the vehicles passing . . .

On higher-end cameras, the audio inputs are XLR connections.

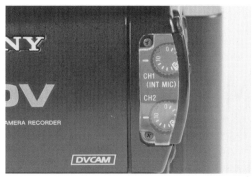

You could have audio input controls to adjust the volume level of the sound being recorded for either the internal mic (the camera mic) or the external mic (the plug-in auxiliary mic).

Ambient sound is often called called *atmos*, which means the background sounds in the local area—the sound atmosphere.

As a standard practice, you should be sure to record at least a couple minutes of atmos at each of your shooting locations, so this background sound can be mixed into your soundtrack and reproduce for your viewers the aural feel of the place. It greatly enriches your soundtrack to have your foreground commentary supported by true atmos, rather than just the sterility of a blank background.

Omnis come in a variety of shapes and sizes, including non-removable camera mics and rugged handheld workhorse versions.

The problem with an omni is that it's entirely undiscriminating. In reproducing everything, it hones in on nothing. Yet most of the time we need to focus on the person speaking, the instrument playing, the sound of the equipment being handled, and so forth.

We don't want the presenter's comments to be drowned out by a passing truck, or the mood of the music to be ruined by the dog barking in the background.

So other types of microphones are needed to do the more focused jobs.

The pick-up pattern of the omni-directional mic.

An omni picks up sound equally from all directions.

Unidirectional

A *unidirectional mic* is designed to pick up sound from the front, and reject sound from the sides and rear. There are ports in the sides which take in the sounds from the sides and rear, but then cancel them out.

These mics are also referred to as *shotgun mics* or *gun mics*, due to their long, thin shape.

Unidirectional mics come in quite a range. Some have a pick-up pattern which is a very narrow-angled cone shape. These are called *super-directional* or *hyperdirectional*.

Others have a much broader angle of receptivity, all the way out to the *cardioid* pattern.

A unidirectional mic is terrific for picking up very specific sounds, and can do so from considerable distances. It's often used in drama or other situations where the mic needs to capture dialogue but be kept out of frame.

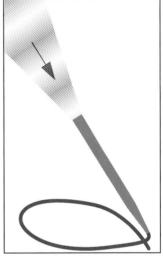

The pick-up pattern of the uni-directional mic.

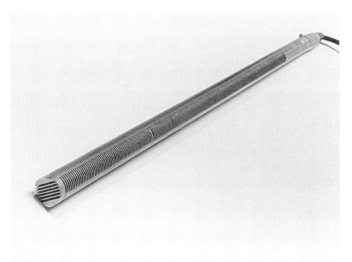

A Sennheiser 816 has a very narrow cone-shaped pick-up pattern. Notice the ports along its side.

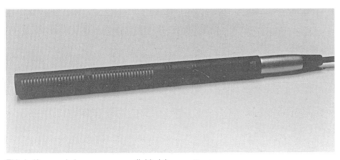

This half-gun mic has a super-cardioid pick-up pattern.

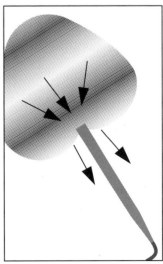

The pick-up pattern of the super-cardioid mic.

On mic   Off mic

The boom handler sways the mic smoothly to avoid mic handling noise. (University of La Verne, California)

The boom operator must constantly monitor the sound quality. Colin Holmes and Shirley Burgess on location for *Promise*.

Gun mics are frequently mounted on booms so they can be moved in as close as possible to the sound source without getting into the shot. They're very sensitive and susceptible to *handling noise*, which is an obnoxious sound that gets recorded when the mic or even the boom is rubbed or jarred.

Gun mics need to be in a shock mount to protect them from transmitting handling noise.

The mic handler or boom operator must take care to point the gun mic exactly at the sound source. A slight error in pointing will cause the recorded sound to be *off mic*. *Off-mic* sound can still be heard, but it's dull in tone, because it's missing the crispness of the high frequencies present in *on-mic* sound.

The *cardioid mic* is a unidirectional mic with a very broad pick-up pattern which looks like an upside-down heart, hence its name. It picks up well from the front and upper sides, and is biased against picking up sound from the rear.

Cardioid mics are frequently used in handheld, on-the-street style interview situations. This mic needs to be pointed towards the speaker's mouth and away from the major noise sources. With skilful positioning and handling, a cardioid can yield good voice recordings and eliminate much of the background noise.

One aspect of the cardioid mic you should know about is called the *proximity effect*. This is an exaggeration of the bass frequencies (the lower tones) in the sound being recorded. It happens when the mic is held very close to the mouth. Some people like the 'close, intimate sound' which this particular distortion produces, and deliberately cause it to happen. If you don't like it, just move the mic further away from the mouth.

Be sure that any unwanted sounds, like traffic, are at the back of a cardioid mic.

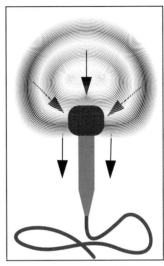

The pick-up pattern of a cardioid mic. It rejects sound from the rear.

There are three simple tricks to remember when using a cardioid. First, make sure you don't nervously rub the mic with your thumb or fingers, because the mic is *hot* all over. That means it reproduces grievous handling noise from any rubbing on it, or any movement of its cord.

Second, make sure you don't get out of sync in your pointing! (This is a surprisingly common mistake.) If you point to yourself when the interviewee is speaking and to the interviewee when you're asking the next question, you'll get worse results than with an omni, because the mic is made to reject sound from the rear.

Anna Ritchie demonstrates mic handling. A cardioid mic, held close, will produce a distortion called the proximity effect. Normal placement is about 15 cm (6 inches) from the mouth.

Good sound—when pointed towards the speaker.

Poor sound—when pointed away from the speaker.

Third, don't lose control of the mic by handing it to your interviewee or letting an enthusiastic or domineering subject grab it from you. It's unlikely they'll handle it correctly, so your recording will suffer. And it's likely their thumb will find the on/off switch and turn the mic off! Using black tape to fix the mic button into the on position before the shoot can avoid some such problems.

Bi-directional

The *bi-directional* mic picks up sounds from its two large opposite sides and rejects sounds from the other two (thinner) sides, and also from the top and the rear. Its pick-up pattern is drawn like a figure eight.

A bi-directional mic is good used on either a table mount or a hanging mount for stationary interviews; it's frequently used for radio shows and other projects based on live interviews.

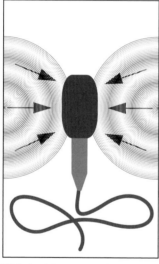

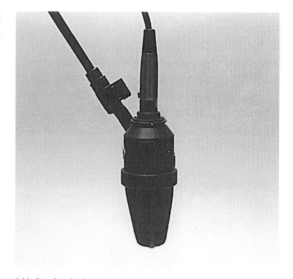

This is the pick-up pattern of the bi-directional mic.

A bi-directional mic.

PZM (Pressure Zone Microphone)

Though the *PZM* (also called a *boundary mic*) looks more like an egg-flip than a mic, don't dismiss it for its weird appearance. There are times when it's extremely useful.

The microphone head is actually very tiny and is mounted *facing downward* towards the large square piece of metal that catches your eye. When the mic is placed upon a wall, floor or table top, all the sounds in the room hit its large plate and are reflected straight back into the little mic head, making it a very efficient sound-gatherer with a hemispherical (half-dome) shaped pick-up pattern.

It's a terrific mic for unobtrusively taping a round-table discussion with several participants, in situations where pointing a mic at people would intimidate them and limit their comments.

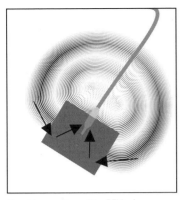

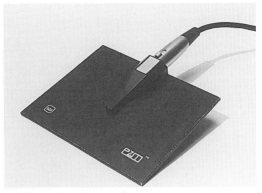

The pick-up pattern of the PZM mic.   A PZM will pick up all the sound in a small room.

It's so sensitive that it over-produces paper rustling and table banging, so for best results people do need to be asked to be as still as they can comfortably be.

Reach

Another important aspect of a mic is its *reach*. This means how far away it can be from the sound source and still bring in a good-quality sound.

Hand-held cardioid mics have a limited reach, and work best if held quite close to the mouth of the person speaking: 15–20 cm (6–8 inches) works well. Other cardioids, like the Sennheiser 416, have a longer reach and can be held out of frame in close shots and still yield a good sound.

The shotgun mic has the longest reach and can be used just out of frame with long shots.

Personally Mounted Mics

Lavalier Mic

You can make your own temporary PZM by using a bit of Blu-Tack to secure a lavalier mic so it's facing *towards* a smooth hard surface, like a desk top. This trick works well and will save you both money and packing space.

Barry Fernandes, Sound Department, AFTRS.

The camera operator has to check that the boom mic isn't seen in the frame. Alla Reynolds and Colin Holmes video Phil Cooper and Claudia Taranto in *Promise*.

The *lavalier mic* (or *lav* or *bug mic*) is a tiny mic which is clipped to a person's clothing or hung around the neck on a short cord.

The lav is actually an omnidirectional mic with a bass cut to counteract the resonance of the chest but, because it has a very limited reach, it excludes most sounds except for the voice of the person on whom it's mounted.

Because the lav is an omni, the speaker can turn his or her head in any direction and it will still pick up a good sound.

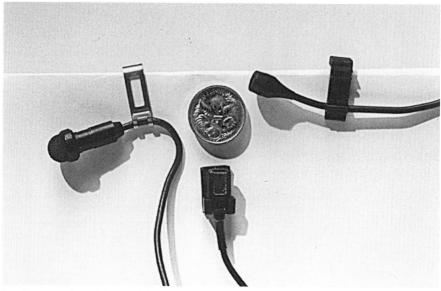

Lav mics are very tiny and clip onto clothing.

A lav mic works well for longer interviews, because the speaker tends to forget about it, relax and speak more naturally. (There's nothing like a mic thrust in your face to make your throat tighten.)

Lavs can either be clipped on the shirt front in plain view, or concealed under an outer layer of clothing, depending on the style of program.

For concealed mics, you can use a little *turtle clip* or *mic cage* to put the mic in when it's being worn. This device hangs around the neck and holds the mic on the mid-chest, like a pendant, isolating it from both skin and clothing contact, thus eliminating clothing rustle sounds.

Mic placement is important with lavs. They should be out of range of necklaces or other jewellery which could clang against them. For softly spoken people, the mic can be clipped higher on the shirt or the record level on the camera can be turned up. For those with louder voices, the mic can be moved lower to achieve the desired recording level.

When the person wearing the lav turns his or her head to the left or right, you can get changes in the recording level. This fluctuation can be reduced by moving the mic a slight bit further away from the speaker's mouth.

Radio Mics

Sometimes you need a very wide shot but also want the mic to be unseen. You can't get a boom in close enough, and you don't want to see cables running across the floor or ground. In that case, you can use a *radio mic*, if you're lucky enough to have access to one. (They're expensive.)

Like lavs, radio mics are tiny and can be pinned to clothing. Instead of sending the sound signal through a cable to the camera, the radio mic has a tiny transmitter with a short antenna attached. This is attached to the mic via a slender cable and is fixed onto the person, somewhere out of sight.

The transmitter sends the sound signal via a radio frequency to a separate receiver, which is tuned in to the transmitter's frequency, and which is kept near the camera, attached via a cable to the camera's *mic in* socket.

A radio mic can allow sound to be recorded under very difficult conditions. For example, dancing, leaping and gyrating performers who also have to sing (!) can wear radio mics. These mics can be concealed on their foreheads just under their wigs or headgear, and the transmitters can be taped inside their costumes in the curve of their lower backs, wrapped in plastic bags to prevent sweating from shorting them out.

Wonderful as radio mics are, they're notorious for giving problems. The batteries wear down very quickly, for one thing. And they're prone to picking up interference, or *fizz*, from large metal objects nearby, like cars. Many sound recordists avoid them whenever possible.

The radio mic (bottom) is clipped to the speaker's shirt and the transmitter (left) can be attached to the speaker's belt or put in a pocket. The receiver (right) is plugged into the mic input on the camera or other sound recording device.

Sound Concepts

Sound is caused by vibration. The speed of the vibration determines the pitch of the sound. A very fast vibration produces the high-pitched *treble* sound. A slow vibration produces the low-pitched *bass* sound.

The vibrating material, whether it's a person's vocal cords, a violin string or the surface of a drum, pushes against the air next to it, sending a wave of sound energy out around it, like the rings in a pool after a stone has been dropped into the water. But whatever the material that's vibrating, it can only move out just so far, then it swings back to its still position and then pushes out an equal distance in the opposite direction. (Just imagine how a drum skin works.)

The skin of a drum moves forwards and backwards, producing the positive and negative halves of each soundwave. Chris Foster, Dorado. (Photo by Ben Lipsey)

When this motion is graphed we see a waveform with peaks and troughs equally distant from the zero position, which represents where the material is at rest.

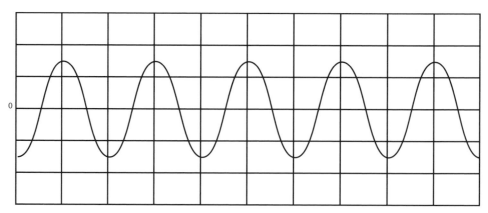

Low-frequency waves produce a bass sound.

One positive and negative section put together (one thrust of the material in each direction) is considered to be one complete wave, or *cycle*.

Sound is measured by the *frequency* of these complete waves—that is, by how many of them happen in a second. In other words, sound is measured by how many *cycles per second* occur.

Another term meaning cycles per second is *Hertz*. Hertz is usually written in its abbreviated form Hz.

So when people talk about sound you'll hear them say things like '100 Hz' (which is a bass sound) or '12 000 Hz' (or 12 kHz), which is a treble sound.

The human hearing range is from about 20 Hz to 20 000 Hz (i.e. 20 kHz), so that's the range we want microphones to be able to reproduce.

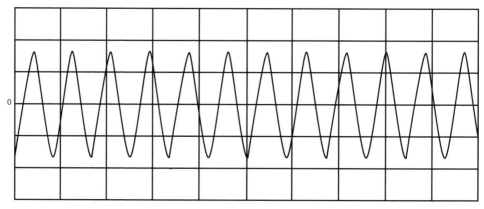

High-frequency waves produce a treble sound.

Microphones pick up these soundwaves and change them into electrical energy, which can then be either transmitted or stored (recorded).

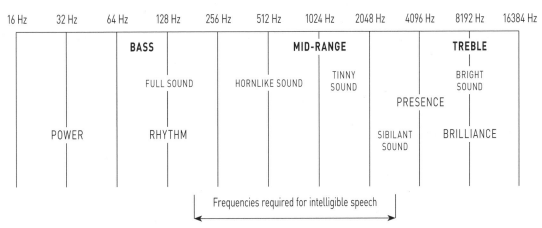

Frequency ranges from bass, mid-range and treble.

Response Characteristics

Microphones are rated according to their *response characteristics*—that is, according to how well they can reproduce sounds of different frequencies. The specification sheet which comes with a mic tells you how good it is at handling different frequency ranges. Usually it will handle some frequencies better than others.

The sibilant sounds, like 's', occur in the higher frequencies of the human voice range. These contribute to the crispness and clarity of the voice, and help us distinguish one word from the next. A mic which is poor in these frequencies yields muddy-sounding recordings that are difficult to understand.

Some mics, often the cheaper ones, exaggerate the high frequencies but are poor at reproducing the low frequencies. These produce thin sounds which are called *toppy* because of the overdose from the top end of the frequency range.

Mics which are very good at the low-frequency end, the bass range, tend to be more expensive. But they do produce a much fuller, richer sound, especially for those deeper voices.

Some microphones have filters which allow the operator to decrease the emphasis of certain frequencies. For example, a *bass roll-off filter* cuts down on the reproduction of bass sounds, and can be handy for reducing the impact of low-level traffic rumbling.

You have to be careful not to over-use the bass roll-off, though, or the recorded sound might be too thin.

Microphone Construction Types

The two major construction types of microphones are the *dynamic* and the *condenser.*

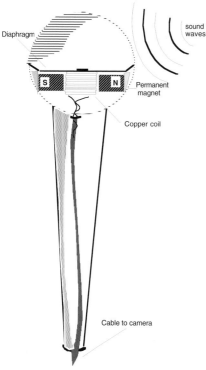

A dynamic mic needs no power supply.

Dynamic

A dynamic mic has a diaphragm (a lightweight membrane), which vibrates when it is hit by soundwaves. A coil is attached to the diaphragm and vibrates within a magnetic field, thus generating a small electrical current. This electrical signal is then output to the record machine.

Dynamic microphones aren't the greatest at reproducing sound subtleties, but they're robust, inexpensive, and they don't require a battery or other power supply.

Condenser

In the condenser mic, a diaphragm and a fixed metal plate act as the opposite poles of a capacitor. Soundwaves strike the membrane and cause it to vibrate. This causes changes in the *capacitance* (stored energy) of the circuit and produces a tiny electrical output.

A condenser microphone requires a power supply to provide electricity for the preamp and the fixed plate.

Sometimes the power supply is a battery inserted within the mic housing—as with the *electret condenser* mics.

Sometimes a separate black box, called the *power supply*, needs to be included in the connection between the mic and the record machine. The power supply can be either battery powered, or it can be an adaptor which uses AC current from the wall.

And sometimes the condensor mic can use *phantom power* supplied by the record machine or audio mixer to which it's attached.

No matter how the condenser mic takes its power, the key thing to be clear on is that it just won't work without it. So always make sure you pick up the battery or power supply when you borrow a condenser mic, and it's a good idea to take a spare battery as well.

Some sound recordists call electret condenser mics *cheap and nasties*. The electret condenser already has a fixed charge on the plates, but this charge doesn't last forever, so they deteriorate in quality over time, and eventually you should throw them away.

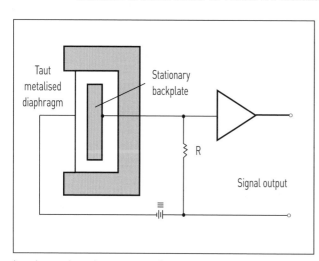

A condenser mic requires a power supply.

Though the true condensers cost more money, it's money well spent—if you have it.

Condenser mics are more sensitive than dynamic mics, and are better at reproducing the subtleties and nuances in sound. They're less shock resistant, and they cost more to buy, but they do give a better recording quality.

Choosing the Right Microphone for the Job

Every recording situation comes with its own set of sound circumstances. In order to choose the right microphone for the job, you need to know as much as possible about the conditions that will apply on the day of the shoot.

It's a good idea for the sound recordist to do a site check of the intended shoot location at the time of day and day of the week when the recording session will occur. Certain loud sounds, like those from aeroplane flight paths, peak-hour traffic, construction sites and school playgrounds, vary considerably according to the time.

> The saying may be that a picture is worth a thousand words, but a video picture without good sound can be virtually useless if you really need to hear what's going on.

Rachel Masters, Corporate Training Coordinator, SBS.

You need a mic that can handle the conditions you'll have to face. You also need a mic that will give the sound quality and sound breadth you require. The right mic for an interview wouldn't be the one you'd use for a broad ambient sound. A super-sensitive condenser will die in front of a big drum or powerful woofer.

Sound recordists try to narrow the choices down to a couple of likely mics, and take them both along on the shooting day to listen to how each one performs in the situation. Then they make their final choice.

By the way, it's prudent to take along an extra mic cable, too. You never know when one will be slammed in a door or just go crackly of its own sweet accord. Always take backups.

Powering the Mic

If you're using a battery-powered mic, it will need a healthy battery to record a strong signal. If you suspect that the sound you're getting is weaker than it should be, put in a fresh battery. It's pointless to record a wimpy signal with a poor signal-to-noise ratio. It will never edit well.

Although some mics take AA batteries, many mics take weirdo batteries that can only be bought from specialist suppliers. So always take spare batteries with you. The corner store near the shoot just won't have the right kind.

Needless to say, you always turn a mic off when you're not using it because it will just go on responding to the sound around it and draining the battery. When you store the mic in its case for the night, take the battery out of it.

Suggestions from Rachel Masters

Sound response patterns vary between microphones. It's a good idea to test the microphone(s) you have access to, and determine what pattern of sound they will pick up. Don't believe what the manufacturer says, test it for yourself.

1. Ask a friend to help you test the sound pattern by having that person talk while walking around the microphone in a circle while you're holding the mic still and pointed in just one direction. Play back the sound and draw a picture of the sound response pattern.
2. Note the variation in quality of sound between different microphones. Assess which microphone would be best for the following situations:
   • a two-person interview
   • recording music
   • recording several voices simultaneously
   • one person speaking in a wide shot.

Keep your notes about the results. They'll help you decide which mic you need for your various future shoots, and they'll also guide you about what angle and position each mic needs to be placed in for it to record sound best.

Looking Further

See Stanley R. Alten, *Audio in Media* (8th ed.), Wadsworth Series in Mass Communication, Wadsworth, Belmont, California.

HAVING THE RIGHT CONNECTIONS

12

It's often said that the screen production industry works on connections—that your next job is more likely to come from word of mouth than from answering an ad. There's a lot of truth in that. And having the right connections is important on more than just the personal level!

When it comes to equipment, it doesn't matter how good your gear is if you can't get the signal to flow from mic to camera or from camera to digital field recorder.

Great performance, but can't connect the mic? This videomaker has a problem to solve!

Being able to put the various bits together relies on your ability to tell one connector from another, and to make sure that you have the necessary adaptors if you haven't got a perfect match.

Sex Lies in Videotape

(Or near it, anyway.)

For every type of connector, there are two models. Video technicians call these models *male* and *female*.

What it comes down to is that the model of a connector that has a prong or a pin or some sort of sticking-out bit (or three) is called male, and its partner version, to which it connects, is called female.

When you go to buy a connector in a shop or ask for it at the media centre, it's important to get the right model. If you get the reverse of what you need, it won't make the right connection for you.

So if you ask for a *female mini* to *male phone* adaptor, you should be given the little adaptor that allows a mic with a mini plug on the end of its cable to connect into the 6.5 mm input on an audio mixer.

An adaptor which could also be called *mini to phone* would look like an inverted model of this, with a hefty receiving dock and a tiny male member. This, called a *female phone* to *male mini*, is exactly the type you'd need to allow a mic with the larger plug to connect into the *mic in* on a camera which has the smaller (3.5 mm) size input.

As a general rule (which indeed has some exceptions), the signal flow goes from the male connector to the female connector en route to its final destination. So the connector-out of most microphones is male, and that is attached to a female connector on the mic cable, which has a male connector on the other end, which attaches into a female connector on the mixing desk.

Got the drift?

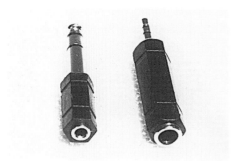

A female mini (3.5 mm) to male phone (6.5 mm).

A female phone (6.5 mm) to male mini (3.5 mm).

Video Connectors

BNC

BNC connectors are the standard video connectors for professional equipment. They're used for conveying the composite video signal—that is, the analogue signal in which the luminance and chrominance signals are composited together and travel along one cable. They're also used for conveying component video—that is, where the luminance and chrominance signals are separated and sent along different cables.

BNC connectors are constructed so they lock together and can't be pulled undone accidentally. This is how:

Once the male and female connectors are joined together, the metal collar of the male BNC is given a half turn so the two little metal nubbins on the outside of the female connector are drawn in along the spiral grooves of the outer metal collar until they slip into two little cut-out sections and the connectors are then locked together.

To disconnect, the metal collar is pushed forward to reposition the metal nubbins back into the spiral grooves and then the collar is untwisted until they're released and the two connectors can be pulled apart.

When you're using a BNC connector, remember that it won't lock on unless you turn the metal collar. Just pushing it straight on will leave the connection susceptible to being pulled off if the equipment is moved. Then you could lose your signal, and will have to go searching for why.

L-R: BNC F barrel connector for attaching two BNC cables together; F BNC; M BNC.

SVHS Y/C Connector

The Y/C connector conveys the SVHS video signal, which is the analogue video signal separated out into the Y/C components. (Y = luminance and C = chrominance.) It's found on SVHS cameras and SVHS edit systems.

This is the connecting cable for SVHS Y/C in an edit system.

IEEE1394 (FireWire or i.LINK)

IEEE1394 is a high-speed serial interface. It conveys lots of signals: video, audio, timecode and device control (allowing your computer to remotely control your digital camera). You'll probably encounter it as the connection cable for putting your digital video signal into your computer.

Your video camera is likely to have both of these cable connections, and they're usually side by side. They're tiny and appear similar, but if you look closely (have to get out those reading glasses, do you?) you'll see the difference. The trapezoidal one carries photographs to a USB connector and the rectangular one is a FireWire connector. You can't fit one of these little doohickeys into the other port. And they're a little difficult—you have to have them lined up exactly straight on their approach to the socket or they won't go in.

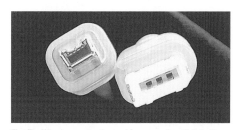

The FireWire connector is used for conveying digital video and HD video into and out of a computer and other equipment.

The USB (left) is used to convey photographs. The iLink (right) is used to connect Sony cameras to computers or hard drives.

UHF

These are now the dinosaurs of video connectors, but if you're into video palaeontology you never know when you might unearth a piece of equipment that has one. They have zigzag edges that fit

Female UHF   Male UHF

together, a thick central pin, and an outer threaded collar which twists on to lock the plug to the socket.

Video/Audio Connectors

RF

The male and female RF connectors look almost the same. The male RF connector has a round metal collar surrounding a bare inner wire, which can be rounded off or quite sharp and raw.

Female RF   Male RF

The female RF connector has a similar round metal collar surrounding a slim connection socket. They're easy to use because they just slip together, but they don't lock into place.

The RF connector appears on RF cables which carry both video and audio signals together, down a single wire. They bring the RF (radio frequency) signal in from your outdoor TV antenna or from your cable TV feedwire and insert it into your TV or VCR. It's also the connector on the RF cable that runs out of your VCR and into your TV.

RCA

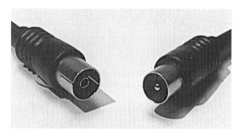

Female RCA   Male RCA

The male RCA connector looks similar to the RF connector, but it can have two or four slits in its metal collar, and its smooth, rounded metal plug projects out beyond the collar. The female looks quite different: it's a streamlined, circular receptor.

The RCA connector is commonly used on home video equipment and on some camcorders. It's easy to attach, but can't be locked into position.

You'll also recognise the RCA as the connector on your home stereo equipment cables. And it's used for line level audio inputs and outputs on VCRs, DVD players, mixers and camcorders.

AV Breakout Connector and Cables

AV breakout connector and cables.

This AV breakout connector sends the analogue picture and sound signals out of a Sony digital camera, and then the cable divides into three: Video, Audio 1 and Audio 2.

Multi-pin Connectors

10-pin, 12-pin and 14-pin connectors are used when a single cable is carrying a variety of signals—video, audio and servo information.

They're used to connect cameras to separate recorders and to connect cameras to CCUs (camera control units) in control rooms.

Their pins must be aligned correctly to the socket pattern before you attempt to connect them together. Locating pins assist in this. Careless connection attempts can result in bent pins and very expensive repairs.

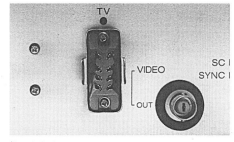

Female 12-pin   Male 12-pin

8-pin Connectors

8-pin connectors transmit video and audio in both directions between a VCR and a TV or monitor. The male is found on the end of cables and the female is mounted on the equipment.

The pins are arranged in groups of six and two, so the connectors can only be attached when they're correctly lined up. They snap on and lock together.

They can be disconnected by pinching in on small metal tabs on the sides of the male connector housing and simultaneously pulling it away from the equipment to which it's attached.

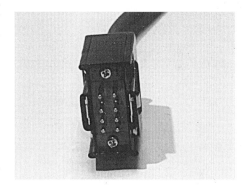

Female 8-pin

Audio Connectors

Mini or 3.5 mm

These carry unbalanced mono or stereo audio signals from microphones to some cameras. They're also used on some headphones.

They're easy to use, but notorious for breaking, and they can disconnect easily by pulling out during a shoot, so they should be carefully watched.

If you can see two black bands on the pin, it's a stereo mini. One black band means it's a mono mini. The black bands are the separators between the signal-carrying contacts and the ground on the pin.

Male 8-pin

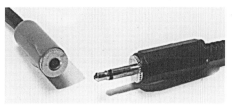

Female mini (3.5 mm)   Mono male mini (3.5 mm)

Female phone (6.5 mm)   Stereo male phone (6.5 mm)

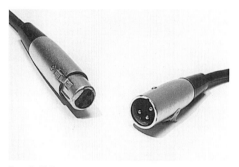

Female XLR   Male XLR

Rachel Masters, Training Coordinator, SBS.

Always be nice to people on the way up . . . 'cause you never know who you'll need on the way down! (I know this isn't what you mean by having the right connections, but I thought I'd mention it.)

Female 4-pin   Male 4-pin

Stereo pins carry two audio signals (channels 1 and 2), and mono pins combine all sounds onto one wire and channel.

Phone or 6.5 mm

These carry mono and stereo audio signals from microphones to some audio mixers. They're found on the end of studio monitoring headphones and intercom headphones. They also carry line level signals between pieces of audio equipment.

XLR (Cannon) 3-pin

These are found on good-quality microphones. They convey balanced audio signals. They're also used on good-quality audio cables, as the audio inputs and outputs on professional camera equipment, on audio mixers and video edit systems.

The XLR connector clicks when you attach it and locks into place. To disconnect it, you push a little metal tab on the outside of the female connector and simultaneously pull them apart.

Electrical Connector (DC)

The DC (direct current) connector looks very much like the XLR, and it's easy to grab the wrong one when in a hurry. But there's no way you can interchange them because the DC connector has four pins (M) or sockets (F) whereas the XLR has only three.

The DC connector (or 4-pin, as it's called) has a large silvery metal housing nearly identical to the XLR, and it can lock into place with a satisfying click. This is good because you certainly want to be assured that your electrical connection is secure.

Like the XLR, the connectors have little push tabs to release them from their locked-on positions.

Audio Adaptors

Because of the variety of audio cables, it's very common to have two pieces of equipment that just don't connect. The mic can't go into the camera or the headphones can't go into the audio mixer, etc. So there's a plethora of adaptors out there. You can pretty much bet there's one for every possible mismatch, though you may not always be able to find it at the shop when you need it. Having a kit bag with you that has a range of adaptors in it is a shoot-saver on many occasions. Here are some handy ones.

Y connector: M RCA to two F RCA.

Y Connector

The Y connector comes in many variations, but it always does the same job: getting two signals through one connector, or splitting one signal on to two cables.

XLR to Phone (6.5 mm)

This adaptor can be a signal changer as well. The pictured one converts the signal from low imped-ance to high impedance, and it's labelled so you know this. There are also XLR to phone adaptors which merely pass the signal unchanged from one style connector to another. Any time an adaptor is a signal changer, it's indicated as such, either with a label or by being red.

Y connector: Stereo M mini (3.5 mm) to two F phone (6.5 mm).

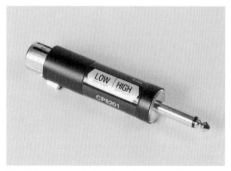

This XLR to phone adaptor alters the signal at the same time, from low impedance to high impedance.

Computer Connectors

Computers have their own ways of linking up and networking, as do computer people.

In computer talk, you don't usually say socket or connection, you say *port*. The *port* is the linking spot on the computer itself, and the right connector is whatever fits into that particular port.

USB

Your computer can have one or several USB ports, through which you can attach a range of devices, including your mouse, keyboard and flash memory drive.

USB male   USB female

The USB connector looks quite similar to the FireWire connector—look carefully before you decide to plug it in: it doesn't have the rounded edge at one end.

USB2

USB2 passes data much faster than USB. People argue about whether it's faster than FireWire. Technically it is, but in practice FireWire usually wins the race.

FireWire

Here it is again, just in case you're looking for it in the computer connections section. FireWire connects your camera to your computer and to external hard drives. It comes in two speeds: FireWire 400 and FireWire 800. The 800 is the much faster one and it's backward compatible.

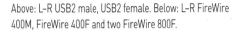

Above: L–R USB2 male, USB2 female. Below: L–R FireWire 400M, FireWire 400F and two FireWire 800F.

Cables

Although at first glance all video cables may look to you like a pile of spaghetti, they're actually quite different, both in how they're made and what they do.

They can be categorised according to the type of signal they carry:

- RF signal
- video signal
- audio signal
- multiple signals.

RF Cable

RF stands for radio frequency. This is the type of signal that's transmitted by television stations through the atmosphere. It enters the TV antenna on the roof of your home, then travels along your antenna cable and goes into the tuner inside your TV set.

If your antenna connects directly into a VCR, then a second, short RF cable takes the signal out of your VCR and into your TV.

The RF signal is also sent through cables in closed-circuit TV systems and cablecast through landlines in cable television systems.

An RF signal contains both picture and sound information, so only one cable is needed to transmit a TV program as an RF signal.

Video Cable

The video is the picture part of the TV signal. Video is usually transmitted on coaxial cable (or *coax*). Coax cable consists of:

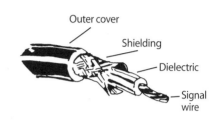

*   an inner wire (or bundle of thinner wires twisted together), which carries the main video signal
*   a surrounding thick wall of high-density foam polythene, called the *dielectric*, which insulates the inner wire from the shielding
*   a plaited mesh of wire, called the *shielding*, that surrounds the dielectric and shields the inner signal-bearing wire from external interference such as radio signals
*   a PVC outer covering which protects the cable from water, dirt and other damagers.

A cross-section of coax cable

Audio Cable

The audio is the sound part of the TV signal. Audio cable is composed of:

*   an inner wire to carry the audio signal (*unbalanced* cable has only one inner wire; *balanced* cable has two inner wires)

Unbalanced audio cable

*   a surrounding PVC insulation cover (much thinner and more flexible than the dielectric in coax)
*   a mesh of shielding (also known as the 'ground'), which conducts unwanted interfering signals to earth

*   a flexible PVC outer covering.

Balanced audio cable

Siamese Cables

So-called *Siamese cables* are two cables which are joined together, although they have separate connectors on the ends. RCA cables often come in Siamese pairs.

It's very handy to have Siamese RCAs because instead of having the snarl of two individual cables, which would normally be used side by side, as in conveying channel 1 and channel 2 audio signals from the same piece of equipment, you have just one double cable. In a video spaghetti situation, this is a help.

You can get Siamese triplets with one connector yellow for video and then red and black (or white) for the left and right audio channels. These joined cables even come in Siamese quads. (That's stretching the image!)

Siamese quads are used when handling a double function which also happens side by side, like connecting your recorder/player audio out to your TV and audio from the TV back to the recorder/player.

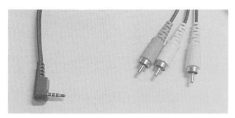

The DV breakout cable is a strange-looking beast—quite different at each end.

The component breakout cable has colour-coded ends to guide you in connecting them: red, green and blue.

Older studio camera cables use multi-pin connectors.

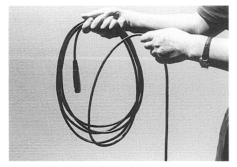

Coil the cables neatly before putting them away.

If you're using a Siamese cable and the connecting points at one end are too far apart from each other for the twins at that end to reach to, the cable is designed so you can gently tear the two ends apart and lengthen their reach.

DV Breakout Cable

This is a hybrid cable that looks like it's trying to be two things at once. On one end there's a plug shaped like a mini connector, which gets inserted into the AV output on a video camera. On the other end there are three cables, one for video and two for audio. This breakout cable is used to connect the camera to a monitor, a VCR, a DVD recorder or another camera.

Component Breakout Cable

The component breakout cable conveys the component signals through this little connector and splits out to the three component cables: red, green and blue (RGB).

Multiple Signal Cables

Some cables carry an assorted bundle of wires that convey video signals, audio signals, signals to operate servos, power signals and grounding. These have multi-pin connectors on their ends.

Connector and Cable Care

- Connectors can be damaged easily by mishandling, so treat them carefully. Re-soldering a plug can be a lengthy and demanding project.
- When attaching multi-pin connectors, be sure to refer to their locating pins to help you line them up right.
- When disconnecting cables from equipment, always grasp the connector by the body of the plug, and pull firmly and straight out.

- Never try to disconnect anything by yanking on the cable.
- If a plug is difficult to disconnect, look for a release mechanism.
- Avoid kinking cables or slamming them in the lids of cases or in doors.
- Don't run over cables with dollies or vehicles.
- Coil cables after use.

Keep on hand a set of the commonly used cables and connectors, and always take spares with you on a shoot.

Jeremy Reurich repairs a cable, technical traineeship, AFTRS.

Checking for Faults

A multi-meter will tell you if a cable is faulty. A soldering iron, some solder and flux, and a very steady hand will allow you to repair it.

Natty movable shelving solution.

Barbara Bishop, Independent Producer.

This equipment room has a system of shelving units on a floor track which can be pushed left or right to reveal the contents of the shelves on the units, like bookcases, so only the solid end shows—it looks much neater. Then they just push the first unit, for instance, to the left, and people can fit between the bookcases to access the equipment. The system is also good for security. When people pass through that room there's no chance of someone taking something off the shelf, a microphone, for instance, because only the solid ends of the bookcase show. I thought it was a good idea for saving space and makes the equipment room look organised.

13 LOCATION SOUND

Sound recording is the Achilles' heel of video. Beginners' video projects are far more likely to have poor-quality sound than poor-quality images.

Why?

This is due to the overwhelming importance the video image *seems* to have.

There's no doubt that getting a beautiful, dramatic or grotesque image is an exciting achievement, and that such images are fascinating to audiences. But their magnetism is short lived.

Unless a program has the additional depth the soundtrack can give, by contributing spoken ideas or enhancing the images with music or sounds, people tire of it quickly. It soon enters the realm of 'video wallpaper'.

Worse still, if the soundtrack is actively bad, due to buzzes, hums, crackles, background noise, muffled speech and distortion, people will refuse to watch it.

Camera operators practise hard-to-get clear focus, steady shots, good composition and smooth action. Good sound recording techniques take similar practice and attention to detail.

Jarrad Kidd prepares for the next take. (Courtesy of Film & TV, Central TAFE, Perth)

Which Microphone Will Do the Job?

Every recording situation comes with its own set of sound circumstances. In order to choose the right microphone for the job, you need to know as much as possible about the conditions that will apply on the day of the shoot.

Again, it's a good idea to check out the shoot location ahead of time, at the same time of day and same day of the week as when the recording session will occur. Certain loud sounds like those from commuter trains, nearby factories, sports facilities and schoolyards vary considerably according to the time and the day, so you need to be sure what you'll have to allow for.

Once you've checked out the location, you need to select (borrow, hire, acquire) a mic that can handle the conditions you'll have to face during the shoot.

When trying new locations, check two or three mics to see which one gives you the sound you like best. Students from the University of Western Sydney.

If you're stuck with using the camera mic, move in as close as possible to the presenter. Favour close-ups over wide shots to get decent sound. In noisy locations, it's better to have an extreme close-up on someone with the camera six inches from their face and hear what they're saying than have a perfectly composed shot and you can't hear what they're saying. Most viewers will put up with crappy pictures a lot longer than they'll put up with crappy sound.

You also need to choose a mic which will give the *sound quality* and *sound breadth* you require.

The right mic for an on-the-street interview in a noisy location wouldn't be the right one for recording a quiet love scene. As discussed previously, a supersensitive condenser mic will just die in front of a big drum or powerful woofer, and it would be no good at all for recording gunshots and explosions.

Try to narrow the choices down to a couple of likely mics, get to the shoot early enough to test them at the location and make your final selection there.

Always take along an extra mic and extra cables and audio adaptors. You never know when a poltergeist will enter yesterday's good connector.

If your audio sucks, your video sucks.

Rich Howley, Video Trainer.

Recording sound is easy, but recording it well takes skill.

Jane Paterson, Sound Editor, AFTRS.

Never push the record button unless you're wearing headphones. Always record sound no matter what you're doing and always listen to the sound.

Tim Rooney, Portland Community Media.

Andy Nehl, Head of Television, AFTRS.

Do not rely on your in-camera mic. Try to use external mics (boom, lavalier clip-ons, etc.) and a separate sound mixer to keep audio levels balanced and clean.

Donna Kenny, The Video History Company and Center for Recording Life Stories.

Don't get more than three times the length of the gun mic away from your subject or the cone shaped pick-up pattern gets too wide and you'll record unwanted sound.

PC Peri, Video Producer.

Don't Use the Camera Mic

The camera mic is almost always an omnidirectional mic. Because it picks up sound equally from all directions, it's terrific for recording a surround sound, but not much good for anything else. Under most circumstances, it's not the right mic for the job.

You'll need to use an *auxiliary* (external) microphone—which just means it's an additional one that you have to plug into the camera.

You can't fix it in the mix! Get good sound now!

Carol Brands,
Curtin
University of
Technology.

You attach the external mic to the camera input labelled *mic in* or *mic*. That input is frequently towards the front of the camera, even next to the camera mic, but on some cameras you need to disconnect the camera mic to reveal the input for attaching the external mic.

If you're out of luck, you'll find that your camera has no place to attach another mic. (That's one of the reasons it didn't cost so much.) If you're deciding on what camera to buy, always make sure it has the capacity to attach an external mic, or you'll be setting yourself up for poor audio recordings.

Get In Close

No matter what sound you're recording, the single most important thing to do is to get the (appropriate) microphone as close as possible to the sound source. Your aim is to record the sound you want at a good strong level, well above the background noise, without your signal being distorted. This is called getting a good *signal-to-noise ratio*.

Signal-to-Noise Ratio

The word 'noise' is used in several ways in video production. It can mean the soft background level of hiss that is generated by any tape during playback; it can mean surrounding sounds that aren't being selected during a shoot; it can even mean the visible graininess that appears in the video part of the signal when the camera is operated on a high-gain setting.

In any of these cases, noise is an undesired part of the signal.

In audio, having a good signal-to-noise ratio means that the desired signal is loud enough to more than dominate the background noise. Once a sound has been recorded, it can't be separated from either the background location noises or the inherent tape noise.

What does this mean for your audio track?

It means that if you record a good strong signal during the shoot, the signal will play back clearly and well on the monitor afterwards, and it will have gusto when being sent through the audio path of an edit system.

If you record a weak sound, you'll be forced to turn the volume of the monitor up during playback, and boost the edit system's audio level during editing. This boosting may let you hear the sound loud enough,

Birgitte Bowen does sound on *The Rainbow Boughquaker.*

but it also brings up the level of the undesired background noise, and it results in poor-quality audio and a muddy edited sound.

> Get good sound! Get good sound! Get good sound! That's the three most important things you can do.

Tim Rooney, Portland Community Media.

How Much Reach is Needed?

You need to be clear on whether it's okay for the mic to be visible in the shot or not. If it's okay for the mic to be shown, you'll usually have no problem getting the mic in close. A lapel mic, or one which is handheld or on a stand, will all do.

When your framing is wide, you need to have a mic with considerable reach, and a boom pole comes in handy. Mariano Aupilarjuk plays skin drum at Rankin Inlet, Nunavut. Albert Kimaliakyuk is sound recordist for *Inuit Piqqusingit: Inuit Ways, Inuit Survival*. (Photo by Kimberley Brown)

But if the mic must be unseen, you need to choose one that can pull in sound over a distance, or that is small enough to be hidden, either on the person or in the set somewhere close to the speaker.

> Always place the microphone as close as possible to your sound source. And be alert to ambient noise that may be recorded in the background during an interview which will be distracting to viewers.

Donna Kenny, The Video History Company and Center for Recording Life Stories.

Recording Levels and Settings

Not all video cameras allow for adequate operator control of audio recording levels.

Many camcorders have no VU meters (VU = *volume unit*) to indicate the level (volume) of sound being received by the camera or to show whether the received signal is so overly loud that distortion is happening during the recording of it.

These cameras rely on their inbuilt *ALC* circuitry.

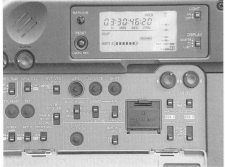

The sound control buttons are sometimes behind a little door, such as on this Sony DVCAM.

Andy Nehl, Head of Television, AFTRS.

Have the headphones over both ears to check audio quality before you shoot, but when you're shooting have the headphones over only one ear so you can hear what's going into the camera and also hear what's happening in the world around you.

ALC

ALC stands for *automatic level control*. The ALC function in the audio circuitry is supposed to ensure that a good level of signal is being recorded by the camera.

Like any auto system on the camera, it works well sometimes, but there are certain circumstances that are too much for it. Overall, it will handle a good signal well, it will clamp down on an overly loud one, and it will boost a low one.

It gets tricky when you alternate between a weak signal and a strong one, because when the ALC boosts the low one up to an adequate level, it brings up the background noise with it, so you end up with a sound continuity problem, where the rising and falling of background noise mars the flow of the recording.

On some cameras, you can choose to use the ALC or turn it off. It's often controlled by one of those tiny buttons hidden behind a secret door on the side of the camera. It pays to snoop over your camera thoroughly to find all these esoteric buttons— knowing what they do and how to use them can make a big difference to your end product.

Always use headphones to listen to the sound coming into the camera. Ideally, you should use headphones with leather padding that encloses the ears, rather than foam ear pads, as foam ear pads allow more external sound into your ears.

Audio Limiter

The *audio limiter* is another sound-control device that can be engaged during recording. Its function is to keep the record level of the incoming signal from going too high, into the distortion range.

When setting an incoming signal level, the audio limiter should always be turned off, so the true (unlimited) strength of the signal can be seen on the VU meter. Then the record level can be set accurately so the audio will be strong but not distorted.

So first turn the audio limiter off, and begin with the audio input level knobs wound all the way over to the off position. Then slowly rotate the knobs clockwise, increasing the incoming volume until the sound is showing at a good level on the VU meter.

After setting the levels, the limiter can then be turned back on and any short, transient loud sounds will be controlled by the limiter, and the main program audio will be at a strong, but not distorted, level.

The main hazard of using an audio limiter occurs if you set the audio input level on the record machine while the limiter is still switched on. Then it's possible to set the audio record level too high, and even when you check the VU meter, the needle won't show any distortion (because the limiter won't let the needle go into the red). However, you'll end up with a very squashed-sounding audio.

Some sound recordists like using a limiter, while others never use them. They prefer to always have full knowledge of the incoming audio, and ride the levels themselves manually throughout the recording session.

Good audio is extremely important in video production. Viewers will tolerate shaky camera work longer than they will an annoying hum or background buzz.

Donna Kenny,
The Video History Company and Center for Recording Life Stories.

Setting the Audio Input Levels

Some camcorders give you no choice on sound levels—the incoming sound is controlled by the ALC, and that's that.

Other cameras allow you to switch off the ALC and adjust the levels however you like. The ones that allow manual adjustment usually have VU meters or *PPMs* (peak program meters) to guide you.

If your camera allows manual adjustment, there's usually a little knob for each channel. You turn the knob until the level of the signal showing on the meter is the level you want to record.

Monitor Levels

In addition to having controls for the audio input levels, the camera may have a *Monitor level* knob.

Turning the *monitor out* knob will raise or lower the volume of the sound you hear through the headphones, *but it will in no way affect the level of the audio being recorded by the camera*. The monitor level is merely an adjustment for the comfort of the operator.

Don't let the loudness or softness of the sound in your headphones distract you from setting the audio level by using the input meters.

As with flying light planes, you have to learn to trust your meters.

Tristian Spillman monitors sound throughout the shoot, Portland Community College.

If the volume knob on your Betacam is turned very low, say pointing to the 9 position on the clock face, you could have problems. Investigate! This is a sign that the input could be overloaded. Usually monitoring conditions from the camera's speaker monitor and headphone-out are so low-level that it can be impossible to pick up distortion. The normal position for the knob is between 11 and 1 o'clock.

Barry Fernandes,
Sound Department, AFTRS.

Selecting the Audio Bit Rate

Paul Sosso,
Editor/
Producer.

If you record 32 kHz audio and import into an editing timeline that's set for 48 kHz audio, you may experience digital artefacts such as clicks and pops, which come from incompatible sample rates.

It may seem like you're saving something by choosing to use 12 bit (32 kHz) audio, rather than going for the bigger number—16 bit (48 kHz) audio. Don't fall into this trap! Forget about using 12 bit audio. The edit systems don't prefer it and it can give you terrible problems of your audio shifting out of sync on the timeline and sound glitches you can neither explain nor get rid of on your audio track.

Mic Handling Techniques

It's easy to think of microphones as being open to sound at their tops, as if they're a sort of vessel, and the sound gets put in that end and sent out the other end to run along the cable to the record machine . . .

Mic Handling Noise

But mics are *hot* all over. This means that touching a mic anywhere on its surface, or along its cord for that matter, can cause a sound to be recorded. These sounds aren't heard through the air by our ears, but they can be detected through headphones attached to the camera, and they can be very loud and obnoxious on a sound recording.

This sort of sound is called *mic handling noise*, and it's unacceptable on a soundtrack.

Shock Mounts

To avoid mic handling noise, microphones can be attached to a *shock mount*, a mic-holding device that separates the surface of the mic from the hands of the operator and buffers the mic against thumps and other movements. A shock mount is definitely worth the price you pay for it.

The shock mount for this gun mic isolates it from handling noise.

Jeremy Reurich,
Technical
Trainee,
AFTRS.

When operating a boom, make sure the mic cable is secured to the boom pole, so it won't cause handling noise when you move the pole.

Internal Shock Mounts

Some microphones have inbuilt shock mounts which invisibly protect their sound recording mechanism from jolts and handling noise. This is often true of mics designed for handheld jobs, like dynamic cardioids, which are frequently used for on-the-street interviewing. Such mics don't need to be put in an external shock mount.

Boom Handling Noise

A *boom* is a special pole made in sections. When you're transporting the boom to the shoot and back, the sections collapse down inside each other to reduce the boom to an easy carrying size, but on location it can be extended out to quite a length.

The boom operator must be steady and noiseless, dressed in soft clothes with no rattling jewellery. Ben Farrawell, TEAME Indigenous TV and Video Training Course, Metro Screen.

The boom is used to get a microphone close in to the action, so good sound can be recorded, while still keeping the mic out of shot. The boom is manoeuvred and held in position for each shot by the sound recordist's assistant, known as the *boom operator.*

The mic is suspended in a shock mount, which is screwed onto the end of the boom; and the mic cable is usually looped around the boom a couple of times to get it back to where the boom operator can control it when moving the boom about.

Boom handling noise happens if the boom operator jiggles the cable or twists or rattles the interconnecting boom sections during recording. Boom handling noise is unacceptable on a soundtrack.

Let's face it, you want your mic to record the program sound and not anything else added in by accident.

Colin Holmes goes the extra mile for good sound on location for *Promise* with Shirley Burgess on camera and Rafael Briant as actor.

Checking Whether the Mic Is Working

In a noisy environment, it's not easy to tell whether the sound you're hearing is coming to your ears through the headphones from the mic, or simply through the air. So how can you tell if the mic is working or not?

The surefire way is to test the mic by picking a sound you know you can't hear through the air. This is very easily done. Just rub your finger gently along the top of the mic or the wind gag over the mic. You can't hear that sound through the air, so if you hear a grating or rubbing noise when you do this, the mic is surely working.

It's not necessary to shout 'Test, test' into the mic, and it's downright stupid to bang it on the side of the table.

Get your mic in as close as possible without getting it in the shot. On the set for *Ash Wednesday*, AFTRS.

Unless you're the person who's going to fix it in post, don't assume that it CAN be fixed in post.

Jane Paterson, Sound Editor.

MONITOR AUDIO. I have been taken to hell and back as a consequence of not monitoring audio during interviews. Audio directors apparently only have one job—and that is to brutally punish operators who don't monitor audio. Background noise can seem innocuous without headphones, but with headphones, any unwanted noise can be easily identified and eliminated. As an added bonus, Howard from audio won't verbally eviscerate you in front of your colleagues, interns and Viv the cleaner.

Gordon Peters,
Cameraman,
Channel 7
News,
Bundaberg.

Monitor Everything

When using an external mic, many things can go wrong:

Unplug the appliances.

Neal Ruckman,
Producer.

1. The mic connection to the camera can come undone. This is most likely to happen with a non-locking audio connector like a mini (3.5 mm) plug. The connector doesn't have to fall out of the camera socket completely for there to be problems. The signal-conducting tip of it just needs to be pulled slightly away from the contact point inside the socket. Sometimes this happens and the mic still looks like it's connected.

Never run a mic cable parallel to an electrical cable because it can pick up an electrical hum. If you're forced to cross a mic cable over an electrical cable, cross them at 90 degrees to each other and separate them if possible. For example, you might be able to run one cable over the seat of a chair and the other one on the floor underneath.

**Adrian
Rostirolla,**
Metro Screen.

2. The mic battery can run down, so the mic output gets too weak.
3. The microphone cable can start crackling when the mic is moved back and forth between the people speaking.
4. The mic extension cable (you know the one that got slammed when you closed the boot of the car?) can ground out and develop a constant buzz.
5. The microphone cable can pick up an electrical hum if it's too close to an electrical cord or a piece of electrical equipment, like a refrigerator or air conditioner.
6. The mic can also pick up a hum or buzz from lighting dimmers, especially the cheaper ones.
7. The extra-long mic cable you got for this special job can start acting like an antenna and pick up a radio station!

Monitor camera audio wherever possible. Just checking VU meters won't tell you if there's mic crackle or distortion.

Philip Elms,
Media Resource
Centre.

So you always check your sound before you start recording. You check it in two ways. First, you listen to it carefully through the headphones. Then you do a 60 second test record of both video and

Bring a *ground lift* with you. This can get rid of electrical hums and isolate the mic from ground interference.

Ben Kreusser,
Producer.

audio, play back the test, and again listen carefully through the headphones.

Some problems, like hums and buzzes from nearby equipment or dying fluorescent lights, can only be heard in playback, so unless you do a test recording you won't know you have a problem until the shoot is over.

Once you've got the sound right, you can begin to shoot, but you can't be sure that problems won't materialise while you're at work. So make sure someone (not too spacey) listens on headphones during the whole shoot.

If you're getting a buzz from a household circuit, try using this inexpensive ground lift.

Five Tips for Using a Cardioid

Though good mic-handling skills aren't automatic, they're also not hard to learn. These simple suggestions can help you greatly improve your recorded sound when doing interviews with a handheld cardioid mic.

When videotaping an interview indoors be aware of ambient sounds from airconditioners, appliances, cuckoo clocks, telephones, answering machines, doorbells and inter-office paging systems.

Donna Kenny, The Video History Company and Center for Recording Life Stories.

1. Keep Your Mic Hand Firm and Still

Make sure you don't nervously rub the mic with your thumb or fingers, because the mic is *hot* all over. That means it reproduces grievous handling noise from any rubbing on it, or movement of its cord.

A nervous thumb can also find the on/off switch which is on the side of some cardioids, and turn it on and off. Imagine what that would do to your interview sound!

2. Always Point the Mic at the Person Who's Speaking

Make sure you don't get out of sync in your pointing! (This is a surprisingly common mistake.) If you point to yourself when the interviewee is speaking and to the interviewee when you're asking the next question, you'll get worse results than with an omni, because the cardioid mic is made to reject sound from the rear.

3. Maintain a Good Mic-to-Mouth Distance

Fifteen to 20 centimetres (6–8 inches) is a good distance to have between the speaker's mouth and the mic. You need the mic close enough so the person's voice will dominate over the background sound, but not so close that the speaker will feel his or her personal space is being invaded.

When Janet Stronach interviews Lucien Cooper on neighbourhood issues, she shows good mic-handling technique by looping the top of the mic cable to prevent wear and tear at the connection point, thus avoiding getting a crackling sound.

Another problem with putting the mic too close is that you may get 'popping' distortions from the force of the speaker's mouth air physically hitting the mic when saying those plosive consonants such as 'b' and 'p'.

A *pop filter* can be used to reduce this form of distortion.

4. Don't Relinquish the Mic

You may find that the person you're interviewing reaches out to take the mic from you. Be assertive about hanging onto it. This is not karaoke time. An inexperienced interviewee won't have developed the handling skills you've had to learn, and the simple act of letting go of the mic may result in sound that is unusable for your project and add up to wasted effort for everyone involved.

Another hazard is that the person who took the mic from you could pass it to another person. You could tape a whole series of people saying their bit, but end up with nothing recorded at all because someone unwittingly switched the mic off somewhere along the way. (This is a particular hazard at heady events like weddings, where everyone wants to—and should—get in on the video.) Using inconspicuous black tape to hold the on/off switch in the *on* position is some insurance against this eventuality.

5. Take Extras

It's prudent to take along an extra mic and an extra mic cable, too (something to do with Murphy's Law).

Using an Audio Mixer

An *audio mixer* is a device that allows several sound sources to be combined into one or two channels of audio.

Mixers come in a range of sizes. The larger ones (with 24 inputs and from two to 24 outputs) generally remain fixed in audio control rooms, outside broadcast (OB) vans and recording studios. But there are smaller, quite portable, ones that are very useful in location work.

Using Several Sound Sources

Sometimes you'll be taping in a situation where you need to use more than two mics simultaneously, yet there are only two mic inputs on your camera. In fact, often there's only one.

With a basic-level portable audio mixer, you can use four separate mics, run them through the mixer, and output two channels (or one channel) of mixed audio into your camera.

You can also take pre-recorded sound—like music—directly from a CD player, another camera, or a mixer split or feed from a house system, input it directly into the mixer, and blend it with your live program sound.

SQN-45 portable mixer.

The volume faders on the mixer allow you to fade the various sources up and down during the recording session.

So in an on-site program taped live, you can open with your program's theme, then fade the music down and bring up the interviewer's mic for the introduction to the segment, and then open the mic of the guest.

Having some mics *open* (their volume faded up) and some mics *closed* (their volume faded down) is usually advisable.

As an example, consider that you're taping a short presentation from several speakers, followed by a discussion. Only the active speaker's mic should be open, so the extraneous noise or muttered comments of the others don't make it onto the soundtrack.

This portable mixer has four inputs and two outputs.

Of course, your sound operator should always be on headphones (and alert). In an unpredictable speaking arrangement, like a round-table discussion, the sound operator's responsibility is to *ride the levels*—in other words, to make sure that only the right mics are open at each point during the recording, and that the open mics are adjusted loud enough to produce an adequate program sound.

Warning: Most people aren't savvy about working near microphones and are unaware that even a whispered comment can be captured if the mic near them is open. On public access programs such as town meetings, which must be broadcast in their entirety, it's not allowable to edit out even damaging comments that were meant only for the person seated next to the whisperer. A wrongly open mic can cause terrible problems!

The camera operator has enough to do concentrating on getting the picture right, so s/he can't be responsible for monitoring and controlling the audio of several mics. Don't let anyone tell you that you can do this job alone!

Mixing several sound sources on location. Jason Troutman in Xishuangbanna, China, for *Dai Women Speak*. (Photo by Michelle Blakeney)

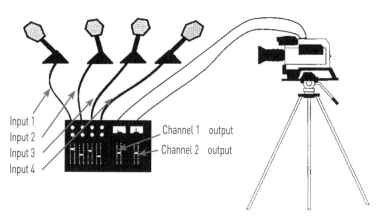

Input 1
Input 2
Input 3
Input 4

Channel 1 output
Channel 2 output

With an audio mixer, you can use several sound sources at once and mix them down to send to your camera.

Only the speaker's mic should be open. Panelists Karene McIntosh and Ross Williams in *Sharing the Road: Disability and Sexuality*, James Cook University. (Photo by Christine Togo-Smallwood)

Ride the levels on the audio mixer so only the current speaker's mic is fully open. (Courtesy of Arlington Community Media Inc. [ACMi])

Mic Level and Line Level

Mixers often have two connection points for each sound source input, one for a *mic level* signal, and the other for a *line level* signal.

These two signals are quite different in strength, so it's important to make sure you attach your sound sources correctly.

The mic level signal is only 2–5 millivolts, and a line level signal can be a full volt.

A mic level signal, sent into a line level input, will barely be heard.

A line level signal, sent into a mic level input, will be totally blasting and distorted.

Generally speaking, an RCA socket indicates a line level input, and a mini (3.5 mm) or phone (6.5 mm) socket indicates a mic level input. But they should be clearly labelled, so you can rely here on your literacy as well as your connector recognition.

Some mixers with XLR inputs can be manually switched between mic and line level.

The mixer outputs can also be either mic level or line level. So check your mixer labels carefully, or read the mixer's specification sheet, so you know whether to connect the mixer to the mic level or line level inputs on your camera or record machine.

If you've only got a line level output from your mixer and only a mic level input on your camera, you can get a signal-changing adaptor (a *pad* or *attenuator*) to cut the signal down from line level to mic level.

Using a Mixer to Control Sound Quality Sent to the Camera

The controls for adjusting audio levels on cameras are often awkwardly placed. Even an alert sound recordist is hard-pressed to tweak knobs that are sandwiched in somewhere between the camera and the camera operator's head! And even if you can get your hand in there, tweaking the knob will often cause the camera to move and put an unwanted jiggle in the shot.

It's also impossible for someone who's holding the mic for an interview to be reaching back to the camera to make audio-level adjustments.

So, for better quality control of location sound, the recordist may choose to use a mixer, even if there will be only one or two mics used during the shoot.

The sound recordist carries the mixer around with a shoulder strap or stashes it somewhere that s/he can attend to it easily.

With sound, there's no headroom in digital. If you get a distortion, the sound's gone. So we're back to having sound recordists on crews, which is good.

Richard Fitzpatrick, Digital Dimensions.

During set-up, the sound recordist sends the calibrated *tone* from the mixer to the camera and then sets the levels on the camera's sound inputs so that tone registers at the level s/he has found to work best for that camera.

Then any changes in audio levels that occur during the shoot can be taken care of at the mixer without disturbing the concentration and smooth work of the camera operator.

Setting Audio Input Switches on Your Camera: Some sound advice from Andy Nehl

Depending on what kind of DV camera you have, you may have external microphone switches that have settings for:

- Mic (microphone level)
- Line (line level)
- ATT (attenuate)
- +48 v (also known as phantom power).

The *Mic* setting is for an audio signal coming from a microphone.

The *Line* setting is for audio signals coming in from an audio mixer, CD player, DAT or some other non-microphone audio source. The *ATT* setting is useful for recording audio levels that are really high. It will cut the audio signal coming into the camera by a preset amount, usually 20 dB. If your incoming audio levels are in the normal range, make sure the audio switch is not set to ATT or your levels will be really low. The +48 v or Phantom Power setting is for use with *condenser* microphones, which do not have their own internal battery and require 48 volts of power from the camera to operate. It should be switched to +48 v for the microphone to work. Some older condenser microphones were built to operate with +12 v (12 volts) of phantom power. These mics will not work with MiniDV cameras. Make sure you know what kind of microphones you're using and adjust the settings appropriately whenever you change mics. If in doubt, check your manual.

Using a Backup System

Jane Paterson,
Sound Editor.

> I would say it's better for sound to use DAT as a primary recording source and use the camera as a backup in case of DAT failure.

Alison Wotherspoon,
Flinders University.

> DATS are very fragile. You have to treat them gently and push the button softly.

Think of using two sound recording systems. As well as your camcorder, you can use a digital audio tape (DAT), a Nagra or a cassette recorder. Your second system may, in fact, give you even better quality sound than the camera will. But the main reason is that almost ANY quality is better than no sound if the first system fails for some reason.

People with high-end equipment, recording to hard drives in the field, still put tape in their cameras (if the cameras take tape) so they make two recordings at once.

Common Pitfalls in Location Sound

Wind

Even a slight breeze can add an unpleasant rumbling noise to your recording. Although we don't hear this wind sound through the air during the shoot, we can hear it through headphones. This is yet another reason to constantly monitor sound during any recording session. Wind noise can range from being an occasional irritant in an otherwise good soundtrack, to being so bad that the whole recording is useless.

Wind noise isn't even always generated by wind, but can be caused by any air movement against the mic. With very sensitive gun mics, just moving them quickly to catch a line of dialogue from another actor can be too much. You can prevent most wind noise by using *wind gags*.

Wind gags are specially designed gadgets that shield the surface of the microphone from contact with moving air.

Wind gags come in many shapes and sizes, and there are wind gags to suit every sort of mic. Many of them are made out of foam; some are made of more sturdy plastic or metal. All are designed to let sound pass through them well, though they can reduce the high frequencies somewhat.

The zeppelin-shaped ones are better than the foam ones, because they preserve a cushion of undisturbed (wind-free) air next to the mic.

Wind gags also come in different capacities—some are okay for breezes, and others are heavy-duty battlers, for the really trying weather conditions.

Some supplementary wind gags are like socks, which fit over those zeppelin shapes.

For the most extreme conditions, there's the *shaggy dog,* which is covered with long fur, like a soft toy. It's a funny sight because it can have two eyes on it, which go on the end of the mic that you point at the sound source.

In windy areas, you need a substantial wind gag over the mic; tav productions. (Photo by Kathy Nixon)

If you're going to be outdoors anywhere, you need to have a wind gag. If you're working in the outback, on the plains, or at sea, wind noise is a major factor and you need super wind gags to counter it.

Background Waves

Any background sound that has a predictable rhythm to it, like ocean waves, a spinning garden sprinkler, passing traffic or cicadas, can pose terrible continuity problems in postproduction.

Although the background sound may seem low level and innocuous—even pleasant—on the day, when the presenter's words or the actors' dialogue are being recut, a break in the background rhythm leaps to the foreground of the viewer's consciousness.

The wave that comes halfway in behind a spoken line and then disappears through a black hole at the edit point, and the wave which seems to be double or triple-crested, are just two of the oddities editors tear their hair over.

Whenever you're taping near a rhythmic background, it's a good idea to use a directional mic and point it away from that sound. Or move to somewhere else entirely.

Luke Barrowcliffe's fluffy wind gag is ready for the wind in Queensland.

Never tape dialogue over cicadas.

Martha Mollison, Video Producer.

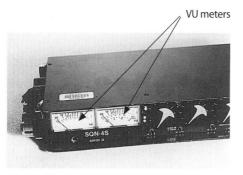

VU meters

The VU meters are your guide to the levels you're recording. Believe the meters, not your headphones.

If you can't move, be sure to record a couple of good minutes of *atmos*—nothing but the rhythmic sound on its own—so the sound editor can smooth out the rough spots in the background during sound postproduction.

More Than One Speaker at a Time

Actors sometimes speak over each other in their enthusiasm. Insist that they don't do this. They shouldn't insert 'Yeah' or sigh out loud or make any other sounds while another actor is speaking. This mars the clean dialogue track. Each person's words need to be separate and pristine. Overlapping for effect can be done in sound postproduction.

Over-adjusting the Input Levels

Scenario: You're taping a drama and didn't notice until the shooting started that the boom swinger isn't able to get the mic quite close enough to the second actor. The mic's sound level from this person is low compared with the first actor. So every time the second person speaks, you assiduously boost the input level. You feel happy that you've managed to record both actors' voices at equal strength.

The problem is, every time you crank up the audio level for the second actor, you also boost the background noise. So the sound editor will collapse at the lack of continuity in the background sound. What else could you have done?

Scenario: You're taping a music concert and you notice that sometimes the needle on the VU meter is reading low and other times it's reading very high. You decide to 'ride the levels' to get a good even sound.

The problem is, every time you adjust the audio level for the fluctuations in the volume of the music, you're eliminating one of the expressive elements of the performance. Music is supposed to get louder and softer at different points.

One of the beauties of a good recording is its dynamic range (the usable range between high and low volumes) which reproduces the experience of varying sound intensities that the people present at the concert felt.

What else could you have done?

Taping Concerts

If you've been asked to videotape a concert, you should arrange to meet with the person in charge of the sound as soon as possible.

If the music will be mixed live and sent out via speakers, sometimes the desk operator will be willing to let you take a feed from an auxiliary output and run it into your camera.

In this case, there are four things to check first:

1. Will you be getting a mono or stereo feed?
2. *Precisely* what connectors will you need to attach your camera to the mixing desk?
3. Will there be two versions done of the mix—one for the desires of the audience, which may require only the vocals to be boosted to compete with the room levels of the bass, and the second a full-mix one for the recording? If there will be two mixes, of course you want to make sure you get the full-mix version.
4. How far away from the mixer's location will you be setting up your camera? Which means, how much cable do you need to run from the desk to your set-up?

Changes in volume level are part of the expressiveness of music. Anita Spring, World Music Festival. (Photo by Michelle Blakeney)

Then you need to consider:

1. Will this person do a good mix? Can s/he be relied upon to give you an undistorted output level? If the feed is too *hot* and overdrives your camera recording, you'll have worse audio than your camera mic would have given you. Included in this question is the need to make sure that if it's a *line level* output, your camera can handle it. Some cameras only have a *mic level* input.
2. Room sound. Though getting a good-quality feed from the mixer is a great boon, it will yield a rather sterile sound. Your video recording

National Aboriginal and Islander Week celebration. (Photo by Michelle Blakeney)

needs to include the presence of a live audience, their clapping and laughter, their soft rustling movements, even their coughs or sneezes.

Doing Your Own Mix at the Camera

To get the ambient sound of an audience, two super-cardioids placed close to the house speakers and aimed *away* from the speakers and *towards* the audience will give you the sound of the live house, without the delay in the music which you'd get if you just placed an omni in the audience.

If the concert's soundperson gives you a good-quality stereo feed, and you set up the cardioids near the speakers, then with a small portable mixer and a second person to help you, you can do a good mix-down of the three or four channels and end up with a soundtrack worthy of the performance.

If you don't feel you can rely on the concert's soundperson, or you're not able to get a feed, an

Can the sound guy give you a good mix, or should you stick with your omni mic? Ian Ross Williams and Friends in performance.

Use a stereo mic for recording music. Your favourite gun mic will record too narrow an angle of sound. You need to capture the full breadth of the live performance sound.

PC Peri, Video Producer.

omni mic may be your best bet for recording the performance. This is because it will capture the PA mix as the audience heard it, and it will also include the ambient sound of the hall.

Though omni mics have only limited uses, this is one case where they can do well. And don't forget your camera mic is likely to be an omni.

Tips for Recording Music

To get a good recording of a musical performance, you need a separate mic for each instrument, and for each vocalist. In other words, you need a mixer.

In a professional recording scene the mixers can be enormous. (Photo by Ben Lipsey)

Mic the singer's voice separately from the guitar. Ian Ross Williams.

Cascading Mixers

Many performances will require the use of a large mixer. But if you can only get your hands on two or three small portable mixers, you can accomplish your ends by *cascading (linking)* them into each other.

For example, the drum kit alone will need a mic for each drum. You could use a six-channel mixer for the mics coming from the drum kit, thus doing a percussion sub-mix. Then you could run the output of that mixer into one of the input faders on a second mixer where you've connected other mics. Get the idea?

Make sure you're careful to notice which are mic and line levels, with both the inputs and the outputs.

Recording an Acoustic Guitar and a Singer

A good trick for recording a full sound from an acoustic guitar is to tape a little omni lav mic inside the sound chamber of the guitar. You can attach the mic to a small piece of foam, and attach the foam to the interior of the guitar. Then the full, resonant sound of the guitar will be the dominant sound into this mic.

You put the singer on a second mic, preferably a directional one that can be pointed straight at the singer's mouth. Aiming it correctly can be tricky because you're trying to avoid most of the sound from the guitar. A boom or mic stand will be helpful for keeping this mic stable and noiseless.

The aim is for the singer's mic to pick up much more of the voice than of the guitar. Then you adjust the pan control on the audio mixer so the guitar and the singer are assigned to separate tracks. Or you just run each mic directly into different channels.

This set-up allows you to vary, in sound postproduction, the levels of the voice and the guitar in relation to each other. Sometimes one sound overpowers the other—in this way, you can make the blend you need, and not be stuck with having both sounds on one mic, with no way to separate the sounds from each other.

Use the Best Recording Space

Don't set yourself up for failure! Before you decide where to record a musician, check out the possible spaces available to you.

Sound ricochets off hard surfaces. A classroom with a tiled floor, smooth hard walls and a low ceiling is a very *bouncy* place. As well as the *initial* sound signal coming into your mic straight from the singer's mouth, you'll be picking up bounced sound (echoes) from all those surfaces, and each different bounce will come with its own delay, depending on where it bounced from. So instead of getting a crisp recording, your sound will be muddied by all the bounced signals.

Sound recording studios are specially designed to be *dead.* (Who thinks up these terms?) This means that the sound is absorbed into the special coverings on the walls, floor and ceiling, so only the initial sound directed to the mic gets recorded.

You can reduce bounce a little by using a carpet and curtains, but if you're serious about good-quality recording, look into how to make your space more sound absorbent.

Because we're used to sound bounce in what we hear, listening to yourself speak in a totally deadened space is quite unnerving. But it's what you need for recording.

Recording studios have special acoustic coverings on the walls to prevent sound bounce. Northern Melbourne Institute of TAFE.

Planning for the Postproduction Mix

As with the picture side of video editing, sound postproduction actually starts in preproduction, and is very dependent on the shoot. It comes down to this—you can't edit what you don't have.

So you need to think very carefully about any sounds you *might* want in the edit, and plan to record them while you're on location.

Clean Dialogue

The uppermost aim is usually to get *clean* dialogue. This means making sure that there aren't variations in the background sound that will make rearranging the order of the shots later on a continuity nightmare.

Donna Kenny,
The Video
History
Company and
Center for
Recording Life
Stories.

When videotaping an interview outdoors, pay attention to common sounds of traffic, sirens, lawnmowers and electric hedge-clippers.

A piece of equipment which was rumbling in the background during part of the shoot, say a lawnmower in the neighbour's yard, can yield an odd result if you have to swap the order of various spoken lines. The lawnmower takes on an inexplicable stop-and-start presence behind the dialogue.

Sound Effects

Although there are some stock sound effects that you can get from sound libraries, it's generally best to record, on location, any audio which could enhance the sound environment you plan for your program.

The creak of the sails and the thud of the rudder that you record on the boat you've videoed will give your soundtrack a life and authenticity that stock FX CDs are unlikely to be able to match.

The Buzz Track or Room Tone

A *buzz track* recording (also known as *room tone*) captures the general background sound present at a location. It's used in sound postproduction to patch and fill those spots where there are gaps in the edited soundtrack.

These gaps can occur for any number of reasons—maybe the director's voice was heard, so it had to be taken out, or the video image needed to be extended with a cutaway or reaction shot, but the next dialogue line couldn't start quite yet . . . whatever the cause, the buzz track is the sound editor's spackle.

So always take the time to record one to two uninterrupted minutes of the ambient sound at each location.

This buzz track is usually recorded at the end of the shoot. With a professional crew, everyone is expected to remain in place and stay completely still and soundless during the recording of the buzz track.

The sound recordist calls out the start and finish times of this recording. Two minutes can seem very long at the end of a hard day, but the buzz track is essential to sound postproduction, and this 'freeze' of the crew is part of the discipline that comes with being committed to making a good product.

All the bits of staging and the arrangement of personnel need to remain the same for the recording of the buzz track, or the acoustics of the room could sound different. Also, it's no good turning the portable lights off until it's finished, because cooling lights generate clicks and other noises that will mar the recording.

The Atmos Track

The *atmos track* is a distinct sound entity, though it's a term often used interchangeably with buzz track. The atmos track gives an overall sound of the location, and is sometimes recorded in the same

There's always time for an atmos track!

Carol Brands, Curtin University of Technology.

place before or after the shoot, while at other times it's recorded somewhere else if the other place gives the right feel for the sound design of the video. The atmos track is mixed into the overall soundtrack during sound postproduction.

Recording Pictures Only

In some video productions, sound and image are combined in the editing process. When people are out shooting the images, they may take little or no care about the quality of the sound they're recording, because they plan to get rid of it in postproduction anyway.

This is the case for music clips and other productions that employ a series of images set to a quite separate soundtrack. It's also true when people are out shooting cutaways which will go with a voiceover.

Some camera operators actually turn off the sound recording when they're doing these shoots.

This is unduly reckless, for two reasons. The plain fact is that you

On location for *Oral Hygiene for Aged Care* for the Australian Dental Association; tav productions. (Photo by Simon Stanbury)

never know what's going to happen next, and suddenly wonderful and unrepeatable sounds can occur when you're out there with a camera. If you're set up for recording sound and you capture them, you may well be able to use them, if not on the current project, then on another one later on.

The other reason is that the soundtrack can be useful as a guide track for locating shots later on, or synching actions (as in dance or music playing) to other recordings of the same piece.

Suggestions from Rachel Masters

PAINTING WITH SOUND

Sound often emphasises little details that can make a story more interesting and creative: the dripping of rain off a roof awning, the school games in a playground, the grating of an old ferris wheel mechanism.

Record some unusual sounds on location, keeping the lens cap on the camera for a while before you record an image of what the sound source is. Test your friends—can they guess the sounds before you reveal the source?

ISOLATING THE AUDIO STRANDS

You don't even need the camera to do this one. Next time you're waiting for the bus or train, or you're in a cafe, at work, out in the bush, at the beach, at your relatives' place, close your eyes for a minute. Imagine you're planning a shoot for this location. What do you hear that would add interest to your shoot?

LOCATION SOUNDS

Great location sound makes for a great production. An interesting exercise is to record location sound without the visual images. Listen to the location sounds on playback—what do they tell you about the location that you didn't notice when you were there?

Practise recording sound at a few locations:

- a shopping centre
- a fun park
- your own house
- outside a school playground.

On playback, listen very carefully to the sounds. Do you hear new sounds you didn't notice before? How can you use these observations in your video making?

SOUND
POSTPRODUCTION

Producing a good soundtrack is challenging and time consuming, but it's a huge factor in the success of your video.

You've probably already worked out that a video made up of just talking heads gets boring very quickly, and you need cutaways of other visuals to liven up the screen. In the same way, your audio track will be thin, plodding and uninspiring if it's limited to someone just jabbering on.

The time to start thinking about sound design is in preproduction. That's when you should determine the overall feel you're going for.

What sound effects could help here? The clink of wine glasses? The sound of birds and flies? (Courtesy of tav productions)

Once the sound design has been agreed upon, you can ask the crew to start capturing useful and unique sounds to further your aims, and you can all be keeping an ear out for suitable music.

Hopefully you'll have a sound recordist with the initiative to record some wonderfully evocative extra sounds during your location shoot (that water fountain, those birds, that train passing, those kids playing baseball . . .). Allowing your sound recordist the leeway to do this will pay off in the edit.

**Rebecca
Gerendasy,**
Producer and
Editor, *Cooking
Up a Story.*

In the stories I produce, I love using a lot of natural sound. That means I have to record good sound when out in the field filming. I use a wireless microphone on my main subject and a small shotgun microphone on my camera and/or a shotgun microphone on a boom pole. When I am editing, I use the natural sound of the video you are seeing, set underneath. When there is a pause in the narration, I bring the natural audio up just a bit, to add to the natural 'pause' in the piece.

Once you get to sound postproduction, your aim is to combine the many audio elements you've gathered to produce a rich sound environment that befits your project. In *sound post* you:

- select and place the best audio takes from the camera footage
- generate voiceovers
- log and organise sound effects from location shoots
- record Foley as needed
- find additional sound effects from stock footage or from the internet
- choose, record or digitally generate music tracks.

Assembling the Audio Bed

Whatever genre you're working in, once the video sequence has been established, the fun begins with constructing the soundtrack.

If you're the sound postproduction editor only, you should be given an edited sequence in which the video with its sync sound has already been assembled in the correct order. If you're doing everything, sound post comes after you've done the basic sequence editing (see Chapter 8, Editing Basics).

Paul Sosso,
Editor/
Producer.

Know what you're going to do before you sit down and start editing.

Your edit system will give you at least two audio tracks to work with, in addition to your field audio, which is sometimes embedded in your video track. Some systems give you many, many tracks, so you have a generous work area for laying out and blending all sorts of audio elements.

How to begin . . .

First you should smooth out the audio which is the basis of the project. At a minimum, this will mean matching the volume from one shot to the next. You carefully adjust the audio levels of all your clips so they match, rather than staggering from loud to soft to loud again.

Adjusting levels is simple—usually just a matter of clicking on the volume line within the displayed clip and dragging it up or down. If you want to change the level of several clips equally, just put them into a group and operate on the group.

You can change the volume of your entire edit in one move, too. Sometimes the entire project is just too soft or it's all a bit too loud.

If, on inspection, your audio track seems empty, you'll have to find the command that will make the volume level appear. In simpler systems, it sometimes appears, surprisingly enough, within the video track. You can usually choose to see the frequency waves as well, and this option is likely to be a separate command.

Seeing the waveform gives you a better grasp of the state of your audio. If one speaker's waveform looks big and fat like a well-fed caterpillar, and another person's waveform looks emaciated, it's obvious that one person spoke louder or was recorded with a better or closer mic. It's now very apparent what work has to be done.

Once you have the overall levels right, you'll need to smooth the changes from one clip to the next. Fading the sound down at the end of one clip and fading the sound up at the beginning of the next is a standard method. You can do this by clicking on the volume line twice near the edit point and dragging the marker closest to the edit point either up or down as needed, so the volume line makes a sharp or languid curve.

Or you can *cross fade* the audio so that, as the outgoing audio clip is lowering, the incoming one is rising. You can do this manually or go to the audio filter section, which most likely has a cross-fade filter that you can drag to the edit point and adjust its duration to suit.

Checking out the audio waveform, a student from Northern Melbourne Institute of TAFE.

Adding Commentary (Voiceover)

After you've got all the clips in the sequence at the correct volume, with the transitions between clips smoothed out, you may decide to add some commentary to link the segments of your project together or to give your audience an overview of the topic.

Some tips from John Sirett, Independent Producer

Because visual communication is many times faster and more effective than verbal communication, the visual dominates. When writing commentary, consider the following:

- If the vision is carrying the story, don't talk over the top of it.
- Minimise the number of words you use to describe anything. Non-essential words should be eliminated and statements rephrased to reduce the word count. It's surprising how much screen time can be taken up with a few small words and how difficult it can be to fit a comment to the appropriate scene, especially if the vision editing is nice and tight.
- Use narration to complement the visuals by mentioning things that are not shown, but are important to the story.
- Don't use commentary to describe something that is on the screen. If you must identify a certain point on the screen, be brief.
- If something should be explained but can't be shown, run this piece of commentary over some unimportant vision. This device is commonly seen on TV news where pertinent information about the highlighted person is detailed while that person is shown merely walking down a long corridor. This makes the viewer's attention switch from the unexciting vision to the commentary.

WRITING THE SCRIPT

What you need is a message that is easily understood and delivered in a conversational style.

- Use spoken English, not written English. Stick with simple vocabulary, and use contractions and other shortcuts as we do in everyday conversation.
- Test-read your commentary by reading it aloud to yourself. Though your script looks good on paper, there could be words that just won't flow together. For example, *Police Constable Nick Kennibody was placed under great stress supporting law and order in the mob.* This could easily sound like: *Police Constable Nick Anybody was placed under great stress supporting Laura Norder in the mob.*
- Make the words flow. Substitute words that don't flow off the tongue smoothly, by using a synonym or simply rephrasing the statement.
- Be prepared to rewrite. You may have to rewrite your commentary many times to get just the right choice of words, phrases and voice flow.

LAYOUT FOR EASY EYE SCANNING

- Use large type (14 or 16 point).
- Double space between words and lines.
- Each line of words should be only half the width of the page. This creates a column effect which is easy for the eye to follow down the page.
- Start each sentence on a new line and don't hyphenate any words. Never carry a sentence ending over to the next page.
- Use phonetic spelling as an aid to ensure correct pronunciation.
- Number the paragraphs for easy reference, especially when someone else is the reader.

THE READING

- Decide how you want the script read—fast, slow, hard or soft—to suit the subject matter.
- Be prepared for retakes. Every line or segment may be repeated several times before everyone (reader, author, director, producer) is satisfied. There's no embarrassment, it's just part of the business. To complete a ten-minute script may take an hour or so. This is regarded as a *read*, and it's charged that way.
- The space: Use a quiet, echo-free and comfortable environment. Some people use a booth lined with papier-mache egg cartons; others sit in their cars and record into their camcorder. It's up to you.
- For a very ad hoc sound booth, put a towel over your head and shoulders. With your face and mic inside, you may be quite pleased with the results.
- Lubricate yourself. (But not with alcohol!) Spend a few minutes loosening up your facial muscles

Allow enough time for your voice artist to deliver the lines in different styles so you have some choices when editing. Media student does reading at Batchelor College, NT.

and your tongue by stretching your jaw, pulling faces and speaking out aloud to yourself. You will find the words you read will flow off the tongue better for this. It's equivalent to an athlete warming up before an event.

- Rehearse each piece several times.
- Experiment with different inflections and emphasis on words to suit your taste, then mark the script to remind yourself when reading.
- Make any last-minute adjustments to the wording.
- Do a test recording to check that your Ps are not popping and your Ss are not whistling. You may need to move the mic or use a pop filter or screen if they are.
- Record your commentary in small, manageable pieces. Not only is this easier to do, it helps you position your voiceover segments on the timeline.
- Act up a little! Let your voice reflect the mood of the subject matter you are reading. This adds to your video, giving the effect of the narrator being part of the action rather than a detached, indifferent voice obviously added later.
- Play it back, and if you don't like what you hear, do it again.

Recording the Commentary

Rules for recording voiceovers:
- Good levels are always #1.
- Make sure your recording space is audio friendly— that is, there's no bounce in the room.

Paul Sosso, Editor/ Producer.

A cardioid mic works well for recording voiceovers. It should be mounted in a floor stand, preferably, and the speaker should be standing close to the front of it. When a person is upright, their voice can be full, rather than somewhat compromised by a slouched position.

Your closet, with all the coats, is a great recording environment. It significantly reduces parallel surfaces. Your car can be pretty good as a recording space, too, but it depends what street you're on.

If your speaker is working from a script, this needs to be held in place somehow at a good reading height, and printed out so there's no need to turn pages during a run of speech.

Once the recording is done, digitise it if necessary and import it into your project.

It's handy to have a folder within your project dedicated to voiceovers. This is where you store the full recording and all the subclips of your best takes.

A good filing system makes editing so much easier! Another folder can be for location sound effects, a third for free stock effects you've imported from the internet, and so on.

If you make the recording using your video camera, show the speaker throughout the recording. The video can help you find the right spots in your recording when you're editing, especially if you include specific visual markers. You can ask the narrator, or an assistant, to hold up a card that tells which segment—and which take—is which. Alternatively, you can use a slate or character generator to mark each take.

A further advantage of using a camera image, rather than a test signal or black, is that it makes your tape identifiable. Having no visually discernible content can put your tape at risk, because you (or someone else) might be tricked into thinking it's an empty tape if you can't *see* a recording when you spot check it.

Needless to say, any voiceover tapes should be clearly labelled as such.

The Spotting Session

The *spotting session* is when the director, musician and sound postproduction person meet together and face the reality of what material is actually at hand. In some cases these are one and the same person, so if you're a Renaissance Person, get used to holding inner dialogues!

Jane Paterson, Sound Editor.

A sound editor should keep good communication channels with the location sound recordist and the visuals editor so s/he can be forewarned of any upcoming challenges (to put it delicately).

The director says what s/he needs for the completion of the project. Then everyone discusses ideas and options. The overall aim is to fix up the bad parts, and achieve the director's goals for the audio track.

One thing to consider is whether the use of music will hide any of the intended sound effects. If so, which should be dropped, the music or the effects?

The decision might be made to add the music first, rather than wasting time putting in effects which no one will ever hear.

The M&E Tracks

Once you're happy that you've got all the words of the field footage and voiceovers assembled in the right order and their levels are corrected, you go over the existing program sound, marking any remaining sounds that need to be fixed (like clipped endings on words) or removed. Then you work your way through the material with the audio equivalent of a fine-toothed comb, removing or repairing all the little audio glitches.

After the tracks have been cleaned up, you then start working on the *music and effects* (M&E).

M&E

In the old days of outputting program masters to videotape with just two audio tracks, the procedure was to put all the dialogue on one track and the mixdown of all the music and sound effects on the other track. That way, programs could be sold to countries where a different language was spoken. The TV station that was purchasing the program would be sent the script, which they would have translated into their local language and have actors dub in the new dialogue. Because the other track, with the music and effects, would work in any language, that was sold and reused as it was.

Atmos

So, to get going with your M&E . . .

Most likely there will be some holes in the background sound in between your dialogue cuts. Silence can be very loud and obvious at times like this! This is where having recorded one or two minutes of *atmos* or *buzz track* at the shoot will pay off. You can fill all these gaps using the ambient sound from the location.

It's best to assign the atmos to its own track, and run it continuously behind all the speech, possibly fading it up slightly in between the speaking sections. Foregrounding location sounds now and then (the magpies, the sports stadium crowd, or whatever) gives your project a feeling of immediacy and presence in the situation, plumping out your soundtrack's depth and body.

Of course, you could also choose to add in atmos and sounds from some other time and place. Sound mixes are often partly fictional constructions.

Dealing with Background Sounds

Certain background sounds are nightmares for sound postproduction.

Beach waves are in this category. Though they may be a balm to the spirit when heard in their full, mind-massaging rhythm, they sound very odd if the crest of one wave sound is abruptly cut off and replaced by a trough, or if two crests are edited in too close together, so the natural sound flow is broken.

When rearranging the words of your speaker on the beach, or selecting the very best drama takes and assembling them, the background rhythm is very likely to be thrown off kilter.

Any background sound that is cyclical in nature is best minimised during the shoot. But you should record it *on its own* for smoothing out the background in the edit.

Other sounds that have to be addressed in post are the *vanishing acts*, like the train or airplane which is travelling along behind the dialogue, and then drops away suddenly at the end of the cut. For the audio track to sound right, that train or plane sound has to either be eliminated or extended beyond the cut and then faded away.

In a perfect world, all dialogue would be *clean*, free of such annoyances. And care taken by the sound recordist on the day makes a *big* difference when editing time comes. Though the director may have all concentration focused on the quality of the acting and be oblivious to background sounds, the sound recordist's job is to halt any take before it begins if a plane drones onto his/her headphones.

If the director can be heard calling 'Action!', that goes. If a crew member coughs, sneezes or dissolves into laughter, out with it. Anything that breaks the spell, gone.

Actors who speak over each other's lines may feel like they're imitating reality, but each speaker's lines should have been recorded separately. Any desired overspeaking is easily produced by

> A lot of sound post is problem-solving, and time-management is very important. As a sound editor, you should assume that technical problems beyond your control can just *happen*, so build enough time into your editing schedule so you can still complete the project on the deadline. With enough time anything can be solved.

Jane Paterson,
Sound Editor.

overlapping two individual audio tracks in postproduction. That's where you'll have the control you need to select which takes to use and exactly how much of an overlap will suit the pace of the scene.

Foley

Sometimes there are sound effects needed in the final edit that weren't shot on location. Maybe they were forgotten, maybe they were impossible at the time, or they were thought of later.

This is where *Foley* comes in. Named after the sound effects artist Jack Foley from Universal Studios, Foley is now the generic term for studio-recorded sound effects. It can include footsteps on wood or on various surfaces (e.g. walking in large trays of sand or gravel). The Foley studio has doors for slamming, creaking or knocking on, and the Foley artist uses inventiveness and imagination to produce a myriad of sounds, from kissing flesh to punching sides of beef for fight scenes and jabbing knives into cabbages for stabbing scenes.

For an oldie-but-goodie humorous look at Foley artists in action, google *Track Stars: The Unseen Heroes of Movie Sound*.

Library Sound Effects

You may not have the time to do your own foley. Or there may be sounds that are too hard or impossible for you to get.

Paul Sosso,
Editor/
Producer.

Check the licence agreements on library music.

In that case, there are many libraries of sound effects, from gun shots to boat whistles to ambulance sirens to rollercoasters . . . Check with your media centre to see what they own.

The student radio station often has a good selection of sound effects, too.

Your edit system will come with a few sound effects, and there are lots available on the internet, some for free, some for a price.

Generally speaking, one gigabyte of hard disk memory will store three hours of mono sound. You may have plenty of room on your system for building a rich library of downloaded effects.

Stitials

This is industry-talk for 'interstitials'. *Stitials* are those additional sounds (whoosh! boink! rrrrrm! ping!) which fit into tiny spots in the soundtrack and add sparkle. They're used heaps in advertisements and cartoons, but they crop up everywhere. Baby crying all night? Dog barking next door? You can turn these annoyances into additions to your Stitials Favourites bin and be building your audio assets as you build your skills and career prospects.

Music

If you want your images to exactly match the music—for example, if you want the pictures to change with the beat of the music—you should record the music track first, and then cut the pictures.

But if you'll be using music for background or mood, you should cut it in after the dialogue track is in place. This is so you can tell exactly where to fade it up and down, so it comes in nicely after the speaking ends and fades down before the next dialogue segment begins.

A common mistake is to record the music track too loud, and find that it drowns out the dialogue track. The dialogue should be recorded good and strong, with the VU meter needle right up near the red (distortion) section, but not in it.

Music sets a tone, music is the emotion, whether it's a 30 second ad or a feature film.

Paul Sosso, Editor/Producer.

Background music, however, should be added at a much lower level. If you find that the relationship of tracks isn't working, first try lowering the volume of the music track.

One major hazard is choosing a music track with words to put under a dialogue track. No matter how much you like the song, the lyrics will fight with the dialogue, and the end result will be an audio muddle and confusion on the part of the audience.

A good trick your radio friends already know is about *back-timing* music. This is handy when your project is to end with a grand flourish, but the music track is longer than the length of your video. Work out how long the available timeslot is, then lay the music track so the end is in the right place and then fade the music up at the beginning of the timeslot. People don't mind music fading in—they hear this all the time, and they LOVE something going out with a satisfying finality.

Sometimes people like to use an *audio wash*, which is a music track so low in the background that it's barely audible, but it adds to the fullness of the soundtrack, and contributes to the mood of the piece.

Kimberly Rabe edits music with assistance from Claire Beach, Edmonds-Woodway High School.

Other people feel that it's manipulative to use music to set mood, and the soundtrack should be composed only of sounds that are inherent to the location.

As you can see, there's both philosophy and craft to the production of soundtracks.

Your project's style and needs may determine whether you put in music or effects first. A good spotting session should predict whether putting in the music or the effects first would be the best route.

Steve Ellingson of Dorado, great for composing that link on keys. (Photo by Ben Lipsey)

If you have left the music until last, once it's clear where the remaining gaps are, music selections can be timed and chosen.

If you have musos for friends, you may have music specially composed for these gaps.

Garage Band

If you don't have musos for friends, become one yourself! Try your hand at writing your own music using the audio loops available in the application *Garage Band*. You can choose from a wide range of genres and rhythms for your percussion track. You can import melodies and sounds into it from elsewhere or dive into writing your own melodies. Garage Band will play whatever you send it, even from your own humming into a mic, it can convert the tune you give it into the voice of any of a wide range of instruments, and you can overlay and overlay tracks until you get worn out.

Garage Band is a good *app* to hang out with when you're not pressed for time, say in between semesters or class projects or other deadlines. It's amazing what you can discover by playing around. And take a moment to save and file your gems—you may want to use them later.

Common Audio Problems You'll Face

The list of possible sound problems seems endless, but there are several quite likely ones.

Paul Sosso,
Editor/
Producer.

The basic rule of thumb is to do it right the first time.

A compressor or limiter is sometimes built into the camera—and is sometimes referred to as a 'Compeller' and at other times may also be referred to as AGC (Auto Gain Control). Basically, the compressor actually compresses the dynamic range of the signal and makes it sound 'fat' or 'beefy'. A limiter limits the output of the signal. This can help avoid clipping.

Sound Recorded at Too Low a Volume

Your edit system will probably let you raise the overall volume up 12 dB. You can do this by dragging the visible audio volume level line in your soundtrack up to the very top of the track space. But in a very low-level recording, this still may not be enough.

Your audio filters may help here. If you have a *gain filter*, you may be able to increase the level by another 12 dB. BUT you will be bringing up all the background noise as well.

Another method is to use the *compressor limiter filter.*

Sound Recorded Too Loud

Distorted sound can be harder to repair and you may have to record it again. Just as you can't make a blurry picture sharp, you can't make distorted audio sound clean.

Buzzes and Hums

Some buzzes and hums are very specific. A buzz from an electrical cable that was too close to your mic cable will be 50 Hz or 60 Hz, depending on what country you're in. A notch filter can be used to delete just this frequency.

Ambient Noise

Some background sounds are much harder to get rid of because they occupy many frequencies, including those of the human voice, which you need to keep for your dialogue sections.

Fans, TVs, radios, street sounds, kid noise, other conversations . . . oh dear . . .

> Go through your recording space before you start shooting and get rid of all excess noises. Close doors, windows, turn off fans, mute TVs and radios—mute mobile phones. Whenever possible, remove anyone not involved with the shoot. I've also found that if there's construction going on, or some noise you have no control over, most people are willing to suspend their noise-making activity for 10–20 minutes while you record, so long as you explain and are courteous.

Paul Sosso, Editor/ Producer.

Wrong Settings on the Camera

Bit rate set too low, sample rate set too low: here are some tips from Paul Sosso.

> Typically two channels of audio are done at 16 bit/48 kHz.
>
> Many ProSumer-level cameras that record to tape have a certain amount of space designated to the tape to record audio. In order to make 'room' on the tape for an additional two tracks of audio, the solution was to lower the bit rate and the sample rate. So the XL1 did four channels of audio at 12 bit/32 kHz.
>
> That's okay if it's your only source material—but once you start getting material from other sources for postproduction, you start to get varying bit rates and sample rates.
>
> Ideally you should be doing EVERYTHING at the highest bit rate/sample rate you can. For most cameras that's currently 16 bit/48 kHz at the very least.
>
> More professional cameras also offer higher sample rates—and added features like AGC/COMPELLERs (Auto Gain Control/Compressor-Limiter) or some such thing that helps keep a check on incoming audio levels.

Wrong Mic Choice

For most recordings, the built-in camera mic should be your LAST choice.

Once the location work is done, you can only influence the choice of mics used for voiceover and Foley.

Still, you should take note of problems from wrong mic choices, keep a record of which ones went wrong and why, and learn from your mistakes!

Wrong Mic Placement

Lavs are not properly set: The lav should usually be attached to the shirt of the speaker, high enough to get a good volume level, but not so high as to cause distortion. Placement requires some trial and error because some voices boom while others are barely there.

Mic is too far away: If the mic wasn't in close enough, there won't be enough level and there will be way too much other noise, including echoing from nearby hard surfaces, like walls, floors and even ceilings.

Additional Audio Filters

Your edit system may provide various filters you can experiment with for either repairing or enhancing your audio tracks.

For repairs, look for: Vocal DeEsser
                             Vocal DePopper
                             Hum Remover
                             High Pass Filter
                             Low Pass Filter

For enhancement: Echo
                             Reverberation
                             Parametric Equaliser

Exporting Audio to Specialist Programs

If you find that your edit system isn't able to give you the results you want for your soundtrack, you can export your audio to specialist software packages.

Jeremy Ireland uses ProTools, AFTRS.

Your decision about which one to use will be influenced by the minimum system requirements of the application. If you're actually buying one, be sure to check carefully that your current computer has the capacity to handle the software you want to install.

Some great applications come bundled with editing programs—you might be surprised if you check your bundle!

It's a good idea to take your time when making the software decision. If possible, visit people near you who have already purchased different systems, and see how easy (or hard) they are to operate. Get comments from the people who are using them.

Popular Sound Editing Programs

- Sound Track Pro (Comes bundled with Final Cut Studio)
- ProTools
- Nuendo
- Logic (geared toward music)
- Adobe Audition (Sound Booth)
- Audacity (a free download)

There are many sound editing programs. In my industry you see ProTools as the defacto app due to its integration with post and its real time FX.

Paul Sosso, Editor/ Producer.

The Basic Process

You locate the track you want to work on (called the *read*) and export it as an AIFF file to the specialist application you've chosen. Export it as one continuous file, not a series of audio edits. Then you process it as a single file.

The democratisation of the process is a good thing, but it means that if you do it by yourself you have to be good at everything: lighting, sound, scriptwriting.

Be sure to leave the original file intact so you can go back to it at any time.

You should take care to use the same settings thoughout the process. Don't swap around with bit rates or sample rates.

Once in Sound Track Pro (or whatever), save the original version, and then make a copy for beginning your experimentation.

Each new edit of the track (each new *pass* or *iteration*) should be saved separately and labelled for what it is—for example, Pass 1, Pass 2, Pass 3, Pass 4 . . .

Once you have the soundtrack as you would like it, import it back into your edit program and insert it into your project but STILL keep your original soundtrack there as well. Either put your new mix on additional tracks within that overall timeline, so you can turn the new or old mixes on and off as needed, or make a copy of your edit, place the new soundtrack and label the new version appropriately.

Of course, another alternative is to hand your soundtrack production over to someone else who's expert at it. This can be your best option at times! Don't feel you have to solve every problem in the universe of your video.

Assessing Production Work

Steve Parris of Edmonds-Woodway High School (Edmonds, Washington) has developed a humorous checklist for students and teachers to assess audio production work, reproduced below.

AUDIO PRODUCTION RUBRIC

	5	4	3	2	1	0
Technical	Recording levels are perfect for each instrument	Levels are appropriate	Some levels are too strong and/or too weak	Something really sticks out too much	Levels are terribly unbalanced	No project
	Signal quality	Signal levels are clear and clean	Signals are mostly clear some are muddy or distorted	Signal quality is uneven and distracts the listener	Signal quality is a major distraction	No project
	Use of effects is subtle and artistic	Effects are appropriate	Something has a distracting amount of effects	Badly needs effects or less effects	Effect use causes major distraction	No project
	Equalisation is wonderful	EQ is well done and fits recording	Most things use EQ well	Something has a major EQ problem	EQ is a huge distraction	No project
	Recording is exceptionally mastered	Mastering has cleaned up and bettered recording	Something should have been cleaned in mastering	Mastering in dire need	No mastering	No project
	5	**4**	**3**	**2**	**1**	**0**
Aesthetic	A well-balanced recording, one doesn't even notice the production	Project is well-balanced and even	Something is too strong or missing	Something is sticking out or distracting	Very unbalanced recording	No project
	Performances are incredible!	Performances are solid and clean	Performances are fine but uneven	Performances are good but clearly by an amateur	Very amateurish performance	No project
	Radio ready—recording will draw interest from discerning listeners	Could be on the radio	Is pretty good, but really isn't ready for radio play	Maybe radio-friendly, but pushing it	Not even close to ready	No project
	Message recording is trying to make is very strong and clear	Message is clear	Message gets a little lost in the translation	Message is largely inconsistent	Message almost cannot be discerned	No project
	Overall gut reaction is overwhelming	Strong gut reaction	Okay gut reaction	Mixed feelings about recording	Poor gut reaction to project	No project

© Steven Parris 2002

Suggestions from Rachel Masters

1. Changing a soundtrack or re-voicing your favourite TV show can be difficult but very entertaining. Record a very small section of your favourite show. In the edit suite, record over the audio tracks only, adding whatever new dialogue or sound effects you choose. Try turning a sitcom into a serious drama, or a drama into a sitcom.
2. Another challenging exercise is to try to entirely change the genre of your favourite show. Turn a comedy into a clichéd horror skit, complete with creaky doors and music of impending doom.
3. Write a short script that is versatile enough to be used in several genres. Working in pairs, design a soundtrack to work with the script in the following genres: romance, horror, action, drama, film noir and science fiction.
4. Try creating your own soundtrack from scratch. Make it tell a story which uses only sound and no dialogue. Listen to a few professional soundscapes or dance music for inspiration.

Looking Further

Jay Rose, *Producing Great Sound for Digital Video,* by CMP Books, Gilroy, California, 2000. Available new and used on Amazon.com.

Track Stars: The Unseen Heroes of Movie Sound, a short film by Terry Burke and Andy Malcolm, distributed by Kinetic Inc., 408 Dundas Street East, Toronto, Ontario, 2022, Canada: Tel +1 416 963 5979 or fax +1 416 925 0653. You can Google this title and watch it on the internet, but for classroom use, the quality is much better if you purchase it.

Explore websites, such as that of the Audio Engineering Society (the only professional society devoted exclusively to audio technology: <www.aes.org>).

Thanks to Barry Fernandes, Jane Paterson and Paul Sosso
for their contributions to this chapter.

15 SAFETY ON THE SET

BY DON BETHEL

Safety should be a state of mind—a top-priority state of mind.
Fortunately, most people *are* safety conscious, yet accidents still happen—
or, rather, are caused.

This croc had his jaws tied shut with fishing line—but it was discovered at the end of the shoot that the fishing line had broken some time earlier! Richard Fitzpatrick with watery mate. (Courtesy of Digital Dimensions)

From the beginning of your training, it is essential that you pursue an awareness of safety codes and practices, which will keep pace with your expanding knowledge of video techniques and your developing craft skills.

Work Environments

Video, television, film, theatre and concert presentation all share a common factor. There is a *continuous state of change* during production. The manufacturing environment can easily alter from safe to high risk.

Our work is considered as an artistic endeavour—but the production process is definitely industrial.

Industrial Safety Standards

Industrial means:

- working as a *team member*
- using *specialised equipment* (tools)
- being in the process of *manufacturing a product* (for further use/distribution)
- being in a temporary, selective, *work environment*.

Warning: There's a subtle shift from regarding video as a home craft to regarding it as an industrial activity.

At first, video production may not seem industrial. After all, domestic camcorders are routinely used at home. But no matter how simply you start out in video production, as your skills develop, your projects will become more ambitious. You'll soon be involved in productions that require a professional level of organisation and craft skills, and an appropriate assessment of health and safety factors.

Tanya Andrea and Sebastion Craig haul gear for a production, AFTRS.

General Conditions

We work under time-related pressure. We accept around-the-clock rostering and mixed day and night shifts as normal.

Work routines are variable and performed in all weather conditions, often for long hours.

We create our own environment, then change it continuously—the location, casts, sets, crews . . . all temporary.

On location shoots the workplace is the world! Not only do we have to operate within our own industry's safety standards, but we 'inherit' all the other environments—where often no standards exist.

Obviously, in this industry an individual's health and safety are at some risk.

> Never work with a director or presenter who's braver than you.

Richard Fitzpatrick, Camera Operator, Digital Dimensions.

A Safety Choice

We can minimise the risk to ourselves by:

1. increasing the intensity of our 'safety first' attitude
2. treating safety as a craft skill. In other words, we should *study* survival needs.

Accidents

The human body is equipped with a wonderful array of healing and repairing mechanisms—reflect on your childhood accidents and how you have survived!

But, irrespective of the type of injury, the sequence was common:

- It hurt.
- Patching and healing were unpleasant experiences.
- It often stopped us from doing what we wanted to do.

As adults, injuries are even more annoying—especially if the accident was the result of carrying out a routine task:

- a knife cut from peeling an apple
- a burn from serving hot food
- a fall over a small stray object
- a splinter from handling a wooden or metal utensil.

Slack Concentration

As adults, we know the everyday risks. So what happened? Were we distracted at the time? Operating on remote?

We tend to leave our personal safety awareness on 'automatic pilot', allowing our senses and past painful experiences to remind us. But usually this is at the last moment, perhaps too late, and we may end up repeating the whole painful episode.

Anticipation and the 'Safety Scan'

We can't expect better results until we increase our intensity of safety awareness.

In new or unusual circumstances the anticipation of danger is the respect we give to our common sense.

Learn to trust your judgment. Use all your senses:

Richard Fitzpatrick, Camera Operator, Digital Dimensions.

Whenever you do helicopter shoots, double check that you're strapped in. And make sure you can get out of the harness quickly if you crash.

If it *looks unsafe* . . . it probably is . . .
If it *feels unstable* . . . it definitely is . . .
If it *sounds odd, loose* . . . it usually is . . .
If it *smells hot, burning* . . . Quick! Switch it off! . . .
And if it *tastes terrible* . . . you've booked the wrong caterers.

Workplace Conditions

We do get bumps and bruises—no matter how carefully we move around. We assemble boxes of gear, load, unload, stack, unpack, tidy up, rehearse, shoot, de-rig, stack, pack, travel and start all over again. There are many opportunities for body contact with equipment.

Lifting

We also do a lot of lifting. Thanks to recent technology, many electronic items have been reduced in size and weight. The equipment now used for *EFP* (electronic field production) is certainly more compact than it was in the past.

But cables, lights, stands, sandbags and other ballast remain the same—heavy, or rather awkward to lift.

HEAVY WEIGHTS

So let's define heavy.

Heavy is *any* weight which you find needs maximum effort for you to move or lift.

Your ability to perform is due to factors of fitness and size—muscle tone, physical build and prior experience.

Don't try to match others who display ease in shifting heavy equipment.

Annie Wright uses a secure plank between two ladders to reattach wallpaper high on the set wall, AFTRS.

AN ACTION PLAN

Take time to plan the lift. Approach the task methodically—start gently, observe techniques, don't struggle—and don't hesitate to ask for help.

Never attempt any labouring duties until you warm up physically.

STRATEGIES FOR LIFTING ON YOUR OWN

Plan the move. Run this checklist:

- How will I hold this object?
- Will it be easy to remove? How do I stack?
- Will my grip be easy to maintain?
- Where is it to go?
- Is the next resting place adequate? Clear?
- Is the floor/ground even? Is there good traction for walking?

Rob Stewart, Coordinator of Television Training Unit, Northern Melbourne Institute of TAFE.

There's lots to carry around when preparing the set. AFTRS.

- How far away is the final position? Are there steps? How many?
- What is the height of the final position?
- Is there enough space in the final position for me to release my grip?
- When the object is taken to the lift position, will my view be obscured?

BASIC LIFT

1. For each lifting operation, stand with your feet slightly apart—in your best/most comfortable balance position. Bend your knees, but keep your back straight. Take the strain gently—let your leg muscles do the work.
2. *Don't lift* and *turn your body* in one movement.
3. If the load shifts and you're losing balance, reverse your lift routine if possible. If not, let the load go. Hard on the equipment, safe for your back.

Don't be afraid to share the load. AFTRS.

LIFTING WITH ASSISTANCE

Some objects are awkward for one person to handle. A long ladder is an example. Another is a box full of cables with no handles on it.

As a team, *discuss the action plan* (all points as before), and decide who will give the guidance cues to lift . . . pause . . . lower . . . change hands, etc.

TRAPS FOR LIFTERS

'I can lift it on my own'—well, maybe not.

You may be able to carry it on your own—but reaching for it, on the back seat or in the boot of a car, imposes a totally different mechanical stress on the back.

Get help to slide/lift the object to your comfortable carrying position—then stagger off with it.

PACKING AND UNPACKING VEHICLES

When packing/unpacking vehicles, consider getting help. Slide pieces into place. Leave heavy objects close to access points. Make use of handles. During packing, remember to position handles for easy grasping when unloading.

LOADS OVER DISTANCES

If gear has to be carried some distance between unload and first set-up, pack and use a trolley whenever it's practical.

Planning Ahead

'Use a trolley whenever it's practical' implies planning ahead.

The first step is to think about the location—the environment. Would it be possible to use a trolley to lessen the strain?

Use a strap to secure heavy items to a hand trolley.
Tony Atkins, Building Maintenance Officer, AFTRS.

Location Surveys (Preproduction Safety Scans)

A location survey has to encompass consideration of the many diverse needs of both the production and the crew.

The suitability of the location for the needs of the script is the important factor, but accessibility for the crew, access to electrical power, likely weather conditions and many other things affect the practicality/viability of the site.

This is the time to think the whole operation through from set-up to pull-down, considering safety as you go.

Assessing the Mechanics

In any production, there are always two major spaces to consider. There's the action area, which will be revealed on screen—this space will be occupied by the performers; and there's the off-screen work area, occupied by the crew with all their equipment. These two areas have different needs. The screen action area may be free of any hazard—but what about space for the boom swinger

This is Big Red, the trolley for moving flats for sets, AFTRS.

Richard Fitzpatrick, Underwater Camera Operator, Digital Dimensions.

We do a lot of first aid and medical training. I've stitched someone up out at sea. When we do shark studies we're 24 hours away from medical help, so we have to carry full medical kits, including morphine and defibrillators. We're all trained in how to do things, but we have to ring up the Royal Flying Doctor Service on the satellite phone and they instruct us on what procedures to take.

who has to follow the action, and what about the space(s) allocated as camera positions?

Check for Changes

If it's an exterior location, how will extremes of weather just prior to your shoot date affect the environment?

This practice of anticipation, of visualising the mechanics of the production, considering the practical aspects of the site that occur *before*, *during* and *after* the shoot, will help you expose some of the safety risk factors.

Combine this with the checklists (e.g. lifting plan) and you get the results of a safety scan—a report back to you for assessing risks. Then you can plan the right actions/precautions to minimise or eliminate those risks.

The Industry's Commitment to Safety

For major production work, a specialist safety officer, contracted by the producer, will prepare a safety report which lists the observed risks on each location and how to minimise/eliminate these potential hazards.

Recognition of Safety Requirements

The production's specified safety person will base his/her recommendations on site investigation, knowledge of local occupational health and safety regulations, the product (script as developed), and casting—particularly if children are involved.

Whenever you ask an actor to take on a risky situation, you have to be sure that you've got safety precautions worked out ahead of time. On set for *Ash Wednesday*, AFTRS.

Introduced Risks

If stunts, firearms, special effects, or activity in or near water are part of the script, extra specialists are required to train/guide/supervise these activities.

Preventive Control

These specialists must go through their own safety scan technique. This will alert them to *further* considerations, until they feel confident of their strategies for risk control. Their recommendations/ guidelines are then adopted by production personnel as best operational safety procedures.

Personal note: Safety guidelines are only effective if they're accepted and applied. The attitude and practice of all crew members are important here.

FM or 1st AD Responsible for Safety on the Set

On the set, the FM (floor manager) or 1st AD (first assistant director) is responsible for maintaining safety standards. Situations do develop in the creative process—situations that vary from the original concept.

If the FM or 1st AD considers the new plan of action involves a change from safe to unsafe, then s/he has the authority to disallow the new plan. Crew members shouldn't disregard or argue with these judgments.

Universal Production Rules

Wherever you work, obey the house safety regulations, such as those requiring the use of hard hats and protective clothing.

Unless it's part of screen action:

- No smoking on set—fire risk.
- No eating/drinking on set—spill damage.

These rules apply to technical areas, too, like edit suites and control rooms. Just think of food particles in the edit machines, a half-cup of coffee (sugared) in a mixing console . . .

Extra Skills Needed

We do need some extra skills to give us the 'edge' in emergencies.

Fire

Do get some training in handling fire extinguishers. Learn to identify the appropriate extinguisher for the different sources and causes of fires.

At your workplace:

- Note the small tag on the fire extinguisher that informs you of the last date it was serviced. If it has been *more than a year*, it's time to get the fire extinguisher recharged/serviced.
- Lift each type of extinguisher—don't discharge it, but carry out, as a rehearsal, the operational instructions.
- Notice how heavy some fire extinguishers are. That doesn't mean they'll last for hours! As a research task, check with your fire safety officer on likely duration/capacity.

Learn how to use the fire extinguishers.
Josh Bullen, volunteer, AFTRS.

First Aid

Consider training in first aid—a must for anyone contemplating location work. A St John's Ambulance course or equivalent is excellent. *A first aid kit should be readily available on all shoots.* Check its stock regularly.

ESSENTIALS FOR SMALL CREWS
- a box containing a blanket and/or a ground sheet
- a first aid kit
- thermos and ice
- strong beam torch
- clipboard with up-to-date *local* emergency numbers
- a second kit containing all of the above *and* a small fire blanket and general-purpose extinguisher.

This is your minimum safety equipment.

EMERGENCY NUMBERS
Professional crews get call sheets with emergency numbers listed for the doctor(s), hospital and police station nearest to the production site. In an emergency, there's no time to hunt these details out.

ON LOCATION
Emergencies don't recognise industry status—so even if it is your group's first location shoot, do the right thing for safety reasons.

Creating a Hazard

Accidents don't *just happen.*

Compounding causes: Consider again the injury in the example of peeling the apple.

Possible factors: Hygiene was observed—the apple was washed. But:

- Hands, apple not thoroughly dry?
  So, not a firm, but a slippery grasp.
- Knife not really sharp, perhaps blunt?
  So, force was needed to cut it.

Result: Natural laws of physics went into action (instability + applied force = . . .) That was a two-factor incident involving one person.

Construction Work

When building sets, be sure to wear hearing protection, eye protection and have no loose hanging clothing that might get caught in the equipment. When sawing, be sure to use the blade guard, and pull the nearly sawed piece through the last bit, rather than pushing your hand towards the blade.

Creating a Risk Factor

Now let's consider cumulative hidden agendas that can stress a group situation into a potential hazard for everyone.

It's a rostered early start—EFP (electronic field production) shoot:

Don't ever tap someone on the shoulder or try to get their attention while they're working with machinery. Hilton Ellingham, Props and Staging, AFTRS.

- Crew member A is late, arriving well after the planned departure time.
- Crew member B, as navigator, hasn't bothered to plan the best route.
- They get lost and get further behind on the production schedule.
- The driver tries to make up lost time, speeds, takes small risks.
- Crew member C knows the vehicle is overloaded but says nothing.
- No one knows the car is overdue for brake service.

All are minor contributors to a possible disaster.

Note: Everyone has equal responsibility for the safety and well-being of the others who share the same work area.

'No Hazard' Checklist

PLACEMENT OF GEAR
- Never clutter the studio with unnecessary items, and never have standby equipment, lighting stands, the odd table, props, camera boxes, and so on, in front of a fire exit, hose reel or extinguisher point—and certainly no gear resting on fire stairs.
- On location, don't block existing emergency exits or fire stairs with any bits of gear just because 'there's nowhere else to put them'. Look again— there has to be!

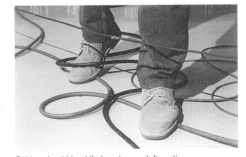

CABLES
- After you connect cables, neaten the scene.
- Don't have easily tripped-over piles or loops of cables.
- Don't have strained cables raised off the floor.
- If cables cross a main foot traffic area, tape them down or place a mat across them, then tape the edges of the mat down.

Cables should be tidied, and never left curling up or stretched above the floor level.

Adrian Rostirolla, Metro Screen.

Never turn on a light that's plugged into an electrical cable which is still coiled up. Uncoil the cable first! A coiled cable can heat up and even melt down.

ELECTRICAL SPOT CHECK
- Cables and connections?
- Damaged insulation?
- Loose connections?
- Connections near water?
- Read *Electrical Practices in the Film Industry*, WorkCover Authority, NSW, or similar publications in your state or country.

LADDERS
- Wooden or fibreglass ladders are safer electrically.
- Check before using it that the ladder is structurally safe.
- Don't carry weights in one hand when climbing. Have someone pass the object to you.
- It's best to treat all ladder work as a two-person job.

Don't try to climb a ladder while carrying gear. Get someone to pass it up to you. Don Bethel assists Rod Bower, AFTRS.

LIGHTING
- Elevated floor stands/supports must be correctly ballasted/tied off.
- Do not place lamps near drapes or the ceiling—they are a fire risk.
- Do not place lamps near automatic fire sprinklers—heat from lamps can activate sprinklers.
- Switch off lamps before repositioning them.
- Check lamps for residual heat before handling them.
- All gear hung above head height needs a second safety fixing.
- If cutting/fitting colour gels, put off-cuts immediately into a waste receptacle. Small pieces underfoot may cause people to slip or fall.

Hold on to the upper section of a light stand when loosening it . . .

. . . or it can collapse on your fingers.

LAMPS CAN EXPLODE
- If one does, duck your head, shield yourself and wait before looking.
- Don't immediately turn and look in the direction of the sound. The housing and the Fresnel lens will usually contain the glass fragments. Most—but not *all*.

During a television rehearsal with the Sydney Symphony Orchestra, a 2K lamp exploded and showered down small fragments of red-hot glass. No one was injured but some musical scores had extra little black 'notes' burnt into their pages.

Grid Work Restrictions

Don't attempt to work on grids or lighting battens unless under the supervision of a qualified electrician.

Lamps suspended overhead need a safety chain in addition to normal fixing. 'Barn doors' must also have a safety chain linked to the lamp housing frame. Check also that safety gauze/glass is in place.

Fire on the Set

If screen action requires a naked flame—lighting a cigarette, candles, kerosene lamps—that action requires a minder in the role of standby props or special FX person, with the floor manager/1st/2nd/3rd AD as backup.

Sharing Space

A crew should observe more care when sharing a location, as when shooting in other people's work areas.

Site permissions are one thing—they're for right of entry only.

A video crew should never 'take over' or impose possible hazards on others.

A video crew is distracting just by being there, so everyone's behaviour should be as unobtrusive as possible—quiet, moderate, businesslike.

To keep an objective perspective on the crew's behaviour, ask yourself this: 'If we needed to reshoot in the same environment, would we be welcomed back?'

Leave a location as you find it. You may have to return for reshoots.

Philip Elms, Media Resource Centre.

Adjusting the Location Site's Lighting Conditions

Work areas lit by fluorescent lights are often a problem for video. The camera has difficulty reproducing correct skin tones/colour balance. In a studio setting, you get rid of the fluorescents—you just switch them off before you start recording. But what if you're in someone else's office space?

If it's absolutely necessary to switch off house/work lights for the colour balance and recording, prior arrangements must be made with area operators and management. Once agreement has been reached, the routine is:

1. Contact personally the on-site workers who'll be affected.
2. Explain to the on-site workers the light-changing procedure you'll be following and the warnings you'll be giving them.
3. Prior to making lighting changes, announce the change clearly.
4. Switch your video production lighting on (assumed).
5. Switch off the house/work lights.
6. At the end of the take, switch on the house lights.
7. At your leisure, switch off your production lights.
8. Say 'thank you'.

Personal Protection

Clothing

- Dress appropriately for an *industrial* environment. Wear low-heeled shoes, in good condition. Never wear thongs (*flip-flops*).
- For location work, take wet-weather gear and any extra items you have decided on from your safety scan. Consider the exercise as you would a two-day bush hike.
- Head gear is essential—a hat for the sun, and a cap for cold nights and windy weather.

Skin Protection

- For protection from sun, wind and insects, use the usual sprays and lotions.
- Apply sunscreens approximately twenty minutes before exposure and reapply regularly.

Gloves

- Not everyone can work wearing gloves, but the light garden type are great for handling and rewinding cables that are dirty or muddy.

Food

- Do have regular meal breaks and eat only nourishing food.
- Once energy is on the wane, concentration decreases— we become less alert, which is a perfect scenario for mistakes and accidents.

Liquids

- Fluid intake is important too. If you're on location and water has to be carried, take more than you think you'll need—and ice.
- Take a thermos of ice—even in winter. An ice pack is a great relief for a bump or a bruise.

Feed the crew! *Uncle Toby's Kebabs*, directed by Mark Tewksbury.

Not Your Scene

Be careful when helping out in craft areas where you are not familiar with the work practices. Helping with stage scenery might be one example, if you are not used to working in the staging area.

Hazards in Helping

Special techniques are needed when handling scenery flats, rostrum tops and bases, etc. If you don't have these skills, ask for guidance/training before giving assistance. Mishandling can cause back injuries.

When two people are carrying flats or other heavy items, they should face each other and have their hand positions in a mirror image of each other. So if one person has their left hand at the top, and their right hand at the bottom, the other person should be the opposite—right hand at the top and left hand at the bottom. If not, the stronger person can overbalance the load and twist the weaker person, resulting in back damage.

Alistair Thornton, Props and Staging Department, AFTRS.

Counterweights

- Don't help yourself to items that may be doing a vital job for other crafts. Removing a sandbag from a French brace, which is holding up a flat, could collapse the whole set.
- If you're asked to 'chuck a sandbag on the brace', the place to put it is in or outside the sharp angle at the bottom of the brace, as far from the flat as possible. This will counterweight the flat so it won't fall. If you put the sandbag closer to the flat, the counterweighting may not be strong enough.
- If you're asked to 'hammer a nail into . . .'—for whatever reason—think about the end result. Will it protrude (at eye level) and cause damage to personnel or equipment?
- And before you strike a blow, do check the striking face of the hammer. If the surface is dirty, it can mishit on the nail—but find your finger(s) an easier target. Then, of course, there are staples and . . . So, take care when helping outside your current area of skills.

When carrying flats, one person's hands should be positioned in the mirror image of the other person's, so the stronger person doesn't overbalance the other one. AFTRS.

Sandbag

Ken Manning repairs a French brace. Note the placement of the sandbag. AFTRS.

Health Hazards

There are some not-so-obvious health hazards—the sneaky ones that build up and eventually cause us personal stress.

Eye strain, lower back pain, RSI (repetitive strain injury), damage to our auditory sense—all of these are due to poor understanding of personal risks.

All computer/screen work, whether typing or editing, when performed over long hours with incorrect lighting/seating and the concentrated use of a 'mouse' control can give us the trifecta of eye strain, back/neck pain and RSI to the wrist/forearm.

Lengthy sessions of loud music (concert conditions or home hi-fi) will decrease hearing sensitivity. Not good for anyone, especially sound recordists and editors.

Publications with specific guidance on *prevention* of these disorders are readily available.

The Broad Issues

Guidelines on health and safety matters that relate specifically to the film and television industry have been developed by the industry and unions. Information on these can be found through the OH&S Safety portal of the Media Entertainment and Arts Alliance (MEAA) website, <www.alliance.org.au>.

Safety guidelines have been developed and endorsed by the MEAA and the Australian Entertainment Industry Association (AEIA) in association with the Musicians' Union of Australia (MUA).

While the guidelines may sound legalistic, they are really helpful and clearly written, with advice on risk assessment, safety induction, key safety issues, and incident and hazard reporting.

A Fact of Life

During production we'll always be working in conditions that require split concentration—one part on the demands of covering the action of producing (in tight timeframes); the other on coping, in a safe manner, with the risk factors inherent with variable and constantly changing location environments. The balance must always be in favour of our health and safety.

Dos and Don'ts

- *Do* read and adopt the valuable advice given by health and safety organisations on health hazard prevention.
- *Do* lift your state of safety awareness.
- *Don't* repeat your early 'accident' experiences.
- *Do* enjoy your craft!

LIGHTING

16

Light is the basic *material* from which you make video images. (I know this is an odd concept, because whether light has substance or not has intrigued physicists for centuries.) But it's the light reflected off objects into the camera lens that forms the video image. Without it, there's no picture.

As a video artist, the different qualities and colours of light are the choices on your palette. As a run-of-the-mill videographer, it's still light that is the *stuff* of your work.

Two Kinds of Light

When people speak of light, they refer to *incident* light and *reflected* light. Incident light is the light as it's travelling from the source. Reflected light is the light after it has hit a surface and bounced off it.

The video image is made from the pattern of reflected light that enters the camera's lens.

As a videographer, your job is to choose the appropriate light sources (incident light) for the visual effect you want to achieve, and then carefully arrange their heights, positions, intensities, colours and reach so the resulting composite of reflected light produces the picture and mood you seek.

Every surface reflects light differently. From some angles, smooth surfaces can reflect an even light, which may be bright or dark depending on the colour of the surface, the intensity of the incident light and the angle of reflection of the light into the camera lens.

For example, a polished black stone surface can reflect a very bright light from some angles, but appear as an even, dark black from other angles.

Other surfaces are textured and reflect a variegated pattern of light interspersed with tiny shadows.

Lighting is about both the areas that are lit and the quality and intensity of the shadows. (Photo by Ben Lipsey)

A softly lit, shadowless curved infinity background emphasises the actions of the two women. (Courtesy of tav productions)

The angle of the incident light in relation to the surface texture is important. Frontal lighting reduces shadowing to almost nothing, whereas side lighting produces dramatic shadows. Knowing this allows you to emphasise or downplay the degree of apparent texturing of any surface in your picture.

So you can choose to make the performer's face look smooth by lighting from the front, or modelled (even craggy) by lighting from the side.

Or you can highlight the folds of a background curtain by lighting the curtain from the side, or make the folds almost unnoticeable by lighting them from the front.

Rachel Masters, Corporate Training Coordinator, SBS.

A good way to see how lighting affects the look of a production is to turn down the colour controls on your monitor for a few minutes. If the images you see then are solid black and white, chances are that the lighting is quite harsh and contrasty. That's great if you want this effect, but generally when shooting video you aim to create a wide tonal variation to add depth and interest.

Curving surfaces reflect a gradation in intensity of light, with some parts bright and some areas falling away into shadow.

As a baby, you had to learn to interpret the meaning of different types of reflected light—you learned to predict hard and soft, sharp and 'comfy', wet and dry, as well as near and far.

As a lighting person, you need to convey similar meanings of texture and depth to your audience—although, because you're working with a flat screen, you have only two dimensions with which to get across the *feel* of things.

In most cases, you should try to use lighting to enhance the illusion of a third dimension. One way to create a sense of depth is by controlling the contrast and shape of the lighting separately in the foreground, mid-ground and background of your scene. For example, if your subject is in the foreground, you might be able to have a lamp lit on a table in the mid-ground and another sort of lighting

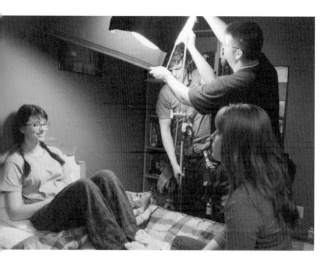

Grips are setting a flag (with a C-stand) to create a diagonal shadow on the wall near the actor's head. Note the placement of black wrap (foil) on the side of the light facing the camera. It was placed there to prevent spill light causing a flare in the camera lens. The light can still reach the subject between the black wrap and the flag. Photographer: Kristin Zabawa; actors: Teresa Decher, Mercedes Rose; grips: Justin Ward, Will Walle.

further back—perhaps a doorway opening to a lit hallway or other room. When this principle of 'contrasts' is applied in its most dramatic form, it is referred to as *chiaroscuro*. This term is borrowed from Italian Renaissance paintings. It refers to the use of alternating patterns of light and dark shade.

Any artificial light sources (such as lamps) which are shown working within the picture are called *practicals*.

To get some ideas, watch some of your favourite films on DVD and pause them as each attractive scene appears. Look carefully and analyse the lighting. Although there's artistry in lighting, you can acquire many practical techniques by careful observation.

Getting the angle right between your camera lens and a critical surface can make or break a shot.

When you set up the lighting for a shot or a scene, you should constantly draw on what you've already learned about reflected light. But don't stop there—take some time and risks to push your skills further.

That's how to lift your shots from mediocre to stunning.

In this intimate scene, depth is conveyed by the placement of two practicals. The floor lamp marks the foreground, the actress is in a softly lit mid-ground, and the bed lamp marks the depth of the space by lighting on the wall. (Courtesy of Film & TV, Central TAFE, Perth, WA)

LIGHTING. In my opinion, easily the most volatile yet rewarding aspect of camerawork. If possible, always light your shots. The difference between lit and unlit vision can be immense. ABC's *Australian Story* is one excellent example of the benefits of lighting. Even a reflector or diffuser can promote a shot from mediocre to something special.

Gordon Peters, Cameraman, Channel 7 News, Bundaberg.

The Quality of Light

Of course, the word 'quality' can mean many things, but when applied to lighting two of the fundamental concepts are *hard light* and *soft light*.

Hard Light

Hard light is the light you get from direct sunlight and from unshielded light sources that are throwing their light in a straight line of sight towards the subject being lit.

With a hard light, you can see a somewhat distorted reflection of the *source* of the light, on the surface of the subject.

Two hard lights on a face can produce deep and unattractive shadows.

A distinct edge to shadows indicates a hard light source. (Courtesy of Metro Screen)

Hard light is very directional. It sharply illuminates the side of the object it hits and causes deep shadows with clearly defined edges on the other side. So hard light is good for dramatic lighting. And it brings out textures well.

Used alone, hard light can look too harsh, and it can over-illuminate areas in the shot, producing *hot spots* (overly bright areas) or causing problems with the contrast ratio.

It can also cause the formation of unattractive shadows, like nose shadows, on your actors. When two or more hard lights are used, there can be many ugly shadows.

Soft Light

Soft light is a bit tricky to define. An indication that a light is soft is the *wrap-around effect*, which means that the incident light wraps around the subject in such a way that there are minimal shadows on the contours of the subject's surface.

With the light source placed behind a large diffusion screen . . .

. . . a wonderful soft light on the child is obtained. (Courtesy of AFTRS)

Another sign of soft light is if the shadows cast behind the subject have soft edges to them.

Whether a light is soft or not depends on its size in relation to the subject. A large source, even if it's a hard light, will wrap around a small subject, and the wrap-around effect increases as the light is moved closer to the subject.

You can say that soft light is much more diffuse than hard light. It's the type of sunlight you get on a cloudy or hazy day. This type of light can be mimicked by artificial light when a light is shone through diffusion material such as silk cloth, nylon cloth, tracing paper or plastic diffusion material (made for such a purpose).

Generally, white material is used in order to minimise shifts in the colour temperature of the light. There will, however, be some 'warming' of the light when using diffusion material. The degree of softness is determined by the thickness of the material (which refracts or scatters the light) and the size of the material relative to the distance from the subject.

Even softer diffused light can be achieved by bouncing light into a semi-reflective white surface that is directed towards the subject. Again, this surface is usually white material to minimise colour temperature shifts. Bounce materials most often used are foam core board, polystyrene bead board, bleached muslin or griffolyn (white plastic material).

This indirect light technique can be used with both artificial lighting and sunlight.

Large white bounce reflectors are often used on exterior locations to fill harsh shadows created by the sun. Large white reflectors are much softer, and therefore more natural looking, than 'silver' surface reflectors. However, they are not as reflective (powerful) as silver surface reflectors.

Soft light is 'pretty' light. It can be very delicate and give a mellow quality to the subject being lit. For this reason, it's often used in portraiture.

Soft light is also less directional: it tends to scatter and is harder to control.

Soft light is usually desirable as fill light because it lightens shadow areas without adding additional distinct visible shadows.

Very broad, soft light produces shadow-free faces. The Tech Club of the The Madeleine School tries out the news desk at KGW, Portland, Oregon.

A strong soft source may be improvised by reflecting the sun off a mirror and through a frame with heavy diffusion on it. The frame can be simply made from 1 inch × 1 inch aluminium tube and removable corner pieces, so it comes apart and stows neatly in a bag.

Tony Mandl,
Gaffer, AFTRS.

Here the main light is directed at Vicki Lucan and also at a sheet of lightweight white polystyrene, so it bounces back to provide a soft fill on the other side of her face.

A key light and soft fill provide gentle modelling of Ruth Pino's face. (Photo by Sharon Howard, capeannweddings.com)

Soft light is not as good for bringing out sharp detail in textures because it produces softer shadows with blurry, indistinct edges.

Combining Lighting on a Set

When you're working out the lighting requirements for a scene or studio set, you'll probably use a variety of lighting instruments and light-control devices to create differences in the quality of light, as well as where light falls. Creating shadow and partial shadow areas is just as important as the areas that are lit. This is sometimes referred to as *subtractive lighting*. You can also enhance the mood or symbolism of a scene by adding selective coloured gels to all or some lights.

Just like a painter, you don't rely on only one type of stroke or size of brush to produce a memorable picture.

The arrangement of the set elements and the positions of some of the lights.

Below: Helen Carter, cinematographer, and Sharon Fulton, designer, conduct a lighting test to work out what lights and what set elements will produce the desired effects within the planned drama scene. (AFTRS)

A gelled light shines on a background flat which is to appear as a brick wall outside the building.

A light shining through a diffusion screen provides a soft light for the actor seated in front of the window frame.

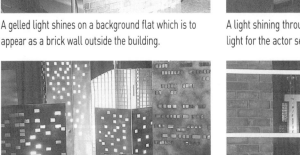

A miniature set made of cardboard has cut-out windows, backlit, to give the impression of a city at night.

A model sits in to test the effectiveness of the lighting.

Contrast Ratio

The contrast ratio is the range that the camera can handle, from the darkest part of the picture to the brightest part.

Video is less able to record high contrast ratios that our eyes can see. The dynamic contrast range (ability to record textural detail in shadows, mid-tones and highlights) of video varies greatly depending on the camera model and whether it is standard definition or high definition. This contrast range varies from approximately five to ten *f* stops. Some of the latest ultra-high definition cameras can record a dynamic range that now rivals the latitude of film.

In a scene that is too contrasty, you'll have to choose an iris setting which suits the brightest parts and leaves the darker areas of the picture looking impenetrably black, or an iris setting which suits the dark areas and makes the bright ones bleached out to white.

Depending on your production, it may be that neither is an acceptable option.

So it's a good idea to steer clear of known troublemakers. White clothing is extremely reflective of light. Black is very absorbent of light. Generally speaking, performers should be advised to not wear white or black. Medium tones will work in much better with skin tones to give a good contrast ratio and a pleasing image. (So now you know why the news readers wear 'TV blue'.)

Sometimes you just can't escape the situation. Your studio guest is wearing something white and it's just too reflective for the lighting you want to use. You can cut the intensity of light reaching that part of the picture by shading it from the light with a piece of card, a *net* or a *gel*.

These methods should bring your contrast ratio into line. If not, maybe you can loan the performer a jacket!

If the problem is that there are areas in the picture which are too dark, try bouncing light into the shadows to lift their light level.

It is often better for lighting and the final image if your actors avoid wearing pure whites and clothing with fine patterns which may cause moire patterns.

Randolph Sellars, Director of Photography.

When shooting HD video, avoid over-exposing (clipping) any sizable elements in the frame. When necessary, under-expose to preserve highlight detail. There's a lot more room in HD to lift shadow and mid-tone detail in post to compensate for the underexposure.

Monitoring Your Light Levels

You can detect the various brightness levels across your set by using a light meter, if you like, and it's good practice to learn to use one.

Video people generally check lighting by looking at the image in a monitor connected to the camera viewing the scene. This shows you hot spots and shadows which you won't see with your eyes until you're very practised at lighting.

When using a monitor to evaluate lighting, it is very important that the monitor is good quality and that it has been calibrated properly for brightness, contrast, chroma and hue. On professional monitors, this is done with the aid of colour bars generated by the camera. If your monitor is significantly off, then your lighting decisions may be adversely affected. If possible, it's most accurate to check light levels with a waveform monitor or use the 'zebra bars' generated by the camera. You can check whether the whites are clipping or not by setting the camera zebra bars to 100 per cent.

Randolph Sellars, Director of Photography.

A good way to set proper exposure for average Caucasian flesh tones is to set the camera zebra bars to 70 per cent. Open or close the iris ring until zebra bars first appear on highlights of a face (nose, forehead, cheekbones).

One trap people fall into is that when their monitor is near bright studio lights, they boost the screen brightness so they can see the image better. But if the screen is cranked up too bright, the lighting person and the director can end up deciding to go with a scene which is actually under-lit.

Actually, if you put the camera temporarily into auto iris and check the *f* stop reading, you'll usually get a good idea of whether the lighting is bright enough.

Lighting and Depth of Field

The darker the scene, the more open your camera iris will have to be to let in enough light to reproduce the image adequately.

The wider the iris opening (the lower the *f* stop number), the narrower the depth of field.

If you want to have a narrow depth of field, you can go ahead and shoot with lower lighting. But if you need clear focus across a broad depth of field, you need to make sure that the scene is brightly lit.

Where this consideration usually comes into play is in videotaping concerts and stage performances.

Stage lighting is often dimmer, overall, than TV lighting, and it's almost always much more contrasty. The contrast is the harder aspect to adjust for.

If you're trying to videotape someone else's performance, you have three possible paths. The first is to convince the person in charge of the performance lighting to use brighter lights on the night you record. (But you're not likely to find agreement on this.)

Another choice is to convince the show to do a command performance for you, with brighter lights. The risk with this is that the lack of an audience could cause the performance level to drop.

The most likely situation is that you'll end up taping the performance with the low light situation.

Now, remembering that when you're zoomed in all the way you also decrease the depth of field, make sure that you get your camera as close to the stage as possible. This way you can work on wide-angle lens to maximise your depth of field.

If you move in close to the performance, you can stay on wide angle and keep a good depth of field.

Otherwise, you could find that the slightest swaying back and forth of the singer will cause him or her to go in and out of focus. Your image quality will be disastrous. (If this section is confusing to you, you may want to reread the Depth of Field explanation in Chapter 2, Image Control.)

Using Location Lighting

There are different opinions on location lighting. Some people prefer to use the natural lighting that exists at a location, as much as possible, and to assist it with bounced sunlight and the occasional portable light, appropriately gelled.

Other lighting people always use artificial light to ensure exactly the quality and control they seek for their image.

The key thing is to be able to work *with* your light sources, rather than have out-of-control elements compromise or ruin your images.

Move the Studio Outdoors

If you don't have access to any decent lights, the best thing might be to move your studio outdoors.

And sometimes the glitter of an outdoor setting enhances your program.

At the right time of day, the sun can illuminate the whole colourful background and the presenter. Travis Johnson interviews Russell Hill. (Photo by Chris Peckham)

Windows

Windows are both a blessing and a bane. They can let in enough light for you to operate entirely with sunlight and bounce cards, but they can be very hard to work around.

Make sure that you notice the number, size and location of windows when you do your site check and find out which direction they face. Will it be a morning shoot with the rising sun flooding in? Or do these windows face west? Will the light be blocked by a clump of trees? Does the building next door shade the room from direct light?

Sunlit site on the Nullarbor Plain. (Courtesy of tav productions)

If you want to use natural light, you have to be able to arrange the set so you can either have the window light at your back, with your performer close enough to the window to be shone upon, or the window at your side and the performer side-on to the window as well. A large white card or piece of polystyrene held at the correct angle on the non-window side of the performer can bounce back a soft fill light to take care of the shadowy side.

Tony Mandl,
Gaffer, AFTRS.

Sometimes you do want to use the view out of a window, to add to the sense of place in your image. Windows *can* be included in the frame if their brightness can be controlled. (A good level is 1–1.5 *f* stops over your exposure.)

In modern office buildings, there may already be neutral density built into the windows, or they may have a heavily tinted film on them. Look around—there may be venetian blinds, or vertical blinds, that can be adjusted to allow the outside to be seen, but not blow out. A piece of neutral density gel may be taped to the glass, and reduce the outside brightness by as much as four stops. Also, the size of the shot, and the amount of the window shown, can be adjusted. This way, the viewer can still see some of the outside, and you can keep the edges of the gel out of shot. The part of the window which is not in shot can still act as a source of light.

Do this.

Or do this.

Do this.

But not this!

Avoid shooting directly into a window unless you can significantly lower the window exposure with heavy neutral density (ND) gel. Without heavy ND gel, the auto iris will respond to the brightness and close way down, giving you a good picture of the outdoors and a silhouette of your performer. If you switch to manual iris and open it up so the performer looks okay, the background will be all bleached out.

Always shoot with the light behind you.

Sue L'Estrange, Video Teacher.

Bright Sky

One of the most common problems with outdoor lighting happens when you try to get a shot of a person with sky behind their head. If you're facing the sunny side of the sky, or if it's a bright hazy day, the auto iris will respond to the brightness of the background sky and close down, leaving your subject as a semi-silhouette.

The first thing to try is simply turning the shot around, so the sunniest part of the sky is at the back of the camera.

If the person still looks too dark, put the camera on manual iris, zoom in so the presenter's face fills the screen and set the iris to give the right result for the face. Then leave the iris setting there, and zoom out. Your picture may now be acceptable. The sky will be lighter, but if it doesn't look too bleached out, you can probably go with it.

If the background is now too glary, change the shot so the background is trees, shrubbery or anything else medium-toned or darker.

If the background is very bright, your subject may become semi-silhouetted.

Here's the shot with a darker background. It's still toppy with eye shadows because the sun was high, but you can at least see their faces. Earlier or later in the day could give a better result. Lucien Cooper and Hayden Barltrop, best mates.

Bough Shelters

Another tricky lighting situation arises with many Indigenous communities.

The bough shelter is a shaded space made using poles as uprights, with a roof of tree boughs, where community meetings take place. Outside it may be very bright and hot, but it's cooler and darker in the bough shelter.

The shelter often has no walls—it's open on all four sides. This is handy for getting differently angled shots of the group, and certainly helps the people in the meeting get a bit of air, but the problem for the person videotaping the meeting is that the surrounding ground is often extremely reflective of sunlight, whether it's red sandy desert or burnt yellow grass.

So whenever the camera operator goes for a wide shot, the very bright ground on the far side of the shelter affects the auto iris and makes it close down, and all detail of the people inside is lost.

One way to avoid this is to stay in on mid-shots and close-ups as much as possible, so the people's faces fill the screen and the outside ground isn't in shot.

Still, it's often desirable to use wider shots to show who's seated near whom (which can be important to the story).

When in this situation, use silver surface reflectors if possible to light the faces under the bough shelter. Use the 'soft side' of the reflector because the light will be less harsh looking.

It would be even better, if possible, to aim the reflectors through diffusion material to soften the light and make it look more natural. In this case, the 'hard side' of the reflector would be stronger and more efficient.

But the reality is that the meeting is what's most important and the more you get into lighting set-ups, the less normal the people at the meeting will feel. It's one of those times when it's important to remember that the video is not the main event, important as it seems.

The bough shelter is a hard location to cover.

Small Rooms and Crowded Spaces

When a room is very small—and often when you go to interview people in their offices you strike cramped space—there's no room for a three-point lighting set-up. However, you can raise the illumination level enough to get a viewable shot by setting up one light and bouncing it off the white ceiling or off the white or pale cream-coloured walls.

On location in Canberra Pharmacy for *Asthma Care*, produced by Owen Murray, University of Western Sydney, Macarthur.

Sometimes on-site shooting has too much stuff in the way to do much of a lighting set-up. Here, too, bounced light can save the shoot.

But bounced lighting is hard to control. A bounce off the ceiling can be very *toppy*, leaving people with shiny heads and dark sockets where their eyes presumably are.

Another factor to watch with bounced lighting is *colour bounce*. Whatever colour the wall is, that colour will bounce onto the surface of your subject . . . Is that person really pink or green or blue?

So first see how you go with using different options, like a single redhead, with spun (a soft white fibreglass material) on it, from one corner of the room.

Beaches, Snow and Water

Other tricky locations are beaches, snowfields and waterways. Sand, snow and water are all extremely reflective and can cause silhouetting of your presenter/actor. In these situations, a neutral density filter is essential to cut down the intensity of the light. Of course, you remember that a neutral density filter doesn't change the quality of the light, only the intensity.

Cloudy or hazy days can be better to shoot on, as they reduce the harshness of the direct and reflected sunlight.

Picking the best time of day is helpful, too—try to keep an angled sun to the back of the camera operator. When it's midday, chill out in a cafe.

Bouncing Light into Shaded Areas

When faced by conditions of harsh light, it can be best to put your performer in the shade. You'll get better colour representation and you can use a flexifill or a big bounce card to reflect the sunlight in at them, if necessary.

Be sure you re-white balance for the new lighting conditions, though. Shade or overcast has a different colour temperature than sunlight.

Aluminium foil provides the strongest reflection. If you use a bounce card covered with crumpled foil, it will diffuse the reflection somewhat. Silver foil gives a colder reflection, gold foil gives a warmer, mellower reflection. White polystyrene gives a soft reflection, as does white cloth. You can even use a white wall if it's nearby.

Both Rosco and Lee sell a fabric scrim with holes in it, which is the most useful soft reflector you can get. One side is a soft silver reflective surface. You can attach it to a board and use it to bounce light, and you'll get a brighter bounce. The other side is black and looks similar to a thick net.

Work out how to get the light where you want it. (Courtesy of Nigel Graves)

You can use the black side in place of ND gel on a window, and you won't get the additional reflection the gel would give you. Because it's a fabric, you can simply lay it on a desk surface, or wherever you need it. You can roll it up to carry it around with you. Its one drawback is that it can be somewhat fragile.

Hat Shade and Brow Shadows

For interviews in sunny places, bounce cards held at the presenter's lap level can do a good job of lifting the light level under a broad-rimmed hat and lessening shadows in deep-set eyes.

Adjusting for Mixed Colour Temperatures

If you use a mixture of sunlight and incandescent lights (portable lights), you'll have to address the problem of mixed colour temperatures.

Say you're doing an interview and you've seated your subject next to a window. But the room is so dark that you've decided to lift the base illumination level by using a couple of portable lights.

The sunlight striking one side of her face has a bluish tinge and the incandescent lights inside the room, affecting the other side of her face, have a reddish tinge. If you white balance for sunlight, one side of her face will look ruddy and her clothing colour on that side may be reddish, too. If you white balance to the portable lights, her indoor side will look fine, but the side towards the window will have a strangely alien blueness to it. Ugh!

There are five strategies to consider:

1. Use a full or half daylight blue *gel* (called *CTB*), which is a special transparent coloured sheet that won't melt from the heat of a light. Attach the blue gel to the front of your portable lights, with wooden clothes pegs, and then white balance the camera to the portable lights. Now the colour contrast between outdoors and indoors won't be too great.
2. Put an amber gel (called *85* or *CTO*) across the window and white balance to the reddish portable lights. Again, both sides will match. But this can be harder because you need the amber gel to be smoothly attached to the window, not torn or wrinkly, so it won't give itself away.
3. Try using a large bounce card so the inside fill light will actually be reflected window light, and therefore will automatically be of matching colour temperature to the sunlight.
4. Close the curtains.
5. Move the shot.

Direction of Light

Simply moving a light to a new position alters the effect of the light. When you have the time, have fun and experiment!

Frontal lighting can make a face look very smooth.

Frontal Lighting

Light aimed from the camera's viewpoint reduces modelling of figures and minimises their surface textures. For some faces, indirect frontal lighting is 'pretty' lighting—it smoothes out face wrinkles and minimises other skin bumps and variations.

Side Lighting

Lighting from the side emphasises texture and modelling. It's good for bringing out interesting surfaces, dramatising facial features and highlighting objects in relief.

Side lighting can produce a more dramatic look.

Edge Lighting or Rim Lighting

A strong lighting highlight restricted to the edge of a person or object can add a glamorous accent to the image.

A dramatic rim light can be striking. Walter Locke as Gonzalo in *The Tempest*. (Photo © T. Charles Erickson)

Night Scenes

When you need to show the audience that the scene is dark, but you still need to show them what's happening, carefully lighting both sides of the actor's head and leaving the front of the face in darkness can achieve this effect.

You have to have some lighting, even for dark night scenes.

Under lighting is great for horror shows.

Overhead lighting can be very toppy and produces dark eye shadows.

So here's the thing—if there's no light on the subject, how can the camera see it?

Francis Treacey, Deakin University.

For those with lots of hair, back lighting is especially effective.

Under Lighting

This gives a wonderful, scary image, good for grotesques. Because it inverts the usual facial modelling and shadowing, it's a device used for mystery stories.

One thing to be careful about—hand gestures may sometimes throw shadows onto the face.

Overhead Lighting

This can leave the eyes looking like deep black cavities. It's not a flattering lighting, but it can emphasise some moods—possibly isolation or desolation. It certainly works well for interrogation scenes.

More often than not, though, overhead lighting is a mistake that happens from not paying attention to the placement of location lighting.

If you seat someone under a ceiling light because that's where the room is brightest, you'll get back to the edit room to discover that your image is dull, disappointing and filled with people with cavernous eyes.

However, a large softlight is sometimes shone from overhead through diffusion material to raise the general light level in a studio set. It can send an overall wash of light into the set, letting individual key lights isolate and accent the actors and important set elements.

Back Lighting

Lighting from behind can outline a figure or object with light. It can be beautiful used on its own. But usually a back light is part of a total lighting set-up, adding its halo effect to separate the figure from the background.

Back light is terrific for illuminating smoke, which tends to disappear with front lighting. You need to have a dark background and the back light set just right, then the smoke will 'materialise' in your video image.

For those for whom the screen dimension is not a smoke-free zone, cigarettes, pipes, 'steaming' mugs of coffee, genies, even guns, can waft and coil their varied spirits for posterity.

Silhouette Lighting

This is achieved by lighting the background but letting no light fall on the camera side of the subject. The subject's outline is apparent, but little or no surface detail can be seen. The background can either be lit from the front or, if there's a translucent screen, the subject can be lit from behind.

Before you record this image, make sure there are no 'hot spots' on the rear wall.

'Until recently this person lived a life of crime...'

Indirect 'Firelight'

You can simulate the flicker of a campfire. To do this, place a shallow tray of water in front of your actor and direct a light downwards onto it. You may decide to put an amber gel on the light, too. Then you have an assistant, who remains out of shot, agitate the water. The light bounces erratically off the wavelets and produces an effect like firelight on the actor's face.

Rippled chrome plastic sheeting (you can get wrapping paper like this) wrapped around a board will give you a similar effect. And it will allow you more flexibility because you can tip it and angle it as needed. With the water tray, you're limited to a horizontal and immobile reflecting body, so you have to get your actors right over close to it.

With ingenuity, you can get some wonderful effects.

Another old firelight effect is achieved by hanging strips of coloured gels from a stick and waving them in front of the light source.

Bouncing the Light to Soften It (Indirect Lighting)

Light is softer if it's coming from a broader area rather than from a point source. So you can soften light by bouncing it off a big white surface, like a large piece of polystyrene or cardboard.

To make a 'soft light', turn your redhead away from your subject, facing a large white surface, and the resulting bright reflected light bouncing off that surface will give a softer, less shadow-creating illumination for your subject.

Pointing a light towards polystyrene will give you a good bounce.

Use a flexifill to bounce light into deepset eyes.
(Photo © Tatiana Boyle)

Another way to soften light is to point it at a reflective umbrella. *Tota* lights come with little silver umbrellas that are designed to be attached to the side of the tota lightheads.

A *flexifill* is a large piece of reflective material, white on one side and silver on the other, which is mounted in a flexible circular frame. It's lightweight and can be handheld by an assistant during a short interview, to bounce a soft light onto the subject's face. Or it can be mounted on a *C-stand* for a longer shoot. When you're done with it, you can twist it down neatly into a small shape to pack it into its zipper bag.

Colour Bounce

Sometimes you may not intentionally bounce light, but may find that the placement of your subject is in the throw of a coloured bounce. Make sure you can live with it before you go ahead and shoot there. An actor who's green around the gills from that house paint on the wall may look more in need of a liver transplant than the adventure he's supposedly on.

A terrible effect comes from shooting under a bluish canopy or sunshade, but people are often expected to cover events under large outdoor tents. The people end up looking like cadavers. (Yes, we can believe it's their 50th wedding anniversary. The question is, are they still alive?)

Coloured Lighting

Lights can be given different colours by attaching gels in front of them. A gel is made of a heat-resistant material which won't melt or burn if placed a safe distance from very hot lights. However, *they can melt if they are too close to a very hot light or the light is spotted.*

Gels are not just coloured plastic or cellophane from the newsagent, and need to be purchased from a supplier.

Gels are expensive, and are usually bought by the roll and then cut off into the sizes needed for each shoot. They're slippery and uncooperative when you try to carry them about, but if they're rolled up, secured with elastic bands and stored carefully at the end of the shoot, gels can be reused many times. It's worth taking care of them and not just crumpling them into the light kit.

Gels can be clamped into metal frames that can either be attached directly to the light fixture or held separately in front of it on a *C-stand*. Alternatively, gels can be pegged to the *barn doors*—those four black metal flaps mounted on the outer front rim of the light fixture—using wooden clothes pegs (not plastic ones, which will melt).

Gels come in any colour. (It's fun to look through the manufacturer's sample book!) The most frequently used colours are blue and amber.

There are special blues that are calibrated to raise the colour temperature of incandescent lights to that of sunlight. You can get them in *half daylight (1/2 CTB)*, *quarter daylight (1/4 CTB)* and *full daylight (full CTB)*. They're useful if you need to match a portable light to sunlight on a location shoot.

> Gels last longer if you don't *spot* the light onto them. And keeping the gel further away from the light helps, too, even if it means you need a larger piece.
>
> **Tony Mandl,** Gaffer, AFTRS.

The darker blues cut down the intensity of the light quite dramatically, so if you want lots of blue light, you'll need heaps of lights. They can give a coolness to the image, and can be used to indicate night time.

The reds are popular when people are taping musicians. They can give a feeling of nightclub or theatre lighting.

Yellows can be tricky. They can make people look rather sallow. But a peach-coloured gel can make people look healthier than they are.

Coloured accent lights, in an otherwise normal-looking scene, can make an image that's quite striking. A swathe of colour hitting only the background wall can look great.

Spot Light and Flood Light

Some lights have movable globes. By turning or sliding a knob you can vary the type of light between *spot light* and *flood light*. The knobs are labelled with arrows showing which way is spot and which is flood.

Spot Light

When the globe is in the *spot* position, it's held well back inside the light fixture's curved metallic reflector. This causes the beam of light to be controlled by the reflector. It produces a limited and intense, direct beam of hard light.

If you watch someone walk across this beam, you'll see that the intensity of it varies. It's bright in the middle, and less bright at the sides.

Flood Light

When the globe is in the *flood* position, it's thrust forward towards the open front of the light fixture's reflector. This allows less control of the light beam, which spills out the sides.

The result is a less intense, broader spread of direct light, with the intensity just dropping off a bit at the edges. It appears more even than a spot light, but the shadows are still sharp.

The ridged lens at the front of the Fresnel controls the throw of the light, whether spot or flood.

Tony Mandl,
Gaffer, AFTRS.

There are no set answers in lighting. It very much depends on the situation you're in. How effectively you light depends on knowing what you can do with the equipment you've got, and relating that to the action you're lighting and the style of the program you're working on.

Shane McNeil,
Flinders
University.

Lighting a scene is like eating potato chips—one light can be too many and a hundred never enough.

Two lighting problems were solved for this shoot: to control the light, the upper windows of the room were blacked out with plastic, and to illuminate the actors' faces, lighting was set up in the middle hole in the table. *Dot Com Dementia*, Boston, Massachusetts.

Fresnel Lights

Fresnel lights have a glass lens with raised circular ridges of glass on the outer surface. This lens is mounted on the front of the light fixture and can be swung aside like a door when you need to change the globe.

On a Fresnel lamp, when you move between spot and flood, the whole inside of the lamp—both globe and reflector—moves forwards and backwards. The focusing of the beam is done by the glass lens, rather than by the relationship between the globe and the reflector.

Basic 'Three-point Lighting'

Some people feel that all you need is *enough* light. So they turn several lamps in the direction of the set and blast the whole area with light. They do have enough.

But the problem is that the effect is flat. There's no modelling or highlighting. Nothing in particular draws the eye of the viewer. There's no sparkle to the scene. What's more, every segment, every show, will look boringly similar. Understanding a few basic concepts in lighting can give you the tools to begin to control the look of your shots and to vary the mood from scene to scene.

Here are the fundamental lighting positions for lighting one person. There is no need to stick with this slavishly, but it's a good theoretical starting point.

Key Light

The *key light* provides the main illumination of the subject. It can be a hard or soft source based on reality or stylistic preference.

A key light near the camera gives almost frontal lighting.

A key light to the side of the model causes much more shadowing on the face.

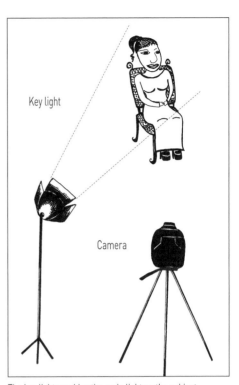

The key light provides the main light on the subject.

The key light is placed to one side of the camera. It's up to you which side you choose. It shouldn't be too close to the camera because then it would be shining into the eyes of the performer and cause discomfort (bad for them) and squinting (bad for the video image).

Once you turn the key light on, you'll see that one side of the person's face is well lit, but the other side is now shaded.

The further to the side of the performer's face that you set the key light, the more dramatic the lighting and the more texture you'll reveal on the face. Position the light according to the effect you want, considering the mood of your program.

Fill Light

You position the *fill light* on the opposite side of the camera to the key light.

The purpose of the fill light is to illuminate the other side of the performer's face, lifting the shadow that is caused by the key light. The fill light is often a softer light, and of a lower intensity than the key light.

You can achieve this by placing it further away from the subject, setting it to the *flood* position and/or putting some spun

The fill light reduces most of the shadows caused by the key light.

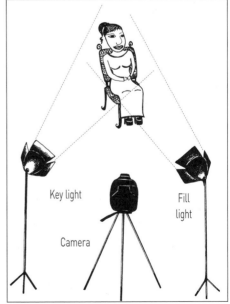

The fill light is positioned on the other side of the camera.

or diffusion material in front of it. You can also use an indirect light or soft light for the fill.

Note: Although spun is still used, it's not as popular anymore. There are better diffusion materials available now.

Back Light

The *back light* is placed to the rear of the performer. Sometimes, but not always, it's on the side opposite the key. Often it's 180 degrees opposite the camera position, but it varies a lot.

The job of the back light is to separate the image of the person from the background.

The back light can be a hard or soft source which should light just the top and side of the head and the top of the shoulders. Light shouldn't be set at so steep an angle as to spill onto the chest or knees of the person. Fresnel lights are often preferred because the barn doors enable you to better control any unwanted spill light—such as light causing a flare in the camera lens.

The intensity of the back light varies with the hair colour of the subject. Blonde hair is very reflective, so it needs a less intense back light. With fluffy, curly hair, the back light can be very glamorising indeed.

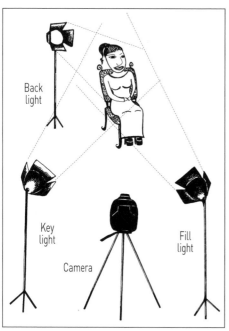

The back light separates the subject from the background.

The back light puts a glamorous halo of light on the hair and shoulders of the subject.

Background Light

The key, fill and back lights illuminate and model the subject with light, but you may also want that person to be situated in a visible background. For this purpose, you use a *background light*, or lights.

If all you want is for the background to be seen, it's sufficient to use one broad soft light placed so its throw of light misses the performer but does illuminate the curtain, flat or wall behind.

If your subject isn't in front of a wall-like backdrop, you can use two or more lights to highlight specific items at different distances away from the camera, giving your shot a sense of depth extending backwards.

Randolph Sellars, Director of Photography.

Sometimes a diagonal shadow thrown across the back wall works well. This can be coloured or white light.

Lighting a Group of People

If you have two or more people in your shot, you can give each person a key, fill and back light.

But too many lights flooding into a small area can cancel out each other's modelling effects.

Barn doors become very useful for restricting each light to striking only the person for whom it's intended. You can ensure that your light paths are distinct by lighting one person at a time and turning the house lights off to check that that person's light is going nowhere except on that one person.

Be aware of excess light spilling onto the floor. Light-coloured floors will bounce plenty of light, which may possibly muddle the effect you're striving for. On the other hand, light hitting the floor is sometimes a good thing; every situation has its own challenges and requirements.

Of course, many people have limited access to lights, and many studios have just a few. So you may have to arrange people in groups and then light each cluster.

For example, with five subjects you might have to use one key, fill and back light for one group of three, and another three-point set-up for the remaining group of two. This lighting won't win you prizes, but sometimes the bottom line is making everyone visible.

Or . . . with careful placement, and the use of a half scrim to vary the intensity of the light, you can have one light perform more than one function. For example, it can be the back light for one person and the key light for another.

When you're short on lights, you can use three-point lighting on small groups, rather than individuals.

You can use a half scrim to send a strong light to one person and a less intense light to the other.

Building Your Lighting Skills

A good way to grow your lighting skills is to find shots in movies that you really like, study the image carefully and then try to achieve the same effects yourself. This skill-building is good for days when you have a few hours to muck about in between projects.

Treat your little camera like a big camera. Do your lighting, sound and composition for a big camera and you'll be amazed what the little camera can give you.

Paul Sosso, Editor/ Producer.

Extensive trial and error doesn't work well on shooting days, though of course there's always some tweaking to do on every set.

Checking out cinematography magazines can help because they often show lighting set-ups from film scenes. It's a good aim that, for every new video you make, your lighting will be better.

Suggestions from Rachel Masters

1. Take an object or a person and light the image in different ways: key light, fill light, high angle, low angle, from under the chin . . . How does the lighting affect the way you regard the image? How does lighting affect the mood the audience feels? How many different moods can you create using just one light?
2. Keep a written log of places you visit: an indoor swimming pool, your parents' house, the football field. Observe the light carefully. How does the colour of the light change throughout the day? Does the quality of the light indicate the time of day? Does the light reveal textures of surfaces? Look at the shadows the light creates—are they long? Soft? Hard? Rippled? Do the shadows affect the scene?
3. What impressions does the light leave with you? How does it make you feel? Use the observations from your log to recreate similar moods and feelings in your video productions.

Suggested Resources

Harry Box, *The Set Lighting Technician's Handbook*, 3rd ed., Focal Press, St Louis, MO, 2003.
Blain Brown, *Motion Picture and Video Lighting*, 2nd ed., Focal Press, St Louis, MO, 2007.
Kris Malkiewicz and M. David Mullen, *Cinematography*, 3rd ed., Fireside, New York, 2005.
American Society of Cinematographers website: <www.theasc.com>.
Australian Cinematographers Society website: <www.cinematographer.org.au/home>.
Australian Film Television and Radio School Workshops: AFTRS website, <www.aftrs. edu.au>.

Thanks to Randolph Sellars for his assistance in the writing of this chapter.
<www.randolphsellars.com>

USING LIGHTING EQUIPMENT

17

There's a huge range of lighting equipment. Unfortunately, most of it is very expensive. *So* expensive that small production companies can find it more economical to rent lights for their shoots, rather than invest in buying them.

So it's no surprise that training courses usually have access to a very limited number of lights, sometimes only a kit of redheads.

Never mind. More isn't always better. With lights (as with other things in life), it's how you use what you've got that counts. Great productions are made by people who are using just the sun and some bounce cards.

Still, whatever lights you *can* get your hands on, you need to use them safely.

Safety with Lights

Lights are the one item in video that can kill you. They carry high levels of electrical current and become life-threatening if used improperly or if they're faulty. Safe practice with lights is essential. People should not use lights without knowing how to use them safely.

RCDs

RCDs (residual current devices)—also called life-saver power boards—prevent accidental injury or death from electrocution. They do this by detecting when electricity is altering its normal pathway and going to earth—for example, when it's taking a path through *you*. Then they instantly switch off the power flow.

In 1993 an Australian university student was nearly killed on a location shoot due to a faulty light. Now that university requires all portable lights to be used only with RCDs. Many of the lights have had their regular plugs replaced with special RCD plugs. Other lights are loaned out with separate RCD power boards in their kit.

Lights are heavy, hot and electrical—take care when using them! (Courtesy of Metro Screen)

Test button

Always use an RCD when you plug in lights, and be sure to test it before you turn the lights on.

Tony Mandl,
Gaffer, AFTRS.

It's important to use RCDs, but it *is* possible to electrocute yourself despite using one. So *always* unplug lights before changing bulbs.

At the beginning of each shoot, before relying on the RCD, you should give it a quick test to make sure that it's working right and will turn off in the event of trouble.

Students should pass a lighting proficiency test, which includes how to test and use RCDs, before they're allowed to borrow lights from the media equipment store.

Calculating the Electrical Load

Portable lights use high-powered lamps. *Redheads* typically have 800 watt bulbs, *blondies* usually have 2000 watt bulbs, other lights may require much more power.

The *six-light*, though each bulb takes only 650 watts, runs in paired circuits that total 1300 watts, and when all three pairs are connected, that lighting unit draws 3900 watts!

In Australia, normal household power circuits carry either 15 amps (older installations) or 16 amps (newer installations).

There's a simple mathematical formula to calculate how many lights you can plug into a circuit without blowing the fuse.

Amps (amount of current) × **Volts** (force driving the current) = **Watts** (power)

or: Amps × Volts = Watts

So a standard 15 amp circuit × 240 volts (household current in Australia) = 3600 watts

Or a standard 20 amp circuit × 120 volts (household current in the USA) = 2400 watts

(Older US houses sometimes still have 15 amp circuits; for them, the wattage is 1800 watts.)

The circuit will carry 3600 watts (USA: 2400 watts), but each circuit is likely to have more than one power point connected to it. Therefore, when each redhead carries an 800 watt bulb, you can plug three redhead lights into one circuit (in the USA, only two lights)—but only if *nothing* else is running off that circuit. (How likely is that?)

Since you can't always be sure what else is running off the entire circuit, it's a good idea to plug in fewer, rather than more, lights per circuit and always have an electrical extension cord with you to run to another circuit for powering additional lights.

The number of circuits available is the same as the number of fuses or circuit breakers marked *power* in the circuit-breaker box of the house.

Some household devices draw large amounts of electricity. For example, little electric space heaters really chew through the power. If you want to run a space heater on the same circuit with lights, be very careful not to overload the circuit capacity. On second thoughts, why not warm up by sitting under the lights?

Plugging In

A general rule of thumb:
1 kW = 4½ amps.

Ian Bosman,
Gaffer, AFTRS.

Most homes built in the last twenty years have at least four electrical circuits—at least two for power, which service the electrical outlets that you can plug things into, and two for lights, which run the fixed lights in the ceilings.

Some fuse-boxes have a circuit map that tells you which power points go with which circuit, but if this isn't available, you can work out which goes to which by using this simple method:

1. Go to the circuit breaker box or fuse-box and turn off the main switch.
   But *before you do this, ask for permission.* Turning off the main power supply can wreak havoc with anything that's got an electronic timer in it, like the microwave, the DVD player or the clock radio, unless they have backup batteries for power outages.
2. Remove a fuse (or flip the circuit breaker) from a position labelled *power.*
3. Turn the main power switch back on.
4. Take a small desk lamp and plug it into each power point in the area where you'll be working.
   If the light turns on, label the power point 'A' (using a marker and masking tape).
   If the light doesn't turn on, label the power point 'B'.
5. Once you've done all the power points in the relevant area, return to the fuse-box and turn the main power switch off again.
6. Replace the fuse you removed or flip the circuit breaker back on.
7. Turn the main power switch back on again.

On				
Main switch	Power 15 amps	Power 15 amps	Lights 10 amps	Lights 10 amps

Congratulations! You now know which power point goes to each of the two power circuits, so you should be able to plug your lights in sensibly, without blowing any fuses or circuit breakers, and begin your shoot with at least one thing going right.

If you do blow a fuse or circuit breaker, re-check your plug-in arrangement to see whether you've mistakenly overloaded it, and look for any hidden electrical load running on that circuit. Refrigerator? Freezer? Sometimes you can get permission to unplug things; sometimes you can't. Try to adjust the load and your lights so the circuit will work.

If you temporarily unplug a location's refrigerator for power or sound-recording purposes, it's bad form to forget to turn it back on before leaving. To avoid paying for replacing food, it's a good idea to leave one's car keys in the refrigerator. That way, one can't drive away without being reminded!

Randolph Sellars,
Director of Photography.

Then rewire the fuse with the correct-strength fuse wire. If it blows a second time, assume there's an electrical fault somewhere. It could be your lights or it could be the house wiring. Call off the shoot until a certified electrician can check the lights and the location and fix the problem.

The globe comes wrapped in foam and paper.

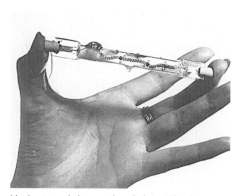

It's okay to touch the ceramic ends, but not the glass.

Handle the globe with the tissue paper still wrapped around it.

Replacing the Globes

1. Always *turn off* and *unplug* a light before you attempt to change the globe!
2. Tota light globes are cylindrical glass envelopes which are held tight in the lamp housing between two ceramic end pieces in a spring-loaded system. In order to remove the spent globe, pry one of the ceramic ends aside and gently lift the globe out. Never just grasp the light and yank, as it will shatter in your hand. Often the springs are very tight and it takes some effort to get the ceramic end to move.
3. Never touch the glass of the new globe with your fingers. Everyone has traces of oil on their skin which can cause the globe to superheat and explode. So leave the paper wrapper around the new globe, then pry aside the end ceramic piece in the light fixture again (it's okay to touch the ceramic ends with your fingers) and put one end of the globe into the other end of the lamp socket, align the globe so it will be in the right place to be connected to the end you've opened, and ease the ceramic end back so it grasps the globe securely. Give the globe a little wiggle to make sure it's correctly positioned. Then pull off the paper wrapper and the light is ready to be used.

Follow a similar handling procedure with all other types of video light globes.

Danger from Water and Other Liquids

Water and electricity don't safely mix. *Never* run light cables through wet areas or puddles. Don't have any watery effects happening near them. Don't set coffee cups and drink containers on the ground near power boards, where they might get knocked over and spilled.

And watch that you don't set up a light beneath an emergency sprinkler system in a ceiling. The heat rising from the very hot light can cause the sprinkler system to go off.

Danger from Heat

Lights are also dangerous because of the very high heat they generate. People adjusting barn doors on lights that are lit should wear thick leather work gloves, or use some thick insulated cloth, to protect their hands from being burnt.

Lights put too close to other items on the set can bubble paintwork, singe woodwork, melt polystyrene, crack glass, and set fire to papers and drapes.

When working with hot lights, it's a good idea to carry a small pair of needle-nose pliers in addition to leather work gloves. The pliers are a handy way to remove hot scrims without burning your fingertips. At a pinch, you can quickly make a 'scrim puller' from a spring type clothes peg. Carefully disassemble and remove the spring. Reverse the wooden legs and reassemble with the tapered legs held tight together by the spring. The tapered legs now look and open like a croc's jaw when squeezed by the 'new legs' formed from the original clothes peg mouth. Happy scrim hunting!

Randolph Sellars, Director of Photography.

Danger from Falling

Lights are also heavy and can be quite top-heavy if they're on spindly stands. If someone trips over them and they fall, a series of results can occur, from people being hurt and set items being damaged to fires starting.

Types of Portable Lights

A Fresnel lamp head has a thick glass lens on its front.

REDHEADS

These are commonly used portable lights. They come in kits of three lights with stands. They use 800 watt globes, which are mounted in a curved reflector. They have attachable barn doors and hooks for securing scrims. Their globes are movable between spot and flood positions.

Some redheads (including Arris) are made from a heat-resistant fibre, so they don't get as hot as metal light fixtures.

FRESNELS

These are lensed lights which can be adjusted between spot and flood. They come in several sizes including 750W–1 kW Babies, 2 kW Juniors, 5 kW Seniors and 10 kW Teners.

Fresnels are good as key lights because they produce a hard light that is easier to shape than the beams from some other light types.

You swing the lens to the side to replace the globe.

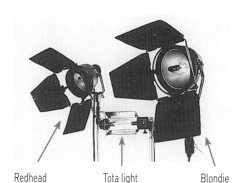

Redhead   Tota light   Blondie

BLONDIES

These are much bigger than redheads and come two to a kit. They use 2000 watt globes mounted in large hemispherical reflectors. They also have barn doors and their globes can be set anywhere between the spot and flood positions.

Blondies (and redheads) are called 'open-faced' lights because they don't have a lens at their front. Their light beam is strong, but not so 'clean' because their reflectors cause multiple-edged shadows. You get more foot candles out of them, but not a clean-edged shadow.

TOTA LIGHTS

These are very lightweight portable lights that come in kits of three or four. They take globes of a variety of wattages (300–800W) and are good for raising the general light level.

A reflector umbrella is a handy way to bounce light and soften it. (Courtesy of Metro Screen)

Tota globes are fixed in one position, so you can't spot or flood them, and they have minuscule barn doors.

They come with reflector umbrellas for softening light.

They're easier to carry than most other portable lights.

HMIs

These are arc lamps that give out an enormous amount of light for their size. Large ones (4–12 kW) can be used to illuminate broad areas. The light they give off is the colour temperature of sunlight, so they're used for providing cloud-free 'sun' for a shot or augmenting the available sunlight.

HMIs are expensive and heavy.

They can damage the eyes because of the UV light they give off, but they come with a glass UV filter for safety.

Small units are often used by news teams. Larger units are usually rented and come with a gaffer and a lighting truck.

Safety tip: HMIs use a ballast (transformer) to increase the voltage to the light. For this reason, extra caution should be exercised when setting up and powering an HMI. Connect the head feeder cable to the light and the ballast first. Then it is safe to plug the ballast into the power source.

Randolph Sellars, Director of Photography.

HMIs come with a 'ballast', which is a transformer that steps up the voltage for striking the light and for running it. The old-fashioned ballast (referred to as a magnetic ballast) has lots of copper wire—and is therefore very heavy. The newer ballasts are solid state and are lighter.

Randolph Sellars, Director of Photography.

Another significant difference is that magnetic ballasts put out a sine wave AC pattern—which means that there are limitations in the shutter angle and the frame rate that you can photograph with when using magnetic ballasts. Usually 24fps, 30fps and 60fps are 'safe' frame rates. But other frame rates (for instance 48fps) are not safe. Shooting at an 'unsafe' frame rate when using an HMI with a magnetic ballast will result in an image with visible light pulsing or strobing. There are published charts with safe frame rates and shutter angles when filming with HMIs with magnetic ballasts. The newer (and more expensive) solid-state ballasts put out a square wave. This enables one to shoot at any frame rate or shutter angle with HMI lights.

PAR LIGHTS (PARABOLIC LIGHTS)

A Par light is a sealed tungsten beam with a shiny silver reflector (like car head-lights). They come with various front lens patterns, ranging from narrow spot to wide beam.

Par lights give off an enormous amount of light and are efficient, but not control-lable. They're often used for night lighting on exterior shoots. Indoors, you can bounce them and they'll raise the overall illumination of a room considerably.

You can attach a lot of par lights to a sheet of plywood to make a super light source.

OTHER SMALL LIGHTS
Mole-Richardson Tweenie II Solarspot (300, 500, 650W)

This is a miniature Fresnel lamp, with a glass lens on the front and the ability to range between spot and flood. It's good for tiny sets or to add lighting details.

Sun Guns

Sun guns are strong portable lights that run off camera batteries or separate batteries. They give a harsh directional light and are used mostly by news crews. The light is a bit nasty and they chew through the juice, but they are better than nothing for a breaking night-time story.

Inkies

For a long time, inkies were the smallest Fresnel lights found on sets. At 200–250W, they can be used to slightly lift the light in a small area, as an eye light, or for any last minute touching up.

Dedo Lights (100W and 300W)

Dedo lights use a special lens that makes them very efficient for a low-wattage light. They give off little heat, which makes them safer and easy to handle. They give a concentrated, even beam of light for small areas. They're good as an accent light on an actor's face or on an important set item.

Richard Fitzpatrick, Camera Operator, Digital Dimensions.

Fluorescent technology's gone through the roof in the last few years. The new fluoros run cooler; the energy's in the light, not in the radiant heat.

This fixture, with banked fluoro tubes, maximises its impact by using mirrors on the inside of the barn doors.

These fluoro tubes are mirror-backed. With their wide reflector, they give a broad, soft light. (Courtesy of Teshome Tesema)

A Litepanels Ringlite Mini encircles your camera lens. (Courtesy of Litepanels)

'Obie' Light

This is a camera-mounted eye light which adds sparkle to the surface of the presenter's eye.

Fluorescent Lights

Fluorescent lights now come in colour-corrected tubes, without the green colour spikes that used to be in them. They come in 3200K tungsten balanced and 55–5600 daylight balanced. They have to be ordered from specialty suppliers and cost more than ordinary fluoros, but if you're doing a shoot in an office space, you can remove the normal fluorescent tubes and replace them with the colour-corrected ones for the duration of your recording session.

Flolight Bank Selectables

Flolight Bank Selectables are fluorescent light fixtures that come in units with two, four, six or eight lamps. You can select how many lamps to have on, depending on your needs. They give the brightness of 500W but each lamp is just 55W. They come in both tungsten and daylight colours and can be mounted on stands or on your camera. They have four-way barn doors, carrying handles and can be attached from below or on the side.

You can also get these light fixtures in dimmable banks.

Kinoflo's Diva-lite

Diva-lite 400 is a bank of soft lights with fluorescent tubes in pairs. They run cool and they're very slim, so you can safely put them right up against a wall, making it easier to get them out of the shot. They come with barn doors and a gel frame, and have a plastic shield for safety.

Diva-lites have a dimmer which can range from off to fully on without changing colour temperature. They can be either tungsten or daylight.

The universal model can be run anywhere in the world, on 100V AC to 240V AC.

LED Lights

For extreme lightweight portable use, the latest LED lights work well if you're working fairly close to your subject. They come as a rectangular array of tiny lights. They draw very little power and run on batteries.

There's an LED mic light that mounts as a circle of lights around your camera mic.

Coloured LED lights can also be used to put a distinct swathe of colour onto your subject. It's definitely worth having a few accent lights in addition to the back-breaking main light kits.

Sticky Pods

Sticky pods are small lights that can be attached with suction cups.

Litepanels

You can get the new LED soft light units (1 foot × 1 foot) which are 100 per cent dimmable, and work in both tungsten colour and daylight colour. They run cool, use little very power, and work on batteries, so no cords to run.

Litepanels Micro is a tiny camera-mounted LED soft light which runs on four AA batteries.

Litepanel Micro. (Courtesy of Litepanels)

Litepanel 1 ft x 1 ft stand-up LED lamp. (Courtesy of Litepanels)

Chinese Lanterns
Randolph Sellars, Director of Photography

Chinese paper lanterns (also called *China balls*) make a great low-cost lighting source that even professionals use.

They come in various sizes and put out a beautiful omni-directional soft light.

They are extremely lightweight, so they are easy to hang. They are often used just out of camera frame to simulate the light coming from a practical source such as a table lamp. They are also a great way to light a group of people sitting around a table. Just rig the light over the centre of the table as low as possible without entering the camera frame. Everyone will be lit with a soft source that 'wraps' nicely but still has modelling.

Since they are soft and omni-directional, they can be a little tricky to control. Use black wrap or black cloth around portions of the China ball to block spill from unwanted areas.

Because they are made from paper, some common-sense safety precautions must be applied. Make sure that the bulb hangs in the centre of the lamp away from the paper sides. Be aware of excess heat put out by higher-wattage bulbs. Use porcelain light sockets instead of plastic ones when using bulbs over 75W. With the smaller China balls, don't use any bulbs higher than 150W. The larger balls can handle up to 300W if they are well ventilated.

A Chinese lantern is used to light three people (third person missing) sitting around a breakfast table. Note the video camera position: barely visible to the right of the boy's head. The white card (on the left of frame) is adding fill light to the actor's faces by bouncing back spill light from the Chinese lantern. (Photographer: Kristin Zabawa; actors: Teresa Decher, Daniel Nelson; director: Randolph Sellars; producer: Sally Spaderna; audio mixer: Dave Scaringe)

A grip adjusts the placement angle of a Chinese lantern (China ball). The Chinese lantern is so lightweight it can be extended (*armed out*) at the end of a C-stand arm without collapsing. This would not be safe to do with any other portable light fixture. Note that the light and arm are still behind the plane of the actors for safety's sake. (Photographer: Kristin Zabawa; actor: Mercedes Rose; grip: Justin Ward; observer: Sally Spaderna)

Cheap Lights

If you can't get a light kit, or can't afford one, the hardware store can provide illumination at a very cheap price.

Workmen's lights from the hardware store can give a broad lift of illumination to an indoor setting, and they're very cheap. Some things to remember with them:

- They must NEVER be directed at people's eyes!!!
- They tend toward the red end of the spectrum.
- Their light stands are rather short.
- The light heads are heavy, so if you add an extension to their stand you have to stabilise them carefully.

You can also buy photo floods and scoop lights from the hardware store and gel them however you like.

Any light is better than no light. Work around whatever problems your lights give. Ray Listing lights the set for *The Meeting*.

More Information on Lights

- Arri <www.arri.de/lighting>
- Mole-Richardson Company <extranet.mole.com/public>
- Barbizon <www.barbizon.com/catalog>
- Kino Flo <www.kinoflo.com>
- Flolight (fluorescent and LED lighting) <www.prompterpeople.com>
- Litepanels <www.litepanels.com>

Additional Light-Control Equipment

There's other equipment to help you manage your lights.

Butterfly or Rag Kits

Rag kits are large sets of cloth material used to block, diffuse or reduce light on a subject. Due to their size, they are generally used outdoors. A standard set usually includes a solid black, a silk, a double net and a single net. They come in various sizes, but the most common are 6, 8 and 12 feet square. They are stretched and tied to collapsible aluminium frames which are mounted onto high stands.

The borders of the nets are colour coded for easy identification. Double nets are bordered by red and reduce light by one *f* stop. Single nets are green coded and reduce light by half an *f* stop.

Sometimes, large nets are set up outside windows (in view of the camera) to reduce the exposure of the background that the camera sees.

Chimera

A *chimera* or *soft box* is basically a black cloth box attached to a light that diffuses the light, but controls the excess spill light. The inside of the box is white or silver for extra reflection. The front of the box usually has velcro tabs for attaching various thicknesses of diffusion material. Sometimes there are extra attachments inside the box to add additional diffusion baffles. A soft box attaches to the light via a speed ring. You just take off the barn doors and slide the speed ring into the barn door holder.

Since soft light is not easy to control, *egg crates* or *grids* are a handy soft box accessory used to control the directionality of the soft light. *Egg crates* are black cloth grids with 1–2 inch square 'slots'. These slots confine the soft light straight ahead by eliminating most of the spread. These egg crates attach by velcro tabs to the front of the soft box.

You can get different egg crates depending on the desired angle spread of the light. Some are 90 degree angles and some are 60 degree angles.

Black Wrap

Black wrap is an opaque, flexible, cuttable, sturdy material which you can use to shape a light path. If you put black wrap over the front of a light, you can cut holes in it so light will fall only on specific patches in your scene—for example, just on someone's eyes.

Grips adjust black wrap (foil) on a daylight colour corrected fluorescent light. In this situation, black wrap is used to block unwanted spill light. (Photographer: Kristin Zabawa; grips: Sam Naiman, Justin Ward, Will Walle)

Pieces of black wrap (left foreground of frame) are being used to create shadows on the actor's legs, comic book and wall (not seen in this photo angle). Note the practical bedside lamp used to 'motivate' the actor's key light. (Photographer: Kristin Zabawa; director: Randolph Sellars; actor: Teresa Decher)

Lifting Heavy Light Kits

Another safety factor with the older light kits is their weight. A kit with three redheads or two blondies in it is very heavy.

You could very easily do your back in if you're not careful when you're lifting light kits.

Working with a Partner

The big kits come with three handles: one on each end and a third one on the top. The extra handles mean that the kit is very heavy and can be more easily (and sensibly) carried by two people.

There's no need to feel that sharing the load is an assault on your physical prowess—whether you're male or female. The alternative could be that you pull a back muscle and are immobilised for the rest of the shoot. Then you're close to useless as a crew member that day. Which is worse?

Solo Lifting

If you're lifting a kit by yourself, never bend over and pick it up by straightening your back. That's how the damage is likely to be done. It puts far too much strain on the muscles of your lower back.

The way to lift the kit is to:

1. Stand beside it, with your side to the kit.
2. Bend your knees until you're low enough to grasp the handle.
3. Lift the kit by straightening your legs—that way, the lifting is done by your leg muscles.

Once you've lifted the kit, the walking isn't too bad, as long as you're not going far. If you are, try to get an equipment trolley.

Never this way!

In and Out of Cars

If you lift the kit up and put it on the outer ledge of your car boot, then you and another person can gently manoeuvre it down into the boot. That works pretty well.

The trick comes when you have to get the kit back out of the boot. Don't do it alone!

If you're leaning way forward and then trying to lift, you're putting your back at great risk. Retrieving a light kit from a boot is never an easy job, but two people can manage this job better than one.

The best way to transport light kits is in a truck or station wagon, so you can lift the kit up to the tailgate and then just

Do this. Sally Don, Roseville College, during work experience at AFTRS.

slide it forward. Unloading isn't a problem—just slide it to the edge again, get a good grip and lift it down to the pavement or the waiting equipment trolley.

Setting Up Portable Lights

Portable light stands are similar to tripods—in fact, their base legs open out to form a tripod.

Like a tripod, they're stored and transported in a collapsed form, and then are opened up when it's time to use them.

How do you open them up? Just like a tripod. Wherever you find a release mechanism, that's where the pole opens up, so the stand becomes taller and taller and taller.

Unlike the tripod, you don't have to adjust the length of each leg separately.

Tighten as You Extend

For each length of the telescoping pole that you pull out, retighten its knob firmly. Though the pole may stand up fine on its own with just a slight tightening, once you attach the heavy light head, one of the pole sections can lose its grip and collapse down into a lower tube. This impact can cause the globe to break. If this happens mid-shoot, it's not great for lighting continuity or the tranquillity of the performers.

Of course, you need to bring an extra globe along, in any case, because these expensive globes can die a natural death at any time.

Watch the Spread of the Legs

The legs on the light stand have a surprising opening action. When you pull them out, they go wider and wider, and then, as you continue to pull them, their bottom ends move inward towards the pole again. So midway open is the widest and most stable position to use them in. If you open them all the way, the base of the stand will have become too narrow for you to put a heavy light way up there and have much (justifiable) confidence in the system.

Be sure to tighten the knob at the bottom of the stand between the legs. That will prevent the stand slowly collapsing down between its legs.

Securing the Light Head

At the base of the light head is a hollow tubular section which slips over the top of the light stand pole. There's a wing nut at the side of this section of the light head, and you screw it in until the pressure against the light stand pole is sufficient to hold the light head securely.

There's only one trick to it. If you don't *unscrew* the wing nut far enough out to start with, the light head's progress down onto the pole will be obstructed by the tip of the bolt, which is meant to squeeze it in place. So the light head will be just resting precariously on the top of the pole, and when you then twist the wing nut to tighten down the bolt it won't really be tightening anything.

The light head has to descend down onto the pole by several centimetres (a couple of inches). If it doesn't, check to see what's wrong.

Stabilising Light Stands

It's a funny thing about portable light stand legs. People just don't see them. Somehow the light head at the top is all their brains register.

Maybe it's because the stands are slim, and they're an unobtrusive silver-grey or black. Yet even the ones with their bottom tripod legs painted red, as a warning, seem to escape the notice of enthusiastic assistants.

People see you putting up lights and they're overcome with the urge to rush over to you (maybe to offer help). Next thing you know, they catch a foot under one of the three outward-slanting base legs and whammo! Either the person or the light—or both—is on the ground.

So you always set the lights up so people won't trip. It's a good strategy to tuck the jutting tripod legs out of people's way. In an auditorium setting, you can get two of the three legs under a row of seats. If you place a rubbish bin next to the third leg, you've effectively protected the no-walk area.

Another way to secure a light stand is to put a sandbag over the horizontal support brace of one of its tripod legs. If the sandbag doesn't fit over the support brace, then fold it over the outside of one of the light stand legs.

Sandbags do a good job, and it's easy enough to use them at the studio, but they're quite heavy to carry around on a location shoot. An alternative is to use waterfilled 'sandbags', which are special sturdy bladders that you can fill once you get to the location and empty before you repack to go home. (Do NOT use the flimsy bladders from wine casks! Water on the set is a grievous danger.)

If you have to walk away from a light stand before you've got it secured, ask someone to help you by standing next to it and holding onto the upright pole. Other people will see the person, skirt around him or her, and not knock it over.

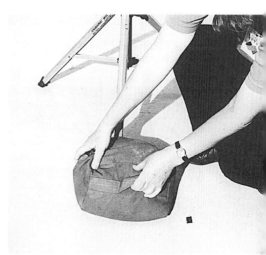

You can secure light stands with sandbags or tough water-filled bladders.

Gaffing Down the Cables

Another hazard with lights is their cables. People can trip over them easily, because you're usually forced to run cables across some portion of the floor area to plug them in.

First of all, you should do your lighting set-up long before non-crew people arrive—like the audience and guests. In general, you should allow at least an hour to set up lights, and they should be fully set up an hour before shooting time.

You can use a person of similar height to sit in for the performer, so you can work out the placement of the light stands and the general throw of the light. Once you're sure where the lights need to be, you should tape down all the cables thoroughly with gaffer tape (that broad, expensive, silver, black or white tape, which is similar to duct tape. Duct tape has a shiny metallic finish and can be used in a pinch, but real gaffer tape holds better.)

Before you tape them, make sure that each cable is hanging straight down the light stand, and run through the legs at the bottom; then run the cord in a short straight path to the electrical outlet. With this cable arrangement, if there's a tug on the cord, the light stand will slide along the floor rather than topple over.

Make sure you leave enough slack in the cable by the stand so you can extend the light to its full height, and so you can adjust the placement of the light head slightly later on.

An accidental tug on the cable wrapped this way won't make the light fall; the stand will just slide towards the tug.

It's good if you can run the electrical cable under a row of seats or some other furniture so people's feet won't be likely to make contact with it. Most of all, never pull the cord outward from the light and through the air, effectively cordoning off a section of the room. That's a real trap for someone.

With your lighting set-up basically placed and aimed, you can use the last hour, while others fuss with the camera and mics, to ensure the lights are giving you just the right effect. Then you can do the final tweaking once your performer is able to be seated.

A room with portable lights on is very bright. If people come in and get seated in a dimmer environment and then you put the lights on, some of them will kick and complain. If you have your lights already on when people arrive, they'll accept the brightness as 'What is, is.' So have the room ready and lit before the audience arrives.

Controlling the Light

Three aspects of light that you'll need to control are its intensity, spread and quality.

Controlling Light Intensity

The *intensity* of the lights can be controlled by moving them away from the subject, or closer to it.

In practice, if you double the distance the light is away from the subject, you cut down to one quarter the intensity of the light. This is known as the *inverse square law*.

For example: If, as the starting point, your distance from the light to the subject equals 1, and the intensity of the light at that distance equals 1, then if the distance between them becomes 2, the intensity is inverted (to half) and squared (to one quarter).

So by doubling the distance, you quarter the intensity of the light.

If you're not into calculating, just remember that moving a light away from the subject diminishes its intensity very effectively.

SCRIMS

Another way to control the intensity of the light is to add a *scrim* to the front of it. A scrim is wire mesh, mounted in a metal frame to hold it straight.

Portable lights are made with hooks or *ears* at the front to hold the barn doors in place. Scrims are inserted in the ears, inside the barn doors, closest to the light.

Scrims come in two densities that affect the intensity of light. They are colour coded on the rim for easy identification. A *double scrim* (red), reduces the light by one stop. A *single scrim* (green), reduces the light by half a stop.

Scrims won't change the light quality: you'll still have a hard light with a hard shadow.

A half scrim (a rim with a half circle of wire mesh) helps if you want to have one half of the light's beam stronger than the other half. A half scrim can be rotated in the ears to any desired position.

The wire scrim keeps shattering glass from flying out and it helps reduce the intensity of the light. (Courtesy of Film & TV, Central TAFE, Perth, WA)

Ordinary fibreglass insect screen mesh makes an efficient scrim. (Disregard slight smoking when new.)

Ian Bosman,
Gaffer, AFTRS.

C-STANDS

A C-stand (short for *century stand*) is a sturdy stand with tripod legs to which you can attach a marvellous range of things.

NETS

A first cousin to wire scrims are *nets*. Nets consist of black bobbinet material stretched and secured on open-ended metal frames. They come in various shapes and sizes and have a metal stem to clasp in a C-stand. Like scrims, their function is to reduce

Jolean Dilorenzo adjusts the barn doors to control the flow of light, TEAME Indigenous TV and Video Training Course, Metro Screen.

Tristian Spillman sets a black flag for interview session, Portland Community College, Portland, Oregon.

light intensity without affecting the light quality (without softening it). Nets also come in double (one stop) and single (half stop) densities, and are colour coded red and green respectively. Nets are more precise than scrims because they can be set with C-stands at various angles and distances from the light to finetune and 'shape' light.

Example: Say you have to light someone who's unfortunately wearing a white shirt. A net could be used to selectively lower light intensity falling on the shirt only.

Controlling the Light Spread

BARN DOORS

Barn doors are hinged plates that usually come attached to a circular ring in sets of four: two rectangles and two trapezoids. They attach to *ears* on the front of light heads. By moving the doors in and out, you can control the spread of the light beam. You can narrow it down or block it off at the top, bottom and sides.

People are often puzzled about how to orient them and ask, 'Which way do they go?' It doesn't matter—do what works for your situation.

BLACK FLAG OR CUTTER

In addition to using barn doors on a light to control the light spread, you can selectively block light from parts of your set by using a *flag* (also called a *cutter* or *blade*). These are metal frames covered with flat black cloth material. They come in various shapes and sizes and have a metal stem to clasp in a C-stand. They are more precise than barn doors because they can be set at various angles and distances from a light source to create finetuned shadows.

For example, you may have an element in your set which is highly reflective, but you don't want to remove it—perhaps a prism paperweight on the executive's desk. Or you may need a dark area next to a bright one, to accentuate a part of the image. In the absence of a proper flag, pieces of cardboard, or polystyrene, or almost

Randolph Sellars, Director of Photography.

When using flags and nets to finetune shadows and for light reduction, it's important to keep in mind distance from the light source. The further away from the light source a flag or net is placed, the sharper the shadow or light *cut*. The closer to the light source, the softer the shadow or light gradation. When controlling soft light, it is often necessary to place the flag or net a few feet from the light source in order to get any definition in the *cut*. When hanging diffusion in front of a light, think of the diffusion as the new light source. Therefore, always set the flag or net in front of the diffusion towards the subject or set area—not between the diffusion and the actual light.

anything else at hand, can be used to block the path of light, and thus control your image. But watch the heat!

Larger flags are often found in the studio for cutting larger light sources.

Changing the Quality of Light

You can soften the quality and the intensity of a light by putting diffusion material in front of it.

There's a gel-like material that is white and *translucent* (which means the light can go through it, but you can't see through it). It's called *white diffusion* and comes in various densities. It is heat resistant and can be attached to the barn doors using *wooden* clothes pegs. (Plastic ones would melt.)

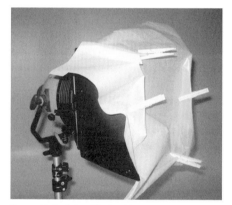 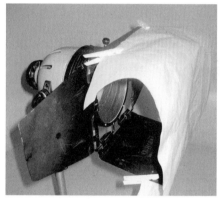

You could attach the diffusion this way . . .

. . . but this would give you more flexibility.
(Courtesy of Film & TV, Central TAFE, Perth, WA)

In the old days, the only diffusion material available was sheets of spun glass (fibreglass). Unfortunately, glass fibres tend to embed in skin. Nowadays there's a safer alternative called *tough spun,* for those who prefer the 'look' of spun glass.

As well as softening, diffusion material and tough spun will warm up the light's colour slightly.

Setting up filters on redhead lights can be a messy affair. Pinning the filters with wooden pegs to the back of the barn doors at the top and bottom allows you to adjust the side doors or slip the filters forward to get more coverage.

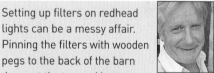

Graeme MacLeod, Film & TV, Central TAFE, Perth, WA.

Diffusion can also be hung well in front of a light by attaching it to a frame and positioning the frame with a C-stand.

A reflective umbrella, with its metallic inner side, is another way to convert a hard light into a softer, indirect light. You shine your light towards the inside of the umbrella, and have it angled so the broad reflection of light bounces back onto your subject.

Studio Lights

Studio lights tend to be bigger and more powerful than portable lights. They're less transportable. They're mounted on heavy stands, often on wheels so they can be shifted around with ease, or they're attached to a lighting grid overhead.

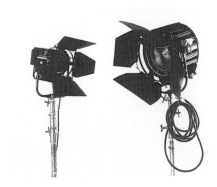

2 kW Fresnel and 5 kW Fresnel.

Lighting Grids

Some basic grids are an arrangement of fixed poles. In order to move lights around, you have to get up there on a ladder, undo them and reattach them somewhere else.

Better grids allow the light-bearing poles to be moved forwards and backwards on tracks, and they have some diagonal movement as well.

Really great grids are computer controlled and have motor-driven batons which will lower the lights down so the globes can be changed from floor level.

Safety Chains

No matter what type of lighting grid you have, every single light which is attached to it must also be attached by a safety chain.

Lights are very heavy; it's easy for one to slip out of the grip of someone who's trying to detach it, or move it to another spot, or reattach it.

And a poorly attached light might lose its grip with no warning.

A falling light could easily crack the skull of someone down below.

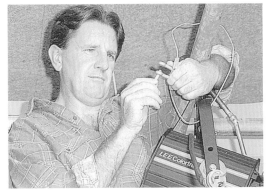

Whenever moving lights, undo the safety chain last, and do it up again first at the new position. Then if the heavy light slips from your grasp, it doesn't drop. Joe Conway, School of Indigenous Australian Studies, James Cook University.

A falling light once missed my head by a few centimetres when I was the guest on a cable TV show. I was sitting in my on-set chair going over my notes while people were still adjusting the lights around me. Suddenly the back light slipped out of the hands of the gaffer up on the ladder, and it came crashing down by my ear. There were no safety chains in that studio. Needless to say, I'm convinced of their value!

Martha Mollison, Video Producer.

Adjusting the Lights

Sometimes grid-mounted lights can be adjusted from floor level using a long pole. The pole has a little hook on the end of it which slips over a thin metal bar inside each large colour-coded adjustment knob on the sides of the light fixture. One knob is for tilting the light, one is for panning it, one is for focus (spot or flood), and one is for turning the power off and on.

Changing Globes

Usually the lights are wired up so their power can be turned on from switches down below at the lighting patch bay. Still, you'd always turn the power off at the light *and* unplug the light if you were going to change the globe.

Who knows—once you're up on the ladder, with your hand in the light, someone else might come along and start flipping switches at the lighting controls below, quite unmindful of your predicament.

Of course, you'd use the same procedure as changing the globes of portable lights.

Never touch the globe with your fingers—always handle it in its tissue wrapper.

Some facilities only allow the technical staff to change the globes of the grid-mounted lights.

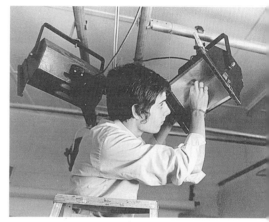

Change the globe on the light after you turn it off. Bryan Mason, Hamilton Secondary College.

Moving the Lights

Because lights are so heavy and difficult to move, studios usually have them set on the grid in an arrangement which suits their major usage patterns.

It's best to think carefully about how you can use the pattern that's there before you launch into undoing the lights and rearranging them.

Sometimes you can get that one additional key light you need by setting up a redhead on a floor stand, rather than pinching lights from the back area of the lighting grid.

On the other hand, sometimes you really do need to do a major rearrangement. You should have helpers to do this.

Some people don't like being up ladders. It's possible to get a ladder-type structure that has a secure standing platform on the top of it, with a surrounding guard rail. If a studio has one of

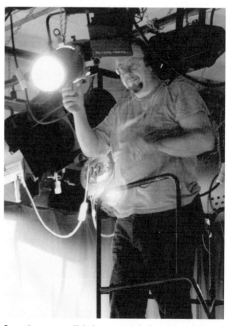

Sometimes a spot light is operated during a show, but often it's set for the rehearsed position and turned on and off as needed. (Courtesy of Portland Community Media)

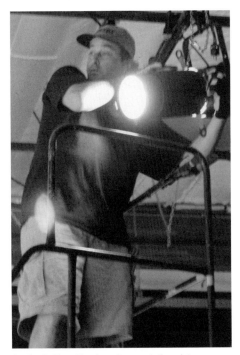

A safety ladder with a fenced upper platform lets more people learn to adjust and move the lights. (Courtesy of Portland Community Media)

Randolph Sellars, Director of Photography.

It's best to use wooden or fibreglass ladders in the studio or on location because they are less conductive of electricity than metal ladders.

these it lets more people learn about lighting and contribute to it.

When removing a light from a grid, it's a good idea to have a person waiting at the bottom of the ladder to grab the light from you, so you can descend safely yourself. Just make sure they're *never* standing beneath the light, in case you lose your grip on it!

When you disconnect the light from the grid, detach the main connection first, always leaving the safety chain attached until you're certain you can manage the weight of the light. When you're reattaching the light, reattach the safety chain first.

Types of Studio Lights

SOFT LIGHTS

These are large lights which use multiple (two to eight) 1000W globes. The globes are mounted facing giant scoop-shaped reflectors. Usually, there are separate switches for controlling each globe.

They're good for lifting the general light level, for illuminating the background curtain or set, and for providing a soft light over a wide area. As with other soft lights, you can't spot or flood them.

FRESNELS

These were mentioned under portable lights, but are also used in the studio.

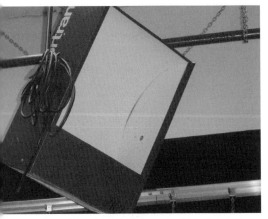

Soft lights on the grid can be used to lift the illumination of a big area of the studio floor.

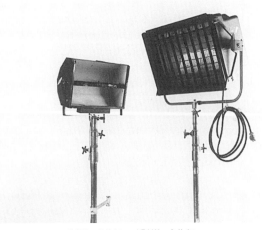

2 kW soft light and 5 kW soft light.

FOLLOW SPOTS

These are hard light sources that provide a bright circle of light. They're used in stage and variety show performances, especially for following guest entrances, and individual dancers and singers as they move around the set.

COLOUR-BALANCED FLUORESCENT LIGHTS

You can lift the overall light level on the set with a soft, virtually shadowless light from banks of colour-balanced fluorescent lights. More direct lights are then used to highlight the subjects.

Fluorescent banks generate much less heat and consume considerably less energy than tungsten soft lights. They don't project their light very far, though.

Spot light

Always use gloves with a hot light.

More Lighting-Control Gadgetry

Graeme MacLeod, Film & TV, Central TAFE, Perth.

SNOOT

A circular attachment that narrows the light beam for a spot light effect. Used in place of barn doors.

GOBO (OR CUCALORIS, OR COOKIE)

A cut-out stencil which can be used in front of a light to cast a desired shadow pattern, like venetian blinds and tree branches. The traditional cucaloris has a random pattern that looks like rounded leaves or clouds.

It can also be a cut metal stencil, inserted between the globe and lens of a pattern spot.

A C-stand can hold a cutter or black flag to shield an area on the set from direct light. Vicki Lucan and Ken Crouch, AFTRS.

DINGLE

Generally, a leafy branch placed in front of a light to give a broken pattern on an otherwise flat surface.

DIMMERS

Controls that allow lights to be gradually faded from full-on to full-off, or anywhere in between. Lights can be assigned to dimmers so they'll fade singly or in groups.

Make sure you cut your filters to the wider extension of the barn doors; cutting them too small wastes a filter.

Graeme MacLeod, Film & TV, Central TAFE, Perth, WA.

GELS

Special coloured transparent sheets that can be placed in front of lights to change their colour or their colour temperature. Unlike normal plastic, they won't melt or burn from light heat—unless they're placed too close to the face of a hot lamp such as a blondie or redhead, or large Fresnel lights such as a 5 kW or above. When necessary, gels mounted in round metal gel rings (placed in the ears inside the barn door) can usually handle the heat of smaller Fresnel lights (2 kW and below). When in doubt, it's best to clip gels onto the outside of barn doors.

Gels let you colour the light. Sarah Moore from Roseville College, during work experience at AFTRS.

Thanks to Randolph Sellars for his help with this chapter.

PRODUCTION OPTIONS

When you're developing the idea for a project, there are some key questions to answer right at the start:

1. Is it a live event that will have to be shot from beginning to end in one go?
2. Or will you have the time and space to do rehearsals with the crew and be able to shoot retakes as necessary?
3. What sort of equipment will you be able to use?
   (a) One camera only?
   (b) Three single cameras on location?
   (c) An outside broadcast van?
   (d) A studio?
4. Will you have the time or equipment to edit the program?
5. Or will you have to do it all with in-camera editing?

> Take a chance and shoot for the moon, because a magnificent failure is better than a conservative success. Risk-taking in a supportive environment is an essential element in learning and, within a course, process is more important than end result.
>
> **Francis Treacey**, Deakin University.

Maybe at first you won't know which method to choose. Each of these production options has its advantages and disadvantages. You have to decide both what you can afford and what you can live with.

The Greys, a production by the Queensland School of Film and Television.

Single Camera—In-camera Edited

Advantages

1. Low cost.
2. Small equipment load.
3. Small crew.
4. Easy to move crew to site and back.
5. Crew can maintain a low profile at the site and have less impact on the people at the location.
6. At the end of the shoot, the program is complete.
7. The program can be shown immediately to the people in it.
8. The program is made of first-generation video (if you're using videotape).
9. The program can be duplicated as is.
10. Copies can be made either at the site or soon.

Check all camera operations carefully before you begin.
Deidre Brannick and Wojciech Marchut on set for *Witchery*.

Disadvantages

1. All shots must be done in the script sequence, regardless of how awkward that is.
2. Shots must be done quickly to keep the camera from going into stop mode and causing a glitch at a shot-change point.
3. Every shot must be done correctly the first time, because to redo a shot eats into the frames at the end of the previous shot.
4. Late ideas are hard to incorporate into a partly shot program.

Single Camera—Postproduced

Advantages

1. Shots can be taken from a variety of camera angles, if there's enough time.
2. Shots can be taken in any order.
3. Last-minute ideas and unexpected shots can be incorporated into the production.
4. Low cost.
5. Small equipment load.
6. Small crew.
7. Easy to move crew to site and back.
8. Crew can maintain a low profile at the site and have less impact on the people at the location.
9. Program can be edited into any shot order, and in a variety of ways.
10. Rough cuts can be shown to advisers for helpful suggestions.
11. Music can be added later.

12. Voiceover can be added later.
13. Titles and graphics can be added later.
14. Field material can be used again for a number of other projects.

Disadvantages

1. Continuity from shot to shot has to be carefully watched. Continuity person needed for this.
2. Lots of cutaways needed to avoid jump cuts in edited footage.
3. All footage must be logged.
4. Editing the project requires a major work commitment after the shoot.
5. Editing equipment can be expensive.
6. Project takes considerable amount of time to complete.

Rebecca Gerendasy surveys footage potential at the Monterey Bay Aquarium.

What you shoot today may be used again in another program, tav productions. (Photo by Neil Smith)

Multi-camera Studio— Live Switching

Advantages

1. Good space for rehearsals.
2. Good technical conditions for producing the program.
3. Access to a range of equipment, including titling.
4. Use of lighting grid.
5. Good sound-mixing capacity, including roll-ins of music and sound effects.
6. Help from the studio's technical director.
7. Constant choice of shots, which are all viewable by the director.
8. All action can be covered from several angles at once—no continuity concerns arising from doing the same action several times for a repositioned camera.
9. Live audience possible—good to inspire better performance and to provide visual and audio reactions.
10. Possibility of getting questions and comments from the live audience.
11. At the end of the shoot, the program is complete.
12. No postproduction time or costs.

John Budzyna, Executive Director of the Arlington Center for the Arts, interviews schoolchildren who were winners of a local art competition. ACA-TV (Courtesy of Arlington Community Media Inc. [ACMi])

During a production of *Dead Air Live*, right to left: Tim Macklin, Mahera Omar, Rachel Eisengart, director Craig Bouchard and Charlie Tesch, technical adviser. Somerville Producers Group.

Treat your crew well! Even if you are paying them, let them know that you appreciate their hard work and dedication to your project.

Judi Kelemen, Producer/Trainer.

Red Shepherd, a multi-camera drama, is shot on *The Canyon* set, Griffith University.

Disadvantages

1. High cost for studio and equipment.
2. Time limits on studio bookings for both rehearsals and the shoot.
3. Large crew needed.
4. Crew needs to be trained ahead of time.
5. Any mistakes made during the shoot (by performers, camera operators, switcher, sound) are in the final product.
6. Good shots may not get selected and are lost.
7. Needs of live audience have to be attended to.

Multi-camera OB Van—Live Switching

Advantages

1. Ability to get to an outside location, even a remote location.
2. Action can be covered from several angles simultaneously—especially good for sports, races, concerts, parades and other live one-off events.
3. Constant choice of shots, which are all viewable by the director.
4. High public visibility for the production and the production crew.
5. The program is complete at the end of the shoot.
6. No postproduction time or costs.

Disadvantages

1. Large amount of equipment to deal with.
2. Lengthy and complicated set-up.
3. High cost for van and equipment.
5. Crew needs to be well trained.
6. Transportation requirements for large crew.
7. Rehearsal time may be limited to the same day as the shoot.
8. Rain or snow can make set-ups difficult and unpleasant.
9. Good shots may not get selected and are lost.

Multi-camera—Postproduced

Advantages

1. Cameras at several angles simultaneously.
2. All shots are captured, so everything is available for use in the final edit.
3. Continuity problems eliminated from action shots.
4. If one camera has problems, all the other cameras' shots are still recorded.
5. Program doesn't rely on the skill of the switcher.

Disadvantages

1. High cost of equipment.
2. Large number of tapes needed.
3. Large crew required.
4. If cameras aren't linked, they may not match in white balance or other signal qualities.
5. Huge amount of footage to be logged.
6. Lengthy and expensive editing.

For series productions, keep a master planning sheet to keep track of your guests, your crew, your B-roll, editing schedules, equipment reservations, transportation, food, etc.

Judi Kelemen, Producer/ Trainer.

Composite Shows

A drama skit being recorded at Methuen High School, Methuen, Massachusetts.

It's also possible to have a show which combines several of the production methods mentioned above. A live magazine-style show can include loosely scripted talk segments recorded live in the studio, pre-recorded on-the-street interviews rolled into the show, rehearsed song or dance performances, pre-edited segments and unrehearsed last-minute live segments.

A show like this needs an exact script order and predetermined time allotments for each segment. The director's assistant will be very busy on this type of production, keeping track of the rundown and carefully timing each piece to make sure there are no time overruns and everything fits into the program's timeslot.

Make the stopwatch your friend.

Sandra Chung, ABC TV Training and Development.

Real-time Productions

When a program is being recorded in just one take, it requires careful planning and a crew with excellent technical skills. There's no second chance.

Some live productions, like orchestral concerts and stage productions, allow for rehearsals. It would be madness to plan to shoot such an event without attending

Thanks to alert media teacher Claire Beach, these ninth graders from Aki Kurose Middle School Academy were among the few local journalists credentialled, through the World Trade Organization in Geneva, to cover the WTO meeting in Seattle.

rehearsals to give yourself a good idea of how things will go.

Usually you can get a copy of the program or script. Sometimes you can get permission to have your crew practise their camera work at a rehearsal. Occasionally, you can get permission to record a dress rehearsal. These shots may save you in the edit the following week!

Other live events, like the visit of an important person, allow for no rehearsals. You should make sure you find out everything you can about the planned schedule for the person, and work out the best places to put your cameras.

You may have to figure on the presence of a large crowd.

Don't forget that your crew may need special passes to get into the action areas, and they may have to get the equipment there very early before streets get cordoned off to vehicles.

Carl Fisher,
Muriimage
Community
Video and Film
Service.

The skills you bring with you—memory, sight, hearing, perspective—are exploited by media technology to communicate your message. As a video producer, how you use them can be good, bad or indifferent. It's up to you.

Production Types

There are many standard types of production. Of course, you may be one of those creative people who develops a new form!

But you could cut your teeth on some of the following well-known formats.

Ben Kreusser,
Producer.

The more you can crystallise your vision for your program, the less footage you'll have to wade through later in editing.

The Lecture

The lecture sounds like it would be easy—just one person speaking for the whole show. But it's deceptively tricky.

Check out the site. Is the person speaking in front of a white wall or whiteboard? This will require care with lighting so you don't end up with the speaker in semi-silhouette.

Or maybe you can add an appropriate backdrop? A plain piece of medium-blue cloth can work wonders on a white wall, and the speaker will look much better.

Will an overhead projector or slide projector be used? If so, where will the images be projected? Will the person be standing in a darkened area much of the time? Or will someone else be changing overheads for him/her?

If you succumb to the temptation to use the fluorescent room lights, you can expect to end up with a person who has black sockets for eyes (from toppy ceiling lighting) and who may look rather sickly despite having robust health.

Does the speaker usually move around or cling onto the lectern for dear life? The speaker can usually tell you this ahead of time.

Someone who stands still can be miked with a cardioid on a table stand. Someone who turns away from the lectern frequently, to talk while looking at projected slides, will need a lavalier (neck) mic. Someone who strides around energetically is better off wearing a cordless radio mic lav. Someone who will be entering the audience and asking them for comments needs a cordless cardioid radio mic, to pick up sound from both audience and self.

Though your speaker will be addressing an audience, you need to have at least a semi-eyeline to camera. Profiles of speakers are hard to watch for long, and they're difficult for people to catch the words spoken with such a reduced view of the lips and face, so position your camera to get a decent shot of the speaker's mouth.

Because lectures are often too long (and boring) for their full length to be shown on TV or video, plan your shooting so you can shorten the piece. To avoid having jump cuts, you can cover the necessary edits with cutaway shots of the audience. You can do these before the speaker starts, but make sure the ones you take are usable. It's pointless taking wide shots that include people arriving if you plan to edit them into the middle of the lecture.

You can get away with tight two-shots and close-ups of people who appear to be paying attention to the front. A good method with cutaways is to shoot them for fifteen to twenty seconds each. Don't just take three to five seconds, because you'll find to your dismay that people tend to do something ridiculous as soon as they notice you're shooting them, and that renders part of your shot unusable.

Set up your camera close enough to have a captivating view of the speaker. Sunshine Dixon of the Urban League, Portland, Oregon.

If your speaker is facing slightly to the left of screen, shoot cutaways that are neutral or facing slightly to the right of screen to underscore that they're facing each other. If your speaker is facing slightly to screen right, reverse this.

Shoot LOTS of cutaways. You'll be surprised how many you need and it looks ridiculous to keep reusing the same ones.

If you can manage, it's better to cover a lecture with two cameras, dedicating one to the speaker and one for cutaways of the audience. That way you get true reaction shots and a more lively and genuine feel to the edited product.

The Panel Discussion

Panel discussions can't be scripted ahead of time because there's no way of predicting who will speak when, or what they'll choose to say.

What can be scripted is the opening by the host or facilitator, and the planned closing remarks. There should also be a general idea of what topics will be introduced, and in what order.

The host should have a good understanding of the topic, and have written details on the names and special titles of each of the panellists, as well as their connection to the topic.

The director needs to decide ahead of time on the best angles for the cameras, and basic coverage strategies—like which two-shots or three-shots work best. Due to the unpredictable nature of the panel discussion, once the show starts the director will have to be concentrating fully on who is talking and who is reacting. There'll be no time then to work out the shots.

Panels need to be carefully miked so everyone's comments can be heard well. Each person can be linked to the mixer with a lav mic, or groups of two can share a table-mounted cardioid.

A riskier set-up is to have a handheld mic that's passed around, but it can work well in some circumstances which benefit from spontaneity.

Mixing a panel discussion live requires a very attentive audio operator who rides the levels and continually raises the mic of the person speaking and lowers all the others.

A handheld mic can help regulate who is the next speaker. (Courtesy of Arlington Community Media Inc. [ACMi])

If all mics are left fully on, some embarrassing muttered comments can enter the soundtrack at full record level. Remember, many panellists are not used to working with mics. Don't bring them to grief through poor sound-recording processes.

The Speak-Out

A wide spectrum of community views can be captured at one event with a speak-out. If your aim is to highlight local opinions by making a grassroots media program, the speak-out can not only get you some good quotes, but it can bring some interesting interviewees to your attention for further videoing later on.

A speak-out needs good miking, good control by a facilitator and good lighting.

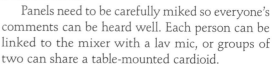

A speak-out can produce lively program material and discover new community leaders. (Courtesy of Portland Community Media)

The Demonstration

Some demonstrators give a very tight presentation and can tell you what the main elements will be and the order in which they'll happen.

An inexperienced presenter, however, is unlikely to exactly duplicate what s/he did in rehearsal. So demonstrations can present surprises and coverage problems.

You need to figure out what your basic shots will be, and hang loose to switch from one to another as the need arises. A demonstration needs at least two cameras.

Essential shots are a good close-up of the demonstration object(s), and a wider shot that includes the demonstrator. At times you can use a close-up of the demonstrator's face, and cut to it while you're refocusing on the omelette in the pan, or the lizard crawling up the assistant's arm.

The Training Tape

The aim of the training tape is to teach something to a target audience. It's very important to work out who the target audience is—the production style you use for senior citizens won't be the same as that which you use for 12–17-year-olds, and a video made about the benefits of housing loans from a certain bank will have a quite different tone and look from one dealing with drink driving or drug use. Unless the members of your audience feel that the message is addressed to them, they'll disregard it.

Training tapes can incorporate a demonstration. They can also use documentary style and short dramas. Training tapes, though the phrase itself may sound boring, are wonderfully malleable in style and quite challenging to produce well.

In general, shorter is better than longer. The message needs to be very clear and simple. Sometimes text on the screen can reinforce the message.

You've no doubt been on the receiving end of some poorly designed training tapes. When you go to make one, think hard about the features of the training tapes which have impressed you.

Documentary

Documentary has the wonderful capacity to take viewers into places they would never otherwise have the opportunity to go.

Because a documentary is made up of footage shot of real people in their actual locations, doing their normal everyday activities—or in some cases doing something extraordinary for them—it has a freshness and vitality to it if shot well.

People shooting documentaries have to be very sensitive and diplomatic. Their presence should be as low key as possible, so their featured people can relax and behave and talk in their normal ways.

A documentary with an overbearing crew, which tries to alter things too much at the location, is really shooting a form of interfered-with reality. A sort of fiction which purports to be true. Sadly, a lie.

One of the benefits of documentary form is that you record people telling their own stories,

Tyler Weymouth shoots a bike repair demonstration by Ryan Brouder in David Shaheen's Advanced Media class, Methuen High School, Massachusetts.

Malcolm Foreman shoots close-ups for an Australian Wholefoods corporate presentation, tav productions. (Photo by Neil Smith)

The Boston Blades, Paralympic Ice Sledge Hockey Champions, on *Dead Air Live*, produced by Jeanne Flanagan and the Somerville Producers Group.

Quvianaktulia (Kov) Tapaungai presents the meaning of the Inukshuk (man made of stone) for *Inuit Piqqusingit: Inuit Ways, Inuit Survival.* Jamisee Pudloo, sound recordist, Cape Dorset, Nunavut. (Photo by Kimberley Brown)

Getting the protest onto video gives you a wider audience. Demonstrators in Seattle.

Jeanne Flanagan, Independent Producer.

I got into video production as a format for teaching exercise. Not just to put an aerobics class on video but to teach about the body and how to use exercise to improve both daily activity and well-being.

Edis Jurcys, Cinematographer.

When you see something in nature or wildlife that's nice, stop and shoot it right then. You may think, 'I can get it later', but later the weather may be different, the light will have changed and you may not even get back there. Do it right away, don't postpone.

Steven Parris, Edmonds-Woodway High School.

When students start getting their feet wet and using the medium for something that isn't corporate or commercial, they get a strong sense of empowerment.

using their own words and patterns of thinking, their own anecdotes and analogies. This can be very powerful, and also very poignant. It can give respect to those people, and gain respect for them from the viewers.

If you decide to do wildlife documentaries, you'll need lots of time, patience and good observation skills, to let the animals tell their own stories.

If wildlife get used to you, you may find new connections will reward your efforts. Edis Jurcys in Turkmenistan for *World of Animals*, Moscow TV.

Trevor Graham, Documentary Producer.

Documentary-making gives you the opportunity to explore the real world and tell a story. I believe that truth is stranger than fiction. Trust is the most important thing—getting to know the people you'll be working with, getting to trust them, getting them to trust you. Everything after that is story, story, story. Finding the story you want to tell.

Oral History/Life History/Community History

By combining photographs, coloured slides, newspaper clippings, super-8 home movies, family videos, drawings and current footage, people make wonderful tributes to their families or friends, or to members of their communities or organisations.

Although these life histories may err on the side of glossing over the hard times or the character flaws, there's nothing wrong with presenting a personal view of someone to an appreciative audience. Such amalgams of visual media take a long time to complete, but by setting your camera up on a tripod in front of photos pinned on a corkboard, you can get very good results. Films can be videoed off a white wall or screen (or a pizza box). Drawings, clippings, cards and other artwork can all be shot directly with the camera—a good time to try out that macro lens?—or you can digitally scan them in and work some magic with Photoshop and/or compositing.

Your town archives can help you take people into the past, show them what has changed and what hasn't in their own locale.

Peter C. Kenny Jr and Peter C. Kenny III, New York, c. 1947. Kenny was decorated by the Russian government for getting supplies through to the Russian people during World War II. Clio Associates videotaped his oral history for a US Merchant Marine project and it's now stored in the USMM Academy archives.

Brewarrina Fish traps, 150 years ago. (Photo courtesy of the Tyrrell Collection, Powerhouse Museum)

Brewarrina Weir now. (Photo by Luke Barrowcliffe)

Drama

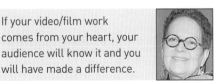

If your video/film work comes from your heart, your audience will know it and you will have made a difference.

Claire Beach, Videographer/ Teacher.

Drama is made up of scenes which are played by actors.

Drama is almost always postproduced—that is, edited from material shot in segments. A director will record a scene several times, often from different camera angles, in order to have a variety of takes to choose from when editing.

Donna Kenny,
The Video
History
Company and
Center for
Recording Life
Stories.

Older people may tire easily,
so keep the on-camera
interview format to no more
than two hours maximum,
with a stretch break after
45–60 minutes. Also be sure
to place a glass of water and
tissues within easy reach of
the person being interviewed
during these long sessions,
regardless of their age.

A major concern with recorded drama is that the actors repeat their lines and actions the same way for each take. Of course, their performance may vary—their voice volume and way of saying their lines may have different emotional qualities—but the basics, of which words were said and where the person was standing when they were said, need to be right on the mark that was agreed to during rehearsals. If not, there can be terrible continuity problems in the edit.

Drama needs to be well rehearsed, and the actors need to be capable of giving a convincing performance. Otherwise it will fall flat. Sometimes you can get good actors from among your friends. Often drama students are very happy to have the opportunity to do a performance for tape because they can use it in their show reel. At other times, it's best to get help from professionals.

Shooting and editing a drama is a huge commitment—don't doom your project to failure (or laughter) by neglecting to get the best actors you possibly can.

Danny Sheehy,
Queensland
School of Film
and Television.

With any production, think
creatively, think critically, think
commercially.

Sets are also important with drama. You can do location shoots or in-studio work. Both have their pluses. Locations can be difficult to light well, and the amount of time they're available to you may be limited.

Studios give you more control, but you have to build a convincing scene from flats and props—this takes time, imagination, and access to materials and building skills.

Dinner table scenes can pose enormous problems!
(Courtesy of Metro Screen)

Docu-drama

Docu-drama is a very popular and frequently used hybrid form. It takes as its subject real people and real events, but uses re-enactments by actors for some or all of the sequences. Parts of the dialogue may be from bona fide sources, and parts may be fictional.

Docu-drama is very useful for presenting educated guesses about events in the past which were not recorded, and for bringing life and interest to moments in history.

The risk with docu-drama is that the viewers take in the whole program as if it's fact, when it isn't. Even for the knowledgeable and careful viewer, it can be hard to separate fact from speculation in a docu-drama. As a program-maker, you may find ways of assisting your viewers in this.

Ficumentary (or Mocumentary)

Sometimes, fiction is shot to look like documentary. By making use of production styles and elements associated with documentaries, like handheld moving camera techniques, on-site interviews and comments, and recognisable real-life locations and passers-by, it's possible to construct a work of fiction and pass it off as 'real'. This can be a great spoof; it can also be a dangerous falsehood.

Program-makers should have ethics that they consult when entering grey areas like this. What is the aim of the program? Who is the audience? Will the audience understand that this is fiction? How much harm can be done if they don't?

There's a traditional form in literature called the historical novel. Such a work tries to bring to life the ambience of a time period, by presenting fictional characters who live out their lives among the events of history as it's been recorded. These characters are informed by the values and common knowledge available to a particular group of people, and they're presented with the likely choices and dilemmas of the day.

> There's no point in trying to show how things look in reality. Video can convey emotion, drama, form, mood, space, etc. by altering reality. How you light, frame and move the camera (not to mention what you do in the edit suite) will play a large part in the overall look of your video. Good video production utilises this principle.

Mark Tewksbury, The Nine Video School.

Ficumentary could be seen as a modern video variation on the historical novel. A ficumentary, clearly labelled as such, can be a thought-provoking work—as long as the audience understands what it is.

The Music Clip

Now this is the form many people want to try! There's so much variation in the music clip genre that there's no point in trying to make up rules of coverage beyond these:

1. Get a good-quality recording of the soundtrack! Don't waste your time with distorted audio or muddy music recordings. It's probably best to record the music in a proper sound-recording studio, then use that recording as the audio bed in your edit.

2. If your music group already has a good-quality audio recording of its track, you can use a video studio to record images of the musicians playing the music. The recording situation is set up so the musicians hear their pre-recorded tape as *foldback* sound, and sing and play along with it. Do make a simple audio recording of this video, though, so you can use it as a guide track to match to the studio tracks recorded beforehand.

3. Other video and graphics can be edited in to make the music clip livelier.

Always base your music clip on the best audio recording possible. Sky Cooper, Dorado. (Photo by Jaime Lowe)

The Use of Commentary

Sometimes you'll choose to supply information to your audience by using a voiceover or commentary. This is a scripted piece that's recorded separately and then added into the program at the editing stage.

Voiceover can be used to tell the whole story. This is sometimes the case in training tapes. Or it can be used to link one segment of a program to the next. This is a common technique in documentary, where there's no field footage to make the link, or where an outside voice is considered better for some reason.

Commentary can be written at different stages in the production process.

Writing Commentary in Advance

If the process to be shown is complex, it can help to work out a description of the process ahead of time. This can assist in visualising the necessary video coverage and in working out the shooting plan.

Writing After the Shooting Is Done

If the commentary is written after the shooting, it will be clear what links need to be made. If the linking voiceovers are recorded before the editing begins, the visuals can be cut to the right length to match them. Sometimes, however, this can lead to awkward shot lengths and a loss of rhythm.

Writing After Editing

If the commentary is written when the program has a definite form, snippets of narration can be written to fill in missing background information, add important details and set the mood for upcoming scenes.

In this case, narration can be written to match the available spaces.

Since everyone speaks slightly differently, it's best to have the intended narrator read the material in the way s/he'll record it, to get an idea of the likely spoken time. It's far easier to tinker with the text, adding or eliminating a few words, than it is to change an already edited sequence.

Suggestions from Rachel Masters

When you organise the shoot and write the recce plan, try to think of as many creative options as possible. Should the shoot be done in the studio or on location? Would a different location be more interesting? Could the light there be different, more atmospheric?

Is it essential to always be at the particular location in the script? For example, will the audience know whether or not you're at the beach if the only shot you need is a close-up of sand? Could you use a sandbox instead?

Make a list of alternative 'trick' locations. When is a hospital not a hospital? When it's a white wall with medical posters and hospital signs instead! Draw your inspiration from the theatre . . . stage and set designers have been using illusion for thousands of years. How could you recreate these scenes: the beach, a garage, a cafe, a spaceship, the moon?

VIDEO FOR EMPOWERMENT

Video is a great tool for capturing the concerns, ideas, perspectives and stories of grassroots people and delivering them to the rest of the world. Unlike print, it's a technology that can be used by people who can't read or write, who are generally excluded from the public debate.

By preserving the personal image, body language, facial expressions and spoken tone of each speaker, along with their words, an immediacy is achieved which promotes the message almost as well as if it were delivered in person to the intended audience.

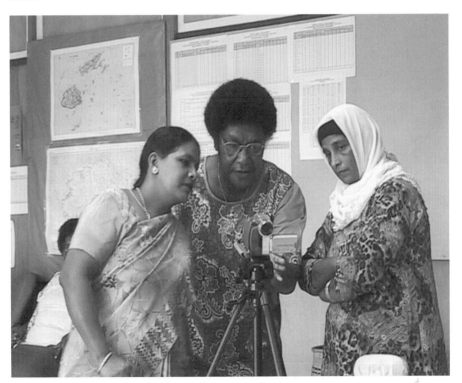

Fijian women checking their empowering images of women at work.

Rural Women's Video in Fiji

By Usha Harris, Lecturer in International Communications, Macquarie University

Usha grew up in Fiji, studied in the United States and now lives and works in Sydney.
<Usha.Harris@mq.edu.au>

Participatory video provides a powerful channel through which communities can reflect their everyday lives and share their success with others. A group of rural women in the small river town of Navua in Fiji produced a series of videos which highlighted their activities in small income-generation schemes. The women were involved in a government-supported pilot project which enabled them to exchange their skills, pool their resources and sell their products via email to civil servants in the city.

When I approached the women about the video workshop, they quickly recognised its benefits to them. The production skills would allow them to make a promotional video which would assist them to expand the market for their products to new clients, such as hotels and tour operators. They could also share their success story with others in the community.

The video workshop was conducted over five weeks with approximately ten women, between the ages of 20 and 60, forming the core team. Other women in the community joined in at times, depending on their circumstances and availability. The women learned about the process of production: how to use video cameras, how to record interviews and how to collaboratively tell stories about themselves and their communities.

The women enthusiastically committed themselves to the workshop despite the challenges facing them, such as walking long distances or taking a bus from remote villages and finding the bus fare to get to classes

There were five phases in the production process: camera training, story development, location shoots, viewing sessions and editing.

Setting the cultural context by using women's craft for the backdrop.

A six-minute promotional video was produced at the end of the workshop. In addition, five longer programs, each featuring one of the five communities where shooting took place, were completed and given back to the communities for their own use.

The women had control of content development and the use of technology during the preproduction and production phases. Editing was done on an Apple laptop using iMovie. Because the women had limited keyboard skills, I edited the footage in consultation with them. Instead of constantly cutting between shots or using short grabs from interviews, the women wanted to show full sequences of actions and interviews. This is in keeping with the format which the originator of participatory video, Canadian community development worker Donald Snowden, described as vertical films, consisting of a series of short segments, each featuring a singular topic or interview. It is in contrast to the 'horizontal' structure of traditional documentaries, which use cross-cutting and montage from different scenes and interviews to represent an issue. The video content does not aim for a polished professional look, but retains the genuine ambience of a community video as it was produced in the field without the aid of sophisticated production equipment and postproduction software.

Instead of using foreign production values, the women developed their own production culture by integrating their own cultural values into the process. This was an excellent example of how technology can be made to conform to people's ways of life.

The producers used their social networks through the women's clubs to create dynamic scenes of community activity for the location shoots. In so doing they gave the women in their community a sense of importance and the ability to represent their lives by displaying their work and talents on camera.

The images the women produced were distinctly in contrast to the stereotyped images seen in mainstream media of rural women, who were usually seen as being within the bounds of their home, in poverty or domestic subservience.

In the promotional video, the women showed themselves as active citizens who made a significant contribution to the family income through the money they earned from their work, and to the community through their clubs. The content reflected their lives, their skills and their communities, and they spoke of these with great ease and delight.

Had the women been brought into a studio to talk, they might have been awed by the technology and the urban environment. Instead the camera went into their life space. The interviews took place in their homes and their community halls, places familiar to them. The cameras rolled as they sat on the floor, where they felt most comfortable, instead of on chairs. Thus location was an important aspect of their representation. After the shoot, the women reviewed their footage and discussed its merits. For many, the experience of seeing themselves on a screen for the very first time was an emotional experience.

The recorded images also created a vital shift in the imagination of the bureaucracy. Suddenly the women's activities, as represented on video, gained in status and importance in the minds of the bureaucrats. People who sat in their offices making important policy decisions could now be included into this world of the women's everyday lives and aspirations.

My aim was to observe how communities engage with participatory media for empowerment, and the implications for dialogue, community-building and representation within Fiji's fragmented multicultural society. During the course of the project, I observed how video production could both incorporate and enhance the social network of rural women, and how the screen images seemed to affirm and validate their lives.

Usha with the Fijian women participants.

So What Is Participatory Video?

Participatory video (PV) enables people to produce and distribute content according to their own needs instead of being reliant on professional producers. When video professionals enter a community to shoot a video about issues facing that community, they are not engaged in a PV process. However, if a video producer is invited into a community and actively engages with them in identifying issues facing their community, training them in the process of content development and production, it is deemed to be participatory video.

Participatory video began 30 years ago, involving Fogo Islanders in Newfoundland under the National Film Board of Canada's Challenge for Change program led by community development worker Donald Snowden and filmmaker Colin Low. The Fogo Process, as it became known, gave birth to the participatory approach and has been practised in its many incarnations around the world.

Video production has gained a favoured place in many development projects. In the area of communication for development, video has been used by non-government organisations, development workers and indeed communities themselves to foster dialogue and to instigate change and empowerment.

Online video blogging sites proliferate as more people gain access to low-cost digital cameras, increased internet capacity and online distribution sites for user-generated content. Content can vary from personalised messages to well-orchestrated social activism campaigns. It must be noted that video has also been enlisted by negative forces in society such as dictators, terrorists and neo-Nazi groups to build up support for their own cause.

Terms such as participatory video, community video, alternative video, process video or direct video are interchangeably used by practitioners and scholars when discussing this field.

Here are some of the key features of PV:

- Participation of communities in message-making is essential.
- Local knowledge and cultural practices are embedded in the documentary process as much as possible.
- The process of production (rather than the finished product) is central to the empowerment of individuals.
- Content is developed according to the needs of the community through a consultation process, and is generally unscripted.
- Participants are involved in the three key activities: shooting, performing (being recorded), and watching the video.
- A feedback cycle of shooting and reviewing is central to the process.
- The video professional is a trained development communicator, and acts as a facilitator rather than a producer or director.
- Communities maintain copyright of the material and distribute it according to their needs.

As a tool for social action, PV has been used by citizens' media collectives to campaign on development issues and to expose injustices around the world. Video activists have captured police violence, exposed the plight of marginalised communities, and highlighted environmental and human rights abuses. Indigenous communities have used it to preserve their knowledge and cultural practices.

Traditional Knowledge

By Luke Barrowcliffe, Goorie Vision
and Chris Peckham, Source Media, Queensland

Luke is a descendant of the Butchulla people of Fraser Island, has an Indigenous Studies/ Communication degree and runs an Indigenous Media Service, Goorie Vision. <luke@goorievision.com>

Chris is originally from Wales, UK and studied TV and Sound Production at Charles Sturt University before working as a TV cameraman and editor across the country. <www.sourcemedia.com.au>

Traditional Knowledge belongs to its people and has been carried through generations by storytelling, dance, song and painting. Culture within communities developed over time through these art forms.

However, storytelling and general society communication have changed form in Australia in the last century. Although many great storytellers still exist within communities, communicating traditionally, the younger generation has become accustomed to other forms of storytelling including television, DVDs, CDs and the internet.

Though similar in many ways, there are great differences in the recording, storage and delivery requirements of stories in the newer formats, and training is needed for those wishing to utilise these new methods.

The affordability of digital technologies allows greater access to new forms of storytelling. Picking up a camera from your home or school has never been easier. We now have the opportunity to record and document our stories from our own perspective and distribute it via TV, DVD and the internet. The technology is in our hands.

Great opportunities now exist for Aboriginal and Torres Strait Islander people to record our culture and traditions, not only to preserve them for their future generations, but also to educate the wider community.

A basic video camera can record interviews, nature and performance.

You can make your own music clip, a documentary on one of your elders, or a video about your community's legends or Creation stories.

Pereiha Poharama capturing a 'behind the scenes' perspective of the workshop process with Uncle Michael Hill, producing the *Gooreng Gooreng Traditional Knowledge* DVD Volume 1. (Photo by Chris Peckham)

Before you start recording, a conscious decision needs to be made by the community as to what the output of the recorded content is going to be. Camera and audio recorder settings need to suit the chosen output, and skills need to be developed in regards to the chosen output.

Traditional knowledge potential outputs include:

- schools, libraries, museums
- film, television, radio, print, DVD
- internet and new media
- archives and database.

Chris Peckham capturing the moment for future generations: Gooreng Dancers Russell Hill, Ray Illin, Pereiha Pomaraha and Travis Johnson dance up the traditional knowledge dust storm at Workman's Beach, Agnes Waters. (Photo by Nokoa Pitt)

Gooreng Gooreng Dancer Russell Hill about to step into the digital history books by pressing the record button. (Photo by Nokoa Pitt)

Cultural Protocols and Knowledge Recording

Consideration No. 1: Beware! There are still spiritual implications if you record something you're not meant to, or are disrespectful to people and places.

Just because you know how to use a camera doesn't mean that you should record everything that's in front of you when on traditional country. The best way to avoid these mistakes is to ask elders what you can, and more importantly what you can't, record, as well as what they would like you to capture.

Consideration No. 2: There are a whole lot of complexities surrounding the recording of traditional knowledge. When you approach any subject, certain care must be taken to ensure that the story and storyteller are the right people you should be talking to.

Ask yourself whether the knowledge is men's/women's business or whether it belongs to a particular family/clan group, and ultimately who should be allowed access to it?

Questions

Generate questions around the theme, subject, person or thing. In relation to recording an elder's traditional knowledge, questioning should start with asking the elder to tell their story. It is always appropriate to start an interview with the interviewee introducing themselves to the audience.

This could include the following.

- *Who* their people are and *where* their traditional country lies. When an interview is done on location at a site of significance, if they agree to the knowledge of that site being recorded, ask them *what* the significance of that site is.

- *How* was the site used and *when*? This will help you gauge whether its use was seasonal or not.
- Is there any reason *why* the site was chosen?
- If you record significant sites or landscapes, make sure to get a range of different shot sizes and angles.

Interviews

Choose the most appropriate location to conduct an interview. Remember to keep in mind these things: noises, wind, sun, shade and a site's significance to the story.

Build a bond with the interviewee prior to the interview so they are comfortable and open up to the audience when sharing their story.

Follow a line of questioning on the subject or theme so the answers provided flow through the story. Listen carefully to their responses because other interesting aspects about the story will come up in their answers. You can generate more specific questions from this, and it shows the interviewee how interesting and important their story is.

Try to get more than just answers. Do they have a song to sing or a dance to dance? Do they have old photos, paintings and documents which add to their story?

Any existing printed photos should be archived using a scanner and PC.

Tressa Hill uses an H4 digital audio recorder to interview Uncle Mervyn Johnson talking about his traditional country and reciting language for their community knowledge archives. (Photo by Chris Peckham)

Different Ways of Recording

Traditional Knowledge comes in various forms and the recording of it can be in different forms also.

An audio recorder is a versatile tool that can be less intrusive than a video camera. It can be used to record oral histories, language, nature, songs and music.

When used for language recording, the words can be transcribed later, but more importantly a word's pronunciation and meaning are documented correctly.

You can use audio recordings to provide additional support for your video soundtracks by recording natural sounds: birds and other animal calls; oceans, creeks, waterfalls and bush sounds. Audio recorders can also be used to record a dance troupe's or musician's songs and music.

Your Audience

The potential recipients of recorded Traditional Knowledge and culture are seemingly endless, from the worldwide viewers of the Chooky Dancers' 'Zorba the Greek' smash hit on YouTube to your local school children using a Traditional Knowledge DVD for your community, local school or library.

Jeff Grinta,
Producer.

In making my documentary *On The Spectrum: Coping With Asperger's & Autism*, I was overwhelmed by the cooperation and assistance participants in the project gave me as far as connections to other interviews, clues to additional related subject matter, and general enthusiasm and moral support.

    The parents of children on the autism spectrum were so happy to see someone portraying the subject of autism in a positive light that they were glad to help me with the logistics of interview set-ups, etc. There was a basis of trust set up which I believed greatly enhanced the production. I definitely wouldn't have made a very interesting film without the guidance and assistance from the enthusiastic parents who greatly helped me with this project. <www.strawbellyjerryfilms.com>

Suriname: Giving an International Voice to Interior Tribes

By Jerry and Machelle Hartman

The Hartmans co-produce documentaries related to human rights and social justice.
    Email for Jerry: Jerry.Hartman@wallawalla.edu, teacher of video and audio production, MFA in Digital Cinema from National University
    Email for Machelle: hartman@whitman.edu, chemistry instructor, MA in Environment & Community from Antioch University

Indigenous Suriname (2008), along with two other related videos, was a joint project of the Organization of Indigenous People in Suriname (OIS) and Eclectic Reel, LLC.

    Indigenous Suriname was a community-directed documentary project based in Suriname, South America, where history is being repeated. Facing exploitive development, including mercury poisoning from gold mining, Indigenous Amerindians struggle to survive in a global society that ignores their existence. In this trilogy of short videos, Indigenous and Maroon people tell their stories about human rights, land rights, development and health.

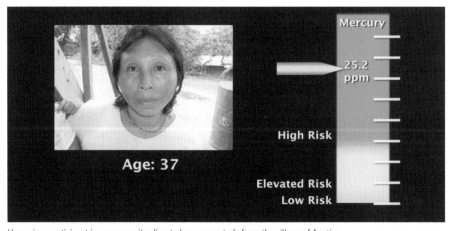

Hanna is a participant in a community-directed mercury study from the village of Apetina.

Community-directed Production

We chose to use a community-directed approach for these documentaries for two reasons:

1. The stories belong to the communities, and always will.
2. As a foreign production team, we understood that our very presence as 'westerners-from-a-developed-country' could be intimidating to the participants and communities. We might be seen as having more power (money, political rights). Since our objective was to empower the tribes of interior Suriname, we needed to minimise our roles and presence in the project.

The community-directed production approach ensured that we maximised the roles of the participants through the following actions:

*   We only recorded in communities where we were invited.
*   Cameras were only turned on once we were given a verbal invitation/permission to begin filming.
*   Community members directed all interviews. We did not ask the questions or prompt the participants about what to say. All content was directed by members of the communities.
*   We distributed small SD video cameras and inexpensive HD video cameras with simple operation instructions so that participants could collect their own footage without us being present.
*   Participants spoke in the languages in which they were most comfortable.
*   We assured participants that they could say anything they wanted on camera. The important element was *their* stories and experiences.
*   We assured communities that they would own all the footage (raw and edited) and final products. If any profit was made from the films, we would return 100 per cent of the revenue (not just the profit) to the communities.
*   In addition to the community-directed content (interviews/footage), the music for the films was produced by community musicians.
*   All final products would be approved by the communities and/or their leaders before they would be released.
*   The communities were the parties that determined where and when the final films would be screened.

Mark Sabajo, board member of the Organization of Indigenous People in Suriname, at a discussion of the future of Indigenous people in Suriname.

The purpose of each of the videos was decided by the communities and their leaders. The first video was intended for an international conference on Indigenous issues; the second and third videos were for international film festivals and to promote global awareness of issues facing the tribes.

To make sure that the final products accurately presented the thoughts and experiences of the community participants, all videos were sent back to Suriname to be approved by communities and/or their leaders. Because the button-pushing editing was being done in the United States, this feedback process usually took several exchanges before the final project met the expectations of the participants.

Postproduction

While it would have been best to be able to be in the community during post-production, this was not feasible. Postproduction was done outside of the country for three reasons: technical feasibility, safety and time constraints.

To begin with, the participating communities lived in very rural locations that usually did not have access to electricity or water. There were no on-site facilities that could accommodate postproduction work. Additionally, the climate of the entire region was not conducive to editing equipment without costly weather/humidity-controlled facilities.

Second, because of the sensitive nature of some of the footage, we wanted it to be out of the country as soon as possible to ensure the safety of the participating communities, the production team and the footage. In fact, we purposely took the footage out of the country in two phases to be certain it would not be taken from our possession during travel. The masters left with the first half of the production team and the backup copies left with the second group.

Finally, time and financial constraints made it necessary to do the postproduction work over an extended period of time. Because the editing was done by unpaid volunteers, considerable time was required to complete each video. The translation alone took more than a year and three different volunteers to complete.

Joan van der Bosch, captain of the village of Pikin Poika, talks about land rights.

These constraints made postproduction a creative challenge. To continue with our community-directed approach, we had to utilise multiple modes of communication to include the participants in the process. Several members of the Indigenous community that we worked with had access to phones, email and the internet. We were able to stay in close contact with them during postproduction and they were able to write and critique narration elements, footage and shot choice. Although our United States-based production team had to manage the technical side of production, the intermediate and final products were shaped by the community leaders and their constant feedback.

Technically speaking, we were able to send footage back and forth via the internet and Fedex. Using the MPEG4 video format, we could compress our footage to very manageable sizes. We ended up using compression rates that reduced the 25-minute video to around 50 MB. While this was too big for email, we were able to post the data files to a website for the community to download and critique. (There are many free websites that will let you post large data files.)

As the narrative unfolded in each of the videos, it became clear that more B-roll footage and interviews would enhance the stories. We mailed small HD cameras to community leaders who were able to collect additional footage and send it back to us via Fedex.

Awards and Distribution

In August 2008, *Indigenous Suriname* aired four times on national television in Paramaribo, Suriname, to honour the International Day of the World's Indigenous People. Also in 2008, the Organization of Indigenous People in Suriname (the organisation that co-produced the video) entered the project in the United Nations Population Fund (UNFPA) Caribbean Population Awards non-media category. For this category, only one winner is selected; OIS won and was awarded $10000 and recognised for outstanding work in population and in improving the health and welfare of individuals.

Resources

For more details on cultural protocols, refer to M. Peckham, *Cultural Recording & Documenting Indigenous Australians Using Video & Audio*. Personal experience, 2007.

S. Crocker, 'The Fogo Process: Participatory Communication in a Globalizing World', in S.A. White (ed.), *Participatory Video Images That Transform and Empower,* Sage, New Delhi, 2003.

A. Gumucio Dagron, *Making Waves: Stories of Participatory Communication for Social Change,* The Rockefeller Foundation, New York, 2001.

U.S. Harris, 'Transforming Images: Participatory Video and Social Change in Fiji', unpublished PhD thesis, Media Department, Macquarie University, Sydney, 2008.

20 SCRIPTWRITING

L ots of people have wonderful ideas. Over a beer or a cappuccino or a Saturday night curry, they can tell you amazing anecdotes from their own lives or the lives of people they've known.

And often someone will say, 'You should write a book!' or, 'That would make a great movie! You should write it down.' But most never do.

For a story to take sufficient form for it to be made into a screen production, it has to be transferred to the page. The script is the blueprint for the production.

People have to be inspired by it, and then realise it in a practical form. This involves a lot of collaboration between the writer, the producer, the director and the other key creative departments.

A scriptwriter is a special kind of writer, a person who's a *visualiser*, who can tell a story or teach a concept through a series of images. A scriptwriter is someone

From your scenes, actions and dialogue, the actors build their characters. Ruth Oliver, Lucien Cooper and Phil Cooper rehearse for *Clara's Curse*.

who can marry images with sounds. It's quite a different form of writing from short stories and novels, essays and reports.

The drama scriptwriter has to imagine and construct a series of scenes that give the actors the opportunity to convey the personalities of their characters, and the meaning of their characters' actions.

Dialogue is a part of the script for a screen production, but it only takes up a limited percentage of the total screen time. The pictures, on the other hand, are always there. They should each speak a thousand words.

Scriptwriting for documentaries has its similarities. Though the characters aren't actors but real people, and the final scriptwriting is done after the footage is shot, still the audience needs to understand where the people are coming from, why they feel the way they do, and what motivates them to take the actions that the video portrays. The scriptwriter shapes the story so its overall message is clear.

In a video or film script, every situation, every scene, should contribute to the underlying aims of the production. It's a very condensed form of storytelling—there's no time to waste on extras. Ninety minutes of screen time is the usual duration of a feature, and most videos are allotted much less than that, so everything in the script must lead to the fulfilment of the project's aims.

Ideas are a dime a dozen. Few can tell a really good story. Good scripts are 10 per cent inspiration and 90 per cent perspiration.

Helen Carmichael, Scriptwriting Department, AFTRS.

Writers write it down.

Mark Stiles, Writer and Filmmaker.

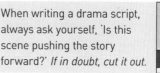

When writing a drama script, always ask yourself, 'Is this scene pushing the story forward?' *If in doubt, cut it out.*

Lester Crombie, Queensland School of Film and Television.

For documentary, write a shooting script that sets out the content of your completed production, prior to starting any shooting.

This should include a narrative structure for the production, enabling you (and your producer) to visualise the different scenes and locations you plan to include in your production. You can even estimate the rough duration of each sequence to make sure you're not trying to include too many elements within the planned program duration.

Of course things may change once you get into production and you many want to incorporate other elements. However, having a structured production outline to begin with puts you in a better position to decide if alternative segments are relevant. Random shooting, without considering how the footage will fit within the program structure, can lead to many weary hours in editing.

David Leonard, Executive Producer, *Race Around the World.*

The Central Theme

You should be able to write the main concept down in a few sentences—sometimes in just one. For example:

This story shows how blood ties win out over everything else.

Know your *characters* because they have to drive the script. If it's the other way around and the plot drives the characters, you're less likely to engage your audience.

Yvonne Madon, Scriptwriting Department, AFTRS.

This story shows how our people need our culture to survive.

This story is about how betrayal ruins relationships.

This story shows how a person with utter determination can overcome an obstacle which seems insurmountable.

What story do you have to tell?

John Lonie, Scriptwriting Department, AFTRS.

Just do it! Get out a pen and paper and write it down. You don't need a computer, you don't need a scriptwriting program.

Claire Beach, Videographer/ Teacher.

If you're going to create something, make sure it moves people. It can make them laugh, cry, doubt, agree, get angry, but the most important thing is that it moves them into action of some significance. We have too much empty airtime. Make it count.

How could using this character affect your story arc?

Asking the Key Questions

Before you begin to write, you need to know your *brief*. What is it that you're trying to do (or being asked to do)?

1. What is the main purpose of the tape? Is it to educate? To persuade? To entertain?
2. Who is the intended audience? What is known about this audience? What are their ages? Their occupations? Their education level? How much do they know about the topic? What sort of screen productions do this group of people generally choose to watch?
3. How will the tape be shown? Will it be broadcast? Will it be part of a teaching module? Will it be used as a trigger tape for small discussion groups? Will it be on the internet?

It's important to get rid of the 'inner editor' when you start writing. Controlling yourself, your emotions and thoughts can limit the creativity of writing. You can put absolutely anything on paper until it's going to be published or released. You can always edit your draft over and over again, either five or 500 times, as well as add, change and cut characters and scenes. Maintain a structure, be clear and use language the potential target audience can relate to.

Antti Hakala, Actor/Comedy writer.

4. Is your project more appropriate to be produced on a DVD? Can it be interactive?
5. What are the main points that must be conveyed?
6. How long should the program be?
7. Where can you get information about the topic? Who are the experts on it? What other people have valuable contributions to make? What about opposing views?
8. How much budget has been allocated for the project? The budget level often determines:
    (a) the number of actors who can be involved
    (b) the number of different locations possible (maybe some locations can be faked in a studio, or presented through still photos or stock footage)
    (c) the amount and type of equipment that can be used
    (d) the number of shooting days
    (e) the amount of special effects and graphics that can be included
    (f) the acquisition of music.

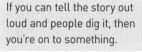
If you can tell the story out loud and people dig it, then you're on to something.

Gypsy Rose Tucker, Writer.

Digital technology allows you to tell stories in different ways, rather than in a linear, fixed-time way, as you're bound to in a TV broadcast timeslot.

Trevor Graham, Producer.

Still, don't feel overly restricted, because there are creative ways around some pretty amazing script requirements. Like the script that called for a herd of elephants to thunder past a house in Africa.

It's really hard to make a good movie out of a weak storyline.

Rob Davis, Editor, Digital Dimensions.

There was no budget for a trip to Africa (or for a herd of elephants, for that matter). The scene was shot in a studio using a set for the inside of the African house. The main character went to a pretend window and exclaimed about the passing elephants he could see, the sound of the elephant herd was rolled in through the audio mixer using a purchased sound effect, and some dust billowed in the window to complete the illusion!

Choosing the Elements

There are many ways to tell any story. You need to work out just what production elements to call for in your script, in order to tell the story *your* way. Be sure to consider what elements are most likely to attract your specific audience to the story.

Would drama be the best way to engage your target audience? Lucien Cooper and Michelle Blakeney in *Clara's Curse*.

Never underestimate the importance of the title.

Miranda Douglas, Publishing, AFTRS.

Will the story be told through drama?

Or will real people tell the story themselves?

Should the dialogue be tightly scripted or ad-libbed?

Should the program include interviews?

Should there be a link person? If so, should the link be a well-known personality (this can be expensive) or just a local person who can present information well?

Will some of the information be supplied through voiceover?

Will there be location shoots?

Will there be graphics?

Will there be animations?

Will photos be used?

What kind of video special effects will be included?

What music would work well?

What kind of audio special effects will be needed?

Training Videos

Make notes of your daily observations, remarks and brain waves. Sometimes a collection of various small stories and events can combine to become a greater one.

Antti Hakala, Actor/Comedy writer.

With training videos, you should be careful to restrict the number of points you're trying to get across. If you need to cover a lot of ground in a subject area, consider breaking the program into several segments. A series of short videos can be more effective than one long one that leaves the audience with their heads whirling with new ideas, none of which is fully grasped, and many of which just whirl out again into oblivion.

If you write several short scripts, the individual segments can then be produced and assembled onto a DVD. The instructor can pause at the end of each segment for class discussion and clarification before moving on, or use just one segment per lesson over a series of classes.

When you're deciding what to include in a script, try listing from one to five main points (no more), and then imagine how you can most effectively get them across visually. Then, having answered the key questions and chosen the points you'll be making, you can begin to design the program.

Check your scenes and dialogue with your target audience. Hannah Westerman and Joe Clover, Methuen High School, Massachusetts.

Designing the Video

The first step in getting any message across is to get the audience's attention. A technique which works well with training videos is to have the presenter, or the main character, look and act like a *member* of the target audience—that is, one of those people who will be watching the tape to learn something. Another technique is to use a person who holds great appeal for the target audience.

Having got the audience's attention, your next challenge is to hold it. That's trickier. If the audience feels that the message is directed to them, they're more likely to continue watching and paying attention. What methods could you use to say—through pictures, sounds, tone and overall look—'This is for *you*'? (And it won't hurt.) Think of scenes with which the target audience will be familiar; think of situations they're likely to encounter in relation to this topic.

Find a way to make your images memorable. *Uncle Toby's Kebabs*, directed by Mark Tewksbury.

Say, for example, you're doing a health promotion video on drink driving. If the scenes you include are unfamiliar to the audience, they'll feel the message is for other people and they'll disregard it. But if they can hear the sounds they usually hear at the pub, if the people are talking in the same style of language, about topics which interest them, they're more likely to be drawn into the video. The right music helps immensely here. And humour is terrifically potent in holding people's attention.

> As James Joyce said, write 'what is in your blood, not what is in your brain'.

Helen Carmichael, Scriptwriting Department, AFTRS.

The next step is to present the information in a way that the audience will understand.

Sometimes people make the mistake that a training video should use big words to sound impressive. The problem is, the aim is not to impress but to teach. Unless the audience grasps the message—easily—the program is a failure. Teachers won't use it, it will sit on the shelf, and the time, effort and money used to make it will have been wasted.

You probably have been made to sit through some pretty dreadful training videos. Analyse them—what made them bad? What made you want to put your finger down your throat? Now you have some distinct ideas about what to avoid.

How do people learn? It helps to present the message in a unique and memorable way. Striking images help people remember things. Surprise can be effective—like putting in a twist at the end of a well-known story format.

But perhaps the most important thing is emotion. You need to move people.

Working Out the Structure

1. How will the program *start*? At the beginning you let the audience know clearly what the program is about.
2. How will it *develop*? The middle section is where you deliver the information of the message. This is where the presenter demonstrates the procedure, or you

Bernadette Flynn, Griffith Film School.

Consider whether multimedia interactivity is the best option for the script. Develop a concept design and pre-visualisation materials to strengthen the idea.

Visit galleries, watch films and look at DVDs to increase knowledge of cultural history and production.

Trevor Graham, Producer.

Research and research and research. Spread your wings and become thoroughly immersed in the subject matter. You need to soak it up. It doesn't matter what it is. The subject can be close to you or quite distant. You can never do enough research. But there comes a point where you have to stop. This is probably when you can talk confidently about your project and when you feel inside that you know enough.

show the cells dividing, or the drama unfolds about the person going for an HIV test.

3. How will it *end?* This is where the main point of your message is reinforced. Sometimes messages are repeated verbally, sometimes they're written on the screen.

4. Sometimes there's an additional *action consequence* message at the end of a training tape, like 'To get your free blood test, contact your local clinic at . . .' This tells the newly persuaded viewer the next step to take.

Research

There are many sources of information for a video project.

You Can Start with People You Know

There are usually people near you who know something about the topic you've chosen or been given. You can speak to them about it and find out what they know.

They can give you leads about other people who could be useful, and they can also send you in the right direction for additional materials.

Maybe they can get permission for you to use a resource centre at their workplace, or maybe they know of a collection of materials held by an institution.

Often your own institution will have at least some beginning materials for you to read. This can get you started. Besides following other people's suggestions, learn to follow your own nose to sniff out a story.

Of course the internet is hugely helpful, but don't rely on it alone. You need to tape original interviews, and dig out opinions and perspectives that will add to the general discourse, not just regurgitate it.

Lies and Video

Once information is made into a video and presented, people tend to regard the information as the truth. It's something about the power of the medium—if you see it on the screen, it has an aura of authority.

So, if you don't research your topic well, and present falsities or half-truths in your video, some people will still believe it because they've seen it on the screen. That's bad in itself.

But there's another consequence as well. Those who know you're wrong will lose confidence in your work. And that affects your long-term reputation.

Script Development

Scripts aren't found under cabbages or delivered by storks. Scriptwriting involves a fairly regular sequence of developmental stages.

No holds barred. Don't censor yourself—go all the way. Where you think you've come to the end may just be the beginning.

John Lonie,
Scriptwriting Department,
AFTRS.

The Outline

This is a brief explanation of what the program will be about. It can be written in point form to show which topics will be covered, which points will be made. It should include:

* the style of the program
* the intended audience
* a list of the main characters.

It needn't be more than a page long.

The Treatment

This is more specific and detailed than an outline, and runs from about one to four pages in length.

This is what people usually use when they're trying to interest others in their project, for funding or some other kind of involvement.

For a drama, the treatment should include:

Careful research pays off when it comes to scriptwriting. Film and Television Institute Library and Resource Centre, Fremantle, WA.

* the theme
* the main story arc (i.e. the overall story development, without going into details)
* the main character arcs (i.e. the changes that each of the main characters will undergo)
* the style.

Ideally, the prose of the treatment should echo the style of the video.

Helen Carmichael,
Scriptwriting Department,
AFTRS.

In describing your characters, you may include a couple of lines of their dialogue.

For a documentary, the treatment presents the major topics planned to be covered. It outlines the sequences expected to be shot and lists possible interviews. Because of the nature of documentary, where you often don't know what you'll find until you get there, the treatment is a guideline but not a total commitment.

The Script

'Script' is a general term that refers to a variety of shooting plans. It doesn't necessarily include either dialogue or narration. For instance, a program can be made up entirely of pictures set to music, but it still needs a script to say what happens and when.

The Draft Script

The draft script is often developed from the original treatment. It includes all the scenes, dialogue and action.

John Lonie,
Scriptwriting
Department,
AFTRS.

No drama, no film.

For training videos, the draft script would set out, in program order, all the elements planned for inclusion in the production. Although some segments can't be tightly scripted because they're interviews or demonstrations, the major points to be made in them should be listed.

For documentaries, the script's structure and content will probably alter during shooting and postproduction. Still, having a good script plan before going on location means the producer, director and crew have a clear idea of what they're looking for, and when the unexpected happens they can make good use of it.

Scripts go through many drafts before they're ready to be used. It's a process of gestation, consultation, rethinking and rewriting.

Throughout this process, the scriptwriter can benefit by consulting other people who have good critical judgment about scripts. The writer hones the focus of the script by taking on board and interpreting some suggestions, and rejecting others.

Brian Williams,
Western
Australian
School of Art
and Design.

A script is never written . . .
It is rewritten and rewritten
and rewritten!

This may involve tinkering with the script here and there, or even turfing out whole scenes and developing new ones.

Scriptwriters need to be able to accept constructive criticism and make use of the perspectives other people offer.

Scripts can go through six or more drafts before they're ready. In fact, a feature film script would almost never go through fewer than three drafts. So take heart and don't let the process get you down. It's a matter of working with a vision and a professional attitude.

After all, what's the gain in shooting something that isn't as good as you can make it?

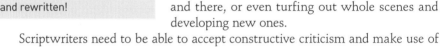

Antti Hakala,
Actor/Comedy
writer.

Show your completed draft to others who you think can be beneficial and get their feedback on how to improve, and use their support to gain more confidence.

The Script Workshop

Sometimes a script benefits from being work-shopped by a director and a group of actors.

This process can include a final reading or performance in front of a live audience. Attending the workshops helps the writer to spot what sections work, so s/he can develop these parts further. It can also help the writer to spot the problem areas. Workshopping is especially beneficial to writers who are at the beginning of their careers.

The Rehearsal Script

This is the final draft script. It may undergo some minor revisions and dialogue polish during the rehearsal period.

The Camera Script

This is the script that will be used during the shoot. It has all the camera directions on it and the shots are marked and numbered. Graphics and captions are also listed, and any special instructions are included.

A scriptwriter directs from the page.

Helen Carmichael, Scriptwriting Department, AFTRS.

An Example of Script Development Stages

Step One: Outline

Charlotte attempts to renegotiate the housemate situation by trying out her new assertiveness skills.

Write from the heart.

Stewart Klein, Scriptwriting Department, AFTRS.

Step Two: Treatment

CHARLOTTE stands at the sink, washing the dishes. ALICE enters the kitchen. CHARLOTTE decides to confront her about the interminable visit by ALICE'S couch-surfing friend PETER.

Step Three: Draft Script

1. INT KITCHEN DAY /

CHARLOTTE stands at the sink washing dishes. 'If U Seek Amy' plays on a CD player on the counter between her and the fridge.
CHARLOTTE turns and looks at the kitchen table which has more dirty dishes. She scowls as she picks them up.
ALICE passes the kitchen sink window, bopping to music on her iPod. She enters the kitchen, takes a slice of pizza from the fridge, and turns off the CD player.

ALICE: How can you listen to that stuff?

CHARLOTTE: Alice, we need to have a talk.

Step Four: Camera Script for a Multi-Camera TV Production

1. INT KITCHEN DAY

__1. C 1 WS kitchen CHARLOTTE who's facing sink.__ /

CHARLOTTE IS
LISTENING TO A
CD OF 'IF U SEEK AMY'. SHE TURNS TO
LOOK AT THE
KITCHEN TABLE.

__2. C 2 MS CHARLOTTE__ /

CHARLOTTE WALKS TO
THE TABLE AND
PICKS UP THE LAST
OF THE DIRTY
DISHES. SHE SCOWLS.

__3. C 1 MLS CHARLOTTE__ /

CHARLOTTE WALKS BACK
TO SINK & PUTS
DISHES IN THE
WATER.
ALICE PASSES
BY THE KITCHEN SINK
WINDOW, BOPPING
TO THE
MUSIC ON HER
iPOD.

__4. C 2 MLS ALICE, follows ALICE from door, to fridge, to
CD player, to table.__ /

ALICE ENTERS, GETS SLICE OF
PIZZA FROM FRIDGE
AND TURNS OFF THE
CD PLAYER.

ALICE: How can you listen to that stuff?

ALICE PLONKS
HERSELF IN A
CHAIR BY THE
TABLE.

__5. C 1 MCU CHARLOTTE__ /

CHARLOTTE: Alice, we need to have a talk.

TV Script Format

Don't take this script format as gospel! Different production houses use different script formats. But within a production house there's usually an accepted scripting style that writers are required to use. (Rather like a school uniform—you gotta get it right.) This consistency helps all the crew to find the information they need quickly, without having to adapt from one day to the next with every new script.

Actors need plenty of white space on a script to add their notes. Lucca Galimberti plans out actions for *Olive Grove*.

Basically, the shooting script needs to include the following elements.

For Each Scene

- The scene number.
- The location.
- Interior or exterior?
- Day or night?

For Each Shot

- The shot number.
- Which camera will do the shot.
- What is the shot size? How will it vary during the shot (zoom out, pan right, pull focus)?
- Who (or what) is in the shot?
- What is the action?
- What is said?
- What sound effects are needed?

Additionally, you find attached to a drama script:

- the scene breakdown
- the cast list
- the crew list
- the shooting schedule.

There are three aims when writing corporate video scripts:

1. aim at the emotions
2. aim for credibility
3. aim to convince.

Danny Sheehy,
Queensland
School of Film
and Television.

Computer Programs for Scriptwriters

There are computer programs which assist writers in doing standard script layouts. They format the dialogue and instructions correctly, and can keep you from going insane with tabs and margins and capitalising character names.

It's very important to know when to stop writing.

Or you could make your own template in your word processing program and save yourself the money.

Helen Carmichael, Scriptwriting Department, AFTRS.

A Simple Script Format for Video Projects

When people are making a script for editing a simple video project, it's not necessary to use the full-on TV format. Often people just use three columns, like this:

TIME	VIDEO	AUDIO
2 minutes	Host opens with details about the upcoming parade.	Host mic only, then roll in music of 1st band.
3 minutes	Two bands pass, then dance group does choreographed routine in front of judges' stand.	Field sound of 2 bands, then voiceover of host describing development of dance routine.
1 minute	Insert pre-recorded tape of lead dancer accepting award.	Pre-recorded sound from awards ceremony

Suggestions from Rachel Masters

Write a three-minute script about a person or a subject that really interests you— someone or something which you feel passionate about. Before you write your script, think about what it is that makes the subject interesting. As you write, try to explore the character, the event or the favourite place. Think visually. What images should be included? What does the person do that reveals their character?

Irony and juxtaposition are two very strong elements which can create a strong impact. Write a script, or plan a soundtrack, which will contrast with the visual images you have shot for your production. Perhaps you could show a woman getting ready for work. At first she appears happy, brisk and enthusiastic. But as she narrates her thoughts, she tells the audience of her unhappiness, boredom and worries about her future. The 'picture' the audience ends with is quite different from their first impression of her. Or perhaps a scene of logging or of a forest being cleared could be overlaid with a poem about the beauties of the bush, and the sound of birds and wildlife. Try to develop tension and contrast between what you see and what you hear.

Resources

A good book is Linda Aronson, *Scriptwriting Updated*, Allen & Unwin, Sydney, 2000.

Also, contact the Jerzy Toeplitz Library, housed at the Australian Film Television and Radio School, to get access via inter-library loan to a wonderful collection of books on scriptwriting, and also to scripts themselves.

See <www.aftrs.edu.au/rd/library.aspx>.

I recommend you read *Screenwriting from the Heart*, by James Ryan (Billboard Books).

Stewart Klein, Scriptwriting Department, AFTRS.

DOING SHORT DRAMAS

BY HARRY KIRCHNER, LATROBE UNIVERSITY

Short drama has undergone a revolution in recent years, driven in no small part by the World Wide Web and the expansion of festivals devoted exclusively to shorts, such as the St Kilda Film Festival, Tropfest and DepicT (UK).

Shorts are, in fact, getting shorter. The maximum length for YouTube movies has been ten minutes. Entries in Tropfest must be no longer than seven minutes. In 2009, the Australian Film Institute and Australia Post co-sponsored a short film competition to tell a story in 200 seconds.

Courtesy of Nash Edgerton

The 'traditional' length for an emerging form, the micromovie, has become 90 seconds. (DepicT; Siemens MicroMovie Award; Berlin Film Festival). Shorts nowadays can be shot on mobile phones or, in the case of Nash Edgerton's *Spider* (2007), on high-end Panavision equipment with a Dolby 5.1 sound mix.

Spider has exhibited at major international festivals and won many international awards; however, viewing it online, it could have easily been shot on a domestic camcorder and edited on relatively inexpensive software such as Apple's Final Cut Pro. It runs just over nine minutes.

Before embarking on any short film, filmmakers should carefully consider their exhibition platforms and any rules regarding length and *delivery items* for those platforms, including competitions and festivals which they might want to enter. The Tropfest people, for example, are not fussy about technical standards. They're more interested in the idea. But there are several other issues which should be carefully thought through during the preproduction stage: entry deadlines, delivery formats, publicity stills, music and actors' clearances and so on.

Spider is a good example of a successful multi-platform film. It works both in a large cinema and 'live' online, on a home computer. (It was also shown as part of an SBS TV shorts season.) It's a good film to illustrate how it is possible to mix camera style, genre and tone.

Spider is a simple story. We are in a car with a young adult couple, Jack and Jill. Jill is driving, clearly angry. Jack turns to her. 'Babe, it was a joke.'

Courtesy of Nash Edgerton

From the outset, the backstory is clear. Jack has played some kind of practical joke, one which Jill did not find funny. There is silence for some time and Jill pulls into a convenience store for petrol. Jack pays and returns to the car with a peace offering of chocolates and flowers. Jill is still frosty but eventually succumbs to a chocolate, which breaks the ice. However, being a practical joker, Jack has been unable to resist planting a fake spider on the sun visor. When Jill pulls down the visor, the spider drops into her lap and she stops the car in horror, jumping out, only to be hit by a passing motorist.

Jack watches in horror as he reflects on his stupidity, with Jill lying helpless on the road. We think this is the end of the film. (We have, in fact, witnessed 'three acts' of story.) The moral is clear: Don't play practical jokes. Until this point, *Spider* would have been an exceptionally fine short film. But there is a tag at the end—a fourth act, if you like. The spider is still amongst Jill's clothing. When an ambulance officer attends to her, he recoils in horror at the spider and accidentally stabs Jack in the eye with a syringe. The final shot is Jack stumbling around in a horrific comedic moment, with the syringe still stuck in his eye.

The camera style is handheld, similar to a documentary. The performances are entirely realistic. The genre is entirely realist (including a very convincing stunt), until the final comedic moment with the syringe, which elevates the film into comedic farce and leads us ultimately to view *Spider* as a comedy.

Let's briefly compare two other (earlier) multi-award-winning short films, both excellent but quite different in story form. Rachel Griffiths' *Tulip* (1998) has a storyline which follows dramatic conventions similar to the ones we might find

Jean Bain and Bud Tingwell as Ruth and   Will has to think of a way to milk Tulip . . .   . . . and he works it out! (Courtesy of Louise
Will in *Tulip*, directed by Rachel Griffiths   Smith)
and produced by Louise Smith.

in a feature film. The second, Jane Campion's *Peel* (1982), displays a quirkiness and open-ended story more typically found in short films.

Tulip is about an elderly man whose wife has recently died, and how the man overcomes the cow's reluctance to be milked. Tulip wants to be milked only by the wife, and despite his determined efforts to milk her, she becomes increasingly bloated until finally the man accidentally stumbles on a solution to the problem. He dresses in his wife's clothing, and the cow, now believing the man to be her old friend, allows the man to milk her. *Tulip* follows the conventions of many narratives. The man is faced with a challenge or obstacle. The man overcomes the obstacle and is also changed in the end in the sense that he comes closer to an acceptance of his wife's death. It has a three-act structure: a beginning, a middle and an end.

Peel is a mini road movie about shifts in power within a family. The family members are on their way home from a drive in the country where they have looked at a scrappy block of land. Everyone is a little disappointed and the son starts throwing bits of orange peel out the car window to amuse himself and annoy his parents. The father stops the car and insists the son pick up the bits of peel. After the son finally accepts the father's ultimatum and returns to the car, he discovers the mother throwing peel out the car window from her own orange. The father and son gang up on the mother, and a stalemate results when the mother refuses to pick up her own peel. We leave the family on the side of the road and ponder the question as to who will eventually give in, in the end.

The endings of many short films are inconclusive. Successful shorts often depend on a clever, sometimes quirky, treatment of their subject matter, often more extreme than we might find in longer pieces such as television dramas or feature films.

But whatever the length or style, they all involve a screenplay (script) which, at some time, somebody has painstakingly written to a set of very specific conventions.

What Drives a Short Screenplay?

The best screenplays, whether they are shorts, teleplays or features, all involve ideas that are both character driven *and* story driven in such a way that it's hard to tell which of these driving forces dominate. Whether something is 'story driven' or 'character driven', they are both sides of the same coin.

Questions to Address

Consider the following theme or story pretexts:

- An injustice to be corrected.
- A danger to be faced.

For the character, these are translated into the following questions:

- What do I want?
- What are the obstacles in my way?
- How am I to overcome these obstacles?
- What are the consequences of my attempting to overcome these obstacles?
- Do I eventually achieve my goal?
- What have I learnt from my journey?

The family and friends in *Alone*, produced by the TEAME Indigenous TV and Video Training Course, Metro Screen.

The answers to these questions go as far back as Aristotle—250 years BC—and are fundamental to the most familiar of all storytelling models, the 'hero's journey', popularised more recently by Christopher Vogler in his screenwriting manual *The Writer's Journey* (Michael Weise Productions, 1992).

Traditional stories fit into what Bordwell and Thompson call the 'classical Hollywood narrative', a term that suggests cause and effect, an audience's acceptance of reality (in the context of the particular genre) and a three-act structure which involves closure.

We know, however, that nowadays this is a very limited view of what possibilities exist in cinema. Audiences are now more sophisticated. The comedic end of *Spider* works precisely because it goes *beyond* what we have been traditionally taught to 'read' as closure, transgressing or perhaps exceeding our expectations.

Style and Tone

Stephen Cleary, who runs the world-famous ARISTA script workshops, suggests that there are very few contemporary films which don't contain a mix of at least two genres. Quentin Tarantino is famous for combining crime and comedy. The Coen Brothers are masters of mixing genres.

While story is often privileged as the most important element in filmmaking, it could be argued that all of the above films would not have worked if the filmmakers had not had an exceptional command of the style or genre elements which best serve their purposes. This can be best learnt in the first instance, perhaps, by choosing a prototype for your own film, an existing film that has *resonances* of style or tone (through editing, camera work, sound design and performances), which you imagine might suit your own short film.

Screenplay Format

In the same way that architects are obliged to follow strict conventions in the expression of their design ideas, so too are screenwriters of drama expected to conform to certain rules. However creatively brilliant any screenplay is, it will nevertheless alienate potential collaborators if it is not laid out properly. Attention to detail is paramount. This extends to whether notation is in upper or lower case, the placement of *parenthetical* instructions (instructions in brackets) in the right spot, the number of spaces between lines, and so on.

Screenplay Layout is Not Rocket Science

Screenplay layout should be easy enough for anyone who's moderately computer literate. It just takes a basic grasp of word processing tools, like justification, line spacing, font formatting, tabulation and the manipulation of headers and footers.

Don't Include Shot Sizes

It's rare for screenplays to contain instructions about shots. Instead, screenplays are similar to stage plays. Regrettably, there are 'how to' screenwriting books still in print which suggest it's acceptable (or worse still, desirable) for the screenwriter to indicate what kind of shot the audience is meant to be seeing: MCU (medium close-up), MS (medium shot) and so on. These days, this is *not* the screenwriter's job. This notation was used once upon a time in the days when writers and directors were contracted to Hollywood studios, and indeed is indicative of how the roles of both writers and directors have changed over the years.

Since the emergence of the *auteur* theory in the 1960s, when the director was beginning to be seen, rightly or wrongly, as the 'author' of the film, directors have gained more prominence as interpreters of the script. Suffice to say, it's up to the director to decide how any particular scene is to be *covered*—that is, what shots are to be used. These days, a writer may imply or suggest what the audience is to see, but not how to achieve it. If the writer is intending to direct as well, the same rules apply and the level of detail should be no more or less than if somebody else were directing.

Layout and Language Conventions

The scene heading is sometimes referred to as the *slug line*.

The Scene Heading (or Slug Line)

A cursory glance at any screenplay will reveal the scene heading to be made up of:

* the scene number (on both sides of the page)
* where the action takes place
    indoors = INT, for *interior*
    outdoors = EXT, for *exterior*

- the location
- the time of day: DAY, NIGHT, DAWN or DUSK.

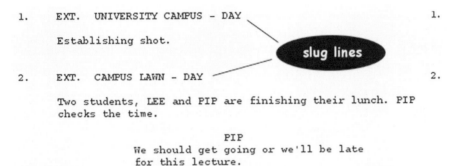

```
1.      EXT.   UNIVERSITY CAMPUS - DAY                          1.

        Establishing shot.
                                            slug lines

2.      EXT.   CAMPUS LAWN - DAY                                2.

        Two students, LEE and PIP are finishing their lunch. PIP
        checks the time.

                                PIP
                    We should get going or we'll be late
                    for this lecture.
```

It can be seen from the example that the body of any scene is normally single spaced. And there are two line spaces between the slug line and the action; and three line spaces between the last line of a scene and the next slug line.

The Big Print

The description of the action is called the *big print*.

The first rule is that the big print should always be written in the present tense: 'Bob comes down the stairs', *not* 'Bob came down the stairs'.

Big print should also be as economical as possible. Screenplay readers don't want to wade through masses of description. Writers experienced in prose fiction often overwrite their big print, finding it sometimes more difficult to adapt to screenplay writing than those who have written little or no creative prose. A screenplay is not a piece of literature.

Timing the Script

A screenplay should read at around the same pace that we might imagine seeing the film. A rule of thumb which is often used is that a screenplay should roughly play out at one minute of screen time per page.

Economy of Phrase

The best big print conveys meaning without being too mechanistic. In Callie Kourie's *Thelma & Louise*, for example, there's a wonderful piece of big print that refers to Darryl, Louise's husband: 'Polyester was made for this man.'

We don't know whether Darryl is short or tall, fat or thin, attractive or ugly. But we get a perfect sense of how the writer wants us to feel about this character.

The best way to get a feel for big print is to read as many screenplays as possible.

Study Your Craft

Teach yourself by reading the sorts of scripts you want to write. Evelyn Lowah works to achieve her dreams, School of Indigenous Australian Studies, James Cook University.

Although it's important to write down the gist of your story while you feel the impetus, it's also advisable to read other work in the screen genre you're planning to use. Nobody in their right mind would seriously sit down and begin to write a short story, or embark upon a novel, unless they had read at least several short stories or novels, yet sometimes people feel they're equipped to write a screenplay once they've familiarised themselves with the layout conventions.

You should study how other scripts are constructed in the genre that interests you. This way, your mind will be tuned in to catch the devices used that make the script live and work.

Actually, it's a good idea to read a broad range of screenplays when you're developing your craft.

Common Errors in Scripting

- Use of *morning, afternoon* or any time of day *other than* DAY, NIGHT, DAWN or DUSK.
- Dialogue centre-justified (as opposed to left-justified).
- Dialogue which extends all the way across to the right-hand side of the page.
- No page numbers.
- Use of more than one font—e.g. page number font different from main text.
- Continuous big print or dialogue which extends over onto the next page.
- Use of shots or camera movement, e.g. 'close-up of', 'zoom in on'.
- Use of backstory in big print—e.g. 'She looks out the window and remembers the time when . . .'
- Use of past tense in big print—e.g. 'Jane was the girl he liked the most at school.'

A Word About Writing Dialogue

First-time writers often enjoy writing dialogue, sometimes finding it fun to write large passages for their actors. There's nothing intrinsically wrong with this. It should be remembered, however, that it's a lot easier for a non-professional actor to remember one or two sentences before the other character replies than to have a character deliver a long passage of dialogue.

The practicalities of filming demand that actors must be able to repeat their lines. The longer the passage of dialogue, the more difficult it is for an actor to repeat lines. Solution? Make your dialogue interactive throughout your script, with short passages for the characters. The longer the passage of dialogue, the more likely you'll have to be prepared to 'go again'. If the drama demands a long passage of dialogue, it's helpful to cover the action in a way that you're able to cut away to a reaction shot so you can use bits and pieces of various takes. If, when you're wearing the director's hat, you want to cover a long passage of dialogue with a complicated tracking shot, you want to be very confident that the actor can remember their lines.

Shooting a Short Single-camera Drama

When shooting a drama in a television studio, several cameras are normally used. In this sense, *multi-camera* television drama is a bit like staging a play. Individual cameras cover different characters and different parts of the action at the same time, so that the vision mixer switches to whichever camera is dramatically appropriate at the time. In short, the shots are cut to tape in real time.

What is Single-camera Drama?

However, feature films and most video dramas are usually shot *single camera*. That is, the same action is repeated several times, with the camera framing a different part of the action each time. Thus, the editor will have a choice of two or more shots to choose from when the scene is edited in the cutting room. This is more time consuming, but allows the editor to try out different ways of interpreting a scene, and to preview cuts before ultimately deciding on a particular course of action.

Even on large-budget feature films, only one camera is normally used. The exception to this is when a shot cannot easily be repeated—for example, an expensive stunt such as blowing up a bridge. In this case, several cameras might be strategically placed to get different angles and shot sizes for use by the editor when cutting the scene together.

In drama, your responsibilities as a camera operator include always scanning the edges of your frame so nothing unwanted, like a mic or boom, is being recorded.

Cathy Zheutlin, Camera person/ Producer.

Sophia Mork shoots her version of 'The Wizard of Oz' with sister Veronica as Dorothy, Portland, Oregon.

As an actor you can never be too prepared. In screen acting it's crucial to know exactly your physical spot on the set, and be focused, follow the script and think of what is really important for the storyline. Good projection and intonation of your voice, as well as exaggerating the usage of facial expressions and body language, can make the performance more colourful, whereas being just 'normal' can seem boring on the screen. Use your experience and imagination to come up with fresh ideas on how to improve, without stepping on your colleagues' toes, of course.

Antti Hakala, Actor/Comedy writer.

Coverage

Coverage is the technical term used to describe the shots a director uses to interpret a scene. In other words, they're the shots which are provided by the director for the editor to cut together in order to create the illusion that the action in the scene is happening in real time. Ideally, an editor will have a choice of more than one shot to use at any one time. Thus, any scene shot by a director will be subject to any number of interpretations by the editor. How is this achieved on set?

Working out camera angles and shots for *We Are Family*: Teshome Tesema with Nigel Graves on camera.

As we have already seen from the drama script example, single-camera scripts look similar to plays, with perhaps a little more detail as to the action and 'business'—the physical things actors do such as picking up a coffee cup. (These movable props are referred to as standby props.) Nevertheless, many scripts leave these physical actions for the director and actors to work out for themselves; this is not only acceptable, but arguably preferable.

Arriving on Set

In student film and video, rehearsal is often considered a luxury, so let's assume the actors, crew and director have arrived on set not having rehearsed the scene. Any good crew will be keen to get working, but in the initial stages, it's important that the director works through the whole action of the scene with the actors *before* addressing any technical matters, or any discussion of shots.

Inexperienced directors sometimes over-prepare. It's good to have an idea of how a scene might be interpreted, but invariably a director will be forced to think on their feet when they discover that the shots they might have imagined are not easily achievable. Storyboards can be useful, but they can also be a trap—especially when a director attempts to shoot a scene *in the same order* in which it appears in the storyboard. This will almost certainly be an inefficient way of shooting any scene.

The Dry Read

The director takes the actors through a *dry read*—that is, without any interpretation of lines (acting). This is to ensure that the actors can actually say the lines—which is sometimes harder than it might seem. (This can be done standing or sitting, but should not address any problems of props or physical movement at this stage.)

Blocking Out with the Actors

The actors play out the scene, sometimes a few times, moving about and using props to their satisfaction, and the director's, until it *feels right*.

It is the director's job to create the most conducive working environment possible for the actors. Respect for the actors is the first lesson in good directing. Performers need confidence, and the director must provide a secure, protected, quiet, concentrated and creative environment on the set.

Tom Kingdon, Emerson College.

At this stage, the camera person is likely to be paying attention to physical movement through the set/location, and thinking about possible shots and implications for lighting. This is called *blocking out the action*, and does not normally involve the overall crew.

Once the action for the whole scene is established, it's time to start thinking about shots, or coverage.

In professional work, the scene may have been rehearsed and blocked before shooting day.

Decide on the Camera Coverage

The director and the camera person now discuss the camera coverage—what shots are to be used in capturing the action—and they arrive at a way of covering the scene. The relationship between camera person and director invariably differs from shoot to shoot. Sometimes a director will defer to the camera person regarding advice on coverage. Sometimes the director will have a clear idea of what s/he wants, in which case it's the camera person's job to advise as to whether this is achievable or not. Please note that the role of the remainder of the crew up until this stage has been marginal—except that they will have been listening quietly, and thinking about their own roles in the process which is to come.

If your actor has to see something out the window, find a reason for her to be at the window in the first place. Joy Saunders in *The Rainbow Boughquaker.*

Explain the Coverage to the Crew

The director then blocks out the shots for the crew. But first, the *blocking out with the actors is repeated*, so the action for the whole scene is played out for the crew. Next, the director stops and starts the action, explaining what shots will be used, and in what order this will take place. (In professional crews, the First Assistant Director usually performs this task.)

Imagine a scene is to be covered in a wide shot, which in this case we'll call the master shot, then a two-shot, then two medium close-ups. That's three shot sizes so far. There might also be

Although alcohol has no place on set during a shoot, blackcurrant juice can make a look-alike prop which will keep your actor happy and hydrated during a sunny scene. John Stephens in *The Rainbow Boughquaker.*

Director Clodine Mallinckrodt explains the next scene to her actors and crew. L–R: Walter Locke, actor; Clodine; Jill Reuers, first AD; David Bachman, actor. On the set for *Dot Com Dementia*.

Remember to count to ten before you call action.

Gill Leahy,
Filmmaker.

Mark every take you do. (Courtesy of Film & TV, Central TAFE, Perth)

a close-up—picking up the telephone receiver, for example. Please note that even if the director has envisaged that the telephone receiver shot might be the first shot the audience sees when the scene is finally cut together, this shot will probably be one of the last shots to be taped on the day. For the purposes of lighting and continuity, the order of shots taped on the day is usually from widest to tightest.

Once the crew is familiar with the entire sequence of shots that will be used to cover a scene, the shooting for the scene can commence.

Shooting the First Slate

A *slate* is a camera set-up. A scene with four shots will have four slates. If an actor makes a mistake, or the director wants to *go again* for technical reasons (camera or sound, for example), this becomes a second *take*. The clapper board (which is also sometimes called the *slate*) would then read: 3:1:2 (i.e. Scene 3: Slate 1: Take 2). Mark every take of every scene you do before you shoot it. When you're editing, it's much easier to find a take visually by these markers than to have to search through the footage and count them out each time.

For student productions, you can make your own slate to write on with a whiteboard marker by covering a piece of cardboard with clear adhesive contact plastic. All the information on the slate should also be recorded on a logging sheet. In addition, you should have somebody mark up a copy of the script, for the editor. To do this, draw lines down through sections of the script, using various colours to indicate which lines and actions have been shot as a single (one actor only), a two-shot (two people in the shot), a master shot (showing the whole action), and so forth.

But first things first. Let's imagine the dry read, blocking and order of coverage have already been explained to the crew, and we're about to shoot the first slate. Crews normally follow a defined series of protocols.

Crew Protocol

1. Shot decided upon by director.
2. Director informs crew—for example, 'We're going to do an MCU of Emily'.
3. Camera person rehearses any camera movement with actor/s while remainder of crew observes quietly. Any cues are worked out during this process.
4. Camera person checks focus—zooms in and focuses, zooms out to required opening frame. *Focus pull* positions are marked if required. Camera calls 'Camera standing by'.
5. Sound person edges microphone in to find edge of frame and, taking into account any camera movement, establishes microphone positioning, leaving sufficient space for *safety*. Sound calls 'Sound standing by'.
6. Director calls 'Ready to go for a take'.
7. Slate person positions slate into shot.
8. Director calls 'Roll camera' or 'Turn over'.
9. Camera person calls 'Camera rolling' after record indicator is displayed in viewfinder.
10. Slate person counts down, e.g 'Five, four, three . . .', etc.
11. Director calls 'Action', and 'Cut' after shot has finished. If the camera operator or sound recordist makes a mistake, they should tell the director immediately at the end of the shot.
12. After the shot is completed, the director asks actors, camera and sound (in this order), if it was okay for them. 'How was that for camera?' Director may decide to go on to the next shot (slate/set-up) or to go for another take. The director informs the crew if the shot was *N/G* (no good, go again), *okay* (possibly go again), or *pref* (preferable, from a number of takes).
13. Slate person marks up the logging sheet and script, and marks up the new slate in advance for the next shot.

In a professional setting, don't try to be friendly. Do the job. Respect will win you more cooperation than niceness.

Sara Hourez, Director.

In a professional crew situation, the continuity person would mark up the script, and the clapper loader (and sound recordist on their own individual sound sheet) would log the shot. Indeed, many of the roles would be highly specialised into departments. Nevertheless, many successful short dramas have been achieved with small crews. The demarcation of roles depends very much, of course, on the budget, goodwill and expertise of the crew.

It should be noted, however, that once roles and jobs have been determined at the outset, it's unwise for crew members to cross over into the areas of other crew members. This is especially important when working with actors, whose job is difficult enough without additional 'help' from crew members other than the director.

Looking Further

The above is a thumbnail sketch of how a short drama production might be approached in terms of conception, scripting and *shooting any single scene*. Production management and scheduling are dealt with in other sections of this book, and although many of the same principles apply to both drama and documentary, *production management* for drama is an especially complicated process. Anyone seriously embarking upon a drama shoot should therefore be prepared to look at additional resources such as the Australian Film Television and Radio School's *Production Budgeting and Film Management* kit.

Other Resources

John S. Douglass, and Glen Harnded, *The Art of Technique: An Aesthetic Approach to Film and Video Production*, Allyn and Bacon, Boston, 1996.
Tom Jeffrey, *Film Business: A Handbook for Producers*, AFTRS, Sydney, 2000.
Linda Seger, *Making A Good Script Great*, Samuel French, Hollywood, 1994.
Christopher Vogler, *The Writer's Journey: Mythic Structure for Storytellers and Screenwriters*, Boxtree, London, 1996.

Screen Productions

Tulip is available as an extra on some versions of *Hilary and Jackie* and as part of a collection from Tribe First Rites on *Australian All Shorts.*
Peel and *Passionless Moments* are available for viewing online through the Jerzy Toeplitz Library: <www.aftrs.edu.au>.
Kitchen Sink can be found on YouTube in two parts.
Spider can be found on YouTube.
DepicT have an extensive archive of 90-second 'micromovies': <www.depict.org>.

BUDGETING

22

'How much will it cost?' That's the first question most clients or sponsors will ask you, once you've told them your great idea for a video.

And it may be the one you feel least prepared to answer.

Explore all funding options! (Courtesy of Metro Screen)

A video production can cost almost anything people are prepared to spend. It can range anywhere from the free piece done by volunteers using public access equipment to the 60 second TV ad, which can cost hundreds of thousands of dollars.

So maybe your first question should be, 'How much will we be able to spend?'

Most sponsors have a certain amount of money in mind when they set out to do a video, but very often the amount isn't based on any experience with the cost of media production, but rather on a 'gut feeling' of what they think such a thing should cost.

For example, it's not uncommon for people to think that a couple of thousand should buy a CSA (community service announcement). Little do they know that it could cost that for the computer graphics.

But then, maybe they don't intend for it to be broadcast at all; maybe they plan to distribute it by sending it around to schools or organisations. It's critical for you to know what sort of distribution method is required because that will help determine the quality of all the equipment needed, from the first shoot right through to the final edit.

What to Include in a Budget

The budget is the financial map used to navigate through the making of the screen production.

Your budget should clearly set out all the expected costs for every aspect of the project.

The five stages of a video production are:

1. development
2. preproduction
3. production
4. postproduction
5. distribution.

Be sure to include all the stages of the production in the budget right from the start. It's no good getting the project shot and not having the money to edit it, or completing it all and having no money left for distribution.

Another good policy is to err on the side of higher quotes. Be conservative. Include the higher quote rather than the lower one whenever you're adding up how much things will cost.

Rachel Masters, Corporate Training Coordinator, SBS.

A constant perceived limitation in video production is the budget and the facilities. At times it may be tempting to cut back, to think small, to abandon your ideas. But there's always another way. You need to ask yourself, 'What are the imaginative substitutes?'

There's no magic to preparing a budget. It's simply a task which requires careful thinking, up-to-date information on costs, and thorough attention to detail. As with preproduction planning, some standard lists can be timesavers and memory prompters. There's really no point in 'reinventing the budget' for every project you do.

And a standard layout, either kept in your computer or on paper, can help you put all the costs down in a readable format.

Some Useful Lists

There's no one budget that suits all projects because every project has its own peculiarities. But there are certain items which are likely to appear for each stage.

The following lists, by no means exhaustive, may serve as a useful skeleton from which you can develop your own budget forms. You won't need all the items listed, and there may be others—not listed—which you'll always need for your projects.

Development

- Develop the concept.
- Write the treatment.
- Write proposals for funding.
- Approach funding bodies.

A good filmmaker makes use of what they have, not what they haven't.

David Opitz,
Metro Screen.

This stage is often unpaid. People develop projects in their own time and then sell them to a funding body, with a budget that begins with 'Preproduction'.

Sometimes, however, there's 'seed money' or 'development funding' available that will pay for the writing of the first one or two drafts of the script, and a round of script editing.

Preproduction

Personnel—fees and wages (including annual leave at 17.5 per cent and superannuation at 9 per cent in Australia):

It's all very well to be an auteur, but it's very hard to get funding, past short film budget levels, without a producer.

Alison Wotherspoon,
Flinders University.

- Scriptwriter
- Script editor
- Producer
- Director (planning, storyboarding, conducting rehearsals)
- Production designer
- Office manager
- Bookkeeper/accountant
- Production manager
- Site scout
- Camera operator (planning and site check)
- Sound recordist (planning and site check)
- Performers (rehearsals).

Put your money on the screen.

Darrell Lass,
Production Designer.

Costs:

- Office costs (phone, stationery, photocopying, postage, electricity, heating)
- Insurance
- Site check (vehicle, petrol, airfare², food and accommodation for site scout)
- Requirements (materials and manufacture of sets, costumes and props)
- Rehearsals: duplication of scripts, hire of rehearsal space
- (Story rights: purchase)
- Music (composition of original music and/or search and selection of existing works).

Believe no one, assume nothing and follow the money.

Marsha Della-Giustina,
Emerson College.

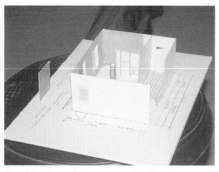

A model of the set helps everyone visualise shots, lighting, actions and possible sound problems.

Wayne Smith, Hilton Ellingham and Ken Manning check out staging plans, AFTRS.

Production

Personnel—fees and wages (including annual leave loading at 17.5 per cent and superannuation at 9 per cent in Australia):

Wayne Smith, Head of Props and Staging, AFTRS.

The designer draws up the plans for the set, then comes and speaks to me. It's important that this happens as early as possible. I work out how much it will cost, and how much time it will take, to construct it as shown, then we look at how much has been allotted for the set in the budget. The next step is compromising, trying to get the best set, as close to the design as possible, with the funding available. Once a realistic redesign has happened, Props and Staging get on with building the set.

- Producer
- Director
- Director's assistant
- Floor manager
- Production manager
- Office manager
- Bookkeeper/accountant
- Lighting director
- (Vision mixer)
- (Technical director)
- Camera operators
- Sound recordist
- Boom operator
- Performers
- (Stunt person)
- Caterer
- (Child care)
- (Animal wrangler—that is, person in charge of care of animals on set)
- Drivers and runners.

Costs:

- Equipment: purchasing or hiring costs
- Stock (videotapes or other recording stock)
- Travel costs (vehicles, petrol, parking, aeroplane tickets, departure taxes, visas, inoculations, medical e.g. malaria pills, accommodation, food allowances)

Stephen Jones, AFTRS.

Never underestimate the value of *chocolate*! . . . Catering is about caring for the crew. So don't underestimate its value. Budget for meals, morning and afternoon teas, and treats on the set.

- Studio rental
- Site fees and permits
- Food catering for all shooting days
- Office costs (phone, stationery, photocopying, postage, electricity, heating)
- Insurance (equipment, site, personnel—check with client as to who is covered by what).

Postproduction

Personnel—fees and wages (including annual leave loading at 17.5 per cent and superannuation at 9 per cent in Australia):

Make sure you include everything! Peter Millyn, Production Accountant, AFTRS.

- Producer
- Director
- Office manager
- Bookkeeper/accountant
- Postproduction supervisor
- Editor
- Assistant Editor
- Sound (tracklayer, mixer; musicians, performers, conductor; voiceover; sound effects—manufacture and/or search and purchase).

Costs:

- Logging (equipment hire)
- Editing (equipment hire)
- Music (recording facilities hire)
- Audio track (sound-mixing suite hire with editor)
- Final cut (online facilities hire)
- Stock (videotapes, DVDs or other)
- Artwork/graphics
- Music rights.

If the budget is tight, beg, borrow and use your imagination.

Darrell Lass, Production Designer.

Distribution

Personnel—fees and wages (including annual leave loading at 17.5 per cent and superannuation at 9 per cent in Australia):

- Office manager
- Distribution coordinator
- Bookkeeper/accountant
- Auditor of accounts.

Budgeting is knowing how much things are going to cost. Production management is getting them done for the price.

Ian Ingram-Young, Academy of Photogenic Arts.

Costs:

- Launch party
- Publicity (advertising, brochure, accompanying material)
- Stock (videotapes, CDs, DVDs)
- Dubbing fees
- Packaging
- Postage.

Budget Layout

Having a clear layout helps project assessors and everyone else to interpret your budget more easily. You may find it useful to set up your accounts with line item numbers. This way it's easier to locate items that are being discussed, and it's simple to separate out the costs of the distinct phases of the production. For example: 1400 for Production, so:

Account	Unit Price	Quantity	Rate	Amount
1401 Camera operator with camera	Shoot days	12	$950.00	$11,400.00
1402 Sound recordist	Shoot days	12	$350.00	$4,200.00
1403 Extra Light kit hire	3 days	1	$375.00	$375.00
1404 DVCam stock	T-64 non chip	30	$16.54	$496.20
1405 Location fees #1	Monastary	1	Gratis	$0.00
1406 Location fees #2	Belleview Mansion	1	$500.00	$500.00
1407 Vehicle costs (Phil's van)	Shoot days	1	Gratis	$0.00
1408 Petrol, parking, tolls	Shoot days	12	$30.00	$360.00
1409 Lunches, morning tea afternoon tea, snacks	Per person day	24	$40.00	$960.00
1410 Childcare	Mothers' sessions	2	$150.00	$300.00
			SUBTOTAL 1400	$18,591.20

And 1500s for postproduction, 1600s for licensing, 1700s for marketing and distribution. Got it?

These costs are for demonstration only—don't take them as the real costs you'll encounter. Prices vary from place to place and time to time. The thing is, when budgeting, try to plan for everything you'll need!

Never use your own money.

Brian Williams,
Western
Australian
School of Art
and Design.

Contingency

Once you've come up with the total cost estimate for the project, add 10 per cent on top of that and label it *contingency*. That means you've allowed some extra money for unexpected costs. You may well need it. If you don't, everyone will be pleased that you've come in under budget.

Don't spend the contingency in your head. If there's an expense, include it in your ongoing accounts. Leave the contingency intact for real blow-outs.

Peter Millyn,
Production
Accountant,
AFTRS.

In-kind Contributions

Not all the costs of a project end up being paid for directly in cash. Sometimes one or more of the people working on a project are receiving their pay from their normal job. This is the case, for example, with many in-house productions, where people within a workplace are producing a training tape for their company or government department. Their time appears to come free. The same may go for equipment costs, editing time, office costs. Many budget items can be invisible when it comes to direct cash payouts.

There are at least three reasons why it's usually the best idea to include these items in your budget anyway, and label them appropriately.

First, it helps both you and your sponsors to see what the true cost of the project is.

Second, it gives credit where credit is due, either within the organisation or to the helpful contacts outside it.

And third, funding bodies often want to see that many of the production costs are being taken care of by someone else.

One way to get helpers for your video is to crew for other people sometimes. Beryl Stephens, always ready to help.

Keep track of the spending as you go, so you can make adjustments if you're having a cost blow-out. Dave Sheridan and Sarah Curnow, AFTRS.

Keep Records

It's a good idea to keep your old budgets filed away. They will help you draw up your new ones more quickly, and they can help you learn from your mistakes. If you find that you under-estimated costs somewhere within a project, make a note of it so you won't be caught out again.

If an unforeseen cost arose, record that too. It may help you foresee it next time.

Stick to the Budget

Although you may find that you spend slightly less in one area and slightly more in another, overall you should make every effort to work within the budget once it's been accepted by all parties.

Monitor your budget progress regularly, so things don't get out of hand without you knowing it. And be sure to communicate regularly and clearly with the producer about the current status of the budget.

Lastly, be prepared to reassess the plans for the rest of the production if significant budget blow-outs have occurred.

Suggestions from Rachel Masters

Time is money. Yet time is often the thing people find hardest to budget. If learning to budget even the smallest production achieves the recognition that people value their time more than anything else, it's well worth it. When you budget a production, often you place value only on the tangible things like equipment and consumables. But the time that you and your friends put into a shoot needs to be budgeted too. Sometimes the opportunity to go into someone's home or to a special event can't be calculated on a monetary basis, but you still need to value the contribution these opportunities make to your production.

Practise including *all* the contributions to your shoot into its budget. It often helps people to be more economical and thoughtful.

PREPRODUCTION

23

The preproduction period is that stretch of time between your commitment—or commercial agreement—to do a video project and the beginning of the shoot itself. Although this phase is less 'visible', and may seem less exciting, than the actual production time, the success of your video project depends largely on the amount of detailed care you take during this preparation period.

Pick a crew that will share your vision, get along with others, do their best and stay with the project until it's done. Deirdre Brannick does camera for *The Rainbow Boughquaker*.

There are five keys to good preproduction:

1. Being able to *determine* what cast and crew, equipment and arrangements will be necessary for the success of the shoot.
2. Being able to *imagine* the possible difficulties in accomplishing the production, and finding the ways to overcome these difficulties or adjusting the production plans so the goals are achievable.

3. Being able to *plan thoroughly*, sorting out all the details. Never assuming things will turn out right by themselves.
4. *Keeping written records* so phone numbers, addresses, dates, quoted prices, location agreements, interview consent forms and all the other details involved in a production can be accessed whenever necessary.
5. *Scheduling* enough *time*, and *people*, to attend to everything.

The Production Timeline

Philip Hayward, Macquarie University.

Ask yourself, *Is it doable?* If not, don't do it.

Your production will go through a number of phases. The first one is development (or *pre-*preproduction)—this is when the skeleton work is done for the project. It includes:

1. Writing the treatment and selling your idea to a funding body or buyer.
2. Writing the script and getting it approved.
3. Nutting out the budget (if you have one!).
4. Lining up a reputable crew (a commitment from a known director or camera operator is a good selling point).

In commercial situations, the development work must be completed before a project is given the go-ahead by whoever is commissioning it. Sometimes people

Clint Ganczak, Videographer.

It's all about problem solving when you have no money.

are able to get grants or payment for this development time. At other times it's a labour of love (or desperation)—it's work time you gamble in the hope that you can sell your idea to someone.

People don't commit money to a formless inspiration floating around in your head, no matter how lit up your eyes are. You have to get at least a treatment in writing in order to sell it.

In a video course setting, you still do this development phase, but it usually has to fall within the semester framework, so you'll have to fit this within your thirteen-week production timeline.

Fixed Deadlines

The first thing to get clear on is how much time you have, all up. Often the one date you'll know for sure is when the project must be delivered.

Tim Rooney, Portland Community Media.

As General Eisenhower said, 'In preparing for battle I have always found that plans are useless, but planning is indispensable.' The plan may only be good until the first shot is fired, but you have to have it.

Once you know this, then you can count up how many weeks or months you have until then. That's the full extent of time you have to work with, and you must fit all production tasks somehow within this limit—or renegotiate the delivery date right away.

Within this time limit, you schedule:

- *Preproduction:* Organising everything necessary for a successful production.
- *Production:* The shooting days, including any travel to and from the locations.
- *Postproduction:* Logging the footage, doing the first edits, possibly doing some minor reshoots (*pick-ups*), producing the soundtrack, getting decisions and approvals for the final cut, getting the needed graphics generated, editing the final cut, and burning or dubbing the necessary copies.
- *Distribution:* Artwork for the DVD and cover, promotional brochures, organising details for the premiere screening—including venue, invitations, catering and press coverage. (For students, this may be simplified to getting your finished video in the box on the lecturer's desk by noon on the day of the screening.)

> Think about the editing before you start shooting.

Julian Lauzzana, Primal Digital LLC.

> You should always shoot the best format you can afford.

Richard Fitzpatrick, Camera Operator, Digital Dimensions.

Production managers often work backwards when constructing the production timeline, marking in the foreseeable deadlines and making best estimates of how long each production phase will take (or can be allowed to take). The way of thinking goes like this:

1. If the project has to be finished by 15 June (for example), and it will take three weeks for postproduction, then the shooting has to be finished by the third week of May.
2. The shoot will take two weekends (so schedule three weekends, to allow for hold-ups like rain, equipment breakdown, performers getting the flu, incorrect shooting time estimate, and so forth), so we have to have everything ready to go by the beginning of May.
3. That means that all the preproduction work (sites found and booked, equipment booked, transport arrangements completed, cast and crew finalised, and so forth) has to be done in April. But people will be away for Easter break in April, so that's going to be a push.
4. Which means the script had better be finished by the end of March, so we know what we're arranging for!

> It is essential that producers allow adequate funding and time to plan their film's publicity, marketing and distribution.

Sharon Taylor, Public Relations and Marketing, AFTRS.

Contingency Time

Though this may seem laughable to students juggling a full semester of coursework, it's a very good idea to allow a little extra time (contingency time) at the end of each section of the schedule.

> Never leave to the day those jobs that can be done the day before.

Don Bethel, Consultant, Television Production Techniques.

You see, even if your production relied solely on you, it would be a good idea to have some flexibility. But when you're juggling the schedules and needs (health, emotional and academic) of an entire crew, things almost never work out entirely according to your original schedule. Being able to adapt quickly, and to imaginatively surmount the insurmountable, is what's required.

Good planning sessions can generate great ideas for your project and build crew morale as well. (Courtesy of Metro Screen)

Some Standard Tasks of Preproduction

Though every shoot has its own particular requirements, there are certain generic tasks which need to be done during preproduction.

1. Finalise the script. Photocopy and distribute it.
2. Draw up the production schedule.
3. Engage the key creative team.
4. Have discussions with the camera operator and the designer about the look of the video and how it will be realised. Order sets to be constructed, props found, wardrobe found or made.
5. Organise insurance coverage, bookkeeping and payrolls.
6. Book the cast, negotiate contracts.
7. Book the crew, negotiate contracts.
8. Conduct preproduction meetings with crew to make sure everyone knows what's going to happen and to allow for their input.

Julie Booras, Offspring Productions.

I think it's extremely important BEFORE shooting video to think about how it's going to be edited together. If you're shooting a talking head interview that you will need to edit down, what material will you use to cover those edits? You might want to think about shooting some interesting cutaways. If you're shooting dialogue between two or three people, do you have the coverage necessary to edit your scene together successfully?

9. Book the equipment, buy the necessary recording stock.
10. Check out possible locations (site checks should be done by the director, camera person, sound operator and safety officer).
11. Choose the locations, obtain permits and clearances where necessary.
12. Book interviews, if needed.
13. Make the arrangements for travel, food and accommodation.

Philip Elms, Media Resource Centre.

Plan postproduction effects in preproduction.

Judi Kelemen, Producer/ Trainer.

For field productions: Do a site search! Check out space, windows and coverings, wall colours, AC sockets (and do they work!), what you can move, what you need to bring in for a set. Who's in charge of the building and can open doors? Do the lights work and will they be enough or do you need a light kit? Make sure you can run light cords to another area if necessary for power.

Crew members can often contribute valuable perspectives and good shooting ideas. Erika Addis, Bernard Purcell and Deborah Klika discuss camera coverage plans for *Bernie's World*.

What designs, colours and sizes of costumes are needed? (Courtesy of Film & TV, Central TAFE, Perth, WA)

14. Arrange and conduct performance rehearsals prior to camera rehearsals, when needed.
15. Generate the storyboard, then photocopy and distribute it.
16. Ensure that sets are being built according to design decisions, and that they'll be completed on time.
17. Get artwork done.
18. Make and distribute call sheets for shoot days—these tell everyone where and when they'll be working.
19. Check that all props have been found, that wardrobe is complete.

As you can see, this list is long, and it's still not all-inclusive.

The point to remember is that anything that's overlooked can give you problems on the shoot.

Do all the costumes fit the actors? What alterations are needed? Enid Holmes in *Clara's Curse*.

Problems to Solve Ahead of Time

The more time and thought in preproduction, the more it pays off in the shoot and edit.

Ben Kreusser, Producer.

Another aim of preproduction is to think ahead, and foresee problem areas so they can be sorted out before the actual shoot begins.

Scripts need to be read carefully for any built-in challenges, and props and staging issues should be tackled early, while there's a hope of managing them.

At Hamilton Secondary College, the video team came up with a superb response to a script which required an under-age driver.

Does your script require a lad at the wheel?

Work out the camera angle you need and then . . .

. . . solve how you'll achieve it. Shooting *And she said . . .*, Hamilton Secondary College. (Photos by Liesl Cosh)

Each of the umbrella categories in the preproduction checklist covers a wide number of individual tasks. A good example of this is the site check.

Nigel Graves,
Scriptwriter/
Producer.

Believe it when you are told not to think you can just wing it on the day. When the time comes you will be so busy, you will have precious little time for doing rewrites on the run.

But here is the catch. Expect the unexpected. Be prepared to have to ad-lib at any moment. You cannot possibly prepare for every occurrence. You need to be willing to compromise in order to get the film shot. The more you plan, the less surprises will happen, but they WILL happen.

Which leads to my next point: Getting good people around you. The more experienced and enthusiastic people you have around you, the more chances you have of finding solutions. Finding a good cast and crew is just as important as your script.

The Site Check

The site check, which is also known as the *location recce* or *reccy* (for reconnaissance), is the careful assessment of the planned shooting location to figure out what problems it could pose to the production. You can expect there will be *some* problems, and you may find there are so many that a better site needs to be chosen.

It's amazing how many beginners blithely grab a camera and rush off to a shoot, with only the sketchiest idea of what the location will be like. Sometimes they're lucky and get great results, but many times they're faced with difficult or impossible conditions.

This could mean a very trying shoot, last-minute changes to the storyboard, unfortunate compromises which handicap the realisation of the project idea, and sometimes outright failure.

So *always* do a site check.

Note: Be sure to do your site check at the time of day, and day of the week, that you plan to do your shoot, because many things at a site change as the time changes.

With outdoor sites, this will be true of sun position, for sure.

Ambient noise level usually varies, depending on what goes on at or near the site, and sometimes there are dramatic external factors, like aircraft flight paths, traffic noise and building construction, which render some sites useless at some times, even though they're fine at others.

It's always easy to rush into a shoot, and if you need to catch a news event, it may be warranted. But taking the time to think about the purpose of the shoot and what you're attempting to achieve can be rewarding in the long run. Go to locations before the shoot and prepare a thorough recce plan.

Rachel Masters, Corporate Training Coordinator, SBS.

Work out what security arrangements might be necessary (e.g. traffic diversions, crowd control, overnight protection of props and equipment) and put these in place.

Colin Holmes, Videographer.

Power

IS AC ELECTRICITY AVAILABLE?
- How many power points are there?
- How far are the power points from the shooting site? (Which means what lengths of electrical extension cable will be necessary? And how many multi-socket connection boards will be needed to plug everything in?)
- Where is the fuse-box? The circuit breakers? Who will be around to help with electrical supply at the time of the shoot? (Make friends with the caretaker.)
- How much electrical load can the circuits carry? Will your proposed lighting set-up overload this?
- What about safety? Will the shoot need a licensed electrician to be present?

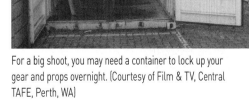

For a big shoot, you may need a container to lock up your gear and props overnight. (Courtesy of Film & TV, Central TAFE, Perth, WA)

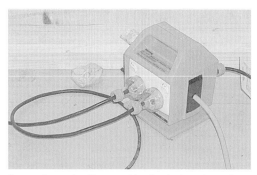

How much capacity will you need for plugging in equipment? Bring along enough extra sockets!

If you're shooting overseas, you may need adaptors for the electrical outlets. AC adaptors can often handle multiple voltage levels, but if in any doubt, run your camera only on batteries.

What time of day will this building work for video? Will reflected sunlight help or ruin your shot?

IF NO AC POWER IS AVAILABLE
- How many batteries will be needed?
- How can batteries be recharged during the shoot?
- Can you use the car battery?

If battery power will be insufficient:

- Can a generator be used instead of batteries?
- Where could you get a generator locally? How much would it cost?
- Can it be positioned out of range of the microphones?

Light

OUTDOORS
- Will sunlight be sufficient for the shoot? If so, where is the sun in the morning? In the afternoon? Does the position of the sun restrict the times when the site is usable?
- If you need any big location feature, like the front of a building, to look its best, at what time of day is the light right for this?
- Where are the shadows at the different times of the day? Will shadows be a problem to the shoot at any time? Will reflector boards be necessary to bounce light into deep shadows? Or will lights be needed?
- Will the sun be so bright that some screening will be necessary? What about an ND filter for the camera?

- Are additional portable lights needed? How large an area needs to be lit? What quality of light is called for?
- Will any colour correction (gels) be necessary due to light sources of different colour temperatures?

INDOORS
- What sunlight will be available?
- What other lights will be available? Are any of the available lights unusable? For example, fluorescent lights often give a green tinge to the image, so they should be avoided if possible.
- Will any wall or ceiling surfaces be useful for bouncing light? Or are their colours wrong?
- How large an area needs to be lit? What quality of light is called for?
- Will any colour correction (gels) be necessary due to light sources of different colour temperatures?

Visuals

- Does the scene contain sacred sites which you should not be videoing?
- Are there electrical power lines strung across the view?
- Is there a building which is inconsistent with the set design?
- Are there billboards or signs which could be a problem? Can you shoot around them?
- Is it possible to get the view you want from the camera? Can the crew safely get to the right position? Check this by going to the spot yourself. Does the view look the way you want it from there?

Sound

You need to think about both the sound you'll want to record, and the sound that's inherent to the location.

AMBIENT SOUND
What are the ambient sounds at the time of day and the day of the week when the shoot will happen?

- Will planes, trains or automobiles cause unacceptable disruption to the sound-recording process?
- Is there a railroad or construction site nearby? A stadium or racetrack with amplified sound? Any other uncontrollable source of sound?
- Are there objectionable sounds which can be avoided by planning ahead? For example, can the airconditioner be turned off, can the phone be left off the hook, can the shoot happen after the nearby playground is emptied for the afternoon, can the street be temporarily closed off to vehicles? What day are the lawns mowed?
- Will the rhythm of unavoidable background sounds cause problems in editing dialogue? For example, ocean waves, crows, cicadas . . .

MICROPHONES
- What microphones will be necessary to capture the sound required by the shoot?
- How many microphones will be needed?
- What sort of batteries go in each mic? (Always take spare batteries and spare cables.)
- Can these microphones be correctly placed, given the limits of the site?
- How much mic extension cable will be needed?
- Will special mic supports or booms be needed?
- Will an audio mixer be needed? If so, will an additional sound operator be required?

Jane Paterson,
Sound Editor,
AFTRS.

Record any wild material you can while on location. That's much easier than coming up with it in sound post-production.

SOUND EFFECTS
- Can all the sound effects be recorded during the shoot? Or will some need to be done at another time?
- Are any needed effects impossible to record at the site? Will Foley effects be required?

Safety

- What potential safety hazards exist at the site?
- What hazards will be created by the introduction of your shoot?

Plan how you'll handle the risks from each scene. Be prepared for what can go wrong. (Courtesy of Digital Dimensions)

When doing commissioned work for overseas companies, there's a lot of paperwork you have to do relating to insurance indemnities. I have to write out protocols for extreme shoots. Be prepared to write out huge standards and procedures, and program risk assessments. It's a nightmare, but it makes you think about what you're going to do. Like when we work with snakes, we have to phone the hospital and make sure they have a supply of anti-venom. We once had a snake bite on a shoot. We had a helicopter on call for the shoot and the snake handler was medivaced out of the Tablelands. You know, we used the sequence in the doco, it was great TV!

Richard Fitzpatrick, Camera Operator, Digital Dimensions.

Access

VEHICLES
- How will people get to the site? Is it near public transport? What are the scheduled arrival times of the trains, buses? Who will pick people up at the station?
- What sort of vehicles will be needed? Four-wheel drive?
- Do crew members have these vehicles or do they need to be rented?
- Who can drive the required vehicles? Do these drivers have valid licences? Does anyone need to get trained and certified ahead of time?

PARKING
- What parking facilities are available?
- Are parking permits needed? What do they cost? How do you get them? Who will get them?
- Is the parking lot supervised or not? Would the attendant be able to give instructions or directions to later arriving crew members?

UNLOADING
- Where can the gear be unloaded from the vehicles?
- Is there a time limit on how long you can stay in the unloading area?
- What's the most convenient pathway to carry equipment to the set? For example, which door is closest to the right lifts or stairways inside the building?

SHELTER
- Where can the cast and crew rest? Should you bring folding chairs?
- Can people get out of the sun, or do you need to bring a tarpaulin or tent?
- Can people and gear get out of the rain?

How will your crew get to the location? Lucca Galimberti and Juan-Carlos Martinez arrive at location for *Olive Grove*.

Do your drivers have valid licences?

How long can this gear stay here? Who will move it into position? (Courtesy of Metro Screen)

TIMES
- Are there restrictions on times of arrival and departure?
- Is the park only open until dusk? Does the building close at the end of business hours? Do the crew have to use the site only when the public are not there?
- Are other times important to consider? Does it matter when the tide is high or low? Does it matter when it's peak hour?

PERMISSIONS
- Is it necessary to get permits for the use of this site? If so, how do you get the permits? What do they cost? How long does it take to get them? Who controls them? Who will get the permits?
- Who holds the key to the building?
- Does the location owner know about the shoot?
- Have the police been advised?

A chain reaction: Video production is a constant process of decision-making. Every decision you make from the preproduction phase affects everything that comes after. Every decision while shooting affects editing decisions, and so it's like a chain reaction. The preceding link affects the following one.

**Mark
Tewksbury**,
The Nine Video
School.

FACILITIES
- Where are the toilets?
- Where are shops for food? Emergency supplies?
- Where can people stay overnight?
- Where is the nearest medical facility in case of an emergency? What is its phone number?
- Is there any suitable place for playback?

How's that for starters? And the site check is only *one element* of preproduction.

Rearranging a Location Set-up

There are times when the site check can alert you to problems which can be avoided by acting early and using some diplomacy. Here's a good example:

> It doesn't matter where you come from or how many times you've done it, always go for local knowledge. Ask around.

Richard Fitzpatrick, Camera Operator, Digital Dimensions.

You've been asked to videotape the wedding of a friend. You're happy to use your new skills to do this, and by now you understand that video skills go far beyond camera operation and include many other things, including good preproduction practices. So you agree, but you say that you'll need to have a look at the wedding site a couple of weeks ahead. It turns out that the wedding is to be held in a relation's home that you've never been to. Since you've made your request early, your friend manages to schedule a visit before all the hoopla begins. Your friend's aunty leads you cheerfully out to the large deck with a lovely view. She beams with pleasure when you tell her it's a beautiful site for a wedding, and how generous of her to offer her home.

'And how will you have it arranged on the day?' you ask. (This is the key question.)

'Well, we thought we'd have the bride and groom standing here facing everyone,' she says, gesturing to the west end of the narrow porch, 'and have the chairs lined up in rows facing them.'

'Oh,' you say softly. Your mind is racing—it's your first wedding and you get the worst-case scenario!

'Hmmm,' you say, looking thoughtful and professional. 'The wedding will be at four in the afternoon, right? And that's the west side of the house. Which means the sun will be shining directly in at a low angle from that side. You know what will happen? The brightness of the sun will make the camera's iris close down and the bride and groom will just be silhouettes.'

'Oh no!' says the aunty, surprised and genuinely concerned.

'We want the video to be good so we can send it to his grandparents, who can't come.'

'What if . . .' you say gently, 'what if we have the bride and groom standing on the east side of the deck facing everyone? Then the afternoon sun will light their faces and all the colours will be beautiful.'

If you're shooting a wedding, you can't do a reshoot. Ensure you know as much as you can about the site and the plans ahead of time. Ron and Doreen Cooper.

Always time-code your tapes before shooting.

Beryl Stephens, Videographer.

Don't forget to charge the batteries.

Walter Locke, Community Outreach Coordinator, Arlington Community Media Inc. (ACMi)

'Of course! Will that fix things?' says Aunty with relief. 'It doesn't really matter which way we set it up. I just pictured it the other way so the frangipani would be in the picture.'

'Well, we'd get that in silhouette, too,' you say matter-of-factly. 'But I could get a beautiful shot of the frangipani for you earlier in the day by looking in at the deck from the west side to show all the flowers and decorations. I could do that before everyone arrives.'

'That would be great. I'm so glad we got this sorted out ahead of time.' And then you have the obligatory cup of tea. The shoot is salvaged from disaster—and you've rescued yourself from considerable embarrassment.

In contrast, can you imagine the other possible scenario?

You arrive at the house twenty minutes before the wedding party does. The aunt is in the kitchen taking headache tablets and fanning herself. She's visibly shaking, but when she spots your camera she quickly ushers you out to the deck. It's been lovingly decorated with crepe paper streamers and baskets of flowers. Sixty folding chairs are facing west towards an arbour of ivy and tiny white blossoms which have been wired onto a large rented arch. And the huge wedding cake is sitting on a table at the east end of the deck. The doorbell rings and the aunt hurries off. You sit down because your knees are shaking. 'It's my first wedding and I get the worst-case scenario!'

Do you:

(a) Rush out and tell the aunt that the video will be ruined unless everything is rearranged to face in the other direction?

(b) Tape the wedding as it is, knowing that the ceremony part will look awful, and try to think of what other shots you can get to partially salvage the situation?

(c) Leave quietly through the back gate?

(d) Awake from this normal anxiety dream knowing that you've done the site check and everything will be right on the day?

When You Have No Control

Sometimes you'll be shooting an event over which you have no control at all. For these you must be totally ready ahead of time.

Choosing the Crew

Video is not a lonely-writer-in-a-garret activity. It's a group effort that benefits from the skills, ideas and commitment of every crew member. For people to give their best, they need to feel that they're working in a well-assembled team, that the director has a clearly focused goal, and that their individual contributions are valued and supported.

Know the exact schedule and be fully set up and ready, in case that train comes through a little early. Jim Adolph for tav productions, South Australia. (Photo by Neil Smith)

Crew Size

The size of your crew depends on the logistics and complexity of your production.

> Everyone has to be passionate about what they want to do.
>
> **Ed Spencer,** Sound man.

Documentary crews sometimes need to be very small, so they can move around quickly, use only one or two vehicles, and not take up too much space on location.

Drama features seem to have a cast of thousands behind the camera as well as in front of it. (Give some thought to the credits at the end of the next feature film you watch, if you want to think mega-crew.)

If your project is small, crew members can sometimes double or triple up on roles. Your production assistant during preproduction might also look after props/wardrobe ahead of time and be a driver on the day of the shoot.

But on larger shoots, many jobs have to be done all at once, so you need a person looking after each role, even if that person will be inactive and waiting around at times. (Patience is not just a virtue, but a requirement in this industry.)

It's a false economy to undercrew a shoot. Trying to fix up things that went wrong because you were short one or two people will cost you much more in money, psychic energy or both than it would have done to book a full crew for the day.

> For professional work, never try to interview someone and also operate the equipment. Thoughtful on-camera documentary interviews require *at least a two-person crew*—one to relate to and handle the interviewee(s) and one to focus on the equipment.
>
> **Donna Kenny,** The Video History Company and Center for Recording Life Stories.

Who to Choose

There are several things to consider when choosing crew members:

1. Does the person have the skill and experience to do the job well?
2. Will the person give a full commitment to the success of your project?

Richard Fitzpatrick, Camera Operator, Digital Dimensions.

In extreme filming, you have to be totally competent at what you're doing before you add a camera to the activity. No one should be filming who's new at the sport. I reckon a person should have a couple of hundred dives under their belt before they try to do underwater filming.

Judi Kelemen, Producer/ Trainer.

Keep everyone involved with your project up-to-date. Use an email list or an online service, whatever you feel is most efficient and safest.

Alison Wotherspoon, Flinders University.

Working collaboratively and developing creative teams is one great thing you can get out of tertiary training.

3. Will the person take direction from you?
4. Will the person get along with the rest of the crew?
5. Will the person act responsibly and professionally on the day?

You should be able to answer yes to all of these questions.

Crew Dynamics

A crew is like a living organism: if one part of it isn't functioning well, the whole being feels sick and is dragged down.

There's a saying: 'People choose friends for their faults, not their good points.'

The idea is that no matter how much you like and admire a person, if he or she has a fault you cannot abide, then you'll never be friends with that person. On the other hand, you can hang around for years with a person who has faults you can live with. Like any saying, it has its truths and its limitations.

Applying this idea to a video crew means that each member should be chosen with an eye to the way they'll interact with the other people you're choosing.

Note that the emphasis is on *the way they'll interact*. Crew members with a professional attitude can function well on a job even when they don't really like another crew member. Being courteous and respectful of each crew member's skill, and getting on with your own job the best way you know how, is part of the discipline of being professional.

A harmonious crew will produce much better work than one torn by irritations, jealousies and intolerances. For someone to deliberately bring ill-feeling to a shoot is unacceptable.

When you choose your crew, use both the information you can get about their job skills and about their people skills. Over time, your experience and intuition will help you make these choices.

Pick your team partly by their ability to get along with other crew members. Michelle Blakeney interviews Toni Janke for *XX Live*.

Sensitivity to the People in Your Video

How would you feel if some people you barely knew came to your workplace—or even worse, to your home—and wanted to ask you a lot of deep and meaningful questions?

You might feel upset and invaded.

If you liked the people, you might want to help them out and do a good job with the interview, but you still might feel nervous and hear yourself giving stiff and awkward replies.

Alternatively, how would you feel if one or two of the video people had visited you a week earlier and had a relaxed discussion with you about their project and why you were chosen to be in it?

What if they'd shown you some of their materials and told you a few stories about why they'd chosen this topic and how things were going for them so far?

What if they told you things about themselves which made you feel that you all had some common interests and values?

What if their manner made you feel an intuitive trust in them, sensing that they would consider you when they did the editing and not show things in a way that would make you lose face?

What if they offered to give you something in return for your time and effort—like a copy of the video once it was done?

Now say you were the videographer in this story. Under which circumstances would you get the best video, with the most natural look and the greatest amount of information coming forth?

Under which circumstances would you enjoy the shoot and go home happy and feeling like everyone else was happy, too?

COMMUNICATE. Dialogue is just as important off-camera as it is on-screen. The more you discuss something, the more you understand it. The most minor details can have a great impact on a project. Little things mean a lot and miscommunication is easily avoided.

Gordon Peters, Cameraman, Channel 7 News, Bundaberg.

Film crews can be so arrogant and they end up burning their bridges in communities. You should always be mindful of people's needs and be as little disruptive as possible. Work around their daily lives.

Richard Fitzpatrick, Camera Operator, Digital Dimensions.

Being from the same culture can help. Camera operators David Poisy and Kimberley Brown with reknowned throat singers Napatchee Pootoogook (left) and Quanaq Makkigak (right), Nunavet.

How can the actions of the crew help to relax the person being interviewed? A production by KINO, University of New South Wales.

Lists and Forms: Building on Experience

Gordon Peters, Cameraman, Channel 7 News, Bundaberg.

PACK YOUR BAGS. I keep a backpack handy for roving location shoots on foot. If you will be shooting off the shoulder, make sure your bag has a single strap. Usually I take camera batteries, spare media, earphones, shotgun mic and cable, radio mic and lapel (plus spare AA batteries), polariser, lens rag (SPUDZ), leatherman and camera lights (tungsten and daylight).

Rachel Masters, Corporate Training Supervisor, SBS.

Why not create your own version of standard production forms, a call sheet, a recce and location plan, shotlist, logging sheet and edit sheet? You can create the sheets using your own invented production company name. With customised sheets you'll look very organised and professional.

David Opitz, Metro Screen.

Get your agreements before you start shooting, not after.

One way to make preproduction both easier and more certain is to develop lists and forms that you can use for each new shoot. For example, compile a list of the video equipment you need for a basic shoot. Your personal list will probably contain the items that you know how to use and have ready access to. It doesn't matter if it's your own camcorder, or the local access centre's gear, or the up-market video hire service's HDCAM rig. This list comprises what is functionally *your* gear.

After listing the basics, like camera, tripod, microphones, headphones and light kit, you list those essential little accessories which must not be forgotten. You'll learn through experience (or even—could it be?—thoughtful foresight) what these bits and pieces are.

For example, it may be that your headphones can't plug into the camera without a *phone-to-mini* adaptor, or your microphone needs an *XLR-to-mini* cable in order to connect it to the camera.

Without these adaptors, your equipment set-up won't be functional, but they're small items and easy to overlook. It's not only easy to forget them when you're booking the gear, there's always the risk of forgetting to take them to the shoot, or forgetting to bring them back with you when it's all over. So this one list can help you check your gear at several different times during the project.

You could make a secondary list of the less commonly used pieces of equipment, under general categories like lighting and sound. This will assist you in drawing up your equipment list for more complicated shoots. That way, during quiet, unpressured times, you can put some good thinking to long-term use. There's no point in reinventing the wheel, or anything else, during actual preproduction —you'll have enough else to do.

Other forms that are useful to have on file are:

- production schedule sheet
- call sheet
- consent forms
- basic contracts.

A Basic Call Sheet

HOSPITAL:	AMBULANCE:	FIRE:	POLICE:

AFTRS
AUSTRALIAN
FILM
TELEVISION &
RADIO
SCHOOL

CALL SHEET:

. . . .

DIRECTOR:

. . . .

PROJECT#: . . . .

DAY:
DATE:
M/U & W/ROBE CALL:
CREW CALL AFTRS:
CREW CALL LOCATION:
PRE-LIGHT:
EST. WRAP:
SUNRISE:
SUNSET:
EST. SCREENTIME:

1300 131 461

SETS LOCATIONS: . . . .

WET WEATHER CALL

SCENE/ PAGE	D/N DUR	INT EXT	SET/LOCATION SYNOPSIS	CHARACTERS	ARTIST	P/U	M/U	ON SET

PROPS:
ART DEPT:
PICTURE VEHICLES:
LIVE STOCK:
ADDITIONAL CREW:
STUNTS/SAFETY:
SFX:
SPECIAL REQUIREMENTS:
CATERING:
MOVEMENT ORDER:
PARKING:
TRANSPORT:
RUSHES   (EXPOSED):
         (SCREENING):
WET WEATHER COVER:
ADVANCE SCHEDULE:
NOTES:

Sample Consent Form

○

Put your own logo here

RE: STUDENT FILM/TELEVISION PROJECT

I . . . .
hereby give my consent to be filmed by [insert your school or production group's name here]. The footage is to be utilised in the making of . . . .

I also agree that [your school or production group] may use the aforesaid film in whole or part in the final version of any motion picture film or television program either as a sequence on its own, or preceded, interlaced or followed by such other material.

Signed: . . . .   Date: . . . .

Name & Address (please print):

. . . .

. . . .

. . . .

. . . .

School or production group name
Address
Phone/fax/email

Performer's Clearance Form

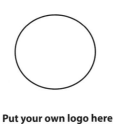

Put your own logo here

TO: [Your Production Company]

RE: [Name of film/video] . . . .

I, ... acknowledge receipt of $ . . /$NIL* as full payment for my contribution and performance for the production of a sound recording for use in the soundtrack of . . . .

I acknowledge that I have no right, title or interest in the sound recording containing my performance.

SIGNED: . . . .

DATED: . . . .

*delete one

School or production company name
Address
Phone/fax/email

Sample Request for Use of a Site

University of Technology, Sydney
PO Box 123
Broadway NSW 2007
Australia
Tel +61 2 9330 1990 Fax +61 2 9330 1551

Media Centre
Faculty of Humanities and Social Sciences
PO Box 123
Broadway NSW 2007
Tel: (02) 9330 2282 Fax: (02) 9330 1041

REQUEST FOR USE OF SITE

The bearer . . . . , Student Number . . . .
is a student in the Faculty of Humanities and Social Sciences. S/he is seeking your cooperation
in carrying out photography; film production; video/audio recording as part of her/his course
work at a site owned, leased or controlled by yourselves namely:

. . . .

Should you grant permission for use of the site, the University's insurance policies cover the
following contingencies and the University will meet claims arising from these, subject to
negligence on your part:

Accident or injury to the student, and to his/her unpaid individuals (whether or not these
persons are students of the University) whilst on the site or travelling to or from the site;

Accident or injury to third parties at the site arising from the student's use of the site;

Damage to the site and to property thereon, arising from the student's use of the site.

Occasionally a student's work may involve potentially hazardous situations. These include, but
are not limited to, use of inflammables, firearms and copies thereof, stunts and any aerial or
marine recording/photography/filming. In these instances, the student is obliged to disclose
fully such situations when seeking permission for use of the site, and to present, prior to use
of the site, authorisation from the University's insurers that the policies apply to their work.

If you require any further information, please contact the undersigned on . . . . or the
Universities Asset Control Officer on . . . . The University will not normally issue any
further documentation regarding the use of the site, except as required by the previous
paragraph.

We request that you state permission for use of site in writing—the form overleaf may be used,
with the original being returned to the student and copy retained by yourselves.

Yours faithfully,   Date . . . .

Officer City campus, No 1 Broadway, Sydney NSW
Campuses City, Kuring-gai, St Leonards

Used with the permission of University of Technology, Sydney.

Sample of Site Agreement

University of Technology, Sydney
PO Box 123
Broadway NSW 2007
Australia
Tel +61 2 9330 1990 Fax +61 2 93301551

. . . . , Dean
Faculty of Humanities and Social Sciences
PO Box 123
Broadway NSW 2007
Tel: (02) 9330 1926   Fax: (02) 9330 1041

AGREEMENT FOR USE OF SITE

I, ...
being (tick one)

            owner of
            lessee of
            a duly authorised person in relation to the site

give permisssion for . . . .
a student enrolled in the Faculty of Humanities and Social Sciences of the University of
Technology, Sydney, and for . . . . unpaid individuals to use the site at:

. . . .

to record, film or photograph in pursuance of his/her course requirements, on dates to be
agreed between us.

Permission is given to the University of Technology, Sydney agreeing to meet claims arising
from accident and damage, as stated in its attached letter.

. . . .

Signature of Authorising Person   Signature of Witness
Date   /   /   Date   /   /

. . . .

Position—if signing on behalf of company, other organisation, government department or
instrumentality.

. . . .

       Name   Witness Name

. . . .

. . . .

       Address   Witness Address

Office City campus, No 1 Broadway, Sydney NSW
Campuses Balmain, City, Kuring-gai, St Leonards

Used with the permission of the University of Technology, Sydney.

Location Survey Checklist

Australian Film Television & Radio School
PO Box 2286
Strawberry Hills NSW 2012
Phone: +1300 131 461

PRODUCTION TITLE: . . . .   INTERIOR/EXTERIOR: . . . .
. . . .   SCENE NO. . . . .
DIRECTOR: . . . .   WEATHER/TIME . . . .
. . . .   DAY/NIGHT/D for N . . . .
REC. BY: . . . .   FILMING DATE(S) . . . .

LOCATION	LOCATION FEE . . . .
ADDRESS	TERMS OF PAYMENT . . . .
FLOOR NO.	
MAP REF	COUNCIL CONTACT . . . .
	PHONE . . . .
CONTACT	POLICE CONTACT . . . .
WORK PHONE	PHONE . . . .
HOME PHONE	OTHER CONTACT . . . .
CONTACT	PHONE . . . .
WORK PHONE	
HOME PHONE	USE OF LOCATION . . . .
	PROP AT PRESENT . . . .
TOILETS	PROPS NEEDED . . . .
PORTABLE?	SECURITY NEEDED . . . .
WARD/MAKEUP	SPRINKLER SYSTEM/
. . . .	HEAT SYSTEM . . . .
. . . .	TURNED OFF . . . .
TELEPHONE	NEIGHBOURS CONTACTED . . . .
ACCESS	SCRIPT FORWARDED . . . . . .
KEYS REQUIRED	INSURANCE POLICY FORWARDED . . . .
. . . .	STRUCTURAL CHANGES OR ADDITIONS . . .
HOURS OPEN FOR BUSINESS	
. . . .	VISUAL PROBLEMS
USE OF PREMISES	NEON SIGNS . . . .
(DAYS)	OTHERS . . . .
(HRS)	NOISE PROBLEMS . . . .
. . . .	
REHEARSAL/PROPS ACCESS	SPECIAL EFFECTS . . . .
. . . .	. . . .
. . . .	. . . .
ELEMENTS RE LETTER OF INDEMNITY	. . . .
. . . .	. . . .

FLOOR PLAN (Windows & Doors)	ACCESS (Parking, Signs, Loading Zones)
FUSE-BOX DIAGRAM (attach photograph for electrician)	NOTES/PICTURES

Insurance Indemnity Form

University of Technology, Sydney
PO Box 123
Broadway NSW 2007
Australia
Tel +61 2 9330 1990   Fax +61 2 9330 1551

TO BE AUTHORISED BY INSURANCE OFFICER
REFER to . . . .

Indemnity

UNIVERSITY OF TECHNOLOGY, SYDNEY (hereinafter 'the University')
in consideration of its having requested and been granted permission by

. . . .
(name of organisation)

(hereinafter **'the receiving organisation'**) for . . . .
(state numbers of staff)

members of the University's staff and . . . . students of the Faculty of
(state numbers)

. . . . , plus . . . . voluntary
(state Faculty)   *(state numbers)*

workers to visit . . . .
(state site and site address)

(hereinafter **'the site'**).

Indemnity period from . . . . to . . . . (inclusive).

HEREBY AGREES that if any such member of staff or any such student or voluntary worker
sustains injury or damage to his/her property or person however caused whilst visiting the
site whether or not such injury results in or contributes to his/her death AND/OR if any act
of any such member of staff or student or voluntary worker causes any damage, or loss to the
receiving organisation AND/OR if any claim is made against the receiving organisation as a
result of granting this permission AND/OR the excercise of this permission if liability would
be attached to the University notwithstanding the terms of this permission THEN IN EVERY
SUCH CASE the University will release and indemnify and keep indemnified the receiving
organisation from and against all actions, claims, damage and loss that have arisen or that
may at any future time arise therefrom.

DATED this . . . . day of . . . . 20 . . . .

State the names of all students,
staff and voluntary workers going   . . . .
onto the site: **AUTHORISING OFFICER**

. . . .
. . . .
. . . .   Office City campus: No 1 Broadway, Sydney NSW
. . . .   Campuses: Balmain, City, Kuring-gai, St Leonards

(Please attach list if space not available)   *Used with the permission of the University of Technology, Sydney.*

Insurance

Schools with media programs usually have insurance coverage for their students while they're out on shoots. It may be required, for coverage purposes, for the shoot details to be lodged with some school authority *before* the students embark on the shoot. When this is required, *be sure to do it*.

Most likely you'll need to list the names of all the crew and performers who will be working on the site with you. School insurance can be organised to cover all members of the shoot, whether they're students of the school or not. But it's essential to list these people on the form before the shoot.

Also, your school administration may be able to give you a printed statement about the insurance coverage available to you and your crew. It may be useful to show this statement to the site manager when you're negotiating the use of a location for your project.

Assuring Competence

Preproduction is the time to make sure that all the performers and crew can do whatever will be required of them. This may seem appallingly obvious, but it's a common oversight.

A True Video Fable
There was once a minor twelve-shot storyboard which called for a whistling person to walk through a field, discover a fire in the brush and run to get a fire extinguisher to put it out. Simple?

The video crew found a willing friend to play the part.

They didn't show him the storyboard. At the beginning of the shoot, it was discovered that he couldn't whistle. The crew adjusted by having him pretend to whistle while someone else held a microphone and whistled into it.

The fire was lit, all sorts of close-ups and long shots were quickly done, while the fire was still containable. The friend was shot approaching the fire, discovering the fire, and then . . . the crew found out that due to an injured ligament in his heel, the friend was unable to run! His slow lope to the fire extinguisher was an irretrievable blow to the project.

But it was too late to reshoot. Enough said?

Unfamiliar Equipment

Always prepare for the worst-case scenario.

It's not only important that people can do what is required of them, but that they can do it with the equipment you've booked. A person can be quite competent at camera handling and camera technique, but if s/he has never laid eyes on the model of camera you've booked, there will need to be time available to go over it, possibly even to read the manual (make sure it's available) and practise a bit. It's very unwise to give a person a new piece of equipment and expect them to use it in the next three minutes.

Richard Fitzpatrick, Camera Operator, Digital Dimensions.

Whenever possible, the operator should have the camera the night before the shoot, to go over it carefully in some quiet place.

Suggestions from Rachel Masters

The more you think about locations, and the difficulties and rewards of using a particular site, the more alternative great ideas will be generated. When planning a shoot, try to think ahead of alternatives in case the weather changes. Make a list of your five favourite places and prepare comprehensive recce reports for these locations. Great locations could be: ocean baths, a country field, a dog obedience training school, a football field, the theatre, an ice-skating rink or your own lounge room.

THE LOCATION SHOOT

24

The big day has arrived! All your plans, preproduction efforts and rehearsals have led to this. Now the challenge is to achieve the best possible results from your shoot.

What do you need for this to happen?

1. You need everyone to get to the site, on time and in good condition, so they can work well.
2. You need all the equipment to be there, in good working order.
3. You need everyone to understand what they're supposed to do, and be up-to-date on any changes that have been made to the plan.
4. You need people to feel enthused about the project and energised for the work ahead of them.

Cathy Zheutlin uses a flexible handheld camera strategy while recording Rami Shapiro for *The Wisdom Keepers*.

Getting the Crew to the Site

Before the day of the shoot, everyone should be given, *in writing*, a call sheet which tells them:

1. the address of the shoot
2. the starting time and estimated finish time
3. the contact phone number at the site, and the mobile (cell) phone number of the production manager
4. emergency details, like the address and phone number of the hospital nearest the shoot location.

Doco crew arrives at the site. Scott Barber, Pat Saunders, Chris Ellis, Brad Francis, Curtin University of Technology. (Photo by Ryan Hodgson)

It should have been determined ahead of time how each person will get to the site. If someone needs to be picked up, there should be a written record of who's picking that person up, and at what time, and the driver and rider should have each other's phone numbers.

If the rider is to meet the driver somewhere other than at home, both people should have, written down, the meeting place details. A rendezvous at 'Central Railway' is not clear enough. Which entrance, on which street? Even if they might finally find each other by checking all the entrances, you don't want people arriving late for the shoot.

Colin Holmes,
Videographer.

Have emergency contact numbers (ambulance, police, fire etc.) in your mobile phone just in case, and on the premise that any adverse happening you are prepared for will never happen.

Know the schedule at the site. If you want shots of the snow being loaded onto the ramp for the snowboard demonstration, you've got to get there early enough. (Photo © Tatiana Boyle)

If people are travelling by bus or train, they need to know for sure which bus or train route to take, and they should have a copy of the timetable for that route. They also need a clear and well-labelled map showing them how to get to the production location from the bus stop or train station. And they need to know how long the trip is likely to take, so they can plan how early in the day to set out.

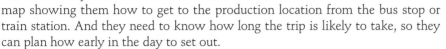
Drive and talk, don't talk and drive.

Gerry Letts, Operations and Facilities, AFTRS

Car parking details should have been worked out during preproduction, so drivers have the necessary permits or entrance money, and if there's a guard on an entrance gate, the guard should have a list of the vehicles that will be involved in the shoot.

And in the best of all possible worlds (which rarely seems to be the case on student shoots), it's a good idea if everyone has had a decent night's sleep and something to eat before the shoot begins.

Take more batteries.

Hart Cohen, University of Western Sydney.

Checking Out the Equipment

This may be the point of greatest resistance for beginners, but it's really very important.

Make sure you put all the equipment together and check that it's all working BEFORE you leave for the shoot.

In fact, the most sensible time to do this is when you pick the equipment up at the media centre, because that saves you lugging it home and then back again if it doesn't work. It also saves you being accused of having broken it yourself.

A number of good things happen when you do a thorough gear check:

For field productions, keep a kit in your car containing gaffer tape, a flashlight, clothespins, 3–2 plug adaptors, AC extension cable, adaptors like phone to mini, BNC to RCA, etc.

Judi Kelemen, Producer/ Trainer.

1. You find out if everything you need is there . . . 'Oh no! We've forgotten the tapes!'
2. You find out if it all connects together . . . 'Hey, we can't plug this microphone into the camera without an adaptor!'
3. You find out if it does or doesn't work, and hopefully have time to do something about it . . . 'Can we book another tripod? This one's had it!' . . . 'This battery is dead!' . . . 'This viewfinder is just hanging on by a thread!' . . . 'This lens is dirty—do we have a lens cleaning kit?'
4. You can leave for the shoot with a modicum of confidence.

Make sure you get everything you need, and that it PLUGS TOGETHER and WORKS. Equipment Store, University of Technology, Sydney.

Florence Onus,
Producer.

ALWAYS check that your
equipment works before you
go to the interview.

Usha Harris,
Lecturer in
International
Communication,
Macquarie
University.

When shooting on location
always take the camera bag
with all the accessories inside
it (cables, extra batteries and
tapes). You may need these
during the shoot. I know of
students who've just taken the
camera while leaving the bag
behind because it was 'too
heavy', and then not had the
right gear when faced with an
emergency.

**Rachel
Masters**,
Corporate
Training
Coordinator,
SBS.

Before getting into the car to
drive for two hours for that
fantastic shoot/interview/
location, don't forget to ask,
'Who's got the blank tapes?'
    Getting to a location
without the tapes can be
very infuriating. Oh, and don't
forget to label the tapes before
the shoot. Erasing material
because you forgot what was
on the tape can almost be a
criminal offence.

**Richard
Fitzpatrick**,
Camera
Operator,
Digital
Dimensions.

When doing extreme location
work, have a checklist. It's no
good doing a dive without a
tape, or a battery!

Now a gear check doesn't just happen. Someone has to agree to do it. It's handy if the person with the car can do the gear check, but whoever it is, they need to be able to spot a problem if there is one.

The person picking up the gear needs to allow an HOUR or so for the gear check.

Careening in to grab the camera on the way to the shoot, and not checking the gear, leaves you open to getting to the site with something disastrously wrong.

It's a totally good idea to get a copy of the list of what you've borrowed. That way you can be sure you pack everything up again at the end of the shoot.

Don't be the only guy in the school who hasn't got what he needs. Richard Fitzpatrick on shark project, Digital Dimensions.

If your shoot is in a remote location, be EXTRA sure you have everything with you. There may not be a chance to duck into a shop for batteries or more tape! Quvianaktulia Tapaungai and Loretta Kanatsiak unload sleds during the shoot of *Inukshuk: Inuit Ways, Inuit Survival*, Cape Dorset, Nunavut.

And what is accommodation en route to the shoot? Cindy Rennie, Kimberley Brown and Jimmie Papatsie hunker down in an igloo for the night on their two-day skidoo trip to the shooting site for *Inukshuk: Inuit Ways, Inuit Survival*, Nunavut.

Getting the Gear to the Shoot

Video equipment is heavy, but it's also delicate. It should never be banged or dropped. It should be packed in well-padded cases before it's transported, and loaded into a vehicle so that it's protected from being flung about. Wrapping it in thick blankets can help protect it, and also hide it from view. Putting it on the floor instead of the back seat of a car is a good idea, so it can't slide off the seat if there's a sudden stop.

Never leave video gear unattended in a car when it's visible through the windows. Insurance companies can consider this negligence, and may not pay for its replacement if you find your window smashed and the camera gone.

Never leave video gear unattended when you're unloading at a location site. Unloading gear to a location which is out of line-of-sight from the vehicle requires three people: one to carry the gear to the site; one to guard the gear once it's at the site; and one to remain with the car that still has equipment waiting in it. Of course, the same person doesn't have to do all the carrying.

If you work in the tropics, build a heat cupboard for your camera and recorder. With the levels of humidity we get in the wet season, going from even mild airconditioning to outdoors can cause condensation that takes an hour to clear!

Debra Kroon, Northern Territory University.

Crew Briefing and Scripts

Smoothly functioning shoots don't begin the instant people jump out of their cars and unload the gear. There needs to be a crew briefing at the beginning so everyone is certain about where they should be, what they should be doing and what changes were made to the plan at 11.00 p.m. the night before.

In the excitement of getting going, it may seem stodgy to have a meeting rather than just launch into things, but it takes a lot longer to round people up later and try to correct their misinformation.

Good communication is essential. Be sure everyone knows the latest plan. (Courtesy of Metro Screen)

SOMEBODY has to know the overall picture. Amanda Liok, Drew White and Lew Keilar working on *Through Tony's Eyes*. (Courtesy of Metro Screen)

Elisabeth Knight, Directing Department, AFTRS.

Always date your scripts.

This is also when the latest version of the script should be available to everyone, and all other versions should be collected or marked as out of date, so some people aren't mistakenly following yesterday's shot list.

If last-minute changes have to be made to job roles and responsibilities, this is the time to make them. No one should begin the shoot unclear about what contribution is expected from them. Any hazy areas or overlaps where more than one person is trying to attend to a single job should be straightened out before there are emotional fireworks on the set.

Peter Watkins, University of Western Sydney.

One camera, one operator!

A well-tuned crew hums along—it doesn't backfire, spit, cough, sputter and stall.

Depending on your crew and the work situation, this could be a sensible time to ensure that everyone has something in their stomachs before the work begins.

Energising the Crew

Brian McDuffie, Director.

A director has to be white hot in the morning, so he can still be red hot by the end of the day. If he's red hot in the morning, he's ash by lunchtime.

The director is the source of inspiration for the whole crew, and it's from the director's zest that crew members get their drive.

If the director is full of fire and raring to go, the crew will catch that wave of enthusiasm.

If the director is dragging around, the crew will slow down, too. Once the crew's energy drops, it's hard to get everyone up again.

Rachel Perkins, Director.

Make sure you get lots of sleep!

Give People Adequate Breaks

Enthusiasm has to be tempered with reality, and with reasonable and safe work practices.

People need to be given breaks now and then in order to keep up their stamina and refresh themselves. The director may be running on pure adrenaline (or fear), but the crew's well-being has got to be considered. Some of the worst tailspins a crew can go into happen when people have been worked too long and not fed. Normal practice is that five hours after crew call there must be a meal break.

There needs to be plenty of accessible drinking water on site, too. And, as no smoking is allowed on set, you may need to consider including smoking breaks for smokers.

Food

Whether you like it or not, food is a big issue on video shoots.

It seems there's always someone who arrives hungry and shaky. It should have been decided in preproduction whether people will be responsible for feeding themselves or whether they'll be fed as a crew. One way or another, they have to eat well to work well.

If they're feeding themselves, it's best if they bring their food with them. Why? Because no matter how close the nearest convenience store or fish and chip shop is, once crew members leave a production site they can be swallowed up into some sort of black hole and not return for ages. Then there are the wildest explanations, if you have time to listen to them.

That's why on commercial shoots the crew is always fed on location, and they're fed *well*, because no one leaves the site until the shoot is over.

On low-budget student productions, where no one has any money, it still may be a good idea for the director to supply a minimum level of calories to keep the crew going—whether it's coffee and tea to start, juice and biscuits for morning tea or sandwiches at lunch time . . . keep them happy and keep them on site.

And it's always a good move to have a wrap party.

Take a break when you need one—it will give everyone a boost. Benjamin Schaaf, Sylvia Pfeiffer and Beryl Stephens, *The Lizard of Oz*.

Adrian Barham, Colin Richards, Jeremy Watkins, Harold Lowah, Imparja TV, Alice Springs.

Allowing Enough Time for a Careful Set-up

Peter Watkins,
University of
Western
Sydney.

Remember to switch off the date/time!

Andy Nehl,
Head of
Television,
AFTRS.

Be aware of the icons in the viewfinder that are usually visible for normal shooting settings. If you see an icon and you don't know what it is or why it's there, find out. If it's not meant to be there, turn it off.

Richard Fitzpatrick,
Camera
Operator, Digital
Dimensions.

When you're loading an underwater camera, don't let anyone talk to you. Go through your checklist methodically, at your own pace, 'cause if you screw up you can flood the gear. Rushing leads to disaster.

Colin Holmes,
Videographer.

Have a good producer who has got all the necessary permits, permissions and authorities beforehand.

People forget things when they're nervous or hurrying, and when they're under stress. They forget little things that they'd normally remember.

Unfortunately, in video there are tiny things that can make or break the quality of the image. Like forgetting to white balance, and having the whole day's shoot come out too blue. Or forgetting to put the camera's audio switch to *external mic* and getting an entire interview with thin, echoey, camera-mic sound.

Then there are the little things that can make or break the equipment. Like forgetting to tighten one of the tripod legs and having the camera keel over when you turn away from it. Or forgetting to gaffer tape the light cable down and watching the redhead crash to the floor when someone's foot gets caught in it.

Make a generous estimate of the amount of time you'll need for set-up. A good rule of thumb is at least an hour for a simple shoot without lights, and an additional hour if there are lights.

Go through the set-up methodically, checking that every piece of equipment is connected right and is working the way it should.

Make sure everything is right before you launch into recording. Jeff Grinta, director of *On the Spectrum: Coping with Aspergers and Autism*. <www.strawbellyjerryfilms.com>

Underwater camera work by Richard Fitzpatrick, Digital Dimensions.

The Test Record

Finally, you do a short test recording—60 seconds should be enough—and play it back to make sure that you have a good picture and good sound (use headphones).

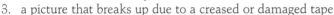

There are some problems you can only discover this way, like:

Always check that the lens is clean before shooting.

Beryl Stephens, Videographer.

1. a 50-cycle (or 60-cycle) electrical hum in the audio—which you can get if a mic cable is too close to an electrical cord or device
2. a rolling line of disturbance in the video—also called a video hum—which comes from an electrical current nearby
3. a picture that breaks up due to a creased or damaged tape
4. a spotty image due to excessive dropout on the tape. (It's common sense to invest in new, good-quality tapes for your original footage.)
5. a half-image or no image at all, due to clogged video heads.

Monitor everything!

Hart Cohen, University of Western Sydney.

Other problems which will show up are:

1. no sound at all, due to the mic being turned off, or a flat mic battery
2. wrong sound quality, due to the mic selection switch being in the wrong position—especially having the camera mic engaged instead of the external (auxiliary) mic
3. mic-handling noises
4. wind noise.

People often feel very rushed and don't take time for a test recording. But ask yourself if you've got the time to lose the whole shoot.

Once you're sure things are recording okay, you can go ahead. But even though you've had confirmation that things are working right at the beginning, you should stay alert to possible changes as the shoot goes along.

For example, the sound should be monitored throughout—mic cables sometimes get pulled out of the camera socket or they develop strange crackling sounds. Location poltergeists abound!

Ask yourself, is doing a 30-second test recording more work than doing this shoot again? In fact, CAN we do this shoot again? David Poisy, Camera Operator, and David Maltby, Director, *Inukshuk: Inuit Ways, Inuit Survival*, Nunavut.

Using a Field Monitor

If the camera's viewfinder is black and white, a field monitor can be useful for checking the colour of your shot, making sure the white balance worked and that the overall look is what you want.

Don't forget to get cutaways and ambient sound.

Colin Holmes, Videographer.

By first adjusting the colour, contrast and brightness to camera-generated colour bars, you can be sure that what you see is what you're getting.

Richard Fitzpatrick,
Camera
Operator,
Digital
Dimensions.

Never let the producer behind the camera! They can have a field monitor, but don't let them near the camera.

There are those who say people should have enough skill to work without field monitors—that they're for wimps. And there are those who have no choice because there are no little portable models in their equipment store.

But there are other good reasons for a field monitor. For some people, it's easier to get a perfect focus if they can look at a bigger image. It also helps to work from a bigger monitor for a long shoot, so you don't develop spasms in your left (or right) eye. And if decisions on shots are to be made by two or more people, it's much more convenient if everyone can view and discuss the shots at the same time.

Possibly the best reason is that after the shoot, it's good public relations to let people have a look at what they've done—to give them back something of what they've given you.

Double check the framing before shooting the scene. Joy Saunders on camera and Beryl Stephens, Director, *Fit As . . .*

If you don't have a monitor, the LCD screen may be good enough to let your actors get feedback on their scenes.

Harry Kirchner,
La Trobe
University.

Inexperienced directors sometimes over-prepare. It can be useful to have a storyboard or a shot list, but you should also be able to think on your feet. You should be willing to acknowledge the practical problems of your original plan as well as new possibilities when you get on location with your actors.

Time Management at the Shoot

It's the responsibility of the director, the director's assistant and the floor manager to keep the activities moving along according to the production schedule. By the end of the day, the planned amount of work needs to have been completed.

When a production hits a snag, it needs to be dealt with as efficiently as possible, and the momentum of the shoot must be kept going.

Variations in Busy-ness

By Don Bethel, Floor Manager and Consultant

There are peak loads at certain stages of production. Everyone should be available to contribute in their main role at these points, undistracted by other responsibilities. So cover these times with an adequate number of crew. This may mean that some support crew members are hanging around for long periods in between with little to do or to interest them, but that's the nature of TV/video-making.

A word here about attitudes. Inexperienced crew members, bored with waiting, can become social and treat the production area with less respect, becoming noisy or inattentive. At best they look amateurish, at worst they detract from the concentration of the crew and cast who are still working.

Such behaviour usually results in a rocket from the director or the floor manager/first assistant and is justly deserved. A crew member's best contribution for the day may be their patience! Everyone needs stacks of it—and stamina, too.

Another consideration in assessing crew numbers is the turnaround factor. During and after each rehearsal and prior to the take, time must be allowed for resetting of props, the repositioning of cameras and booms, and for wardrobe changes. Slates/idents have to be recorded, makeup patched, continuity checked. Time is wasted if crew numbers don't match the workload. Further time is lost if these functions are not efficiently coordinated. This is one of the responsibilities of the floor manager/first assistant.

A complete pull-down (strike) and movement to a new location presents another time-management challenge. You may have to consider booking additional assistant camera, lighting, sound, props or wardrobe crew.

The production manager or floor manager, while preparing the production schedule, mentally rehearses these turnarounds or transitions and makes a judgment on estimated time and crewing requirements.

As your product increases in complexity, so does the need for planning. Early attention to detailing

Have someone mark off the shots as you take them.

Make sure the kids know who to go to with their questions and concerns. *Good Relations* community service announcement shoot, Murriimage.

Unless you enjoy buying cartons of beer for the rest of the crew, turn off your phone during filming.

Philip Elms, Media Resource Centre.

the mechanics of production gives you more time to attend to performance values on your recording day.

Anticipation is the name of the game.

Richard Fitzpatrick, Camera Operator, Digital Dimensions.

Producers and directors are always pushing for time, always want to move on to the next site. Resist their rushing you, make sure you get enough cutaways. They'll come back to you later and say thank you. At the end of the day, it's your reputation on the line.

THE GOOD DIRECTOR

You don't have to think for or direct everyone in their skill area—let your crew feel they're supporting your production idea by getting on with their jobs.

But you must make it clear what you want. If you have to make a change, be sure everyone thoroughly understands the new direction—otherwise there'll be much confusion and flack heading your way!

Explain the choreography so all crew members understand how to handle the changes in actors' positions. (Courtesy of Portland Community College)

Sara Hourez, Director.

Plan everything and be flexible enough to cope with sudden cast absences, relocations or camera breakdowns.

THE CREW AND PROFESSIONALISM

If you commit yourself to a crew position, recognise that you will need patience—lots of it—while you wait for some other crew member to rehearse his/her bit again, or change to a better position, or change batteries, or . . .

Video production calls for long spans of concentration, long hours of waiting, and then having to perform your task under pressure. It requires a sensitivity to the difficulty that others are experiencing, and an understanding of the shared frustration when it all falls apart and has to be redone.

It requires a great deal of empathy and energy from every single member of the crew in order to be supportive, but that's what being 'crew'—a team member—is all about.

Welcome to the challenge!

Treat all locations as you would your own house.

David Opitz,
Metro Screen.

Wet Weather

Water wrecks video equipment. If you strike rain on the day of your shoot, cancel the shoot if you can. If you can't cancel, move inside. If you must be outside, cover the camera with a garbage bag and have someone holding an umbrella over the camera operator, the mic and the camera.

The wind ruffling the garbage bag will put terrible noises into a camera mic. A handheld mic wrapped in plastic will record the sound of the raindrops that hit it.

Never run cables through puddles!

If you're near the water, use a splash protector for the camera. (Courtesy of Digital Dimensions)

Quality of Work

Take a second shot just for safety's sake.

Philip Elms,
Media Resource
Centre.

The director decides when a take is good enough. If the director wants another take, the crew does another take.

Sometimes it may seem that it isn't worth the effort, that the problem was minor, but no matter what the crew thinks, it remains the director's job to assess the take, and the overall situation, and decide if the extra effort is necessary for the final product.

To be able to do this, the director must carry in his or her head a vision of the finished whole. The director's reputation relies on the final cut, and any compromise on quality at the shoot lessens the possibility of achieving that vision in the end.

Still, the director can't know everything about what's happened, and s/he needs to make quality decisions based on as much information as possible.

When taping flags, be sure they're flying in the correct direction. With an American flag, the stars are supposed to be in the top left. Depending on the wind direction, the flag may appear to be flying 'backwards' with the stars on the top right. If that's the case, the camera person has to change position to the other side of the flag to get it flying in the right direction. Getting the flag right is very important to many people in veterans' organisations. *Another hint:* unless you're trying to create an artsy shot, try to have the flagpole straight, which means parallel to the left side of your viewfinder.

**Barbara
Bishop,**
Independent
Producer.

The director needs to be told anything that has gone wrong so the shot can be taken again. (Courtesy of Metro Screen)

Remember *you* have to edit it.

Phil Hayward,
Macquarie
University.

Ian Ingram-Young,
Academy of
Photogenic
Arts.

Never rely on postproduction to put things right. This is a myth which seldom works—and never without extra expense and some compromise to the quality of the program. Get it right at the time of shooting if possible.

There will be enough to fix up in post in any event.

Great preparation and direction can be ruined by a glitch in the camera work or the sound recordist not alerting the director to a passing jet. (This should be done before or right after the shot has been completed, not during the shooting of it.)

So it's important for crew members to let the director know if they realise something has gone wrong. It's in the nature of video that even when each crew member is striving to do his or her best, mistakes can be made, an unforeseen difficulty can get in the way, or a shot just doesn't work. Directors know this.

It's no good covering up a problem—it will show up in the editing room and then it will be much harder to fix, maybe impossible.

Covering up lowers a crew member's professional reputation, and that affects their future work chances.

Quality of Personal Relations

You need to be careful about the quality of your interactions with your crew, as well as the quality of the video you're recording.

Be considerate and professional in your criticisms. Wherever possible, speak to people quietly and privately about what you'd like them to do differently.

You need a good flow of information from your crew. If people feel that they'll be given a public dressing-down, or spoken to in an arrogant or humiliating fashion, they're not likely to tell you much.

On the other hand, praise goes a long way towards making people feel happy to be on the job. And a crew that feels you value them will usually go the extra distance for you when the chips are down.

A successful shoot relies on the skill, care, cooperation and good energy of everyone involved. Make sure you let everyone know you appreciate their work. The crew of *And she said . . .*, a full-length feature shot at Hamilton Secondary College. (Photo by Mark Pilla)

Making TV programs and videos involves teams of passionate creative people all working together, and can be very rewarding and a lot of fun. It can also be very stressful when resources are less than ideal, personalities clash and things don't go as planned. If you find yourself getting really stressed out, no matter how worthwhile and important the project is, it's not worth giving yourself a heart attack over it. Just remember . . . at the end of the day, it's just dots on a screen.

Andy Nehl, Head of Television, AFTRS.

Keeping Perspective

What if your shoot is of an event that's happening apart from your own efforts? A concert or conference, a religious ceremony, an awards presentation, a sports competition?

When you're the documenter, rather than the initiator, your role and the degree of control and influence you have over the action are quite different from when you're doing a drama or even an interview.

Sometimes it's hard to remember that the video itself is not the event, that there are other interests at least as important as your own, that the show will go on whether you're ready or not, and if you're not—that's just tough.

Are you the show or are you documenting it? Students from the National Recording Studio Training School.

Documenters should not change the event they're covering. Of course, the mere presence of any camera does change things a bit. But sometimes video crews walk in like they're the main item. They string cables and lights all over, regardless of how difficult or uncomfortable they make things for the guests or the audience;

Rebecca Gerendasy, Producer and Editor, *Cooking Up a Story.*

I like to edit what I shoot because while I'm filming I'm editing in my head. I know what shots I need to tell the story. I like to build sequences and I do this by getting a variety of shots while the action is happening.

Philip Elms, Media Resource Centre.

Shoot with 'handles' on the start and end of each shot. This helps for pre-roll in linear editing and for batch capture or transitional effects in non-linear editing.

Harry Kirchner, La Trobe University.

It's okay to look back over your material when you're on location, but decide whether it might not be just as easy to go for another take. If you want to review your last shot, that's fine, but don't fast forward into blank tape or you will end up with a timecode break. Continuous timecode on your DV tape will save a lot of headaches during postproduction.

Rob Davis, Editor, Digital Dimensions.

If your timecode restarts on a tape, due to ejecting the tape, a battery, or whatever, the computer can't tell which shot is which and may capture the wrong shots or not anything.

they set their cameras up in front of people who have a right to their own view; and they even take handheld cameras into the performance area.

High praise for a video crew is for someone to say, 'We hardly knew you were there.'

What's more important . . . the event or the video?

Keeping a low profile, working discreetly and efficiently, may mean you'll be the one group that gets asked back.

Shooting for Editing

Be in record mode for about ten seconds before each shot begins and for at least a few seconds after the end of the action. This video padding, or buffer, is referred to as *handles* in digital editing.

These handles give you the added frames you need for slightly varying your in and out points in the edit, and for adding digital shot transitions without eating into the frames in your shots proper.

If people are disciplined and quiet on the set, these added seconds will also give you some spare ambient sound for patching up holes in your soundtrack.

You can avoid timecode breaks in your tapes by putting timecode on them ahead of time. In the same way that, in the old days we used to stripe the tapes by recording black on them, you put the tape in the camera and run it in record for its full length—an hour? This will put continuous timecode on it, so you can take it out of the camera, put it back in again and restart recording without a fresh timecode automatically starting up at zero again.

When you go to batch capture your footage, there will only be one run of timecode, so there will be no mistakes of capturing the wrong shot which had the same numbers to it.

Guidelines for Shooting an Interview

Here are a few suggestions to consider before doing an on-site interview.

The eyeline of your interviewee has to be correct for the camera. Control the eyeline by taking care where the interviewer sits or stands. Donna Kenny interviews a client. (Courtesy of Clio Associates)

Preproduction

- Visit the person whom you'll be interviewing before the day of the shoot and establish, as much as you can, a feeling of trust and rapport with him/her.
- Ensure your interviewee is comfortable before you start the interview. When interviewing Elders, always ask them where they would like you to conduct the interview.
- Visit the intended site ahead of time, so you can plan how you'll set up the shots and figure out what difficulties there may be.
- Brief your crew, ahead of time, about the interviewee(s) and the site.
- Research your topic carefully, and know how the interviewee is connected to the topic.
- Have a well-organised list of questions, written out clearly, and held neatly and reliably on a clipboard.

Most Elders feel more comfortable at home, so be prepared to go to them.

Florence Onus, Producer.

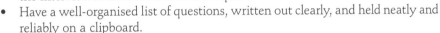

BE CONSCIOUS OF YOUR BACKGROUND. If possible, try to make the background of your interview/standup relate to the topic. For example, if interviewing a musician, try to position their instrument in the background (or set up a light to cast a silhouette of the instrument on the wall behind your musician). If talent is presenting to camera, the same rule applies. If you get really stuck, use a light with barn doors to cast a strip across the background. Use a gel if appropriate.

Gordon Peters, Cameraman, Channel 7 News, Bundaberg.

- Find out whether direct questions are culturally appropriate or considered downright rude in the culture of the person you're going to interview. In some cultures, information and knowledge are shared differently, so be sure to find out how to do an interview correctly with that person.

For interview composition set-ups, watch your backgrounds. Keep an eye out for unwanted background debris like poles or tree branches growing out of heads. Keep an eye out for bright objects and colours that may distract the eye. Avoid getting too close to walls that will get you with pesky shadows. Go for depth in the background which can then be de-focused for a nice narrow depth of field look. If you see walls keep them angled off axis to the camera which will add an interesting sense of depth instead of a flat mugshot look.

Erik Fauske, Videographer/ Teacher.

Donna Kenny,
The Video
History
Company and
Center for
Recording Life
Stories.

Prepare your questions—
many more than you can
realistically use—before you
interview someone on camera.
Have the questions written in
large print on index cards
which can be held quietly on
your lap during the taping. Do
your research ahead of time
and know how to pronounce
key words, names and terms
that may come up.

**Rebecca
Gerendasy**,
Producer and
Editor, *Cooking
Up a Story*.

One of the most important
things to remember while
interviewing someone:
LISTEN. Be prepared, know
what you'd like to talk about,
try to keep from reading the
next question as they answer
the one you just asked, and
listen. You might be surprised
what you hear. And, by all
means, don't be afraid to ask
a follow-up question!

Help your interviewee to feel comfortable and relaxed
before you begin. Terrance Burton interviews Jacqueline
Ehlis, Portland Community College.

Setting up

- Set up as quickly and unobtrusively as possible. Don't let the technical processes dominate the interviewee's experience of the interview.
- Never argue with the crew or shout at them. (This goes for *any* shoot.)
- Try to sit down quietly somewhere with the interviewee, away from the setting up.
- Have an easy chat, if possible. Maybe a cup of tea.
- Don't talk the subject out before the camera rolls. Give a general idea of the outline and flow of the interview, but don't rehearse the actual questions and answers. People answer most vibrantly when they're engaged by a question. Their answers are often shorter, less detailed and lacklustre when they're repeating an answer they've already given.
- If the interviewee is worried about making a mistake or leaving something out, give your assurance that any answer can be started again or entirely redone at the interviewee's request.

Rolling

- If a hand mic is used, keep it in the hand further from the camera.
- Start off with a couple of easy questions to get your subject relaxed and warmed up. You don't have to use these answers in the final edit, but it will help ease the tension.
- Aim for clear and precise answers, but avoid 'closed' questions that can be answered by a one word answer or a 'yes' or 'no'. Aim to draw as much useful information out of the interview as you can.
- Keep in mind that you're not in a competition and don't have to prove that you know more than the interviewee. In fact, if you appear to know only the basics of a topic, your guest can feel prompted to elaborate.
- Although your questions are written down, don't read them out. Refer to your notes and then look at the guest and ask the questions naturally.

- Always listen to the answers. If something unexpected but interesting is said, follow up on it. You needn't feel obliged to rush straight on to the next question.
- If you're going to edit out the question, ensure that the interviewee speaks in full statements, rather than in short responses to your question. For example: 'I was born in Wagga.' Not: Q. 'Where were you born?'; A. 'In Wagga.'

Learn from your mistakes.

Carl Fisher, Murriimage Community Video and Film Service.

- Maintain good eye contact, if it's culturally appropriate to do so. The interviewee is usually more nervous than you. If you look at him or her directly and nod in affirmation from time to time, the interviewee will gain confidence.
- Avoid punctuating the interviewee's answers with 'I see' or 'Uh-huh'. These utterances can be irritating to the viewer, and make it difficult to edit the taped sequence, especially if you make these sounds while the other person is speaking.
- Leave quiet space at the end of each answer for the editor to make a cut, if necessary.
- Remain aware of the director and the camera operator, who may be signalling some kind of message to you.
- Maintain an air of respect for the interviewee.
- Don't be afraid to stop if things aren't going well. If you're dealing with a hostile interviewee, it often pays to pause for a while and allow time for everyone to blow off steam.
- Don't go on forever in the hope of getting the answer you want. Interviewees tend to burn out after awhile. If you haven't got all the information you'd hoped for, you might be able to add it in later with a voiceover or with an interview with someone else.

Ask your questions and then step out of their way. Be quiet. Omit all 'um-humms' and other verbal supports. Especially if the interviewer is off camera, he/she can use body language—nods, smiles, raised eyebrows, leaning forward, etc.—to encourage the interviewee's responses.

Donna Kenny, The Video History Company and Center for Recording Life Stories.

At the Wrap

- Always thank the interviewee cordially for their time and assistance.
- If appropriate, invite the interviewee to watch a playback of the interview on your field monitor or their TV.

The Idiot Check

When the end of the shoot comes, the work isn't over. First of all, the performers should be thanked for their participation and their performance (hopefully enthusiastically, but at least courteously), the crew should be thanked, and the site should be returned to the state it was in before the shoot.

A double check should be made that all tapes or other recording media are accounted for and labelled correctly.

If you're not sure what's missing, refer to your checklist. What's missing from this shot? See the end of this chapter.

Martha Mollison, Producer.

Thanking someone for an extra effort or a particularly good piece of work is a form of recognition and reward, even when you know you can't write anyone a cheque at the end of the day.

Philip Elms, Media Resource Centre.

Thoroughly clean camera equipment after shooting on the beach, as salt spray residue can damage lens coatings and electronic circuitry.

Hart Cohen, University of Western Sydney.

To err is human; to bring back broken equipment is unforgivable.

If there was anything wrong with the gear, tell the equipment store people about it when you return. Student discusses a mic with Dmitri Mazin, Media Store, University of Techology, Sydney.

And the equipment needs to be packed away carefully, making sure that every little cord, adaptor and doo-dad is found and put in its rightful case. This is when you pull that photocopy or printout from the equipment store out of your pocket and start ticking off each item you borrowed as it's rounded up and packed in the car.

Once everything is checked off against the equipment list, loaded into the vehicles, and the crew have packed up their personal items and prepared to leave, someone should do an 'idiot check'.

The idiot check is when the entire shoot area is carefully looked over, one last time, to find anything that has been left behind without anyone noticing.

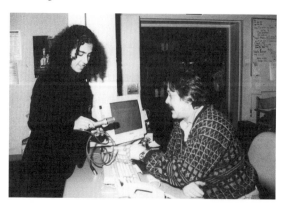

That's when small bits and pieces are found—like the little black camera battery atop the black piano, or the tiny lav mic on a chair, even though the case has already been packed away.

Clean the car! Return it clean and don't be mean.

Gerry Letts, Operations and Facilities, AFTRS.

When equipment is returned to a media centre or hire store, anything that didn't work right, or was broken during the shoot, should be pointed out to the person checking in the gear. That saves the next borrower from copping it unrepaired.

Protecting Your Original Footage

You should safeguard your original material so it will stay in the best possible shape.

Transfer your footage to your computer or to a storage drive as soon as is feasible.

Your camera originals should be carefully labelled as such and put away in a safe place. (*Remember:* Cool, dry, dust free and away from magnetic fields.)

Never risk playing original footage in any VCR because you can't tell when the universe will frown on you and some cranky machine will just eat your tape. There's too much work involved in a reshoot and too little time at the end of a semester to play roulette with your original material.

Sometimes you'll have material that is so valuable to you that it's worth also making a *security dub*. This is a copy of your original footage which is also never used, and stored in a different safe place, so if anything goes wrong and you lose your original footage, you'll have a good-quality copy to fall back on.

Of course, you should use new, high-grade tapes for security dubs, and you should take care that you copy the audio levels well when you make these dubs so that you don't end up with low-level or distorted audio if you need to rely on them in the end.

Don't be disappointed if your first production isn't Academy Award material. It's a learning process, and even great directors make stinkers from time to time.

Keith Smith, Edith Cowan University.

At the end of the day, let's hope everyone was glad they were part of it. Actors and crew of *Promise*, shot in Berrima, NSW.

Be sure you keep a list of exactly what you borrowed.

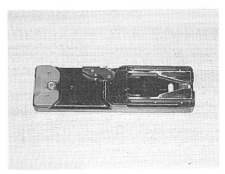

This is what was missing! The base plate for the tripod.

25 STUDIO LAYOUT AND EQUIPMENT

Studios come in all sizes. Some are large enough to hold a symphony orchestra, with room to spare. Others are tiny rooms with a chair for a presenter and a minimal background set.

Whether your studio has access to the latest high-tech equipment with all the bells and whistles, or you have the most rudimentary of set-ups, your studio layout and the principles behind your equipment hook-up will be similar.

And with imagination and tenacity, you can achieve good results under almost any conditions.

Not every organisation has the luxury of a studio floor which serves only one purpose. In many schools, the studio doubles as a classroom. In public access cable TV stations, it can have all manner of functions!

Multicamera TV studio at Northern Melbourne Institute of TAFE.

The Studio Floor

The studio floor is the area where the cameras face the performers.

Although it's possible to do a single-camera shoot in a studio set-up, studios are usually organised for the simultaneous use of two, three or more cameras.

Studio production at the University of Southern Queensland.

The Lighting Grid

It's helpful if the studio has a lighting grid above the studio floor so lights can be mounted in a variety of positions without getting in the way of the cameras' movements and without having their stands be in the frame of some shots. But a studio can work with portable lights only.

Flats/Scenery/Props

Some studios have flats that can be used for simple backgrounds or hooked together for more elaborate sets, like mock-up rooms.

Lots of useful props can be collected over time. In fact, some remarkable items can be scrounged from the local tip (dump).

Risers

Some studios have risers, which are movable platforms upon which presenters and performers can be seated. With the performers on risers, the camera operators can stand comfortably upright and still get a neutral shot into the presenter's and guests' eyes, rather than a high shot which looks down on the seated people and subtly diminishes their impression of authority.

The background should be planned and working for each intended camera angle. (Courtesy of Arlington Community Media Inc. [ACMi])

At Wakefield Community Access TV, there are audio and video 'outlets' in the lounge so they can just plug in an audio mixer and camera and use that room as a studio as well. The 'outlets' are connected into their second control room, which doubles as an audio studio for voiceovers.

Barbara Bishop, Independent Producer.

At Wakefield Community Access TV, the studio triples as a classroom and meeting area. Tables are set up for a public meeting. One wall of the studio is painted in the sponge technique and works well as a background. Part of another wall is painted chroma key blue. (Photo by Ruth Stegner)

The cyclorama can give your set a neutral background. Erika Addis adjusts cyc at AFTRS.

All cables should be coiled and put away when the studio floor is not in use.

Walls

Studio walls are sometimes painted with good basic background colours or patterns, or chroma key colours.

Some studios have a chroma key blue or green wall, or a portable chroma key set-up.

Floors

Dark floors can be an advantage because they won't give off lots of uncontrollable bounced light from the studio lights hung from the overhead lighting grid. Some studios paint and repaint their floors, based on the needs for the current set.

The camera operators should wear rubber-soled shoes so their footsteps on the tiles aren't audible.

Rollable carpets can be used to dress sets, and can help reduce sound bounce from the floors. Rugs can be picked up quite cheaply at charity shops or for free through freecycle.org.

However, the camera dollies work best across smooth tiles or linoleum.

Curtains

The *cyclorama*, or *cyc*, is a long curtain attached to little rollers which run in the grooves of a curving track. The track is mounted high up along three or four walls of the studio. When the cyc is pulled open, it makes a good generic background, hiding the bare studio walls (and a myriad of oddments) with soft folds of cloth. Cycs are frequently black or deep blue, but they can be almost any colour, including chroma key blue and chroma key green, for use in chroma key effects.

Soundproofing

The studio floor should be able to be isolated from passing noise and interruptions. Usually it's a large room with a double-door system for soundproofing.

On-Air Light

Outside the outer door, there's often a red light that is lit up during recording sessions so people are warned not to enter and spoil the take.

Airconditioning

Most studios are airconditioned, which is good for the equipment and also good for the people arranging the set and rehearsing for the show under the hot lights. However, someone must remember to turn the airconditioner off before the actual recording begins, because it puts terrible background noise onto the audio.

At Portland Community Media, Studio B has a multi-purpose trolley providing the floor area with a monitor, a clock and microphone storage drawers.

Studio Cameras

Studio cameras are usually the best-quality cameras the institution can muster. Most places try to limit the use of these cameras to just the studio, plus maybe the OB van.

But it's also possible to hook field cameras into a studio system, either as the mainstay cameras or as auxiliary stationary or roving cameras for more complex shoots.

Studio cameras have larger viewfinders, so the camera operators don't have to put their eye to them and can stand back and comfortably frame and focus their shots. Such viewfinders have an on-air light (called a *tally light*), which lets the operator know when that camera's signal is being used in the program.

The camera's zoom and focus controls are connected to *servos* (cables which allow remote control) and are mounted on the tripod's control handles. This allows the operators to make zoom and focus adjustments with their fingers while still having complete control of the pan and tilt of the studio cameras.

Headsets allow the camera operators to receive instructions from the director or DA and to talk back to the control room when necessary, but for the most part camera operators don't speak once the show begins.

Camera operators control zoom and focus by servo controls mounted on the tripod handles. Northern Melbourne Institute of TAFE.

Studio camera for *Call to Serve*, Methuen Community Access TV. (Photo by Nancy Clover)

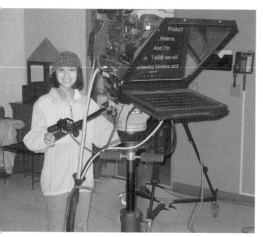

The camera used for the host of the show can have the teleprompter mounted on it. Christina Tapiero works on *Product Reviews* for Arlington Middle School Producers, Arlington Community Media Inc. (ACMi)

The better the viewfinder, the easier it is for the camera operator to get a well-focused shot. (Courtesy of Arlington Community Media Inc. (ACMi))

The studio camera may have a teleprompter on the front of it. If so, when rehearsal time comes, the presenter looks towards that camera. The words have to be large so the presenter can read them at a distance. Generally, the words roll up the screen so the reader's eyes aren't seen to be tracking left to right again and again.

Signal adjustments, like white balance and iris setting, are not done by the camera operators. They're controlled by the TD operating the CCUs (camera control units) in vision control.

Camera Mounts

Studio cameras are mounted on camera pedestals or on tripods with dolly wheels.

The camera pedestal is designed to move the camera quickly, smoothly and quietly around the studio floor. A sideways movement is called *tracking* or *trucking*. A forward or backward movement is called *dollying*. When a stationary camera is needed, the brakes can be locked on.

The camera pedestal can also smoothly raise or lower the height of the camera. This camera action is called *ped up* and *ped down*. Some camera pedestals are controlled by a steering wheel mounted horizontally beneath the camera. You turn it in the direction you want the camera to go in, give a push and away it goes. The camera is mounted on a pan/tilt head, which is controlled by four knobs.

Tilt Lock

This knob locks or loosens the tripod head's tilting action (which allows the upward and downward swing of the camera lens). The tilt should always be locked before the camera operator walks away from the camera.

Tilt Friction (Tilt Drag)

This knob allows the camera operator to adjust the tension control on the tilt action. The ease of movement of the tilt can be varied from very fluid to quite firm, depending on the requirements of the shot and the ability of the operator. The tilt friction should never be used to lock off the tilt—this can strip the control and render it useless.

Lightweight camera pedestals at Northern Melbourne Institute of TAFE.

Pan Lock

This knob locks or loosens the tripod head's panning action (the swivelling of the camera to the left or right). The pan should be locked before the camera operator walks away from the camera.

Pan Friction (Pan Drag)

This knob allows the camera operator to adjust the tension control on the pan action. The ease of movement of the pan can be varied from very fluid to quite firm, depending on the requirements of the shot and the ability of the operator.

> In Australia, camera operators get to their use-by date at 30 years of age, and should think about moving on to floor managing or directing.

Chris Fraser, Cinematography Department, AFTRS.

If the pan friction is on too tight, the panning action might lose its smoothness and become jerky.

The pan friction should never be used to lock off the pan—this can strip the control and render it useless.

The Control Room

The main control room is where the director is during a production, and where the vision mixer (VM) sits at the switcher (or vision mixing console), electronically selecting the chosen camera shots and executing the visual special effects which are needed.

All input sources can now be shown on one screen. (Courtesy of Arlington Community Media Inc. [ACMi])

In this control room, the crew can use either the TV monitors or the glass window to check what's happening on the studio floor. Northern Melbourne Institute of TAFE.

The director and vision mixer work in front of a bank of monitors, each of which presents them with an available video source. There's a monitor for each studio camera and for each of the other possible inputs, like the video playback machines, the teleprompter, the titler/graphics computers, and remote sources (like an OB van or microwave link) and the telecine.

In some control rooms the individual monitors have been replaced by a single large display screen that shows all the sources.

There's usually still a large colour Program Out monitor which shows the signal that is currently being sent to *line*, either to record or broadcast (or both). And there's a Preview monitor next to it which lets the director look at the upcoming shot and make sure it's right.

During studio production at the University of Southern Queensland, Toowoomba.

Also present in the control room are the DA (director's assistant), the TD (technical director) and the lighting director.

In larger productions, other crew members such as the designer and the wardrobe supervisor may be in the control room as well. The makeup artist would work from the studio floor.

Program sound is heard over loudspeakers by everyone in the control room. There's a talkback microphone into which both the director and director's assistant speak, linking them to the floor manager and the camera operators on the studio floor, and to audio control and videotapes.

Donna Rose Garrett helps Jacqueline Ehlis with that shine from the hot lights. Portland Community College.

Quite often, there's a huge soundproof glass window between the control room and the studio floor, so the director and DA can see what's happening in there. But sometimes there's no window, and the two rooms may even be in separate parts of the building. In that case, the floor manager is essential as the eyes and ears of the director, and the only view the director has is what the camera operators provide.

Vision Control

Vision control may be in the main control room, or nearby.

Each studio camera has a long thick, multi-pin cable that carries signals in both directions. Besides sending the video signal to the control room equipment, it carries the genlock signal to the camera. It can handle intercom signals and also *return video*, so the camera operators can check which shot is selected at any moment by the vision mixer.

Usually each camera cable plugs into a patch bay on the studio wall, and from there it's connected to its own CCU (camera control unit). But in some set-ups there's just a hole in the wall, and the camera cables run through it.

Each camera is set up by adjusting its CCU in vision control.

The TD (technical director) sets up all the cameras so their signals are within the required range and their images match each other in colour, brightness, contrast and black level. White balancing is done at the CCUs, as well as some tweaking to adjust luminance levels, video gain, the black pedestal, and the blue and red signals, if need be. Without this matching, the look of the picture could change from shot to shot, distracting the viewers.

The camera signals are fed into the vision mixer.

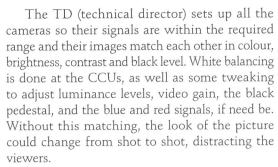

Every row of buttons is called a bus.

The Vision Mixer (or Switcher)

The vision mixer is a device with a counter-mounted panel with buttons on it, which allows the operator to electronically preview and select program video from the array of camera shots and other video sources which are patched in to it.

The chosen button lights up, so the current choices are clear to anyone at a glance. The line output of the vision mixer is routed either to a recorder or to broadcast or both.

It is also used to set up and execute visual effects and transitions.

For details on the operation of the vision mixer, see Chapter 28, Operating the Vision Mixer.

When the light's on, that source is selected. (Courtesy of Northern Melbourne Institute of TAFE)

Audio Control

Audio control may be in the main control room, but it's better if it's separate from the general frenzy and noise so the sound operator can hear the program sound well and pick up on signal problems, like buzzes or crackling cables. Often it's in a nearby room; sometimes it's viewable from the main control room through a large window.

All the studio mics are plugged into a patch bay on the studio wall, and from there audio cables are run to audio control and connected to the input sockets at the back of the audio mixer.

Audio control also contains various playback machines for audiotapes, DAT, DVD and CD. Maybe even a phonograph player.

The responsibility of audio control is to test, adjust and control the volume and quality of each sound source, and insert each one into the program correctly, according to the director's calls.

For each input sound, there's a corresponding fader control which allows the operator to set the volume of that sound and to fade it in and out, as required.

Operating the audio mixer, Northern Melbourne Institute of TAFE.

Each fader controls the volume level of the signal attached to the one sound input.

There's also a master output fader (or two) for volume control of the mixed sound as it is sent onward for recording, broadcast, or both.

The sound operator must ensure that the signal output from the mixing desk is strong enough and that the sound levels are consistent throughout the program.

Sometimes the sound operator works alone, and sometimes there's an assistant who helps by playing the needed discs, tapes and cassettes for program music and special effects.

On more complex mixers, the sound quality can be manipulated by using equalisation controls for bass, mid-range and treble frequencies, the sound can be selectively assigned to any combination of outputs, the gain can be adjusted, inputs can be

Audio control ensures the consistency of the levels of all the sound sources in the program. Valerie Giarrusso at Methuen Public Access TV. (Photo by Nancy Clover)

Updating the credits for tonight's show. (Courtesy of Portland Community Media)

Martha Mollison, Producer.

Store a template of the standard end-credits for your show, including your copyright announcement. Then for each new program you only need to adjust for any changes in crew names and guests. No need to retype the whole thing each week!

The teleprompter screen can be mounted on the host's camera or it can be free-standing. Tom Gradzewicz prepares for recording *Call to Serve*, Methen Community TV, Massachusetts.

muted if necessary, and any single source can be listened to on its own (solo).

For more about the audio mixer, see Chapter 29, Operating the Studio Audio Mixer.

Titler (Character Generator or CG)

Titlers have a range of fonts and font sizes, can do special effects on the lettering (like drop shadow, bold and outline), generate coloured letters and backgrounds, and store several pages of credits in memory.

They can also present the pages of credits in a variety of scrolls (where the words roll upward or downward across the screen) and crawls (where the letters move horizontally across some section of the screen—like on CNN), and some can produce a virtual circus of alphabetic feats.

Teleprompter

A teleprompter is basically a combination of a computer and a display system. The word entry is usually done from the control room, and the display screen is on the studio floor. It can be mounted on the host's main camera, or it can be freestanding.

Whatever the presenter has to say—the news, the weather, the commentary, anything—it can be typed in advance and saved to a file.

In the control room, the operator of the tele-prompter works out what's the best speed for the presenter to read the words aloud, and makes a note of it, with the variations needed for handling long, hard words, or quickly spoken phrases.

Graphics Computer

The graphics computer is connected to the vision mixer and used as a flexible source for imaginative program content.

Graphics can take a long time to produce, but they can be generated well ahead and then input live into the program.

There are lots of free graphics on the internet. Maps are especially handy to pull down and use.

Graphics can be presented on their own, or mixed or wiped into combinations with live video from the studio cameras or from pre-recorded video.

Some crew members may excel at generating graphics that will wow your viewers. (Courtesy of Portland Community Media)

The Lighting Mixer

The lighting mixer is operated by faders which allow the brightness of each light in the studio to be set, so some lights can be on at full strength while others are slightly or seriously dimmed.

The lighting director decides what combination of lights and light strengths to use for each scene. As the lighting director is setting up the faders on the lighting mixer, the lighting assistant is on the studio floor, adjusting the positions and throws of each light, as directed.

Once the combination of lights and intensities has been chosen, a master fader will raise and lower the entire lighting group, simultaneously getting each light in the arrangement to its assigned output level.

Kevin Smith designs yet another intro for *Madeleine Morning News*, The Madeleine School, Portland, Oregon.

If there's a need for some lights to change within a scene (for a spotlight to come on and go off, for example), some lights can be assigned to be *independents*, and are then operated singly rather than in the main group.

Lighting consoles usually allow more than one lighting set-up to be held in memory at once, so there could be set-up A and set-up B. These set-ups can be activated either manually or by a computer. This makes it possible to do a slow or quick crossfade from one lighting arrangement to the next, giving a smooth transition from scene to scene on the same set.

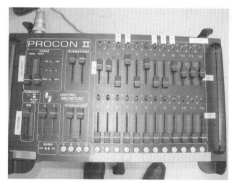

The lighting set-up can be worked out well ahead of the live show. Lightboard at Arlington Community Media Inc (ACMi).

As there are frequently more lights on the studio grid than there are ports on the lighting mixer, the lighting mixer is usually serviced by a patch bay.

Whatever lights are needed for the production are attached to the patch bay during set-up time, and then the patch bay should be cleared at the end of the production.

Genlock

Video cameras have to be able to generate their own timing pulse (or sync) so they can function independently and record a stable signal on their own.

Some cameras can also receive a sync pulse from an external source and use that pulse as the timebase for the signal they produce. When cameras (or other video-generating devices) are sent the same sync pulse from an external source, they operate to exactly the same timing, and they're said to be *genlocked*.

Their video signals can then be used sequentially on the vision mixer in cuts, dissolves, wipes and other effects without causing any signal breakup or glitching due to differences in timing.

Any video signals that are input into a vision mixer need to be from sources which are *synchronised* (*synchronous* with each other, having the same *timebase* as each other). Synchronisation can be achieved through genlock or, in the case of some smaller vision mixers, the synchronising of the incoming signals is done within the mixer itself and genlock cabling isn't necessary.

When the *NS* light comes on during a mix or wipe on a vision mixer, it means that the two sources are *non-synchronous*, and they can't be combined smoothly until they're synchronised.

Sync Pulse Generator

The sync pulse generator is the drum major of the studio or OB van. It *genlocks* all the equipment by providing a stable timing pulse (*sync pulse*).

Timebase Corrector (TBC)

The *timebase corrector* (TBC) receives the video output from the playback machines, strips the signal of its unstable sync (timebase) and then attaches that signal to a 'rock solid' timebase and outputs it to the vision mixer, where it can then successfully be combined with other signals.

Playback (Videotapes)

Also located in the control room, or in its own separate room, is Playback (Videotapes). This section has a range of playback devices, usually mounted in racks.

Frequently during live shows, the director wants to insert material which has already been taped and edited. This could be on-the-street interviews done on the topic the program is addressing, or it could be public service announcements (PSAs), or even advertisements, depending on what the station is allowed to do.

Someone has to operate the playback machines. The videotapes or DVDs must be cued up and ready to roll in an instant, at the director's request.

The playback video signals must be synched with the live video which is being generated by the cameras, so the signals can all be intermeshed without glitches as they pass through the vision mixer.

Black Generator

Playback has to keep up with all the possible formats people are using—an ever-increasing challenge. (Courtesy of Portland Community Media)

The black generator comes either as a device on its own, or it can reside inside the vision mixer. It produces a clean black signal with solid sync pulses. It's used to produce the black for the beginning and end of shows, and its composite video out signal can also be used to genlock the studio.

Patch Bay

Patch bays are the ultimate for allowing the user choice in connections. They are available for both video and audio signals, and also for assigning lights to the lighting mixer.

Patching in a video cable. Colin Kemp, Engineering Department, AFTRS.

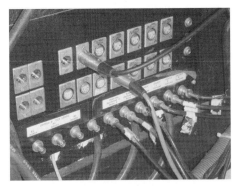

Audio and video signals can be routed through this patch bay. (Courtesy of Portland Community Media)

A patch bay has a row of inputs and a row of outputs. It's rack mounted and the cables coming from and going to the various pieces of studio equipment are labelled and connected at the back. The back is usually accessible to the technicians only.

At the front are connecting sockets for every in and out position, and each socket is (hopefully) correctly and legibly labelled. (We're talking about the best of all possible worlds here!)

The patch bay allows anyone to connect any input to any output by the use of short cables or attaching devices.

The patch bay allows much more flexible use of equipment by giving the operator the ability to quickly and easily set up whatever signal paths are desired. No need to climb in behind the rack and reconnect everything—and make a total mess of the studio hook-up. Any signal paths can be set up by one user, and then unplugged at the end of the shoot so all the wiring is intact for the next user and all the options are still available.

DV/Analogue Bi-directional Converter

If you're using a mix of digital and analogue sources in your studio, you'll have to be able to convert signals. For this you need a digital/analogue converter.

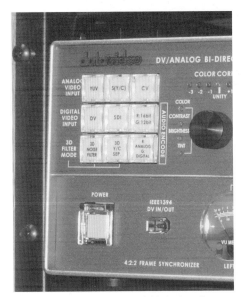

This bi-directional converter is useful for both studio recording and postproduction work.

Video Distribution Amplifier

A *video distribution amplifier* (VDA) is a simple device that takes a video signal in at one port and outputs the same signal, at full strength, to four or six outputs so the same signal can be sent simultaneously to several studio devices, without its signal level being lowered (attenuated).

A typical distribution of a video signal would be that the camera signal is taken out of the CCU and sent simultaneously to:

- the patch bay connected to the waveform monitor and vectorscope
- the camera monitor
- the vision mixer.

A VDA is essential to a video copying set-up, where several VCRs need to receive the same signal at once.

Routing Switcher

The routing switcher works in reverse to the VDA. A routing switcher is simply a row of buttons, when viewed from the front. At the back it has a row of BNC sockets which allow several video signals to be input into it, and it has one or two video outputs.

The routing switcher is used to assign a variety of video sources to a single piece of video test equipment, like the waveform monitor or the vectorscope, or to a monitor, a recorder, or whatever is desired.

The routing switcher lets you select a signal and send it to whatever equipment you choose.

The TD (technical director) can select any source s/he wants to view or adjust by pressing the labelled button at the front which corresponds to that source's input; that signal is then allowed to passed out of the routing switcher and is sent along to the desired device.

Routing switchers are usually rack mounted so the input cables at the back are inaccessible to all but the technicians. This is so the cables stay connected to the right positions and the routing switcher remains reliable for the next operator.

Waveform Monitor

The waveform monitor is a signal testing device that has several different selectable displays.

The waveform monitor shows information about the luminance signal, including the brightness peaks and the black pedestal.

The technical director (TD) uses the waveform monitor to check specific aspects of the video signal, like the *sync pulses*, the *luminance level* and the *pedestal* (black level). It's helpful in diagnosing problems, matching signals from different sources, and ensuring that the studio output signal conforms to broadcast standards.

Although it may mystify you at first, it's a helpful tool and not that hard to read. You'd be wise to learn it so you can use it when the TD can't be there.

Find out anything you can to do with timecode, the vectorscope and waveform monitor. Learn the difference between dropframe and non-dropframe.

Kimberley Brown, Editor/Camera Operator.

Vectorscope

The vectorscope is another signal testing device, used for analysing the properties of the colour portion of the video signal.

It shows *colour phase* and the *chroma amplitude* (strength of the colour signal). It's especially useful when operating in NTSC, where the colour from a camera can be out of phase, and therefore mismatched to the next one.

Suggestions from Rachel Masters

Try to create an opportunity where you and your friends can observe the workings of a television studio. Often television stations need audiences. Phone your local station for tickets and be a part of the show, while observing what's going on behind the scenes. Making television is fun—even though everyone often looks very serious. Try not to be disappointed when you see that all the glamour is in front of the cameras.

26   STUDIO ROLES

Some studio crews number twenty or more people, and other wizards pull off a good production with only two or three people doing all the studio jobs. So when we talk about studio roles, it's as a general guideline only. You have to work with what you've got and whoever is there to help you. However, it does help, when dividing up the work, to have a general overview of all the jobs that need to be done. So here goes.

The Producer

The producer is the head of the production team and is responsible for the successful completion of the project.

The producer decides on the program concept, chooses the director and other key production personnel, like the heads of design, photography, lighting and sound, and may be involved in the selection of other crew and performers.

Every studio role is important and contributes to the end product. (Courtesy of Metro Screen)

The producer has the final say on artistic and editorial policy, and controls the budget. The producer also has overall responsibility for the quality of the program. However, once the major decisions on program treatment have been made, the producer hands the artistic realisation of the production over to the director in the studio.

In a drama production, the producer does not usually sit in the control room and dictate ideas on how the shots should go.

In broadcast news and current affairs, where stories are sometimes being included and dropped up until the moment of transmission, the producer is present in the control room to make those last-minute decisions.

The producer is responsible to the television station or to whomever has commissioned the project.

PTT: Passion transcends technology! The tools will continue to change, but passion will always remain the soul of the film.

Claire Beach, Videographer/ Teacher.

The producer is at the top of the chain of command for the production. Julianne Palazzo, Methuen High School, Massachusetts.

The Director

The director is responsible for the creative vision behind the production, and for guiding the program designers in realising that vision through sets, costumes, lighting and sound. It's the director's responsibility to decide the final visual and audio treatment.

The director needs to keep the DA (director's assistant) up to date on any changes to the program. The DA then informs the rest of the crew.

It's the ideas that count. The producer's business is content.

Gilda Baracchi, Producer.

As a director, you have to stay flexible, because control room procedures vary from place to place. For example, in Sydney the DA calls the shots, and in Melbourne s/he doesn't. As a freelance director, you have to adapt to the crew you are directing.

Sara Hourez, former Director of *Neighbours*.

The director explains the project to the performers. (Courtesy of Portland Community Media)

Directing involves being able to live in two worlds—the world of your inner vision, and the day-to-day world where your inner vision is given life.

Kathryn Brown, Director.

The director is responsible for explaining the production to the performers and the technical crew, rehearsing them until they're ready to give a good performance, and directing them through every step of the actual recorded or broadcast program.

The director must enthuse the whole team, so everyone is committed to the success of the project.

As a result of all this responsibility, it's usually the director who gets the overall credit or blame at the completion of the project. The director is responsible to the producer.

Be ready for any eventuality—and don't be afraid to ask! If you don't know what's going on, how can you tell everyone else?

Anna Lang,
Directing
Department,
AFTRS.

The Director's Assistant

The director's assistant (DA, or producer's assistant), performs a wide range of tasks which help the director to organise and run the production.

The DA ensures that the scripts and rundown are copied and up to date with last-minute changes, and distributes them to all crew members.

Take one step at a time!

Sandra Chung,
ABC TV
Training and
Development.

The DA acts as the director's go-between with every department involved in the production, and ensures everyone knows exactly when and how the production will proceed.

For the actual performance, the DA alerts Videotapes (Playback) to record, times all segments and the program itself, prepares cameras for their upcoming shots, uses the character generator, watches continuity, liaises with external program sources such as an OB van or satellite feed from another site, alerts the director to snags or timing problems, and may type in the credits.

The DA needs excellent communication skills, diplomacy and a good knowledge of every role in the production process. The DA may need special qualifications if working on productions such as music or dance.

The director's assistant is responsible to the director.

DA Anna Lang times a studio segment, AFTRS.

The Designer

The designer is responsible for the overall look of the production, and is in charge of staging and properties, wardrobe and makeup.

In response to the producer's brief, the designer draws up a proposed set. Once s/he has received the go-ahead, the designer draws up and delivers floor plans to the producer, the director and the technical director.

Anyone can design with a million dollars. It takes a clever designer with a hundred dollars to make it look like a million.

Darrell Lass,
Production
Designer.

The designer arranges for the construction of staging and any other necessary set elements, and makes sure that they're built according to the approved specifications and delivered on time.

The designer also makes sure that all props are procured, and that the performers are dressed appropriately, in the correct period of wardrobe and makeup.

The designer is responsible to the producer and the director.

The Floor Manager

The floor manager (FM) is in charge of everything that happens on the studio floor, during preproduction times, rehearsals and the production itself. He or she is the director's right-hand person and representative on the studio floor.

The floor manager also attends site checks for location shoots.

The FM is particularly concerned with safety, crew morale and contentment, performance achievement and discipline—where necessary.

The floor manager compiles a workable schedule that allows for the creative needs of the director and performers, and the practical needs of the technical and support crew. This schedule would include the amount of time needed to do special effects, for example. At the beginning of a production, the FM welcomes the performers and guests to the studio and looks after their comfort and needs.

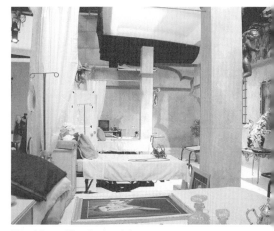

This elaborate Victorian hospital set . . .

. . . and its waiting room . . .

The FM makes sure presenters are comfortable, understand the hand signals to be used during the production, and have water and adequate breaks. (Courtesy of Portland Community Media)

. . . were built by Ken Manning, Annie Wright, Wayne Smith and others in the Props and Staging Department of AFTRS.

Don Bethel,
Floor Manager
and Consultant,
Television
Production
Techniques.

Anticipation is the name of the game.

The FM puts tape markings on the floor to help the performers know where they should stand, or to stop their movement, and assists performers to achieve the right positions and eyelines.

During rehearsals, the floor manager can give the director information about possible difficulties with the stage directions planned, and during performance the FM remains alert to anything that might get in the way of achieving the desired shots, remedying whatever is possible.

The floor manager gives the countdown to the actors so they know when the show begins.

FM Erik Vaage Teigen gives countdown to the band Mech, Griffith University.

The FM remains in constant contact with the director, via headphones *with talkback*, and conveys the director's instructions to the performers and crew.

The FM also discreetly relays to the director the needs of performers and crew, making sure that the director is aware of the mood on the studio floor, and that people get rest breaks when they need them.

At the end of rehearsals and the production, the FM thanks the performers and crew, on behalf of the director.

The floor manager is responsible to the director.

The Technical Director

The technical director (TD) is in charge of the booking and operation of all technical resources, and liaises between the director and the technical crew.

The TD/camera operator uses controls like these to manoeuvre and operate robotic studio cameras from within the control room at KGW Portland, Oregon.

It's the responsibility of the TD to ensure that each camera's picture is technically lined up and that the signals from all the cameras are correctly white balanced and match in colour, brightness, contrast and black level. This is done by adjusting the CCU (camera control unit) for each camera. The CCUs are all housed in the vision control room, where they're linked to signal test equipment—a waveform monitor and a vectorscope—so their signals can be analysed.

The TD also makes sure that the system is correctly set up for special effects, like chroma key.

The technical director is responsible to the director.

The Vision Mixer (Switcher)

The vision mixer (VM) inserts each shot into the program by operating the vision mixing console according to the instructions of the director.

During rehearsals, the VM works out how to achieve the shot sequences and special effects that the director may require. On air, the VM sets up and programs any effects required and switches the cameras and other sources to line.

In a harmonious working relationship, the VM could alert the director to problems related to effects or shot sequences. The VM needs to be able to follow a script and/or rundown and to constantly think one step ahead. In most cases, the vision mixer is responsible to the director.

The vision mixer is meant to follow the director's instructions, but can sometimes save the day by alerting the director to upcoming problems. (Photo by Nancy Clover)

The Sound Supervisor

The sound supervisor might be working alone or overseeing a sound crew. In either case, s/he ensures that all elements of the desired soundtrack for the production are ready, and that each one gets correctly mixed into the program.

This includes:

1. Making sure any necessary pre-recorded music and effects have been procured, and the necessary playback machines have been hooked up to the audio mixer. Also that the corresponding mixer faders have been labelled, the sources are cued up and that sound checks have been done to find the correct levels to achieve the program's needs.
2. Selecting the right mics and making sure they're placed so the desired sound can be captured.
3. Participating in rehearsals and alerting the director to any problems with boom moves, in relation to lighting, or to the performers.
4. Mixing all sound sources (from mics, VCRs, CD players, tapes, DVDs, OB van and remote sources, special effects equipment, etc.) into the program soundtrack.
5. Ensuring that the program sound level is consistent and neither too high nor too low.
6. Returning all sound equipment to its proper storage at the end of the production.

The sound supervisor is responsible to the director.

Staying on top of all sources! Barry Fernandes, Sound Department, AFTRS.

The Lighting Director

The lighting director is responsible for designing the right lighting look and for achieving it.

This includes deciding on the type and strength of all lighting fixtures to be used, drawing up a chart which shows where each light will be hung or stood, and planning for the appropriate use of gels, spun and reflectors. It also includes working out the details of special lighting effects, like helicopter lights.

The lighting director oversees the installation of the lights for the production, and works with the sound supervisor to solve problems relating to boom access or boom shadows.

The lighting director makes sure that the script for the program lighting is correct, that the lighting board or computer control is properly programmed, and that the lighting operation is adequately rehearsed and correctly performed during the production.

The lighting director is responsible to the director.

The Videotape Operator (Playback)

The videotape operator is responsible for cueing up all media inserts and rolling the sources quickly when requested to do so.

In small studios, the same person may also operate the device to record the program (be it tape or hard drive).

In a tape-based studio, s/he must load the correct record tape, put the VCR into and out of record mode as instructed by the director, and play back segments so they can be checked.

The videotape operator makes sure everything is recording correctly by referring to the record monitor and the video level meter, and watching the audio VU meters to make sure the sound is reaching the record machine and that it's strong enough but not distorting.

After the program, the videotape operator is sometimes asked to replay the program for viewing by the director, the crew and possibly the performers.

The videotape operator is also responsible for correctly labelling the record media and delivering the recording to the director.

In a production facility, the videotape operator's job is complex and involves many important functions, including editing. But to a student just beginning to learn studio work—whose only duties are to start the recorder, watch the levels and stop the machine at the end of the shoot—being put in this job slot can seem like a set-up for a boring class. Still, when you come right down to it, what good is everyone else's work if it doesn't get recorded? Which sometimes happens. This is a critical position.

The videotape operator is responsible to the director.

The Camera Operators

The camera operators should be totally familiar with the cameras and pedestals they're using. The standard studio set-up has four or five cameras, three on pedestals, and one or two handheld that are able to rove.

Although shot sizes are roughly standardised, each camera operator should be sure to learn what the current director means by each shot size.

They should rehearse each shot they'll be required to produce, according to the planned script, and they should make sure that their camera cards, which list their shots, are correct and up to date on any changes.

The camera operators should practise any difficult camera moves and let the floor manager or director know of any anticipated problems. They should get to know whether the director wants them to offer up shots and, if so, then to do so (the director's feelings on this become obvious pretty quickly!).

During the production, each camera operator should go directly to the next scripted shot as soon as the last one is no longer being used. If the shots aren't totally scripted, the camera operators should follow the general coverage instructions they've been given (like 'stay mainly on the host' or 'keep to long shots').

The camera operators are connected by head-phones to the control room. They can talk back to the DA or the director during rehearsals, but should usually refrain from speaking during the production. If camera operators make a mistake, they should keep going regardless and *never* stop the production.

The camera operators are responsible to the technical director, and they work for the director.

Teshome Tesema operates a studio camera at North Sydney TAFE.

The real buzz of being a camera operator is not the money. The biggest reward is having the skill to interpret what the director wants and achieving it every time.

Chris Fraser,
Cinematography Department, AFTRS.

Mike Beshara works on *Call to Serve*, Methuen Community TV, Massachusetts.

The Boom Operator

The boom operator guides the boom to pick up the needed sound for each part of the production. The boom may be handheld or it may be mounted on a movable dolly. The boom operator is connected by headphones to the control room.

The boom operator should rehearse all moves carefully, watching for problems like boom shadows being cast on the set, or potential collisions with moving cameras, lighting fixtures or other set elements.

The boom operator is responsible to the sound supervisor and to the director.

Jeremy Reurich demonstrates studio boom rig at AFTRS.

Lena Adams operates handheld boom for *The Spirit of Our Land*, School of Indigenous Australian Studies, James Cook University.

Carol Brands rehearses Ben Air, Katie Air and Sam Talbot-Dunn, Curtin University. (Photo by Judy Wheeler)

The Performers

The performers should arrive on time for rehearsals, follow the directions of the director and the floor manager, be clear about whatever needs they have which can be accommodated, and put out the best performance they can.

Performers should watch their energy levels, giving less energy to early rehearsals so they have reserves left for building up to full performance level for the final rehearsals and the production.

Other Roles

In large studios, the production team would include many other positions, such as costume designer, makeup artist, stage hands, continuity (or script supervisor), electricians and gaffers, camera assistants and grips.

Production Manager

The production manager books the studio facilities and looks after a myriad other production details long before the day of the shoot. The production manager, in some cases, even does the budgeting.

Production Secretary

The production secretary types and photocopies scripts, and does other things to help the production run smoothly.

Makeup artist preparing a performer for *Uncle Toby's Kebabs*, directed by Mark Tewksbury.

The Script Supervisor (Continuity Person)

The script supervisor makes sure that all the necessary takes are recorded and marks off the script accordingly. She or he makes a note of each actor's physical position (Sitting? Standing? Near the door?) at the beginning and end of each shot so they can return to the right spot for the next shot.

The script supervisor also makes sure that visual aspects of props and sets are managed to make sense from scene to scene. So a glass isn't mysteriously more full of liquid in a shot following an actor drinking it down, that jackets remain on or off, sleeves remain rolled up or down, chairs stay in the same places and so on. As there are so many variables on a set, the continuity person takes digital photos to keep track.

Since dramas are often shot out of script order, the continuity person has to make sure that every shot has been recorded before the production moves on to the next set. (Photo from Metro Screen)

Casting Director

The casting director works in consultation with the producer and director to find the appropriate performers for the production. This person's job is to understand what the director is after for a particular role and draw on their own knowledge of actors to present a list of suitable available choices for the director to consider.

The casting director then arranges for the director to meet the actors for a chat or audition and offer any advice or knowledge to help the director make his or her decision.

Aysha Ahmed helps out as a volunteer production assistant, AFTRS.

Rob Stewart,
Northern
Melbourne
Institute of
TAFE.

You're only as good as your
last job.

Once a performer is decided upon, the casting director will negotiate with the actor's agent to contract the artist.

Productions that cannot afford a casting director, and have no money to pay performers, could approach organisations/drama schools or local theatre groups to seek out actors. These places do not act as agents (i.e. offer suggestions for each role), but will usually allow you to put up a notice with your requirements so that actors can contact you for an audition—a children's theatre company for juveniles, adult amateur theatre groups for others. Often these people are keen to get the experience; however, the quality of their performance skill is variable.

Suggestions from Rachel Masters

Learning to cooperate but not to compromise on standards is a good rule when working with your friends. Making friends may be easy, but keeping them can be hard when everyone is striving to make the production a success and some people are losing their tempers under the pressure. Before the production, organise a production meeting and decide on the roles you will need on the shoot day. Decide, as a group, who will be the director, the producer, the director's assistant/continuity, the editor, the sound recordist, the lighting person. You may need to double up on roles. Then the next time you shoot a production together, rotate the roles so that everyone gets to understand the responsibilities and duties of each role. Eventually, you may have your personal preferences, but learning that each team member's contribution is integral is also invaluable. When you work as a team, don't forget to follow the plan.

'What plan?' you say. Exactly . . . don't forget to have one that's written down.

STUDIO PROCEDURES 27

Studio work requires the smooth coordination of a team of people who are spread out over two, three or more rooms. Everyone needs to know what's happening, and everyone needs to be up to date on whatever changes have been made by the director.

Recording a Business Studies unit for satellite replay throughout WA, Western Australian School of Art and Design.

Studios use talkback systems which allow the director and director's assistant to converse with the floor manager on the studio floor, all the camera operators, the sound supervisor in audio control, and the playback operator in the record area. The sound supervisor can also communicate with the boom operator via headphones.

Audio control can leave a boom mic *open* during preparation times so the director can hear what's happening on the studio floor, and anyone on the floor can speak to the director through this mic if necessary.

Kevin Noakes hosts *A Blackcurrent Affair*, School of Indigenous Australian Studies, James Cook University.

A Word to the Director

Carol Brands,
Curtin
University of
Technology.

> Remember the 7 Cs: Clear Concise Communication is the Cornerstone to Creating a Capable Crew.

Pam Carsten,
Portland
Community
Media.

> Make sure everyone shuts off their cell phones!

The main point to remember when directing a production is to promote effective communication. You have to make sure that everyone knows what you want to happen, when you want it to happen, and what you want it to look like.

All crew involved in the production must be kept constantly informed of any changes.

A new shotlist for cameras, changes to the script, different camera moves, different choreography for the actors, a change of running order—everything must be communicated to everyone involved.

In the heat of the moment, it's easy to forget that you, as director, are the source of all action. The rest of the crew have to act on your instructions. Keep them informed, and always give them plenty of warning.

The Floor Manager

The floor manager is pivotal in studio communication. The FM is in charge of relaying messages promptly and accurately to anyone on the studio floor who is not wearing headphones. This includes the performers, obviously, and any other helpers, like those arranging the set or adjusting lights.

Once the floor manager puts on headphones and establishes initial communication flow with the director, the FM should never break that link by taking the headphones (*headsets* or *cans*) off. If that link is broken, the production will soon grind to a halt.

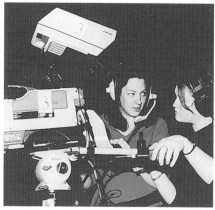

FM Clare Mowday discusses the shot list with camera operator Kira Morsley, Edith Cowan University. (Photo by Keith Smith)

Camera operators should keep their headphones on throughout the rehearsal period. Robin Cowburn, TEAME Indigenous TV and Video Training Course, Metro Screen.

During rehearsal, if the FM must leave the studio floor, the headphones—and the floor manager's duties—should be delegated to an assistant until the FM resumes them.

Because the FM also needs to be in contact with the people on the studio floor, a good trick is to wear the headphones with one earpiece on—to listen to the director—and one earpiece off—to listen to the people on the studio floor.

Establishing Comms

During the set-up period, time should be allowed for a routine communications check:

The floor manager gives a countdown cue, Northern Melbourne Institute of TAFE.

1. The director speaks to the floor manager, and the floor manager responds.
2. The director speaks to each camera, and each camera responds in turn.
3. The director speaks to audio control, and audio control responds. (The boom operator has a *split* of director's comms and program sound.)
4. The director speaks to the videotapes (playback) area, and videotapes responds.
5. The director speaks to the lighting area (if it's separate), and lighting responds.

The technical director also has communication with the technical areas, to establish program levels, and so forth.

Sometimes the DA and director share the same mic. A balance should be established early on, because the DA's shot-calling and instructions need to be heard at the same volume level as the calls of the director.

It's good if the director and director's assistant have noticeably different voices, such as one male and one female, so everyone on the intercoms can easily identify which person is speaking.

Using Talkback Systems

In most speaking situations, we're face to face with the one or two people we're talking to, so it's obvious who's speaking and who's being addressed; people take turns to speak and outsiders don't butt in. These are the communication rules we were taught at a young age. Telephone conversations follow a similar pattern because they're still one to one, even though we don't have eye contact.

Learning to use the intercom is key to functioning well in a studio team. Danny Boy, Arlington Community Media.

But when you hook up many people to a talkback system—where they can't see each other—many people could have something to say at the same time. When everyone is hearing messages that are not addressed to them, and most people are under pressure, good communication can break down quickly.

The director sets the mood during the production, so the director's talkback manners have a big impact on the overall feeling within the crew.

For good talkback:

1. Use the same courtesies of speech that you'd use in person.
   Director: 'Let's go for a rehearsal. Would everybody please stand by?'
2. Always specifically address the person to whom you're speaking, before you give your message.
   Director: 'Camera 1, could you give me the opening shot, please? A little tighter, thanks. Yes, that's fine.'
3. Don't speak unless you have something to say that is relevant to the production. People should not be chatting about other things over the talkback system—the 'airwaves' need to stay clear for necessary production communication.
4. Stay quiet. There's nothing worse than someone adding useless noise into everyone's ears. So refrain from humming, whistling, clicking, grunting, burping, and so on.
5. Speak in a normal tone. Not all headsets have volume controls, and being constantly screamed at is enough to set people right on edge.

The DA instructs each camera operator to line up their next shot. Julie Nimmo, SBS TV. (Photo by Anna Warby and Arne-Romy Berg)

PTT (Push to talk)

To cut down on the amount of noise that would go through the talkback system, many headsets—especially those worn by the camera operators—have a good feature called a PTT button. This means that what you say is only transmitted into the system while you're pushing that button; the rest of the time you can't be heard.

Mute

The talkback mic in the control room usually gives the director a number of options about who can hear what's being said. The director can choose to speak only to the floor manager, or only to the camera operators. It's also usually possible for the director to speak to everyone on the studio floor through an intercom speaker, or to mute the whole system and speak only to those in the control room.

Never switch off control room communications to the floor. Your floor crew may think that you're talking about them and paranoia will reign. Also, don't joke in the control room because if the performers on the set see the camera operators laughing, they may think you're laughing at them.

Sara Hourez,
Director.

In times of crisis, it may be best for the director to mute the talkback system and sort out the problem in private. No point sending aggravation out to everyone. But it's important to get back on line as soon as possible, because crew feel very nervous if they're cut off for long.

Before muting the comms, the director should always explain that this is about to happen and give a time estimate of how long the mute will last.

'Sorry, we need to sort out a question here. We'll be back in about three minutes.'

If the problem takes longer, the floor manager should be advised.

'This will probably take another ten minutes. Let everyone have a break.'

Don't leave people just hanging and wondering.

Check in regularly with your camera operators if you need to mute their comms while solving a problem in the control room. Leo Roy does camera for *Call to Serve*, Methuen Community TV. (Photo by Nancy Clover)

Regrettable Speech

Talkback demands another element of self-discipline. A person should *never* say something over talkback that is meant as a private comment. Everyone hears what is said, and the words can't be recalled.

It's especially important to not rudely criticise anyone's work in public like this, or to make derogatory comments about a crew member or performer. Such speech is unprofessional, unkind and also capable of being accidentally sent out over a speaker or recorded.

Technical Difficulties

Talkback systems vary in quality, and some can be quirky and discouraging. Successful productions have been put together with only a couple of headsets working on the day, with the floor manager whispering shot directions to a camera operator, or with no one able to talk back to the director at all.

In times of necessity, people rely on hand signals and dramatic facial expressions sent through the window between the studio floor and the control room.

Control Room Dialogue

Directors need to make their messages simple, clear and polite, and use as calm a tone of voice as can be mustered under the circumstances. There should be enough time for people to give their replies.

Here's a sample of the way a director would speak during a rehearsal.

Director (this message is relayed via the floor manager): 'Stand by everyone.'

Control room in action, Methuen Community TV. (Photo by Nancy Clover)

'We'll be going in about 30 seconds.'

'Everyone okay?'

Note: Audio control should have left one of the studio microphones open so that people on the floor can talk back to the director if they need to.

Director (over headphones talkback system): 'Stand by studio.'

'Stand by audio.'

'Stand by videotapes.'

'Stand by opening titles.'

Floor Manager (after checking that the floor is ready): 'The floor is standing by.'

Audio Control: 'Audio standing by.'

Videotapes: 'Videotapes standing by.'

Titles: 'Titles standing by.'

Director: 'Opening shots please.'

'Videotapes, roll to record.'

Videotapes: 'Tape is rolling' (or 'We're recording').

Director: 'Ten seconds . . .'

(Either the DA or director will count down from 10 to 0.)

'After titles, we're opening on Camera 2.'

'Go theme . . .'

Audio control brings up the opening music to be played under the titles.

Director: 'Take titles.'

'Ready 2 . . .'

Audio control has all the music and effects cued and ready.
Broadcasting students, Batchelor College.

For the director's assistant: Don't worry about the closing titles when you're rolling the opening titles.

Sandra Chung,
ABC TV
Training and
Development.

As the production proceeds, the director is responsible for telling the vision mixer exactly what images to put to line. The director tells the VM (vision mixer) when to cut, dissolve, set up for an effect, do an effect, and so forth.

They may be working from prearranged shots notated on a script, or ad-libbing. In either case, the director needs to watch what's happening on the camera monitors and the preview monitors because things don't always go to plan. It's pointless to put a camera to line if the shot isn't ready, no matter what the script says.

In scripted work, the director's assistant prompts each camera to get ready for the next shot.

Director's Assistant: 'Camera one, a mid-shot of the guest, please.'

Director: 'Stand by to take [camera] one.'

'Take one.'

Camera operators need warning that their picture is about to be used.

Director: 'Camera two, can you get me a close-up of the host?'

'Focus?'

'Good.'

'Stand by, two.'

'Take two.'

The same procedure applies to videotapes, to the titler (CG or character generator) and to any slides or graphics being used. The director's assistant makes sure each source is ready, and the director calls the take.

Director: 'Take videotape.'
　　　'Take character generator.'
　　　'Take slide.'

If these sources are available on preview monitors, the director may refer to the number of the monitor instead of the actual source.

In multi-camera, once you've committed yourself to a shot, let it go to air or tape. Look ahead to the next shot and ensure that it is what you want. In high-turnover television (over 25 minutes screen time per day), you do not have the luxury of revision and perfecting.

Sara Hourez,
Director.

In multi-camera television drama series in studio, you usually use and camera script to three cameras. You might, without warning, need to rescript for two cameras.

Cuing Audio

Sound must be cued by the director whenever it's needed. The sound operator should be ready to bring in the next music or effect by reading the script, but the exact time and the pace at which the music is brought in is a creative decision made by the director. After several rehearsals, the sound operator will have a pretty good idea of what's required, but it's still up to the director to give the cue.

Never assume, always ask—for example, are there any reflective surfaces on the set? As drama crews know the set backwards, clarification of this will mean no time wasted on a reshoot.

Lighting

Lighting changes must also be cued, unless there's a standard format to the show that is always followed. Usually a stand-by is given to the lighting operator, with a description of the next lighting needed.

Performers

Instructions for the performers are passed on through the floor manager. When the director wants the performers to begin talking, or moving, or taking any particular action, s/he says:

Director: 'Cue performer.'

Then the floor manager makes the appropriate signal, taking care to be in the current eyeline of the performer. Of course, the floor manager never speaks out loud, as their voice would be picked up on the studio microphone. Once the performer has received the director's cue:

Relax—enjoy it—it's not brain surgery!

Director: 'Take one' (or whatever), and the shooting sequence begins.

Leone Adams,
NSW ABC TV
Training
Coordinator.

Silent Communication on the Floor

The floor manager uses a vocabulary of hand signals that should be well understood by the production crew.

Before the start of the show, the FM (floor manager) should demonstrate to any front-of-camera participants the signals that are likely to be used and where s/he will stand to give the signals.

This way the performers won't just stop talking and look stunned when confronted with an incomprehensible hand sign or waving of arms.

Make sure that the signals are always repeated in the same form and in the same spot.

Types of Cues

There are three major types of cue a floor manager handles:

- time cues
- performance cues
- written cues.

Time Cues

Time cues let the performers know how long it will be until the segment starts, when to begin speaking, and how much time is left until the segment ends.

Standing by

Start

Standing by (further away from performer)

Start (further away from performer)

We're on-line (or) everything's okay

Wind up (move finger in circular motion)

Stretch (move hands as if to pull on elastic)

Cut!

Cut! (used when performer's eyeline is directly to camera)

5 minutes

30 seconds

30 seconds (at a distance)

15 seconds

10 seconds

5 seconds

Performance Cues

Performance cues give the performers directions about where and when to move, how to change speaking or singing level, the limits of the frame to which the performers are working (this takes considerable skill on the part of the floor manager), and which camera to direct the performance to. The floor manager can even use cues to direct or correct the performer's eyeline.

Come closer

Move back

Stop!

Speak up

Tone it down

Walk in that direction

Go from this camera...

...to this camera

Go from this monitor...

...to this camera

No good

Applause!

Dan Dow (director, floor manager and camera operator!) counts in the next sequence for the comedy *A Blackcurrent Affair*, School of Indigenous Australian Studies, James Cook University.

The floor manager must be acutely aware of which camera is being used and the eyeline of the performer to whom s/he is signalling.

The floor manager must always signal messages from a place that will allow the performer to continue speaking or acting *without being seen to have been given a message*. On television, when eyes move even slightly left or right (*hunting*) the uncharacteristic glance is completely obvious.

In practice, this means the floor manager stands right next to the camera the presenter is working to or, if there's a conversation going on with a studio guest, the floor manager's signals are offered in the eyeline of the presenter—but, of course, out of frame of the camera's shot and also not casting shadows into the shot.

Signal along the eyeline of the presenter.

Whatever is required, the floor manager signals along the eyeline of the performer, but never intrudes on the active shot.

Complications in Sending the Signals

Sometimes the floor manager has to give directions to more than one actor, and isn't physically able to get to the next signalling position in time. This problem should usually be spotted during rehearsal and can be solved by working out a plan for *bouncing* signals. In such a case, the floor manager receives the director's cue over the headphones and signals the assistant floor manager or other designated floor crew member (who's positioned correctly), or even another actor who won't be on camera for that shot but will be in the eyeline of the performer, and the signal is received and then sent on by the *bouncer*.

Another complication is when the performer is unable to see a signal given by anyone. For example, the performer might have to begin an action from a face-to-the-floor position. In this case, the floor manager could work out that the performance would begin a certain number of beats of time (counted silently by the actor) after a spoken signal is given by the floor manager.

Sometimes a signal must be bounced.

Or an off-camera physical signal, like a tap to the bottom of the foot, could be used. Floor managing often requires quick thinking and ingenuity—coupled with common sense.

Elaborate signals are never preferable to clear, concise ones. Which brings us to style. A skilled floor manager gives signals in an unambiguous style which neither confuses nor distracts the performer.

For example, time signals should appear at the correct time and then be finished. A cue for 'two minutes left' which is hanging in the air for ten to fifteen seconds becomes less usable because it's less accurate.

This can lead to a bit of a quandary. If the floor manager must finish a signal as soon as it's received by the performer, the performer must have some subtle way of letting the floor manager know that the signal has been received.

If the performer is off camera at the time, that's not so hard—a minor hand movement or nod will do. But when the performer is on camera, this kind of message acknowledgment is part of the craft of competent actors and floor managers.

Written Cues

There are times when a presenter needs to be prompted with a name, a title or some non-signable information. When this happens, the marker and large white card, strategically placed, can save the day.

It's a good idea to not rely too much on written instructions, however. Presenters can get too dependent on them, and it's hard to disguise the fact that they're being read.

Book more than one band. If one flakes on you, hopefully the other will show up.

Neal Ruckman,
Producer.

Rehearsal Routines

Marking a Position

Once a position for the performer has been lit and approved on camera, the floor manager will see that appropriate and discreet floor marks are placed down (using floor-marking tape), thereby targeting or 'locking in' the preferred action area.

Studio Calls During a Rehearsal

The floor manager conveys the stages of production to those personnel not in headset contact with the director by using these standardised calls:

'Quiet please, we're standing by for a *stagger through.*'
   This signals the first attempt at coordinating all production elements—performers, cameras, audio, lighting, etc. At this stage, everyone expects stops and starts and repeating the action several times.
   Performers will speak their lines but there will be no performance yet.

'Quiet please, we're standing by for a *run.*'
   This means a *continuous* rehearsal of the segment or scene, hopefully with few interruptions. From this the crew should get an indication of pace and a recognition of performance. Rehearsals continue with improvements until:

'Quiet please, we're going for a *final run.*'
   This signals the last rehearsal. Everyone gives their top performance.
   Then:

'Quiet please, we're going for a *take.*'
   Commitment!

Throughout the rehearsal period, it's important that the floor manager indicates to performers, as soon as possible after each stop, the recommencement point:
'We'll pick it up from . . .'

Sometimes spectators are allowed in the control room, but they must stay silent. (Courtesy of Portland Community Media)

Live Transmission

Live transmission is called in as:
   '[number of] minutes to air.'
   All communication in the production environment should be clear and concise, avoiding confusion and wasted time. The floor manager, in the coordinating role, is the key figure in the passing on of accurate information. So say what you mean, and mean what you say!

The Floor Manager's Toolkit

Before rehearsal begins, make sure you have a talkback headset with sufficient cable length for adequate movement (a radio headset is preferable) and that you have access to:

- slates and identification boards
- cue cards
- markers and white board
- floor-marking tape, gaffer tape, double-sided tape
- cloths
- staple gun, hammer, screwdriver, pliers, clips.

The Floor Manager's Survival Guide

Preparation

- Study script and floor plans carefully.
- Assess problem areas.
- Discuss problem areas with your director.
- Liaise with technical and support staff.
- Schedule appropriately.
- Check progress on all work prior to the production period.

Production

- Be early. Check that everything and everybody is ready.
- Start rehearsals on time.
- Give adequate and timely refreshment breaks.

Overall

- Use common sense.
- Be calm and courteous.
- Maintain a quiet discipline.
- Anticipate the director's needs.
- *Care* for the cast and crew.

Production Identification on the Tape

Every production must have some form of identification recorded before the program itself. This can be done either by using the character generator or by an ID board.

A program ID should include:

- program title
- director
- date of recording.

It could also include:

- the producer
- the name of the client who commissioned it
- the place where it was made.

Segment Identification

Every segment of a program should be identified just before the beginning of the segment. Generally this is done by recording this information from a character generator. When a character generator isn't available, the floor manager is responsible for providing the identification for each segment. This is done by speaking the information while using an identification slate or clapperboard, as in film production.

Information should be complete and include:

- the segment or scene number
- the take number
- the script line reference.
- the program title.

Rolling-in Sequence

The lead-in to a recording can be:

- 30–60 seconds of colour bars
- fifteen seconds of tape identification
- ten seconds of black
- ten seconds of countdown
- program begins.

All tapes should be properly labelled with production name, roll number, time code and date.

Serge Golikov,
Postproduction,
AFTRS.

Assessing Studio Work

Steve Parris of Edmonds-Woodway High School in Washington has developed this humorous sheet for students and staff to assess studio production work.

EWTV STUDIO PRODUCTION RUBRIC

	5	4	3	2	1	0 (no show at all)
Technical	Camera composition is consistently beautiful	Solid composition looks good throughout	Camera shots have a few weak shots with poor framing	Shots are consistently outside of prescribed composition guidelines	No shots use quality composition	Show didn't make deadline
	Switches are timed and create a fluidity without any errors	Switches are well-timed and clean	A couple of switches are early or late or use inappropriate wipes	Most switches are out of sync with the show script	Switches cause major distraction	Too little, too late!?!
	Audio quality is flawless and perfectly equalised	Audio is clear and well equalised	A couple of audio distractions, okay EQ	Audio mishaps, poor EQ	Major audio dropouts or distractions; draws attention away	My dog ate our tape
	Talent makes NO errors, with clear, professional delivery	Talent speaks clearly; good eye contact, posture and language	Inconsistent eye contact; can't hear some words; weak presence	Poor eye contact, speaking and presence	Talent is using the opportunity to grandstand their own ego	Just five more minutes!?!
	Lighting is very inviting, flattering	Lighting looks good, no glaring shadows	A few shadows, light uneven	Many shadows, very uneven	Very distracting lighting	We don't have a show because _____ .
	Gear is stored better than it was	Gear is put away as prescribed	Room is a bit messy	Cables lying around uncoiled, stuff laying around	Messy Marvin City!	Show is a no show
Aesthetic	Show has a smooth continuity and rhythm	Show is well made without any glaring errors to draw away from message	A few hiccups in flow and continuity	The show stops and starts like an old Buick	This is a show?	We punt!
	Maintains a high level of interest in viewers (they can't stop watching)	Viewers stay interested!	Viewers say: 'Yeah, that was okay…'	Show was pretty lame	Show is REALLY, REALLY LAME!	Crew abducted by aliens? Yeah, right…
	The show touches us in a meaningful way!	The show has important content	Some stuff that we could care less about	Lots of fluff	WHO CARES!	'Show is missing… with Elvis…'
	GUT FEELING	GUT FEELING	GUT FEELING	GUT FEELING	GUT FEELING	No show? No score, Baby…

Caring for the Studio Space

A studio is a shared space which is used by different groups of people, who may never meet, but are joined by the desire that their program will be done as well as it can be.

As a user of this space, you want it to be clean and functional when you arrive. So does everyone else.

Somerville Community Access TV, which services a wide range of public access groups, has developed this studio checklist that all groups are expected to fill out when they arrive and when they leave.

Somerville Community Access TV
Studio Checksheet

Producer _____ Date _____

Staff In _____ Staff Out _____

	In	Out
Chairs/tables/risers/flats properly stored		
Rugs rolled and stored/Props in bins		
All lights on grid with safety chains attached		
Lighting board: masters/lights and all faders off		
Program/intercom/CAM 4 cables on hook		
XLR cables neatly coiled		
All four Lavalier mics, clips and batteries in cases		
Cabinet neat: mugs, headphones, gels, gloves		
All three studio cameras:		
Three wheels locked		
Lens cap on		
Tilt and pan locked		
Cable on hook		

Comments:

_____

_____

Thanks to Don Bethel for his major role in the preparation of this chapter and for demonstrating the floor manager's signals.

OPERATING THE VISION MIXER

The vision mixer (*switcher*) takes in all the video sources available to the program. It has rows of buttons, and sometimes some T-bars, which the operator uses to combine signals for various transitions, and it has other buttons to select the desired output signal for *program out* (*line out*).

Vision mixer at Portland Community Media.

The vision mixer can make clean cuts from one signal to the next, passing on any input signal unaltered, or it can impose effects on the signal and combine two or more signals together.

The vision mixer signal output goes to a video recorder, to a transmitter for broadcast, to an external cable network, through an in-house closed circuit system, or any combination of these.

Vision mixers are used in video studios, edit suites, OB vans and portable multi-cam set-ups.

All the video signals in a vision mixer must be *synchronous*—that is, they all need to have exactly the same underlying timing pulses. If two signals aren't *in sync*, you can't do any effect that involves both of them simultaneuously, and if you try to cut from one to the next, you'll get a glitch at the cut. On some vision mixers, a warning *NS* light comes on, which means the signals are *non-synchronous*.

Some vision mixers can handle synching up a small number of signals by themselves. With a large studio vision mixer, all the sources are genlocked to a sync generator or other timing supplier.

Learning to Use a Vision Mixer

For most people, vision mixers are a bit mind-boggling at first—they have so many buttons and moving levers.

A good way to start is to have a session or two with someone who already knows how to use the equipment pretty well. That person can run you through the basic knobs and show you how to get some of the effects you've always wanted to achieve.

Then it's great fun to play around with the equipment by yourself, especially when using your own footage. The more you play, the better you'll understand the vision mixer and the larger your own personal bag of tricks will be.

When you get an effect you really like, it's a good idea to jot down the positions of the knobs and faders. That way you should be able to reproduce the effect later on, whether it's to show someone else or to use it in one of your own projects. (There's many a frustrated beginner who just can't figure out how to get back to that deadly effect s/he got on the first day!)

You could even try following the steps suggested in the equipment manual. You may come across effects you'd never discover on your own. Perhaps even effects nobody else at your school has learned yet. After all, who reads manuals?

Padraig Gillen operates the vision mixer for the weekly multi-camera live show, *Madeleine Morning News*, The Madeleine School, Portland, Oregon.

Standard Vision Mixer Functions

There are certain basic things you can rely on finding in a vision mixer.

The Bus

A *bus* is a row of buttons. It may be three buttons long or ten or many more, depending on the mixer. (I don't know why it's called a *bus* since all those little buttons in a row look more like a train to me.)

Each button is connected to a different input video signal. By pressing a button down, the vision mixer operator selects the signal to be used. On many mixers, the button that has been selected lights up.

On all but the most basic mixers, there are at least two buses. One is used for selecting the signal for 'program out', so it's called the *program bus*.

The other bus is used for checking a signal before it's put into the program, so it's called the *preview bus*. Preview is used to make sure the next image (camera shot or whatever) is framed, focused, steady and ready to be used in the program. This is especially important if you're trying to set up an effect, to make sure it's right before you go with it.

The buttons on each bus correspond to those on the buses above and below it. So if the program bus goes, from left to right, camera 1, camera 2, camera 3, DVD player, graphics computer, titler, colour bars, colour, video black and effects, then, to avoid confusion, all the buses on the mixer are connected up and labelled in exactly the same order.

Obvious as this may seem, it's important for each button to be clearly labelled. New users shouldn't have to puzzle over the meaning of half-scratched-off labels.

When you're doing a remote multi-camera shoot, you'll be assigning the inputs to the mixer yourself. A strip of masking tape stuck beneath each bus works well for temporary labelling.

Both the program bus and the preview bus are connected to monitors, so the vision mixer operator can see what's current on each one. In a studio situation, although the control room's camera monitors may be black and white, the program and preview monitors are almost always in colour.

These monitors should be clearly labelled, too. A classic mistake is for a director to get confused between the two monitors and start calling the program shots according to what's on the preview monitor!

Whatever button you select will light up. (Courtesy of Northern Melbourne Institute of TAFE)

The program bus controls the signal which goes to the vision mixer's program output.

Every bus is labelled the same.

Some mixers have a *take* button which, when pushed, sends whatever is on the preview bus to the program bus. Other mixers let you toggle (switch) between the two buses by moving the T-bar (fader) handle forward or backward.

In a two-camera studio, because most switching is done between camera 1 and camera 2, pressing the take button makes operating the mixer a piece of cake for a beginner, as long as the show is made up exclusively of cuts.

You can see at a glance what sources are active. (Courtesy of Northern Melbourne Institute of TAFE)

Don't get confused about which monitor is showing your program out signal. Methuen Community Television. (Photo by Nancy Clover)

Cut

A *cut* is when one entire signal instantaneously and completely replaces another. It's a clean live edit between the two sources.

Plenty of buses to take your image where you want it to go.

The T-bar is the T-shaped handle that takes you from the A Bus to the B Bus. Sometimes the T-bar can separate into two pieces, for doing more complex tricks.

Many programs are made up entirely of cuts, and many others have only a small number of shot transitions using other effects.

More is not always better when it comes to video effects. The overall look of the program is important to consider when deciding what style of shot transitions to use.

Other Buses

There are several other standard shot transitions on a vision mixer. They are:

- mix/dissolve
- fade
- wipe.

Vision mixers usually have at least two more buses, called *effects buses*, to allow the operator to set up these other shot transitions.

The effects buses are often named the *A bus* and the *B bus*. (How's that for wildly imaginative nomenclature?)

To use an effect in your program, you select the button labelled *effects* on the program bus. Once that's selected, whatever source is chosen between the two effects buses will automatically be sent to program out.

How do you set up the effect? It's pretty simple once you get the hang of it. There's a T-Bar handle which moves between the two effects buses. This handle can be positioned to select the signal which is assigned to the A bus or the signal on the B bus. It can also be set anywhere between the two.

Mix/Dissolve

A *mix* (also called a *dissolve*) is a blend of the images from two sources. As you do a mix, one whole picture fades away as the other picture gets stronger on the screen. In mid-dissolve, both pictures are viewable at half-strength.

Ratana Salam does a dissolve, School of Indigenous Australian Studies, James Cook University.

To do a mix, select the *mix* button from the effects-mode choices section. Then select one of your desired signals on the A bus, and the other one on the B bus. As you move the T-bar handle from the A position towards the B position, you'll see the A picture becoming fainter and the B picture overlaid on it and becoming stronger. When you get all the way to the B position, the B picture is full-strength and the A picture is completely gone.

When you move the handle from the B bus back to the A bus, the dissolve is reversed.

If you want your next shot transition to be a dissolve to a different source, select the new source on the inactive effects bus, and then move the fader to that bus when the time comes.

Cutting on an Effects Bus

Once you've completed a dissolve (or fade or wipe), you can stay working on the active effects bus, cutting from shot to shot as long as you like by just pressing the buttons on that same bus for the shots you require. Each shot will automatically go to program out, as long as *effects* is selected on your program bus.

Then you're well positioned to do another effect when you need to. Or you can return to cutting your shots on the program bus if you prefer.

Just remember to reactivate the *effects* button on the program bus when you need to do your next mix, fade or wipe.

Fade

A fade is like a dissolve, but it goes from a picture to black, or white, or to a plain colour, all of which are internally generated by the vision mixer.

You do it in the same way as a mix, by selecting the picture on one effects bus, and the black or colour button on the other bus, then moving the T-bar from one to the other.

You can also fade up from black (or any other colour).

Choosing the Colour

On mixers that have internally generated colours, you'll have three standard controls affecting the colours:

- *Hue* selects what we normally call the colour—like red, blue, green and so forth.
- *Saturation* selects the intensity of the colour, ranging from pastel to vivid.
- *Luminance* selects the brightness of the colour, from very dark to nearly white.

By playing around with the three controls, you'll discover quite a range of colours, from muted sepia-like tones to garish chartreuse. You can use anything you want, from the restrained to the outlandish. These colours can be used in fades and wipes, and other effects like *superimpose* and *key*.

Wipe

A wipe is a transition effect which causes one picture to replace another by moving across the screen in any one of many selectable geometric patterns.

A wipe is done much the same way as a dissolve or a fade.

You start off by selecting the *wipe* button from the effects-mode choices. But then you have to deal with another whole range of choices! Are you up to it? You'll find an array of buttons with geometric patterns on them, each showing the wipe it will give you. Or you'll have a numeric keypad for entering the number of the wipe pattern you want.

Choose your wipe pattern—maybe you want to start with a wipe that replaces the picture diagonally from top left to bottom right across the screen.

Then you assign your two signal choices to the A and B buses respectively. As you move the effects fader handle you'll see the wipe happening.

On some vision mixers, you choose your wipe pattern by number.

And there's your wipe!

Wipe Direction Controls

Some mixers have a way for you to select the direction of the wipe, regardless of the direction in which you're moving the fader handle. You can assign the wipe function to always go in one direction (from left to right, for example, or from centre to edge).

Or you can choose for the wipe to always go in the other direction. Or you can choose for the movement of the effects fader handle to correspond to the changes in wipe direction, so if you move the handle down, the wipe goes one way, and if you move it up, the wipe goes the other way across the screen.

Another setting is called N/R, which means normal/reverse. With this selected, the wipe will alternate directions each time, regardless of the way you move the T-bar.

Positioner Joystick

Look for a little handle sticking out like a gearshift in a racing car. This is the positioner. It does nothing unless you turn it on—there'll be a switch labelled *positioner on/off*. Once you turn it on, you'll find that the positioner affects the starting position of certain wipes—usually the ones that open from the centre of the screen.

For example, if you're using a circle wipe, you can make it start from the top right of the screen or the bottom left, or wherever you want it to. You can even colour it and move it around—anyone old enough to remember 'follow the bouncing ball'?

Framing for a Live Effect

When you're preparing and rehearsing an effect for a live production in the studio, your camera operators need to be clearly told what you're trying to achieve. Usually they like the challenge—it makes the shoot more interesting for them.

They can press the *return video* button, which is generally a tiny button on the underneath side of one of their servo tripod handles, so they can see the combined image that is being produced by the vision mixer, and adjust their shots accordingly.

If the cameras don't have return video, a monitor in the studio can help them line up their shots.

If the studio doesn't have a monitor (some studios work with skeleton equipment), the camera operators can crane their necks and look through the control room window at the program monitor.

Robby Paul vision mixes for the drama *The Spirit of Our Land*, directed by Janice Stevens, with Chandini Jesudason on lighting. School of Indigenous Australian Studies, James Cook University. (Photo by Jason Troutman)

If the control room doesn't have a window, they have to listen very carefully to the director's instructions through their headsets.

If there are no headsets . . . it's one of those crews that knows how to fly by the seat of their pants, and they'll find a way. (Maybe they don't have a wipe button either.)

Framing for a Postproduction Effect

When you're planning to do an effect in postproduction, you need to be sure you frame your shot correctly at the location shoot.

For example, if you want to open your show with a child's head appearing in a circle wipe at the centre of frame, you should take care to shoot the original footage with the child's head in the centre of your shot, and it should be the correct size to fit into the circle wipe you intend to use. It's no good having a T-shirt logo in the centre rather than an elfin grin.

Although with digital editing video can be reframed and resized, as with everything else, it's going take less time and generally give better results if you shoot it right to begin with.

Unless you're very careful about framing during the location shoot, your split-screen may make your performers look even more fragmented than they seemed on the day of the shoot, or your title graphic may be just too big or too small or too high or too low for the effect you worked out so carefully on the storyboard.

Do you have the time to reshoot?

Wipe Borders

On some mixers, you can also choose to put a border on the edge of your wipe. There'll be a switch labelled *border on/off*. When you flip it on, suddenly a border appears, clinging to the edge of your wipe, and it moves across the screen as your wipe moves.

Now this border has its own set of controls:

* *Colour*, to adjust the hue, saturation and luminance of the border colour.
* *Width*, to make the border wider and thinner.

Wipe Edges/Border Edges

As if that's not enough, there's another knob that you can turn to make the edge of the wipe or the edge of the border either hard—like a straight line—or softer and softer until it's blurry like a mid-dissolve or vignette.

Moving Edges/Moving Borders

Now, for the people who gravitate to the psychedelic, you can also choose to make the edges or borders oscillate in a wave pattern. There's a *modulator on/off* switch to get this happening. And then you can really let loose. The waves can be made to be deep or shallow, by turning the *amplitude* knob, and they can be made to be many or very few, by turning the *frequency* knob.

If you've got a mixer that lets you oscillate borders, you'll probably be transfixed for some time.

It might be a good idea to stop here and try these basic mixer moves.

Vision Mixing Round Two

You're back for more? Well, moving right along, we still need to cover:

* Superimpose
* The key effects

- Luminance key
- Chroma key
- Internal key
- External key
- Downstream key.

Superimpose

When you *superimpose* something, you make it appear over the video image. This effect is used for putting titles or graphics onto a picture.

You can superimpose a title by stopping a dissolve midway, but better results can be obtained by keying if the mixer doesn't have a button labelled *super*.

Key Effects

The key effects cause parts of the video image to disappear and be replaced by another video signal. The resulting effect is as if a cutout stencil were being applied to the screen. The different key effects operate by being connected to different aspects of the video signal. So for each type of key, different video information is used to determine the shape of the holes that the key stencil cuts.

And now for key effects.

LUMINANCE KEY

The *luminance key* is connected to the brightness part of the video signal. When using the luminance key, you can make any area of the image disappear that is *above* a certain luminance level (brightness level). You can vary the level of brightness at which the key becomes active by adjusting the *clip* and *level* knobs in the section of the vision mixer labelled key effects.

Wherever the initial image disappears, another video signal will replace it. You can choose whatever signal you want to supply the replacement video. You can use the signal from a camera, or from the vision mixer's own internally generated colours, or you can use colour bars, black, a pre-recorded image . . . It's up to you, and there's enormous scope.

So, for example, all the white shirts and bright parts of faces can be replaced with purple or black or colour bars or some moving image.

You can also switch the luminance key to *negative* and have the initial signal drop out sections of the image that are *below* a designated brightness level. So all the dark hair and black pants can suddenly be replaced with whatever you decide.

> For the best key results, go for the biggest luminance contrast. Black and white work best.
>
>
>
> Jim Tumeth,
> Training
> Development,
> AFTRS.

White-on-black captions can be inserted easily and well using luminance key. To engage luminance key, you need to use the *lum* knob at the *key effects* section of the mixer panel, and you also have to select *key* at the *effects mode* section on the panel.

CHROMA KEY

Keying can also be done in connection with the chrominance (colour) of the signal. You do this by selecting *chroma key* with the key effects choices dial on the vision mixer. Then you have to tell the mixer what colour you want to eliminate from the signal.

Some colours tend to work better than others. Red can be a poor choice for a chroma key because red is a component in skin tones, and usually the aim is not to have parts of people's faces eaten away, though maybe you'd go for that effect in some cases.

Often with chroma key, the aim is to get rid of the background of the shot and replace it with something entirely different.

Your guitarist can appear to be playing music in the wildflowers on a mountainside in Switzerland, or your love scene can be played out in a cafe with the Eiffel Tower in the background.

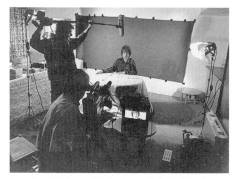

Interview with chroma key background, for *Asthma Care*. University of Western Sydney, Macarthur.

To make the effect happen, you have one camera pointed at the actor, who's positioned in front of a plain-coloured background. You delete that background colour from the image using the chroma key function, and you insert in its place an alternative background which is being supplied by another camera, aimed at a carefully lit scene from a postcard, picture book, or painting that is mounted on a graphics stand.

You can use pre-recorded footage. Say you have an interior car scene happening and you need to supply movement outside the windows. That can be shot ahead of time.

Another possible background source is a computer-generated image supplied by a graphics computer linked in to the vision mixer. With computer-generated backgrounds, you can let loose your fantasies.

Laudie Porter and Anna Ritchie stand in front of chroma key wall during their tour of KGW TV, Portland, Oregon.

Madeleine School Tech Club girls are miraculously transported to the Oregon seacoast, via chroma key, at KGW, Portland, Oregon.

The camera that shoots the chroma key window is called the *source camera*. On some vision mixers, there's only one input for a chroma key source camera, so only one camera at a time can be used as the chroma key source. Save yourself some frustration by finding out if this is the case with yours! (To do this, look at the cable connection at the back of the vision mixer.)

Any other camera can be used to supply the *fill* video (to fill in the holes), but the stencil for the chroma key must be *cut* with the source camera.

Chroma key can be a fiddly process—you have to check your image carefully before you record it. Watch for craggy edges around hair, or incomplete keying in shadow areas. Watch out for tell-tale glare from the glossy page you're using as the replacement background image.

Chroma key blue, which is a very vivid blue, is frequently used for chroma keying because it's a colour that can be avoided deliberately in clothing and it isn't a skin tone. Sometimes you can run amok with it on close-ups of blue-eyed people, though.

Consider what your shots will be before you make your key colour choice. Bright green is also commonly used for chroma keying.

When using chroma key in Final Cut Pro, sometimes the blue/green choice works the best.

Screens and studio curtains can be bought in chroma key blue. Because the shadows in the folds of the curtains can give problems in getting a clean key effect, you'll probably need to pull them out flat.

Special paint can also be bought in chroma key blue. It's expensive, but if used only as necessary it can allow you to create some terrific effects. You can paint it on chairs, boxes, wooden structures . . .

Once there were some students at the University of Technology, Sydney, who were crazy about *Star Trek*. For their final project, they painted boxes with chroma key blue and carefully placed them at the front of their set, and put a blue screen at the back. Then they performed their actions in between the two blue surfaces.

The vision mixer operator did a chroma key, inserting a freeze frame of the control room of the *Starship Enterprise* as the replacement signal. The blue on the boxes dropped away to be replaced by the front of the spaceship's control panel. The Trekkies stood behind it, speaking in Klingon, and behind them the blue screen dropped away and was replaced by the rear wall of the spaceship control room, complete with a window out into the universe.

The effect worked so well that they forged ahead and managed to insert one of their number into a scene with Spock himself!

INTERNAL KEY

Internal key is a luminance key. It uses as its key source a signal which is on the A or B effects buses. This is frequently one of the studio cameras, but it could be any signal that is connected into the effects buses.

With internal key, the luminance signal from one of the buses cuts the key stencil and that same signal fills in the resulting 'holes'. The signal from the other bus supplies the rest of the picture.

Like the other key effects, it's controlled by the clip and level knobs in the key section of the vision mixer.

EXTERNAL KEY

External key is also a luminance key. The difference is that the external key source is not available to be selected on either of the effects buses; there's no button there for it. It's a video signal that is connected only to the vision mixer's input, labelled *external key in*.

With external key, the stencil is cut by a source which cannot otherwise be called up for the program. The 'hole' which the external key source cuts is filled by the video from one of the effects buses, and the rest of the picture is from the signal on the other effects bus.

Again, it's controlled by the clip and level knobs in the key section of the vision mixer.

DOWNSTREAM KEY

This was once used for inserting titles into a program from a camera that was permanently set up and aimed at a graphics stand. Now titles are done usually by computers.

If your mixer has this feature, it's called *downstream key* (DSK) because it performs the key function on the signal just before it reaches *program out*. Because this effect happens after the signal has passed beyond the effects circuits in the vision mixer (in other words, downstream of those circuits), it leaves the main effects system free for constructing other effects.

Titles

Titles can be done either by artwork, a character generator (CG) or by computer.

Aspect Ratio

If you're making your titles by hand-drawing them or using stencils or pre-punched letters like Letraset, it's important to set them out in the right proportions on the page or the cardboard. So find out whether your program will be using 4:3 or 16:9 screen dimensions.

When printing them out from a computer, choose the *landscape* mode.

Meredith Quinn, Publishing Department, AFTRS.

Allow plenty of time for doing your credits. Often there are surprising disputes about whose name goes where and in what size type—and never assume you know how to spell every name.

Safe Titling Area

When framing title artwork (or any graphics), don't forget the *safe titling area*.

Because not all TV screens have the same amount of image cut-off at the top, bottom and sides, the titles will appear differently placed when viewed from screen to screen. Now, you don't want any part of your lettering to disappear off the left or right sides of the screen, or for your subtitles or people's names to be hanging off the bottom of the frame, so make sure your titles are placed with plenty of screen space all around the lettering.

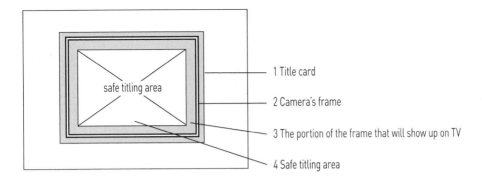

1 Title card

2 Camera's frame

3 The portion of the frame that will show up on TV

4 Safe titling area

Live Switching

During rehearsals for a program, the vision mixer works out how to achieve the effects the director asks for. Once a decision has been made to use an effect, the vision mixer notes it on the production script.

During the actual program, the vision mixer works from the production script, making the prearranged transitions. But s/he is not supposed to execute any shot change or effect until the director calls for it.

Suggestions from Rachel Masters

Script a scene that involves a two-person conversation. Then video the scene with one person holding the first half of the conversation and standing on the far left of the frame, but talking to the right side of the frame (as if someone were there). **Don't move the camera.**

Now ask the *same* person to play the other part in the conversation and be at the right side of the frame, talking to the left side. Time the pauses in the conversation carefully to allow for the other part of the dialogue to fit in. Then, if you run the two recordings into a vision mixer at the same time, and make a split screen wipe down the centre of the frame, you can make the conversation appear to be happening in real time!

The practicalities of this idea take a bit of practice. You'll need to keep the camera perfectly still so the split screen line down the centre doesn't move. The line in the frame between the two people should be invisible. You'll also need to record each half of the conversation in one take and time it exactly. If you did an edit in either half of the conversation, you'd get a jump cut. Changes in lighting will also give the game away. Give it a go. It can be very odd to have a conversation with yourself and see it on screen—unless you're an identical twin, in which case you probably know the feeling already.

29 OPERATING THE STUDIO AUDIO MIXER

The first glimpse you get of a *studio audio mixer* will either delight you—if you're a buttons person—or give you a fright.

It's a bit like walking into the cockpit of a plane. 'How can anyone learn all these buttons?'

Mixing live is definitely a challenge. Griffith University.

Well, the big relief is that the *desk* is full of repetition. Once you've learned the buttons related to one sound input, all the other input rows are basically the same!

The function of the audio mixer is to take in a variety of sound sources, blend them together, and send them out through either one or two master output channels.

In a studio situation, it would be usual for some of the inputs to be used for live mics from the studio floor, some for rolled-in music from digital audio tapes, CDs or tapes (even—*gosh*!—phonograph records), and some for rolled-in sound accompanying pre-edited video inserts from tapes, DVDs, Blu-ray discs and computers. There could also be telephone feeds, sound from a remote site, and special effects.

It looks hard at first glance...
(Courtesy of Northern Melbourne Institute of TAFE)

...but don't panic. Operating the studio audio mixer at Northern
Melbourne Institute of TAFE. (Photo by Shane Fox)

The person operating the mixing desk, who's also called the *audio mixer* or the *sound desk operator*, has to be constantly alert to make sure that all the sounds are flowing through the mixer at the right volume.

Each sound needs to be loud enough but not distorted. And each sound needs to appear and disappear at the right times.

Studio audio mixing desks can also used for doing sound postproduction for video edits.

Inputting the Sound

The sound enters the audio mixer at the back of the mixing desk, which is the opposite side from where the operator sits, and is usually kept almost inaccessible.

This arrangement contributes to the athleticism of the operator. In times of confusion or full-on crisis, the operator may have to scrabble through a small space under the desk and arch his/her body upward in the darkness, hand-tracing the snarl of cables to check whether the connections have been correctly made, or alternatively do a full-body sprawl across the top and hang upside down, trying to read the input labels and tugging at the wiring to check that it's secure.

Akila Padmanabhan operates sound for *Golden Opportunities* at Arlington Community Media Inc (ACMi). (Photo by Walzo)

In practice, most technicians who maintain a studio would like to get their hands on midnight cable swappers. A hint for survival in a media centre environment: ask the resident technician to make any cabling changes you need.

> Remember, this is a *system*. It's only as good as the sum of its parts. A good mixer connected to worn-out mics isn't going to give you the best sound.
>
> **Ed Spencer,** Sound man.

For now, let's assume that no clown has been in there rearranging things the night before it's your turn to operate.

The Inputs

Each *input* (or *input channel*) is made up of the connection socket, where a sound signal enters the mixer, and the row of control buttons and switches that can be used to affect that particular sound signal.

A 6/2 channel mixer has six inputs and two *outputs*, whereas a 16-channel mixer has sixteen inputs and could have any number of outputs, from sixteen to two to one.

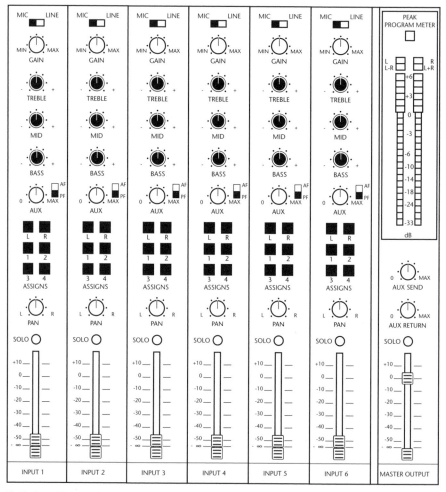

The knobs and buttons of one input row are repeated for every input row across the mixing desk.

Once you learn the controls on one input, you know how all the others work. So, in one fell swoop, you'll have learned most of the mixer's buttons.

At the back end of the audio mixer, for every input row there are usually two connection sockets, a 6.5 mm (*phone*) connection and an XLR (3-*pin*) connection. However, you may strike a mixer with RCA sockets for inputs.

This dual capacity means that it's possible to assign two different cables to each input, effectively doubling the number of signal sources which can be wired into the mixer, but of course only one connection for each input can be used at a time. Usually one socket for each input is used for a *mic level signal* and the other one is used for a *line level signal*.

A digital audio board doesn't have specific sources directly connected to each input. Instead of XLR and phone input sockets, it has CAT6 connectors, which are a bit like Ethernet connectors.

You'll probably use a different mic for each singer and each instrument. *Country Ebony*—Gus Williams, with Warren Williams (standing) and Clyde Williams (kneeling). (Photo by Michelle Blakeney)

A digital audio board is like a huge patch bay. Repatching is done just by typing in a new number and all the sources change instantaneously. Each show's mic configuration can be stored and called up as needed. We can store up to 99 different show configurations.

Byron Minger,
Director/Audio
Operator.

Mic Level vs Line Level

What's the difference?

A mic level signal is the audio signal level which is output from many microphones. It's a lower-voltage signal (usually from 2 to 5 millivolts).

A line level signal is a higher-voltage signal (up near 1 volt or even higher), and is usually output from a piece of equipment, like a VCR, a tape player or a CD or DVD player.

Now, in this case, the expression *higher voltage* is a relative term. In no way is this voltage dangerous to the operator. But the mixer's circuitry is very sensitive to these differences in voltage.

MIC ☐ LINE

The switch with the greatest effect on the input signal is the mic/line selector.

The first choice the sound operator makes in setting up a mixer for the project at hand is to select whether the input signal is mic level or line level.

If the operator makes an error, and a mic level signal is assigned as a line level source, the volume coming through the mixer will be far too low. Even moving the input's volume fader up to maximum level may not yield an adequate signal.

On the other hand, if a line level signal is assigned as a mic level source, the volume will be blasting and distorted, even when the volume fader is only moved up a little way.

Radically low or high volume is a good indication that the input signal has been incorrectly designated.

With certain editing set-ups, you're seeing a removal of the 'board' altogether! We did this purposefully to reduce error as the entire SFX library is now digitised (no more CD input required) and the music library is now in download form from our distributor. Should we need CD input, we just use the CD/DVD ROM drive on the computer!

Paul Sosso,
Editor/
Producer.

Phono

On some mixers, there's another kind of input, labelled *phono*. This input is designed for use with a phonograph player (record player—ever heard of one?) and this input will automatically amplify an incoming signal because the phonograph signal is weaker than line level.

If your mixer doesn't have the mic/line switch, it may have a small lever to flip between the phono input and the line level input.

The *gain* knob is for initial gross volume control.

Gain

Moving systematically down from the mic/line switch (which is the correct order to follow when adjusting an input signal), the second choice the operator makes is the signal's gain level.

The *gain* knob (also called *trim* or *sensitivity*) allows the operator to boost or diminish the raw volume of the incoming signal. If the signal is very *hot* (high in volume), it can be reduced at this point. If it's coming in low, it can be boosted here.

Equalisation

The third section in the line of buttons, in our mixer example, is the equalisation section.

Equalisation allows the operator to affect the *quality* of the sound coming through the mixer by selectively emphasising or diminishing the relative strength of different parts of the sound.

Very basic mixers have two equalisation controls: treble and bass.

Bigger studio models also have a control for the mid-range frequencies. Some mixers have several mid-range knobs.

The equalisation knobs have a passive position (the *detent* position), sometimes marked right above them by a zero. When the white line on the face of the knob is oriented straight up and down in relation to the column of buttons in the input, it's lined up with this zero, and the knob is therefore in the detent position. Some knobs also settle into a little grooved resting place in this position.

When the knob is in this zero position, the signal is allowed to pass through this part of the input circuitry unaffected.

The *equalisation* knobs let you alter the quality of the sound.

Turning the knob towards the *min* (–) will reduce the volume of the frequencies affected by this knob. Turning the knob towards the *max* (+) will increase the volume of the frequencies affected by the knob.

TREBLE

The *treble* knob affects the high frequencies in the sound. Turning the knob towards *min* (–) will separate out and reduce the volume of the high-frequency elements within the sound signal. It reduces the presence and the impact of the high-frequency section of the sound.

Turning the knob towards *max* (+) will increase the volume of those frequencies.

Why would you adjust the treble? If your recording is very *toppy* or *hissy*, you'd reduce the treble frequencies.

MID-RANGE

The knob labelled *mid* is the one for adjusting the mid-frequencies of the sound. This one controls the main components of the human voice. There are times when tweaking this one will help you out.

When employing equalisation, your best method is to first try to take away something instead of adding something. So if the audio is 'muddy', take away some of the low end before you try adding to the high end. If the audio is too 'crispy', take away some of the high end before pumping up the low end.

Paul Sosso, Editor/ Producer.

You might want to decrease the higher mid-range if you're equalising the sound from the mic of a speaker with an overly sibilant voice—the sort who makes annoying little whistles with their dentures when pronouncing *s*, for example.

On the other hand, you'd probably try to increase the high mid-frequencies if the voice you were recording (or had recorded) sounded a bit muddy—that is, if you found it lacking in clarity and crispness—the sharpness of a *t* or *s*, for example.

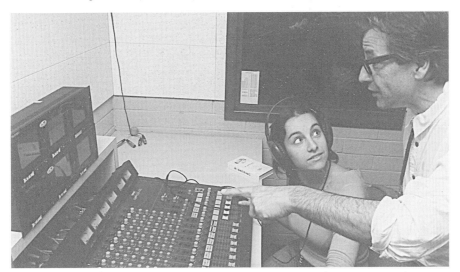

George Karpathakis explains equalisation to Daniela Fego, Edith Cowan University. (Photo by Keith Smith)

BASS

The *bass* sounds are the low frequencies, including what you know as the bass in human voices and in the sounds produced by some musical instruments, like drums.

Bass also includes the low-frequency rumble from traffic and the 50-cycle (and 60-cycle) electrical hum that can be picked up sometimes by mic cables.

You may well have a pre-recorded on-the-street interview that would benefit from having the bass frequencies diminished.

When would you increase the bass frequencies? Well, some people like to add bass to male voices, in the belief that it makes them sound sexier, or scarier, or more authoritative.

Any time you encounter a thin-sounding voice, you could try adding a bit more bass, to see whether this improves it.

Equalisation On/Off

Some mixers have EQ (equalisation) on/off switches. To compare whether the equalised signal is better or worse than the unequalised signal, switch between EQ on and off, listening carefully to the difference. EQ, like salt, can be quite effective in small doses.

Also, always check that the EQ switch is off when you first start your recording session, or you may hear, and even record, a voice that's drastically different from reality, just because someone else's EQ from a previous session wasn't turned off.

In fact, the first thing to do, whenever you arrive at a session, is to go over the mixer carefully and check that all the knobs are in the off or detent positions. That way, you start with a clean slate (to use a nineteenth-century expression).

CONSISTENCY IN EQUALISATION

One trap that goes with altering the sound of a person's voice is that later you may not remember exactly how much treble or bass you added or subtracted.

If you're doing more than one shoot with the same people, you'll need their voices to sound the same on each recording.

So if you do employ the equalisation circuitry, carefully draw a picture for yourself of the equalisation knob positions, or write down the relevant numbers if it's a digital system, so next time you can set the adjustments exactly the same.

If you're doing a number of shoots for a project which will be edited later, it's generally a good idea *not* to equalise the voices, but to record them as they are. Then the equalisation, if needed, can be done in one go in sound postproduction.

Make sure his voice is always recorded the same.
Sky Cooper, Dorado. (Photo by Jaime Lowe)

It's very odd to have an actor or presenter who sounds like a different person from one scene to the next.

Auxiliary

The *auxiliary* button controls an output which you may or may not want to use.

Beside it there's a tiny switch with two possible positions, labelled *prefader* and *postfader*. It's critical to understand the function of this little switch.

If the switch is set on *prefader*, the sound that is sent out of this output will be unaffected by the position of the main volume fader (which is the sliding button at the bottom of the input row that controls the volume level of the sound being sent to the main output channels).

An example of using the prefader position would be if the presenter wants to hear his/her own sound in foldback even when the program sound has been faded out—say, during a commercial break or a pre-recorded insert.

If the switch is set to *postfader*, the sound that is sent out from this output will be at the volume level that is being specified by the volume fader at the bottom of the input row.

As with the gain switch, this knob controls the volume of the signal, but in this case it's the signal *after* the equalisation has been applied, and in direct relation to the position of the volume fader.

AF = prefade (antefade)

PF = postfade

AF

PF

0   MAX

AUX

The position of the *prefader/postfader* switch is a key concern.

IFB = Interruptable foldback: this kills the program out sound going to the performers and lets audio control speak to them directly.

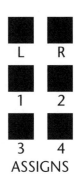

Byron Minger, Director/Audio Operator.

Assign Buttons

The *assign* buttons control the pathways the signal will take once it leaves this input. You can assign the signal to the left and right channel outputs, and most likely you would. You might also assign the signal to other outputs going to other record machines, or to foldback to the studio floor.

There are also times when you'd decide to group several inputs into a *subgroup*, which is then controlled by one volume fader, and from there sent to the master outputs (the left and right channels).

An example of this would be if you had separately miked several drums from a drum kit, and you wanted to be able to raise and lower the overall drum volume separate from the rest of the mix. It's a lot easier to have five drums assigned to a subgroup, which is controlled by one fader, than to be trying to raise and lower five faders at once while keeping their volumes still correct in relation to each other!

L   R

1   2

3   4

ASSIGNS

With the *assign* buttons, you can send several inputs to a subgroup, so you have fewer faders to move when you're mixing.

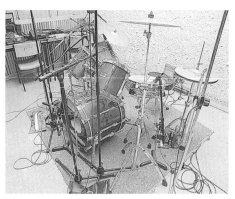

Assign all the drums to one subgroup. Music recording studio, Northern Melbourne Institute of TAFE.

L   R

PAN/BALANCE

Turning the *pan pot* knob can make footsteps travel from the left speaker to the right one.

So the *assign* buttons are for establishing subgroups, as well as sending the signal to either the left or right channel, or both.

An important thing to remember is that the sound from any individual input won't go *anywhere* unless it is assigned to a subgroup or output.

Pan Pot

The *pan pot* (pan potentiometer) knob allows the mixer operator to apportion the percentage (amount) of sound from each input channel to each output channel—that is, to adjust the balance.

So some sounds can be assigned entirely to the left output channel, and other sounds can be assigned entirely to the right output channel.

When the *pan pot* knob is in the middle position, it assigns the sound from that input channel equally to both left and right output channels.

Why would you want to split the sounds into distinct channels? There are numerous reasons, but let's take a simple but frequent scenario as an example:

You're recording a friend singing a terrific song she's written for your project. Another friend will accompany her on an acoustic guitar. This pleases you because they're both good at what they do, and you feel that at least this part of your project will seem professional.

During the recording session, you tape both the vocal and the instrumental sounds at the same time. You notice that the guitarist is playing unusually energetically, but you think it will be okay.

Later you decide that the guitar is just a bit too overpowering at some points, and you think the song would have a better feel if you could lower the level of the guitar in relation to the singing voice.

If the two sounds have been assigned to separate tracks, you can change the balance between them in postproduction. But if both sounds have been assigned equally to both output channels, you're stuck with what was recorded on the day.

Solo

At the bottom end of this whole column of control knobs and buttons on the input channel, there's a little press button labelled *solo*.

When you hold this button in, you can hear the sound from that input exactly as it is on its own, unmixed with any other audio input.

Solo is a good tool for finding where an audio problem is. If there's a hum or crackle coming from somewhere in the mix, checking the solo sound for each input channel can locate the culprit channel (and sound source) easily.

One thing to know: Some solo buttons will stay on without being held in. If a mixer has a solo button engaged, the headphones and the monitor speaker will only output the sound from that input. The program sound will not be heard again through the headphones until the solo is disengaged. So, if you can't figure out where your program sound disappeared to, check the solo buttons before you panic.

Solo doesn't affect the main output sound, however.

SOLO

Solo lets you hear each input sound on its own, with no regard to the volume fader's position.

Volume Fader

The *volume fader* is the last control for each input. It's a sliding button which glides up and down within a groove.

The groove has numbers along the side of it, ranging from the very bottom position, which lets no volume pass out of the input, up through numbers like –50, –40, –30, –20, –10, to 0, then on to +10.

Each fader controls the volume of the sound that is sent out of its input channel into the overall mix.

All the other previously mentioned input buttons should be set before the studio production or sound post-mix begins, but it's during the production itself that the volume faders are moved up and down.

This is when the sound desk operator responds to the director's instructions, such as:

'*Cue music*' (by raising the correct fader for the desired music).

'*Cue presenter*' (by raising the fader for the studio boom mic or presenter's lav mic).

'*Roll insert*' (by lowering the studio mics and raising the fader for the pre-recorded roll-in).

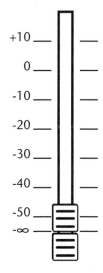

During the show or the mix, the volume faders are the only buttons you should need to be moving.

Seriana Lui raises faders for Mics 1 and 2, the host and the guest, during a studio production at the School of Indigenous Australian Studies, James Cook University.

I prefer to turn the individual mics on and off during a live shoot because that way it maintains my levels and I don't have to keep searching for levels.

Byron Minger, Director/Audio Operator.

If the volume fader on your mixer is raised less than one quarter of the way up, you could have problems. Investigate! Try winding back the gain knob at the top of the input row, so you can bring the fader up further. Or try switching a pad in. That way the quality of the sound should be much better.

Barry Fernandes, Sound Department, AFTRS.

You can expect that each source may need to be raised to a different level. How will you keep track? (Courtesy of Northern Melbourne Institute of TAFE)

Byron Minger, Director/Audio Operator.

Do your pre-flight check. Go through your rundown sheet and make sure all the sources are working and get a sound check not only for level but for quality, then EQ (equalise) if you have to.

Don't start a show without labelling your sound inputs. (Photo by Gordon Peters)

Paul Sosso, Editor/Producer.

If the breakout box for a video system has enough I/O (in/out), there's no need for a mixing board in many instances (particularly the home studio).

'*Fade to black*' (by lowering the master output sound fader).

It's the desk operator's job to *ride the levels* during a mix, so if someone in the studio starts talking louder or softer, their fader can be nudged subtly up or down to maintain a consistent sound level for the program.

Labelling the Inputs

During a live production, it's essential that the sound operator is clear on which fader operates which sound source. It's no good raising the level on the music feed instead of the studio host!

It's common practice to use masking tape to make temporary input labels for your production. People also use tape to mark the volume levels they want to achieve for each studio mic, so they don't overshoot and distort the sound when *opening* any mic.

It's good manners to pull off your labels when you're cleaning up at the end of the show.

Outputting the Sound

Once all the input sounds have been checked and the sound levels and equalisation have been adjusted where necessary, the mixer is ready to blend the various sounds together according to the volume fader positions.

After passing through the mixing circuitry, the sound is sent to the outputs. Studio audio mixers have a minimum of two audio outputs, which can be connected by cables to the two sound inputs on the studio recorder.

The output sound is *line level*, so it should be connected into the recorder at the *line in (audio in)* input, not the *mic in* input.

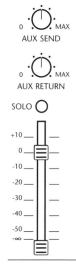

Master output.

Portable audio mixers for field use sometimes output mic level sound, so be careful that you remain clear on the differences when you're connecting pieces of equipment together. If you're in doubt,

Jake Perry mixes sound for *Madeleine Morning News*, The Madeleine School, Portland, Oregon.

check the output—it should be clearly labelled as either *line out* or *mic out*.

Some studio audio mixers have more than two outputs. These auxiliary outputs can be sent to the *PA* (public address system) for the audience, or to foldback to the presenter or singer. Sound can also be sent out to another piece of recording equipment, or sound can be sent to special effects equipment, for reverberation—or other tricks—to be added. Then the sound can be brought back into the mixer and re-added to the mix.

In most cases, there will be at least two master output volume faders, one for all the sounds the operator has assigned to be output as channel 1, and the other for the channel 2 combination.

Digital audio is carried on BNC cables. There are XLR-to-digital converter plugs for taking audio out of older equipment, like an earlier CD player, so there's no need to buy all new equipment even if you do move on to a digital audio board.

Byron Minger, Director/Audio Operator.

Phantom Power

Phantom power is 48 volts DC power sent from the mixer out along the mic cables to power the mics that are connected to the inputs.

If your mixer has phantom power, you won't need to set up separate power supplies for each of the mics that normally require them.

If you have problems, first check if there's the appropriate power to the microphone. Maybe there's a flat battery or phantom power isn't arriving.

Barry Fernandes, Sound Department, AFTRS.

Colin Kemp,
Engineering
Department,
AFTRS.

Don't use phantom power on a dynamic mic.

Byron Minger,
Director/Audio
Operator.

Rechargeable batteries have no 'slope'. An alkaline battery will trail off as it runs down—it will run for a while with a hissy, poor signal. But with rechargeables, it's a sheer cliff, they're either on or off. Always have spare batteries; always send spares out with the presenters doing the remote sends.

VU

When the VU meter needle passes beyond the 0, the sound is distorting.

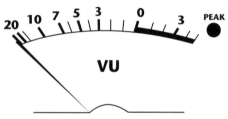

John Waikart,
Satellite News
Gathering,
KGW TV.

The biggest difference between the analogue and digital worlds is the difference of the levels you mix to. With analogue it's 0, with peaks +4 to +6, with digital you mix to −20 dB, with peaks to 0.

But be very careful you don't apply phantom power to mics that don't take it, like dynamic mics, or you could damage them.

You should be able to turn phantom power on and off with a switch somewhere on the mixer. Put on your detective mindset for this one.

VU Meters and PPM Meters

On a good audio mixer, there will be a *VU* (volume unit) meter for every input, so the operator can see the level of every individual sound source at any given point.

The operator should take care to keep the signal levels right. Generally speaking, sounds such as dialogue should be kept good and strong. The VU meter's needle should be reading up between 5 and 0, but not in the distortion range past the zero—that is, right up near the red, but not in it.

It's better to have a strong initial signal available from each input than to have to boost the sound too much with the volume faders. If you're having to run your faders way up at their top limit, go back and boost the gain at the input so you're working with a more substantial signal.

Even if there are no input VU meters, there will be output meters. These show you the level of the sound departing through the outputs.

On some mixers, the output meters are PPMs (peak program meters). These are made up of lines of LED lights—green ones for up to the 0 level, and then red ones to indicate distortion levels. Some will give you orange when you're getting near the distortion level.

PPMs are more sensitive to sudden loud sounds (transients) than VU meters are.

For the output channels, it's essential to make sure the mixer is passing along a good strong signal. Don't rely on cranking up the levels at the recorder. If you're boosting a

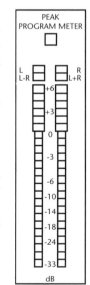

The peak program meter will show you red lights if the sound is too hot.

weak signal further down the line, you may get it loud enough, but you'll have an undesirable amount of background noise or hiss with it.

Watch the levels!

On the other hand, be careful that you're not sending out a distorted signal, either. Even if it's recorded at a low volume level, the distortion in the sound will be recorded, and you'll be stuck with it on your master.

Jim Tumeth,
Training
Development,
AFTRS.

Not all VU meters are equal. That's because consumer-grade audio is calibrated to –10 and pro audio is calibrated to +4. So if you take your cassette deck from home—and the meters are really good—and then you plug that into a pro board, the levels will be low. Yet the cassette deck still displays 'normal' levels.

VU ballistics differ too regarding how they're calibrated. So the 'peak' (PPM) indicator is usually calibrated to start blinking/holding 6 dB before peak—or sometimes 4 dB before peak.

Paul Sosso,
Editor/
Producer.

It depends upon who's doing the calibration. Sometimes these can be programmed by the user so they can indicate different things to different people. Some newer video cameras allow you to set the peak too.

Level-setting Order

Always set sound levels starting from the source and following the entire signal path to the final recording machine.

If you like, you can think of the signal flow like water going down a stream. Start from the headwaters and move to the sea.

The *last* machine to set levels on is the program recorder.

Monitoring the Sound

The mixer will have a headphones outlet, so the operator can listen to each sound without the distraction of whatever control room noise is happening at the time, and so the other people trying to sort things out in the control room don't have to listen to every step of the sound checks.

Close to the headphones outlet, there's usually a volume knob labelled *monitor*. This controls the level of the sound sent to the headphones, but doesn't affect the master output sound in any way. This knob is for your own personal comfort (yes, someone cares!) so adjust it to suit your ears and head on the day.

Make sure you're not sending too much level to the headphones or you'll deafen yourself.

Jeremy Reurich,
Technical
Trainee,
AFTRS.

But remember that the monitor sound out isn't the same as the *program* sound out. Take care that you watch the output meters to gauge the levels of your program sound. Don't be tricked by thinking it's loud enough because some wax-eared or iPod-deafened person before you left the monitor sound turned way up.

Other Possible Features

Studio audio mixers may have many other features, including:

- a talkback system
- an inbuilt speaker
- *aux send* and *aux return* monitoring controls
- the facility to do four or more submixes in them.

Despite the cringe that the following comment usually elicits, it's a good idea to thoroughly read the manual for your audio mixer. You may find out that your mixer can do all sorts of things no one at your media centre ever knew about!

Normalising the Mixer

Before you set out to do anything with the studio audio mixer, you should *normalise* it.

This means putting all the input knobs to their zero (passive, detent) positions, so you can hear every sound fresh and unaltered by any electronic circuitry.

It can be alarming to do a sound check and hear your great guest singer's voice sounding way too thin or too bassy. You can add minutes to your life by getting rid of any *EQ* (equalisation) left on the mixer from someone else's mix before you start judging your sound sources.

And after all, a signal that sounds good unaided can probably best be left that way! No need to tweak knobs for the sake of it.

It's good audio manners to renormalise a mixer when you've finished working with it, too.

Chris Hall does audio mix for Arlington Middleschool Producers Group at Arlington Community Media Inc. (ACMi). (Photo by Walzo)

Doing a Sound Check

Part of setting up for a studio production is doing a sound check. The aim of this is to find the right operating level for each input fader.

You can usually set the levels for roll-in music and other pre-recorded material during rehearsals.

When the time comes to set the levels for guests or actors using studio mics, it's good to have a helper.

First, the assistant pins the mic to the person's shirt, or seats the person and sets the mic on its stand in the planned program position. Then, when the desk operator is ready, the assistant asks the guest to speak in their normal speaking voice.

Because people are often nervous about the whole studio thing, they can get hung up trying to think of what to say. No one wants the people around them to think they're buffoons. It usually works to give them an easy task, so you could suggest that they tell you how their trip to the studio went, or tell you their name, address and other fairly automatic details.

They're more likely to speak up naturally if they're not nervous about what they're saying.

The guest can say *anything*, as long as it's in a normal speaking voice. Contrary to popular belief, it's not a great choice to ask them to count. It's too staccato a sound, with none of the usual nuanced tones.

Always check for *air gaps*. Is everything plugged in?

Barry Fernandes, Sound Department, AFTRS.

As each person you're checking is speaking, the desk operator brings the input volume fader up to the right level for program sound. S/he could mark this spot with a bit of masking tape so that during the program it's clear what level to take each fader to for the right sound volume. Please, no indelible markers!

The desk operator should also take care to adjust the gain so there's some room to move the fader up during the program if needed. Though most people tend to speak louder once they get going on a topic, there should be some correction leeway in case they speak softer for some reason.

Once the sound check has been done on all sources, you're nearly good to go.

Lining Up Tone

Set the tone as quickly as possible because the sound of the tone annoys many people.

Colin Kemp, Engineering Department, AFTRS.

There's still one more job to do. You need to send *tone*, so the person operating the recorder can set the audio input levels correctly. Find the button on the audio mixer that switches on the calibrated tone, the standardised line-up signal. Then adjust your master output faders so you're sending tone out at 0 volume level, a good strong signal level, just below the distortion level.

The recorder operator should then set the audio input VU meters on the master recorder so they're reading the tone at 0 as well.

From then on, the adjustments to program sound should *all* be done at the audio mixer.

You can cram so much more audio into the higher end with digital without getting distortion.

John Waikart, Satellite News Gathering, KGW TV.

The person watching the record machine shouldn't be making independent decisions about program sound level. If something appears to them to be wrong—for example, if there's no sound arriving at their recorder, or it's too low, or it remains distorted—the audio desk operator should be told at once. But corrections should be done at the mixer, *not* at the record machine.

Many of the newer/smaller audio mixing boards no longer generate tone. Many ProSumer cameras do! Good idea to set bars and tone prior to recording.

Paul Sosso, Editor/ Producer.

Operating Tips

Assign Mics to Inputs in a Sensible Pattern

It often helps to have a logical connection between what you can see through the control room window and what you're doing! Have your sound assistant set up the studio mics so their inputs correspond to the same left-to-right order as the seating arrangement of the studio guests and host.

So if, during the program, you forget who 'Melissa' is, you can at least raise the fader of that person on the far left whose mouth is moving.

When you're plugging or unplugging sources from a mixer, ensure that the channel fader is at a minimum and the monitoring level is set to low.

Colin Kemp,
Engineering
Department,
AFTRS.

Keep in Contact with the Studio Floor

Not all studios have enough talkback headphones to go around, and they tend to be passed out first to the camera operators.

But the sound assistant needs to be in contact with the audio desk operator, and vice versa. This can be managed by leaving the boom mic fader up during set-ups, otherwise known as *leaving the boom open*.

The sound assistant can then go over near the boom mic and speak quietly to audio control, and audio control can speak back via the PA system to the studio.

In the absence of boom mic and PA, a good set of hand signals can get messages across, providing there's line of sight between audio control and the studio floor.

With a hybrid set-up where we're using analogue mics and digital cameras, we have to insert delays for the analogue to digital because the digital video comes in slower due to extra processing. We check the delay during the set-up of remotes by putting a metronome in front of the camera. If we get the delay wrong, we get 'lip flap'.

Byron Minger,
Director/Audio
Operator.

Resource

Tom Lubin, *Shaping Your Sound with Microphones, Mixers and Multitrack Recording* (DVD).

STUDIO INTERVIEWS 30

The studio interview is a simple, low-cost and efficient way of getting information across. It can also be entertaining and humorous, with the right host and guest combination. It's worth aiming high and being imaginative when you're searching for guests.

Your choice of set furniture influences the dynamics of the interview. (Courtesy of Portland Community Media)

The interview can stand on its own, as just *talking heads*, or it can be interspersed with pre-recorded video segments. It can also be livened up if the guest shows things s/he's brought in, or gets up and does a demonstration.

The Set

In the interview, the guests and what they have to say should be the focus of attention, so the set is usually kept quite simple. Frequently the cyc curtain is drawn across the background, so the interview is in an indeterminate location with a soft background.

Faye Starr is interviewed by Vicki Lucan, AFTRS.

Martha Mollison, Producer.

I know of an interview done once in front of a banner with 'MASS' on it, which was the old-time abbreviation for Massachusetts. The speaker's head was in such a position that the M was blocked out so every close-up had 'ASS' next to his head, but this wasn't noticed until the edit.

Still, adding simple but appropriate artefacts, which reflect the culture of the guest or the content of the interview, can enhance the look of the program.

Because camera operators usually stand, the comfortable height for their cameras is higher than the eyeline of seated guests. For this reason, the interview set is elevated on *risers* (movable platforms) when possible. This makes the camera angle neutral in relation to the host's and guest's eyelines.

A standard interview set consists of a chair for each guest and one for the host. Sometimes a low table is placed in front of them, so items which will be discussed can be at hand for close-ups.

Chairs should have fairly straight backs, because people look better and less paunchy if they're not slouching.

Rotating chairs are a potential disaster because nervous guests tend to swivel in them during the shoot, and they can also introduce squeaks, clunks and other undesirable sounds into the audio track.

It's important that the set doesn't get in the way of camera moves, and that it doesn't look peculiar from any anticipated camera angle.

Check that background details and designs don't appear to grow out of anyone's head, and watch that unexpected words don't appear when someone's body blocks out sections of background lettering.

Lighting the Interview

Simple three-point lighting set-ups work well for the studio interview, and they're easy to achieve because there's usually a high ceiling and adequate space around the seated people.

If there are plenty of lights, each person can have a key light, a back light and a fill light of their own.

However, when two people are sitting side by side, it's workable to light them both with the same key and fill lights, and give them each their own back light. Sometimes the back light can be shared as well.

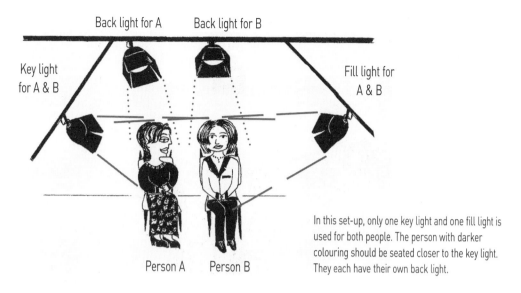

Back light for A   Back light for B

Key light
for A & B

Fill light for
A & B

Person A   Person B

In this set-up, only one key light and one fill light is
used for both people. The person with darker
colouring should be seated closer to the key light.
They each have their own back light.

If two people are facing each other, it's possible for the key light of one person
to be the fill light for the other and vice versa.

Key light for A

Fill light for B

Key light for B
Fill light for A

Person A   Person B

Sometimes the key light of one person can be the fill
light for another. A half-scrim on the key light can
help you achieve this.

It's also possible for both people to share a key light and each have their own
fill and back lights.

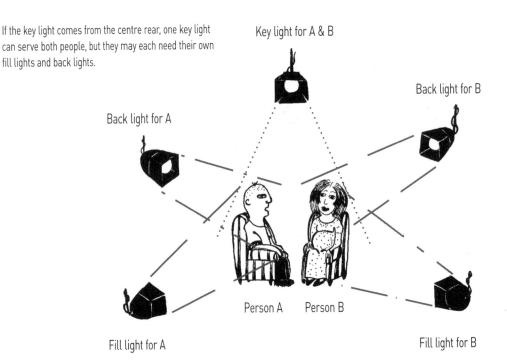

If the key light comes from the centre rear, one key light can serve both people, but they may each need their own fill lights and back lights.

Indirect frontal lighting can be soft and shadowless. Combined with a strong back light on the head and shoulders, this lighting set-up can give a very pretty effect.

Indirect frontal lighting from floor stands can get in the way of camera shots and tracking moves, though.

When lighting an interview, take care to control the light intensity that falls on each face. Lighter-skinned people tend to look bleached out fairly easily, while darker-skinned people can handle a stronger light intensity. When lighting two people together who have quite different skin tones, seat the darker-skinned person closer to the light.

Guests should be advised to arrive in clothing that is neither very pale (white is especially reflective and difficult) nor dark (black is a problem, too), as these contrast too starkly with skin tones and make lighting very difficult. Medium tones, especially blues and rose, work well. Green can make a person look sickly.

Coloured gels can be used for throwing mood lighting on the cyc, but should usually be kept off the skin and hair of the guests.

The person who designs the lighting can make it soft and flattering, or stark and dramatic, depending on the tone of the program.

Good lighting adds greatly to the aesthetics of an interview, so allow enough time to get it right, and don't cut corners.

Setting the Sound

Let's face it, talking heads with poor sound is a waste of everyone's time. No one will watch it, not even your mother!

First of all, you should use the best mics you can get your hands on. Second, you should never accept buzzing or crackling sound. Find the source of the buzz and remedy it. Change to another cable to get rid of the crackle.

Third, if the sound level is too low, replace the mic batteries with new ones. If you can't get an adequate level, change mics.

If you have only one mic, you need to place it so the sound is of equal quality from both—or all—the speakers. This probably means positioning it closer to the more softly spoken person.

Because interviews aren't totally pre-scripted, and people can jump in with a comment at any point, it's very difficult to mic them with a super-directional boom mic. It works best if each person has his or her own mic, either a clip-on lav or a directional mic, which is out of shot if possible.

Once the mics have been placed, a sound check is done to find the right record levels for each voice. The floor manager or studio sound assistant asks each person to talk in their normal speaking voice. Giving them something easy to do, like talk about their trip to the studio that day or the weather, helps them to speak fluently for long enough so the person operating the audio desk can get a good sample of their voice volume and mark their fader at the right program level for them. Although people often ask their guests to count to thirty, the staccato bursts of sound from counting make it a less reliable way of setting levels.

Each participant's voice level should be set so the VU meter needle on the mixer is up near the red, but not in it.

Bear in mind that people tend to speak louder once they get revved up, so it may be necessary to lower their level slightly during the actual interview.

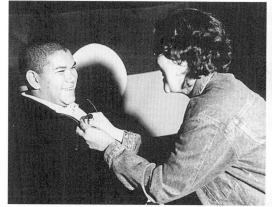

Michelle Fullerton attaches lav mic to Kris Flanders, TEAME Indigenous TV and Video Training Course, Metro Screen.

I have particularly enjoyed the live format of our productions because they are less formal and more interactive than a pre-recorded and edited program structured to get the maximum information into the shortest time.

Jeanne Flanagan, Independent Producer.

Research Preparation

The success of an interview depends on both the skill and the preparedness of the host. A person's ability to be lively and entertaining on camera isn't always matched by a knowledge of the relevant issues.

Someone needs to do good research and become thoroughly grounded in the facts, opinions and controversies surrounding the subject to be discussed.

Florence Onus,
Producer.

Research and preparation are the key to an effective interview. By the time you sit down to do the interview, you should know as much—or even more—about the topic than the interviewee.

This person may be the host, or it may be another crew member acting in the role of researcher. Either way, the end result should be that the host is thoroughly familiar with:

- the main aspects of the issue
- the names of key people active in the area to be discussed
- the main arguments held by proponents and opponents of the show's guest.

Lester Bostock, director of TEAME Indigenous TV and Video Training Course, with actor Lee Willis, Metro Screen.

Cultural Awareness and Sensitivity

People from different cultures ask questions in different ways; they also ask different questions. In some cultures, direct questions are downright rude or only certain people have the right to ask certain questions.

Body language varies, too. Looking straight into the eyes is respectful for some and insulting for others. The list goes on and on.

Claire Beach,
Videographer/
Teacher.

An open heart and open mind opens doors of possibilities.

You need to be as knowledgable as possible about the culture from which your guest comes. This way the risk of giving offence to your guest or to members of your audience is lessened.

And it's quite amazing how much more positively many people respond if they feel you've taken the time to try to understand where they're coming from.

A seemingly small gesture, like greeting a person in the *hello* of their first language, can make a huge difference to the results of your interview.

Questions

The interview should be structured around a list of key questions or topics. The director, researcher and host should have a preproduction meeting in which they discuss the questions/topics ahead of time and decide the order in which they will be addressed, usually starting with easy areas designed to put the guest at ease, and building to the real stingers which should bring out strong reactions and statements from the guest.

Florence Onus,
Producer.

Always ask your interviewee what his/her title is and how s/he would like to be addressed during the interview.

The host should have this list written down on handheld prompt cards or on a clearly readable script held on a clipboard. The director should have a copy of the list, so if necessary s/he can prompt the host to ask one that was missed out.

Part of the art of interviewing is to know when to follow a lead. The guest may say something which opens up a whole unexpected area. The host needs to make a decision on the fly about whether to follow an unplanned line, or return to the prearranged plan.

To a certain extent, the director needs to trust the interviewer to follow his or her instincts in this.

Treat your guests with respect; this means respecting cultural diversity.

Marjorie Anderson, National Coordinator, Aboriginal Employment and Development, ABC TV.

Hospitality

The guest is the most important person in the program—in fact, there is no program without the guest. The guest should be warmly greeted and treated well during the entire time he or she is there.

Hospitality for the guest is primarily the responsibility of the floor manager, but all the crew should be polite and considerate of the guest. It's unprofessional to ever make a guest feel unwelcome or belittled, no matter what you may think of his or her line of argument.

The flow of the taping session should be clearly explained to the guest. The floor manager should not only go over all the hand signals that might be used during the show, but should make sure the guest is comfortable in the set's chair, and promptly explain the reason for any hold-ups and the expected duration of the delays.

On long shoots, the floor manager should make sure that the guest gets drinks and rest breaks at comfortable intervals.

At the end of the recording session, the guest should be thanked and accompanied to the door. If possible, the guest should either be allowed to view the playback right away or promised a copy of it at a later date.

Listening: Always conduct your interview with an open ear. If you're not listening to what the person is saying, you can miss the opportunity to pick up on things you were unaware of.

Florence Onus, Producer.

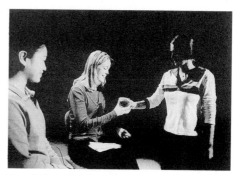

Those lights get hot! Floor Manager Christine Parlevliet gives water to Dianne Bain, while Sunshine De Luna looks on, Edith Cowan University.

You don't need to be an expert in the subject—*they* are—but you do need to know the right questions to ask to elicit their most informative and dynamic responses.

Donna Kenny, The Video History Company and Center for Recording Life Stories.

In the studio, people are much more relaxed if they know the show is being taped, not live. 'We can redo it if you make a mistake.'

Pam Carsten, Portland Community Media.

Coverage Guidelines for the Director

1. When setting lights and planning out camera shots during rehearsal, use other people to stand in for your guests. It's not a good idea to tire guests out, and they would benefit more from having a relaxed chat with the show's host in another room.
2. Establish the physical relationship between the host and guest at the beginning of the interview. A wide two-shot can do this.
3. During the interview, it's important for you to listen to the content as well as look at the shots.
4. The pace of switching between shots will depend on the mood of the discussion. Lively, controversial interviews benefit from quick cutting. More personal or reflective interviews suggest longer and more intimate shots, slow zooms and thoughtful reaction shots.
5. Medium close-ups and close-ups are the lifeblood of interviews.
6. Make sure that the shots of your host and guest match in both size and framing. Never intercut between shots in which the interviewer appears larger on the screen than the guest does.
7. When either the guest or host is gesticulating, either zoom out to include a full view of the hand motions, or zoom in and lose the hands entirely. Never let the gestures be only partially seen at the bottom of the frame.
8. Name captions should be superimposed over medium shots, not close-ups. Writing across a person's chin looks bizarre.
9. Tape or film inserts, photographs, graphics and props can make an interview more interesting. But the timing and order of these additions should be scripted ahead of time so that they flow into the program smoothly, everyone knows when they will appear and their usefulness is maximised.
10. If the guest or interviewer is to give a live commentary to a pre-recorded tape segment, s/he needs to preview the tape and have one or two rehearsals, preferably in a quiet place away from the studio. Once on the set, the commentator needs to have an unobstructed view of the monitor that is showing the segment.

Never say 'We're ahead of schedule.' You're asking for it!

Sara Hourez,
Director.

A Selection of Basic Camera Set-ups

The arrangement of the chairs on the set has a surprisingly signficant impact on the way the guests feel, and therefore how they act and speak. This, and the positioning of the cameras, affects the way the audience perceives the interview.

So don't just automatically plonk people into the chairs as you find them; rather, think carefully about what the dynamics of the interview will be and arrange the set to underscore the alliances or conflicts you hope to show your viewers.

Use whatever camera resources you have to give you the flexibility you need for good coverage. It's almost always possible to connect an additional camera into the studio mixer, using a cable from the camera's video output. So don't be shy to go for a second, third or fourth camera if you need it.

One Camera, One Guest

Covering an interview with only one camera demands skill on the part of the camera operator. Every camera move must be done well because that camera's shot is always on show.

The majority of interviews are done with people who are known for their interest in a subject, or their specialised knowledge, but whose ability in front of a camera is an unknown quantity.

As a director, you need to arrange the shoot so your program host can carry the interview if necessary.

Sean McLean from Arlington Middle School Producers. (Courtesy of Arlington Community Media Inc. [ACMi])

SUGGESTED COVERAGE IF HOST AND GUEST SHARE EQUAL PROMINENCE

When the guest's speaking ability is unknown, the guest and host can be given equal screen importance.

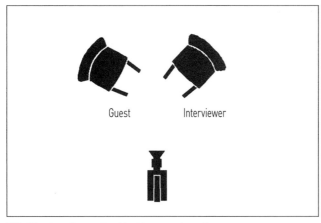

Guest   Interviewer

With this set-up, the guest and host have equal prominence.

- You could begin with a medium shot of the host, who looks directly down the camera lens to give an introduction to the piece.
- As the host turns to introduce the guest, zoom or dolly out to reveal the guest, until both are framed in a tight two-shot. Stay with this two-shot for a while (maybe until the guest is answering the second question), and then tighten the shot to a medium shot of the guest only.
- As long as the guest is performing well, you can stay with this one-shot, varying it from medium shot, to medium close-up, to close-up, depending on the content and emotional quality of the answers.
- For variety, pan to the host for a question or reaction shot. But do this only from a medium shot, never from a close-up.

Speak clearly, in short sentences that the interviewee and audience can understand.

Florence Onus, Producer.

- Also for variety, sometimes widen out from the guest to a two-shot. You may choose to do this if the guest is faltering and you think the footage would benefit from the additional image and body language of the host. Take care to stay with your two-shot for a decent amount of time, because frequent zooming in and out is annoying to the viewer.
- At a prearranged signal, return to a medium close-up of the host, who again looks directly to camera for closing remarks.
- Fade studio audio, fade up program end music, and slowly widen to a two-shot of host and guest quietly talking to each other as you roll credits over the screen. For an arty effect, fade down the frontal lights and show the host and guest silhouetted against the background.

SUGGESTED COVERAGE IF THE GUEST IS CAPABLE OF CARRYING THE INTERVIEW

When the guest is capable of carrying the interview, the host can be shown in partial profile in the two-shots. This bolsters the screen importance of the guest.

- Begin with a medium shot of the host, who turns his or her upper body around to show full face to the camera.

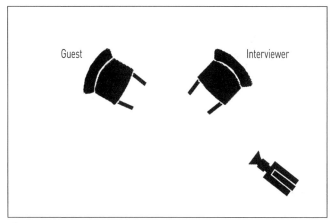

With this set-up, the camera emphasis in on the guest.

- As the host introduces the guest, pan left to a two-shot with depth, or track back slightly to include the guest in a wider two-shot. You can stay with this two-shot until the guest has answered the first question.
- Then either zoom or dolly to tighten to a medium shot of the guest. As long as the guest is performing well, you can stay with this one-shot, varying it from medium shot, to medium close-up, to close-up, depending on the content and emotional quality of the answers.
- Towards the end of the interview, widen out to a two-shot again, or pan to a single of the host and have the host turn to the camera again for the closing.

Florence Onus,
Producer.

Double-barrelled questions: These often confuse the interviewee. For example, 'Where is the conference going to be held, and who's going to be there?'

Two Cameras, One Guest

Having the second camera gives you a great advantage, because now you can adjust one shot unseen while your viewers are looking at another one that is steady and well focused.

SUGGESTED COVERAGE FOR A RELAXED STYLE OF INTERVIEW
When the relationship between the guest and host is relaxed and friendly:

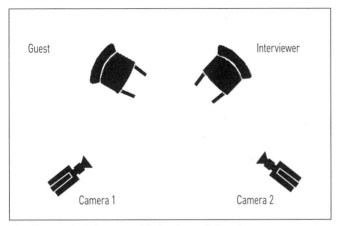

With this set-up, both the guest and the host have a dedicated camera.

It's a convention that cameras are numbered from left to right across the set. Although this isn't totally necessary, it does help to reduce the director's and vision mixer's confusion, and there's definite benefit in that!

- Camera 2 can start off with the establishment two-shot.
- Then Camera 1 can be used in a medium shot for the host's initial remarks.
- Camera 2 reframes to a medium shot of the guest, and the director cuts to the guest during the introduction.

As the interview proceeds:

- Camera 1 covers all single shots of the host.
- Camera 2 covers all single shots of the guest.
- Either camera can be asked for a two-shot.

However, this is more likely to be asked of Camera 1, because Camera 2 will be used for the greater amount of screen time, leaving Camera 1 more opportunity to dolly or rearrange shots.

- Camera 1 can dolly to a more central position to pick up an evenly balanced two-shot of the guest and host.
- Camera 1 can also be used to cover close-ups of objects the guest wants to show.
- Camera 1 can turn left to get shots of graphics on a pre-lit graphics stand.

SUGGESTED COVERAGE FOR A CONFRONTATIONAL STYLE OF INTERVIEW

For a 'hard-nosed' interview where there could be a feeling of confrontation between the guest and the host, a table can be used in between them.

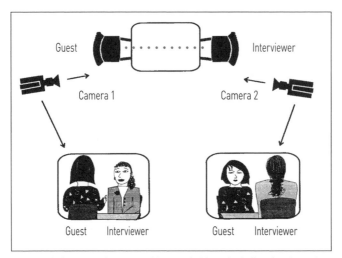

A table or desk between the guest and host can heighten the feeling of confrontation.

- The two cameras need to be positioned almost directly opposite each other, but still out of each other's shot. Each camera should have a good over-the-shoulder shot.
- Cameras should take care not to cross the action axis line, drawn in dots in the illustration above.

The two camera shots should be carefully balanced by:

- matching the lens heights of both cameras
- matching the camera positions in relation to their subjects
- matching the framing of both shots.

As with all interviews, it's best to have a neutral-angle shot of both guest and host. This is done by setting the camera lens at the eye level of each person. Elevating the guest's chair on risers, or lowering the camera height, will achieve this, with the first option being the preferred one for the comfort of the camera operators. Especially in a confrontational type interview, you don't want to diminish the authority of any speaker by looking down at that person from a high camera angle. Nor do you want to artificially aggrandise one or the other by looking up at that person from a low camera angle. As with the previous set-up, the bulk of the screen time will go to Camera 2, so Camera 1 is the camera to ask to dolly out to a more central position for a two-shot, or to cover any extra shots, like objects and graphics.

The over-the-shoulder (OS) shot allows a direct view of each person's face, despite the fact that they're facing each other. (Courtesy of Portland Community Media)

Two Cameras, Two Guests

There's more than one way of looking at the idea of having two guests on a show. Some say that unless each person can make a distinct contribution to the interview, you should go with just one guest—that it's pointless to have a second person who says little and is basically a rubber stamp of the first. On the other hand, some say that asking people to appear in a studio interview is a very big request, and that many people find the thought quite frightening. By allowing a second person who holds a similar position on the subject to come along, you give your guests some moral support, and you cover yourself if your primary guest goes speechless.

SUGGESTED COVERAGE FOR AN AMIABLE INTERVIEW WITH TWO PEOPLE

When there are two guests who concur on the subject, they can feel more comfortable if seated together.

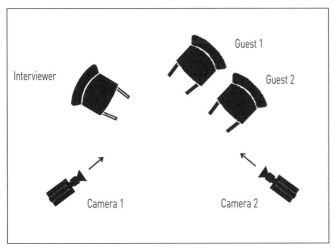

Guests who take a similar stand on an issue are usually happy to sit side by side.

- Camera 1 is responsible for covering each of the guests, using both two-shots and singles. This means Camera 1 will be very busy, and will be asked to change shots frequently and rapidly. It makes good directorial sense to put your better camera operator on this camera.
- Camera 2 covers the host during opening remarks, questioning, reaction shots and the final wrap-up.
- Camera 2 can also be asked to dolly back and get a three-shot, or track left for a three-shot.
- For variety, Camera 2 can track right and get a deep profile shot of the two guests.

SUGGESTED COVERAGE FOR AN INTERVIEW OF TWO PEOPLE WITH OPPOSING VIEWS

When there are two guests who oppose each other on the subject, it may be better to seat them on either side of the host.

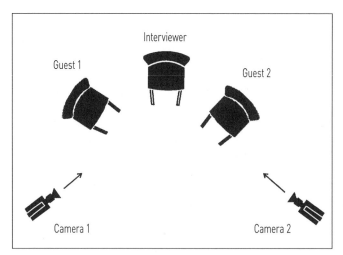

Guests who take an opposing stand on an issue may prefer to be seated separately.

The role of the host could be minimal in this interview because the two guests are likely to fuel each other, and each will have plenty to say. Most of the camera coverage will go to the guests. Still, the host needs to keep control of the show.

The opening of this interview is tricky because each guest needs a good shot for their moment of glory—the introduction. One possible way to handle this is:

- Move one of the cameras to a central position and open with an establishing three-shot, then zoom in to a medium shot of the host, for opening remarks.
- Cut to the other camera, which has a medium shot of the first guest to be introduced.
- Cut to your first camera, which is now on a medium shot of the second guest, for the second introduction.

Alternatively, you could do this:

- Open with a medium shot of the host.
- As the first guest is introduced, widen out with that camera to a two-shot that includes the first guest.
- Cut to the other camera for a medium shot of the second guest for the second introduction.

It's critical for everyone to be clear on which guest will be introduced first. It doesn't matter whether Guest 1 or Guest 2 is the chosen one, as long as everyone knows the game plan.

Coverage can proceed with successive single shots of the guests, interspersed with shots of the host for variety.

Two-shots are also good showing the host and a guest framed together. Just don't jump from one two-shot to another, or the host will appear to leap from side to side of the frame.

SUGGESTED COVERAGE FOR TWO OPENLY ANTAGONISTIC PEOPLE

Where the two guests hold strongly opposed views, providing them with a physical barrier might be a good idea.

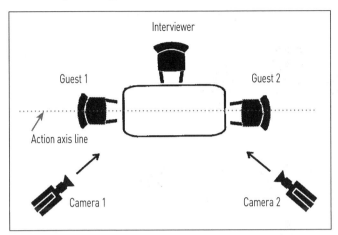

Sometimes the drama is heightened by emphasising the difference between the two guests.

- Inserting a table between the two guests does physically separate them, giving them each their own space, while also acting as a psychological barricade (and possibly stopping them from slugging it out!).
- The director needs to be especially aware of eyelines when cutting between singles, so people don't seem to be looking the wrong way.
- There's a good opportunity for over-the-shoulder shots, but take care to keep both cameras to the front of the action axis line.
- Again, you shouldn't cut from one two-shot to another, because your host will appear to leap from side to side of the screen.
- Camera 2 can open, either with:
  - an establishing three-shot that zooms in to a medium shot of the host
  - a medium shot of the host
  - a medium shot of the host that widens out to a three-shot.
- Coverage continues with each camera dedicated to cover the singles of one of the persons on the set.
- Camera 1 covers Guest 2 and can also be asked for two-shots of the host and Guest 2, and for occasional three-shots.
- Camera 2 covers Guest 1 and can also be asked for two-shots of the host and Guest 1, and for occasional three-shots.

Body language is important when conducting an interview. You can acknowledge the interviewee by nodding your head rather than by saying 'yes' or 'uh-huh' or grunting. This appreciative silence will save you lots of heartache when editing. There's nothing worse than a tape splattered with off-camera sounds, which can't be explained later without being forced to show the interviewer.

Florence Onus, Producer.

Three Cameras, Two Guests

SUGGESTED COVERAGE WHERE EACH GUEST CAN HOLD THEIR OWN

You can use your cameras to maintain the distinctness of each guest.

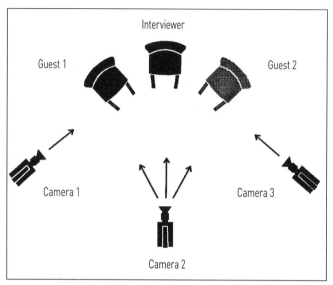

The third camera greatly increases your flexibility.

- Camera 2 can open with one of these shots:
  - an establishing three-shot that zooms in to a medium shot of the host
  - a medium shot of the host, or
  - a medium shot of the host that widens out to a three-shot.
- Coverage continues with each camera dedicated to cover the singles of one of the people on the set.
- Camera 1 covers Guest 2 and can also be asked for two-shots of the host and Guest 2, and for occasional three-shots.
- Camera 2 covers Guest 1 and can also be asked for two-shots of the host and Guest 1, and for occasional three-shots.
- Camera 3 covers the host and can also be used for:
  - a safety two-shot
  - a safety three-shot
  - graphics from a pre-lit graphics stand
  - shots of guests in partial profile, if tracking is possible.

SUGGESTED COVERAGE WHERE THE TWO GUESTS GIVE EACH OTHER SUPPORT
You can seat the guests so they feel each other's support.

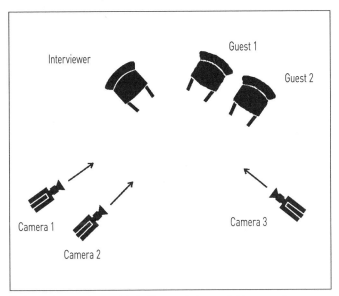

Each guest is covered separately, but they can feel supported by one another.

- Camera 1 covers most singles of Guest 1, and can be asked to track left to get shots of either guest over the shoulder of the host.
- Camera 2 covers most singles of Guest 2, and can get two-shots of the guests. Camera 2 can also get a profile of the host, if needed.
- Camera 3 covers the host and can get a three-shot with depth.
- You may need to use one of your cameras for graphics, or for covering a close-up of something one of the guests has to show. The camera you choose will depend on which cameras you're using leading up to the shot. This is where planning ahead will definitely help you troubleshoot.
- You may need to release one of your cameras for use on the next segment in your program. If so, give this camera ample warning and plenty of time to reach its new studio position so it can frame and focus before you have to use its shot. Don't wind up one segment before the first shot of the next one is ready!

Once you have completed your interview, replay a small segment of it to ensure:

1. that you have it.
2. that the sound quality and levels are good for broadcast.

Florence Onus, Producer.

Ethics and the Interview

It's easy to influence the tone of a studio interview. The director does this by choosing the seating arrangement, and selecting the content and order of the questions.

The interviewer does this by tone of voice when asking the questions, and by changes in facial expression and body language.

It's also possible for the director to use camera shots to subtly, even subliminally, influence the viewing audience.

A high camera angle looking down on the guest can be interpreted as reducing his or her authority.

A very tight shot of the guest, intercut with loose relaxed shots of the host, can seem to put the guest in the hot seat. If the guest is able to see his or her image in a studio monitor (which is almost never a good idea), s/he can feel squeezed and under attack by such an image. This can affect performance, especially in a guest who's started a downward spiral.

A close-up reaction shot of the host with a slightly raised eyebrow or tiny smile may imply that the guest is not telling the truth.

Don't succumb to underhanded tricks like these. Camera shots and angles should remain neutral and people's credibility should stand or fall on their words and their own performance.

Otherwise it can be justly said that the guest has not had a fair go.

Suggestions from Rachel Masters

If you can record an interesting one-person interview, you're well on the way to becoming an accomplished videomaker. There are many different variations on the one-person interview, but they all revolve around the same idea: the interviewee should be the focus of the interview. Your friends may be budding current affairs journalists, but their face on camera may not always be needed, and it can be distracting. Record a one-person interview which, when edited, will run for about four minutes. Remember to include cutaways and reversals. If you don't have access to a studio, don't worry—there are lots of appropriate places to do interviews. Perhaps you can do the shoot on location. Look around your neighbourhood. Who are the local celebrities?

Resource

Lester Bostock, *The Greater Perspective*, 2nd ed., SBS, 1997. Available from SBS. This style manual gives information on how to go about doing screen productions within Australian Indigenous communities. It is a must to read.

Lester Bostock, author of
The Greater Perspective.

THE H.O.T. STUDIO (HOST OPERATED TELEVISION)

31

Although it's usually easier to do video as part of a group, some people do productions on their own, perhaps for an assignment, as a community service or as a hobby.

People in remote communities, working in tiny broadcast stations, can find that they're the only ones around with the skills and interest to do video, and therefore their community expects them to carry the whole load.

If you're making programs for yourself, the HOT studio is for you. Sharon Thomson. (Courtesy of Portland Community Media)

It is feasible (I didn't say easy) to go out alone and interview someone, then return to base and edit the piece together, eliminating the blips and repetitions, inserting some cutaways, and adding opening titles and closing credits (sometimes called *tops and tails*). This results in a finished video that can then be distributed, donated or sold.

Democratising the Means of Production

But the idea of doing a full-scale studio production single-handed could seem impossible.

However, with a nifty design and a minimum of equipment, a single person can produce finished video shows that look like they were done by a whole team.

Not only can the show have multiple sources, but it can be done LIVE for broadcast, and can include phone calls into the studio from the watching audience! It's not exactly a smoke and mirrors act, but most viewers are probably tricked by it.

The Room Layout

All you need is a small room—4 × 5 metres (12 × 15 feet) would be enough.

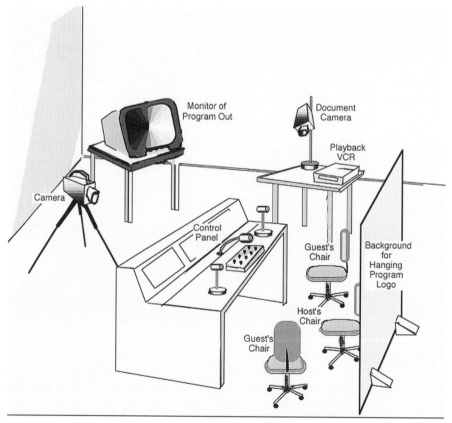

With very little gear and a small room, you can have a HOT studio that works for community broadcasting or your own home productions.

For fire safety reasons, the room should have two exits. Check with the local fire regulations to see whether you need to add a door to the exterior. Remember, the design idea is HOT, but we're not building an oven to cook anyone in!

You'll also need to consider ventilation and cooling.

A small room running studio lights will become very warm very quickly. However, the noise of an airconditioner or a fan can do terrible things to your audio by adding an obnoxious background hum. You need to think carefully about the temperature conditions in your community, and allow for quiet room cooling, or you may limit yourself and your facility to rather short shows.

Lighting

If you have the luxury of planning ahead and making the HOT studio part of a purpose-built facility, be sure to call for quite high ceilings. This is so you can have a small overhead lighting grid. The grid can be made of criss-crossed poles and suspended from the ceiling.

A lighting grid can only be used if you have a high ceiling because the studio lights run very hot, so they have to be sufficiently lower than the ceiling so they don't melt it, burn it or cause harmful gases to be heat-released from ceiling materials.

The electrical wiring for any TV studio needs to take higher-power electricity than normal household circuits provide. Have a separate circuit installed to supply the lighting grid. The sockets for the grid lights can be up along the grid poles, too, so there's no need for the electrical cords from the lights to hang down and get in the way.

A basic set of lights can be attached to the grid, and they can even be wired so they can be turned on by ordinary light switches next to the entry door. One or two frontal lights to light the host and guests, a back light to separate the people from the background, and a background light to illuminate their signage or backdrop would do.

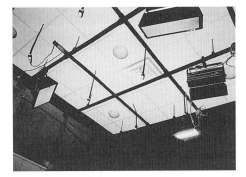

In a HOT studio, try to keep things COOL! A small room heats quickly and airconditioning ruins a sound track. Somerville Community Access TV.

Using the new colour-correct fluorescent lights would be a good idea because they run at much cooler temperatures.

For those artistes who need more complicated lighting, the grid is there for adding whatever lights they choose. Even attaching coloured gels to the front of some lights can go a long way towards changing the look of a standard set. A gobo (cucaloris or cookie) can give a new background in an instant.

If you're working with a room in your existing building, or even in your own home, a lighting grid may not be possible. Don't worry, you can use lights on floor stands—it will just be more cluttered at floor level. Take care to stabilise them with sandbags so you don't trip on a stand leg and knock over a light.

Camera

The most basic camera will do, since there's no need to genlock it in a HOT studio.

This is the easiest part. Your portable camera can be mounted on a tripod and set up facing the end of the room where your host will sit. You will need to take the signal out of this camera and send it to the little vision mixer on your studio desk. This is done by running a connecting cable from the *video out* or *AV out* port on the camera to one of the *video in* inputs on the vision mixer.

If you're a tiny operation, you can have the camera connecting cable attached to the desk and reconnect the end to the camera whenever you use the HOT studio. If you have more than one camera, you could dedicate one to the HOT studio and not have to be plugging and unplugging every time.

The Host Desk

This is where the HOT studio comes together. Whatever you put into the host desk determines the technical capacity the host will have to assemble a show.

The host desk is fairly broad, as it faces the camera. It has a rising section at the front, which the camera sees as a nicely painted or panelled desk-front, but which secretly holds most of the studio operating equipment.

You should decide on the design of the host desk yourself, keeping in mind what your own shows will be like and what your community needs are. But here's an example.

First you need a vision mixer, which allows you to switch from one video signal to another. This should be set into the tabletop of the desk so you can operate it without appearing to reach around and push buttons.

A very simple vision mixer has inputs from only four sources, but that's enough for you to make quite an impressive show. Let's consider what you would connect to it.

Each different piece of equipment is known as a *source*. Each source is attached to a different input on the vision mixer.

The most obvious source is your camera. You can connect that to the input labelled source #1 on the vision mixer. Then whenever you press the button marked #1 on the vision mixer, the camera's signal will be broadcast, or sent to your record tape, or both.

In the rising part of the desk, at the front of your work surface, you can have a monitor that shows you the signal from your main camera. This way you can be sure that the picture is well framed and in focus. If it isn't, you need to adjust your camera before your show starts. Pretty essential stuff!

Another handy source for your program is a VCR or DVD player. This allows you to play any video that you've shot and edited before the show. Or you might have a video someone else has sent you, perhaps from another community like yours, or from a national organisation that deals with your topic.

So a very simple show could open with your personal on-camera introduction, then go to a pre-recorded video, and after that insert has finished, it could go back to you for the wrap-up comments.

Therefore, you could connect a VCR or DVD player as source #2.

From the front, the host desk looks like nice furniture. Nancy Grabowski and Debby Higgins produce a live call-in show on special education. Somerville Community Access TV.

Another handy source is a document camera. This is another portable video camera, mounted in a stand facing downwards towards a flat surface (you can buy these stands or make one). This camera can be used to give a close-up view of anything too small to show well with the main camera. The document camera should be close enough for you to reach easily, maybe just off-camera to your right.

So you could connect the document camera as source #3.

Source #4 could be a computer, which can provide graphics and credits for your show.

Also hidden on your desk you could have a small computer monitor displaying your script or rough running sheet, or you could be low-tech and use a regular sheet of paper for that. Which means you could use the monitor screen for something else. How about having a live phone-in capacity?

Everything the presenter needs is within easy reach. Somerville Community Access TV.

If you can link this screen to the computer in the front office of your building, and manage to get someone to agree to take your calls, then people can phone in to your show. Your telephonist can answer the calls and send the basic information on to you discreetly via the computer screen in your desk. So your screen might say:

Line 1: Jennifer from Brockton
Line 2: Michael from Haverhill
Line 3: Hot Lips from *MASH.*

This option certainly makes local shows much more exciting and involving for the community of viewers! It means, though, that your desk will need another little box with buttons that allows you to select the phone line you want next. Then once you make the choice, you're on your own!

You rig your audio system so the caller's voice is sent out via a speaker into the studio; that way your audience can hear both sides of the conversation, and you

This HOT studio is hot to trot. It's ready to go wherever the show needs to be and can get there on its own wheels. Wakefield Community Access TV.

don't need to be fussing around with a telephone handset.

A final necessary monitor in the host desk shows the output of the vision mixer, so you can always see what your show looks like, and be sure that you've pushed the right button to get the signal you want into your show.

The vision mixer needs to be patched or wired in to your broadcast system, so you can send your video feed live to cable or live to air.

Additionally, you most likely would choose to have a record device, this one attached to the outputs of the vision and audio mixers, so you can capture your program. This is good for checking your work, and it gives you finished programs for reruns.

Sound

Barbara Bishop, Independent Producer.

This is a HOT studio. It allows one person to produce an entire show. They have push–pull levers which control the intensity of lights, and all kinds of other features. Great Northern Video in New Hampshire is selling these packages for use at municipal meetings. They can be connected to permanently wall-mounted robotic cameras, and the cabinet can be locked with a padlock. This allows one person to complete a very sophisticated production with a minimum of lugging of equipment. Nice!

The mini-mobile unit at Portland Community Media.

It makes sense, when you're designing your HOT studio, to think of what possible uses both you and others might make of it in the future.

So although you may start off thinking of it as being just what you need for *you* to make a show on your own, the day might come when you decide to have a guest. Maybe two guests. Maybe more.

Where would they sit? How would you capture their voices well?

You could have three cardioid microphones attached to long bendable necks: one in the middle of the desk for the host, and one on each end for whoever else might squeeze onto the show.

Each microphone is wired into the audio mixer (sorry, yet another box with buttons to operate!) and can be turned on and off. If only the host is on the show, only the middle mic needs to be activated. If there's one guest, then one end mic gets turned on as well. And so forth.

Background

The background may be simple to decide upon. For example, your community station may decide that the Aboriginal or Torres Strait Islands flag should be behind all your shows. Or the local TV committee may decide that every show should have its own look. One simple solution is to have a plain or textured cloth background, in some medium tone, hung on the wall behind the host's chair. A medium blue works well on TV.

The worst thing you can have is a glossy white wall behind the host. This reflective background will make the auto iris on the main camera close down, and anyone seated in the host's chair will look semi-silhouetted. As a general rule, the darker the skin tone of the host, the darker the background should be. So think of your range of producers when deciding on your background.

Ideally, the cloth should be backed with cork or some other such material, so things can be easily attached to the background with pins. But if not, if it's cloth over a hard surface, velcro tabs work well.

With this generic background, anyone using the studio can put up their own posters or artwork, their show sign or tapestry, and they've quickly and easily established the look for their show.

Label Everything

Even with a relatively simple set-up like a HOT studio, it's important to label all your cables at both ends—for example, DVD L&R audio out to audio mixer L&R input 2.

Way too much time and energy can be wasted if somebody has reconnected a cable or two for their own clever purposes or misguided ideas of fixing up a fault. Faults do happen—no system is perfect. But not all enthusiastic fixers are sensible.

When things stop working and it becomes necessary to trace unlabelled cables, it often involves climbing under the mixing desks and behind cabinetry with a finger running along a cable which can keep disappearing into a bundled clutch of cables. In dire cases, you'll need to cut the bundling straps. Cable tracing generally requires two people, one giving a tug at one end while the other tries to work out if that's the same cable s/he is holding on to at the other end, and then deciding whether the cable is running from the right output to the right input and, if so, why it isn't working.

A video RCA cable mistakenly attached to an audio input will generate a strong buzz in the audio mixer. An audio RCA cable mistakenly attached to a video input generates no picture.

Thanks to Somerville Community Access TV, Wakefield Community Access TV and Portland Community Media.

32

COPYRIGHT

What do you own, what can you sell, and under what circumstances can you reproduce someone else's work? Every filmmaker needs a working knowledge of copyright to keep out of hot water.

Although copyright laws vary from country to country, those nations that are members of the *Berne Convention* of 1886, the *Universal Copyright Convention* of 1952 and which signed the *World Intellectual Property Organisation* (WIPO) treaty of 1996 will have copyright protection in countries that are also co-signatories. The majority of OECD countries adhere to these agreements. The information in this chapter broadly covers the situation in Australia, Canada, New Zealand, the United States and the United Kingdom in particular.

In Australia, information and legal advice on copyright for filmmakers can be obtained through the Arts Law Centre <www.artslaw.com.au> and from the Copyright Council <www.copyright.org.au> (see their information sheet on film and copyright). The Arts Law Centre also offers a set of handy contract templates for film and video producers.

The Canadian Artists' Representation/Le Front des Artistes Canadiens (CARFAC) offers an online introduction to copyright, 'Demystifying Copyright' and other handy information and training programs: <www.carfacontario.ca/>. The Toronto-based Artists' Legal Advice Services offers free legal advice to Ontario-based creative artists: <http://alasontario.com/>.

In New Zealand, the Creative People's Centre is both a community and web-based service for people involved in the arts and creative industries. It offers 'legal factsheets' which provide a detailed insight into specific legal issues encountered in the creative industries <http://creativepeoplescentre.co.nz/>.

In the United States, the Volunteer Lawyers for the Arts (VLA) runs frequent workshops on legal questions, amongst many other topics, and their website offers an excellent list of online resources: <www.vlany.org/>.

For the United Kingdom, the UK Copyright Service has a website with information and guidelines: <www.copyrightservice.co.uk>. *The Writers' & Artists' Yearbook*, A&C Black, published annually, contains a clear explanation of both British and US copyright law, as well as other useful information for filmmakers and other artists. See also the online guide to legal advice and information at Film London Artists' Moving Image Network: <http://flamin.filmlondon.org.uk/>.

Claiming Copyright on a Work

To be the legal copyright owner of a work, just three requirements must be met:

1. The work must exist in a material form. That is, it must be in writing, exist as a digital file, or be recorded on video, audiotape or film, or in some other form. You cannot copyright an *idea*; it must exist as a work.
2. The work must be original. This means it must be the product of your own skill and effort and not copied from someone else. It doesn't mean it has to be very creative or imaginative; it just has to be *your work*. The exception to this is where you've produced the work in the course of your employment, in which case the copyright belongs to your employer unless agreed otherwise. This proviso generally relates to paid employment, but if you've produced the work while a volunteer for an organisation it would still be wise to check ownership rights.
3. You must be a citizen or resident of a country that is a signatory to international copyright conventions, and which has copyright laws.

That's it. At the basic level, it's very simple. If you made it, you own it. No one else can copy it without your permission.

In Australia and New Zealand you cannot register your copyright, but you should always put the copyright symbol and your name and the year the work was first produced on any script, video, song or sound recording you create. Like this: © Sky Cooper 2010.

This alerts others to the fact that you're claiming copyright on the work, and it lets them know from whom they need to get permission if they want to use any part of it.

In the United States, Canada and the United Kingdom, contrary to popular belief, there's no requirement to register your work with the copyright office in order for your copyright to exist. Just include a notice of copyright on all publicly distributed copies of your work, either by using the © symbol or the word 'Copyright', with the year of first publication and your name.

However, in the United States you must register your work with the US Copyright Office before an infringement suit can be filed in court. For up-to-date information, check <www.copyright.gov>.

In Canada you can register your copyright in a work at the copyright office: <http://strategis.ic.gc.ca/sc_mrksv/cipo/cp/cp_main-e.html>. In the United Kingdom you can register your work with the UK Copyright Service.

Moral Rights

This is a legal right separate from copyright that prevents someone from using or altering an artist's work in a manner which might hurt their reputation.

Under moral rights legislation, the artist must be identified as the creator of his or her work. The work must not be described as unaltered if it has been altered, and the work cannot be treated in a derogatory way. For example, footage from your film can't be used in a cigarette or alcohol advertisement unless you've specifically agreed to this use.

You can waive your moral rights, but if you do so, you cannot sue for infringement of your moral rights if you don't like what is subsequently done with your work.

Community Ownership of Creative Materials

Sometimes a creative work is understood by a community to be looked after by certain members of a clan group.

Indigenous communities have songs, stories, designs, drawings and dances that are part of their culture and have been passed down by their ancestors for untold generations.

Certain people are the traditional custodians of these works, but they may not *own* them in the personal way that a non-Indigenous lyricist might own the words to a song s/he wrote. Nevertheless, the community asserts its past, current and future ownership rights to this material. This is a sense of ownership that hasn't been addressed much in non-Indigenous legal systems.

There are many gnarly questions that can arise when it comes to copyright and ethics.

When a story is understood to be the common property of a clan group, but a particular person writes it down, who owns the rights?

Dancers, L–R, top: Shaun Edwards, Earle Rosas, Jenelle Gray; bottom: Tamara Pearson, Colin Lawrence and Tanya Reading from the show *Ignishin* by the Cape York Indigenous Theatre Troupe.

When a dancer allows the recording of a traditional dance, or a singer records a traditional song, to whom should the copyright be assigned: the individual performer or the community or clan group?

Or what about when someone produces a painting that is the reproduction of a traditional design or story?

I guess for me copyright for Indigenous people is very important, and we as a people must work to protect our copyright as a human right.

Most of what we promote as artists is from the old people and it's very old. We must remember that Indigenous art and dance is part of a structure that worked. It made sense, and for thousands of years. It's worth protecting because it worked for so long.

Shaun Edwards, Kokoberrin person, Staaten River, West Coast Cape York Peninsula.

Indigenous copyright and methods of safeguarding the cultural rights of Indigenous people are being hotly debated around the world. Because of differences between cultures in the understanding of *ownership*, there have been many times when Indigenous people have felt that their cultural heritage has been unfairly used for the profit of others.

Of course, Indigenous people, like anyone else, may produce works that are entirely the result of their own creative effort, and therefore they may have sole rights to these works.

If you are working with Indigenous people or if you would like to use something from an Indigenous culture in your work, you need to take particular care to find out in advance the culturally appropriate way of doing this.

Joint Ownership

What if someone's personal story is recorded by someone else? What if two or more people create a work?

Wurringu (The Women) painted by Karen Doolan, and dedicated to her mother and sisters. Her mother's people are the Gwamman and Tagalaka of North Queensland and her father's people are the Waka Waka and Gurrang Gurrang from further south around Woorabinda. Karen works as an artist in Townsville.

Oral Histories

When someone tells his or her life story to someone else, the question is, who owns the work? In such cases, it's advisable to figure out a fair apportionment of rights before the project begins.

Joint Authorship

When a work is produced by more than one person, there can be conflict over copyright unless there's an established understanding from the beginning. For example, when a person or group of people produces the text and others produce the artwork, who should have what rights? It's also good to clarify in advance whether anyone holds rights to the entire work.

To avoid misunderstandings and later problems, for a work of any substance it is advisable to establish these issues at the beginning of the project in writing, by a contract signed by all parties or some other written documentation.

The Protection of Confidential Information

As copyright law only protects works that exist in a material form, if you need to tell someone in confidence about an idea you have for a project, you can protect your idea by asking the other party to sign a *confidentiality agreement* before you tell them your ideas. You can purchase a template for a confidentiality agreement at <www.filmtvcontracts.com>.

What Rights Are Included in Copyright?

In the law, copyright is considered to be a kind of property right. It's in the class known as *intellectual property*.

Although a video script or a song isn't the same sort of sturdy object as a house or a car, the *right to copy it* is still regarded as a true property. The copyright holder has the exclusive right to do certain things, and to authorise or prevent others from doing certain things.

In a video production, these things include:

1. *Making a copy of the video.* Only the copyright owner has the right to make a copy of the video. If someone purchases a copy they can own it and use it themselves, but copyright laws generally do not permit them to make a copy of it to give or to sell to someone else. This includes making a digital copy.
2. *Broadcasting the video.* This includes via television, radio and some satellite broadcasts.
3. *Streaming or other methods of downloading* a video from the internet.
4. *Holding a public screening* of the video.
5. *Adapting the work,* for example cutting part of it, or having it translated into another language.

How Long Does Copyright Last?

In Australia and the United States, copyright in a new film or video lasts for 70 years from when it was first released. In Canada the duration is 50 years after the death of the creator. In the United Kingdom the duration is 70 years from the end of the calendar year in which the last principal director, composer or author dies, or 70 years from when it was first released in public. After that, the work enters the public domain and anyone can copy it without infringing copyright.

This also applies to underlying rights in new work commissioned for use in a film or video, such as music or artwork.

The duration of copyright in older works can vary from country to country according to when they were first created. Check with a reliable source if you want to incorporate footage from an old film or an old artwork or music in your video.

Transferring Your Copyright Ownership

Because copyright is a property right, the copyright owner can sell, lease or bequeath any or all of the rights related to any work.

If you *assign* (sell) your copyright, the new owner usually buys all the rights to the work and they can do what they want with it.

Alternatively, you can sell only some of the rights—like the right to make your video into a computer game. You can also limit the assignment of right by *time* (as 'for a ten-year period') or *territory* (e.g. 'international rights only').

Another approach is to *license* (lease) your copyright, which means that the licensee (the user) has the right to use the work, but does not actually own it. The licence needs to be clear about what it includes:

1. Is it exclusive or non-exclusive?
2. What is the period of use?
3. In what territory does the licence apply?
4. Exactly what uses are being licensed? Videotapes? CD ROM? DVD? Blu-ray? Video games? Book? Broadcast? Video streaming?

Both an assignment of copyright and a licence of all or partial rights must be in writing to be enforceable.

Objecting to Someone Infringing Your Copyright

If you think that someone has infringed copyright on your work, you need to act immediately.

- You should have evidence that you own the work in question.
- If possible you should obtain the product that you believe infringes your rights.
- You should inform the alleged offender in writing that s/he is infringing your copyright and ask him/her to cease immediately.
- If the person persists in using your work, you then take legal action. *Note:* You will need proof that you have contacted the offender about this before entering into a legal action.

To help in your documentation against unauthorised use, you should keep copies of all correspondence (including emails) with other people who have access to your work.

Acquiring Rights

Just as no one is allowed to copy your work, you're not allowed to copy anyone else's work without permission. Videos and films are generally made up of many different copyright elements: a script, music, footage and artwork. You need to obtain permission to use any work belonging to a third party not engaged in your project.

This includes downloading images and music from the internet. Yes, it's so easy to do and possibly very tempting, but legally problematic.

So what happens if you want to use someone else's script? Or include a music recording in your video? Or if someone else wants to screen your video in public?

To Use a Script or Adapt a Literary Work

The first place to check is the publisher, because publishing contracts can include exclusive licence to film rights.

If the publisher doesn't own the film rights, or the work is unpublished, contact the writer or his/her agent or, if the writer is deceased, his/her estate.

Writers' associations generally provide samples of options and purchase agreements. In some instances they may also be able to assist in tracing writers.

Australia
The Australian Society of Authors (ASA), <www.asauthors.org>.

Canada
The Canadian Authors Association (CAA), <www.CanAuthors.org>.

New Zealand
New Zealand Writers' Guild (NZWG), <www.nzwritersguild.or.nz>.

United Kingdom
The Writers' Guild of Great Britain, <www.writersguild.org.uk>.

United States
The Writers' Guild of America (WGA), <www.wga.org>.

To Use Music

If you wish to use pre-existing music, whether it's library music or commercial music, you'll need two licences, one from the copyright owner, or his/her representative, and one from the owner of the recorded music, which would be the music library or a record company.

The copyright licence, a synchronisation licence, is normally granted by the original publisher. However, it might be helpful for you to use the services of the relevant mechanical rights organisation. Some of these rights organisations have the authority to grant the synchronisation rights themselves; and some of them will contact the original music publisher. Finally, if you wish to reproduce the video, you'll need a licence from the same organisation.

Australia and New Zealand
Australasian Mechanical Copyright Owners' Society Ltd (AMCOS), <www.amcos.com.au>.

Canada
The Canadian Music Reproduction Rights Agency (CMMRA), <www.cmrra.ca>.

United Kingdom
Mechanical-Copyright Protection Society (MCPS), <www.prsformusic.com>.

United States
Harry Fox Agency, <www.harryfox.com>.

Public Performances

If your video is to be played publicly, for example on free-to-air TV or cable/pay TV, or shown in clubs or other gatherings, performance rights become an issue. However, the licence for public performances of the musical copyright does not have to be procured by you (as the producer of the video), but by the TV station or organisation that wishes to play the video.

Australia and New Zealand
Australasian Performing Rights Association (APRA Ltd), <www.apra.com.au>.

Canada
Society of Authors, Composers and Music Publishers of Canada (SOCAN), <www.socan.ca>.

United Kingdom
Performing Right Society (PRS), <www.prs.co.uk>.

United States
Broadcast Music Inc (BMI), <www.bmi.com>.
American Society of Composers, Authors and Publishers (ASCAP), <www.ascap.com>.

Copyright of the Actual Sound Recording

Australia and New Zealand
Contact the record company direct, or the Australian Record Industry Association (ARIA), <www.aria.com.au>.

The Australasian Music Industry Directory (Immedia, Sydney) has an up-to-date and comprehensive listing of record companies, music publishers and music associations for Australia, New Zealand and the Asia-Pacific region.

Canada
Society of Authors, Composers and Music Publishers of Canada (SOCAN),
<www.socan.ca>.

United Kingdom
Contact MCPS, <www.prsformusic.com/productionmusic>.
The *Music Week Directory* is a valuable resource for the UK and is available in print
and online.

United States
Contact BMI (Broadcast Music Inc), <www.bmi.com>.
Or ASCAP (American Society of Composers, Authors and Publishers), <www.
ascap.com>.

Other Sources

- *Recording Industry Sourcebook*.
- *Yellow Pages of Rock* (out of print but some editions are available online).
- The *International Buyers Guide* (Billboard, NY) carries detailed US and international
  listings and is available online, <www.billboard.biz/bbbiz/directories>.
- For classical music, the British and International Music Yearbook,
  <www.rhinegold.co.uk/directories/>.

Performer's Release

One last thing—you need to check whether the record company has obtained the
performer's consent for the recording to be used on video or film. If not, a performer's
release will have to be obtained from each performer. Your national arts copyright
centre should be able to provide a pro forma agreement for this purpose.

Fees for the Use of Copyright Music

Fees are usually set for 30-second segments of the music for commercial use.
Fees can be waived. If you're using the music in a video that you're making for
a charitable project or for a student assignment, it's worth asking for either a fee
waiver or a reduced fee.

To Use Part of a Film, TV Program or Videotape

Whenever you use someone else's film or video footage, you must get permission
from the copyright holder.
   If the footage used includes *underlying rights* to music, script or artwork, you
must also get permission from the owners of those rights.

What About Videos Made for Class Assignments?

You don't need to get permission to copy parts of videos, films or recorded music if you're making a video for the purposes of study and research, as long as the use is considered *fair*. Fairness is determined partly by how much you copy.

If a class assignment video does include copyright material for which permission has not been obtained, the screen production may not be exhibited publicly, either with or without an admission fee.

An earlier version of this chapter drew on 'Copyright and Other Legal Matters', Ian Collie, *Film Business*, ed. Tom Jeffrey, AFTRS and Allen & Unwin, 1996, and research by Meredith Quinn. With thanks to Dr Ekke Schnabel of BMI for his comments and contribution, to Kay Hawley of APRA for her assistance, and to Ian Collie for his additional comments.

Later additions to this chapter have been made by Martha Mollison.

33

DISTRIBUTION

Once you've finished your video, most likely you'll want other people to see it. How will you distribute it? Will you show it by invitation at small screenings? To the monthly meeting of the school or organisation it promotes? Will you sell copies to interested parties? Will you put it out over the internet? Will you schedule it to be broadcast or cablecast on a public access channel?

Will you sell it to a TV network?

Hopefuls at Sydney Video Maker's Video of the Year night: Trevor and Joy Saunders, Beryl and John Stephens.

You could enter it in festivals and see how it rates against other works of its kind.

Festival exposure takes some form filling and deadline meeting on your part, but there are benefits. You could have your ideas appreciated by people far away, or get asked to work on another project. You could even win a prize! Somebody has to.

Perhaps you'll just send copies to friends or family. It doesn't matter—it's your work, you know your audience, and any audience is fine.

Although the distribution facet of videomaking comes at the end of this book (and at the end of the process, for many people), the major questions about distribution (Who is the target audience? How will the video be delivered to them?) *should* be answered before the video is even made—during the planning and preproduction stages.

That way, the video is more likely to be well designed to appeal to the right people. And it will be made on an appropriate video format.

Archiving and Distributing

Once your video is completed and you want to distribute it, first and foremost hold on to your master! It's taken you too many hours of editing to risk having it 'eaten' by an erratic tape machine (even a normally reliable one, even if it's your best friend's), or misplaced, dropped on concrete, left behind on a bus seat or accidentally dubbed over.

Don't hand someone else the drive with the source media and the only digital file of the edited version, and make sure you keep a couple DVDs of your program on the shelf for yourself.

As soon as you've finished editing your project—or say within the next week if you had to pull an all-nighter to complete it—output a master to your preferred archival system—which could be tape, or one of your own portable drives, DVD, Blu-ray or your workplace server. Another possibility is internet storage space. One cyberspace option is Apple computer's archival server which you can access via the internet.

If your project is currently sitting on the school's server, you may have to act quickly. Ask the media centre about the deadline when all course projects get cleared from computer lab drives or when the work of graduating students is purged from the server.

Save not just your program, but your EDL (edit decision list or timeline) and all the graphics and rendered files.

If you archive to tape, *erase protect* the tape, label it clearly as a master tape and store it safely. It's prudent to make two copies and store them separately. The primary master should never be played but the secondary one can be used for making dubs, if needed.

I know this next piece of advice is hard to live by, but don't even give your master out for the big screening night; instead, give an additional copy.

Distribution copies should be run off directly from the host computer/server or from a reproduction facility to which you've given the saved edit file, or a DVD you've burnt and checked to make sure it's error-free. Hard as this will seem, you have to sit and watch the completed disc all the way through, while paying complete attention, not on the phone ordering pizza at the same time. You surely don't want to pay for hundreds of copies with glitches!

Actually, before sending something to be reproduced, it's sensible to have someone else's hawk eyes check it over for any small errors your own bleary eyes missed. Spelling mistakes and unintended omissions in credits are particularly likely flaws.

Your video work will be known by the quality of your distribution copy, so never send something off that isn't the best it can be. When checking, be sensitive to all three: picture quality, sound volume and sound quality.

Anonymous

> I could burn the scones in no time, but it took me a whole weekend to learn to burn the DVD.

There are two methods of putting video on DVDs. One is the burn method, which computers can do. This works well for small copy runs. Be warned, though: you may find you're getting glitches on the DVDs if you try to make too many, one right after the other, without letting the burner have a little rest.

The other copy method is called *replication* (or *DVD manufacture*). Replication takes more time at the start because a glass mastering process is used to make a metal stamper with the video information on it, and it has a higher initial cost. However, replication is ultimately faster and better when large numbers of DVDs are needed (1000+).

A correctly spelled label—possibly with a bit of artwork and pizazz—gives your copy a more professional look.

Video Festivals

Video festivals have become very popular. There are hundreds of festivals around the world, with more cropping up locally each year and some now on the internet.

The web is a good source of information about festivals. You can search by locality (city, state or province, country) or genre (comedy, short films), time of year (January) or focus (disabilities) or do more advanced searches tailored to your project.

Tropfest

Tropfest is probably the best-known screen festival in Australia and has become the largest short film festival in the world. Entries have to somehow make use of the TSI (Tropfest Signature Item) which is different each year and deliberately ambiguous, like rock, hook, bubble, spring or dice. Some constraints with Tropfest are that the video must have been made for Tropfest, must be no longer than 7 minutes, and can't have been publicly shown anywhere before the Tropfest festival. <www.tropfest.com/au/>

SASDVF

The US-based SASDVF (Short Attention Span Digital Video Festival) is an international festival that features the work of both undergraduate and graduate students from around the world. The festival accepts films in all genres: Animation, Fiction, Documentary, Performance, etc. For more information: <sasdvf.org>.

Directories

Two festival directories accessible online are:

- *Directory of International Film and Video Festivals*, <www.britfilms.com/festivals>
- *Film Land Festivals*, <www.filmland.com/festivals/>

Don't forget about getting your film into libraries. Libraries have a yearly budget to purchase DVDs and I've had great success there.

There are specialised distributors who deal exclusively with libraries, which will save you having to spend time contacting them individually yourself. Keep in mind that when you sign with a distributor, they will take about 50 per cent of your suggested retail price so be sure that you are charging enough to make it worthwhile.

Jeff Grinta,
Producer.

Public Access

Public access is defined as *a common carrier, available on a first-come, first-served basis*. You can understand this definition by thinking about a public road. Anyone can travel down it, and the first one who gets to it is allowed to ride down it first. Then all others can use it in the order in which they arrived.

Your locality could well have *public access TV*—that is, TV broadcasting channels to which any member of the community has access. Check it out if you don't know about it yet.

In Australia, public broadcasting occurs in Sydney (TVS on UHF 31), Melbourne (C31), Brisbane (QTV) and Perth (Access 31), all of which have been granted permanent licences for community broadcasting.

In addition, there's Adelaide (C31) and Lismore (LINC TV, Ch 68).

There are active community broadcasting groups in some regional areas: Bushvision in Mount Gambier (<www.bushvision.com/>), Queanbeyan Canberra Television (QCTV) in Canberra, Hunter Community Television in Newcastle, Illawarra Community Television (ICTV) in Wollongong and WARP Television in Bathurst.

For more information, or to start your own local community channel, contact the Australian Community Television Alliance (est. 2008), which is the national organisation for community television.

In the United States, public access channels are usually on cable TV and are provided by the local cable TV company. Check with the company that is the licensed provider in your area.

Your Own Showreel

If you're enamoured with videomaking now, why not consider it as a career path? Or use video skills as one aspect of an IT hunter-gather income?

The delivery of screen productions has mushroomed with the new platforms, for example video content delivered to mobile (cell) phones. For sure a lot of this content is not part of the money economy, but some of it is.

If you apply for a job in video, you need to provide a snappy showreel. It shouldn't be longer than five to ten minutes. Always put your best stuff first—prospective employers could well toss it in the reject pile after the first 60 seconds if they're not impressed. And don't linger on any single production for more than 30 to 60 seconds. You should show a variety of productions to verify your breadth of skill and experience.

Don't expect there to be jobs waiting for you. Start working for your job from Day 1. That means networking.

Alan Hills,
Queensland School of Film and Television.

When starting a videography business:

- Consider doing some free jobs for friends and family in exchange for using their productions as demo material to show your first paying customers. Spend time building a solid business infrastructure.

- Have your rates written down clearly and simply so when a potential client calls, you can inform them efficiently and confidently about your standard rates.
- Practise stating what you do in a cogent sentence or two.

Remember the three As essential to business: availability, affability and ability.

Donna Kenny,
The Video History Company and Center for Recording Life Stories.

- Aim for consistency in the look of all your marketing materials. Use the same font, colours, logo and design for all your business cards, flyers and pamphlets.

Live Video Via Webcam

The simplest, no-work way of sending live video over the internet is by using a web camera connected to your computer. A web camera is a tiny video camera specifically designed for sending moving images over the internet.

You may hear them called either *PC videocameras* or *webcams*.

Webcams come bundled with software that allows them to capture video in a format which is ready for transmission via the internet. They can be attached directly to your personal computer, usually by a USB or USB2 connection, and can send video live out into cyberspace or home to your mother, depending on whether you're broadcasting or doing a private communication.

You can use webcams to do basic videoconferencing.

Webcams can capture and send a 640 × 480 image, and if your HD videocamera can link in, you can get 720 × 480.

You can receive a full-screen image if you reset your computer screen to 640 × 480, provided that the person sending to you has the capacity to send an image of that quality. But if they can only send 320 × 240, their image will fill about half of your screen.

Most people are more sensitive to image motion than to pixel count. This is determined by the connection you have from your computer to the internet. If you're stuck with using a modem, the number of frames that can be transferred per second will be very low, producing a jumpy picture. But if you have a cable or DSL connection, you should be able to send video at fifteen frames per

Stephanie Millard, Sam Neilson and Jeremy Pau from Pimlico State High School, Townsville, have fun with webcam at the Croc Festival in Weipa, Queensland.

second, which is about half the speed of normal video, so it will look quite good to most people.

The cost of webcams has plummeted; some sell for less than $20. But as always, if you want to pay more, there's a model there for you. For example, if for some reason you want to operate your webcam using a remote control, and you want it to have a zoom lens, and you want it to be wireless so you can have it well away from your computer, more dollars will readily be accepted by the manufacturer.

Maybe you want your webcam pointed at the baby in the playpen, so you can keep an eye out from the other room, or you want to monitor the activity going on anywhere else from which you can get a connection. You want to use it as a security camera? That's fine, some webcams come with motion detection software. Using it with a laptop? You can get them with both stands and clips for versatility. It's up to you.

Webcams can come with inbuilt microphones to add audio life to the image you're sending. In other cases, you can use the inbuilt computer mic but sometimes you'll have to buy an additional mic.

Besides USB connections, there are FireWire, Ethernet and PCI varieties. Check your computer's available ports before buying, so you're sure you can attach it. Hopefully your PC will automatically detect the webcam once you plug it in, and will go ahead and install the driver software. If not, you might need to use an installation disc.

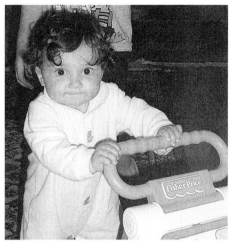

Wouldn't your relatives still like to watch her play, after they've had to fly back home?

Internet Broadcast Methods

Video is delivered through the internet in two distinctly different ways: *progressive downloads* and *video streaming*.

Progressive Downloads

Progressive downloads are also referred to as *progressive streaming*, and that second word is the cause of some confusion.

With progressive download, video is sent over the internet and as soon as a specified amount of data has arrived at the receiving computer, the video can start to play. The faster your modem, or the better your cable link, the quicker the process will be.

Progressive download will play back smoothly unless the rate at which the video arrives is slower than the playback rate, in which case the video will stop and start whenever the sending video needs to play catch-up.

Ultimately, the entire video is downloaded to the computer drive and can be saved there and manipulated like any other video file, and you can save it to DVD, tape or whatever.

This isn't *always* the case, however. Although YouTube uses progressive download, you may not realise it because the videos that YouTube plays are only temporarily stored on your computer and then thrown away as you browse to other content.

While the video is downloading, it used to be that the viewer couldn't jump ahead to view another part, but that aspect now depends on the server. If the server allows you to disrupt the delivery of the data and resynchronise at a different time offset, you can skip further through the video and the server will deal with it. (The boundaries between streaming and progressive download have become fuzzy.)

Video Streaming

With video streaming, the receiving computer is also able to begin playback of the video once a small amount of data has arrived. But, unlike progressive downloads, with video streaming the file isn't usually stored onto the computer. This method has been preferred by those who wanted to protect their video from piracy.

However, for anything that a computer receives, there are tools that allow you to save the content, so streaming is only safer in theory than progressive downloads are.

With video streaming, the viewer can jump ahead in the video to view any other parts as desired, unless it's a stream of a live event, like a horse race or ball game.

As things have evolved, streaming is mostly used for live events these days.

Do You Need a Dedicated Server?

(Why does this sound like a household helper dressed in formal gear?)

With progressive download, you can send and receive video from your own computer, as long as the computer is set up as a web server.

But in order to get into *video streaming*, you need to have a more specialised, dedicated video server to handle the media streams, and you need to install A/V server software onto it, which means additional expense to you. It may make more sense to outsource this job to an ISP (internet service provider).

Video streaming is well suited to longer videos and the broadcasting of events, lectures, training sessions, corporate functions and so on.

Video streaming is more like a broadcast situation. But, unlike normal TV transmission, you can also jump ahead or backwards to any location on the video as you please, provided it's not a live event.

There are other more advanced features in real-time streaming as well. Real-time streaming allows for admission control and multi-stream multimedia content. Some of the software programs allow you to get detailed reports on who requested which streams. You may like this feature if you're a provider.

On the other hand, you may worry about this detailed reporting if you're the consumer! What will people do with the information about you which they get kicked back to them once you receive one of their videos over the net?

Video that has been encoded for streaming tries to keep pace with the connection speed at the user's end so as to minimise disruptions to the program flow, like stalling. Sometimes this method falters, due to web congestion.

One of the great things about video streaming is that it allows lots of people to be downloading the same file at almost the same time. This makes it very suitable for broadcasting on the internet. Many users can be accessing the video all the time.

The person sending the video needs to consider how many users there are likely to be. The more users, the greater the bandwidth needed at the sending end.

Direct your readers to the Apple website, which is currently <http://www.apple.com/support/finalcutpro/>, but could change.

Harry Kirchner, La Trobe University.

If you're expecting thousands or millions of people to be wanting to see your video, you have to get it set up on a server with serious capacity!

Putting your Program on the Net

Before you encode your video for *direct delivery* to clients or your audience, you need to make some important decisions.

Quality (Resolution) vs File Size

If you want a better quality of video, you'll end up with a larger file size. Large files take a long time to download, and people usually want the downloading process to be quick.

Because ISPs generally base their charges on downloading size, huge files can become a financial issue for your viewers.

If most of the people who'll receive your video have limited computer capacity, you need to decide in favour of practicality and keep the files sizes small, which means lower-quality video. If you don't, the people you want accessing your programs are unlikely to be willing (or even able) to download them. It's a case of low quality being better than no video at all.

However, if you know your client audience is more concerned with quality, and has high-speed network connections and the latest computers, you can go for huge files and impressive quality.

You will be asked to make choices about:

- the data rate (e.g. for 56K modem)
- the frame rate (e.g. ten frames per second)
- the size of the video on the screen (e.g. 240 × 180 pixels).

Alternatively, if you want people to access your videos themselves, from your own website, you'll need to have enough storage, bandwidth and the installation of a video player. You transcode your videos to the Flash video format and publish them using a Flash video player on your website. Good Flash players that are available are Flowplayer (<http://flowplayer.org>) and jwplayer (<www.longtailvideo.com>).

On the other hand, if you're going to upload your video to a social video network like YouTube or Vimeo, that site will transcode your video to its standard format. Thus, you can send them a high-quality piece and your video will still not take up more space than other people's—but it might look better. The upload doesn't

Cathy Zheutlin,
Producer/
Camera
Operator.

> There's way too many choices in compression, as far as I'm concerned.
>
> Both YouTube and Vimeo have very good instructions on how to compress for their sites.

usually cost you anything in bandwidth, since ISPs typically only charge for download volume.

Conduct Trials

Do some *trials* first, and get some friends or colleagues to report back to you on how your video downloads and plays on their computers. Unless you get feedback, you could happily feel that your video was out there for everyone to see, yet people could be terminating the download in impatience or disgust, or be distinctly unimpressed by what they watched.

Getting feedback is a critical step in putting video on the internet! But you can get by with the help of your friends.

Bernadette Flynn, Griffith
Film School.

> Build in extra time/ contingency for compression and testing. Test across a range of platforms and with the intended audience.

The Wizard Interface

You may find that your encoding software offers you a *wizard interface* (sometimes called a Set-up Assistant). It's like an 'encoding for dummies' routine. It's fine to start off with that, to have the rush of getting your first video on the net, but the Wizard interface doesn't always give great results—in fact, sometimes they're downright disappointing.

So once you get your confidence up, move on to create your own settings. Then, when you find what you like, *as with everything else in video*, SAVE IT! You can use that cluster of settings again for your next video, and tweak it as need be.

Allow Enough Time

When you're starting out encoding videos, it will take you much longer than you expect, and you'll find that you're way back again at that steep learning curve. Never mind, you've been there before. Just have patience, and don't promise to deliver anything too soon!

Uploading Procedure for YouTube

By Dr Silvia Pfeiffer, CEO Vquence Pty Ltd <www.vquence.com>

Let's go through a detailed publishing process using free video publishing sites. Assuming that you will publish the video in Flash format to YouTube:

1. Register a channel with YouTube by filling in the form at <www.youtube.com/create_account>. You will need to own an email account for this. Assuming your account is called 'someuser', you will be able to send a link to all your uploaded videos at <www.youtube.com/someuser>.
2. You can improve the look and feel of your channel by logging into YouTube and going to your account design at <www.youtube.com/profile>, where you can

change colours, background image, and so on. Further changes can be made at <www.youtube.com/account>.

3. When you want to upload and publish a video, you log in and go to <www.youtube.com/my_videos_upload>. The video that you upload should be your final version and you want to have it exported from your video editing software to a single file. YouTube prefers as input files MPEG2 or MPEG4 videos, preferably using the H.264 encoder. The video should be in 16 × 9 HD layout, e.g. 1280 × 720 resolution, or alternatively at 640 × 480 for 4 × 3 SD layout. Keep your original video frame rate and set a fairly high-quality bit rate. The audio should be stereo MP3 or AAC at 44.1 kHz sampling rate (see also <www.google.com/support/youtube/bin/answer.py?hl=en&answer=132460>).

Select your video and upload it, also providing the requested meta-data in the form. Note that your video has to be less than 1 GB in size and less than ten minutes duration for YouTube. Other video-hosting sites such as Vimeo, MySpace.TV, Metacafe or Dailymotion have other limits.

4. If you want to use the uploaded videos on another site (e.g. your blog), YouTube provides you with an embed tag, which is a piece of HTML code that you can copy from your YouTube video page and then paste into your own web page. If you paste it into a blog, for example, you can turn your blog into a vlog (a video blog).

This is a sequence of steps on how to publish to YouTube. Steps for uploading to other sites such as Vimeo, MySpace.TV, Metacafe or Dailymotion are similar.

As most of your dramas will be longer than ten minutes, I would recommend people to upload to Vimeo, which is explicitly for amateur filmmakers. Their recommendations for upload video formats are at <http://vimeo.com/help/compression>.

Who's Doing It?

Charles Sturt University in Bathurst, New South Wales, incorporates video streaming into its main TV journalism course.

Lecturer David Cameron says it's partly because the university has been lucky enough to get access to the technology, and partly because in a rural city like Bathurst there aren't the opportunities for students to do live broadcasting in other ways, as the students in the urban centres can.

They're video streaming shows several times a semester. The shows are composites, with some live segments and some pre-recorded inserts. Sometimes they do joint shows with CSU Wagga Wagga.

Their news show is received at the CSU Bathurst student union, the Union Bar and on the web at <www.csu.edu.au/faculty/arts/commun/mc_webstreaming.html>.

Students at Charles Sturt University, Bathurst, have the adrenaline rush of live webstreaming of their shows.

Tips from David Cameron, Charles Sturt University, Bathurst

WHEN SHOOTING VIDEO FOR THE WEB

- A steady shot with minimal camera movement helps produce a smaller file. Avoid excessive pans, tilts and zooms, and use a tripod if available.
- Shoot for a smaller screen. Consider avoiding wide shots. Stick to closer shots that show detail even when reduced in size for the desktop.
- Excessive detail or unnecessary movement in the background will soak up valuable bandwidth.
- Consider shooting in front of a plain background, with gelled lighting to provide a suitable wash. The simpler the better—for example, avoid leafy trees.
- Consider using a composite shot to reduce the file size. Shoot in front of a blue or green screen, then add a static image for the background. Compositing is a snap with software like Final Cut Pro.
- Don't forget the audio—your audience won't forgive you if they can't hear what's going on. Get the best possible recording your gear allows, and avoid unnecessary background noise.

WHEN EDITING VIDEO FOR THE WEB

- Avoid fades and wipes. The slower frame rate of video compressed for the web can turn your snazzy transition into an ugly splash of pixels.
- For clarity, consider using a subtitle approach for your titles. Add a black bar (letterbox) along the bottom of the screen, and add your titles as large white text.
- Avoid mixing music and voice unnecessarily, as this can make it harder to compress the file without losing sound quality for one or both elements.

WHEN NAMING FILES AND FOLDERS FOR THE WEB

- Avoid eXCesSIVE CaPITalS. The web is case sensitive.
- Use underscores (_) instead of spaces.
- Use only numbers, letters, underscores (_), and dots (.). Avoid !@'#$"%^&*()-+=?<>{\}}{/;
- Avoid rude or embarrassing file names—you don't know who might see them on the web.
- Use correct file extensions to indentify the file format (e.g. file.gif, file.mov, file.html).

Video on Phones

Metro Screen has done a serious (funded) investigation into the development of video content for mobile (cell) phone delivery.

David Opitz,
Facilities
Manager, Metro
Screen.

It's an imprecise science. There are so many variables in carriage services and individual phone capabilities. Some phones are more video capable than others are.

Working on the cutting edge with micro movies, and aiming for delivery to mobile phones with differently shaped screens, has been both exciting and challenging.

Here's a protocol they've worked out for sending video to phones. This is dependent on using Quicktime, which you can get as a free download off the net, if it didn't come bundled with your edit software or computer. From there, you can upgrade to QTPro for a small fee.

QuickTime Pro exports directly to iPhone.

So here goes:

1. Open QuickTime Pro.
2. Open your project.
3. Choose Export settings 3GP (3GPP).
4. Choose format:
   a. MPEG4
   b. H263 (this worked better for some phones)
   c. H264 (they preferred this for most phones).
5. Start with a data rate of 64 kbits/sec or up a little (goes to 20 Mbits/sec).
6. Standard image size is 176 × 144 pixels.
7. Standard frame rate is 15 frames/sec.
8. For audio, use mono so you don't double the audio data component:
   a. AAC is good for music
   b. AMR is good for speech.
9. Do tests using a range of phones to find out what works best.

To calculate the file size of your video:

1. Multiply out the pixel dimensions, so   176 × 144
2. Times the frame rate   × frame rate
3. Times the colour depth (use 20 bits/pixel)   × 20 colour depth.

Some tips: Keep the background simple, with not much movement in the shot. Stick largely to talking heads, probably not more than two people in the shot use mid-shots and closer.

The good news is that Final Cut Pro now comes bundled with Compressor. So when you finish your video:

1. Export it to Compressor.
2. Pick the folder 'Other work flows'.
3. Choose 'Mobile devices'.
4. Pick 3GPP GSM or whatever is the best local network (Edge? CDMA?).

Once everyone has made their movie, we get them to experiment with formats, frame rates, image size and give it a real-time test.

Start with a base level and scale it up until the phone or service can't handle it well. Start by scaling up the data rate until you get to maximum quality.

David Opitz, Facilities Manager, Metro Screen.

At Metro Screen, they shared the micro movies either by using Bluetooth to put them on someone else's phone or by putting the video up on the web and downloading it to a phone.

Check out some phone movies at the Metro Screen website:

<www.metroscreen.com.au/_blog/Mobile_Movies>.

Other Internet Video Options

There are several other methods for sending short videos over the internet.

Email

A *small* Quicktime or AVI (video for Windows) video can be electronically *attached* to an email and sent along with it. So you could efficiently send a very short video to lots of people, providing they can decode it at the other end.

As some ISPs limit the size of emails which can be sent, file size may be a problem.

Don't try to send anything bigger than 10 MB.

Newsgroup

A newsgroup is an internet information site, formed around an agreed-upon topic, which allows people to post messages for all the visitors to the newsgroup site to read. Anyone can send a message in to a newsgroup, and it will usually be posted for everyone to read. You could send a text message with a video attachment, and people who are browsing through the newsgroup may see your message, download it and watch your video.

Some newsgroups have a person who sorts through the incoming messages and orders them into some preferred sequence, so there isn't a 100 per cent guarantee of getting your video posted.

A newsgroup limits your audience to those who visit the newsgroup site and choose to download your file.

Mailing Lists

A mailing list is like a newsgroup, but it always has a *moderator* (minder). Mailing lists are also based on common interests, but the messages sent in aren't public. The moderator culls the messages and sends all the relevant ones to the individual mailboxes of the subscribers.

So with a mailing list, everyone could be advised of your video—though of course they'd still choose whether or not to download and watch it.

Home Page or Blog Site

Your home page can offer your videos to anyone who finds your site and wants to click on them. In theory there's no reason why your home page couldn't have ads, soapies, documentaries—whatever you want.

If your web presence is more active, in the form of a blog (vlog) site, you can keep people returning by regularly posting mini videos—about your trip, your family, your job, your music, your art, your psychological state . . .

Good Sites to Check Out

- *2-pop*—'The Digital Filmmakers Resource Site': Forums, blogs, news, features.
- Creative COW (Creative Communities of the World): 'Support communities for digital video, video editing, and media production professionals in broadcasting, motion graphics, special FX . . .'
- <www.StreamingMedia.com>: an international web magazine for media. Among its many features it maintains a directory of service providers for video streaming.

Thanks to Bill O'Donnell, David Cameron, Silvia Pfeiffer and David Opitz for their help with this chapter.

GLOSSARY

A-Roll A term from analogue days; it means the top-priority material for the edit, like the footage of the interviewee.

A/B roll Analogue video edit set-up that has two player VCRs feeding into the control system, so dissolves and wipes can be done.

AC Alternating current. This is the type of electrical current which is supplied through the wiring in buildings. In Australia, New Zealand and the United Kingdom, the AC is 240 volts. In the United States and Canada, the AC is 120 volts (sometimes 110 volts).

AC adaptor The device which converts AC to DC, so your camera can use wall current (AC) as well as battery current (DC).

Action
(i) Any movement which takes place in front of the camera.
(ii) The cue for performers to begin the scene.

Ad lib Unscripted dialogue or movements.

Address track A track on some video formats that can be used for recording timecode or userbits data.

ALC Automatic level control. A system built into some cameras which automatically keeps the input audio signal below the volume level that would result in distortion. When ALC is turned on, the operator cannot control the audio levels manually.

Amplitude The volume of sound, indicated by the height of the soundwave on the graphic display. The bigger the amplitude, the louder the sound.

Analogue A continuous signal. Analogue video systems generate a video signal by fluctuating current or voltage.

Analogue to digital converter A device that changes an analogue signal into a digital one. It may also be able to convert digital signals to analogue.

Angle
(i) The line along which the camera looks at the subject.
(ii) The view available to the camera via the particular lens being used—for example, *wide angle* or *telephoto*.

Animation A series of images (drawings, computer graphics, photographs) shown in a quick sequence to create the illusion of movement.

Aperture The adjustable opening which allows light to enter the camera. The size of this opening is indicated by the *f* stop setting. (The bigger the number, the smaller the hole.)

Aspect ratio The relationship between the width and height of a television picture. Standard definition is four units wide by three units high (4:3). Widescreen is 16 units wide by 9 units high. HDTV is also 16:9.

Atmos A recording of the ambient sound at a location.

Attenuate Reduce the amplification of a signal.

AVCHD High-compression HD video format.

B-Roll A term from analogue days but still in use. B-roll refers to footage shot for cutaways and other support material for the edit.

Back focus In the zoom lens, the focus adjustment at the rear of the lens barrel, just before the light reaches the image-gathering surface. Back focus affects the view at wide angle.

Back light Lighting which comes from behind the subject and is used to outline the subject and visually separate it from the background.

Backdrop The curtain used in the background of a shot.

Background (b/g) Anything beyond the main area of interest in a picture.

Background light A light used to illuminate the background in a shot.

Balanced audio A balanced audio cable has three conductors: two centre wires and a braided shield. Balanced is preferred because the signal is more protected from interference from radio signals and electricity.

Bandwidth Capacity of a communication channel, for example, the amount of data per unit of time (megabytes per second) that can be handled. Wider bandwidths can deliver signals faster, with more detail and better quality.

Barndoors Four adjustable metal plates attached to the front of light heads, used to limit and control the spread of the light beam.

Bass The low frequencies in a sound. Low-pitched drums, traffic rumble, thunder and electrical hum are all in the bass range 30 to 240 Hz.

Batch capture To transfer to the computer editing system several shots in one go.

BCU Big close-up. A shot that shows the human face framed from mid-chin to mid-forehead.

Best Boy The assistant to the gaffer or the grip in a film crew.

Bi-directional mic A microphone which picks up sound from two sides, and not from the top, rear or other two sides. Good for two-person interviews, especially in radio.

Bit The basic unit used in digital data. Only two bit characters are possible in a binary system: *on* and *off.*

Bit rate The number of bits that can be processed in a unit of time—for example, bits/sec.

Blocking Planning out the moves for either the performers or the cameras within a scene or production.

Blu-ray Optical disc made using a blue-violet laser. Blu-ray discs can store much more data than DVDs.

BNC This lock-on connector is a standard video connector on professional video equipment.

Boom pole A special lightweight telescoping pole used for holding a microphone close to the performer, but out of frame.

Bounce down To combine several audio tracks into one track.

Bounced light Light directed at another surface so it will be softened and reflected back onto the subject.

Breakout box A device used to convert signals from analogue to digital, and from digital to analogue.

Breakout cable An AV cable with a single connector on one end, which goes into a digital camera, and three connectors on the other end, to transmit video and two audio tracks for connection with a piece of analogue video equipment, like a monitor.

Browser The section in a digital edit program where the shots are listed for selection into the edit.

Burn To encode data onto a CD, DVD or Blu-ray disc.

Byte A sequence of eight adjacent bits, used as a unit in digital data.

Cable TV A system of transmitting television via a network of wires directly connected to homes, rather than through the air to antennae.

Camera card A list of the shots, movements and repositions for each camera in accordance with the shooting script. Camera cards are usually held in a mount on the studio camera pedestal.

Camera left/right Directions given to performers, always described from the camera's point of view.

Camera script The final script with all camera shots and positions noted for the recording.

Cans Headsets or earphones worn by the crew on the studio floor so that they can hear the director's instructions from the control room.

Call sheet Written information about the performers, crew, start and finish times, and locations for a shoot. It should also include emergency phone numbers, nearest hospital, and so forth.

Canvas In Final Cut Pro, the onscreen viewing section that shows whatever is on the timeline—for example, the edit so far.

Capture To load video into a non-linear edit system, changing it from an analogue to a digital signal in the process, if necessary.

Cardioid mic A directional microphone with a heart-shaped pick-up pattern. It picks up sound from the front and sides, and rejects sound from the rear. It's very useful, handheld, for on-the-street interviews.

Catwalk A walkway set above a studio, for use by lighting and maintenance technicians.

CCD Charge-coupled device. A sensor for scanning images, used in video cameras in place of the older video tube. A CCD stores light information as packets of minute electrical charges.

CCTV Closed circuit television. A video system which is linked together by coaxial cable; its signals are not broadcast beyond the range of its physical connections.

CCU Camera control unit. A remote-control device that adjusts the signal sent from a camera. In a multi-camera studio, the CCUs are all in the vision control area, so the technical director can set up each camera to the desired signal levels and match their signals to that of the other cameras being used.

CD-ROM Compact disc read-only memory. A compact disc that stores digital files, whether text, video, audio or graphic. It can't be overwritten.

CG Computer generated. CG backgrounds can be added to the video of characters shot in front of chroma key backgrounds, to make a composited image.

Character generator A device used to type in and store the credits and captions used in a video program. Character generators (CGs) have a variety of fonts, can store many pages of information, and present words page by page, in rolls, crawls and other dynamic screen motions.

Chip A collection of related circuits designed to work together on an electronic task. Some video cameras have one chip for image-gathering; some have three chips.

Chroma key Electronic special effect that eliminates a selected colour from a video image and replaces it with the image from another source. Chroma key is often used to add a separately produced background to a studio shot.

Chrominance The colour information in the TV signal (also *chroma*).

CMOS Complementary metal oxide semiconductor. CMOS is the type of sensor which is replacing CCDs in newer cameras.

Coaxial cable (coax) A shielded cable used for the transmission of RF (radio frequency) signals and also for video and sync signals.

Codec Compresser/decompresser or coder/decoder. A device or computer program that can encode and decode a digital signal or data stream.

Compact disc (CD) A small disc that can carry digital signals. CD-R and CD+R can be recorded on only once. CD-RW and CD+RW can be re-recorded.

Component signal

(i) A separated-out part of a composite video signal—for example, the luminance only, or the R (red), G (green) or B (blue) part.

(ii) The entire video signal, but sent out on a separate cable for the red, green and blue parts.

Composite video   A complete video signal containing all necessary picture and sync information, sent on just one cable.

Compositing   Combining different shots and video elements into one screen image.

Composition   The arrangement of picture elements within a scene.

Compression   A formula for reducing the amount of data in an image file.

Condenser mic   A microphone which uses an electronic component called the capacitor to respond to sound, and requires a power supply to operate it. It's generally more sensitive to a wide range of frequencies, more delicate, and more expensive than a dynamic mic.

Continuity   Keeping production factors like lighting, sound, costumes, props, makeup and performance levels consistent so they flow smoothly from one shot to the next in the final edit.

Contrast ratio   The comparison of the lightest and darkest sections of a picture.

Control room   The room from which the TV program is directed and coordinated and the vision mixing is done.

CPU   Central processing unit. The integrated circuit that controls computer programs.

Crane   A large mechanical 'arm' on which the camera can be mounted and which can be raised, lowered and manoeuvred through space.

Credits   The names of the contributors to a program.

C-stand   A metal stand with a three-legged base used for holding lighting controls like cutters, bounce cards or polystyrene, and frames with spun or gel in them.

CU close-up   A tightly framed shot of the subject. When referring to humans, it usually means a head-and-shoulders shot.

Cue   Visual or audio signal given to performers or technical operators for them to commence, alter or stop an action.

Cut
(i)   Instant switching from one camera to another in the vision mixer.

(ii)   The join that is the end of one shot and the beginning of another in the editing process.

(iii)   The director's signal to stop the action.

Cutaway   A shot that shows something related to the main action or topic, but which is a view of something other than the action or the speaker. Cutaways are used in editing to conceal the edits necessary to reduce the time a sequence takes on screen, from real time to program time.

Cut-in   A shot which shows a detail within the frame of the action or the interview. A cut-in is used to cover edit points, so the real time of an action or interview can be reduced in the editing process.

Cyc, cyclorama   A large curtain, sometimes attached to rollers, that is hung on a high track suspended around the edges of the studio, and which can be drawn behind the performers to make a background for a set.

DA   Director's Assistant. A studio role with many responsibilities, including advising camera operators of their upcoming shots and timing the progress of each segment of a production.

DAT   Digital audio tape. A tape system which records and replays audio using a digital signal.

DC   Direct current. The type of electricity supplied by batteries. Portable video cameras are designed to run on DC so they can be battery operated. To plug them into the wall current, you need an AC adaptor to convert the AC to DC.

Decibel (dB)   Measurement of the sound volume or signal strength of an audio signal. A dB meter gives a visual display of this signal strength.

Definition   The level of detail in an image, often measured by multiplying the pixel count in the height times the width. High definition TV has far more data (hence detail) than standard definition TV.

Degauss   To demagnetise. Audio heads need degaussing from time to time to reduce the hiss on tape recordings. Monitor screens also

need to be degaussed at times to improve functioning.

Depth of field   The distance between the closest and furthest objects that are in clear focus to the camera's image-gathering surface. Depth of field is affected by the angle of the lens (*wide* or *telephoto*), the aperture setting (*f* stop) and therefore indirectly by the amount of available light.

Detent position   The neutral position of a knob on the equalisation section of an audio mixer. In this position, no equalisation (change in volume to selected sound frequencies) is applied to the signal.

Diffusion material   Spun-glass cloth, or other material, which is placed in front of a light to soften the quality of the light and make the shadows produced by it less hard.

Digital   An electronic signal that is made up of discrete (separate) pieces of data, as opposed to a continuous flow of information. Digital video, like computer information, is encoded into a binary code, made up solely of *on* and *off*.

Digital video   A video signal that is recorded in a binary code, and can be copied through many generations without any loss in signal quality.

Digitise   To change a signal from analogue to digital. This word is also used to mean the process of entering an analogue video signal into a non-linear edit system.

Dimmer   Device connected to a light, or a lighting system, which varies the light output (brightness) by changing the voltage supplied to it.

Diopter   The lens in the viewfinder of a video camera, which can be adjusted to suit the eyesight of each camera operator.

Directional   Receptive from only one direction, as in *directional microphone*.

Director   The person in charge of deciding the overall camera coverage and the camera movements, and who guides the actors' performances in the making of a production.

Dissolve   Transition from one shot to another by a process of cross-fading, during which the image of the incoming shot is temporarily superimposed over that of the outgoing shot.

Dolly
(i) Movement of the camera towards or away from the subject.
(ii) The support on which the camera tripod is mounted. It has little swivelling wheels so it can be moved in all directions.

Down-convert To change a video signal to a format with lower definition, for example, to change an HD signal to a standard definition signal.

Download To take data into your computer from the internet.

Dropout Loss of signal due to damage to the tape or dirt on the tape or record head, preventing proper recording or playback.

Dry run Rehearsal without cameras.

Dub
(i) A copy of a videotaped or audiotaped signal. An analogue dub is not quite as good as the original material, because it's *down a generation*.
(ii) To make a copy of a signal.

DVD Digital versatile disc. A DVD can hold seven times the information that a CD-ROM can. Feature-length films can be delivered on DVD.

DVR Digital video recorder. This device records video in digital format to a hard drive.

Dynamic mic A microphone of the moving coil type. A dynamic mic doesn't require a power supply and is generally more robust and less sensitive to some frequencies that a condenser mic.

ECU Extreme close-up. A shot that enlarges a detail to bigger than life size.

Edit The process of putting video material into a scripted order to form a final program.

EDL Edit decision list. This is a record of all the in and out points of an edit.

EFP Electronic field production. The term applied to recording drama on location with a video camera rather than a film camera.

ENG Electronic news gathering. The term applied to recording the news on location.

Equalisation To change the quality of a sound by adjusting the volume of selected sound frequencies. Equalisation is done on audio mixers for recording purposes and on playback equipment according to personal listening preferences.

Establishing shot A shot, often a long shot, that gives the viewer an idea of the larger surroundings in which the action is occurring.

EVF Electronic viewfinder, the small monitor in the camera which shows the shot the camera is seeing.

Exposure Quantity of light being admitted to the camera.

Eyeline The line along which a person is looking, especially in relation to the framing of a picture. For example, the director may decide that the subject's eyeline should be to the left of frame or to the right of the camera position.

F stop Calibration of the size of the camera aperture (the hole which lets light into the camera). A large *f* stop number means a small opening and greater depth of field. A small *f* stop means a large opening and a shallower depth of field.

Fade in (or up)
(i) To increase the volume of the audio signal.
(ii) To make the picture appear gradually from a black, white or coloured screen.

Fade out (down)
(i) To decrease the volume of the audio signal.
(ii) To make the picture go gradually to a black, white or coloured screen.

Fader The control which can be moved up and down, or rotated, to adjust the volume level of a signal.

Feedback
(i) In audio: an effect that occurs when a microphone is placed too close to a speaker and a loud howling sound is produced.
(ii) In video: a visual effect produced by videoing a camera signal from a monitor that is showing the image from the same camera. An endless multiplication of the image is produced, like

looking down a tunnel, with ever-smaller images.

Field One half of the picture information within a frame of video. A field is one scan, from top to bottom, of the image-gathering surface of the camera, entailing all the odd lines or all the even lines.

Fill light
(i) A light that illuminates the subject from the opposite side of the camera to the key light.
(ii) A light which gives general illumination to a scene, or a part of a scene. Fill lights are often diffused light.

Filter
(i) A glass device that attaches to the front of the camera lens to alter the image during recording.
(ii) Video and audio controls within an edit program which can be applied to alter signals during postproduction.

FireWire The trademark name for the connection (and connecting wire) for putting video into a computer. Also called iLink and the IEEE 1394 interface.

Fish pole A microphone suspended from a pole, held either from the catwalk or the floor, and used to cover sound in areas not reached by the boom.

Flare Areas of super-brightness in the video image caused by light reflections off polished objects or dirt or tiny particles on the surface of the lens.

Flash memory Solid-state storage device, often used for transporting data from one computer to another using a flash memory stick. Some video cameras record to flash memory.

Flat
(i) A piece of standing scenery.
(ii) Dull image quality; even, not contrasting, usually referring to lighting.

Flexifill A handy cloth device for bouncing light. White on one side and metallic on the other, the cloth is large when being used but twists to fold into a small bag for packing away.

Floor The studio space where the actors and cameras are located.

Floor plan   A diagram of the studio floor, showing the positioning of scenery and properties, the entrances and exits, and the available technical facilities such as power points.

Fly   Studio objects or scenery hanging from above.

FM   Floor manager. This is a production role that occurs both in the studio and on location. The floor manager has many responsibilities, including keeping all the people on set in a productive and harmonious mood, and relaying directions from the director to all those who are not on headsets.

Focal length   The distance from the optical centre of the lens to the photoelectric surface in the camera.

Focus   To adjust the lens to obtain the sharpest image.

Foley   Sound effects produced in a studio for use in the production of a soundtrack.

Foot-candle   A unit of the measurement of light. It means the brightness of light one foot away from one candle. Some domestic camcorders can obtain a usable signal from only three foot-candles of light, but other cameras require much more light.

Footprint   The geographical area on the Earth's surface that receives a satellite's downlink signal at a useful strength. Because footprints don't align with national borders, satellite signals can be received in countries whose governments don't necessarily approve of the program content, yet who have no regulatory control over the broadcasters of the signal. This is one of the benefits—or hazards, depending on your point of view—of satellite TV.

Foreground (f/g)   The part of the picture nearest the camera, usually that which is between the subject and the camera.

4:3   The aspect ratio (relative screen dimensions) of standard definition television (SDTV).

Frame
(i) The vertical and horizontal edges to the video image.
(ii) To use the camera to set up a shot with a particular

composition of visual elements.
(iii) One complete television picture scan comprising two fields in interlaced video (as in 1080i) and just one scan in progressive scan video (as in 720p and 1080p).

Frame capture   The process of digitising a frame of video.

Frame rate   The number of frames shown per second, expressed as fps. NTSC = 30 fps; PAL and SECAM = 25 fps; CD-ROM and internet video can be 15 fps.

Frame store   A device that can store a frame of video as a digital signal and allow various electronic adjustments and manipulations to be done to the signal.

Freeze field   A motionless image caused by the repeated scanning of just one field of video. A freeze field is needed when there is fast motion in the video.

Freeze frame   A motionless image caused by the repeated scanning of one frame of picture information.

Frequency   The number of electromagnetic cycles that pass a given point in a second. Frequency is measured in cycles per second, usually referred to as Hertz (Hz).

Frequency response   The reproduction characteristics of microphones or other audio equipment.

FX   Abbreviation for *effects*, meaning special effects.

Gaffer   A person who assists with lighting.

Gain
(i) The volume level of the audio signal.
(ii) The amplification level of the video signal.

Gel   A transparent or translucent coloured sheet, which is heat resistant and can be placed in front of a light to alter the colour of the light beam.

Generation   A recording of a signal. The original recording is called the first generation, a copy of the original recording is called the second generation, a copy of the copy is called the third generation, and so on.

Genlock   Linking different video sources (such as studio cameras,

playback machines and remote sites) to the same synchronising pulse, so their signals are in exactly the same timing. This is to prevent rolling of the picture when one shot is switched to another in the vision mixer.

Gigabyte   One billion bytes (USA), one thousand million bytes (Australia). Video editing storage systems are rated in gigabytes.

Grandmother clause   When a newer model of equipment, or a computer program, will correctly play back the data of products recorded by an earlier version.

Graphics   Artwork such as drawings, maps, photographs and titles.

Grid   The overhead suspension system used for mounting the hanging studio lights.

Grip   A person who assists with the camera, and is responsible for mounting it on the tripod and other camera supports.

Handling noise   Unwanted sound which is introduced into the signal path between a microphone and the recorder. This noise can be caused by the hand that is holding the microphone, by careless operation of the boom, or by movement of the microphone cable or its extension lead.

Hard disk   A rigid plate with a magnetic coating that can store digital data. Frequently refers to the drive(s) within a computer.

HDTV   High definition television; 1080i and 1080p are formats of HDTV.

Head   The device that transfers the picture or sound signal onto magnetic tape. It also *reads* the signal from the tape during playback.

Head room   The space on the screen between the top of the subject's head and the top of the frame.

Hertz (Hz)   The unit of measurement of electromagnetic signal frequency. It means *cycles per second*.

High angle (H/A)   Any shot taken above normal eyeline.

High definition TV   See HDTV.

High key   High-intensity illumination; generally refers to a brightly lit set but can also mean a bright performance.

Hot

(i) When a portion of the video signal is overly bright, as when there are hot spots on the wall due to a poor lighting set-up.

(ii) Receptive to recording sound. A microphone is hot all over its housing, so it will transmit handling noise if it's rubbed or knocked anywhere on its body.

Hot swappable When an external drive can be plugged into, recognised and used by an edit program which is already running.

Hue The word used in television vocabulary that is the equivalent of *colour* in normal speech.

Ident (ID)

(i) Station identification.

(ii) A board used at the beginning of every taping sequence, containing details of what is about to be taped.

IEEE 1394 Institute of Electrical and Electronic Engineers standard for inputting signals into a computer. This standard connection is also known by the trade names FireWire and iLink.

iLink The trademark name for the connection (and connecting wire) for putting video into a computer. Also known as Firewire and IEEE 1394.

Image compression The reduction of video file size by reducing the number of data bits per second of a signal. Compression can be done in various ways, including reducing image size, frame rate and colour depth.

Impedance Rating of the resistance characteristics of audio components, such as microphones. Different impedance levels are expressed as *high impedance* or *low impedance*.

In the can A finished television recording, a show ready for broadcasting.

In-camera editing Shooting a video program, exactly in script order, in one shooting session, moving between *record* mode and *pause*, and never putting the camera into *stop* until the program is done. At the completion of the shoot, the program is ready for distribution if all goes well. In-camera editing is used by people with no access to editing equipment, or no time to use editing equipment. In-camera editing requires a high level of skill to make a good product.

Intercom Audio communication system used by studio floor and control room personnel.

Interlace When a horizontal line of picture information from one field of video is followed by a horizontal line from another field of video, ultimately resulting in two fields being combined to make one frame. Interlaced video is designated by 'i', so 1080i is a high definition interlaced format.

Iris (diaphragm) The circular opening and closing mechanism that controls the amount of light which reaches the camera.

Joy stick

(i) Gearstick-like device on the vision mixer panel for controlling the placement of wipe effects.

(ii) Gearstick-like device on the edit controller, for controlling videotape movement.

JPEG Joint Photographic Experts Group. A standard for the data compression of still images. JPEG converts image files to a smaller size.

Key An electronic stencil effect which subtracts some part of the video image and allows another image to show through at the deleted places when the key is superimposed over the other image. See *Chroma Key*, *Luminance key*.

Key frame In digital edition, a frame at which a change occurs. A motion key frame, for example, would be the position at which some alteration of the motion begins to happen.

Key light The main source of light on the subject or the scene.

Lavalier (Lav) A small omnidirectional microphone, usually worn clipped to the clothing.

LCD (liquid crystal display) screen The flipout screen on a video camera that gives the camera operator a larger view than the tiny viewfinder does.

Lens Optical system that collects and focuses light and transmits it to the image-gathering surface of the camera.

Level

(i) A description of the intensity of audio and video signals.

(ii) To *set levels* for a production is to adjust sound levels on the audio mixer and recorder to obtain the best-quality recording.

Line level The level of an audio signal that is sent from an amplified source, like an audio mixer, a CD, DVD or BD player or a monitor. A line level signal is usually around 1 volt in strength.

Line monitor The monitor that shows the pictures going to air, or being recorded on tape.

Lip sync When sound and picture are played back in correct relation to each other so the movement of lips matches the words spoken.

Live

(i) A *live* microphone is one that is transmitting a signal.

(ii) A *live* show is one that goes straight to broadcast.

Location Any place outside of the studio where material is recorded.

Log

(i) The written breakdown of a day's program schedule.

(ii) The list of the material which has been recorded.

(iii) To make a list of what's been recorded.

Loose shot A shot slightly wider than the standard shot size.

Lossless compression After compressing the video, then decompressing it, you wind up with exactly the same data with which you started.

Lossy When you compress the video and then decompress it, you do not get back to exactly your original data.

LS Long shot. A shot framed to show the whole body of the subject.

Luminance The brightness part of the video signal. The luminance signal is the main part of the video signal, and on its own gives the black and white reproduction of the image.

Luminance key This key effect can be used to delete the brighter or darker parts of an image.

Macro A lens setting used for taking shots of objects that are less than a metre away from the camera.

Mark To put a small piece of masking tape on the studio floor to indicate positions for the performers and scenery, or camera stopping points.

Mask
(i) A shield placed before a camera to cut off some portion of its field of view.
(ii) To conceal, by use of scenery pieces, any portion of the background.
(iii) When a performer or object is blocking the view to some background performer or object.

Master The first generation of a recording, or the first edited version of a program. The master should be kept safely and used only for the production of copies, never for routine playback.

Master control Control centre through which all television production and playback areas are routed.

MCU Medium close-up. A shot which shows the subject from mid-chest up, with a small amount of headroom in the frame above the head.

Megabyte (MB) One million bytes of information.

Mic level The level of the audio signal that is sent from many, but not all, microphones. It is 1 to 4 millivolts in strength.

Microphone A device for converting soundwaves to electrical energy. This energy can then be transmitted and recorded as an analogue signal, or digitised and transmitted and recorded as a digital signal.

Mid-range Sound frequencies higher than bass and lower than treble: 250 to 4000 Hz.

Mix To combine audio signals from several inputs down to one or two output channels.

Mixer
(i) In video: a device for selecting or combining video signals.
(ii) In audio: a device for combining audio signals.

MLS Medium long shot. A shot that frames the subject from about knee level to just above the head.

Monitor A video display unit that looks like a home television set but receives its picture and audio information through line inputs. It's sometimes unable to receive an RF signal.

Motion path A defined route along which a video shot, or an element, will travel within a video frame.

MPEG Moving Picture Experts Group. A standard for digital image compression. MPEG1 is used for CD-ROM; MPEG2 is used for DVD and TV; MPEG3 is used for audio; and MPEG4 is used for multimedia.

MS Mid shot. A shot showing the subject from the waist up to slightly above the head.

Multimedia A computer-based system for working with text, video, film, audio, graphics and animation.

Narrator Reader or speaker who adds information to a program and who can be either seen or unseen.

ND filter Neutral density filter. A filter that reduces the amount of light that gets to the camera lens, but doesn't alter the colour of it.

Negative image An image where the lights and darks are reversed for special effect, or where the colours are reversed.

Noise Unwanted interference in either the audio or the video signal.

NTSC National Television Standards Commission. The SD video format used in the United States, Japan, Canada, Mexico and many other countries.

Off-air signal Any RF signal broadcast through the air and available for public reception, for free.

Omnidirectional mic A microphone that picks up sound equally well from all directions.

Opacity The degree to which the image can be seen through. The opacity of an image can be varied, so it can be made more and less transparent. Altering opacity is a method of combining images.

Order wire A sound link set up between two sources distant from each other.

O/S Over the shoulder. A shot taken from behind, looking over someone's shoulder at another person or an object. This shot is often used for a cutaway in edited interviews.

Out of frame Out of the camera's view.

Pacing The flow and speed of an edited video piece, including length of shots and types of transitions.

PAL Phase alternate line. The name of the SD video standard used in Germany, Australia, New Zealand, the United Kingdom and many other countries.

Pan To move the camera left or right in the horizontal plane.

Parallel action Intercutting shots showing two different actions at two different locations. This allows the edited program to convey a sense of two things happening at the same time, and the cut from one scene to another works in editing in the same way as a cutaway does, allowing the editor to reduce time from real time to acceptable screen time.

Patching Directing various audio, video or light cables through a patch bay to send specific signals to specific inputs (e.g. your chosen channels on a mixer).

Pause mode The mode on a camera recording system in which the recording has stopped, but the tape is still in contact with the record heads. Pause is used between shots, and is especially useful for in-camera editing.

PCM Pulse code modulation. A system of digitising a sound signal.

Peak Highest level of signal strength, as on VU meters.

Pedestal
(i) A rolling mount for a camera, used in the studio.
(ii) The black level in the video signal.

Phantom power A method of sending electrical power from a studio audio mixer to condensor microphones, so individual microphone power supplies aren't needed. Computers can also phantom-power devices connected to their inputs.

Photoelectric Able to change light energy into electricity.

Photosensitive Responding to or sensitive to light. The video image is made when light is changed into an electrical current at the photosensitive CCD or CMOS.

Pixel Individual dots or picture elements in a video or computer image. The screen image is made up of thousands of pixels.

Plotting Planning of camera shots, deciding camera and boom positions.

Portable drive (External drive) A freestanding drive that can be connected into an edit system to provide additional storage space and which can also be used to transport files to another edit site.

Pot Abbreviation for potentiometer. This refers to any equipment control knob that allows continuously variable output, as with the *pan pot* on an audio mixer.

POV Point of view. A shot where the camera shows what one of the characters would see.

PPM meter Peak program meter. A type of meter used for reading the volume of sound. PPMs use a display of lights, rather than a swinging needle, to indicate sound levels.

Pre-amp An amplifier which comes before the main amplifier, used to raise the signal to an appropriate level.

Premix To combine several audio tracks to form one track, which is then input into a further audio mix.

Preview
(i) View a production on the preview monitor before it is sent to broadcast or recorded.
(ii) View a caption or a special effect on the preview monitor in the control room before placing it into the production.

Program monitor The studio monitor that shows the signal being sent to broadcast or record.

Program out The signal being sent to broadcast or record.

Progressive A non-interlaced video signal, designated by 'p', as in 720p. Progressive video uses all horizontal lines sequentially, so there are no separate fields, just complete frames.

Proximity effect An exaggeration of bass frequencies which occurs when a cardioid microphone is placed very close to the speaker's mouth.

Though it's a form of distortion, the particular sound yielded is considered desirable, even sexy, in some instances.

Public access A policy which means that everyone has the right to broadcast on a public TV or radio channel, on a first-come, first-served basis (just as everyone has the right to travel down a public road).

PZM Pressure zone microphone. A microphone with a hemispherical pick-up pattern, which can reproduce room sound very well, but isn't selective.

Quicktime A widely accepted video compression format. You can use Quicktime files for burning video to a DVD and for posting video on the internet.

Radio mic A mic which transmits its signal through the air, using a radio frequency, rather than sending it through a cable.

RAID Several hard disk drives linked together but seen by the computer as one entity.

RAM Random access memory. A memory system in which data can be accessed in any order, with equal speed. The contents of RAM disappear when the computer is turned off.

RCA A slip-on cable connector that is often used on home equipment for both audio and video cables.

Reach The distance over which a microphone can pick up a good signal strength. A shotgun microphone has a longer reach than a cardioid, which was designed for handheld interviews.

Real time Time as we experience it. Most edited programs show actions that have been reduced from real time to a shorter length.

Recce (reccy) A visit to a site to check out its potential for a video shoot and to determine its inherent problems.

Receiver/monitor A video display unit that can display signals received either via broadcast (RF) or via direct line inputs.

Render To have the computer generate the new frames needed to combine signals and produce the desired video outcome, as with a composited image.

Resolution A measure of the amount of detail that can be recorded within the video image, by a particular camera or with a particular format.

RF Radio frequency. A modulated video, audio and sync signal. RF signal is used to broadcast television through the atmosphere. Television receivers are designed to decode RF signals.

RGB Red, green and blue, the primary colours of the video image. The R, G and B signals can be viewed separately with video test equipment, and the relative strengths of these three signals can be adjusted during shooting and postproduction to produce certain effects.

Roll The director's signal to start the video recording or to start a replay.

ROM Read-only memory. Memory that cannot be overwritten.

Run down The list of proposed content for a program.

Run-through A rehearsal of action and/or camera movement.

Sampling Taking a reading. When a high sampling rate is used, the collection of data has greater accuracy. So in audio a higher sample rate is usually preferable.

Saturation The richness of the hue (colour) in the colour TV signal. A very saturated hue is like a vibrant cartoon colour; a not very saturated hue is pastel.

Scanner A device that converts images to a digital form.

Scene The shot or assemblage of shots that make up a unit of a program.

Schedule A listing of all information regarding the recording day, with dates, times, locations, scenes, actors and crew.

Scrim A wire mesh put in front of lights to slightly diffuse the beam. A scrim is also useful for catching flying glass if the globe explodes.

SECAM Système Électronique Couleur Avec Mémoire. The standard definition signal used in France, the former Soviet Union, former Eastern Bloc countries, and some other countries.

Servo control Remote control of the zoom and focus on a studio camera, operated by switches mounted on the pan handles of the camera pedestals.

Set The arrangement of scenery and props which make up the environment shown in a shot or scene.

Set up
(i) To install a set in the studio.
(ii) To get all cameras and equipment positioned and ready to operate.

Shock mount A microphone holder that isolates the microphone from any handling noise.

Shooting ratio The relationship between the amount of footage shot and the length of the final edited product. Drama usually has a much lower shooting ratio than documentary because the shots can be more carefully planned out ahead of time.

Sibilant Having a high-pitched sound, like that produced by *s*.

Signal-to-noise ratio The strength of a signal compared to the background noise. A high signal-to-noise ratio means a better recorded result.

Site check A visit to a shooting location, done ahead of the shooting day. A site check is for obtaining useful information such as the position of the sun, the accessibility of the site, the possibility of using AC power, environmental noise factors, and so on. Also called a *location reccy*.

16:9 The aspect ratio (relative screen dimensions) of widescreen TV and high definition TV (HDTV).

Snow Random black and white dots shown on the television screen. Snow can be due to poor reception or a dirty VCR head. It's also the image you see if you play an erased tape or a never-recorded tape.

Soft light A light which produces little or no shadowing. It's often an indirect light, possibly bounced off another surface before it hits the subject.

Special effects (SFX) Creation of illusions by mechanical or electronic means.

Spotlight A light focused or restricted to cause it to send a narrow beam.

Spun A fabric made of spun glass, which is put in front of

lights to slightly soften the beam and reduce its intensity.

Standard definition The TV standard used before the introduction of HDTV.

Still (freeze) A motionless image caused by the repeated scanning of one frame of picture information.

Storyboard Shot-by-shot drawings and accompanying text indicating the major points in the content of a scene or program. Audio content may also be listed. A storyboard looks rather like a cartoon strip, but of course it's much longer.

Superimpose (super) Electronic overlapping of two or more pictures on the screen—for example, captions or credits over an image.

Surround sound The sound of a location, recorded by an omni-directional microphone, used to give presence and authenticity to the scene.

Sync Electronic timing pulses that control the recording and replay of the video image.

Sync generator A device that produces electronic synchronisation pulses. All studio equipment can be linked to one sync generator so there will be no timing differences between the signals from the various sources. This is called *genlocking* the equipment.

Synopsis A brief description of the program's storyline or plot. A scene synopsis lists all scenes with a short description of the plot movement in each one.

Take
(i) The director's signal to cut from one camera to another.
(ii) The completion of one part of a production.

Talent The term once used to refer to all performers and actors. This term now has a derogatory flavour to many people, and is no longer considered acceptable. It should be replaced with *performer* or *actor*.

Talkback A speaker or headset system that connects the studio to the control room and allows the crew on the studio floor to communicate back to the director and DA.

Talking heads The term applied to close-up shots showing people

speaking. Talking heads are commonly part of a TV program, but they quickly become tiresome, so cutaways related to what the speakers are discussing are used to liven up the content.

TBC Timebase corrector. A device which corrects the timebase (sync) of a video signal and makes it synchronous with other devices, like a vision mixer.

TD Technical director. The person in the studio whose job it is to set up and balance the signals from all the cameras.

Telecine A device for the transfer of film to video.

Telephoto A lens designed to narrow the field of view and enlarge the subject. The focal length is longer than usual—for example 150 mm. Used for close-ups that are shot from a distance.

Terabyte A thousand gigabytes.

Test pattern Specially designed chart to test resolution and colour balance in a video picture.

Texture mapping The process of wrapping a 2D image onto a 3D object.

Thirds A concept in shot composition that divides the screen into three sections, vertically or horizontally.

Tilt To tip the camera up or down, as you would look up or down with your head.

Timecode A system which gives a unique number to each frame of video.

Timeline The section of the edit program where you assemble your clips and effects to make a program.

Track (or **truck**) To physically alter the position of the camera in the horizontal plane, either handheld or on a dolly. Often done in a motion parallel to a moving subject.

Tracking The movement of the video heads, or the hi-fi audio heads, along the recorded signal path on the tape. If the heads aren't riding right on top of the signal tracks, the replay picture or audio quality will be poorer, and you will have what's called a *tracking problem*. This can usually be fixed by adjusting the tracking knob on the player.

Transition Any method of getting from one shot to the

next in an edit. Transitions are commonly cuts, wipes or dissolves.

Treatment   A brief description of the film idea, including the theme, characters, story arc and style.

Treble   High-frequency sounds—4096 to 16 KHz.

Two-shot   A shot including two people.

Unbalanced audio   Not shielded. An unbalanced audio cable is not recommended for professional use because it's subject to electrical interference.

Unidirectional mic   A microphone that picks up sound only from a cone-shaped area to the front of it. Some unidirectional mics have a broader pick-up range than others. The ones with a very narrow range are called *hyperdirectional*.

Up-convert   To change a video signal into a higher-definition format, e.g. from standard definition to HD.

Up-link
(i)   The transmission system sending a signal to a satellite.
(ii)   The signal sent up to the satellite.

Upload   To put data—like your video—onto the internet.

Upstage
(i)   Away from camera, towards the back of the set.
(ii)   To walk towards the back of the set, causing the other actor(s) on set to turn away from the camera. This is a trick to focus the audience's attention on oneself and

away from the others. This move is not very popular with the other actors.

Vectorscope   A device that graphically displays information about the colour part of the TV signal.

Video   The picture component of the television signal.

Video streaming   A continuous stream of video data sent via the internet and displayed on a viewing device in real time.

Viewfinder (EVF)   A small monitor screen in the camera eyepiece which shows the operator the camera's view.

Virtual reality   Interactive electronic media which give the illusion of immersion in an artificial world that exists inside the data space of the computer.

Vision mixer   A device for selecting or combining video signals.

VLOG   Video blog. A type of website to which video is posted regularly and usually frequently.

VLS   Very Long Shot. A shot in which the full body of the subject takes up about half the height of the screen.

VM   Vision mixer. The person who operates the vision mixer.

Voiceover   The voice of the narrator or another person, used without the accompanying image of that person.

VU meter   Volume unit meter. A meter with a moving needle that indicates the audio level in the camera, recorder or mixer.

Walk-through   A rehearsal, usually preceding camera

rehearsal, where performers and crew note the major action.

Waveform monitor   A device that graphically displays information about the signal strength and sync characteristics of the video signal.

Wavelength   The length of one cycle of an electromagnetic signal.

Webcam   A camera connected to a computer and used to send video images over the internet.

White balance   To adjust the camera's colour rendition for any new lighting situation.

Wide angle   A lens, or a setting on a zoom lens, that maximises the width of the background in a shot.

Wipe   A visual effect where one picture appears to push another off the screen, following some geometric pattern.

WS   Wide shot. A shot showing a broad view of the surroundings, often taken with a wide-angle lens.

XLR   This lock-on three-pin connector is used on cables carrying balanced audio signals. It's the standard audio connector for professional microphones, mixers and recording equipment.

Y/C   The abbreviation used for the SVHS signal, which is separated out into its luminance and chrominance components.

Zoom lens   A lens with a movable element that enables the selection of various focal lengths. A 12 mm/120 mm lens has a 10:1 zoom ratio.

INDEX